DATE DUE

Korean Attitudes Toward the United States

Korean Attitudes Toward the United States

United States

CHANGING DYNAMICS

Foreword by Robert L. Gallucci

DAVID I. STEINBERG, Editor

An East Gate Book

M.E.Sharpe
Armonk, New York
London, England

An East Gate Book

Copyright © 2005 by M.E. Sharpe, Inc.

Library of Congress Cataloging-in-Publication Data

Korean attitudes toward the United States : changing dynamics / edited by David I.
Steinberg.
  p. cm.
 Includes bibliographical references and index.
 ISBN 0-7656-1435-9 (alk. paper)
 1. United States—Relations—Korea (South)—Congresses. 2. Korea (South)—Relations—
United States—Congresses. 3. United States—Foreign public opinion, Korean—Con-
gresses. 4. Public opinion—Korea (South)—Congresses. 5. Anti-Americanism—Korea
(South)—Congresses. I. Steinberg, David I., 1928–

E183.8.K6K678 2004
303.48′25195073—dc22
                                  2004003612

Printed in the United States of America

Contents

Part III. Alliance Perspectives

Part IV. Civil Society Perspectives

Foreword

Robert L. Gallucci

The Republic of Korea remains of vital interest to the United States. Although over-shadowed through much of 2002 and 2003 by the nuclear crisis with North Korea, its policies and peoples are intimately intertwined with the North and are of enduring importance to the United States because of growing strategic, economic, cultural, and institutional ties between our two states. The relationship is both strategic and sym-bolic and reflects the growing interchange between us.

The fifty-year alliance between the Republic and the United States has, in the early period of the new century, been buffeted by internal gales in both states and from North Korea. This has been reflected in growing anti-American sentiment in South Korea, which, not so long ago, Americans would have thought virtually inconceiv-able. These concerns have influenced the 2002 Korean presidential election and are likely to play an even greater role in relations between the two states if this phenom-enon is not better understood.

For this reason, the Asian Studies Program of Georgetown University's School of Foreign Service planned and brought together a major conference on this subject—the first such meeting devoted specifically to this issue—although it inevitably is raised, peripherally but significantly, at virtually every international gathering. The premise behind this meeting and this volume is that the issue in all its complexity must be directly addressed and understood if effective policy decisions are to be made to continue the close relationship that has existed in the half-century of the alliance and that is in the interests of both states. Although there have been the inevitable tensions, and more will no doubt occur, a more comprehensive understanding of the problem should enable policy makers on both sides to mitigate the worst aspects of the problem.

The School of Foreign Service has been pleased to have the support, moral and financial, of a variety of individuals and institutions that have offered assistance to the meeting and its deliberations. I would like to thank ambassadors Donald Gregg, Richard Walker, and Yang Sung Chul for giving talks at the meeting. Ambassador William Gleysteen had agreed to attend, but his untimely death prevented us from partaking of his wisdom. Those others who played important roles in the conference include

Young-Dal Chang of the Korean National Assembly, Nicholas Eberstadt of the American Enterprise Institute, Sung Min Jang of Duke University, Mitch Kaneda of Georgetown, Don Oberdorfer of the School of Advanced International Studies of Johns Hopkins University, Bonnie Oh of Georgetown University, John Oh of Catholic University, Gilbert Rozman of Princeton University, and Stephen Rounds of the U.S. Embassy in Seoul.

We would like to thank our donors, who generously supported the meeting and participated in it. The Pacific Century Institute, specifically Spenser Kim, has been most kind in this as well as other meetings at Georgetown, and his presence added to the event. The Korea Society supported the gathering, and its President Ambassador Donald Gregg was actively involved; contributions were also received from the U.S. National Intelligence Council, Mr. Mark Gaston, and the Asian Studies Program of the School of Foreign Service.

We believe that this conference and volume will contribute to explication of the issues connected with this trend and reflect Georgetown's interest in participating in the policy dialogue on critical foreign policy issues.

Introduction

Anti-American Sentiment in the Korean Context

David I. Steinberg

Setting the Stage

The year 2003 was a significant milestone in Korean-American relations. It memorialized both the centennial of Korean immigration into the United States and the fiftieth anniversary of the Korean-American security treaty.[1] It was, apparently, a time for celebration and was so treated in innumerable conferences, seminars, and speeches reaffirming the strong, officially proclaimed ties between the two nations. But all the talismans were not so positive. Growing concerns over the behavior of North Korea the previous year had all but erased the progress in North–South Korean relations that had been so apparent in the 2000 summit in Pyongyang between President Kim Dae Jung of the Republic of Korea (ROK) and Chairman Kim Jong Il of the Democratic People's Republic of Korea (DPRK).[2] Many in Korea attributed this to American policies toward North Korea as well as to North Korea's surreptitious breakage of North-South, DPRK-U.S., and International Atomic Energy Agency agreements and the North's secret nuclear program. There were growing rifts between the United States and the South over the most appropriate and feasible policies to be pursued toward the North as well as internal debates on these issues within both South Korea and the United States.

The history of the alliance is now shrouded in myth and in the euphoria over its longevity. The shared blood and agony of the Korean War and the close friendships built over the years between the (generally older) citizens of the two nations, as well as official pronouncements by both governments, have partly masked the constant tensions, were inherent even at its inception, and are inevitable in this long relationship. There is thus a tendency to ignore or submerge those problems in the face of a common enemy, and this was especially so during the period of the Cold War. But "anti-Americanism is growing at a startling rate in South Korea, potentially escalating into a serious problem that could jeopardize the future of the U.S.–Korean alliance."[3]

In 2002, President Roh Moo Hyun was elected in South Korea on the hitherto absent political platform of greater equality of that American relationship, one coming under growing skepticism among younger voters, who are more nationalistic in an environment where such attitudes have been pervasive and increasing in intensity. Complaints that Korea had given up critical elements of its sovereignty in the alliance, as is true in any such relationship, were increasingly articulated at official and unofficial Korean levels. Tensions over a grievous accident that brought tragic deaths to two middle school Korean girls who were run over by a U.S. military vehicle surfaced with massive, generally peaceful demonstrations against the United States when the two soldiers involved were found innocent in a U.S. court martial just prior to the voting and again in June 2003 on the anniversary of the girls' deaths. The causes, immediate and historic, of anti-American sentiment have, since the summer of 2002, been the subject of diverse and intense policy reviews and media explorations by both Koreans and Americans. These sentiments have caused a negative reaction to U.S. troop deployment in Korea in some, generally conservative, American policy circles. But President Roh has expressed his belief that the problem is not serious, saying that he has confidence in his own ability, courage, and morality to handle the situation and that he would not succumb to popular pressures on this issue (as he has not done in the case of Japanese relations).[4] On the other hand, Mr. Kwon Young-ghil, president of the Democratic Labor Party and a previous presidential candidate on the left, attributes such sentiments to three factors: the U.S. support of military dictatorships, perceived U.S. obstructionism to national unification, and U.S. infringements on national sovereignty and independence.[5]

However, in spite of its immediate presence and increasing strength, anti-American sentiment in Korea is nothing new. Although it may have reached a new level of intensity and visibility, it has been evident for long periods, sometimes forced underground under authoritarian Korean governments that viewed their relationship with the United States as essential for their security against a potentially belligerent North and also, and importantly, as a protective mantle invoking a degree of political legitimacy to regimes that came to power through unconstitutional means or stayed there through questionable tactics. Such was the early, positive U.S. political influence, which has since quite obviously waned. The National Security Law pervasively allowed the state to control public expressions that seemed to threaten any administration and its orthodoxy, including views that questioned the appropriateness of the alliance. Thus, to publish on the issue in Korea before political liberalization in 1987 was both difficult and dangerous. The democratization of Korea since that time provided the freedom to express these concepts, and incidents since then have exacerbated the problem.

To this writer as well as to many other observers, the causes of such anti-American sentiment are complex, involving historical, social, psychological, economic, political, and cultural elements too often ignored for a variety of reasons. To many in successive South Korean governments, to raise the issue for serious discussion and debate was likely in their view to intensify the problem, which might have both negative security and political ramifications for their administrations.[6] To Americans before 2002, the issue had not reached crisis levels negatively affecting the global and regional security interests of the United States; thus these tensions either went unrecognized or were ignored as being of lower priority than other international crises. As long as Korea was ruled with an iron fist, public sentiment could, it was believed, be disregarded. Many on both sides of the alliance considered that unfortunate incidents exacerbating the problem were like cold sores—ugly and bothersome but soon to subside and thus of evanescent concern. Korean anti-American issues seemed, on a worldwide scale of violence and vituperation, of marginal intensity.

The existence, growth, and intensity of anti-American sentiment, however, had been of concern to this observer and others for quite some time.[7] To draw out the causes and effects, he began in May 2002 to organize and seek support for the conference that has led to the publication of this volume.

The following hypotheses prompted the call for a conference:

- The Korean-American relationship is important to furthering the national interests of both the Republic of Korea and the United States, even though these interests are overlapping rather than completely congruent and may further diverge over time. The relationship is also important for the regional stability of Northeast Asia.

- Measured discussion and analyses of the issues would help both states and their peoples better to cope with the problems associated with the relationship and diminish its intensity. Conversely, avoidance of the issues, like ignoring a cancer, would allow expansion of the problem.

- Overt expressions and concerns about anti-American sentiment, however defined, may peak and diminish at any given time and over any particular incident. But according to a multitude of opinion polls, the strength emotion has perceptibly increased and encompasses broader elements of the Korean populace, with (since the conference) an apparent political impact in Korea.

During the period from January 30 to February 1, 2003, a distinguished group of scholars and officials met at Georgetown University to discuss these issues. Their revised papers, often expanded and edited, together with some other commissioned papers, form this volume. Its purpose is to elucidate the complexities, present influence, and potential of anti-American sentiment, so that the Korean-American alliance can contribute to improved relations between these two states and to progress in regional East Asian affairs.

The alliance between South Korea and the United States is in effect both a pillar and a facade of the bilateral relationship. Official U.S. and Korean statements consider the alliance strong and firm—the basis of the superstructure of other multiple relationships. But others, especially Koreans, consider it a facade, hiding tensions, antagonisms, a variety of emotions that are both positive and negative and that vary by a complex miscellany of experiences, backgrounds, demographics, regions, and many other factors.

Anti-American sentiment in Korea has its own historical roots, which are well known to the Korean people, but it is also a part of, and related to, a worldwide trend that has resulted from both the growth of American military, economic, and even cultural power and the diminishing of other alternative international hegemonic influences.[8] This introductory chapter considers that issue and follows it with a consideration of definitions of the term *anti-American sentiment* or *anti-Americanism*. It then considers the role of the press in this process, the efforts by the United States to enhance democracy in Korea, categorization of this phenomenon, anti-Korean reactions in the United States, and the organization of the conference and the volume itself.

Anti-American Sentiment as a Worldwide Concern

By 1988 a growing body of literature began to appear devoted to the worldwide phenomenon of anti-American sentiment, however defined. This was demonstrated by volumes that explored this issue regionally. There had been strong anti-American movements among the left and intellectuals in Europe for decades.[9] One author has noted that over two centuries, anti-American sentiment, originating in Europe but spreading worldwide, has passed through "five major layers or strata, each of which has influenced those that succeeded it." These are as follows: the new world as physically degenerating; the United States as intellectually inferior; the United States as a mixed (not pure and thus superior) racist society; the United States as a materialistic and spiritually empty society; and America as the site of catastrophe (*katestrophenhaft*; from Heidegger).[10] Perhaps it was the fall of the Shah in Iran and the holding of the U.S. hostages in Teheran at the close of the Carter presidency that prompted more global consideration of the issue. Perhaps it was globalization itself, which many feel is a surrogate for U.S. influence. The problems have been exacerbated by the unipolar nature of U.S. power and the fall of the Soviet Union. In some sense, the military and economic strength of a democratic United States together with the rise of other, new democracies, of whatever stripe, around the world have prompted the need for such states to listen to their own people, who may be more nationalistic and less inclined to follow blindly the policies of their administration, thus making the issues that the United States must address more complex. Governmental fiats are no longer sufficient to satisfy various populations. By coincidence, the political liberalization of Korea in 1987, to which the United States contributed, gave intellectual stimulus to dialogue about that problem within Korea and, indeed, to the spread of this phenomenon.

From the early nineteenth century, beginning with de Touqueville, observers have noted that Americans were concerned with foreign views of their society. They wanted to be admired, and, as we say today, even loved.[11] This characteristic of U.S. society, which continues to this day, is in marked contrast to the attitudes of other major "imperial" powers, which have been satisfied with being feared. But democracy tempers imperialism, even as it did (rather unsuccessfully) in later-nineteenth-century England. The irony is that as some in the United States proclaim a virtual imperial role as policy, the United States has fostered, with relative degrees of success, democracies and democratic deepening in many parts of the world; these two policies are often in direct conflict. Further, after the tragic attacks of September 11, 2001, the U.S. government has become more aware of the growth of anti-American sentiment and at the same time less tolerant of its vigorous expression.

Thornton, in his worldwide 1988 study, raises several issues, two of which are germane to the Korea question. The first is that attitudes toward the United States often result from the ways in which individuals see their own countries; the second is whether all foreign criticism of the United States is to be counted as anti-Americanism. The latter is summarily dismissed, both in that study and below. The need to define anti-American sentiment is thus apparent.

Definitions

In an attempt to allow the participants to explore the full range of issues, the conference organizers did not attempt to define anti-American sentiments, anti-Americanism, or any other aspects of this phenomenon in advance. However, reflecting on the conference itself and on the somewhat meager literature on the subject as it relates to Korea, a variety of definitions have become apparent. Yet it must be noted that criticism of an American administration or person and/or his or her actions or policies does not itself constitute anti-Americanism, and that anyone may hold conflicting views on the United States at the same time; for example, extolling the American educational system and wishing to participate in it while deploring U.S. policies, arrogance, or cultural intrusions. Such differences need not be seen as cognitive dissonance but rather as parallel or supplementary positions that are not necessarily contradictory.

In the broadest context, "Anti-Americanism can be defined as any hostile action or expression that becomes part and parcel of an undifferentiated attack on the foreign policy, society, culture, and values of the United States."[12] The authors distinguish four types of anti-Americanism: issue-oriented, ideological, instrumental (mobilizing domestic support by using the United States as a scapegoat), and revolutionary (seeking to overthrow a pro-U.S. government). Woo-Cumings, quoting Paul Hollander (Chapter 5), notes "Anti-Americanism is a *predisposition to hostility* toward the United States and American society, a relentless critical impulse toward American social, economic, and political institutions, traditions, and values. . . ." Ceaser believes that "Anti-Americanism rests on the singular idea that something associated with the United States, something at the core of American life, is deeply wrong and threatening to the rest of the world."[13] Donald Clark suggests that "The anti-Americanism at issue here is systematic hostility toward Americans and their institutions in Korea, criticism that goes beyond understanding to attack the motives and ideas of Americans, and attacks by Koreans on other 'pro-American' Koreans in a manner reminiscent of attacks on former Japanese collaborators after the Second World War."[14] Hyun Syng-il draws a distinction between anti-American sentiment and criticism of America: ". . . anti-Americanism is a form of criticism combined with hatred toward the United States."[15]

John Oh defines it as "significant manifestations of anger and hostility toward the United States and its policies, practices, institutions, and citizens—either military or civilian."[16] Stephen Linton goes further:

> It is more of a "background anti-Americanism" that inclines Koreans to see what is valuable in their way of life under constant pressure from a dominant American-led western culture. This sense of "cultural victimization" predisposes Koreans to sympathize with whoever opposes America in a dispute. Because this form of anti-American sentiment has clear racial undertones, by its very nature it is more difficult to address through policy initiatives than any other form of anti-Americanism.[17]

It seems evident that the key concepts are systemic and undifferentiated, but individual issues or incidents—or, more broadly, ideological or cultural factors—can seriously affect alliances and attitudes that help shape political reality, especially in democracies, which ironically seem more vulnerable to these tendencies or at least their expression. Various contributors to this volume define the terms with different emphases.

Yet anti-Americanism has sometimes served an internal political purpose. "The Chun regime did little to discourage anti-American expressions so long as they served to deflect and dissipate some anti-regime fervor."[18] It effectively used the press to support its positions, with some of which the United States strongly disagreed.

Meredith Woo-Cumings in her chapter takes a different approach, essentially arguing that the most apt analogy for anti-American sentiment conceptually is that of European anti-Semitism, which vilified a whole people and their culture. If that analogy were to be applied to Korea, she argues, then anti-Americanism does not exist there. She forces us to consider a relative degree of anti-American sentiment and thus perhaps to eschew attaching the *ism* to the term, thus giving it this all-encompassing meaning. But, as Jean Paul Sartre reminded us in *Anti-Semite and Jew,* if anti-Semitism did not exist, we would have to invent it to deal with the "other." Perhaps Koreans have a need to define themselves by what they are not, and the United States is an obvious, tempting target.

On the Press

> I read the newspapers with lively interest. It is seldom that
> they are absolutely, point-blank wrong. That is the popular
> belief, but those who are in the know can usually discern an
> embryo truth, a little grit of fact, like the core of a pearl, round
> which have been deposited the delicate layers of ornament.

> —Evelyn Waugh, *Scoop* (1938)

There is a widespread belief, certainly in American circles but also among Koreans, that the Korean media have played an important contributory role in exacerbating anti-American sentiment in Korea. Efforts were made, unsuccessfully, to have papers on this subject for this volume, but to exclude the subject is to ignore an important component of the problem. Although no Korean government has strategically used the press or the media to foment such responses, tactically it has used public information and disinformation to pursue its own ends, in some cases falsely or inappropriately aligning the United States with its official position on an issue, which because it was unpopular with a significant segment of the Korean populace, thus resulted in increasing anti-American sentiment. Kwangju is a prime example of this issue.[19]

Lee's study carefully documents daily press stories that manipulated the press to identify the United States with Korean state suppression of the Kwangju revolt. Mass media were "somewhere near the center of the conflict, at times as mediators and observers, but more times as participants—in most cases, as agents of the ruling regime which attempted to manage the entire gamut of public communication with an extremely intense desire for legitimation."[20] Ironically, the democracy that resulted from the June 1987 reforms that the United States had wanted and to which it had contributed in the spring of 1987 resulted in the growth of anti-American sentiments because of the new freedom to express such views: "The rapid expansion of anti-American sentiments after the collapse of the authoritarian regime in June 1987 was, in a sense, a natural phenomenon, resulting from the incorporation of anti-American articulations by the establishment media under the increasing hegemonic pressures from the oppositional forces."[21]

To understand the role of the media, which have become increasingly independent of the state but are still subject to its formal and informal influences,[22] the history of the press and attempts to control it are important. Each government since independence has had a Ministry of Information (at times a Ministry of Information and Culture) that has supported newspapers that conveyed its position to internal and external audiences, controlled television networks, and attempted to influence directly and indirectly how its actions were presented to the people. In the most rigorous period of command, under the Yushin period of Park Chung Hee's regime (1972–79), Korean CIA officers sat in editorial offices and stringently controlled what could be printed. President Chun Doo Hwan, following his coup of December 12, 1979, purged the media of hundreds of reporters and writers and consolidated the news agencies to ensure greater government control. Even under the liberal government of President Kim Dae Jung, the state went after the opposition newspapers with tax audits, fines, and convictions designed to stifle criticism of his government.[23] This simply hurt the credibility of his administration. President Roh, soon after his inauguration, instituted procedures that limited reporters' contacts with ministerial officials, thus insulating the press from the informal contacts that breed news stories. Even after liberalization, other legal means were sought to control the press.

> With the democratization of Korean society since 1987, government officials realized they could no longer use illegal, extralegal, and irrational methods to silence the press, and they seized on libel law, which is still listed in the Criminal Code as

well as in the Civil Code, to punish members of the press. During the past six years, the Korean press has continuously been challenged by complaints of criminal defamation and civil libel suits filed by public officials. Korean law concerning political libel and the Korean courts have favored public official plaintiffs.[24]

The role of the press cannot be separated either from pressures to conform to state policies, orthodoxy, or from Korean nationalism.[25] Following President Kim Dae Jung's trip to Pyongyang in June 2000, in August of that year a large group of South Korean publishers also went to Pyongyang, where they promised that they would not publish articles that were critical of the North and that might harm or destroy the "Sunshine Policy" of the South Korean government. The Kim Dae Jung administration was singularly silent on human rights abuses in North Korea, although he himself had suffered from such abuses under South Korean regimes.

When Korea seems confronted with disputes with other states, there is an understandable but intense response to support the orthodox Korean position, and in some cases to manipulate information to that purpose. There is no definitive general study on this phenomenon, but in a speech prepared for this conference, Stephen Rounds[26] explored press reporting on the sale of new fighter aircraft to the South Korean government, maintaining that these and other inaccurately reported stories contribute to anti-American sentiment.

> The point is that the problem [press bias] is cumulative: the one-sided press reporting forms and drives a vicious circle, in which reporters who are persuaded of U.S. ill will or arrogance fight back by slanting their stories. These stories are read by others, who come to believe that they, too, should contribute to "the national interest" by creating or passing on one-sided reporting. Thus, a significant part of Korean anti-Americanism has probably been caused by the fact that Koreans carry with them a whole inaccurate history of the details of our relationship because so much of the coverage of day-to-day events has been inaccurate. The accumulated misperceptions it has communicated form a heavy burden on the relationship.

The dilemma for any Korean administration, if a close relationship with the United States is deemed a priority, is how to encourage accurate, balanced reporting on the inevitable disputes that will arise in the future without engaging in press control or censorship.

Professor Auh Taik Sup[27] distinguished between two tiers of anti-American sentiment: those sentiments (diffused, emotional, passive) that concern hegemony, egocentrism, materialism, and so forth, and those that reflect an ideologically oriented and cognitive reaction to the United States, its ideals, politics, and dominance. His findings were that both were ambivalent, polarized, and evolutionary, having progressed from prevalence in smaller groups to a broader public. The Korean media can set the agenda, give primary focus to an issue, and frame the material, thus strongly influencing public opinion. In using the Status of Forces Agreement (SOFA) case as an example, he concludes that the media coverage was episodic using a single (negative) frame, and a "falsifiable consensus emerges when debate is curtailed, making it extremely difficult even to describe the situation in a different way," and that "its problem definition, casual interpretation, moral evaluation, and treatment—the spiral of silence resides not only in the minds of the general public but in the news media and the working journalists." Thus, there is a belief that the SOFA is not only unfair to Korea but is harsher than similar U.S. agreements with Germany and Japan.

The role of other media should not be ignored. According to a January 2001 survey, 74 percent of the population got its news from television, 13 percent from newspapers, and 8 percent from the Internet. However, the credibility of these media was newspapers, 17 percent; television, 75 percent; radio, 5 percent; and Internet, only 3 percent.[28]

The role of the U.S. media in portraying anti-American sentiments should also not be ignored. The American media have certainly played up Korean discontent with U.S. policies and graphically portrayed it by reporting on demonstrations and through "investigative journalism," such as the television program *Sixty Minutes*. The U.S. media, supported by administration officials from John Foster Dulles in the 1950s to President George W. Bush, have had a "binary" approach to foreign policy—"If you are not for us you are against us"—thus exacerbating the differences that are inevitable in any bilateral relationship where national interests are concerned.

Democracy, Human Rights, and the United States

If there is one area in which, according to popular American impressions, the United States should be given credit by Koreans, it is that of encouraging democracy and human rights. Americans perceive this as part of their core values and have institutionalized this approach with a bureau devoted to it within the Department of State. Yet from a Korean vantage point, that is not how many Koreans feel. College students, an obviously volatile group, believe that the United States has had a negative effect on human rights (41.9 percent compared to 22.5 percent), and an even more intensely negative effect on democratization (60.2 percent believed it to be negative while only 10.1 percent thought it positive).[29] Clearly the perception has been that the United States has been more supportive of dictatorships than of democracy because U.S. objectives in Korea have been, in priority order: security, an economic "level playing field," and finally democracy. This disparity of views on such a primordial value as democracy is one core element of tensions in the relationship.

Korean writers have downplayed the important role of the United States in effectively denying to the Korean government the potential use of its own military, through imposition of martial law or garrison decree, during the massive public demonstrations in the spring of 1987, resulting in the June 29 political liberalization. At the same time, although U.S. influence has been important for both democratization and improvement in human rights, this has not been because of official policies but rather informal and unofficial U.S. influence on the society as a whole.[30]

Categorization of Crises and Events

It may be helpful to consider those specific incidents that have materially contributed to the rise of anti-American sentiment. Some of these were events that stirred the official community and have led to a sense of distrust of the United States, thus providing a milieu in which anti-American sentiment could build more broadly, and some have been those affecting the public. Of course, the boundaries in any such delineation are often indistinct.

State concerns about the reliability of the United States as an ally began with the armistice itself, which President Syngman Rhee opposed. The coup of 1961 led to an intense period of mutual mistrust between the United States and General Park Chung Hee, since Park overthrew a popularly elected government supported by the United States. It was a rift that was never completely overcome although the United States perceived that it needed Park for security considerations. The Guam (or Nixon) Doctrine of 1969 precluding the United States from fighting further land wars in Asia, further exacerbated the feeling that the United States could not be trusted or relied upon in an emergency. This resulted in the buildup of Korea's armament industries (and a nuclear capacity that the United States effectively vetoed in 1974) so as to avoid too great a dependence on the United States. Trade disputes involving manufactured goods after that time were continuous as the United States tried to open a highly protected Korean domestic market and the United States accused Korea of dumping goods into the United States.[31] Subsequently, the requirements to open Korean rice and beef markets have created a continuing storm of anti-American demonstrations in the rural sector, which, although small, is quite vocal and has a disproportionate influence (as in Japan) in the legislature. The Kwangju rebellion created both state and popular distrust of the United States, but with different interpretations of U.S. culpability, while the bilateral negotiations between North Korea and the United States leading to the Agreed Framework of 1994 created palpable unease in official Korean circles at the highest levels. The financial crisis of 1997 and the subsequent International Monetary Fund (IMF) conditionality was interpreted by the state and the people as surrogate requirements of the United States, which was seen as intent on buying up Korean businesses and industries at bargain prices, thus creating an explosion of popular nationalism.[32] Some of these incidents may be attributed to a generalized antiforeign sentiment rather than focusing directly on the United States. For example, in a survey conducted in July 1997, just when the Asian financial crisis hit Thailand but had not yet affected Korea, a large number of Koreans did not want any foreigners to own Korean land or businesses, and an even larger number did not want them to own larger parcels of land or larger businesses—just the conditions the IMF imposed on Korea a half-year later.[33]

To these more structural problems have been added issues connected with military incidents involving U.S. personnel. They have included environmental waste issues, a controversial U.S. military firing range, and personal assaults, culminating in the tragic deaths of the two Korean middle-school girls in June 2002 and the subsequent stir to revise the SOFA and the effect on the December 2002 Korean presidential election. The revelation of the Nogun-ri Korean War massacre of South Korean civilians by U.S. troops created a major controversy, even though it was the Associated Press, through detailed investigative journalism, that uncovered the story, which then was picked up by the Korean press. In many of these incidents, two cultural-legal Korean-American differences continue to contribute to anti-American sentiment. The first is the issue of an apology—required in Korean customary usage in a moral sense but which, in official U.S. circles, seems to carry the stigma of guilt and responsibility, including financial liability, and is thus eschewed by lawyers. The second is that someone should be responsible for tragedies and thus take the blame, even if it is only symbolic. This is not American practice, and thus the acquittal of the two U.S. soldiers in 2002 was seen as unfair and inappropriate from a Korean standpoint.

The latest polling available (May–June 2003) indicates that "South Korean dislike of the United States was deeper than [that of] any other U.S. ally": 58 percent said they were disappointed that Iraq did not put up more resistance to the United States, and only 24 percent support the U.S. war on terrorism.[34]

"Anti-Koreanism" in the United States

As a result of Korean protests against the United States in 2002 and the very visible burning of American flags and vigils around the U.S. Embassy, and in spite of large pro-American counter rallies, there has grown up in some circles in the United States a counter, anti-Korean sentiment.[35] If there is little "anti-Americanism" in Korea, then there certainly is no "anti-Koreanism" in the United States, although anti-Korean sentiment is apparent. Although these incidents were seen by Koreans as peripheral to the message being conveyed of concern and generally not of a violent nature, these events had important repercussions in the United States. Beginning with the second Bush administration and the insistence of President Kim Dae Jung on coming to Washington in March 2001, before the Bush team was really ready to receive him and against the administration's advice, trouble began. The resulting summit was disastrous, and since then differences in approaches to North Korea have led to a mistrust of the South Korean position on peninsular relations in Washington, especially in the Defense Department, which ironically has been the traditional bastion of pro-Korean sentiment and the alliance. Anti-Korean attitudes reside essentially in that department. Since the tragedy of September 11, 2001, the United States is far less tolerant of anti-American demonstrations of any sort.

The United States wants to be loved and respected, and the result has been a number of newspaper articles by well-known conservative commentators that if the South Koreans are against our presence, we should withdraw all our forces from Korea. A slanted segment of the widely popular television program *Sixty Minutes* featured anti-American demonstrations without analysis and probably affected a large element of the American public, who always thought of Korea (if they did at all) as a loyal and essentially subservient ally. Although anti-American sentiment would be applauded by a small segment of the Korean public, no government and the majority of the Korean people have never wanted the precipitous withdrawal of U.S. forces from Korea.[36] That would create a sense of abandonment and intensify the vulnerability Koreans have historically felt over their position in East Asia.

Organization of This Volume

This volume is organized into the following sections: global, regional, and comparative perspectives; anti-American sentiments as structural phenomena; alliance perspectives; civil society perspectives; and economic and legal dimensions. It thus proceeds from the general to the regional and then to specifically Korean issues.

Global, Regional, and Comparative Perspectives

John Ikenberry reviews the anti-American phenomenon in a global perspective. The U.S. order was built on force and consent, and thus legitimacy, but the United States has shifted away from legitimacy and more toward force. He notes the disparity in power between the United States and other nations, but considers that there was little in the U.S. environment to discipline its exercise of power. He points out that the United States was experiencing a "legitimacy deficit and anti-Americanism in East Asia," western Europe, and other areas, noting the need to distinguish between foreign anger and disapproval of U.S. policies and the United States itself. Majorities around the world, even in some democracies, do not like American ideas and values, but the United States does not appear to be willing to play by international rules. U.S. unilateralism seems out of control, and the United States is viewed as "undisciplined" and as a "rogue state." Ikenberry notes three types of U.S. power: (1) system-structural power (capitalism, democracy—manifest in the basic logic of globalization); (2) political-institutional-hegemonic power—people see the presence of the U.S. military and economic power as intrusive; and (3) unilateralism and neoimperialism. Ikenberry believes that the new strategy "attaches little value to international stability." This situation is not irreversible, as the United States could become a benign hegemon and work with multilateral institutions. "The United States must rediscover those elements that help reconcile American power with stable and legitimate international order. . . . There are aspects in the American experience—institutions and strategies—that can help the United States legitimate its power and reduce the instabilities that are manifest as anti-Americanism."

Kent Calder focuses on the Japanese Peace Treaty signed in San Francisco in 1951. The interrelated politicomilitary and economic commitments between the United States and its Pacific allies gave the United States a security role in exchange for opening its markets to the newly developing economies, especially Japan. With the rise of Japan and improved relations with China and the end of the Cold War, disaffection with the political aspects of the relationship (SOFA, etc.) became apparent. Quoting the Pew Memorial Trust survey, Calder notes that the United States had the least favorable rating in Korea among other Asian states: Philippines, Japan, Vietnam, and Indonesia. Most Koreans were against the war of terrorism; they believe that the United States considers others least and is little concerned with the threat of nuclear weapons. "Korean attitudes toward the United States, in sum, seem to be substantially more critical than those of Asians generally, resembling most closely those of Islamic nations like Indonesia. . . . Korea's differences at the popular level with the United States, it can be argued, are the psychological residue of the San Francisco System." It was designed to "enrich and stabilize Japan, [Korea's] longtime nemesis. Not surprisingly, that systematic orientation stirs resentment in Korea." Important as well has been the rise of competitive party politics in Korea and the growth of civil society—most importantly the increase in protest activism from the early 1980s until the early 1990s—more than twice as rapid as in Japan. Also, the increasing autonomy of local government in Korea has no parallel in East Asia. Pressures for revision of the San Francisco system are likely to continue. "Nationalism and democratization are eroding the San Francisco System." To keep the alliances, do we need to eliminate the bases? Korea resembles the Philippines more than Japan. The civil society movement is important in both the Philippines and Korea, where it has exploded, and far more than in Japan.

Brad Glosserman reviews anti-Americanism in Japan. He considers it as taking three forms: left, right, and "opportunistic." Marxist thought was ideologically important since before World War II. Right-wing anti-Americanism obviously predates World War II and was sharpened by U.S. attempts to delink the present from Japan's imperial past. The Japanese charge that Japan's economic troubles were caused by the United States. But the roots go back to the opening of Japan; there is an often overlooked but critical tension between modernism and traditional Japanese norms. This has been glossed over. Placing the blame for World War II on a small number of people allowed the Japanese to disclaim responsibility. The right wing has argued that the United States forced Japan to go to war. The perception of U.S. influence in Japanese policy making is important; *gaiatsu* (foreign pressure, usually American) can be used by Japanese for their own ends. There are specific triggers of anti-Americanism, such as the Okinawa rape case and the sinking of the Ehime Maru. Important in Japanese perceptions have been the shocks resulting from the U.S. failure to consult with the Japanese on critical policy issues. "There is speculation that such tactics have been deliberately used to 'manage' the relationship; if so, it has been a terribly short-sighted approach." There is increased impatience in Japan with the way the alliance has been managed. Special problems are associated with the overwhelming presence of U.S. forces in Okinawa, which disproportionately bears the burden within Japan for the U.S. presence. Okinawa has been the poorest prefecture of Japan, discriminated against by other Japanese, yet in part it is dependent on the U.S. forces for its economic well-being. It may be significant that anti-American sentiment in the Philippines seems to have diminished with the removal of the U.S. bases from that region.

Yoichi Funabashi discusses the new dynamics of anti-Americanism in Japan, which, before World War II, was the most anti-American country in the world. However, after its defeat, it became the most pro-American country. Japan became a "good loser" while the United States was the "good winner," supplying food during the occupation in time of need, preserving the symbol (not the power) of the old order by retaining the emperor, and supporting the "stake-holding" peoples (such as women, labor, and farmers) by ensuring their rights. The Peace Treaty of 1951 provided an element of trust toward the United States, as it was fair and generous, but the show trials of war criminals created anti-American sentiment among some groups. One source of anti-Americanism in Japan was the resort by the United States to "hard power" rather than "soft power." The rise of economic nationalism has been directed toward the United States, the idea of a "Japan that can say no" is focused on the United States, and antiglobalization translates into anti-U.S. sentiment, although sometimes Japanese business failures are incorrectly blamed on the United States. The most serious problem between the two states is alliance management, as other states feel powerless in the face of U.S. strength. The United States plays a masculine role in the alliance while Japan plays a feminine role. The problem with the economic and alliance system is that the winner takes all, with indifference to the loser. In a sense, Japan is a model of the good loser. One way to improve relations is to increase educational exchanges, as U.S. higher education is the most advanced worldwide and is admired; the Fulbright program, for example, has sent some 7,000 Japanese to the United States and some 3,000 Americans to Japan.

In the course of the discussion, Funabashi draws attention to the differences in support for U.S. troops in Japan and Korea. U.S. forces in Japan are better housed, can often bring their families, and have better facilities; thus the level of frustration among the military seems lower and relations with local communities are generally better (except perhaps in Okinawa).

Meredith Woo-Cumings considers the issue of anti-American sentiment in the broad historical context of European anti-Semitism and concludes that the term *anti-Americanism* is inappropriate as applied to Korea. She considers the cultures too far apart to result in the "loathing" with which anti-Americanism is associated in Europe, where it has become endemic to the intellectual establishment in a number of countries. She notes that the statistical rise of anti-American sentiment coincided with the Agreed Framework with North Korea in 1994 and policies of the Bush administration, both of which gave rise to South Korean insecurity and rising apprehension that the U.S. unilateral approach to foreign policy and the use of force could jeopardize the Korean people of both the North and the South. She charges the U.S. Treasury with insisting on the breakup of "Korea Inc." in the aftermath of the Asian financial crisis of 1997 and related economic issues that negatively affected perceptions of the United States in Korea. Woo-Cumings quotes George Santayana that rejection is a form of self-assertion, and that anti-American sentiment is the obverse in the Korean case of pride in Korea's obvious accomplishments.

Ronald Meinardus reviews the German experience with anti-Americanism in a comparative analysis. Anti-American thought in Germany historically was rooted in a fearful reaction to modernity, with the United States considered by traditionalists

and conservatives alike as the heaven of modernity. After World War II, a great majority of West Germans were pro-American: although the country was defeated by the
Americans militarily, many greeted the U.S. forces as liberators. Attitudes turned
slightly more negative during the Vietnam War. Following that episode, the deployment of U.S. missiles on German soil became a controversial issue. For the first time,
sizable portions of the population perceived a cleavage between U.S. and allied interests and "national" West German interests. Today, there are strains on Iraq policy.
Still, in spite of differences on policies, 68 percent of Germans consider themselves
to be basically pro-American. The Korean and German experiences have major differences. Although both nations were divided, the division was accepted as a fait
accompli by a majority of West Germans; in Korea, the divide is considered an open
wound. The United States invested heavily in both countries—both militarily and
economically. More recently, demographic change in both states has occurred, with
the younger population tending to ignore the benefits their parents derived from U.S.
assistance and support. In South Korea, many youngsters accuse the United States of
prompting division of their country. This has never been the case in West Germany,
also for the simple reason that unification was not considered a realistic option. Korean nationalism, Meinardus argues, is stronger than German nationalism. This has
an immediate impact on the intensity of negative attitudes toward the United States.
U.S.-German relations have been structured through NATO; historically, this has al-
leviated political friction between the two states, as the governments in Bonn participated on an equal footing in most strategic decisions. On the other hand, there is no
such multilateral structure in Northeast Asia. U.S.–ROK relations are more problematic because they are reduced to the bilateral sphere, and "structurally, bilateralism
has opened the door to the accusation of unilateralism." In reviewing Anti-American
sentiments in both countries, one must take into account the evolution of democracy:
today, fortunately, the Germans and the South Koreans are entitled to elect their governments freely. Thus, political leaders have to take their people's attitudes into consideration as they devise their policies.

Structural and Strategic Phenomena

Bruce Cumings concentrates on "structural" aspects of anti-American sentiment, including the division of Korea, the foreign bases that are part of an "archipelago" of
such bases around the world, the Combined Forces Command, the unexamined assumptions and history that are now being revisited and reinterpreted, and racism. In
his view, there is a difference between "anti-Americanism" and "anti-American policies." The question was asked whether Koreans were more critical of the United States
now in contrast to the 1980s and previous periods, or whether they now are simply
more able to express their opinions. The 1980s may have been the high point of
virulent anti-American sentiment, but evidently the policies of the Bush administration have exacerbated this feeling. During the Clinton administration, anti-American
sentiment (e.g., the 1997 Asian financial crisis) was against globalization, of which

the United States was the surrogate. The Koreans now see the United States, under the Bush administration, as standing against Korean integration, and in their view the United States has botched Korean policy. But what does anti-American sentiment mean? It is usually about policies, not people, and the demonstrations in Seoul concerning the trial of the soldiers who were acquitted in the deaths of the two Korean middle-school girls were well organized and peaceful, with older participants as well as young ones. Certain U.S. responses to these protests (e.g., Richard Allen) seem petulant, condescending, and surprised, as when calling for the withdrawal of U.S. troops. Yet the troops were there to perpetuate the division of the peninsula and to constrain and restrain South Korea as well. The United States does not like the idea of the two Koreas being alone together. Racism, certainly evident in earlier dealings with Korea, is still evident, even if expressed in different forms, such as "All Koreans are. . . ." Important also has been the growth of civil society.

Victor Cha considers five structural trends in the forward presence of the United States and its impact on anti-American sentiment, suggesting that changes in the U.S. force composition stationed in Korea are inevitable. These five trends are as follows: (1) the forward presence of the United States has successfully deterred threats (yet noting that such forces need to be far more flexible); (2) the allies of the United States in the region are far stronger than they once were; (3) democratic and social changes have taken place, which will affect policies, especially since the population is also younger; (4) there have been important changes in U.S. military technology, with the development of U.S. capacity to conduct long-range and precision military strikes; and (5) there have been exogenous shocks and unintended consequences on the peninsula. These include the Sunshine Policy, the effect of the worsening perceptions of the U.S. presence, and the "failure" of the Sunshine Policy, which has led to the United States being used as a scapegoat for this failure. It is unfortunate that there is no serious dialogue on this, but simply buck-passing. There is thus a weakening of the foundations of the ROK–U.S. alliance. A broader vision of the alliance is needed, such as regional stability and facing the issue of quasicontainment of China or peacekeeping in the region. After unification, the geopolitical landscape will not be favorable to the United States, as Korea will seek accommodation with China and more tensions will develop between China and Japan. A demographically older Japan will be more uncomfortable with the U.S. relationship, and this will go against U.S. interests. This sequence of events may lead to regional nuclear proliferation, and the United States should try to shape the outcome differently. The ROK–Japan–U.S. alliance should go beyond the Cold War and stand for something positive—have a broader meaning (such as antiterrorism, etc.). There are four requirements for revision of the alliances and forces. These are (1) a flexible presence; (2) a rapidly deployable force; (3) a credible force; (4) and an unobtrusive force. U.S.–ROK relations are "a train wreck in slow motion"—there is no connection in policies. Korea is not anti-American, but it has a solidarity and heightened nationalism, and opinions there are different from those in the United States. The ROK people are not concerned about the North Korean nuclear issue. The two sides do not meet. The United States sees images in North

Korea and considers them real, while South Koreans see the images and believe them to be marginal and insignificant. Rethinking the alliance thus is necessary.

Chung-in Moon discusses the spectrum of attitudes toward the United States, noting that it is nothing new in Korean history. He discusses the changing attitudes toward the United States—*banmi* to *sungmi*—anti- and worship. There is a dualistic phenomenon: "Many South Koreans show a very strong pro-American attitude in person, but in public or in a group, they take an anti-American tone." There are three dimensions to the issue: (1) left-wing ideology, especially in the 1980s; (2) attitudes that fluctuate along with events and changing circumstances (e.g., trade); and (3) rejection of American exeptionalism, justified "in the name of national security" (meaning that the United States need not obey Korean rules and norms). Anti-Americanism "has become more salient than before." The factors prompting this are unilateralism and cultural insensitivity; emerging disjuncture between power and status; and rejection of or opposition to pro-American forces, "who monopolized material and positional values in (Korean) society"; lack of knowledge and understanding of the United States. There is a strong rejection of U.S. unilateralism, especially the Bush administration's policies. Korea needs the status comparable to its economic power. There is a growing feeling within Korea against Korean societal elements that monopolize power through U.S. connections (such as U.S. education). At the same time, Koreans look for scapegoats, such as the United States. The United States has not played the role of "honest broker" in the North-South relationship. The current problems could have been avoided. There are no easy solutions; one cannot get rid of anti-American attitudes, they are part of the Korean psyche. But we can minimize them and maximize pro-U.S. or know-U.S. attitudes. There is a need for centers for American studies, which are lacking in Korea at the university level.[37]

Alliance Perspectives

Chung Min Lee feels that South Korea was in a state of deep strategic denial about North Korea. North Korean key behavior has not changed since the start of the Sunshine Policy, and he deplores the payment of $200 million to North Korea to facilitate it. The December 19 Korean presidential election was a cultural revolution with important implications for policies toward the United States and North Korea that Roh has to deal with. Roh has become a combination of Tony Blair and Perón. The Korean people, however, are looking for a new security architecture. The anti-Americanism is not a majority view but rather that of those in power, who see the United States, not North Korea, as responsible for the lack of unification. The Sunshine Policy has not yet produced behavioral change in North Korea. If such changes were to have taken place, they would have already happened. There has been a new, cumulative rise in Northeast Asia: China, a nuclear North Korea, and a resurgent Japan. There is also a new strategic awakening in East Asia of which the United States is not aware. There are three key choices for South Korea: (1) universal values; (2) autonomy or independence; and (3) a unified Korea. But what kind of future do they envision? Some South Koreans believe that if the North has nuclear weapons, they will someday belong to the South and thus are not something to worry about. This is the time to make critical policy choices. There should be a 2 + 2 meeting (ROK–U.S.), including both defense officials and diplomats, and a more precise definition of issues should result. The ROK may choose to live with a nuclear North Korea and will sweep it under the carpet, as the North has tied its nuclear program to regime survival.

> Although the top political leaderships continue to emphasize the importance of sustaining the alliance even after Korean unification, neither Seoul nor Washington has paid enough attention to building a new strategic framework. In part, this absence stems from the persistence of the North Korean threat—albeit in more varied forms than before; but it would be a mistake to assume that the alliance can be sustained without paying greater attention to articulating a new and more credible strategic framework.

Kim Sung-han feels that South Koreans consider inter-Korean relations as between brothers (and thus closer), while they view South Korean-U.S. relations as between friends. Before the Pyongyang summit, there was competition between North Korea and the United States versus South Korea and the United States; now, South Korea and the United States are competing over North Korea. When President Clinton left office, 50 percent of South Koreans did not feel the North to be a threat, so the South Korean people could not understand President Bush's policy toward the North, and they see any preemptive strike against the North's nuclear facilities as leading to another Korean War. South Koreans believe that the United States wants North Korea to remain a "rogue state" so as to justify the U.S. missile defense system. The most recent origin of anti-Americanism arose after the June 2000 summit and was also exacerbated by the inequity of relations under the SOFA, the "axis of evil" remark, and so on. The United States believes that the ROK–U.S. alliance faces two major challenges: the North's attempts to drive a wedge between the United States and the South, and the South's growing anti-American sentiment and potential demands for troop withdrawal. South Korean people have romantic nationalistic feelings toward peninsular relations, and the United States should then be relegated to observer status.

James Feinerman considers the SOFA a cardinal point of contention and calls for its continuing revision. The SOFA covers U.S. forces at the ninety U.S. bases in Korea, and it is uncertain whether SOFA will continue in its present form. In perspective, the United States has coerced countries through security concerns into accepting U.S. concepts of common law and the U.S. legal order for U.S. military personnel overseas. There are strong congressional pressures within the United States to keep U.S. citizens under the U.S. legal system. Criminal jurisdiction is the highest-profile legal issue for U.S. military personnel, but others may be important, such as customs, labor, civil claims, environmental issues, sanitation, and so on. U.S. soldiers committing crimes on or off duty are not tried in Korean courts. Perhaps there is a need for more professional soldiers and not relying on a volunteer army.

Hahm Chaibong traces the historical roots of anti-American sentiment but first concentrates on those aspects of the relationship that bring the two nations closer together: education, religious influences, values, and economic systems. Hahm noted the festivities associated with the 2002 World Cup that gave Koreans a sense of pride in their national accomplishments, not only in sports. Strong nationalist sentiment was evident in the event and its aftermath. The end of the Cold War and the fall of the Soviet Union resulted in one of the rationales of the strong American connection to disappear—a midterm cause of the rise of anti-American sentiment. Revisionist arguments and ultranationalist sentiments were more widespread and could be disseminated along with the democratization movement in Korea in 1987. The long-term issues relate to the perceived threats to Korean-ness. "(In this sense), anti-Americanism . . . is an expression of a deep-seated sense of anxiety regarding Korean identity. It is a reaction to yet another chapter in their history where Koreans are forced to adapt to a new civilization." Thus, anti-American sentiment is "part of an effort to articulate a sense of national and cultural identity on the part of Koreans, who have had to go through major civilizational shifts."

Civil Society Perspectives

Katharine Moon considers the rise of civil society and the American military presence. She charges that anti-American sentiments were not new, that these were not Korean-made issues but were regional in character. *Anti-Americanism* is probably a misnomer—*America bashing* is probably a better term. This sentiment is both organized and unorganized, and in part based on a U.S.-Korean relationship that is fraught with violence, tensions, and frustrations. Why does this occur now and with such intensity? Democratization is one factor. Another is the dichotomy between the wealthy Koreans and the camp towns around the bases—both the U.S. and ROK governments have treated them with neglect. Decentralization has affected these towns, which now have more authority and can press their grievances; there are newly empowered citizenries around the bases. A late-1990s law required transparency in local autonomy and allowed claims if such transparency were not provided. If there is transparency within the Korean government, should there not be the same in the administration of American bases? There is a need to take local grievances seriously; they have been built up over time against the bases and against the local police. There are now attempts to get redress for past problems, exemplified in Korea in the "comfort women" movement, the Nogun-ri incident of U.S. troops killing Korean civilians in the Korean War, and Kwangju (as in the case of the black community in the United States and slavery). The growth of Korean civil society has been important, and through its growth and contacts, social capital has developed in the peripheral areas in conjunction with those in Seoul. The anti-American movement has brought these groups together for the first time. The legacy of authoritarianism lives on in the anti-American movement. The United States demands gratitude for past assistance, but this has no place in Korea.

Scott Snyder, in an oral presentation, considered that anti-American sentiment as a proxy for the discussion of the role of class and access in Korean society and the elites and elitism that have access to the United States through education and other benefits. The United States is seen as favoring elite interests by its association with the establishment. By some, Lee Hoi Chang was considered a puppet of such groups. Although the United States may see itself as promoting democracy, Koreans may see it differently. This problem is fostered by the Korean education system and overcompetition, where the top elite use their financial advantages to continue elite status via the U.S. education system. English is required, multinational corporations offer good jobs, and privileges divide Korean society. Is the Koreanness of those associated with the Americans questioned, and what are the implications of this? In the past (when economic opportunities were limited), U.S. bases were magnets for economic opportunity, but times have changed. To get a U.S. visa, one must demonstrate financial assets, and all this creates jealousies. The rich-poor gap has widened since 1997, and there is likely to be less mobility as the elite continues its domination.

Uichol Kim approaches the issue of anti-American sentiment through a psychological survey of middle school, university, and adult populations. His findings indicate that there is a negative view of the American people and society and their influence on Korea and the world. The current results challenge the commonly held assumptions that the younger generation will have a positive view of the United States and emulate its values and norms. In terms of attitude, junior high school students had the most negative view of the United States and its influence on Korea; university students were mixed; and older students were least negative. Most had had no contact with the United States, but those with more contact had a more balanced view. "It is likely that Korean respondents have developed anti-American sentiments largely from the media and through informal contacts." First, these sentiments are susceptible to change, since they are not based on accurate information or personal contacts. Second, since people are likely to process information to be consistent with their beliefs, anti-American sentiment will likely increase. Third, "the anti-American sentiment in South Korea is driven by neither ideology nor tradition. They reflect a growing confidence of the younger generation in themselves and their nation." Fourth, Koreans want to maintain a strong bilateral relationship. They are angry because they feel neglected, abused, and betrayed by the unilateral policies and decisions of the United States. For some, the anger has turned into hostility, since Koreans are accused of being irrational and ungrateful, as evidenced by the U.S. threat to withdraw its troops from South Korea. In order to reduce anti-American sentiment, Koreans must be listened to, since they and Americans often view reality differently, in terms of different cultural assumptions. With family reunions, the evil image of North Korea has partly been transformed, and the anti-Japanese movement is over. Koreans view the United States as a superpower and feel themselves to be victims, especially with the Bush administration's policies toward North and South Korea. They are motivated to be closer to the United States, but existing structural barriers (such as the sheer difficulty of obtaining a U.S.

visa), psychological barriers (such as the perceived injustice of the death of two young girls), and perceived U.S. unilateralism are fueling anti-American sentiments. The recommendation is to provide more accurate information to Koreans about the United States using existing media, and especially educational institutions. Allowing Koreans to travel and study in the United States (by providing nonvisa exemption status) and further strengthening the bilateral ties would be the most effective means for modifying Korea's anti-American sentiments.[38]

William Watts's presentation is based on survey data on Korean attitudes toward the United States. Roh Moo Hyun, the newly elected president of the Republic of Korea, faces a major problem that he surely neither wants nor needs: a rising tide of anti-Americanism that has assumed proportions previously unseen on the Korean peninsula. There has been an enormous negative shift in views toward the United States. China is regarded as the most important country for Korea in the next ten years, replacing the United States. The United States is regarded as the principal beneficiary of the ROK–U.S. relationship. Security is most important to the Koreans. The problems with the United States involve hegemony, unilateralism, creating dependency status for Korea, the "axis of evil" remark of President Bush, and lack of attention to other countries. Although the United States is respected in some fields, such as science and technology, Koreans are against the war on terrorism and the missile shield, but they do not want the U.S. troops to withdraw at this time. U.S. opinion is generally favorable to South Korea, although if defending the South from a North Korean attack were to fall on the United States alone, the U.S. public would be against it, while those considered informed would strongly favor it.

William Drennan refers to the Kwangju incident of May 1980 as the "tipping point" in anti-American sentiment. He details the problems connected with negotiating with the Korean government of Chun Doo Hwan, and the important distinction between the "command" (under Koreans) and "operational control" (under Americans) of forces under the Combined Forces Command. He distinguishes between Kwangju the event and Kwangju the myth. "In the eyes of many Koreans today, the U.S. was the 'wire puller' behind Kwangju and therefore bears ultimate responsibility. Kwangju was not caused by U.S. manipulation. In one sense, it was not 'caused' at all; it 'happened.'" Unless and until Koreans recognize that "Kwangju was about Koreans killing Koreans . . . the United States will remain the scapegoat, the ROK–U.S. alliance will remain hobbled, and the ghosts of May 1980 will continue to haunt Korean society." Although the legal responsibility for Kwangju rested clearly with the Koreans, did the United States have a moral responsibility to protect the Kwangju citizenry from the Korean government?

Brent Choi feels that the problem is not anti-Americanism, but "anti-baseism," exacerbated by a generational shift in Korea and concern over the Bush administration's policies toward North Korea and the treatment of Kim Dae Jung by President Bush at their summit in Washington. The wounds Korea suffered as a result of the 1997 financial crisis and declines in the stock market were overcome by the national pride illustrated at the World Cup. These may have been the largest demonstrations in Korea since Sam Il (the March 1, 1919, independence movement). Korea (North and South) are viewed as a family, and have different concepts of law; in Korea, someone is always guilty and intent is not as important as in the West. The United States should understand that the generational shift in Korea is more important than the demonstrations. The Pyongyang summit humanized Kim Jong Il. We are witnessing the signification of Korea as the South moves further from the United States. Sensitivity toward Korea is critical and was exemplified by the head of the American Chamber of Commerce, whose language and manner stopped demonstrations against that institution.

Economic Dimensions

Dennis McNamara, in considering economic issues, analyzes the changes in identity issues of the company, the state, and the people (labor and consumers) through analysis of the automobile industry as foreign firms began to participate in it. "Borders give identities. Globalization undermines existing borders but also stimulates emergence of boundaries." He noted the importance of the auto industry in terms of employment and in the downstream industries; the Korean automotive industry as a 'full-set' industry, producing all elements of the machines. There has been strong state intervention, controlled labor, and encouraged consumption. There is strong consumer nationalism. "Transitions in Korean auto manufacturing provide a window on the reconstitution of social capital. . . . The study comes to a focus in solidarity and flexibility, testing the borders of closure to permit flexibility yet solidarity and identity." The chapter raises the issues of foreign (i.e., U.S.) investment in prestigious Korean firms and such actions in relation to identity, national sentiment, and antiforeign feeling without reaching a specific conclusion.

Notes

1. Signed in 1953 and ratified in 1954.
2. A cloud hung over that summit when it was revealed in 2003 that President Kim Dae Jung authorized a payment of some $500 million to the North in relation to the summit.
3. Kim Seung-Hwan, "Anti-Americanism in Korea," *Washington Quarterly* (Winter 2002–3).
4. Personal interview, Seoul, June 2003.
5. Personal interview, Seoul, June 2003.
6. When I wrote an op-ed for a Korean paper on this subject in the mid-1990s, I had a personal telephone call from the foreign minister complaining about my raising such an issue.
7. See, for example, David I. Steinberg, *Stone Mirror: Reflections on Contemporary Korea* (Norwalk, CT: EastBridge, 2002). Specifically see "On Rising Anti-American Sentiment" (pp. 251–56). This is a collection of selected op-ed columns that have appeared in the *Korea Times* since 1995 under the title "Stone Mirror." See the bibliography at the end of this chapter for a list of the more salient publications on this subject as they relate to Korea.
8. In East Asia, China traditionally had the "soft power," being the cultural attraction at the center of that world. It was aptly known as the Central Kingdom. The United States has in the past century played a similar role, and in part the ambivalence toward the United States is a

product of the clash of the soft power and hard power that the United States obviously has, and the growth of nationalism in Korea.

9. See Chapter 5.

10. James W. Ceaser, "A Genealogy of Anti-Americanism," *Public Interest*, no. 152 (Summer 2003).

11. Thomas Thornton, "Preface," *The Annals of the American Academy of Political and Social Science* 497 (May 1988): 9–19.

12. Alvin Z. Rubinstein and Donald E. Smith, "Anti-Americanism in the Third World," in *Annals of the American Academy of Political and Social Science* 497 (May 1988): 35–45.

13. Ceaser, "A Genealogy of Anti-Americanism."

14. Donald N. Clark, "Bitter Friendship: Understanding Anti-Americanism in South Korea," in Donald N. Clark, ed. *Korea Briefing 1991* (Boulder, CO: Westview Press, 1991). On the growing trend of Koreans criticizing other Koreans for being too pro-American, see David I. Steinberg, "On *Mikguk Nemsae*," *US-Korea Tomorrow* 6, no. 2 (April 2003). In December 2002, "Never had so many people exhibited neutral sentiments or feared being ostracized by others for holding pro-American sentiments." Byung-Kook Kim, "An Anti-American Americanized Generation? The Paradox of Democratization, Globalization and Antiterrorism in Korea," paper presented at the Weatherhead Center for International Affairs and the East Asia Institute, Harvard University, February 14–15, 2003.

15. Hyun Sying-il, "Anti-Americanism in Korean Student Movement," in Tae-Hwan Kwak and Seong Hyong Lee, eds. *Forty Years of Korea-U.S. Relations, 1948–1988* (Seoul: Kyung Hee University Press, 1990).

16. John Kie-chang Oh, "Anti-Americanism and Anti-Authoritarian Politics in Korea," in Ilpyong J. Kim, ed., *Two Koreas in Transition: Implications for U.S. Policy* (Rockville, MD: In Depth Books, 1998).

17. Stephen W. Linton, "Impact of Anti-American Sentiments in the ROK on the U.S.-ROK Security Alliance." Conference on the 2002 Presidential Elections in the Republic of Korea: Implications and Impacts. Asian-Pacific Center for Security Studies, Honolulu, April 2003. It was apparent in the Korean response to the 1988 Olympics held in Seoul that a very large and vocal element of the audience cheered for any opponent to any American team.

18. John Kie-chang Oh, "Anti-Americanism and Anti-Authoritarian Politics in Korea," in Ilpyong J. Kim, ed., *Two Koreas in Transition: Implications for U.S. Policy* (Rockville, MD: In Depth Books, 1998).

19. The definitive study of control and misuse of the media in Kwangju is Jae-kyoung Lee, "Anti-Americanism in South Korea: The Media and the Politics of Signification," unpublished Ph.D. dissertation, University of Iowa, 1993.

20. Ibid., p. 205.

21. Ibid., p. 51.

22. See Kyu Ho Youn, *Press Law in South Korea* (Ames: Iowa State University Press, 1966).

23. The government claimed that these papers, specifically *Chosun Ilbo*, *Dong-A Ilbo*, and *Joongang Ilbo*, which together represent some 70 percent of newspaper circulation, were evading taxes and by law had to be audited at least every five years. Whether this was true is unclear to this writer, but as one sage American correspondent quipped, "You don't get into a fight with people who buy ink by the ton." These papers were critical of president Kim's "Sunshine Policy" toward North Korea—a policy that became the hallmark of his administration.

24. Taegyu Son, "The Law of Political Libel and Freedom of the Press in the Republic of Korea and the United States," Ph.D. dissertation, University of North Carolina, 2002.

25. In one conference, I was asked by a Korean institution to write a paper on the role of the American press in improving relations on the Korean peninsula. I replied that this was a Korean, not an American, question, because from an American vantage point, there was no such

role of conforming to administration policies, while in Korea the practice has been for the media to support the state when the latter is in dispute with foreign nations.

26. Stephen Rounds, "The Korean Media and Anti-Americanism: A Case Study" [unpublished paper].

27. Auh Taik Sup, professor of mass communications, Korea University at a seminar in Seoul in 2002 on "An Overview of Korean Perceptions of the United States and U.S.-Korean Relations."

28. Personal interview, former director, KBS, Seoul, June 2003.

29. Gi-wook Shin, "South Korean Anti-Americanism: A Comparative Perspective," *Asian Survey* 2936, no. 8 (1996).

30. For a study of the U.S. role, see David I. Steinberg, "U.S. Policy and Human Rights in the Republic of Korea: The Influence of Policy or the Policy of Influence," in the U.S. Institute of Peace study on U.S. influence on human rights worldwide (forthcoming 2004).

31. Such disputes are too numerous to chronicle, but include steel: selling Hanbo Steel, Daewoo Motor, and Hynex semiconductors. Other issues were forcing U.S. cigarettes into the Korean market at the time when the United States had declared them a health hazard at home, the pricing of imported pharmaceuticals that affected the Korean health system, and so on. Other issues involved zoning for housing the U.S. Embassy in downtown Seoul. See Yang Junsok, "Anti-Americanism in Korea?" *US-Korea Tomorrow*, April 2003.

32. See Chapter 5.

33. Doh C. Shin, *Mass Politics and Culture in Democratizing Korea* (Cambridge: Cambridge University Press, 1999).

34. Kim Sung-han, "Realignment of U.S. Forces in Korea and Korean Attitudes Toward the United States," Korea–U.S. Opinion Leaders Forum, July 11–12, 2003, Washington, DC, Korea Economic Institute of America.

35. This was the subject of a talk by Dr. Curt Campbell, former deputy assistant secretary of defense, at the CSIS-Pacific Forum seminar on Korea, May 23, 2003.

36. According to Byung-Kook Kim's study "An Anti-American Americanized Generation?" the percentage of Koreans who want immediate withdrawal of U.S. troops has been constant for a dozen or so years at under 10 percent, while about 45 percent want staged withdrawals.

37. Don Oberdorfer notes that the Koreans and Americans do not talk against the U.S.–ROK alliance as such, but they do not seriously examine it either. Even President Carter did not do this in his advocacy of U.S. troop withdrawals. Some felt that Koreans wanted the United States to save them from dictatorships, which was not done because of the security priority. Although earlier Korean students were anti-American because of a radical ideology, this is not presently true. The seeds of disaffection are broadly shared, with no sense of threat from the North among the college students interviewed. Whatever the United States does, it does without the consent of Korea, and this strains the alliance to the breaking point. The United States must take account of Korean attitudes, for not to do so will affect Northeast Asia and mean the further rise of China.

38. Jae Sung-min commented that the United States emphasizes human rights, respect for property, and the rule of law, but the Korean people believe that the United States is moving away from these ideals. There is a clash of policies between the ROK. and the United States on North Korean issues, and now one must distinguish anti-U.S. sentiment from anti–Bush administration sentiment. The Bush administration is characterized as arrogant. There was no such anti-U.S. feeling during the Clinton administration, he claimed. In fact, Bush has empowered Kim Jong Il by calling him "evil." There is a Korean saying, "Even if she is ugly, dance with her."

Bibliography

Annals of the American Academy of Political and Social Science 497 (May 1988).

Auh Taik Sup. "An Overview of Korean Perceptions of the United States and U.S.-Korean Relations." Seminar, Seoul, 2002.

Bond, Douglas G. "Anti-Americanism and U.S.–ROK Relations: An Assessment of Korean Students' Views. *Asian Perspective* 12, no. 1 (1988).

Bong, Young-shik. "Anti-Americanism and the U.S.–Korea Military Alliance." In *Confrontation on the Korean Peninsula*. Washington, DC: Korea Economic Institute, 2003.

Brown, R.A. "The Development of Anti-American Attitudes Among Korean University Students: An Exploratory Survey." Research Note. *Journal of Northeast Asian Studies* (Winter 1990).

Choi, Seung-Kwan. "Policy Proposals for the Revision of the ROK-US Status of Forces Agreement." *Journal of East Asian Affairs* (Fall/Winter 2000).

Clark, Donald N. "Bitter Friendship: Understanding Anti-Americanism in South Korea." In *Korea Briefing, 1991*, ed. Donald N. Clark. Boulder, CO: Westview Press, 1991.

Hoffman, Diane. "Culture, Self, and 'Uri': Anti-Americanism in Contemporary South Korea." *Journal of Northeast Asian Studies* 12, no. 2 (1993).

Hwang, Balbina Y. "The Implications of Anti-Americanism in Korea for the Future of the U.S.-ROK Alliance." *Korea Observer* 34, no. 1 (Spring 2003).

———. "Defusing Anti-American Rhetoric in South Korea." *Heritage Foundation Backgrounder*, no. 1619, January 23, 2003.

Hyun, Syng-il. "Anti-Americanism in Korean Student Movement." In *Forty Years of Korea-U.S. Relations, 1948–1988*, ed. Tae-Hwan Kwak and Seong Hyong Lee. Seoul: Kyung Hee University Press, 1990.

Kim, Byung-Kook. "An Anti-American Americanized Generation? The Paradox of Democratization, Globalization and Antiterrorism in Korea." Paper presented at the Weatherhead Center for International Affairs and the East Asia Institute, Harvard University, February 14–15, 2003.

Kim, Jinwung. "From 'American Gentlemen' to 'Americans': Changing Perceptions of the United States in South Korea in Recent Years." *Korea Journal* (Winter 2001).

———. "The Nature of South Korean Anti-Americanism." *Korea Journal* 34, no. 1 (1994).

———. "Recent Anti-Americanism in South Korea." *Asian Survey* 29, no. 8 (1989).

Kim, Seung-Hwan. "Anti-Americanism in Korea." *Washington Quarterly* (Winter 2002–2003).

Kohut, Andrew. "Anti-Americanism: Causes and Characteristics." YaleGlobal Online Magazine. December 10, 2003.

Larson, James F. "Quiet Diplomacy in a Television Era: The Media and U.S. Policy Toward the Republic of Korea." *Political Communication and Persuasion* 7 (1990).

Lee, Aie-Rie. "Culture Shift and Popular Protest in South Korea." *Comparative Political Studies* 26, no. 1 (April 1993).

Lee, Jae-kyoung. "Anti-Americanism in South Korea: The Media and the Politics of Signification." Unpublished Ph.D. dissertation, University of Iowa, 1993.

Lee, Man-woo. "Anti-Americanism and South Korea's Changing Perception of America." In *Alliance Under Tension: The Evolution of U.S.-Korean Relations*, ed. Man-woo Lee et al. Seoul and Boulder, CO: Institute for Far Eastern Studies, Kyungnam University and Westview Press, 1988.

Lee, Sook-Jong. "The Roots and Patterns of Anti-Americanism in Korean Society: A Survey-based Analysis." Paper presented at the U.S.-Korea Academic Symposium on "The United States and South Korea: Reinvigorating the Partnership." Asia/Pacific Research Center, Stanford University, October 23–24, 2003.

Lee, Won-sup. "Changing Notion of Anti-Americanism." *Korea Focus* 5, no. 1 (1997).

Linton, Stephen W. "Impact of Anti-American Sentiments in the ROK on the U.S.–ROK Security Alliance." Conference on the 2002 Presidential Elections in the Republic of Korea: Implications and Impacts. Asian-Pacific Center for Security Studies, Honolulu, April 2003.

Liu, J., and R. Hughes. "Growing Resentment. The Rise of Anti-Americanism in South Korea." *Harvard International Review* (Fall 1995).

Manyin, Mark. "South Korean Politics and Rising 'Anti-Americanism': Implications for U.S. Policy Toward North Korea." Washington, DC: Congressional Research Service (RL 31906), May 6, 2003.

Moon, Katherine H.S. "Korean Nationalism, Anti-Americanism, and Democratic Consolidation." In *Korea's Democratization*, ed. Samuel Kim. Cambridge, UK: Cambridge University Press, 2003.

Oberdorfer, Don. "Korea and the United States. Partnership Under Stress." *Korea Society Quarterly* 3, nos. 2 & 3 (Summer/Fall 2002).

Oh, John Kie-chang. "Anti-Americanism and Anti-Authoritarian Politics in Korea." In *Two Koreas in Transition: Implications for U.S. Policy*, ed. Ilpyong J. Kim. Rockville, MD: In Depth Books, 1998.

Shin, Gi-wook. "Marxism, Anti-Americanism, and Democracy in South Korea: An Examination of Nationalist Intellectual Discourse." *Positions: East Asia Cultures Critique* 3, no. 2 (1995).

———. "South Korean Anti-Americanism: A Comparative Perspective." *Asian Survey* 36, no. 8 (1996).

Shorrock, Jim. "The Struggle for Democracy in South Korea in the 1980s and the Rise of Anti-Americanism." *Third World Quarterly* (October 1986).

Snyder, Scott. "The Role of Media and the U.S.–ROK Relationship." Paper written for the Center for Strategic and International Studies, Washington, DC: 2004.

Steinberg, David I. "On *Mikguk Nemsae*." *US-Korea Tomorrow* 6, no. 2 (April 2003).

———. "U.S. Policy and Human Rights in the Republic of Korea: The Influence of Policy or the Policy of Influence." In *Implementing U.S. Human Rights Policy*, ed. Debra Liang-Fenton. Washington, DC: United States Institute of Peace Press, 2004.

Yang, Junsok. "Anti-Americanism in Korea?" *US-Korea Tomorrow* 6, no. 2 (April 2003).

U.S. Embassy Cable #7396, 12/31/85. "The Fifth Republic, President Chun, and the U.S.: The Ambassador's Reflections at the End of 1985." Declassified.

Part I

Global, Regional, and Comparative Perspectives

1

Anti-Americanism in the Age of American Unipolarity

G. John Ikenberry

Introduction

The United States is increasingly unpopular around the world. The era of good feelings about America that followed the collapse of the Berlin Wall and the end of the Cold War is over. The momentary sympathy for the United States that followed the terrorist attacks of September 11, 2001, has also passed away. Recent public opinion data gathered from dozens of countries indicate that while many people around the world admire America—its ideals and open society—they have growing misgivings about its policies and role in the world. Anti-Americanism has also become part of presidential elections in various parts of the world. Schroeder in Germany, Lula in Brazil, and Roh in South Korea—all these recent election victors drew upon themes that involved opposition to the United States and its policies.[1]

What accounts for this wave of anti-Americanism? Is it about American power or American policy? Is it a deep and inevitable outgrowth of the changing global power structure, in which the United States increasingly towers above everyone else? Or is this global anger and resentment at America a more focused reaction to current American foreign policy? How earthshaking is this recent upsurge in anti-Americanism? Is it a passing tempest in the American hegemonic teapot, or is it the prelude to a more basic fracturing of the American-led international order?

The driving forces of this global reaction to the United States are the everyday frustrations and worries that are produced by sharp power disparities between America and the rest of the world. Because of America's size, small shifts in its policy can have huge consequences for other states. At the same time, there is little in America's environment to discipline the exercise of Washington's power. If America sneezes, the rest of the world catches a cold. It is hard for the world to ignore or work around the United States regardless of the issue—trade, finance, security, proliferation, or the environment. But while the world worries about what America does next—or neglects to do—the United States needs to worry very little about what the rest of the world does. In such a benign and unchallenged environment, American foreign policy tends to be driven by domestic politics or the current policy tastes of its leaders. The sad fact is that in a world of unipolar power, Americans need to know very little about what other governments or peoples think, but foreigners must worry about the vagaries of congressional campaigns and the idiosyncratic prejudices of senate committee chairmen.

This paper argues that recent shifts in the international power structure have altered general perceptions of the United States. The American system is increasingly experiencing a "legitimacy deficit"—and anti-Americanism in East Asia, western Europe, and elsewhere is a reflection of this development. The American-led international order has always rested on a combination of force and consent; but in the eyes of many people, the balance has shifted toward force. To some extent, this development is rooted in the changing distribution of global power, and any American president would confront this new reality. But while some of today's anti-Americanism is inevitable, its character and intensity are not. American policies and postures matter.

Three considerations are important in placing current anti-Americanism in perspective. First, it is important to distinguish between foreign anger and disapproval of American policy and America itself. The enormity of American power clearly worries people around the world, but American policy can either mitigate or exacerbate these worries. American policy today—whatever its merits or justifications—is tending to exacerbate these worries.

Second, reactions to the United States vary widely around the world. Public approval of the United States is high in some regions—such as eastern Europe—and low elsewhere. This is another way of saying that American power and foreign policy are not experienced in the same way in all places. The American imperium is variously a threat and an opportunity. The United States continues to offer its European and Asian partners both markets and security protection. There continue to be overwhelming reasons for governments in Asia and Europe to work with the United States—to engage it and attempt to alter the most untoward aspects of its policies—rather than resist or balance against it.

Third, the United States is not newly powerful. It has been at the apex of world power for most of the twentieth century. There is a historical record that demonstrates how the United States can provoke anger and resentment among foreigners but also friendship and esteem. At various historical moments, the United States has been able to wrap its unrivaled power in the clothing of shared values and cooperative security—thereby eliciting support and acquiescence from other peoples and governments. There are insights in this historical record that indicate how the United States might do the same again today.

Varieties of Anti-Americanism

The most striking aspect of today's anti-Americanism is its variability. Attitudes toward the United States vary widely across countries, but these attitudes also are focused on a variety of aspects of the United States—its political system, values, and foreign policies. Untangling these complex attitudes is important in order to make sense of the magnitude and shifting character of anti-Americanism.

Recent public opinion polling by several different groups bears out this variability. In a Pew Foundation poll of forty-four countries, the findings show that there are majorities in most countries that have a favorable view of the United States: 61 percent of Germans, 63 percent of the French, and 75 percent of the British had such views—and, overall, majorities in thirty-five of the forty-four countries liked the United States. It is primarily in the Muslim world—Egypt, Pakistan, Jordan, and Turkey—that majorities dislike America.[2]

Majorities—or at least large minorities—in most western and Asian countries do not like the ideas and values that the United States spreads around the world. This finding is true even in western countries that share the same liberal democratic traditions. American political culture enshrines an antistatist individualism and laissez-faire market society, while European political traditions privilege communal liberalism and social democracy. These divergent traditions give play to more specific differences over a host of issues, such as environmental protection, regulatory policies, corporate rules, and social welfare. Others see the values disagreement hinging on religion. The United States is more prepared to embrace "traditional values"—religion, family, country—thus inclining it more toward older-style nationalism and to see the world in terms of good and evil. Europeans tend toward more "secular-rational" values. "In America," the *Economist* reports, "even technical matters become moral questions. It is almost impossible to have a debate about gun registration without it becoming an argument about the right to self-defense. In Europe, even moral questions are sometimes treated as technical ones, as happened with the controversy over stem-cell research."[3] These differences have been around for a long time, but the loss of a common Soviet threat and the rise of new transnational issues give salience to value splits.

Some see a deeper philosophical divide between the United States and the outside world—including western Europe. Francis Fukuyama argues that the disagreement is over the locus of liberal democratic legitimacy. In his view, the United States tends to see the source of democratic legitimacy in the constitutional nation-state. This, in turn, places severe limits on the willingness of the United States to cede power to higher international or supranational authority. "To the extent that any international organization has legitimacy, it is because duly constituted democratic majorities have handed that legitimacy up to them in a negotiated, contractual process. Such legitimacy can be withdrawn at any time by the contracting parties. International law and organization have no existence independent of this type of voluntary agreement between sovereign nation-states." In contrast, Fukuyama argues, Europeans tend to believe that democratic legitimacy flows more from the will of the international community. "This international community is not embodied concretely in a single, global democratic constitutional order. Yet it hands down legitimacy to existing international institutions, which are seen as partially embodying it."[4]

These differences tend to reinforce the view that the United States is not just the most powerful country in the world—but that it also sees itself as exceptional and therefore not fully willing to play by the rules that others must play by. Europe and other countries are committed to building an international order that binds individual nation-states to global rules and authority, while the United States clings to its sovereignty and the primacy of the nation-state. Europe and the rest of the world community seek a rule-based international order, and the Americans seek a world made safe for national polities. This split has potentially far-reaching implications for the myriad issues that the United States and the rest of the world struggle over—peacekeeping, the United Nations, the use of force, the World Trade Organization (WTO). These struggles are not just over divergent interests but also over philosophical principles.

America's rise as a unipolar power is a critical aspect of the recent wave of anti-Americanism. On the one hand, the Pew study did find that majorities in most countries said that a world with a rival superpower would be less safe than today's unipolar system—and this was even true for Russians.[5] But there is growing nervousness and anger in many quarters about the way the United States exercises its power. When Europeans were asked if the United States should remain the only superpower or the European Union (EU) should become a military and economic superpower like the United States, 65 percent of European respondents want the European Union to rise to superpower status. But the vast majority of these Europeans—nine out of ten—indicated that they support this as a way for Europe to better cooperate with the United States, not to compete with it.[6]

America's position as a lone superpower that can project force around the world—seemingly without restraint—is an important aspect of today's disquiet. It is revealing that in the recent public opinion polls, Europeans were willing to agree to the use of force in Iraq by a clear majority if the United Nations sanctioned the war. If it were to be unilateral American intervention, opposition to the use of force dominated. The world worries about American power—about the way it is used to promote ideas and values and about its disassociation from the rules and norms of the international community.

Three Types of American Power

Is it possible to isolate more clearly the various sources of anti-Americanism? In this regard, it is useful to distinguish between three forms or levels of American power: system-structural, political-institutional, and policy-related power. Each is a distinct type of power that offers a complex array of threats and opportunities to governments and peoples around the world. Each can be seen as a type of domination with its own type of politics.

System-Structural Power

The most basic and diffuse form of power is system-structural. This is power as manifest in the global structures of American-led capitalism and democracy. In effect, the global spread of modern western systems of politics and economics is a process in which power is being exercised. Power is manifest in two ways. One is "power through integration"—that is, power is manifest through the spread of capitalism and democracy, which displaces local and nonwestern social and political structures. As more and more parts of the world are absorbed into this American-dominated order, weak and vulnerable societies lose aspects of their autonomy and distinctiveness. The structures of global order act on them. The other way is "power through subordination"—that is, power becomes manifest as these newly integrated societies find themselves increasingly shaped and constrained by the more powerful societies at the core of the system, particularly the United States. The spread of modern western order creates new forms of superordinate and subordinate relations.

In this sense, today's domination—manifest in the extension of American-led modern western politics and economics—is only the more recent chapter in a long history of European and western domination of the non-West. The rise of western power in the last three centuries, the expansion of western ideas and practices to the rest of the world, and spread of the western state-system itself—these are all part of the longer-term process of modernization and westernization that creates the circumstances for American domination.

An analogy for this type of system-structural power might be a small shopkeeper who builds a way of life around owning and running his own store, only to be bought up and absorbed by an international conglomerate. To survive and prosper, he must give up the autonomy and security of his local store and operate as a subordinate unit within a vast corporate structure. It imposes pressures and incentives on the shopkeeper and in his resulting placement within the evolving hierarchical structure.

This form of power has been described most recently in *Empire,* by Michael Hardt and Antonio Negri. In a sweeping neo-Marxist vision of world order, the authors argue that globalization is not eroding sovereignty but transforming it into a system of diffuse national and supranational institutions—in other words, a new "empire." Whereas European imperialism was built on notions of national sovereignty and geographic cohesion, this empire has no political center or territorial limits. Nor is the new order simply a creation of American hegemony. Rather, power resides in the rules and logic of the global order itself, which in turn is rooted in the transforming capitalist system of production. The new empire has a great capacity for "oppression and destruction," but its power stems from the unrelenting logic of global capitalism more than from individual states or leaders. Part of this system-structural domination is manifest in the rise of juridical order and the merging of domestic and international law.[7]

System-structural power is what many activists have in mind when they attack American-led globalization. This power is manifest not in the policies of the International Monetary Fund (IMF) or the U.S. Department of the Treasury but in the basic logic of globalization itself. Indeed, it is the headless and diffuse character of globalization that makes it such a threat to many people. As Thomas Friedman has observed, no one is really in charge. Despite this, the United States—along with its neoliberal doctrine and the multilateral economic institutions it leads—is at the epicenter of this system and, as a result, is frequently the target for those seeking to resist structural domination.

Two types of responses are possible for peoples and societies seeking to escape this form of domination. One comprises the transnational social movements that have become organized in recent years to protest at global economic gatherings. The IMF-World Bank annual meeting, the G-8 summit, ministerial meetings of the WTO—these are events that attract this sort of grassroots protest. The specific demands of these groups are often vague and incoherent precisely because the structures of global capitalism are seen as the ultimate threat. But these social movements do express a sense that the global economy needs to be brought more fully under the democratic political control of the weak and powerless people who come under its influence.

The other response to the structural domination of American-led global capitalism is for governments to take radical steps to disengage from the system. Some have argued that the Russian and Chinese revolutions of the early and mid-twentieth century, as political movements, were driven in part by attempts to chart a nonwestern capitalist path to modernity.[8] No countries are actively attempting to do this, for understandable reasons: the costs are great and in most societies there are powerful local groups and elites that have an enormous vested interest in remaining connected to the global economy. Some countries, such as Malaysia, are seeking more selective controls on their exposure to the world economy.

Political-Institutional-Hegemonic Power

A second type of power is exercised through the American military-political system. This is a view of the United States as a global hegemonic power. This is power that is manifest as the United States builds on its postwar order-creation efforts—dating back to the 1940s—and as it extends and defends it today. The United States sees its global role as enlightened leadership—providing markets and security protection to Europe and East Asia in exchange for cooperation and partnership from countries in these regions. But peoples and governments in these regions can see the presence of American military and political power as intrusive and domineering. This expression of American power is relatively stable over the postwar era. But the circumstance in which America's extended order is perceived and experienced does change. Obviously, the end of the Cold War has altered the character of the threats that Europeans and Asians encounter—and this alters the way the United States is seen and appreciated as a security provider. Political change inside partner countries—and the turnover of generations of leaders—also alters the way American power is perceived.

The American hegemonic order is a product of two order-building exercises after World War II. One is familiar and commonly seen as the defining feature of the postwar era. This was the containment order, organized around superpower rivalry, deterrence, and ideological struggle between Communism and the free world. Truman, Acheson, Kennan, and other American foreign policy officials were responding to the specter of Soviet power, organizing a global anticommunist alliance and fashioning an American grand strategy under the banner of containment. America's strategy was to "prevent the Soviet Union from using the power and position it won . . . to reshape the postwar international order."[9] This is the grand strategy and international order that was swept away in 1991.

But there was another order created after World War II. Here American officials were working with Britain and other countries to build a new set of relationships among the Western industrial democracies. The political settlement among these countries was aimed at solving the problems of the 1930s. This was a political order whose vision was articulated in such statements as the Atlantic Charter of 1941, the Bretton Woods agreements of 1944, and the Marshall Plan speech in 1947. Unlike containment, there was not a singular statement of strategy and purpose. It was an assemblage of ideas about open markets, social stability, political integration, international institutional cooperation, and collective security. Even the Atlantic Pact agreement of 1949 was as much aimed at reconstruction and integrating Europe and binding the democratic world together as it was an alliance created to balance Soviet power.[10]

The importance of American power in the building of postwar order was most evident in the occupation and security binding of Germany and Japan. American troops began as occupiers of the two defeated states and never left. They eventually became protectors but also a palpable symbol of America's superordinate position. Host agreements were negotiated that created a legal basis for the American military presence—effectively circumscribing Japanese and West German sovereignty and made necessary in the early 1950s by a growing Cold War. These could only be achieved by binding Germany to Europe, which in turn required a binding American security commitment to Europe. Complex and protracted negotiations ultimately created an integrated European military force within NATO as well as legal agreements over the character and limits of West German sovereignty and military power. A reciprocal process of security binding lay at the heart of the emerging American-led system. John McCloy identified the "fundamental principle" of American policy in the early 1950s: that "whatever German contribution to defense is made may only take the form of a force which is an integral part of a larger international organization. . . . There is no real solution of the German problem inside Germany alone. There is a solution inside the European-Atlantic-World Community."[11]

Japan was also brought into the American hegemonic order during the 1950s. The United States took the lead in helping Japan find new commercial relations and raw material sources in Southeast Asia to substitute for the loss of Chinese and Korean markets. Japan and Germany were now twin junior partners of the United States—stripped of their military capacities and reorganized as engines of world economic growth. Containment in Asia would be based on the growth and integration of Japan into the wider noncommunist Asian regional economy—what Secretary of State Dean Acheson called the "great crescent" in referring to the countries arrayed from Japan through Southeast Asia into India. Bruce Cumings captures the logic: "In East Asia, American planners envisioned a regional economy driven by revived Japanese industry, with assured continental access to markets and raw materials for its exports."[12]

This strategy would link threatened noncommunist states along the crescent, create strong economic ties between the United States and Japan, and lessen the importance of European colonial holdings in the area. The United States would actively aid Japan in reestablishing a regional economic sphere in Asia, allowing it to prosper and play a regional leadership role within the larger American system. Japanese economic growth, the expansion of regional and global markets, and the bilateral security ties generated by the Cold War went together.

Behind the scenes, America's hegemonic position has been backed by the reserve and transaction-currency role of the dollar. The dollar's special status gave the United States the rights of "seigniorage": it could print extra money to fight wars, increase domestic spending, and go deeply into debt without fearing the pain that other states would experience if they did the same. Other countries would have to adjust their currencies, which were linked to the dollar, when Washington pursued an inflationary course to meet its foreign and domestic policy agendas. Because of its dominance, the United States did not have to raise interest rates to defend its currency, taking pressure off its chronic trade imbalances. In the 1960s, French President Charles de Gaulle understood the hidden source of American hegemony all too well and complained bitterly. But most of America's Cold War allies were willing to hold dollars for fear that a currency collapse might lead the United States to withdraw its forces overseas and retreat into isolationism.

This American-led international order has been extraordinarily successful. It has remained relatively stable and continued to expand outward to more parts of the world over the decades. It has also withstood the end of the Cold War and radical shifts in the international distribution of power. But European and Asian states within this hegemonic order are in a subordinate position. They rely on the United States more than it relies on them. They are forced to adjust to Washington more than Washington adjusts to them. Power relationships exist within even a relatively open and benign American hegemonic order.

The most evocative view of American hegemony that emphasizes its coercive and exploitive character is that of Chalmers Johnson. In *Blowback,* Johnson argues that the United States is the last imperial power and that the experience of American empire around the world has been not unlike that of past colonial peoples who have experienced empire. Asians and Europeans during the Cold War were willing to tolerate the abuses and disruptions caused by the presence of American troops, but today this is not necessary. "For any empire, including an unacknowledged one, there is a kind of balance sheet that builds up over time. Military crimes, accidents, and atrocities make up only one category on the debit side of the balance sheet that the United States has been accumulating, especially since the end of the Cold War."[13] In Johnson's view, world politics in the twenty-first century will be driven by "blowback from the second half of the twentieth century—that is, from the unintended consequences of the Cold War and the crucial American decision to maintain a Cold War posture in a post–Cold War world."[14] It is America's imperial project that is the object of growing resistance and counterattack.

There may be limits to what the United States can do when confronted with opposition to its global political-military hegemonic role—at least limits short of reducing that role and retreating back into its borders. After all, the reaction to the United States at this level is against American power—manifest in its global hegemonic order—rather than to specific American policies. But there are ways that the United States can—and has—made its hegemonic order compatible with the interests and purposes of people in other countries. The basic idea is to make American hegemony open and "user-friendly" to other countries, that is, to make American power as legitimate and acceptable as possible. This entails creating institutional limits on the exercise of indiscriminate and arbitrary power by the United States. We look more closely at this logic in the next section.

American Policy: Unilateralism and Neoimperialism

A more proximate source of anti-Americanism stems from the specific policies of the American government. At this level, people around the world are reacting not to the United States as such but to the Bush administration and its foreign policy agenda. If a different American president—with a different style and different policies—were in office, the reaction would be very different. There is some reason to suggest that some of the reactions are focused on Bush foreign policy. To be sure, the Clinton administration also provoked antagonism and anti-Americanism during its term in office. By the late-1990s, there was a great deal of foreign criticism of American neoliberalism. Secretary of State Albright's description of the United States as the world's "indispensable power" provoked Asians and Europeans to claim that the United States was acting in an increasingly arrogant and self-interested manner.[15]

But the Bush administration has provoked widespread and persistent criticism for ushering in what many people think is a basic shift in America's hegemonic orientation. In particular, the Bush administration has signaled a deep skepticism of multilateralism in a remarkable sequence of rejections of pending international agreements and treaties, including the Kyoto Protocol on Climate Change, the Rome Statute of the International Criminal Court (ICC), the Germ Weapons Convention, and the Convention on Trade in Light Arms. It also unilaterally withdrew from the 1970s Anti-ballistic Missile (ABM) treaty, which many experts regard as the cornerstone of modern arms control agreements. More recently, spurred by its war on terrorism and confrontation with Iraq, the Bush administration has advanced new and provocative ideas about the American unilateral and preemptive use of force.[16]

Unilateralism, of course, is not a new feature of American foreign policy. In every historical era, the United States has shown a willingness to reject treaties, violate rules, ignore allies, and use military force on its own. But many observers see today's unilateralism as practiced by the Bush administration as something much more sweeping—not an occasional ad hoc policy decision but a new strategic orientation. Capturing this view, one pundit calls it the "new unilateralism." "After eight years during which foreign policy success was largely measured by the number of treaties the president could sign and the number of summits he could attend, we now have an Administration willing to assert American freedom of action and the primacy of American national interests. Rather than contain power within a vast web of constraining international agreements, the new unilateralism seeks to strengthen American power and unashamedly deploy it on behalf of self-defined global ends."[17] Indeed, Richard Holbrooke, former U.S. ambassador to the United Nations, has charged that the Bush administration threatens to make "a radical break with fifty-five years of a bipartisan tradition that sought international agreements and regimes of benefit to us."[18]

The leading edge of this new unilateralism concerns the American use of force in fighting terrorism and rogue states that seek weapons of mass destruction. Here too the Bush administration has articulated an assertive, go-it-alone-if-necessary doctrine. In a June 2002 speech at West Point, President Bush put it succinctly when he said "the military must be ready to strike at a moment's notice in any dark corner of the world."[19] The United States stands alone poised to act preemptively to attack terrorists wherever they lurk. The Bush administration's recent National Security Strategy document captures the new view on the limits of concerted or multilateral use of force: "While the United States will constantly strive to enlist the support of the international community, we will not hesitate to act alone, if necessary, to exercise our right of self-defense by acting preemptively against such terrorists, to prevent them from doing harm against our people and our country."[20] The United States will invite other states to support the American antiterror campaign, but it is prepared to go forward alone.

America's "new unilateralism" has unsettled world politics. The stakes are high, because in the decade since the end of the Cold War, the United States has emerged as an unrivaled and unprecedented global superpower. At no other time in modern history has a single state loomed so large over the rest of the world. But as American power grows, the rest of the world is confronted with a disturbing double-bind. On the one hand, the United States is becoming more crucial to other countries in the realization of their economic and security goals; it is increasingly in a position to help or hurt other countries. But, on the other hand, the growth of American power makes the United States less dependent on weaker states, so it is easier for the United States to resist or ignore these states.

This is the realm of American power where the most flexibility exists for responding to anti-Americanism. Policies and strategic orientations can be adjusted. People in various European and Asian countries have the view that American power is not being put to work in ways that serve their interests. A hard-line, assertive unilateralism toward North Korea unsettles people across the political spectrum in South Korea. American resistance to an international agreement to reduce global warming generates huge amounts of antagonism in Europe and elsewhere. Across a variety of issues, it is possible to see how the United States can adjust its policy—and signal a more cooperative and benign hegemonic orientation—without sacrificing American interests. We can look more closely at the ways in which American power and policies can work with rather than against others.

Domination and Resistance

Anti-Americanism is built into the latent character of the global power distribution. Power can be muted, disguised, or rendered legitimate—but it is still lurking in the shadows. When it is exposed and is expressed as domination, it invites a response. Georges Clemenceau, who was a young left-wing republican during the Franco-Prussian War, said of the settlement: "Germany believes that the logic of her victory means domination, while we do not believe that the logic of our defeat is serfdom." American power allows the United States to dominate, but others will look for ways to resist.

The terms of American hegemony—or the way in which that hegemony is perceived and experienced around the world—do appear to be undergoing a change. Perry Anderson describes the shift in terms of a set of post–Cold War developments—that together are making it harder for the United States to legitimate its global power. First, of course, was the end of the Cold War and the rise of the United States to a preeminent and unchecked position.

> For once the Communist danger was taken off the table, American primacy ceased to be an automatic requirement of the security of the established order *tout court*. Potentially, the field of inter-capitalist rivalries, no longer just at the level of firms but of states, sprang open once again, as—in theory—European and East Asian regimes could now contemplate degrees of independence unthinkable during the time of totalitarian peril. Yet there was another aspect to this change. If the consensual structure of American domination now lacked the same external girders, its coercive superiority was, at a single stroke, abruptly and massively enhanced. For with the erasure of the USSR, there was no longer any countervailing force on earth capable of withstanding U.S. military might. The days when it could be checkmated in Vietnam, or suffer proxy defeat in Southern Africa, were over. These interrelated changes were eventually bound to alter the role of the United States in the world.[21]

At the end of the 1990s, the United States still enjoyed a great deal of legitimacy as a global hegemonic power. Anderson argues that two changes occurred in the past few years that have altered this perception. The first was the shock and aftermath of September 11. This mobilized American power and nationalism, and it reinforced the assertive unilateralism of the Bush administration. The second change, according to Anderson, was the Revolution in Military Affairs (RMA), which has changed the nature of warfare. The United States now has the political and technological ability to pursue its goals around the world without much resistance. Anderson argues that along with these changes in circumstances—the inflaming of popular nationalism in the wake of September 11 and the new latitude afforded by the RMA abroad—there has also been an ideological shift in Washington.

> Where the rhetoric of the Clinton administration spoke of the cause of international justice and the construction of a democratic peace, the Bush administration has hoisted the banner of the war on terrorism. These are not incompatible motifs, but

the order of emphasis assigned to each has altered. The result is a sharp contrast of atmospherics. The war on terrorism orchestrated by Cheney and Rumsfeld is a far more strident, if also brittle, rallying-cry than the cloying pieties of the Clinton-Albright years.... The new and sharper line from Washington has gone down badly in Europe, where human-rights discourse was and is especially prized. Here the earlier line was clearly superior as a hegemonic idiom.[22]

What has unsettled a great deal of world opinion is the seeming shift in American foreign policy away from its previous alliance-based, multilateral orientation toward a more unilateral, even neoimperial strategic orientation. This new orientation is captured in the recently released National Security Strategy, and it is expressed in the speeches and policies of the Bush administration as it wages war on terrorism and confronts Iraq and other rogue states. In this new strategic view, America is to be less bound to its partners or to the rules and institutions of the world community while it simultaneously steps forward to play a more unilateral and anticipatory role in attacking terrorist threats and confronting rogue states seeking weapons of mass destruction. The United States will use its unrivaled military power to manage the global order.

This new grand strategy is organized around a fundamental commitment to the maintenance of a unipolar world order where the United States has no peer competitor or where any coalition of great powers could achieve it together. The United States will not seek security through the more modest realist strategy of operating within a global system of power balancing nor will it pursue a liberal strategy where institutions, democracy, and integrated markets reduce the importance of power politics altogether. America will be so much more powerful than the other major states that strategic rivalries and security competition among the great powers will disappear as an option, leaving everyone—not just the United States—better off.[23]

The new orientation also holds that the Cold War concept of deterrence is outdated. The threat is not other great powers that must be managed through the statecraft of the balance of power. It is now transnational terrorist networks that have no home address. They cannot be deterred either because they are willing to die for their cause or because they can escape retaliation. The old defensive strategy of building missiles and other weapons that can survive a first strike and be used in a retaliatory strike to punish the attacker will no longer ensure security. The only option now is a relentless offense: deterrence, sovereignty, and the balance of power work together. When deterrence is no longer viable, the larger intellectual edifice starts to crumble. The use of force will increasingly need to be preemptive, and this plays havoc with the old international rules of self-defense and United Nations norms about the proper use of force.

As a result, the new grand strategy involves recasting the terms of sovereignty. Because these terrorist groups cannot be deterred, the United States must be prepared to intervene anywhere at any time to preemptively destroy the threat. Terrorists do not respect borders, so neither can we. Moreover, countries that harbor terrorists either by consent or because they are unable to enforce their laws within their territory effectively forfeit their rights of sovereignty. As reported this past spring in the *New Yorker,* State Department Policy Planning Director Richard Haass has hinted at this notion:

> What you are seeing in this administration is the emergence of a new principle or body of ideas—I'm not sure it constitutes a doctrine—about what you might call the limits of sovereignty. Sovereignty entails obligations. One is not to massacre your own people. Another is not to support terrorism in any way. If a government fails to meet these obligations, then it forfeits some of the normal advantages of sovereignty, including the right to be left alone inside your own territory. Other governments, including the United States, gain the right to intervene. In the case of terrorism, this can even lead to a right of preventive, or preemptory, self-defense. You essentially can act in anticipation if you have grounds to think it's a question of when, and not if, you're going to be attacked.

Another element of this new grand strategy is a general depreciation of international rules, treaties, and security partnerships. One reason for this relates to the new threats themselves: if the stakes are rising and the margins of error are shrinking in the war on terrorism, multilateral norms and agreements sanctioning and limiting the use of force are just annoying distractions. The critical task is to eliminate the threat. But the emerging unilateral strategy is also informed by a deeper suspicion expressed by some influential voices inside and outside the Bush administration about the suspect value of international agreements themselves. Part of this view is a deeply felt and authentically American belief that the United States should not get entangled in the corrupting and constraining world of multilateral rules and institutions. American sovereignty is politically sacred. For some Americans this leads to a preference for isolationism. But the more influential view—particularly after September 11—is not that the United States should withdraw from the world but that it should operate in the world on its own terms.

Finally, the new grand strategy attaches little value to international stability. There is an unsentimental view in this camp that the traditions of the past must be shed. Whether it is withdrawal from the ABM treaty or the resistance to signing formal arms control treaties, the conviction is that the United States must move beyond outmoded Cold War thinking. Administration officials have noted with some satisfaction that America's withdrawal from the ABM treaty did not lead to a global arms race that critics warned of but actually paved the way for a historical arms reduction agreement between the United States and Russia. This is seen as a validation that moving beyond the old paradigm of great power relations will not bring the international house down. The world can withstand new—even radically new—security approaches, and it will accommodate American unilateralism as well. But stability is not an end in itself. The administration's new hawkish policy toward North Korea might be destabilizing to the region, but that might be the necessary price to be paid for dislodging a dangerous and evil regime in Pongyang.

The new ethos is "going after the threat" or "getting the job done." It is decidedly not about following multilateral norms or tending to the sensibilities of allies. Proponents of this new grand strategy are willing to take big risks to reduce the risks of catastrophic terrorism. After all, the clock is ticking. They are willing to throw American power around even if this makes old relationships with Europe and the rest of the world more coarse and antagonistic. Reflecting this view, one prominent adviser to the administration said at an international gathering last year: "If the United States is going to get crucified as a hegemon, it might as well act like one."

This new strategic orientation has altered the way the world looks at American power. The question today is whether the United States will exercise its power in old-style hegemonic terms or in fact move toward a more coercive imperial strategy. The new strategic ideas coming out of the Bush administration show that at least some officials are pushing the United States in the imperial direction. These new imperial ideas are at odds with the bargains and institutions established across the Atlantic and the Pacific in the postwar era. At least some of the anger and resentment being expressed today comes from the fact that the United States is violating—or threatening to violate—the norms and understandings that have guided American relations with its European and Asian partners over the decades.

Taming American Power

Anti-Americanism today is a reaction to American power and policy. The United States started the decade as the world's only superpower and it proceeded to have a better decade than any other power. Disparities in economic and military power between the United States and the other major states widened during the 1990s. Between 1990 and 1998, United States's economic growth (27 percent) was almost twice that of the European Union (15 percent) and three times that of Japan (9 percent).[24] The weakness of the euro today is ultimately a result of these divergent European and American economic trends. While Europe and Japan have struggled with economic restructuring, the United States has ridden the wave of the "new economy" and rising productivity. The United States also reduced defense spending at a slower rate after the Cold War than the other major powers, resulting in greater relative military capabilities by the end of the 1990s. In fact, it has come close in recent years to monopolizing military-related research and development, spending roughly 80 percent of the world's total.[25] These developments have resulted in an extremely lopsided distribution of world power.

While these brute material disparities might normally be hidden below the surface, recent developments have rendered them salient and provocative. The American-led NATO air campaign over Kosovo in 1999 provided at times dramatic—and to many countries, such as China and Russia, disturbing—evidence of America's military and technological advantage. The squabble between the United States and Germany over the leadership of the IMF also gave the impression that the United States had acquired a taste for dominance. The United States similarly bullied Japan during the East Asian financial crisis, opposing Tokyo's plan for an Asian Monetary Fund and insisting on American-approved remedies. Bipartisan support for a National Missile Defense—despite the opposition of the other major states and its unsettling consequences for world security relationships—is another source of rancor. America's confrontation with Iraq puts American power and unilateral impulses on full display around the world. In the meantime, the expansion and integration of world markets, unfolding under the banner of globalization, are seen by many as a Washington-directed phenomenon that spreads American values and disproportionately favors American interests. For these and many other reasons, it is widely believed around the world that the global distribution of power is dangerously out of balance.

But a global backlash to American power is not inevitable, particularly if the United States remembers its own political history. Our leaders have the ideas, means, and political institutions that can allow for stable and cooperative order even amid sharp and shifting asymmetries of power. The United States faced this problem after World War II and solved it by building what might be called "stakeholder" hegemony. It can do this again today.

A critical ingredient in stabilizing international relations in a world of radical power disparities is the character of the United States itself. The United States is indeed a global hegemon, but because of its democratic institutions and political traditions it is—or can be—a relatively benign one. When other major states consider whether to work with the United States or resist it, the fact that the United States is an open, stable democracy matters. The outside world can see American policy making at work and they can even find opportunities to enter the process and help shape the way the overall order operates. Paris, London, Berlin, Moscow, Tokyo, and even Beijing—in each of these capitals officials can readily find reasons to conclude that an engagement policy toward the United States will be more effective than balancing against American power.

The United States in large part stumbled into this open, institutionalized order in the 1940s as it sought to rebuild the postwar world and to counter Soviet communism. In the late-1940s, in an echo of today's situation, the United States was the world's dominant state—accounting for 45 percent of world GNP as well as leading in military power, technology, finance, and industry and brimming with natural resources. But the United States nonetheless found itself building world order around stable and binding partnerships. Its calling card was its offer of Cold War security protection. But the intensity of political and economic cooperation between the United States and its partners went well beyond what was necessary to counter Soviet threats. As the historian Geir Lundstadt has observed, the expanding American political order in the half century after World War II was in important respects an "empire by invitation."[26] The remarkable global reach of American postwar hegemony has been at least in part driven by the efforts of European and Asian governments to harness American power, render that power more predictable, and use it to overcome their own regional insecurities. The result has been a vast system of America-centered economic and security partnerships.

Even though the United States looks like a wayward power to many around the world today, it nonetheless has an unusual ability to coopt and reassure. Three elements matter most in making American power more stable, engaged, and restrained. First, America's mature political institutions organized around the rule of law have made it a relatively predictable and cooperative hegemon. The pluralistic and regularized way in which American foreign and security policy is made reduces surprises and allows other states to build long-term cooperative relations. The governmental separation of powers creates a shared decision-making system that opens up the process and reduces the ability of any one leader to make abrupt or aggressive moves toward other states. An active press and competitive party system also provide a service to outside states by generating information about American policy and determining its seriousness of purpose. The messiness of a democracy can, indeed, frustrate American diplomats and confuse foreign observers. But over the long term, democratic institutions produce more consistent and credible policies—policies that do not reflect the capricious and idiosyncratic whims of an autocrat.

This open and decentralized political process works in a second way to reduce foreign worries about American power. It creates what might be called "voice opportunities"—it offers opportunities for political access and, with them, the means for foreign governments and groups to influence the way Washington's power is exercised. Foreign governments and corporations may not have elected officials in Washington, but they do have representatives. Looked at from the perspective of the stable functioning of America's hegemonic order, Choate was actually describing one of the brilliant aspects of the United States as a global power. By providing other states with opportunities to play the game in Washington, it is drawing them into active, ongoing partnerships that serve the long-term strategy of the United States.

A final element of the American order that reduces worry about power asymmetries is the web of multilateral institutions that mark the postwar world. After World War II, the United States launched history's most ambitious era of institution building. The UN, IMF, World Bank, NATO, General Agreement on Tariffs and Trade (GATT), and other institutions that emerged provided a more rule-based structure for political and economic relations than anything seen before. The United States was deeply ambivalent about making permanent security commitments to other states or allowing its political and economic policies to be dictated by intergovernmental bodies. The Soviet menace was critical in overcoming these doubts. Networks and political relationships were built that—paradoxically—made American power not only more far-reaching and durable but also more predictable and malleable.

In effect, the United States spun a web of institutions that connected other states to an emerging American-dominated economic and security order. But in doing so, these institutions also bound the United States to other states and reduced, at least to some extent, Washington's ability to engage in the arbitrary and indiscriminate exercise of power. Call it an institutional bargain. The United States got other states to join in a western political order built around economic openness, multilateral management of trade and monetary relations, and collective security. The price for the United States was a reduction in Washington's policy autonomy. Institutional rules and joint decision making reduced American unilateralist capacities. But what Washington got in return was worth the price. America's partners also had their autonomy constrained but in return were able to operate in a world where American power, channeled through institutions, was more restrained and reliable.

The array of postwar multilateral institutions does provide constraints on America's actions in the world. But the United States gets something significant in return. Secretary of State Dean Rusk noted this in testimony before the Senate Foreign Relations Committee in 1965: "We are every day, in one sense, accepting limitations upon our complete freedom of action. . . . We have more than 4,300 treaties and international agreements, two-thirds of which have been entered into in the past 25 years. . . . Each one of which at least limits our freedom of action. We exercise our sovereignty going into these agreements." But Rusk argued that these agreements also create a more stable environment within which the United States can pursue its interests. "Law is a process by which we increase our range of freedom" and "we are constantly enlarging our freedom by being able to predict what others are going to do."[27] The United States gets a more predictable environment and more willing partners.

Conclusion

The United States must rediscover those elements that help reconcile American power with stable and legitimate international order. Think of the United States as a giant corporation that seeks foreign investors. It is more likely to attract investors if it can demonstrate that it operates according to accepted accounting and fiduciary principles. The rule of law and the institutions of policy making in a democracy are the political equivalent of corporate transparency and accountability. Sharp shifts in policy must ultimately be vetted within the policy process and pass muster by an array of investigatory and decision-making bodies. Because it is a constitutional, rule-based democracy, outside states are more willing to work with the United States or—to return to the corporate metaphor—to invest in ongoing partnerships.

Today, if the United States were a giant corporation, many people around the world would liken it to Enron. But this perception is not inevitable. There are aspects in the American experience—institutions and strategies—that can help the United States legitimate its power and reduce the instabilities that are manifest as anti-Americanism.

Notes

1. This chapter builds on several previous essays: Ikenberry, "America's Imperial Ambition," *Foreign Affairs* 81 no. 5 (September–October 2002), pp. 44–60; and Ikenberry, "Strategic Reactions to American Preeminence: Great Power Politics in the Age of Unipolarity," National Intelligence Council report, Summer 2003.

2. Data reported in "Living with a Superpower," *Economist*, January 2, 2003.

3. Ibid.

4. Francis Fukuyama, "The West May Be Cracking Up," *International Herald Tribune,* September 8, 2002.

5. "Living with a Superpower," *Economist*, January 2, 2003.

6. German Marshall Fund of the United States, "Europeans See the World as Americans Do, but Critical of U.S. Foreign Policy," press release, September 4, 2002.

7. Michael Hardt and Antonio Negri, *Empire* (Cambridge, MA: Harvard University Press, 2000).

8. Theodore H.von Laue, *The World Revolution of Westernization: The Twentieth Century in Global Perspective* (New York: Oxford University Press, 1987).

9. John Lewis Gaddis, *Strategies of Containment: A Critical Appraisal of Postwar American National Security Policy* (New York: Oxford University Press, 1982), p. 4.

10. See Mary N. Hampton, "NATO at the Creation: U.S. Foreign Policy, West Germany, and the Wilsonian Impulse," *Security Studies* 4, no. 3 (Spring 1995): 610–56; and Hampton, *The Wilsonian Impulse: U.S. Foreign Policy, the Alliance, and German Unification* (Westport, CT: Praeger, 1996).

11. Quoted in Thomas Schwartz, *America's Germany: John J. McCloy and the Federal Republic of Germany* (Cambridge, MA: Harvard University Press, 1991), p. 228.

12. Bruce Cumings, "Japan's Position in the World System," in *Postwar Japan as History*, ed. Andrew Gordon (Berkeley: University of California Press, 1997), p. 38.

13. Chalmers Johnson, *Blowback: The Costs and Consequences of American Empire* (New York: Metropolitan Books, 2000), p. 5.

14. Ibid., p. 229.

15. Although the Clinton administration articulated a foreign policy strategy of "assertive multilateralism," its record was more mixed. In June 1997, the Clinton administration declined to join most of the world's countries in signing the Ottawa Convention on the Banning of Land Mines. In 1999, the U.S. Senate rejected the Comprehensive Test Ban Treaty, ignoring warnings from experts that such a move would weaken global nonproliferation norms, and it signaled its opposition to the Kyoto Protocol and the International Criminal Court (ICC). The Clinton administration did not await UN Security Council approval for its 1998 bombing of Iraq, nor did it seek such approval in the American-led bombing campaign by the North Atlantic Treaty Organization (NATO) against Serbia in the spring of 1999.

16. For an excellent summary of recent multilateral agreements rejected by the United States, see Stewart Patrick, "Multilateralism and Its Discontents: The Causes and Consequences of U.S. Ambivalence," in *Multilateralism and U.S. Foreign Policy: Ambivalent Engagement*, ed. Stewart Patrick and Shepard Forman (Boulder, CO: Lynne Rienner, 2002).

17. Charles Krauthammer, "The New Unilateralism." *Washington Post*, June 8, 2001, p. A29.

18. Quoted in Todd S. Purdum, "Embattled, Scrutinized, Powell Soldiers On," *New York Times*, July 25, 2002, p. 1.

19. President George W. Bush, speech at West Point, June 2002.

20. Bush administration, "The National Security Strategy of the United States," text released by the *New York Times*, September 20, 2002.

21. Perry Anderson, "Force and Consent," *New Left Review* 17 (September–October 2002), 6–7.

22. Ibid., pp. 13–14.

23. I summarize these ideas in Ikenberry, "America's Imperial Ambition," *Foreign Affairs* 81, no. 5 (September–October 2002).

24. Calculated from OECD statistics (July 1999 Web edition). GDP measures are figured at 1990 prices and exchange rates.

25. See International Institute for Strategic Studies, *The Military Balance 1999/2000* (London: Oxford University Press, 1999). For additional measures indicating an intensification of American power, see William C. Wohlforth, "The Stability of a Unipolar World," *International Security* 24, no. 1 (Summer 1999).

26. See Geir Lundestad, "Empire by Invitation? The United States and Western Europe, 1945–1952," *Journal of Peace Research* 23 (September 1986): 263–77.

27. Quoted in Edward C. Luck, *Mixed Messages: American Politics and International Organization, 1919–1999* (Washington, DC: Brookings Institution Press, 1999), p. 61.

2

Pacific Co-Prosperity?

The San Francisco System and Its Implications in Comparative Perspective

Kent E. Calder

On September 6, 1951, just over half a century ago, forty-nine nations met at the San Francisco Opera House to conclude the peace treaty with Japan following World War II. The treaty and the political-economic arrangements attached to it are highly distinctive in comparative context and have stirred diverse reactions throughout the Pacific. In Japan they were applauded, while in Korea and China they were widely condemned. Together, the provisions of the treaty and related agreements have structured the conduct of trans-Pacific affairs to a remarkable degree for the past half-century. Indeed, the political-economic order they created is so closely tied to the momentous agreements made then that it deserves to be known as the "San Francisco System."[1]

More concretely, the San Francisco System, as the term is used here, refers to the comprehensive, Japan-centric structure of interrelated political, military, and economic commitments between the United States and its Pacific allies that was initiated by the San Francisco Peace Treaty of September 1951. The system is in reality a complex maze of treaties and administrative agreements, mainly bilateral, concluded between the United States and various Pacific nations over the 1951–1954 period, in the shadow of the Korean War. It was originally unified by a common yet contradictory purpose: ensuring the nations of the region against a revival of Japanese aggression while simultaneously ensuring sufficient economic opportunity for Japan that it could serve as an engine of growth for the broader Pacific region as a whole.

The new framework ultimately transformed Japan into an affluent yet broadly pacific nation running huge trade surpluses with the world. It did not, however, accomplish the same magic for other nations. Some, such as China, were excluded, although they gradually found their way in. Others, such as Korea and Vietnam, suffered through wars that ultimately brought Japan prosperity; thus they came to resent a political-economic order that the Japanese found much more positive. Despite these divergent reactions, the San Francisco System continues to define the broad profile of

Pacific relations in highly distinctive ways, with major implications both for international relations and for local attitudes toward the United States.

Anatomy of the San Francisco System

The classic San Francisco System, as it emerged in the 1950s, had seven salient features:

1. It included a dense network of *formal security alliances*, mainly bilateral, between the United States and key nations of the Pacific, such as Japan, South Korea, the Philippines, Australia, and New Zealand.
2. Apart from ANZUS (a treaty between Australia, New Zealand, and the United States of America), the San Francisco System *did not create a multilateral security structure*. To the contrary, it established a "hub and spokes" network of bilateral ties radiating from Washington.
3. The San Francisco System was highly *asymmetrical* in both its security and economic dimensions. It offered military protection and economic access to non-U.S. participants while failing to impose analogous collective defense obligations on most of them. South Korea, unique among the participants, confronted heavy, direct defense commitments due to its exposed position confronting North Korea.
4. The system offered *special precedence to Japan*—ironically the defeated power—in terms of both economic opportunities and security obligations. This precedence contrasted sharply to circumstances of the Republic of Korea (ROK), which found itself on the front line, in defense of a Japan-centric system dominated by its former colonial master.
5. The San Francisco System *involved remarkably narrow consent and participation by the nations of the western Pacific*. Neither Korea was a party to the agreement. Ultimately the only Asian nations that categorically supported the treaty were Pakistan and Ceylon—neither of which had been significantly involved in the war against Japan.
6. The system offered *extensive economic benefits* to security allies of the United States, although not in the form of direct reparations from Japan, for which most of the Allies had originally hoped. These incentives were partially embodied in bilateral treaties of commerce and navigation, offering open access to the U.S. market for Asian firms. Yet reciprocity was rarely enforced.
7. *Unsettled boundaries within Northeast Asia* were a major element of the system. These issues, of course, had been dormant for half a century prior to 1945, since Japan ruled the entire region, without meaningful boundaries. Since the San Francisco Treaty disposed of territorial issues concerning both the home islands of Japan and its former colonies, including Korea and Taiwan, however, that treaty had the potential to either clearly define the postwar contours of the various Northeast Asian nations or to leave them in ambiguity.

Ambiguity in the treaty over what constituted the Kuriles, for example, estranged Japan and the Soviet Union from one another. Similarly, ambiguity as to who held sovereignty over Takeshima/Tokdo, in the middle of the Japan/East Sea, complicated Japan–Korea relations. Lack of clarity regarding whether the Senkaku/Diaoyutai islands were part of Okinawa or Taiwan likewise estranged Japan and China. The treaty also failed to resolve the North–South territorial division in Korea, not to mention relations across the Taiwan Straits, thus enhancing prospects for future intraregional conflict along multiple geopolitical dimensions.

The intraregional conflicts among Northeast Asian nations created by treaty ambiguity ultimately enhanced the geopolitical leverage of the United States, particularly with an anxious and defensive Japan and a war-torn South Korea. These dependencies definitely served the geostrategic purposes of Secretary of State John Foster Dulles. They also helped neutralize the diplomatic consequences of his indulgent approach to Japanese economic recovery and obviated any prospect that the prewar "Co-Prosperity Sphere" might be revived. They also, at least initially, defused local resentments in most nations of the region toward the United States, directing them more toward traditional regional adversaries.

Comparative Alliance Perspectives: A Skewed Economics for a Security Bargain in the Pacific?

The San Francisco System is clearly distinctive relative to other recent alliance structures. Its integrated security and economic features contrast sharply with virtually all pre–World War II alliances, which tended to have a more exclusively military character.[2] The conciliatory economic steps taken to rehabilitate Japan, a former enemy, contrast very sharply with the punitive Versailles settlement with Weimar Germany after World War I. In forcing Germany to cede massive reparations, the Versailles Treaty helped trigger its own early collapse.[3]

These steps obviously helped to reinforce positive attitudes in Japan toward the United States. The San Francisco provisions also contrast with post–World War II American policies toward Germany. For example, the United States provided less direct economic assistance to Japan than it had to Germany. Yet America accorded Japan unusually favorable (and highly asymmetrical) trading arrangements. The United States likewise insulated Japan from the reparatory demands of its neighbors, which it did not do for Germany or Italy. It thus encouraged resentments against the special treatment of Japan; these were especially pronounced in countries like Korea, which had suffered at Japanese hands.

Virtually all the bilateral arrangements of the San Francisco System embodied a distinctive bargain: unusual and asymmetrical U.S. *economic* concessions to the host nation in return for unusual and asymmetrical *security* concessions from the United States. The system involved, in short, definite economic measures in return for security trade-offs, which implies sharply more asymmetry between the economic and security arenas than was common in other U.S. alliance relationships of the early Cold War period. This asymmetry was particularly great in the case of Japan and much less so with respect to Korea—a natural source of resentment in Korea toward both Japan and the United States.

Many Pacific allies also agreed to provide substantial offset payments (host-nation support). These escalated steadily over the years, to over $20,000 annually per U.S. soldier in Japan, more than four times the maximum achieved in Germany.[4] In Europe extensive host-nation support was a rarity after the occupation years, even in West Germany, where offset arrangements in support of U.S. forces were terminated in 1976.[5] Asian partners also acquiesced in Status of Forces Agreements (SOFA) that allowed U.S. military personnel substantially greater autonomy from host-national control in Asia than they commonly enjoyed in Europe.

On the economic side of the equation, the San Francisco System exhibited a "trade more than aid" bias. The United States supplied much less direct financial aid to its Pacific partners than the $13 billion it provided to Europe through the Marshall Plan. Most of that was exclusively earmarked for Japan and was provided at levels much lower than those for Germany.[6] Even war-torn Korea received relatively little in comparative terms.[7]

Yet the United States tolerated huge asymmetries in trade and investment access, especially with Northeast Asia, that it did not readily accept with Europe. It tacitly accepted large-scale Asian protectionism while opening American markets quite flexibly to Asian exports. These asymmetries ultimately came to have fateful competitive significance for U.S. and East Asian firms, creating "co-prosperity" for some and bankruptcy for others, although most effects were not evident until the 1970s and after.

The crucial difference between Asia and Europe was the "China factor," which had no parallel in Europe. In order to wean Northeast Asia away from its traditional reliance on China—newly emerging Cold War antagonist and archenemy of Korea—the United States offered virtually unfettered access to its own market.[8] It also proved hospitable to such investment funds as impoverished East Asia was able to muster.[9]

Yet the United States demanded remarkably little in the way of economic reciprocity. In contrast to strong pressures against the Europeans for trade and investment opportunities for American capital, the U.S. government was generally more passive in economic relations with allies in Asia. This was often true even where U.S. firms expressed clear interest in penetrating the Japanese, Korean, and Taiwanese markets. The local political result was, naturally, business support for prioritizing relations with the United States, which were proving to be so lucrative for local elites.

Striking Persistence over Time

The durability of the San Francisco System has been remarkable. To be sure, certain features—notably the exclusion of mainland China and the Soviet Union—have been gradually modified since the early-1970s, beginning with the loosening of long-standing strategic embargoes dating from 1948 to 1951.[10] Indeed, with China's December 2001 admission to the World Trade Organization (WTO), the traditionally pronounced economic discrimination in favor of U.S. strategic allies and against prospective opponents, which was an original hallmark of the San Francisco System, has virtually disappeared. Vietnam, ostracized by the United States for two decades after the fall of Saigon, became a WTO observer in 1995 and ratified a favorable bilateral trade agreement with the United States in November 2001. It too is expected to join the WTO by 2005.[11]

The United States also countenanced a substantial deepening of economic relations between North Korea and America's South Korean ally during the late 1990s, although it grew more ambivalent with the coming of the Bush administration in 2001. Multilateral bodies like Asia-Pacific Economic Cooperation (APEC), never envisioned by Dulles, have grown more important in the economic arena as bilateral economic arrangements have atrophied. Since early 2002, Japanese Prime Minister Koizumi Junichiro and Defense Minister Nakatani Gen have made important new proposals for expanded Association of Southeast Asian Nations (ASEAN)/Oceania cooperation, involving both economics and security. China has also made major new overtures toward ASEAN.[12]

Yet the fundamentally asymmetrical and bilaterally oriented "hub and spokes" security framework, with a forward-deployed U.S. military presence at its core, still persists to a remarkable degree. Indeed, Japan and South Korea alone today host nearly as many U.S. troops as they did twenty years ago and more than one-third of all the U.S. troops deployed outside the United States before the September 11, 2001, terrorist attacks on the United States.[13] This situation leaves Asians divided and at odds with one another, thus undercutting tendencies toward resentment at the asymmetrical structure of power relations between the United States and any one Asian nation.

Asian Popular Responses: Korea in Comparative Perspective

The San Francisco System, as the foregoing analysis suggests, has presented the nations of Asia for the past half-century with several stark, asymmetrical trade-offs between economic advantage and national autonomy. Broadly speaking, the system has offered the prospect of privileged access to the U.S. market, the largest and most affluent on earth, in return for security cooperation, typically including access for U.S. military forces. Not surprisingly, the popular response to this implicit bargain has varied sharply throughout the Pacific.

From the outset, it should be stressed that public opinion in any nation is embedded in broader political-economic systems. Its broader political significance is related profoundly to the structure of those political systems themselves. Generally, the stronger the local pattern of political pluralism, the more consequential popular opinion becomes for public policy.

Public sentiment toward the San Francisco System, and to the role of the United States more generally in Pacific affairs, has evolved substantially over the past fifteen years in almost all countries of the region, responding to broader post–Cold War geopolitical changes. The sharpest transformations seem to have occurred in the na-

Table 2.1

East Asian Perspectives on the United States

I. General Opinion of the United States	Philippines	Japan	Vietnam	Indonesia	ROK
Favorable	90	72	71	61	53
Unfavorable	7	26	27	36	44
II. View of U.S.-led War on Terrorism					
Favorable	82	61	62	31	24
Unfavorable	17	32	29	63	72
III. U.S. Considers Others					
Great deal/fair amount	74	36	80	41	23
Not much/not at all	15	59	8	49	73
IV. Source of Differences with U.S.					
Values	26	61	24	66	41
Policies	71	34	68	31	53
V. Greatest Global Threat: Nuclear Weapons	32	44	17	11	14

tions where actual military conflict occurred during the Cold War: Vietnam and Korea. Strongly estranged from the United States in the late 1980s, reflecting the bitter heritage of past conflict, Vietnamese public opinion appears to have grown much more positively inclined toward the United States. Conversely, the waning of Cold War confrontation seems to have made it easier for Koreans to feel and express dissatisfaction with a San Francisco System incorporating many features, including a pro-Japan orientation, that they find uncongenial.

Table 2.1, drawn from survey data gathered by the Pew Global Attitudes Project in late 2002,[14] suggests the sharp current variation that prevails across East Asia in attitudes toward the United States. General attitudes toward the United States appear to be most favorable in the Philippines, Japan, and—surprisingly—Vietnam. They seem to be much more unfavorable in South Korea. Indeed, opinion of the United States was lower in Korea than in Muslim Indonesia and lower in Korea than in all but two of the forty-five nations in which the study was conducted.[15]

General views toward the United States across East Asia appear to correlate closely with views regarding a U.S.-led war on terrorism. This effort is strongly supported in the Philippines, Japan, and Vietnam but not in South Korea or Indonesia. Interestingly, Korean attitudes correlate closely with those of the only Muslim nation in the sample. Indeed, Korean views of the United States are even more skeptical than Indonesian, perhaps reflecting the inclusion of North Korea in the "axis of evil."

The *origins* of anti-Americanism are more difficult to ascertain from the Pew study than the broad profile of such sentiments. It appears that the causes are to some extent country specific. In Japan, for example, nuclear issues and perceived value differences with the United States are more substantial concerns than in most other nations of the region. In Korea, by contrast, neither of these concerns are major irritants in popular perceptions of the United States. Instead, Koreans appear to feel—more strongly than any of the other Asian nations considered—that the United States systematically *neglects* their national concerns. This "neglect" variable correlates much more closely with anti-Americanism in Korea than it does in Japan or indeed than in any other Asian nation considered, suggesting that resentment of American "imperial pretensions" may be particularly strong in Korea. Indirectly, this attitude may well reflect the embedded Japan-centric character of the San Francisco System itself.

One final issue is raised indirectly by the Pew study: the impact of U.S. bases on attitudes toward the United States. The issue was not directly considered in the study itself, but it is noteworthy that two of the three nations where attitudes toward the United States are strongly favorable (Vietnam and the Philippines) are countries that have previously expelled U.S. military bases. Although Japan is an outlier, in both hosting U.S. bases and having a generally favorable attitude toward the United States, attitudes appear to be substantially more negative in parts of Japan with a heavy concentration of U.S. military installations. In Okinawa, which hosts 75 percent of all U.S. forces in Japan, for example, local attitudes toward the United States appear to be close to those in Korea, although their political expression is moderated by heavy central government financial assistance and related local government reticence in pressing for retrenchment in the U.S. presence. The generation gap in attitudes toward the United States also appears to be less pronounced in Okinawa than in Korea.

Korean attitudes toward the United States, in sum, seem to be substantially more critical than those of Asians generally, resembling most closely those of Islamic nations like Indonesia. The reasons for anti-Americanism in Korea, however, appear to be substantially different from those in the Islamic world. Koreans do not view their differences with the United States as a "war of civilizations." Indeed, they subscribe much more strongly to common Judaeo-Christian values than does Japan.

The Regional System as an Element in Korean Frustrations

Korea's differences at the popular level with the United States, it can be argued, are the psychological residue of the San Francisco System, as suggested above. They are, ironically, the delayed response to a Cold War architecture intended by John Foster Dulles to protect Korea but also, more importantly, to enrich and stabilize Japan, its longtime nemesis. Not surprisingly, that systemic orientation stirs resentment in Korea.

While nations further south, such as the Philippines and Indonesia, were largely beyond the ambit of the San Francisco System, Korea has been deeply affected by its transformation over the past fifteen years. With the gradual tacit admission of China, the relative benefits to Korea have declined. Yet the Japan-centric bias and the discrimination against North Korea have grown more visible. And as North Korea weakens, the U.S. security guarantee to South Korea, for which Seoul has sacrificed some political autonomy, becomes less self-evidently valuable, especially for younger people lacking memories of the Korean War.

The Institutional Dimension

Public opinion, of course, must be mediated through institutions and political processes to affect public policy. A comparative cross-Asian examination of relevant institutions lends further insights into why recent expressions of anti-American sentiment in South Korea place unusually strong political pressures on public policy. It is not only that the San Francisco System disadvantages South Korea relative to other nations in the region, particularly Japan, and that Koreans are frustrated by this. In addition, recent domestic institutional developments in Korea magnify the policy impact of public sentiment more than is true in the other four Asian nations under examination here.

Three particular Korean institutional changes seem important in comparative context. The first and probably the most influential is the transition to competitive party politics that has occurred since 1988. This has no parallel, of course, in Japan or Vietnam, where one-party dominance has continued. The closest parallel to Korea's democratic transition might be in the Philippines, following the downfall of the Marcos regime in 1986; there, pluralistic democracy led to strong anti-Americanism and to the withdrawal of U.S. military forces in 1992.

A second distinctive institutional change in Korea, seen in comparative context, is the rapid expansion of the activities of nongovernmental organizations (NGOs). According to the World Values Survey, South Korea had the most rapid increase in protest activism in the world from the early 1980s until the early 1990s—an increase more than twice as rapid as in Japan.[16] Korea's absolute levels of NGO activism by the mid-1990s were already in the top quartile of the World Values Survey global sample, together with those of Scandinavia, Germany, and the United States, and substantially ahead of Japan's.[17] And that was before the advent of two Korean presidents highly supportive of such activism: Kim Dae Jung and Roh Moo Hyun.

A final distinctive institutional development in Korea—highly synergistic with the other two—has been the increasing autonomy and policy activism of local governments. This change was instrumental in forcing revision of the U.S.–Korea SOFA in 2001, and in magnifying other political pressures against U.S. bases in Korea. It has no exact parallel anywhere else in East Asia over the past decade.

The closest analogy to Korean local government activism on U.S.-Korean issues may be the efforts of Okinawan Governor Ota Masahide, who agitated strongly against U.S. bases there. But Ota was defeated for reelection in 1999, in the face of strong economic pressures from the Japanese central government. Korea's central government does not have the regulatory and financial tools that its Japanese counterpart used to help bring Ota down, even if it should want to pressure recalcitrant local government in analogous fashion.

South Korea thus stands out, in comparative perspective, along two related dimensions. First, the level of popular anti-American sentiments appears to be quite high, with its roots in resentment of the asymmetrical bargain implicit in the San Francisco System. Second, recent institutional developments in South Korea help to magnify the political pressure that rising anti-Americanism creates for revision in the terms of the San Francisco bargain. Pressures for revisions in the privileged U.S. security presence in Korea are especially severe and may be expected to continue.

The Future of the San Francisco System

The central bargain implicit in the San Francisco System has traditionally been *economics for security*: the provision of asymmetrical economic incentives to Asian nations to persuade them to participate in an asymmetrical security alliance system favoring and led by the United States. This complex economics-for-security bargain is growing increasingly untenable at the dawn of the twenty-first century, as the Cold War in Asia wanes and as the Pacific political economy globalizes.

To be sure, overwhelming American military strength, so convincingly demonstrated in the wars in Afghanistan and Iraq by 2001–2003, may well be making security ties with the United States attractive on their own merits for would-be Asian allies. Yet deepening nationalistic trends across much of the Pacific, reflecting resentment of American preeminence worldwide, make security alliances difficult to justify politically, just as their economic dividends are simultaneously eroding. Nowhere, of course, is this contradiction—implicit in the San Francisco System as it evolves— more salient than in South Korea in the wake of the 2002 presidential election. There, resentment of the United States has risen to record levels, particularly among the younger generation.[18] Yet simultaneously, trade with China—never a real member of the San Francisco System—has grown much more rapidly than trade with the United States and has generated large and profitable surpluses for Korea.

Developments in the Middle East, to be sure, are arresting the practical expression of anti-American sentiment at the policy level. As major energy importers with energy-intensive economies, the nations of East Asia have much to lose from conflict with an American colossus that not only provides markets and capital but now also has a powerful influence, through its occupation of Iraq, on both global oil production and postwar reconstruction contracts. The increased moderation in President Roh Moo Hyun's pronouncements, over his first six months in office, no doubt relates in part to this sudden reinforcement of the San Francisco System through American influences in the Middle East.

The San Francisco System, despite its remarkable durability over the past two generations, is thus gradually and precariously evolving. It is changing into a softer, more ad hoc, more security-centric system, largely shorn of the blatant economic favoritism toward alliance members and the discrimination against outsiders that had been characteristic of earlier years. "Hub and spokes" bilateralism, while still central to military deterrence in flash points like Korea, is also gradually being supplemented by a more multilateral approach.

Three basic forces are slowly transforming the San Francisco System, simultaneously undermining both its economic and political logic. Most crucial perhaps is the steady emergence over the past decade of a truly global economic order. Successive international trade rounds and the coming of the World Trade Organization have gradually reduced the level of trade discrimination between members and non-members of trading blocs worldwide, thus eroding the benefits of membership in U.S.-sponsored discriminatory economic schemes. China—a potential U.S. adversary with strong competitive economic advantages vis-à-vis many U.S. Asian allies—is becoming more and more deeply involved in these globalist economic undertakings. This development has significantly reduced the *economic* dividends for such allies of bilateral security ties with the United States. Pacific alliances are inevitably coming to be judged ever more definitively in terms of their not inconsiderable *security* merits alone.

Globalization and systemic risks have increasingly forced the United States to ameliorate the economic frailty even of long-time military adversaries like Russia, China, and at times North Korea. Long subject to a categorical strategic embargo dating from the Korean War, North Korea had, since September 1999, some limited opportunity to trade and engage in financial transactions directly with the United States,[19] not to mention a broad range of other nations. However, the 2002–2003 nuclear crisis brought an end to this.

Nationalism and democratization, too, are eroding the San Francisco System by sapping the political capacity of host-nation governments to confer asymmetrical security advantages on superpowers like the United States. In South Korea, for example, grassroots protests against U.S. forces have *already* led to a recent renegotiation of the SOFA agreement governing U.S. forces in Korea and arguably influenced the outcome of the 2002 presidential election.[20] Parallel grassroots trends, including pressures for SOFA revision, are also observable in Japan, especially in Okinawa, as noted previously.[21] Other changes in bilateral security arrangements, such as new limits on host-nation support, may well be in prospect.

Since 1993, multilateralism has slowly emerged to cover the gap in the regional security framework created by some erosion of the "hub and spokes" bilateral arrangements originally fashioned by Dulles. APEC has become more vigorous and ventured gingerly into some security discussion. Multilateral development banks have become more active, albeit persistently constrained by an American veto.[22]

Among the most important recent multilateral innovations in economic policy coordination has been the "ASEAN plus Three" (APT) process, born at the Kuala Lumpur APEC Summit of 1997.[23] Comprising Japan, China, South Korea, and the ten nations of ASEAN, it excludes both the United States and its Anglo-Saxon Pacific allies, thus clearly contradicting the San Francisco System. Conceived in the course of the Asia-Europe Meeting (ASEM) dialogue, beginning in 1995, and further catalyzed by the trauma of the 1997–1998 Asian financial crisis, the APT has undertaken some substantial initiatives, including the May 2000 Chiangmai currency-swap agreement. Lingering historical rivalries and complex domestic politics in key nations, however, make it unclear just how far the APT can ultimately go in undermining the San Francisco System in its security dimensions. In a lasting tribute to Dulles's handiwork, the deepest problems the APT now confronts in fashioning an alternative to that U.S.-centric system concern the integration of Japan, privileged beneficiary of American support at San Francisco, against which many others in Asia continue to harbor unresolved claims.

Conclusion

Much international relations theory, particularly that of a realist persuasion, presents politics among nations as a fluid, shifting pattern of alignments. Nothing could be further from the reality of Pacific political-economic ties across the past half-century. Indeed, the basic pattern of political-economic relations in the Pacific remains remarkably close to what it was when the San Francisco System was inaugurated in the early 1950s, particularly when that pattern is contrasted to the greater fluidity of international relations elsewhere in the world.

The San Francisco System has been remarkably stable thus far, this research has suggested, due to the congruence of the underlying economics-for-security bargain at its heart with key domestic political interests in major nations of the region. Most importantly, the opportunity to pursue economic interest largely unimpeded by complicating security concerns has strongly appealed to the conservative Northeast Asian business and political elites. Conversely, the opportunity to pursue national security goals unchallenged by the most economically and technologically advanced nations of Asia has appealed to American leaders as well. This complementarity of elite interests on both sides of the Pacific has been reinforced by rising trans-Pacific capital flows. These have offset the effects of shifting trade competitiveness that naturally flow from the asymmetrical political-economic bargain at the heart of the San Francisco System.

To be stable is not necessarily to be universally appreciated. Political and business elites across Asia, together with the middle class in many nations, have found the San Francisco bargain congenial for the stability and prosperity it has created. Yet populist opinion is criticizing the old San Francisco "economics for security" bargain on nationalist as well as pragmatic grounds, in both Asia and the United States.

Nowhere is this criticism more strident than in Korea. Seoul was arguably disadvantaged by the original Japan-centric San Francisco System, and Korean popular resentments are magnified politically by rising local political pluralism as well. The massive surge of foreign investment into Korea since the Asian financial crisis—more than $50 billion during 1998–2001 alone—has provoked new affluence among young westernized businesspeople, but new, nationalist resentments as well.

The rise of China, and its gradual inclusion in a political-economic order long reserved for security allies, is also corrosive of the San Francisco System as traditionally constituted. The interaction of China and Korea under the new, reformist Roh Moo Hyun administration could put strong pressures on the remaining fabric of the San Francisco System, despite the formidable embedded political-economic strength of the U.S.–Korea bilateral relationship. A lessening of North–South tension on the peninsula, whatever its complex uncertainties, could accelerate this process still further.

The prospects thus appear strong for somewhat greater volatility in trans-Pacific alliance relationships than heretofore, with such prospects being markedly stronger in Korea than the regional norm. Both domestic and international systemic pressures in key nations combine to make this true. The key question is whether leaders with vision, holding an ability to communicate to their broader publics, will have the ability to look beyond the immediate circumstances to forge a renewed strategic bargain, as their for-bearers did so ably, if controversially, in a simpler world more than half a century ago.

Acknowledgments

The author expresses special thanks to Edna Lloyd for assistance in preparation, and to Min Ye for research assistance.

Notes

1. For an early discussion of this concept from a political-economic standpoint, see Calder (1996), pp. 151–52, 174–75, and 195.

2. Liska (1962).

3. The analogous Allied treaties of St. Germain with Austria-Hungary and Sèvres with the Ottoman Empire were similarly vindictive and destabilizing for the vanquished. See Lamb and Tarling (2001), pp. 23–34.

4. Sandars (2002), p. 172.

5. Ibid.

6. Precise comparisons are obviously difficult. During 1948–49, however, the U.S. Army asked Congress for a "Little Marshall Plan for Japan" in order to finance U.S. exports to Japan. Congress granted $165 million under the Economic Recovery for Occupied Areas (EROA) program, compared to roughly $400 million under the analogous Economic Recovery Program (ERP) for Germany. See Borden (1984), pp. 74–75.

7. The high point was 1957, when South Korea received $383 million in economic assistance, $400 million in military aid, and $300 million for the costs of U.S. forces in Korea. Overall, Korea received about $12 billion from the U.S. Treasury for the entire 1945–65 period, a time frame far transcending the war-reconstruction era itself. See Cumings (1997), pp. 306–7.

8. Textile quotas introduced during the mid-1950s were a partial if relatively minor early exception to this pattern, although they were followed by more substantial import restrictions on steel in the late 1960s and automobiles in the 1980s. See Borden (1984).

9. The U.S. government, for example, raised no objections to the 1957 establishment and subsequent expansion of the Alaska Pulp Company, Japan's first major foreign investment after World War II. The venture, headed by Sasayama Tadao of the Industrial Bank of Japan, was financed by Dillon, Read, and Company. See Davis and Roberts (1996), p. 73.

10. See Zhang (2001), p. 288. U.S.–China trade, virtually nil from 1951 to 1971, rose from $12.9 million in 1972 to $4.8 billion in 1980.

11. "Vietnam Looks to WTO Membership by 2005," *People's Daily Online*, March 6, 2002; available at http://english/peopledaily.com.cn/200105/11/print20010511_69668.html; and *World Trade Organization Website*; available at www.wto.org.

12. See, for example, Nakatani Gen, "Perspectives on Multilateral Security Cooperation in the Asia-Pacific Region," paper presented at the IISS Asia Security Conference, Singapore, June 2, 2002.

13. See International Institute for Strategic Studies, *The Military Balance*, 1980–81, 1985–86, 1990–91, 2000–2001 editions.

14. All the Asian national polls were conducted in July and August 2002. See Pew Research Center (2002), pp. 75–79.

15. Views of the United States were more unfavorable only in Argentina (49 percent) and Bangladesh (47 percent) than in South Korea (44 percent). See Pew (2002), p. 55.

16. See Pippa Norris (2002), p. 201.

17. Ibid, p. 199.

18. *Washington Post,* January 9, 2003.

19. *Korea Times,* September 17, 1999.

20. See Center for Strategic and International Studies, International Security Program (2001).

21. On recent trends in Okinawan opinion coupled with concrete suggestions for Japanese and U.S. policy reform, see Eldridge (2002), pp. 48–50.

22. On Japan's new role in promoting multilateralism through such institutions, see Yasutomo (1995), especially pp. 61–118.

23. See Stubbs (2002), pp. 440–55.

References

Border, W.S. (1984). *The Pacific Alliance: United States Foreign Economic Policy and Japanese Trade Recovery, 1947–1955.* Madison, WI: University of Wisconsin Press.

Calder, K.E. (1996). *Pacific Defense: Arms, Energy, and America's Future in Asia.* New York: William Morrow.

Center for Strategic and International Studies, International Security Program (2001). *Path to an Agreement: The U.S.-Republic of Korea Status of Forces Agreement Revision Process.* Washington, DC: Center for Strategic and International Studies.

Cumings, B. (1997). *Korea's Place in the Sun: A Modern History* New York: W.W. Norton.

Davis, G. and Roberts, J.G. (1996). *An Occupation without Troops: Wall Street's Half-Century Domination of Japanese Politics.* Tokyo: Yen Books.

Eldridge, R.D. (2002). *Okinawa and U.S.-Japan Relations in the Twenty-first Century: Bilateral and Trilateral Approaches to a Sounder Okinawa Policy.* Tokyo: Research Institute for Peace and Security.

Lamb, M. and Tarling, N. (2001). *From Versailles to Pearl Harbor: The Origins of the Second World War in Europe and Asia.* London: Palgrave.

Liska, G. (1962). *Nations in Alliance: The Limits of Interdependence.* Baltimore: Johns Hopkins University Press.

Norris, Pippa (2002). *Democratic Phoenix:* Cambridge: Cambridge University Press.

Sandars, C.T. (2002). *America's Overseas Garrisons: The Leasehold Empire.* Oxford: Oxford University Press.

Stubbs, R. (2000). "ASEAN Plus Three: Emerging East Asian Regionalism?" *Asian Survey* 42, no. 3: 440–455.

Yasutomo, D.T. (1995). *The New Multilateralism in Japan's Foreign Policy.* New York: St. Martin's Press.

Zhang, S.G. (2001). *Economic Cold War: America's Embargo against China and the Sino-Soviet Alliance, 1949–1963.* Stanford: Stanford University Press.

3

Anti-Americanism in Japan

Brad Glosserman

Anti-Americanism in Japan is a thick cord that is composed of several strands. It is a constant in contemporary Japan—as in much of the world—but its appeal ebbs and flows with events. This chapter first examines the forms of anti-Americanism that have surfaced in postwar Japan and then looks at the various roots of the phenomenon. It then explores the factors that have influenced—and continue to influence—its development and periodic resurgence. Finally, it offers thoughts on how supporters of the U.S.–Japan alliance can combat anti-Americanism. It will be an uphill battle. Successive U.S. administrations have shown little inclination to treat Japan as anything but a junior partner in the bilateral relationship. (Japan is complicit in this arrangement.) Moreover, America looms disproportionately large in the Japanese mind. As long as that is true, the United States will be a convenient target whenever Japanese are unhappy with their own government or unsettled about their future. Nonetheless, the United States can do more to minimize some frictions (some it cannot); nothing more is required of Washington than to give an ally the respect it is due.

Forms of Anti-Americanism

Traditionally, anti-Americanism in Japan has taken three forms: left anti-Americanism, right anti-Americanism, and what can be called "opportunistic" anti-Americanism, which reflects no ideological bias but is the result of circumstances and is used to prop up whatever cause is near and dear to the heart of the advocate.

Left anti-Americanism is a product of Japan's Marxist-pacifist heritage. In the Marxist variant, the United States is condemned for being the representative of international capital. Marxism dug deep roots in Japan's intellectual community during the 1930s, despite—or perhaps because of—repression by the imperial authorities. The U.S. occupation released leftists imprisoned during the war years, and they assumed prominent positions in intellectual life and politics until the intensification of the Cold War forced the Americans to reverse course in the late 1940s. (The politicians were marginalized; the intellectuals and other public figures, such as some union officials, maintained considerable influence.) This "betrayal" of the left has been one source of anti-American sentiment, and it has been propagated through the influence that Marxists have had in teachers' unions and in universities. The end of the Cold War, the demise of the Soviet Union, and the virtual disappearance of the Japanese political left have undermined the political appeal of Marxist anti-Americanism, but it survives in another form.

The pacifist strand can be confused with the Marxist variant—understandably, given the "peace-loving" rhetoric of Cold War Marxism—but it should be treated separately. The atomic bombings of Hiroshima and Nagasaki provide the physical and historical foundations of this argument, although the imagery has been appropriated by most anti-U.S. movements in Japan at one time or another. The chief complaint among the pacifists is that the "entangling alliance" with the United States has obliged Tokyo to compromise the "no war" idealism of the Japanese constitution. Here too disillusionment probably intensified the anger—the constitution and its famous Article 9 were given to Japan by the United States, and their repudiation by Washington looked like betrayal.

Washington's efforts to push Japan to remilitarize during the Korean War provided the first opportunity for protest.[1] (At that time, the police forces were transformed into a nascent military, the precursors of today's Self Defense Forces.) The anger and unease reached its apogee in the violent protests that marked the 1960 revision of the U.S–Japan Security Treaty. Many Japanese feared that the revised treaty with the United States would tie Japan more closely to Washington's military and foreign policies. (That the revisions were engineered by a prime minister, Kishi Nobusuke, who had been affiliated with the imperial regime, added to the anger.[2])

Fears increased in tandem with Cold War tensions. Hopes that the end of the superpower standoff would lead to a peaceful "new world order" were dashed. The pacifists blame the United States for the creep of Japanese military capabilities and security commitments since the Persian Gulf War. More recently, pacifists' concerns have been rekindled by adjustments to the bilateral security treaty—in particular, the Defense Guidelines' provisions involving "contingencies in areas surrounding Japan"—that they worry will drag Japan into war.

Right anti-Americanism predates World War II, but it has been sharpened by U.S. attempts to break postwar Japan's links to the imperial past. For Japanese conservatives, the occupation and the bilateral security alliance emasculate the Japanese national spirit. They argue that responsibility for World War II has been unfairly foisted upon Japan; history's verdict has been rendered by the victors. The postwar constitution, and in particular the war-renouncing Article 9, are attempts to permanently deny Japan the means to assert itself internationally. Japan's subordinate position to the United States within the security alliance is proof of that proposition. In recent years, this critique of the United States has dovetailed with complaints about globalization, which is also condemned by conservatives as an attempt by the United States to smother national identity through the imposition of "universal values."[3] Susumu Nishibe, a former professor and social critic, argues "since reform of Japan has been discussed only from the American perspective since the end of World War II, I oppose most of the reforms made. . . . The reforms being conducted in the [contemporary] Heisei era will eventually lead to the submersion of Japan."[4]

Finally, there is what I call "opportunistic" anti-Americanism. It is opportunistic because it pops up whenever it can be used to cloak some other complaint. The underlying problem has no intrinsic relationship to anti-Americanism—at least to most observers. In simple terms, it is scapegoating.

For example, several analysts and commentators blame the United States for Japan's economic ills. It was reported in the *New York Times* that "All week, Japan wrestled with fears that America Inc. was plotting to buy Japan Inc.—at a deep discount. According to the conspiracy talk, Heizo Takenaka, the new economy chief, was doing the bidding of American 'vulture funds' by planning to knock over shaky banks and force bankruptcies of companies that are insolvent on paper. . . . 'Agent of the Americans' screamed one tabloid headline about Mr. Takenaka, the minister of economy and of financial services."[5]

The theory may sound ludicrous, but it is not new. Several years ago, a "popular economic theme among both the editors and directors/producers was that the Japanese financial bubble of the late 1980s had been touched off by the Plaza Accord of 1985, the implication being that Japan's 'lost decade' was caused—intentionally or otherwise—by the United States."[6] The *Yomiuri Shimbun,* Japan's largest newspaper, rang in the New Year with a critical series on the United States. In it, Ota Hiroshi, deputy chief officer of the Yomiuri Research Institute, argued that Japan has made numerous attempts to help the United States out of its difficulties. Ota believes that Japan's troubles are attributable to those efforts and that it is time for Washington to reciprocate.[7]

Roots of Anti-Americanism

The roots of anti-Americanism are deep in Japan, since the phenomenon reflects fundamental questions about Japanese national identity. In one sense, its origins can be traced back to the arrival of the "Black Ships" in the nineteenth century and the challenges posed by modernization. Since Commodore Perry, the Japanese have had to assimilate foreign ideas and technologies to achieve the national goal of claiming a place among the leading nations of the world. Externally, the effort was successful: the country quickly assumed international prominence. Internally, however, Japanese society was strained by the accommodation of western ideas. The tension between modernism, as represented by western behavior and thinking, and traditional Japanese norms was glossed over at best. It erupted in the 1930s and led eventually to war.

In the aftermath of defeat, antiwestern sentiment focused on the United States. This was only natural given the U.S. role in the defeat of Japan and the subsequent occupation. Occupation policies made perfectly clear the "artificiality" of the postwar regime, since they were designed to break the link between pre- and postwar Japan. Japan was "modernized" on western terms (although scholars debate the continuity that exists in a range of fields). Defeat in war made that possible, but it raised questions and issues that were certain to reemerge in time—and have done so. Many of the issues raised in this chapter go to the heart of Japanese national identity in the twenty-first century. I believe that Japan is the most confused nation on the planet, since so many basic questions about the nation's place in the world are unanswered; as the foregoing discussion makes plain, anti-Americanism colors many components of the identity question as it is debated across the political spectrum.[8]

While modernization raises a host of questions, there is the more specific problem created by the occupation: the question of war responsibility. The U.S. decision to spare the emperor from being held responsible for the war waged in his name meant that any attempt to find justice was going to be difficult to justify. The eventual decision to hold a small number of individuals responsible, charging that they "hijacked" the state, allowed the rest of the Japanese people to disclaim any responsibility for the war and even to consider themselves victims as well. In this light, Article 9 is not only a declaration of Japan's future intent but also protection against future attempts to victimize the Japanese people by the authorities—a hedge against the re-creation of another authoritarian state.

For conservatives, the entire procedure smacks of victor's justice and unfairly discredits the imperial system and the ideals behind it. Conservatives also argue that it is wrong: It disregards the circumstances that forced Japan to go to war. In this reading of history, the United States is as guilty as Japan; at the very least, Tokyo's behavior was no worse than that of any other aspiring great power.

The foregoing may seem like a digression, but the decision to prosecute a virtual handful of individuals cuts off debate about the meaning of nationalism within Japan. Attempts to discuss national pride and patriotism inevitably founder on the question of war responsibility, since there is the perception that honoring the state is what got Japan into trouble in the 1930s. There are even questions about which symbols of the state are free of taint: The national anthem and even the flag raise associations with the imperial regime. In other words, there is no easy answer to what the patriotic Japanese should be proud of. And since the United States is perceived as the instrument of postwar justice—even though the trials were held by an international tribunal—the debate invariably includes the United States. And, it seems, the United States is always wrong: Either it unfairly blames Japan for the war, it is holding Japan back, or it is pushing Tokyo to be more militarist and to turn its back on the constitution's promise to be peaceful.

The perceived influence of the United States in Japanese political decision making is a third factor in explaining anti-Americanism in Japan. The United States looms large in the Japanese mind. As the junior partners in the U.S.–Japan security alliance, postwar governments in Japan have always worked to accommodate the United States. That makes sense, given the imbalance in the relationship and the vital role the United States played in defending Japan.[9] Handling the United States and ensuring that relations functioned smoothly has been the benchmark by which Japanese governments were evaluated. (This has changed somewhat in recent years, but it is still a key concern.)

The perception of U.S. influence over Japan's destiny has been encouraged by the structure of Japanese politics in the postwar era, in particular the absence of a real opposition party to challenge the government. To fill the vacuum, the United States has emerged as the primary voice for change in Japan, and there is a word, *gaiatsu,* or external pressure, that is used to describe U.S. attempts to bring about reform.

While the perception is that the United States intervenes in Japan's domestic affairs, in fact Japanese politicians use *gaiatsu* for their own ends.[10] Recognizing the strength of the United States and cognizant of their own relative weakness, reformers ally with U.S. interests—usually letting the United States lead—as they push for change. The interests under attack are inclined to see the United States as their enemy and to let loose, charging it with arrogance and interference.

This process has become apparent in other ways in recent years. In the past decade, the U.S.–Japan bilateral relationship has become more pluralistic on almost every level—political, economic, and even social. As a result, debates that were once closely held have become more public as more groups participate and more individuals and interests are involved. For example, in the past, security issues were handled primarily by the Japanese Foreign Ministry; now politicians and bureaucrats from other ministries demand seats at the table. Issues that were handled quietly are now very public. Again, U.S. interests are used to validate a position, creating the impression of interference or undue influence over Japanese decision making.

Triggers of Anti-Americanism

It is clear that anti-American sentiment always exists in Japan. The question is when does this feeling become an issue in Japan—what triggers outbursts of anti-Americanism and turns it into a political force?

The most famous incident was the September 1995 rape of a twelve-year-old schoolgirl by three U.S. servicemen in Okinawa. Within weeks of the rape, 85,000 Okinawans had taken to the streets, demanding the withdrawal of all U.S. forces and bases from the island. That feeling was echoed by other citizens throughout Japan. The rape created one of the most serious crises in U.S.–Japan relations in the postwar era, and it was several years before the aftershocks had quieted. (The Okinawa problem is discussed in more depth below.)

More recently, the sinking of the *Ehime Maru,* a Japanese fisheries training vessel, by a U.S. nuclear submarine in 2001 set off another outburst of anti-Americanism. Nine high school students and their instructors were killed in the accident, which occurred off the coast of Hawaii. The subsequent discovery that the ship was carrying out risky emergency surfacing procedures while visitors were on board distressed many Japanese. It was a dangerous political combination: the death of Japanese high school students—always tragic but even more so at a time when birth rates are declining—by a U.S. military vessel. The controversy had the potential to derail U.S.–Japan relations, but it was defused by a sensitive and speedy U.S. response that included apologies and extensive efforts to find the bodies of the dead. The episode can be considered closed only now, as the two families of victims that had been holding out finally accepted a settlement from the U.S. government.

Perhaps the most widespread and intense round of domestic disputes occurred a little over four decades ago during demonstrations against revisions of the U.S.–Japan Security Treaty. The riots resulted in the death of a college student and the cancellation of a visit by President Eisenhower; it stunned Japan. While the unrest was set in motion by the treaty amendments, there were other important factors: most notably the way the bill was rammed through the Diet by a government headed by Prime Minister Kishi, a former alleged war criminal. Thus, a more nuanced view of the AMPO crisis (as it is known in Japan) would put less emphasis on its anti-American component and more on the Japanese domestic politics involved.

Another bout of anti-Americanism was set in motion during negotiations over the FSX (Fighter Support Experimental) plane in the 1980s. This episode, discussed in detail elsewhere,[11] was exacerbated by a nasty confluence of issues, in particular rising concern about declining U.S. economic prospects and the rise of Japan. The United States took a hard-line position during the negotiations, and even reopened— "clarified" was the term the diplomats used—the agreement after an initial deal had been reached. Those tactics and the images of U.S. congressmen crushing Japanese electronics on the capitol steps (in response to another scandal involving the export of Japanese products that could be used to support the Soviet military) prompted a predictable anti-American backlash in Japan.

Anti-American sentiment has also been evident throughout the latter half of the 1990s, not in response to a particular incident but because of a host of concerns about the security relationship generally and the ability of the United States to manage the alliance properly. These worries have grown in tandem with a rising sense of realism within Japan about security risks in Northeast Asia. The 1990s were a turbulent decade for the region: The Persian Gulf War was followed by the North Korean nuclear crisis of 1993–94; the Taiwan Strait crisis of 1996; and the 1998 launch of a *Taepodong* missile by North Korea, which traveled over Japan; and the current North Korean nuclear crisis.

In some cases, Japanese—and others, it should be pointed out—worried that the United States was provoking a crisis. In other instances, there was fear that the United States was insufficiently attentive to Japanese concerns. President Bill Clinton's 1998 trip to China, during which he flew over Japan without stopping on both legs, sparked fears of "Japan passing," and the Clinton administration's focus on Pyongyang's nuclear program prompted speculation that U.S. and Japanese interests diverged in dealing with the Korean Peninsula's security issues.[12] Some security specialists note rising fears of abandonment in Japan, which have resulted in an increasing tendency to "hedge" in security planning[13] as well as a greater willingness to criticize the United States for its management of the alliance. It is worth noting that these events can prompt anti-Americanism on both ends of the political spectrum: the first set of issues, which revolves around the "entangling" alliance, encouraged "left" anti-Americanism; the second involves "abandonment" and set off the right.

Anti-Americanism can also be triggered by nonsecurity issues. Throughout the past thirty years, Japan has repeatedly experienced "shocks" as a result of U.S. decisions. In 1971, President Richard Nixon abruptly ended the Bretton Woods exchange system, which drastically revalued the yen against the dollar, and then revealed his overtures to China and his readiness to open relations with that country. Washington's apparent readiness to treat an ally with such disregard has not been good for the relationship. There is speculation that such tactics have been deliberately used to "manage" the relationship[14]; if so, it has been a terribly shortsighted approach—especially since these shocks have raised resentment toward and doubts about the United States in Japan. "Taken together, there is increasing impatience among Japanese citizens with the way the alliance is managed."[15]

The Special Case of Okinawa

Any discussion of anti-Americanism in Japan must address the Okinawa question. This island chain south of the mainland is a particular sore point for the relationship, but the problem extends well beyond relations with the United States. In fact, the real Okinawa issue centers on relations between the islands and Tokyo rather than those between Japan and the United States. One prominent Japanese who has worked extensively on the problem has noted that "an insurmountable distrust of mainland Japanese lies at the heart of the Okinawa issue."[16]

Okinawa was an independent kingdom until the latter half of the nineteenth century, when it was integrated into Japan as a province. The island was the only battlefield within Japan during World War II, and the losses were horrific. Some 200,000 Okinawans died during the ferocious battle for the islands—nearly one-third of the residents. Many of the victims were killed or forced to commit suicide by Japanese.

After the war, Okinawa was placed under U.S. control and was turned into a virtual military fortress, a situation that continued even after Japan regained its independence. Many Okinawans believe—with good reason—that Okinawa was sacrificed to the Americans as the price of Japan's renewed independence.[17] Today, 70 to 75 percent of U.S. exclusive-use facilities in Japan are in Okinawa, which makes up only 0.6 percent of the land area of Japan; 19 percent of the main island of Okinawa comprises military facilities; only 14 percent of the bases in the prefecture were reduced in the postreversion (1972) period (as compared to 60 percent on the Japanese mainland).[18] "Compared with the Japanese mainland, U.S. military bases are concentrated 200 times more heavily in terms of land area in Okinawa and 300 times more heavily in terms of population."[19]

Discrimination has imposed a heavy burden on the Okinawa people. The military presence, always onerous, is considered to be an even greater offense because of the "peace loving" nature of the island people. Military accidents have occurred; inconveniences are created; prime real estate is denied the community. And then there is crime. According to prefectural statistics, since the return of Okinawa to Japan in 1972, more than 5,000 incidents (both minor and major) have occurred, including approximately 510 "particularly heinous crimes" such as rape and murder.[20]

While security issues—and the U.S. bases—are the focus of Okinawans' complaints, the real problems are much greater. The unemployment rate on the islands is twice the national average and the income of the prefecture is the lowest in Japan.[21] The local economy relies on government subsidies to survive. The crux of the Okinawa problem is that the islanders do not feel that mainlanders understand the reality of life in Okinawa; that they do not appreciate the special role that the islands play in Japan's security and the burdens it creates.

The 1995 rape incident galvanized public sentiment in Okinawa. Local politicians used the crime to make their case vis-à-vis the national authorities. Okinawa Governor Ota Masahide used the courts to challenge national laws concerning Okinawan land use; he traveled to the United States seven times to make his case for a withdrawal of the U.S. military presence on the island. He also met with then Prime Minister Hashimoto Ryutaro seventeen times to try to negotiate changes in the U.S. troop presence.[22]

Ota rode popular sentiment in Okinawa and on the mainland to unprecedented visibility. And while his efforts may have won a wider audience for Okinawan views and greater sympathy on both sides of the Pacific, they did not yield the policies he advocated. Instead, adroit security policy makers in Tokyo and Washington created an administrative structure, the Special Action Committee on Okinawa (SACO) that addressed Okinawan concerns.[23] SACO, along with some important concessions—most significantly the decision to move the Futenma Marine Air Station—took the wind out of the antibase movement. In the 1998 Okinawa gubernatorial election, Ota was defeated by a more conservative mainstream candidate who argued for a more conciliatory approach to Tokyo.

The problem did not go away, however. Crimes and incidents continued, and new Governor Inamine Keiichi was forced to issue a public statement complaining about the inability of the U.S. military to control its troops. The prefectural assembly then passed a resolution demanding the removal of the U.S. Marine Corps from the island. The senior marine general generated his own firestorm when an e-mail he wrote, which referred to local politicians as "wimps" and "nuts," was leaked to the press. The terms of the Status of Forces Agreement (SOFA) continued to be a focus of local resentment, especially after another rape incident. The sense of powerlessness engendered by the SOFA magnifies Okinawan sentiments. "The frustration among local residents in Okinawa stems from a lack of access to the policymaking process regarding the bases."[24]

Anti-Americanism Today

Events of the 1990s have created a more realistic security mindset among Japanese than ever before. This has helped the U.S.–Japan alliance. After reaching a nadir in 1995, views of the alliance have improved. Two years ago, 62.1 percent of Japanese agreed that the U.S.–Japan alliance contributes to regional security (only 23.6 percent said no). Despite their anger at the burden they have to bear, even Okinawans accept the need for the security alliance. More than 85 percent of Okinawans believe the alliance is vital to Japanese security.[25] Ambivalence exists, however: 44.5 percent of Japanese trusted the United States, while 41.8 percent did not. Significantly, 52.5 percent want fewer U.S. forces in Japan and 14 percent want them removed completely.[26] There is widespread agreement across political parties and among all Japanese —not just Okinawans—that the burden should be better distributed. A recent poll shows that 72 percent of Japanese like the United States; 37 percent want to see the security pact maintained, 33 percent would like a friendship agreement, and only 14 percent want to see the security treaty abrogated or Japan to become neutral.

There is the foundation for a strong partnership. Over half of Japanese—55 percent —believe that the United States and Japan "will be able to work together to adopt the same common values of democracy and a market economy." The same number believe the U.S.–Japan relationship is more important than their country's relationship with China.[27] Japanese views about the United States are the most positive in all of Asia except for the Philippines; 72 percent of Japanese have a favorable impression of the United States.[28]

This goodwill can be squandered, however. Virtually every opinion survey taken anywhere in the world shows growing concern about U.S. unilateralism and arrogance in its foreign policy. A Gallup International poll released on the first anniversary of the September 11, 2001, attacks showed that in most countries "the population is more likely to say U.S. foreign policy has a negative rather than a positive effect on their country."[29] Despite positive views of the United States overall, only 36 percent of Japanese think U.S. foreign policy considers Japanese interests; 59 percent say that it does not. Nonetheless, a solid majority (61 percent) supports the U.S.-led war on terrorism; only 32 percent oppose it.[30]

The unease that has grown out of the U.S. execution of the war against terrorism has been magnified by specific concerns in Japan. In addition to the security-related issues already mentioned, there is the more general problem of malaise in Japan. The people have lost faith in the country's political class. A decade of economic stagnation, endless scandals, and a rhetoric of change that is out of touch with reality have raised fundamental questions about the quality of national leadership in Japan. The alliance invariably suffers. "Citizen attitudes toward the alliance are more intimately linked with public frustration in Japan about the ability of political leaders to come up with workable solutions to policy problems."[31]

The United States cannot improve the quality of Japanese leadership, but it can do more to minimize the concerns raised by the U.S. presence. Alliance management is critical. The handling of the *Ehime Maru* incident was rough at times, but a speedy and sensitive response kept a tragic situation from undermining the alliance. The United States must be perceived as responding to Japanese concerns even as it protects its own national interests. The two are not incompatible.

In practical terms, the United States must be a better neighbor. Efforts have been made. The good-neighbor program in Okinawa has helped,[32] but there is more to be done. Community outreach is essential. Military personnel must become better public relations officers. The SOFA must be implemented with more efficiency and with better explanation. As Japanese participate in United Nations peacekeeping operations, a comparison of the legal procedures concerning Japanese soldiers overseas would be helpful and diminish public concern.

Ultimately, the U.S. footprint must be reduced. There is already discussion of this delicate subject, but politics always seems to push consideration to the future. This habit must stop before events force the two countries to make decisions that are not in the alliance's best interest.

Friction is inevitable in any alliance relationship, especially when the two partners are as unevenly matched as the United States and Japan and when the terms of the partnership create visible inequities. Anti-Americanism is also inevitable in Japan, given human nature and the country's history. Properly tended, the alliance can surmount this sentiment. Ignored, it could be overwhelmed by it.

Postscript

This chapter was presented in another format, one that deserves consideration here. During the conference session, I argued that anti-Americanism in Japan could be conceptualized in three dimensions: as a domestic political issue, as a security issue, and as a national identity issue. Since the substance of these issues is examined in detail in the preceding sections, I provide only the schema here.

When examined as a *domestic political issue*, anti-Americanism arises on two levels. First, as a result of *gaiatsu*, or foreign pressure, which is, in turn, a product of Japan's failure to create a homegrown opposition party. Second, in relation to the Okinawa question, the critical features are the historic divide between Okinawa and the mainland and the lack of access to policy making on an issue—the U.S. military presence—that is of overwhelming significance to Okinawans.

As a *security issue*, anti-Americanism arises from rising concern in Japan about national security and doubts about Washington's commitment to protect Japan. The controversy surrounding the response to the 1998 *Taepodong* launch put this issue in the sharpest relief. Alliance management issues have been exacerbated by the failure of the Japanese leadership to solve pressing national problems (primarily economic) during the 1990s. Ronald Meinardus's point that the structure of U.S.–Republic of Korea security relations contributes to anti-Americanism is also relevant here (see chapter 6). Meinardus argues that Germany's relations with the United States are embedded within a multilateral security framework that diffuses anti-American sentiment. Korea, like Japan, operates within a bilateral structure, in which "important policy decisions are clearly identified and identifiable as solely U.S.-inspired."

Finally, anti-Americanism is a product of the *national identity* debates in Japan. Japan is still grappling with questions raised by modernization, westernization, and globalization, to name just three of the forces at work. For many in Japan (and elsewhere in the world), the United States, by virtue of its size and its role in the post–Cold War world, is the source and the symbol of these forces. Anti-Americanism is a convenient shelter for Japanese facing basic questions about who they are and their role in the twenty-first century.

Notes

1. Mike M. Mochizuki, "U.S.-Japan Relations in the Asia-Pacific Region," In *Partnership: The United States and Japan 1951–2001*, ed. Akira Iriye and Robert A. Wampler (Kodansha, Tokyo and New York, 2001), pp. 14–15.

2. Mark Gallicchio, "Occupation, Dominion, and Alliance: Japan in American Security Policy, 1945–69," in *Partnership: The United States and Japan 1951–2000*, ed. Akira Iriye and Robert A. Wampler (Kodansha, Tokyo and New York, 2001), p. 124.

3. Susumu Awanohara, "Japanese Attitudes and Approaches toward U.S. Policies and Presence in the Region," in *East Asia and the United States: Current Status and Five-Year Outlook* (National Intelligence Council, September 2000); available at the NIC Web site, www.cia.gov/nic/.

4. Cited in Brian J. McVeigh, "Postwar Japan's 'Hard' and 'Soft' Nationalism," Japan Policy Research Institute (JPRI) Working Paper, no. 73, January 2001.

5. James Brooke, "Japan Fears Its Weakened Economy Is Becoming America's Prey," *New York Times*, November 3, 2002.

6. Awanohara, "Japanese Attitudes."

7. Hiroshi Ota, "Weaker Yen May Be Cure to Lead Nation to Fiscal Health," *Daily Yomiuri 7*. Online edition, January 3, 2003.

8. See, for example, Akira Ishikawa, "Can Japan Say No?" at www.siue.edu/EASTASIA/yuki_102199.htm.

9. "Introduction," in Michael Blaker, Paul Giarra, and Ezra Vogel, *Case Studies in Japanese Negotiating Behavior* (Washington, DC: United States Institute of Peace Press Perspectives Series, 2002), pp. 12–15.

10. C. Fred Bergston et al., *No More Bashing: Building A New Japan–United States Economic Relationship* (Washington, DC: Institute for International Economics, 2001), p. 17.

11. See, for example, Richard Samuels, *Rich Nation, Strong Army: National Security and Technological Transformation of Japan* (Ithaca, NY: Cornell University Press, 1994), pp. 213–44.

12. Awanohara, "Japanese Attitudes."

13. Michael J. Green, *Japan's Reluctant Realism* (New York: St. Martin's Press, 2001).

14. Michael Blaker, "Negotiations on Orange Imports," in Michael Blaker, Paul Giarra, and Ezra Vogel, *Case Studies in Japanese Negotiating Behavior* (Washington, DC: United States Institute of Peace Press Perspectives Series, 2002), p. 19.

15. Sheila Smith, "Japan's Uneasy Citizens and the U.S.-Japan Alliance," East West Center, *Asia Pacific Issues*, no. 54 (September 2001): 1.

16. Haruo Shimada, "The Significance of the Okinawa Issue," in *Restructuring the U.S.-Japan Alliance: Toward a More Equal Partnership*, ed. Ralph A. Cossa (Washington, DC: CSIS Significant Issues Series, October 1977), p. 90. The following discussion relies heavily on Shimada, who served as chairperson of the Cabinet Minister's Task Force on Okinawa Problems.

17. Gallicchio, "Occupation, Dominion, and Alliance," p. 120.

18. Robert Eldridge, "Okinawa and U.S.-Japan Relations in the 21st Century: Bilateral and Trilateral Approaches to a Sounder Okinawa Policy" (Tokyo: Research Institute for Peace and Security Occasional Paper, March 2002), p. 10.

19. Shimada, "Significance of the Okinawa Issue." p. 91.

20. Eldridge, "Okinawa and U.S.-Japan Relations." p. 4. While the crime rate is a problem, U.S. officials say the numbers should be put in perspective. A Marine Corps representative argues, "The baseline adult population [for U.S. personnel] on Okinawa is approximately 40,000

and approximately one-third of those personnel rotate throughout the year. It is safe to say that throughout any given year, roughly 50,000 U.S. service and family members set foot on Okinawa. Of those 50,000 during 2001, 70 criminal cases resulted. Seventy cases out of 50,000 people comes out to roughly 0.0014 percent of our folks being involved in a crime." Cited in Eldridge, "Okinawa and U.S.-Japan Relations," note 14, p. 6.

21. Ibid., p. 92.

22. Sheila Smith, "Challenging National Authority: Okinawa Prefecture and the U.S. Military Bases," in *Local Voices, National Issues: The Impact Local Initiative in Japanese Policy-Making*, ed. Sheila A. Smith (Ann Arbor: University of Michigan, Center for Japanese Studies, 2000), p. 75.

23. See Shimada, "Significance of the Okinawa Issue" for a detailed description of the SACO process.

24. Smith, "Japan's Uneasy Citizens," p. 4.

25. Eldridge, "Okinawa and U.S.-Japan Relations," note 34, p. 10.

26. *Yomiuri Shimbun*/Gallup survey, conducted December 22–25, 2000, cited in Smith, "Japan's Uneasy Citizens."

27. Harris Poll, April 21, 1999.

28. *What the World Thinks in 2002*, The Pew Global Attitudes Project, December 4, 2002.

29. Gallup International, *Voice of the People*, September 7, 2002.

30. *What the World Thinks in 2002*.

31. Smith, "Japan's Uneasy Citizens."

32. Eldridge, "Okinawa and U.S.-Japan Relations," note 4, p. 3.

4

A Japanese Perspective on Anti-Americanism

Yoichi Funabashi

The recent wave of virulent anti-American sentiment, far from being confined to the Islamic street, has also surged through countries traditionally allied with the United States. I focus here on the new dynamics of anti-Americanism among American allies, primarily dwelling on Japan's case. In doing so, I draw lessons from Japan's post–World War II experience that are pertinent to halting the tide of anti-Americanism today.

In the late 1930s and early 1940s, Japan was perhaps the most anti-American country in the world. Even before World War II, the entire English and American vocabulary imported from the Meiji era onward was erased from the language, down to words such as "strikes," "balls," and "strikeouts" in baseball.

After Japan's devastating defeat, anti-Americanism in the country could conceivably have mushroomed. After all, around 2 million Japanese citizens had been killed in a conflict that reached a climax of suffering in the atomic destruction of Hiroshima and Nagasaki. Unconditional surrender was followed by seven years of occupation under a military bureaucracy that enjoyed the colonial life to the full. The essential ingredients for anti-Americanism were present.

Yet in the event, Japan's postwar history took an entirely different course. Indeed, Japan has turned out to be probably one of the most pro-American countries in the world. What led to this remarkable turnaround?

Anti-Americanism Contained

Good Loser, Good Winner

In defeat, Japan very consciously set out to play the "good loser," in the words of Shigeru Yoshida, Japan's prime minister at the time. The United States, for its part, reciprocated by playing the role of the "good winner," engaging and generous. General MacArthur wanted to make the occupation of Japan the most successful occupation in world history. Accordingly, when, for instance, Japan confronted a serious food crisis, MacArthur ordered the import of emergency food supplies from the United States. This had a hugely positive effect on the attitudes of many Japanese toward the United States.[1]

Showing the vanquished in an occupied area solid evidence of the occupying forces' ability to ensure stability and security can greatly increase confidence in the overall success of the operation. General MacArthur managed this convincingly, as John Dower has noted: "In an occupation that lasted from 1945 to 1952, there was not one instance of Japanese terror against the occupation forces."[2] It is a record America should aspire to emulate today.

The decision to retain the emperor and absolve him from responsibility for the war formed another spoke of a strategy designed to elicit the cooperation necessary for reform and the development of policies. The United States, in other words, pledged to preserve the regime's symbol as a means of radically overhauling that regime.

Many Japanese felt as if they had been liberated. The advent of labor unions, women's suffrage, land reform, and so forth built new stakeholder constituencies for reform, in turn ensuring rock-solid support for the postwar regime.[3] Before long, 90 percent of the Japanese public felt that they belonged to the middle class.

Gaiatsu/Naiatsu

The cardinal rule to be distilled from Japan's historical experience is that America must follow regime change by concentrating on generating a political base for reform in countries such as Iraq and Afghanistan. This has to galvanize domestic pressure (*naiatsu* in Japanese) for reform. Reform is born out of the nexus of *gaiatsu* (external pressure) and *naiatsu* and is then free to progress under its own steam.

The general perception that the reform of the occupation period was simply imposed from above by MacArthur's administration is in fact a misperception. It was actually reignited from the embers of reform proposals from the Taisho Democracy in the 1920s. Democratic practices and movements had flourished until immediately before the 1931 Manchurian incident, and the postwar Higashikuni and Shidehara cabinets[4] pushed for the legalization of trade unions and land reform.[5] The American administration was thus able to harness the extant democratic legacy. This proved an extremely effective strategy for containing anti-Americanism.

Trust and Reconciliation

The geopolitical environment framed a crucial backdrop to the new partnership between Japan and America. Confronted by a common threat and mutual enemy, the United States and Japan forged an alliance between loser and winner. Furthermore, the ideological nature of the Cold War battleground meant that even right-wingers became pro-American. Anti-Americanism in Japan during the Cold War was therefore essentially of an ideological nature, a reaction to perceived American imperialism.

More significantly however, the San Francisco peace treaty of 1951 provided the impetus for the development of a relationship founded on trust and reconciliation—a chance to "start over." By the time Japan achieved independence in 1952, "occupation fatigue" had crept in. Revealing an antidemocratic tendency, the occupation regime forbade criticism, and pictures of Hiroshima and Nagasaki had even been banned from publication. Yet the San Francisco Peace Treaty of the same year was both fair and generous.

The Tokyo Tribunal trying those accused of war crimes (April 1946–November 1948) had previously come in for much heavier criticism. A highly politicized affair, cynically manipulated by the Soviets in particular, it was roundly condemned as a kangaroo court by many Japanese. The anti-American sentiments provoked by this "show trial" linger even now. Although it undoubtedly left many Japanese feeling unsatisfied with the "San Francisco Treaty system" by denying Japan's government the right to challenge the verdicts, the treaty nevertheless made it possible to draw a line under the tribunals as a fait accompli. Above all, it therefore laid the foundations for a process of trust and reconciliation between victor and the vanquished; hence its influence is still felt today.

"Soft Power"

The picture of an unbalanced America utilizing military power to excess has greatly contributed to the surge of anti-Americanism. What can be done to improve America's image? It seems to me that that the answer lies in placing much more emphasis on soft power: extolling the power of example in preference to hard military means. The most effective means of debunking demonizing myths surrounding the United States is to expose people to American society and American education, particularly higher education.

The first thing the Japanese and American governments did after Japan's independence, after all, was to mutually launch the Fulbright Program in 1952. I, for one, was a beneficiary of this program as one among 7,000 Japanese Fulbrighters sent to the United States, and 3,000 Americans have visited Japan in the past half-century. We celebrated the fiftieth anniversary of this large human network of peace and understanding last year.

Even though it sounds like a very minor initiative, another suggestive source of soft power is found in the American Centers. These appeal to a broad range of people worldwide. When the Berlin wall fell, the United States lost no time in establishing American Centers throughout eastern Europe. Lines stretching to a thousand people formed even at 6 a.m. when a new center opened in Leipzig in the former East Germany. I myself remember regularly visiting the American Center in Fukuoka, Japan, thirty-some years ago, when I was stationed there as a young reporter. That was the place where I first read *Foreign Affairs* magazine, which I have come to regard as my indispensable guide to world politics, never missing an edition. There was a program arranged by a director of American affairs under which I was invited to take part in a discussion with Fred Ikle, later undersecretary of defense. That was my first experience of having a discussion on policy issues in English with an American intellectual.

America must highlight the real opportunities for international collaboration by building on the esteem with which its institutions are regarded in the Middle East—perhaps the strongest weapon in Washington's soft-power arsenal.

A striking example of this appeal emerged in the wake of the U.S. bombing of the Chinese embassy in Belgrade during the Kosovo War. One day, tens of thousands of angry demonstrators took to the streets of Beijing to shout anti-American slogans.[6] The following day, however, applicants for student visas formed a long line at the U.S. embassy.

Anti-Americanism Transformed

Since the Cold War's end, anti-Americanism has mutated and branched out in several directions in Japan.

Economic Nationalism and Asianism

Economic nationalism along the lines trumpeted in *The Japan That Can Say No*, the 1989 best seller by Akio Morita and Shintaro Ishihara, has praised Japan's technological and economic prowess.[7] Palpably alarming many Americans, this was indeed a kind of harbinger of anti-Americanism to come. During the Cold War, trade disputes played second fiddle to the supreme consideration of security; however, the Cold War era containment effect has been found unequal to current realities.

Japanese economic nationalism, in turn, contributed to the rise of Asianism. Perhaps Morita and Ishihara's most admiring reader was Prime Minister Mahathir of Malaysia. He went on to publish his own book, entitled *The Asia That Can Say No*,[8] where "no" always means no to the United States. This anti-American upsurge (although in Mahathir's case, it is usually a broader antiwestern sentiment based on historic anticolonial resentment) was sharpened by the 1997–98 Asian Financial Crisis and erupted again in the wake of the antiterror war.[9]

Cross-fertilization between Japanese economic nationalism and Asianism also came to the fore when Malaysia's East Asian Economic Conference (EAEC) proposal was aborted. Ministry of International Trade and Industry (MITI) Minister Ryutaro Hashimoto was then able to successfully use the "Asia card" against Mickey Kantor when the United States tried to impose a settlement on Japan, winning with the support of almost all his Asian counterparts.[10] Kantor backed off.

Base Politics

In terms of both symbol and substance, the single most explosive issue driving anti-Americanism in Japan now revolves around U.S. forward bases, most acutely those in Okinawa. The anti-American antibase movement is omnipresent, but it has changed its tack since the end of the Cold War. The Okinawa rape incident of 1995, in which a twelve-year-old schoolgirl was raped by three American marines, caused tremendous outrage and has had a lasting impact.[11] More generally, a wide array of issues comprising human rights, women's rights, the environmental movement, and the debate over local government autonomy have now coalesced, with the bases as their focal point.

A further complicating factor that could bear on Japan's politics regarding bases is the restructuring of American forces on the Korean peninsula. Although relocation of American bases in South Korea is inevitable and is on balance likely to be a positive development, it could be detrimental to the U.S.–Japan alliance if it is poorly handled and seen as a diminution of U.S. commitment to Korea. Worse still, if the United States were to completely withdraw from its Korean forward bases, Japan would be left feeling singled out, overburdened, and vulnerable. While on the one hand seeing herself as uniquely and unfairly burdened, at the same time she might suspect that Korea would turn more neutral. The exclusive U.S. presence in Japan could stoke entrapment fears in Japan, fueling anti-American feeling in Okinawa particularly and in the process transforming the trilateral relationship.

The U.S.–China Dynamic

Since President Richard M. Nixon visited China in 1972 without notifying Japan until three minutes before the official announcement, Japan has been preoccupied with the prospect of the United States and China joining together to "gang up" against her. This has been evident on both the security and economic fronts.

Particularly in a society that values loyalty as the supreme virtue, the visit to China by President Bill Clinton in 1998 served to encourage anti-Americanism and strain Japan–U.S. relations. Without even calling in on his Japanese ally, he upgraded the U.S.–China relationship to a "strategic partnership." This "Japan passing" came hard on the heels of joint China–U.S. criticism of the weak yen, which both countries complain is harmful to their trading interests. China's and the United States' castigation of Japan's economic travails is a continuing embarrassment.

As Japan perceives it, weakening the U.S.–Japan alliance is a strategic priority for China, while the United States stands to gain leverage over Tokyo by playing on fears that it is moving closer to China and conversely devaluing its alliance with Japan. Such perceptions remain pervasive among Tokyo's policy makers.

America and China have also found common cause over nuclear issues. Japanese anti-American sentiments were severely exacerbated by America's indication that China should denounce North Korea for its nuclear activities by employing the rationale that there could be a possible domino effect in terms of Japan's nonnuclear stance. Japanese suspect that the United States wants to cap the bottle on Japan, limiting it to a purely defensive role, and has found a mutual interest with China in doing so. This perception could breed mistrust and lead to a more anti-American bent in Japan, which could be dangerously detrimental to the U.S.–Japan relationship and lead Japan into pursuing a more individual course.

Anti-Globalism and Anti-Americanism

Anti-globalism movements have readily translated into anti-Americanism. Furthermore, in Japan there has traditionally been a tightly closed circle entwining politicians, bureaucrats, and protected industries. The regulated and the regulator have historically closed ranks together against market-opening forces. Typically, these forces of resistance blame the United States for "their problems"; in fact, they are often merely cynically using the United States as a scapegoat for their own policy failures.

Likewise, anti-Americanism is also in currency as a domestic political ploy. The "Takenaka bashing" response of the protectionist lobby to Minister for Economic and Fiscal Policy and for Financial Services Heizo Takenaka's recent attempts to reform the banking system and deal with "zombie companies" is a clear example of this. The "forces of resistance" have castigated him as "nothing better than an agent for foreign vultures," caricaturing his reforms as an American multinational "plot to buy bankrupt Japanese banks and firms on the cheap."[12]

In the past, the protectionist nexus formed by the agricultural and fishing industries, retailers, and construction companies, all sponsoring pork-barrel politics, were able to successfully defend their turf and resist change. The reality now in Japan, however, is that losers and potential losers are increasingly mainstream. Even the elite class—bureaucrats, bankers, steelmakers, educators, and university professors, for example—are threatened.

No Viable Alternative

There is a sense of having been deprived of an alternative to "the American way." Younger politicians, including members of the ruling Liberal Democratic Party (LDP), are attracted by the more communitarian and social-democratic tradition of the European Union model.[13] This can also be seen as a hedging strategy. The Enron and Worldcom scandals have served to undermine the platform of those reformers who seek to emulate the American paradigm. Nonetheless, as yet no viable alternative to the American model has emerged. People feel the lack of an alternative vision but at the same time feel overwhelmed by the American way. The biggest challenge is to find a means of compensating those who have suffered losses due to globalization.

The Difficulty of Alliance Management

The increasing difficulty of alliance management has entailed a corresponding deepening of frustration. Constant irritants are chipping away at the foundations of the relationship. Possibly the most critical of these is the enormous capability gap between the United States and its ally. The Gulf War, the Kosovo War, the Afghanistan War, and the Second Gulf War were fought with the newest arms, such as microwave weapons. Present-day U.S. military prowess represents the culmination of a long-term trend.

U.S. allies resultantly feel a growing sense of impotence. They resent being constantly reminded of their powerlessness in a lopsided relationship. This perhaps lies at the root of European irritation and the tinge of anti-American sentiments lurking behind the criticism of it as a *hyperpower*. Indeed, my interview with Hubert Vedrine, who famously coined the term *hyperpower*, left me with the impression that he was more frustrated with the impotence of Europe than with American power as such.[14] Robert Kagan has also pointed to the widening capability gap as one source of American unilateralism. He observes that in the Balkans, "As some Europeans put it, the real division of labor consisted of the United States 'making the dinner' and the Europeans 'doing the dishes.'"[15]

Can the division-of-labor model work? Taking Japan's case, we have turned to global civilian power and defensive military power. We have no choice but to play the complementary "feminine role" to the "masculine role" of the United States. But Japan is constantly being reminded of the "free rider" criticisms that boiled over during the First Gulf War. These are spurred by the lack of mutuality in the alliance and compounded by Japan's constitutional constraints on the use and projection of military power.

If the United States is visibly seen to be exploiting this, anti-Americanism will erupt as it did at the time of the First Gulf War, when Japan had to raise taxes to contribute $13 billion to the coalition's campaign. The contemporary anti-American crowds saw this as both "guilt money "and "extortion money." The Bush administration pressured Japan to commit militarily, even though it knew perfectly well that this was a constitutional and political impossibility. On the one hand, the United States calls on Japan to shoulder more of the burden for its own defense; on the other, it maintains the status quo. In this way, it is able to extract concessions.

Japan must overcome the constitutional and political constraints on its involvement in the United Nations and other forms of collective defense. The alternative is to be constantly constrained by the accusation that Japan is a "free rider" protected by a lopsided defense arrangement. Japanese, in fact, feel that they already do enough by virtue of the military bases they provide and their host-country status; they feel exploited by these taunts. However, as long as the current situation persists, Japan has no answer to the American criticisms. If she wants to shake off this constraint, which eventually feeds into anti-Americanism, she must gradually correct the imbalance in the U.S.–Japan relationship and assert her right to collective defense.

Compensating the Losers

America's greatest challenge is to find a way to help compensate the losers. The most dangerous image of the United States and American capitalism is that it inherently has "winner take all" characteristics. A further source of anti-U.S. sentiment feeds on the perception that the world's most powerful country is indifferent to the losers, who have been mass-produced by seemingly unstoppable globalization, which the United States itself has propelled.

The most fundamental challenge to the United States in the coming century is therefore this: How can it aid in compensating the losers and reincorporating them into the mainstream of their society and the world? In searching for an answer to this critical question, Japan's postwar experience remains extremely pertinent.

Iraq Through the Lens of Japan's Experience

As I have said, General MacArthur and the postwar Japanese leaders were fortunate in being able to draw from the well of homegrown ideas. In the same way, fostering the citizens' own sense of ownership is similarly vital in Iraq most immediately, as it will be in comparable situations that America may confront in the future. It will furthermore require considerable creativity where indigenous traditions are not available, as they were in Japan.

To dwell further on a comparison of the Iraqi and Japanese occupations, it is interesting that General MacArthur himself harbored suspicions that the Japanese remained too immature to sustain democracy. "Measured by the standards of modern civilization," he said, "they would be like a boy of 12 as compared with our development of 45 years." Understandably disheartened by the Iraqi émigrés' state of confusion and the lawlessness that followed the collapse of the Baathist regime, many Americans may also be tempted to believe that the country is ungovernable. The Iraqi people, however, are blessed with enormous resources and talent groomed in a splendid civilization. Once liberated, they can be left to themselves. The supposedly pubescent Japanese public, let us remember, managed its own miracle.

Moreover, the international community confronts battles for "trust and reconciliation" on two fronts in Iraq. First, it needs to find ways to bring reconciliation to Iraq's international relationships, particularly with the United States. Second, there is the job of healing the ethnic, tribal, and religious wounds that have been exacerbated by Saddam's divide-and-rule policy. These are not challenges for the faint hearted. But international society should not—and cannot afford to—shy away from them. America also facilitated Japan's reconciliation with "free world" East Asian countries, particularly South Korea. This kind of international peace strategy should accompany reconstruction in Iraq, particularly vis-à-vis the elusive Palestinian-Israeli peace settlement. Democracy cannot be generated in a vacuum; the regional peace structure must be addressed too.

U.S. Resolve

In the last analysis, perhaps the most important question to emerge from a comparison of the Iraqi and Japanese cases hangs not over Iraqi characteristics but over the way in which America's identity may have changed since 1945. Put simply, the key question is this: Does America in 2003 still have the will to commit itself to this effort? In World War II, U.S. planners began to prepare for the occupation three years in advance of Japan's defeat. Thousands of Americans underwent a program of historical and linguistic training to form the main administrative pillar of the occupation. In peacetime, a number of these went on to contribute greatly as scholars to laying down the intellectual foundations of mutual understanding with Japan—Edwin O. Reischauer, Donald Keene, and Edward Seidensticker, to name a few. Particularly after events in Afghanistan, many conclude that the answer is that America is no longer in the "nation-building business."

The United States must prove in the coming years that the pessimism about its resolve in Iraq and in other countries is unfounded. The potential gap between America's level of commitment then and now points to the most valid historical lesson that Japan's occupation can teach. In order to succeed in Iraq, America must commit as it did to Japan, reprising its role as the good winner in a prolonged curtain call. What is more, it must do so multilaterally, in concert with U.S. friends and allies— and most importantly, in partnership with the United Nations. Establishing jurisdiction for the Japanese occupation, one should recall, was one of the debut acts of the United Nations.

Notes

1. Richard B. Finn, *Winners in Peace: MacArthur, Yoshida, and Postwar Japan* (Berkeley: University of California Press, 1992), pp. 113–14; John Dower, *Embracing Defeat: Japan in the Wake of World War II* (Norton, 2000), pp. 93–94; Hisahiko Okazaki, "U.S. Must Learn Lessons from Occupation of Japan," *Daily Yomiuri*, January 19, 2003.

2. "Lessons from Japan about War's Aftermath," *New York Times*, October 27, 2002.

3. The Labor Union Law was passed on December 21, 1945; the Universal Adult Suffrage Act was passed December 15, 1945; and the revised land reform bill won approval in October 21, 1946.

4. August 17 to October 5, 1945, and October 9, 1945, to April 22, 1946, respectively.

5. See Okazaki, "U.S. Must Learn Lessons": "Japan had nowhere to go back except for the Taisho Democracy, once the war had been brought to an end. The first postwar Cabinet, led by liberal Prince Higashikuni as prime minister, threw its support behind full guarantees of freedom of speech and association—despite the Occupation's worry that some radical reforms would have a negative impact on public peace and order. . . . The subsequent administration, headed by Prime Minister Kijuro Shidehara, rallied Shidehara's allies from the Taisho Democracy days and launched a set of democratic reforms that had been pending since the Taisho era."

6. See "Protesters lay siege to embassies," *Guardian Unlimited*, May 10, 1999; available at www.guardian.co.uk/Kosovo/Story/0,2763,207156,00.html.

7. Ishihara Shintaro, *The Japan That Can Say No* (New York: Simon and Schuster, 1991).

8. Published in English as *The Voice of Asia: Two Leaders Discuss the Coming Century*, by Mahathir Bin Mohamad, Shintaro Ishihara (contributor) (New York: Kodansha International, 1995).

9. Mahathir's opening speech at the annual World Economic Forum in Davos in January 2003 is illustrative of his brand of Asianist anti-Americanism: "It is blasphemy to say anything against democracy. If you do, if you resist then you will be considered a heretic and starved to death, or bombed out of existence. . . . [Regarding 9/11:] The worm finally turned. The weak have now hit back in the only way they can. Groping for the enemy, the strong hit out blindly in every direction, in every part of the world. No one is free. Fear rules the world." See "World War Has Begun: Malaysia's Mahathir Assails U.S. at Davos Opening," *Reuters*, January 24, 2003; available at www.commondreams.org/headlines03/0124–05.htm.

10. "Hashimoto Keeps World Guessing," *Asian Business* 32, no. 10 (October 1996): 24–25.

11. See also Yoichi Funabashi, *Alliance Adrift* (New York: Council on Foreign Relations, 1999).

12. From Richard Katz, "Japan's Phoenix Economy," in *Foreign Affairs* (January–February 2003). See also "Tokyo's Bank-Reform Advocate Could Lose Post," *International Herald Tribune*, May 29, 2003, and "Koizumi Faces Cabinet Critics," *Asian Wall Street Journal*, May 29, 2003.

13. See "Datsuseichou shugi, moderu wa oushuu. Kokkai no wakate 101 giin ni chousa," *Asahi Shimbun*, August 3, 2002.

14. "Hyper-realism Paints a Surreal U.S. Face," *Asahi Shimbun*, January 14, 2003; available at www.asahi.com/column/funabashi/eng/TKY200302070196.html.

15. See Robert Kagan, *Policy Review Online*, "Power and Weakness," (2002); available at www.policyreview.org/JUN02/kagan.html.

5

Unilateralism and Its Discontents

The Passing of the Cold War Alliance and Changing Public Opinion in the Republic of Korea

Meredith Woo-Cumings

In a December 2002 survey of national attitudes, conducted in forty-two countries by the Pew Research Center, a stunning 44 percent of South Koreans were found to hold unfavorable views of the United States. This level of disaffection topped France's 34 percent, Germany's 35 percent, and in fact, any country in Europe or East Asia. In the non-Muslim world, only Argentina, whose economy had been in ruins for two years (arguably done in by the neoliberal nostrums pushed by Washington) was shown to harbor more unhappy sentiments vis-à-vis the United States.[1] A Korean Gallup Poll, conducted around the same time as the Pew Research Center survey, confirmed as much and more, reporting that some 53.7 percent of South Koreans held "unfavorable" and "somewhat unfavorable" views of the United States. Most of these malcontents happened to be young and included upward of 80 percent of the college students polled.[2] This situation gave a rise to much hand-wringing about South Korea, once the most loyal of the American allies, becoming implacably "anti-American."

In the United States, the reaction to the alleged South Korean "anti-Americanism" was one of shock and petulance. Jacques Barzun once remarked that Americans were people who valued popularity more than any other kind of success, and that it was galling and inexplicable to them that there should be a widespread dislike of the United States around the world—above all, we might add, in places like South Korea, where more than 53,000 Americans lost their lives so that the freedom of the South Korean people could be preserved. Soon, American reporters were sending dispatches back from Seoul, dismayed that South Korean students did not seem to know much about their own history, including the fact that it was actually North Korea that invaded South in 1950, and that the United States was the deus ex machina that had saved South Korea from communist invaders. Instead, the students seemed resentfully focused on the fact that it was the United States that, before the Korean War, had divided Korea in half in the first place.[3]

If South Koreans could not figure out who their friends and enemies were, some Americans argued, it was about time that the United States and South Korea called it quits. "South Korea has tired of the Americans," columnist Robert Novak wrote, "and the Americans have grown impatient with South Korea." It would be best if the United

States pulled the plug on South Korea, brought the 37,000 troops home, and made the ungrateful Korea "responsible for itself, at long last." [4] Or, as Richard Allen put it on the op-ed page of the *New York Times*, if South Korea cannot decide between the United States and North Korea, U.S. troops should be withdrawn from Korea, out of harm's way. And he meant by this harm the anti-American student protesters on the streets of Seoul.[5] The Washington D.C.–based U.S. Chamber of Commerce also issued a warning that anti-American sentiments, if continuing unabated, would lead U.S. investors to boycott South Korea.[6]

What is this "anti-Americanism," a sentiment that is purportedly held by South Koreans and that so provokes the ire of many Americans, who feel that the Koreans have just bitten off the American hands that have so long fed them? The premise of this edited volume is that there is such a thing as anti-Americanism in South Korea, which is as palpable as it is measurable, and that it has been gaining strength since the early 1980s, only to erupt in full force in the past couple of years. In this chapter I argue against this presumption. I argue, rather, that the charge of "anti-Americanism" is false, misleading, and dangerous for several reasons.

The historic occurrence of anti-Americanism, or at least what is construed as such in the more familiar European context, bears little resemblance to the decline in the popularity of the United States as portrayed by public opinion polls conducted in South Korea. Of course, if the current Korean disaffection toward the United States looks different than the tried-and-true European anti-Americanism, that does not preclude the possibility that Koreans, too, could be anti-American in some unique Korean way. But I argue that Koreans are not anti-American in the sense that the term is usually defined, derived from the European experience of America-envy and America-loathing—and in a curiously circuitous way, anti-Semitism, as we shall see later.

Paul Hollander, in his influential book *Anti-Americanism*, defines the subject like this: "Anti-Americanism is *a predisposition to hostility* toward the United States and American society, a relentlessly critical impulse toward American social, economic, and political institutions, traditions, and values; it entails an aversion to American culture in particular and its influence abroad, often also contempt for the American national character (or what is presumed to be such a character) and dislike of American people, manner, behavior, dress, and so on; rejection of American foreign policy and a firm belief in the malignity of American influence and presence anywhere in the world."[7]

Elsewhere he also emphasizes the *irrational* aspects of anti-Americanism, to distinguish it from any kind of *rational* disagreement that one might have with the policies of the United States. "[A]nti-Americanism implies more than a critical disposition: it refers to critiques which are less than fully rational and not necessarily well founded. It usually alludes to a predisposition, a free-floating hostility or aversion, that feeds on many sources besides the discernible shortcomings of the United States. . . . Among the sources of such anti-Americanism we find nationalism (political or cultural), the rejection of (or ambivalence toward) modernization and anti-capitalism."[8]

There are probably some Koreans, of course, who do in fact harbor anti-American dispositions, defined as a free-floating hostility or aversion toward the United States. In fact, it would be amazing if that were not the case. The United States and South Korea have had an extraordinarily close relationship, and many Koreans have lived cheek by jowl with Americans, near so many U.S. military installations. Because this closeness is also predicated on a terrific asymmetry in power relations—with the dominant party providing protection in return for submissiveness and munificence for gratefulness—it has tended to generate all sorts of predictable pathologies. Max Scheler once used the term *ressentiment* to refer to a lingering hate, one that stems from a sense of frustration and impotence, against a dominant party that has provoked such a feeling. It is a term borrowed from Nietzsche in the *Genealogy of Morals* but used in different ways to mean a persistent feeling of hating and despising, which occurs in certain individuals who feel themselves to be impotent, accompanied by hidden feelings of "self-disvalue."[9]

But an individual feeling of *ressentiment*, regardless of its source and even depth, does not add up to collective anti-Americanism. Koreans, for all their intense and close involvement with the United States in the past half-century, do not possess the kind of historical and cultural vocabulary others have employed for ridiculing and despising America. There is an absence of a tradition, or historical precedent, that could serve as a well-sustaining collective resentment. And this absence is simply a function of the fact that the American and Korean cultures are still too wide apart to develop the truly intense loathing that comes from intimate knowledge of each other. To understand how this may be the case, we have to take a peek at the European sources of anti-Americanism.

"Paltry Republicanism": Resenting America in Europe

"It is a complex fate to be an American," Henry James once observed (and infinitely more complex if one happened to be an American of color abroad, as James Baldwin eloquently contemplated[10]—and it is often American minority servicemen that the Koreans encounter on the streets). The sheer complexity and heterogeneity of the United States aside, however, there are certain themes that rear their ugly heads in the European depiction of the more nefarious aspects of the American character. Below, I pick some at random, simply to underscore the vast difference between the tried-and-true European anti-Americanism and America-loathing and what is (mistakenly) construed as Korean anti-Americanism. European anti-Americanism is almost an art form, which feeds off many sources. Not being a scholar of European culture, I cannot presume to have expert views on the history of the European disdain of the United States, but even a cursory look at my own library shelf yields a trove of insults and contempt exchanged between peoples of the same western cultures (and who, therefore, should get along famously, according to Samuel P. Huntington).[11]

My limited and random sample can be organized into three categories. The first one is cultural, thriving on disparagement of the putative American national character —rude, aggressive, moneygrubbing, sly, and hypocritical—and the examples of this abound from Stendhal (*Love*) to Graham Greene (*The Quiet American*). Still, nobody gave his venomous best to this scurrilous charge more dramatically than Charles Dickens. In *Martin Chuzzlewit* and his *American Notes,* Dickens depicted Americans as disgusting and brutish hypocrites. His American characters were preachy types, mouthing off liberty and equality while maintaining slaves; nor did Dickens see any virtue in the American penchant for "smart dealing," which only resulted in swindles and gross breaches of trust. Americans were people devoid of subtlety and irony who only insisted on "miserable, wretched independence in small things; the paltry republicanism which recoils from honest service to an honest man." Dickens was often accused of being anti-American, not without justification; but he managed to turn the tables by pointing out that it was the American national character that could not bear to be told its faults, while always exaggerating its virtues and wisdom.[12]

The second category of anti-American writings is more political in nature and somewhat more thoughtful than the Dickensian spleen-venting (which, when all is said and done, is based on the "narcissism of small differences," as Freud put it, between the English and American people). This variety is based on a critique of American liberal democracy and individualism as practiced in the nineteenth and the early twentieth centuries. Poets and scholars decried the many nefarious and raucous consequences of mass democracy and liberalism in America, such as massive political corruption, a licentious press, conspicuous consumption, and the unique brand of American conformism that seemed to thrive side by side with the much-vaunted American individualism—in other words, all the pathologies that occurred when the Gilded Age met up with mass democracy. Heinrich Heine spoke of the United States as a "colossal jail of freedom, where all people are equal," the same old "boors"; Jacob Burkhardt equated the ahistorical and antihistorical nature of the American society with barbarism, or the "ahistorical *Bildungsmensch.*"[13] Max Weber saw the corruption of machine politics, ward heelers, and party bosses as the predictable outcome of American mass democracy.[14] Most tellingly, it was none other than the founder of psychoanalysis, Sigmund Freud, who saw in the United States the worst excess of what was wrong with modern civilization, a place that had "no time for libido," an "anti-Paradise," which was governed by the "dollar." Freud, who hit the jackpot when his *Civilization and Its Discontents* became a best seller in America, saw the United States as a gigantic collective manifestation of an enemy he often said he could not do without.[15]

To be fair, it was not only the Europeans who trucked in negative traits alleged to be American. An American no less prominent and thoughtful than George F. Kennan also thought there was something to the European charge of political immaturity inherent in American liberalism. In his autobiography, he wrote about Americans in sunny California: "Here it is easy to see that when man is given . . . freedom from both political restraint and want, the effect is to render him childlike . . . fun-loving, quick to laughter and enthusiasm, unanalytical, unintellectual . . . given to seizures of aggressiveness, driven constantly to protect his status . . . by an eager conformism. . . .

Southern California, together with all that tendency of American life which it typifies, is childhood without the promise of maturity."[16]

The last category, in my view, is anti-Americanism as a parallel manifestation or a veiled form of European anti-Semitism. The coupling of anti-Americanism with anti-Semitism is analytically useful, I think, because if not everyone agrees on the meaning of anti-Americanism, at least there is a greater agreement about what anti-Semitism has historically meant in Europe. The writings on anti-Semitism should provide some purchase on how we might think about the *anti-* in *anti-*Americanism.

Jean-Paul Sartre's 1948 book, *Anti-Semite and Jew*, opens with the following trenchant paragraph: "If a man attributes all or part of his own misfortunes and those of his country to the presence of Jewish elements in the community, if he proposes to remedy this state of affairs by depriving the Jews of certain of their rights, by keeping them out of certain economic and social activities, by expelling them from the country, by exterminating all of them, we say that he has anti-Semitic *opinions*."[17]

In other words, an anti-Semite is a person with a particular disposition toward the Jew, such that he constructs a history—mostly of injury and misfortune—based on that disposition and prejudice. It is not history that determines his prejudice, but his prejudice and his conception of the Jew that determine history. A person is not an anti-Semite for disagreeing with the policies of Israel, for instance, any more than he is an anti-American for disagreeing with the policies of the United States. If anti-Semitism is a passion, an anger against the Jew without provocation, then I think it reasonable to consider anti-Americanism in the same light, as a passion against the United States, taken up of one's own free will and without provocation. One then thinks about anti-Americanism the same way one thinks of anti-Semitism, "a comprehensive attitude that one adopts not only toward Jews [or Americans] but toward men in general, toward history and society; it is at one and the same time a passion and a conception of the world."[18]

Some, like the philosopher Andre Gluckman, have argued that anti-Americanism in Europe has often drawn from the same well as anti-Semitism. Just as some Europeans are quick to suspect Jewish plots everywhere and behind everything, so they see American plots behind everything. What undergirds both anti-Americanism and anti-Semitism is, in this rendering, a suspicion and paranoia about political and financial power that is both ubiquitous and clandestine.[19] But others have also claimed that the connection isn't simply coincidental, and that "anti-Americanism has always been the more high-minded and socially acceptable form of anti-Semitism in Germany and all of Europe"; the events of 9/11, for instance, provided some in Germany with a measure of *Schadenfreude*.[20]

This sort of free-floating and comprehensive resentment against an ethnic group is not what one encounters in Korea. At least I have not encountered it, and this fact is not insignificant, because at some level, the judgment on the quality and existence of anti-Semitic or anti-American sentiments is based on one's knowledge of the society or the groups that harbor such sentiments. The growing sentiment of distance that some Koreans feel toward the United States is not based on cultural differences that are more pronounced for being close (like the one that Dickens professes) or on differences of political tradition (between the feudal tradition in Europe and the liberal tradition in America), nor is it based on an idée fixe such as the notion of the American (or the Jew) and what he is likely to do and not do. And to the extent that there is a small minority of Koreans who give extreme expression to their fear and loathing of the American culture, it is mostly based on massive cultural incomprehension and ignorance—and probably of "western" culture in general rather than just the culture of America. In any event, there is no reason why the anti-American sentiment based on cultural incomprehension should have reared its ugly head *now* and not before. A hostility that is culturally based is presumably relatively consistent, and to the extent that there is change, it should be in the direction of attenuation along with increased modernization of the Korean society. But the vicissitude of cultural likes and dislikes of the Untied States are treated elsewhere in this volume and therefore need not concern us here.[21]

The notion that there is "anti-Americanism" in Korea—and it is the American media that are largely responsible for this—has consequences that go beyond noting the pique-of-the-month prevailing in South Korea. The concept of "anti-Americanism," constructed through the measure of like/dislike toward the United States, is based on a binary distinction between the friendly and unfriendly, between friends and enemies. Pro-American people are friends of the United States, and anti-Americans are the enemies of the United States. This kind of binary distinction is often at the core of national security-oriented mobilization, and in the aftermath of 9/11, this has become truer than ever before. During the Cold War, for instance, the United States had an enemy that was identifiable through a concrete set of ideologies entertained by it. After 9/11, the enemy is no longer identifiable through what it affirms; it is identifiable only through what it loathes—the United States. The enemy is a motley collection of anti-Americans: nihilistic, irrational, and seething with the most intense loathing of everything the United States stands for.

Perhaps nobody understood the political power of such binary distinction better than Carl Schmitt, a leading thinker in Weimar Germany, who argued that the ability to distinguish correctly between friends and enemies was at the core of what he called "political." By *enemy* Schmitt meant a collective hostile entity that invokes concrete antagonism, expressed in everyday language and culture, that defines the collective "we" against the alien "other." The enemy need not be morally evil or esthetically ugly and he need not appear as an economic competitor; it may even be advantageous to engage with him in business transactions. But he is, nevertheless, the stranger, the Other; and it is sufficient for his nature that he is, in a specially intense way, existentially something different and alien, so that in the extreme case he can be killed.[22]

There are people around the world who are clearly anti-American and who are, in the Schmitt sense, enemies of the United States. These are people who willingly blow themselves up themselves and blast the lives of those around them, just so that they can give expression to the intense loathing they feel toward the American way of life and American power around the world. But South Koreans they are not—and therefore to call the political sentiment in South Korea "anti-American" is a profligate misuse of the term. How else, then, should we understand the recent Korean outpouring of discontent vis-à-vis the United States?

The Politics of Insecurity and Rising Apprehension Toward the United States

Some observers of Korean civil society have suggested that the current disenchantment with the United States is not a new phenomenon, and that it traces back to the mid-1980s[23]; furthermore, they hold that such sentiment is not a fringe phenomenon but has become mainstream and well integrated into various sectors of the Korean society.[24] This suggestion is quite plausible, and one can see how studies of South Korean civil society and activist groups would lead to such conclusions. The trouble is that there seems to be a gap between qualitative data grounded in deep knowledge of the civil society and the evidence from the large aggregate public opinion research. Public opinion in Korea with regard to the United States has fluctuated wildly over time, especially in the past fifteen years or so.

According to *Opinion Research*, conducted over the past decade by the Office of Research at the U.S. State Department, public opinion in South Korea was remarkably upbeat toward the United States in the first half of the 1990s through 1994, with anywhere between 54 and 67 percent of the people holding a favorable view of the United States. But even this pales in comparison with the favorable view held by the public between 1996 and 2000, when these ratings were at their historic peak, in a range between 60 and 73 percent.

In other words, the massive public disaffection toward the United States is a sudden phenomenon that began around 2001. A survey by the same State Department outfit, conducted in July 2002 using a sample of 1,514 South Koreans above age twenty, showed that some 46 percent of those polled expressed an "unfavorable" and "somewhat unfavorable" view of the United States. The principal reason cited for this was American unilateralism (described as "U.S. acts on its own without consulting others"); the second reason was economic and trade pressures from the United States, at 50 percent and 47 percent, respectively. At the time of this July survey, relatively few people chose U.S. policy toward North Korea as the primary grievance. In a few months, however—that is, after the escalation of tension caused by the North Korean admission in October that it was proceeding with uranium enrichment—South Korean sentiment toward the United States took a worse turn. According to the *Sisa Journal* poll of 1,013 adults above age twenty, some 62.9 percent of those polled said that the Bush administration's policy was not helpful for the stability of the peninsula; an amazing 57.6 percent of South Koreans blamed North Korea and the United States equally for the interruption in the dialogue. Some 24.2 percent of those polled said that the United States was more at fault than North Korea.[25]

The only other time in the past decade when public opinion turned so decisively against the United States was during another nuclear standoff. In 1994, there was also a massive drop; in fact, the drop in 1994 in the State Department Survey was arguably even bigger than the drop in its survey of July 2002. From late 1994 through 1995, some 57 percent of those polled expressed misgivings about the United States. This was a marked change from the atmosphere in the early 1990s, which had remained friendly to the United States, and also quite different from 1996–2000, when opinions remained quite favorable.

The decline in 1994–95 was accounted for by a confluence of the usual factors—trade frictions and public outrage over incidents involving U.S. military personnel. But the one unusual factor was the tension and unease caused by the U.S.–North Korea nuclear talks. (There is a bit of a time lag here, with the disaffection caused by the U.S.-North Korean standoff continuing through early 1995, after the Agreed Framework was signed in late 1994.) This is highly interesting. Trade frictions as well as anger at criminal action and misdemeanors on the part of the U.S. military personnel continued unabated throughout the 1990s and into the most recent years. But the tension caused by the U.S.-North Korean nuclear standoff happened twice in the same time period—between 1993 and 1994 and between 2001 and the present time—and in both cases the South Korean view of the United States ended up taking a nosedive.

This close fit between Koreans' angst over their security and their disenchantment with the United States calls to mind an analogous situation that prevailed in another divided country, West Germany. In the 1980s, "anti-Americanism" in West Germany came like a lightning bolt out of the blue. The West Germans were in profound disagreement with the United States over the plan of the North Atlantic Treaty Organization (NATO) to install American Pershing II and cruise missiles in Europe, and the massive German protest over this weapons deployment was swiftly denounced by the U.S. media and political establishment as a thinly veiled attack on the American way of life—and slandered as being irrational and unreasonable. Since chapter 6 in this volume makes a sustained comparison of West Germany and South Korea, I limit my discussion here to those aspects of what was construed by the U.S. media as West German "anti-Americanism." This may throw some light on the South Korean predicament today and help us think through the real and serious issues that dwell in the shadows of jingoistic name-calling.

The basic problem in the U.S.-West German relationship in the 1980s was a structural one, which left West Germany vulnerably sandwiched between the United States on the one hand and East Germany and the Soviet Union on the other. Just how vulnerable this West German position was became clear even before the election of Ronald Reagan and went back to the Carter administration's repudiation of détente with the Soviet Union. The end of détente increased the likelihood that the West Germans, with their policy of *Osthandle* and *Ostpolitik*, would be at loggerheads with the United States. This, of course, calls to mind the differences that the Bush administration had with the policies of the Kim Dae Jung administration's "Sunshine Policy," which was a repudiation of the previous policy of forcing the collapse of the North Korean regime. In any event, the differences between the United States and West

Germany became more fully blown in the 1980s, with the inauguration of President Ronald Reagan. Then, over time, the United States noted with some bitterness the West German passivity and acquiescence toward the Soviet invasion of Afghanistan and the crisis in Poland, which led to the outlawing of Solidarity—all the while massively protesting against NATO's plan to install the Pershing II. The West Germans were seen as weasels and appeasers where the East was concerned, but they tended to get their backs up where the United States were concerned. The 300,000 West Germans who spilled into the streets in protest of U.S. policies were also chastised for their galling ingratitude for all the help they had received over the years from the United States.[26] When, by 1986, more West German citizens were professing to like and trust the leader of the Soviet Union than the president of the United States, it became clear to many Americans that the youth of West Germany had become hopelessly anti-American.[27]

Whether the West Germans were ungrateful or not, the West German conundrum was based on the very simple fact that Germany was the central flash point for the East–West conflict; as such it was also slated to be the obvious first casualty should the Cold War turn hot. The arrival of American missiles in Mutlangen, Neu Ulm, and Heilbronn therefore represented a huge increase in the likelihood of a nuclear war on German soil. The former Chancellor Helmut Schmidt once remarked: "Living that close to the Soviet Union, we were careful in not provoking anybody. We don't like provocative behavior on the Western side, either."[28] So, what was labeled as anti-American was in fact the diffuse fear—*Furcht*—of war caused by the imminent missile deployments and bellicose rhetoric of the Reagan administration. This situation, of course, bears a close resemblance to the diffuse fear that the South Koreans have felt since early 2002, when President George W. Bush gave North Korea pride of place as one of the three in the "axis of evil," along with Iraq and Iran. Later in the year, President Bush would argue, in the National Security Strategy of the United States, that the rogue states who form the axis of evil might very well provide weapons of mass destruction to the global terrorist network, and that this had to be forestalled with unprecedented methods. Thus, preemption and unilateralism came to replace the former American strategy of containment and deterrence. There was also a new emphasis in the National Security Doctrine on "regime change," which meant that existing governments of rogue states might be overthrown and replaced by regimes friendly to the United States. The implication of this for the security of South Korea was enormous. It meant that South Korea could be at the receiving end of the American effort to change the regime in Pyongyang, which could invite a massive North Korean retaliation aimed at Seoul.

The West German predicament was one that stemmed directly from the fact that it sat on the global geopolitical fault line, and this fact alone goes a long way to explaining why West Germany was the only country in Europe that ended up producing a powerful and vibrant peace movement—the Greens—that was as politically viable as it was influential. South Korea, likewise, has produced one of the most vibrant, rambunctious, and well-organized civil societies in East Asia, owing in part to the precarious geopolitical position in which South Korea finds itself. The peace movement in South Korea forms a part of the civil society coalition that includes peace activists, religious activists, law professionals, environmentalists, academics, radical students, trade unionists, nongovernmental organizations (NGOs), reunification activists, local government officials, common villagers, members of the national assembly, and the media. Katharine Moon, an astute observer of Korean civil society, observes that this coalition is remarkably effective in pulling together human, financial, and political resources so as to have a larger impact on society.[29]

The Greens in West Germany also distinguished themselves from the mainstream through their support of German strategic neutrality—this allegedly with the ultimate goal of reunification with the East. Among the Greens, an overwhelming majority (some 82 percent) supported German political and military neutrality, as opposed to some 35 percent in the rest of the country.[30] Comparable data are not available for South Korea, but we can get some sense of the South Korean view by noting that among those holding unfavorable views of the United States, some 45.8 percent supported the withdrawal of U.S. military bases, as contrasted with 31.7 percent among those who expressed favorable opinions of the United States. A majority (51.5 percent) of those over twenty years of age also said that South Korea must aid North Korea, regardless of the nuclear issue.[31] Presumably it is this group that would be more critical of the hawkish positions held by U.S. policy makers.

This leads us to the final point of our comparison, namely the relationship between anti-Americanism on the one hand, and national identity and nationalism on the other. Here the comparison with West Germany is far less straightforward. It has often been noted that the West German anti-Americanism after 1945 reflects a profound anxiety about what it means to be German. The West Germans were people who suffered a "quadruple loss" of identity, including the loss of the Imperial German identity that was mangled in the killing fields of Belgium and France; the Republican identity; the Nazi identity; and the socialist identity of the Democratic Republic of Germany. This profound crisis over German identity has often led the Germans to define themselves indirectly and surreptitiously through the images they held of the United States. When the Germans saw America in a positive light, it was to erase and forget the broken nature of the German identity; when America was seen in negative light, it was to accentuate the fantasy of what it meant to be German or what it *would have* meant to be German save for freaky accidents of history.[32]

Korean identity, too, has been robbed multiple times in the twentieth century, through the collapse of the independent nationhood, Japanese colonialism, national division, fratricidal war, and the Cold War. But, the violence imposed upon the Korean identity was not self-inflicted, nor was it accepted as the wage of its past folly and crime, as was the case with postwar West Germany. So when the young West Germans defiantly spoke of *Deutschland als Opfer* ("Germany as a victim") in the context of the NATO double-track decision and the rise of Ronald Reagan, it could only be understood as a kind of historic doublespeak, a gallows humor that nonetheless contained, from a certain angle, elements of truth. But the Koreans are most clearly victims of a history not of their own making, and thus they could express their aspirations for reunification, their hopes for the restoration of a complete nationhood, without looking over their shoulders for fear of seeing the past catch up to them. Nationalism and democracy could go hand in hand in South Korea in ways they never could in West Germany—an important point that Jurgen Habermas noted in differentiating Germany's progressive intellectuals from their South Korean counterparts. "In Korea, where there is the memory of Japanese imperialism," he argued, "political and social criticism can also turn outward and combine with a strong national consciousness. . . . A German has good historical reasons to be cautious in handling national themes."[33]

Because of the relatively unproblematic nature of Korean nationalism (in comparison with places like Germany or Japan), South Koreans are less hesitant to openly air their differences with the U.S. government, especially where North Korea is concerned. The profound anxiety that the South Koreans feel whenever there is a big nuclear standoff between the United States and North Korea is not *just* for the security of the South Korean people; it is also for the security and lives of the North Korean people. This is why, in the aftermath of the terrible famine in North Korea in 1995–98, South Koreans no longer feel that economic sanctions would be a useful tool for inducing change in North Korea; the cost of the sanctions policy is too severe in human terms, inflicting unacceptable suffering on people who are, after all, Koreans. And such pressures do not collapse the state.

Beyond Opinion Polls

A broad contour of opinion polls suggests a connection, I have argued, between security-related anxiety on the one hand and the South Korean apprehension toward the United States on the other. At the end of the day, though, it is also true that opinion polls can also be misleading. They often capture fleeting sentiments, which are liable to manipulation by the media *and* by the types of questions asked in the surveys, and this makes it hard to use opinion polls as a reliable gauge of public sentiment that is more than skin deep. The South Koreans, for instance, reserve their bitterest feelings against America for the most frivolous of incidents that nonetheless inflame the Koreans' love of their country and pride in it. In the *Sisa Journal* poll in early 2002, for instance, some 65 percent of the respondents said that the Korean attitude toward the United States had deteriorated; they cited the "gold medal theft" in Salt Lake City as the primary reason for the perceptional deterioration. (This refers to an incident in the 2002 Winter Olympics when the Korean speed skater, a gold medal hopeful, was disqualified and an American, Antonio Ono, was awarded the medal. In spite of the fact that the judge was an Australian, the Koreans took it as another instance of American prejudice against Koreans.) In this case, the opinion polls were measuring an emotion that did flare up against the United States but had very little bearing on the state of the U.S.-South Korean relationship. This was an emotional combustion without meaning, a stupid pique that nonetheless went some distance in adding fuel to the anger at President Bush's "axis of evil" remark.

There are also incidents that would have disappeared from the radar screen of public consciousness save for the persistence of grassroots activists who were hellbent on parlaying them into big political issues—or, in the Korean-English patois, *isshyu-wha*.[34] The death of two young girls, crushed by a U.S. armored vehicle whose drivers were subsequently cleared by the U.S. military court, is a case in point. Inexcusable as the circumstances leading to the deaths were, the way the story unfolded is illustrative of the way grassroots politics works in South Korea. Initially the incident attracted very little notice and the public reaction was quite muted until the issue was seized by an upstart Internet news service called *Ohmynews.com*. It relies on "citizen reporters" and prominently features reader feedback and chat-room discussions. Daily calls for protests went out to the readers, running in the millions and mostly young, in a country that is one of the most wired in the world, more so than Japan. By December, the fuse was lit, and soon the Koreans were doing what they do so well: protesting. In this case, the opinion polls reflect neither instant antagonism toward the United States nor a well-thought-out position on the U.S. military presence in Korea but rather a long "blanquist" campaign that bore fruit in stirring up passion and mobilizing the population.

Then there are serious issues that never become big political issues. And I think it is such incidents, which do not become contentious, that are in some ways more telling than those that receive great media attention. In 1999, a major international story broke, alleging that during the Korean War, at the little hamlet of No Gun Ri, U.S. forces massacred upward of 400 South Korean civilian refugees—mostly women, children, and old men. A team of Associated Press (AP) journalists who led the investigation was able to prove—through declassified documents and military records as well as through interviews with more than forty disparate people whose recollections meshed down to small details—that U.S. forces had received orders in the early days of the Korean War to shoot South Korean refugees because they were, to the Americans, indistinguishable from the enemy. The story was sent to AP worldwide news wires, making major headlines in newspapers from New York to Paris, and the declassified communications telling troops to shoot refugees were available on the AP Web site for all to see.[35] But this story—the "story that no one wanted to hear"— did not gain the traction in South Korea that, three years later, the deaths of two little girls would. The U.S. massacre of South Koreans at No Gun Ri did *not* become an inflammatory issue and it did *not* lead to massive mobilization of the people. In fact, throughout the No Gun Ri revelations in 1999 and 2000, the United States was enjoying an exceptionally high level of popularity in South Korea. Why might this have been the case?

The reason, I think, lies in the differences in the way in which the U.S. administration approached the management of relationships with allies. After the AP broke the news, President Clinton issued a statement that was as eloquent as it was sincere, expressing profound sorrow for the tragedies that are perpetrated in the confusion of the war. Even the U.S. Army, after years of dismissing the South Korean villagers' story about the massacre, finally came around to affirming that American troops did in fact kill civilians (if without assigning blame). The Clinton administration approached South Korea as an ally, equal in dignity and equal in sovereign rights, in the essential Westphalian sense (although, as we shall see later, its economic policies were far more imperious and high-handed). It also treated the regime in North Korea, however abhorrent it might be, as a sovereign regime that had to be engaged. In other words, when the U.S. government was ready to accord some respect to a smaller ally and show willingness to manage conflicts before they got out of control, South Koreans did respond in kind, appropriately and predictably. And it is this mutual respect that went out the window in the period of unilateralism that was ushered in in 2001.

In any event, by 2002 the South Koreans were upset with the Bush administration's policy of unilateralism, and they were saying so with their feet, in ways that would have been difficult to imagine twenty years ago. Democratization is undeniably part of the explanation for how this situation came to be, but it is not all of it. Buried under the mound of some petty and some not-so-petty grievances that mark the extraordinarily close and involved relationship between the United States and Korea, there may also, over the past couple of decades, have been a tectonic shift. The rhetoric of war against terrorism and rogue states, it is true, triggers profound anxiety in South Korea, but this anxiety is, in turn, predicated on the Korean perception of the change in the U.S.-South Korean alliance—and of what kind of an ally the United States really is. I think that the current Korean perception is simply that the United States is no longer the protector and patron of South Korea and that it could, in some self-serving way, sacrifice the well-being of the Korean people if need be.

Samuel Huntington said in *The Clash of Civilizations,* his social science potboiler, that in the Cold War states used to relate to superpowers as "allies, satellites, clients, neutrals, and nonaligned." In the post–Cold War world, countries "relate to civilizations as member states, core states, lone countries, cleft countries and torn countries."[36] The trouble with South Korea is that the Cold War is now over, and so it can no longer relate to the United States as ally and client. But it does not know how else to relate to the United States or where to find its place in the overall Huntingtonian scheme of things—save, perhaps, as a "cleft" or "torn" country. But finding out, more than a half-century after liberation from the colonialism and the Korean War, that one's country is still divided—and therefore "cleft" or "torn" in the way it relates to the world—hardly makes for a happy sentiment. To understand how things got to be that way, we must go beyond the opinion polls and examine the unraveling of the Cold War alliance between the United States and South Korea.

The Passing of the Cold War Alliance

The Cold War alliance between the United States and South Korea was predicated on the most extraordinary kind of patronage, which was in turn based on the following three pillars. Politically, Washington supported political stability in Korea, even if that meant supporting a military dictatorship. Economically, the United States sponsored Korean development by providing vast aid, offering tutelage regarding the open economy and export-led growth, and opening its vast and lucrative market to Korean exports. Militarily, the United States guaranteed the security of Korea, the best example of such commitment being the presence of 37,000 American servicemen, to assure instant American involvement in the event of a conflict on the Korean Peninsula.

Over the past twenty years, this structure of patronage has become almost completely unstuck. U.S. support for the political stability in South Korea became a nonissue after that country went though democratic transitions and consolidation. U.S. sponsorship of Korea's economic development came to an end a bit earlier than that, but the most dramatic example of the changed relationship did not come until the Korean financial crisis (1997–98)—and I must dwell on this aspect at some length. Finally, the U.S. guarantee of South Korean *security* seems to have been replaced, within the first year of the Bush administration, with policies that were fraught with tension and increased *insecurity*. It is in the context of this evaporating U.S. patronage that we have to understand the Koreans' fear for their security, which in turn feeds Korean discontent with the U.S. policy of unilateralism. The remainder of this chapter traces the changes in the U.S.-South Korean relationship; it ends with a discussion of the U.S. military presence, which is the last vestige of the long-standing special relationship between the two countries.

Political Change

The political dimension in the changing U.S.-South Korean relations is well chronicled in this volume, especially in chapter 17, on the Kwangju Rebellion, by William Drennan, and we need not revisit it. There are, however, a few additional points deserving comment, which bear directly on my argument about the changing political dynamics between the two countries. One is the way in which the United States support for political stability in South Korea created, in the minds of ordinary South Korean citizens, a permanent linkage between the U.S. military and authoritarianism in South Korea, and that this was *not* a case of paranoia. According to Donald Clark, "a dismaying by-product of the Kwangju Rebellion is the fact that so many Koreans believe that the United States government had some connection with what happened, and countenanced it. So many people believe that there was—or should have been— an American role somewhere in the incident," and that it was this suspicion that has given rise to "a palpable anti-Americanism in Korea."[37] But this Korean paranoia had a cause, and a good one. The 1948 National Security Law had linked the U.S. military with the Korean military dictators, as if they were two peas in the same pod. And under Article 7 of the 1980 National Security Law, anyone who had written or disseminated materials criticizing the South Korean government *or* the presence of U.S. armed forces in South Korea was punishable by imprisonment, and Amnesty International noted that many people were held political prisoner under those pretexts.[38] It was forbidden to criticize the U.S. military and/or the U.S. government or to question the status of the U.S.-South Korean relations.

The second point worth mentioning is that Kwangju was a reminder of the moral failure of the United States. The United States was complicit in the massacre, not so much on technical grounds—whether the Combined Forces Command (CFC) did or did not have operational control over combat troops in Korea in any meaningful way—but on grounds that the United States failed precisely at the moment when the South Korean citizens needed her most. While it was indubitably true that Americans may have had little influence on routine Korean politics, including the decision to use the CFC command structure for domestic political purposes, Americans did yield tremendous influence in moments of crisis—and it was this American failure to use U.S. influence for democratic and moral ends that cut deep into the Korean psyche. American representatives in Korea also came across as either callous or indifferent and most comfortable in the company of authoritarian rulers who ran interference for them, cordoning them off in the comfort of diplomatic compounds, away from the madding South Korean crowd.

This takes us to the last point—namely, that Washington seems to have had a far cozier relationship with the dictatorship of Chun Doo Hwan than with the democratic administration of either President Kim Dae Jung or President Roh Moo Hyun. With the passing of military dictatorship in South Korea, the era of American support for the dictatorship too has come to a close, but consolidation of democracy and democratic norms in South Korea seems to provide little comfort to Washington. The Bush administration has been in profound disagreement with Kim Dae Jung's Sunshine Policy, which it sees as little more than appeasement of North Korea. It has also expressed deep misgivings about Roh Moo Hyun, who comes from the ranks of human rights activists, in the period running up to the December 2002 election. And it sees South Korean civil society as raucous, rambunctious, irresponsible, and afflicted with a terminal case of democratic distemper.

End of the Bilateral Economic Relationship

I have stated that the United States had sponsored the economic growth of South Korea in the period leading up to the 1980s. This relationship of economic sponsorship came to an end, many thought, around the mid-1980s, when South Korea began to record trade surpluses vis-à-vis the United States, and trade conflict between the two countries became more frequent. But in reality this relationship of patronage never did end in the 1980s; it continued right through the financial crisis of 1997, until it was shown in a dramatic way that the economic relationship that had prevailed in the days of the Cold War had been completely turned on its head. In the moment of Korea's direst financial need—caused, some would argue, by the very reckless policy of capital account liberalization spearheaded by the United States[39]—the U.S. Treasury Department chose to turn its back on Korea and used the occasion of the crisis to settle the old, nettlesome trade accounts with Korea.[40] This is a long and involved story, but the main point is that Korea now held interest for the American economic policy makers only to the extent that it provided markets for U.S. exports, which had in the 1990s become important as an engine of growth. The fact that Korea was an important strategic ally played very little role in the decisions of the International Monetary Fund (IMF) to bail out of Korea. Quite to the contrary; the desire of some American policy makers to use IMF conditionality to crack open the Korean financial and commodities market ended up in a huge mishandling of the initial bailout. All of this requires some explanation.

As is well known by now, the Korean system of industrial financing was largely based on the banking sector, which doled out loans to the hugely leveraged corporate sector. As a consequence, the banks were saddled with loan portfolios that contained massive amounts of nonperforming loans. So long as the economy was growing and corporations were able to service their debts, the perennial problem of nonperforming loans could be papered over. In a global downturn, however, an economy as exposed as South Korea's was likely to have trouble with the huge fixed cost in the form of interest payment, and predictably, South Korea would slip periodically into severe financial crisis. The catch, however, was that South Korea was blessed with an economic guarantor of last resort, the United States, with which it had a special relationship based on military security. One of the great cushions to the Korean economy was the Cold War, such that any serious economic crisis also invoked security concerns or even transformed economic crises into crises of security. The United States always stood ready to help out in the event of trouble, even as it slapped the Korean wrist now and then for maintaining market barriers and not liberalizing enough. So, at any time before 1989, Seoul could expect Washington and Tokyo to step in and help it out bilaterally, with the best example being the crisis of 1979–80, which was probably the worst financial crisis in the South Korean history.

During the economic debacle of 1979–80, for instance, the United States acted swiftly to stabilize Korea, sending signals to the international financial community that Korea—the assassination of Park Chung Hee and the Kwangju Rebellion notwithstanding—was a sound investment for more loans. The United States also exerted pressure on Japan to "share burdens" in bailing out Korea, and the ensuing Reagan-Suzuki agreement stipulated, in effect, that the maintenance of peace on the Korean Peninsula was important for the security of Japan, which meant that Japan would have to ante up. After much back and forth to adjust the total bill, Korea got from Japan about $4 billion in government and EXIM (Export Import Bank) loans. This was nearly 13 percent of Korea's net external debt, more than 5 percent of its gross national product (GNP), and almost one-fifth of total investment in 1983. (A comparable figure today— i.e., 5 percent of GNP—would be approximately $25 billion.)

In November 1997, when the South Korean minister of finance called on Washington for *bilateral* help, the refusal was swift and decisive. The Korean political economy had been a kind of leftover Cold War artifact, good for an era of security threats and close bilateral relations with Washington but of questionable use in the global "world without borders" of the 1990s, and Washington's refusal to help South Korea on grounds of international security finally laid to rest the long relationship of economic patronage that inhered between the two countries.

To be sure, there was a big debate within the U.S. administration as to what to do about the impending default of South Korea. National security and foreign policy heavyweights pleaded with the U.S. Department of the Treasury that South Korea needed to be bailed out, using bilateral means, and that the United States could not just walk away from Seoul at such an hour of need. Paul Bluestein, the *Washington Post* reporter who covered the Asian crisis and subsequently wrote a fine account of it, writes that James Steinberg, the deputy national security adviser, argued with the Treasury team that "this president is not going to look like Jimmy Carter," referring to Carter's proposal in the 1970s for a major troop withdrawal. "By failing to show strong support for Korea, the United States risked stirring an anti-American backlash in Seoul that could lead to pressure for the removal of U.S. troops," he argued. National Security Adviser Sandy Berger wondered whether North Korea might cause mischief if the South Korean economy collapsed, and Secretary of State Madeleine Albright was most emphatic in favor of a bailout, even in the face of derision by Treasury officials, who thought she knew little about economics.[41] In the end, the members of the foreign policy and national security establishment lost the argument.

There were a number of reasons why the tried-and-true national security argument did not gain traction in Washington. One was intellectual: the argument that South Korea was too important to be allowed to default was one that Secretary of the Treasury Robert Rubin hated because, as Assistant Secretary Tim Geithner explained, "you can't let some perceived imperative of action dictate your choices, and you may not have alternatives that are a plausible response to the problem."[42] There were other, deeper reasons. Rubin, Lawrence Summers, and their lieutenants saw the crisis as the perfect opportunity to break up Korea Inc. once and for all, and to do this they wanted the IMF to impose conditions on South Korea that went far beyond the Fund's traditional boundaries. Thus the Treasury kept steady pressure on the IMF officials to extract more and more concessions from South Korea, including instant resolution of all *trade*-related issues, in favor of the United States. The exasperated Koreans were soon accusing the IMF of always raising new issues at the behest of the United States—something that the IMF officials readily acknowledged.[43]

Foremost in the mind of Treasury officials was also the interest of Wall Street, especially American financial services firms. Joseph Stiglitz has argued that the origins of the Korean financial crisis rested, in the first place, with the excessively rapid financial and capital market liberalization that the Treasury had pushed on Korea, on behalf of Wall Street and over the dead body of the Council of Economic Advisers, of which he was the chairman. "At the Council of Economic Advisers we weren't convinced that South Korean liberalization was a matter of U.S. *national* interest, though obviously it would help the *special* interests of Wall Street." (Italics in the original.)[44]

The IMF conditions served the brokerage firms on Wall Street far better than the needs of South Korea. Americans demanded, and got, the right to establish bank subsidiaries and brokerage houses in the Korean market by mid-1998; the ceiling on foreign ownership of publicly traded companies raised to 50 from 26 percent; and the ceiling on individual foreign ownership raised from 7 to 50 percent. From that point on, accounting in Korean corporations would adhere strictly to international standards, with large financial institutions required to submit to audits by internationally recognized firms. In addition, there would be large-scale restructuring of the financial sector, including a revision of the Bank of Korea Act, to provide for central bank independence, "with price stability as its main mandate." "Other Structural Measures" in the Letter of Intent with the IMF covered trade liberalization, including old sticking issues like transparency of the import certification procedures, complete capital account liberalization, corporate governance and corporate structure, and labor market reform.[45]

By signing the December 3 Letter of Intent, South Korea practically gave away the store. The trouble was that the massive concessions did not save the day for South Korea, and it slid into deeper trouble as the month wore on. Part of the problem was the American refusal to send a credible signal to the world that the United States was now firmly behind the deal providing the more than $55 billion promised to South Korea. The $55 billion package consisted of $35 billion that would come from the two Bretton Woods Institutions and the Asian Development Bank and another $20 billion, called the "second line of defense," which would come from wealthy governments. The trouble was that South Korea could avoid default only if it could obtain all the loans in the package, and the Treasury never intended to permit disbursal of the "second line of defense," lest it catch flak from Congress. The market could see that South Korea was running out of reserves, and as the financial analysts peered through the $55 billion hype, they realized that "there was no there there." Exit rush began, and by December 12, the IMF and Treasury were contemplating the unthinkable, to allow Seoul to default.

In the end, the method chosen to rescue the failed rescue was a "bail in." That meant rounding up banks that had loaned big to South Korea and asking them to reschedule the debts—or else allow South Korea to default. Once the decision for bail in was made—and it did take an inexcusably long time to make this decision, with Rubin and Alan Greenspan, chairman of the Federal Reserve Board, holding out until the last minute—the bankers moved extraordinarily fast. Korea was an ideal case for a bail in. It had a sound economy, good macroeconomic fundamentals, a good payment record, and it owed almost all its money to banks, which are more easily organized in a collective action situation, and not to mutual funds holding bonds. Why, one might wonder, as the bankers who rescheduled the Korean debts eventually did, had it taken so long for Washington to accept the call for a bail in? Many were calling for it, including the Germans. As the German secretary of finance put it, the plan should not have waited until the last minute.[46] Had Washington asked American banks from the beginning to roll over Korean debts, the situation would not have gone out of control in South Korea.

If the whole point of the exercise had been to teach South Korea a lesson, then the Treasury succeeded brilliantly. The Koreans learned their lesson the hard way, through the massive bankruptcy of large and small firms, and a recession that contracted national income by 7 percent brought wages for the average worker down by 10 percent and sent the jobless rate to nearly 9 percent. But along the way they also learned another kind of lesson. The Koreans learned in the hardest way possible that in the moment of their financial ruination, the United States had chosen to further its parochial self-interest rather than help an ally. The economic basis of the U.S.-South Korean alliance was now standing on a very different footing than it had before.

Guarantees of Security into Guarantees of Insecurity

The security calculus that undergirded the U.S.-Korean relationship has also been dramatically altered over the past decade. Examples of this change may be dated to 1994, when the United States began bolstering its military presence in South Korea in preparation for a possible strike against the nuclear facilities in North Korea. The Clinton administration came within a hair's breadth of war in Korea without so much as consulting with its South Korean ally on an action that would have devastating consequences for the nearly 70 million people on both sides of the demilitarized zone (DMZ). In the event, the war was averted by the signing of the 1994 Agreed Framework, through which North Korea agreed to mothball its nuclear facilities for producing and reprocessing plutonium in return for alternative forms of nuclear energy production and, eventually, diplomatic recognition. But the agreement was in trouble from the get-go. Two weeks after it was signed, Republicans swept the Congress and almost immediately began raising hackles about whether it was proper for the United States to have sat down and negotiated with the North Koreans in the first place. When the Bush administration was inaugurated, it took the position that all bets were off and that it would not negotiate with any state that was deemed to be terrorist. The way the whole thing looked from Seoul, it appeared that the security of Korea and the fate of 70 million people in the Korean Peninsula were held hostage to the vagaries of changes in the U.S. administration and the whims of congressional politics.

The basic difference in the way the United States approached the North Korean issue and the way that South Korea—and, for that matter, Japan and China—approached it was that the East Asian countries wanted the problem to be *managed,* and the only way to do that was through negotiation. Washington, on the other hand, wanted *moral clarity.* As George Bush put it in his West Point commencement speech, "Containment is not possible when unbalanced dictators with weapons of mass destruction can deliver those weapons on missiles or secretly provide them to terrorist allies. . . . Because the war on terror will require resolve and patience, it will also require firm moral purpose. . . . Moral truth is the same in every culture, in every time, and in every place."[47] But obviously *moral truth* looks very different when you have tens of thousands of artillery guns facing you, and the South Koreans have tended to think that avoidance of war ought to take top priority, even if that meant purchasing peace outright with cash payments—as the Kim Dae Jung administration did by funneling hundreds of millions of dollars to North Korea.[48]

The bellicosity of the rhetoric of *moral clarity,* in turn, has given rise to the perception that the United States may very well become the party that provokes war in

Korea. To what extent this perception has contributed to the renewed focus, at least on the part of civil society activists, on the U.S. military bases is hard to say. The military bases in South Korea are profoundly troubled places, more so than such bases in Okinawa or Germany. They have their own singular pathologies and marked propensity toward crime that exasperate local citizens, for reasons independent of the larger picture involving national security. South Korea is one of the two "non-command-sponsored tours," meaning that the U.S. Department of Defense will not pay for the travel and living costs of family members. In 1991, only 10 percent of the 40,000 troops were accompanied by their family members. Korea is also a "hardship tour," due to its status as a war zone and also because of the living arrangements, language, and cultural differences. It is also a "short tour," usually about 1 ½ years long. This contrasts hugely with the situation in Germany, which is a "plum post," mostly for married men with their families, and where they can all have their "European experience."[49] As James Feinerman describes in chapter 12, the enlisted men also tend to come from the bottom rung of the social stratum in the United States, often from broken homes, and facing unemployment were it not for the option of entering the military service.

The very difficult position of enlisted men in places like South Korea and even Japan results in the perpetration of crimes that top the rates of such crimes reported at military bases within the United States. Chalmers Johnson has noted that since 1988, Navy and Marine Corps bases in Okinawa have had the highest number of courts-martial for sexual assaults of all U.S. military bases worldwide, which is 66 percent more cases than the number-two location, San Diego, with 102 cases but more than twice the personnel. Also, bookings at the Okinawan Prefectural Police Headquarters between 1972 and 1995 show that U.S. servicemen were implicated in 4,716 crimes. Thirteen years at 365 days per year adding up to 4,745 days, American servicemen were thus committing just under one crime a day in Okinawa.[50] One can imagine what the picture might be like, if charges against U.S. military personnel were allowed in South Korea as freely as in Okinawa.

It is well known that the United States commands the armed forces of the Republic of Korea in times of external crisis and has done so since 1950. Less noticed is the historic extraterritoriality of the United States—whereby, since 1945, when the American occupation began, Americans have for the most part lived in Korea outside the processes of Korean law. Extraterritoriality was, in the words of one author, "one of the most offensive aspects of Western imperialism in East Asia." Furthermore it was an American invention, first inscribed in its treaty with China following the Opium War of 1839–42. "Extra'lity," as it was called, meant that if a European, American, or Japanese committed a crime in China, he or she was turned over to his or her own consular officials rather than being tried under the law of China, the country of the victim, where the crime had occurred. It is not an exaggeration to say that the Chinese Revolution—in both its communist and nationalist versions—was in part fought to be rid of this demeaning practice.[51]

By the early 2000s, then, the main political, economic, and military underpinnings for the Cold War alliance had been thoroughly weakened. But the United States still maintains its military presence—and it is this military presence that serves as the lightning rod for anti-Americanism in Korea. It is a lightning rod because Koreans imbue the U.S. presence with all kinds of highly charged and ambivalent emotions that reflect their own troubled feelings about national identity, sovereignty, and history. They are conflicted about whether the U.S. troops are in Korea as guarantors of security or as occupiers; whether they are facilitators of reconciliation between the two Koreas or the main stumbling block to such efforts. Meanwhile, every fracas that involves American servicemen is a reminder that Korea is not a wholly sovereign country and that the United States operates in its military bases a sovereign state-within-a-state, unbeholden to the laws of Korea. If the military presence is not the lightning rod, there are grassroots and civil activists making sure it is—and that another mishap involving U.S. servicemen or the U.S. bases would likely mean, to borrow from James Baldwin, "the fire next time."

In June 2003, Undersecretary of Defense Paul Wolfowitz journeyed to Korea to inform the Seoul government that the United States would soon begin moving its 15,000-odd troops between Seoul and the DMZ south of the Han River. (The Han River offers a useful natural defense line, but the heart of Seoul is north of it.) In some respects this move is a good idea: first, the American public never liked the idea that a "tripwire deterrent" would involve Americans in any new war in Korea; a majority of the American public has consistently expressed opposition to the use (let alone the automatic use) of U.S. forces if North Korea attacked South Korea.[52] U.S. public opinion has been remarkably stable on this score. According to the 1975 foreign policy survey of the Chicago Council on Foreign Affairs, the most prestigious and comprehensive of such surveys, 65 percent of those polled said that they opposed the use of U.S. forces if North Korea attacked South Korea. In 1999, again, 66 percent said they opposed it. Second, this redeployment will finally get Americans out of the venerable (Japan set it up in 1894) Yongsan base, smack in the middle of Seoul and flypaper for any number of Korean activists who like to protest outside its gates. But, of course, Koreans worry that the United States wants this pullback so that its own forces will be under less direct threat should a conflict break out over the North's nuclear program.

Conclusion

In this chapter I have endeavored to show that "anti-Americanism," to the extent that one insists on calling it that, is a ubiquitous phenomenon around the world. In some quarters in Europe, it is de rigeur, part of the culture, to disparage the United States. The Bush administration's unilateralism and its general unwillingness to accept binding restraints on its sovereignty has merely brought this culture out into the open again, and the decision to go to war in Iraq without the endorsement of the United Nations Security Council made it spread and bloom. Predictable as it might be, the spread of anti-Americanism, particularly in Europe, has been so alarming to the foreign policy establishment that every issue of *Foreign Affairs* since the fall of 2002 has carried an article or two dealing exclusively with anti-Americanism in Europe and the Middle East.[53] This concern with anti-Americanism must be seen in the broader context of anxiety over the deteriorating relationship with the old European allies within the Atlantic Alliance[54] and, as we have seen, with Asian allies such as South Korea.

Koreans, however, have never shared European biases about the inferiority-cum-barbarity of American civilization. I have instead argued that contemporary Korean apprehensions about the United States have played out against the backdrop of fundamental shifts in the U.S.-Korean relationship in the past twenty-five years, illustrated by long-term support for dictatorship, the Kwangju Rebellion, the Korean financial crisis, and the changing perception of military (in)security provided by the United States since the crisis of 1993–94. Of course I recognize that my arguments will leave some readers still unconvinced; they will insist that the majority of South Koreans today do indeed entertain anti-American emotions, or even that they may have a profound need to express such emotions. If so, that is not entirely bad either. George Santayana once wrote that rejection is also a form of self-assertion. "You have only to look back upon yourself as a person who hates this or that to discover what it is that you secretly love."[55] In the end, is it so surprising that a country colonized, divided, and then devastated by war in the past century, only to remain divided, should look upon this century and say "Isn't it high time for the eleventh-ranked industrial power in the world, which is also one of the most interesting mass-based democracies, to revel in what its people truly love, and to express its justifiable pride in itself?"

Notes

1. "Awkward Allies," *Economist*, April 19, 2003, pp. 11–13.
2. Gallup.chol.com, December 14, 2002; also see Sisapress.com, January 16, 2003.
3. *New York Times*, December 2002.
4. Robert Novak, "The Real Crisis for South Korea," *Chicago Sun-Times*, January 6, 2003.
5. Richard Allen, "Seoul's Choice: The U.S. or the North," *New York Times*, January 16, 2003.
6. *Korea Herald*, January 11, 2003.
7. Paul Hollander, *Anti-Americanism: Irrational and Rational* (New Brunswick, NJ: Transaction, 1995), p. 339.
8. Hollander, *Anti-Americanism*, p. 7
9. Max Scheler, *Ressentiment*, trans. Lewis B. Coser and William W. Hildheim (Milwaukee, WI: Marquette University Press, 1994). In this 1914 investigation into resentment, the term *ressentiment* retains the nuance of a lingering hate that our English word "resentment" does not always carry.
10. James Baldwin, "The Discovery of What It Means to Be an American," in *Price of the Ticket: Collected Nonfiction, 1948–1985* (New York: St. Martin's Press, 1985).
11. Samuel P. Huntington, *The Clash of Civilizations* (New York: Simon and Schuster, 1996).
12. See Charles Dickens, *Martin Chuzzlewit* (Oxford: Oxford University Press, 1989), xxvii; *American Notes* (New York: St. Martin's Press, 1985), p. 249.

13. The quotes are from Andre Markowits, "Anti-Americanism and the Struggle for a West German Identity," in *The Federal Republic of Germany at Forty*, ed. Peter H. Merkl (New York: New York University Press, 1989), p. 39.

14. Max Weber, "Politics as Vocation," in *From Max Weber: Essays in Sociology*, ed. H.H. Gerth and C. Wright Mills (New York: Oxford University Press, 1958).

15. See Peter Gay, *Freud: A Life for Our Time* (New York: Norton, 1988), pp. 563, 570.

16. George F. Kennan, *Sketches from a Life* (New York: Pantheon Books, 1989), pp. 149–50, quoted in Hollander, *Anti-Americanism*, p. 394.

17. Jean-Paul Sartre, *Anti-Semite and Jew* (New York: Schocken Books), p. 1.

18. Sartre, *Anti-Semite and Jew*, p. 17.

19. Andre Gluckman, the French philosopher, argued that anti-Americanism has the same contours of classic anti-Semitism; his statement is quoted in Hollander, *Anti-Americanism*, p. 337.

20. Andrei Markowits, "Terror and Clandestine Anti-Semitism: Thoughts on German and American Reactions to September 11, 2001," *Partisan Review* 69, no. 1 (Winter 2002): 14–18.

21. See chapter 9.

22. Carl Schmit, *The Concept of the Political* (New Brunswick, NJ: Rutgers University Press, 1976), p. 27.

23. See for instance, Gi-Wook Shin, "South Korean Anti-Americanism: A Comparative Perspective," *Asian Survey* 36, no. 8 (August 1996).

24. Katharine Moon, "Korean Nationalism, Anti-Americanism, and Democratic Consolidation," in *Korea's Democratization*, ed. Samuel Kim (New York: Cambridge University Press), pp. 135–58.

25. Sisapress.com, January 16, 2003.

26. Andrei Markovits, "The Minister and the Terrorist," *Foreign Affairs* 80, no. 6 (November-December 2001): 132–46.

27. Andrei Markovits, "Anti-Americanism and the Struggle for a West German Identity," in *The Federal Republic of Germany at Forty*, ed. Peter H. Merkl (New York: New York University Press, 1989), p. 36.

28. Andrei Markovits, "On Anti-Americanism in West Germany," *New German Critique* 34 (Winter 1985): 3–27.

29. Moon, "Korean Nationalism, Anti-Americanism, and Democratic Consolidation."

30. Ibid.

31. http://service.joins.com, January 16, 2003.

32. Sander Gilman, "Introduction," in *America in the Eyes of the Germans: An Essay on Anti-Americanism*, ed. Dan Diner (Princeton, NJ: Markus Wiener), p. xvii.

33. Jurgen Habermas, "National Unification and Popular Sovereignty," *New Left Review* 219 (September/October 1996): 8.

34. I quote the term from Moon, "Korean Nationalism, Anti-Americanism, and Democratic Consolidation."

35. For accounts of this, see Martha Mendoza et al., *Bridge at Nogunri* (New York: Henry Holt, 2001).

36. Huntington, *The Clash of Civilizations*, p. 135.

37. Donald Clark, "Commentary: Interpreting the Kwangju Uprising," and Don Oberdorfer, "Introduction," in *The Kwangju Uprising*, ed. Donald Clark (Boulder, CO: Westview Press, 1988), pp. 6, 69.

38. Amnesty International, "South Korea: Prisoners Held for National Security Reasons" (September 1991), p. 6, quoted in Moon, "Korean Nationalism, Anti-Americanism, and Democratic Consolidation."

39. Joseph Stiglitz, *Globalization and Its Discontents* (New York: Norton, 2002).

40. See Paul Blustein, *The Chastening: Inside the Crisis that Rocked the Global Financial System and Humbled the IMF* (New York: Public Affairs, 2001).

41. Ibid., *The Chastening*, p. 138.

42. Ibid., p. 137.

43. Blustein relates that one former IMF economist was quoted as saying "the U.S. Treasury guys were incredible hawks, wanting us to raise interest rates sky high. They hid behind our skirt. They were willing to let the Fund take all the blame, and never made it clear that if things were left to them, interest rates would have been raised substantially higher" (ibid., p. 157). Even Michel Camdessus, the executive director of the International Monetary Fund complained of U.S. pressure on the IMF to get tough on South Korea. Informed that Americans were dissatisfied, Camdessus snapped back: "They are always unhappy" (ibid., p. 147).

44. Stiglitz, *Globalization and Its Discontents*, p. 102.

45. International Monetary Fund and the Republic of Korea, Letter of Intent, December 3, 1997. See also Blustein, *The Chastening*, p. 149.

46. Blustein, *The Chastening*, p. 199.

47. George W. Bush, "West Point Commencement Speech," Council on Foreign Relations, *America and the World*, pp. 366–67.

48. The same approach to terrorism exists in Japan. In fighting terrorism, the Japanese have preferred negotiation and ransom paying rather than insisting on principles such as "never negotiate with terrorists." In later 1990, Japan paid some $2 million to $5 million to the Islamic Movement of Uzbekistan, which is closely linked to Al Qaeda, to win the release of four Japanese geologists who had been taken hostage. See Peter Katzenstein, "Same War, Different Views: Germany, Japan, and the War on Terrorism," *Current History*, December 2002: 427–35.

49. Katharine Moon, *Sex Among Allies: Military Prostitution in U.S.-Korean Relations* (New York: Columbia University Press, 1997), p. 36.

50. Chalmers Johnson, "The Okinawan Rape Incident and the Rekindling of Okinawan Protest against the American Bases," in *Okinawa: Cold War Island*, ed. Chalmers Johnson (Cardiff, CA: Japan Policy Research Institute, 1999), p. 114.

51. Johnson, "The Okinawan Rape Incident," p. 117.

52. See Selig Harrison, *Korean Endgame* (Princeton, NJ: Princeton University Press, 2002), p. 189.

53. See for instance, Barry Rubin, "The Real Roots of Arab Anti-Americanism," *Foreign Affairs* 81, no 6 (November/December 2002): 73–85; John Waterbury, "Hate Your Enemies, Love Your Institutions," *Foreign Affairs* 82, no. 1 (January/February, 2003): 58–68; Walter Russell Mead, "On French Anti-Americanism," *Foreign Affairs* 82, no. 2 (March/April 2003): 139–42.

54. Pundits like Francis Fukuyama have written of "deep differences" within the Euro-Atlantic community; Jeffrey Gedmin, director of the Aspen Institute Berlin, spoke of the old alliance being irrelevant in U.S. global strategic thinking; Robert Kagan has written that it was time "to stop pretending that Europeans and Americans share a common view of the world, or even that they occupy the same world"; and Charles Krauthammer has declared, "NATO is dead." See Philip Gordon, "Bridging the Atlantic Divide," *Foreign Affairs* 82, no. 1 (January/February 2003): 70–83.

55. George Santayana, "My Father," *The Background of My Life* (New York: Scribner, 1944).

6

Anti-Americanism in Korea and Germany

Comparative Perspectives

Ronald Meinardus

German Definitions of Anti-Americanism

Anti-Americanism and the related debates have a long tradition in Germany. There, as in other parts of the world, the term *anti-Americanism* is often used in an undifferentiated and therefore confusing manner. While the term—in general—refers to negative opinions, sentiments, and/or concepts that individuals or groups have regarding the United States of America, a clear distinction should be drawn between (1) negative attitudes regarding certain elements or the totality of U.S./American policies at a given time, and (2) a "political attitude, that does not only defame the primary and guardian power of the West, but at the same time questions the membership of the Federal Republic of Germany in the community of countries sharing Western values."[1]

Critical and negative attitudes toward the United States tend to be limited in duration and scope and may therefore be called transitory. Often, these negative attitudes come hand in hand with positive attitudes on other aspects of the American reality. One example: Today, Germans are highly critical of Washington's policies in the Middle East. At the same time, they share a general admiration for the political and economic order in the United States. In contrast, anti-Americanism may be called a deep-rooted national stereotype. It is a mind-set based on a total rejection of the principles and values for which the United States stands.

In his much-discussed book *Feindbild Amerika. Über die Beständigkeit eines Ressentiments* (translated as: "America Conceived as the Enemy. On the "Endurance of Resentment"), the historian Dan Diner argues, "the phenomenon of anti-Americanism is virtually a matter of mentality." For Diner, "the anti-American resentment primarily does not refer to what the United States do [sic], but what they are."[2]

In his historical essay, Diner retrieves—and explains—the century-old tradition of anti-American ideology in Germany. He shows that anti-Americanism has been used as a political instrument in various periods of German history. On the other hand, it becomes evident that the anti-American ideologues speak more on their own behalf and that of intellectual elites, rather than representing the vox populi in the sense of the numerical majority of the German population at any given time.

Diner argues German anti-Americanism throughout its 200-year history has been rooted in what he calls a reactionary and antimodern state of mind: all anti-American ideologues, he states, are stirred by a "hostile and fearful reaction to modernity." They join hands in "lamenting the demise of grown and tried and tested values and traditions caused by the United States."[3]

Richard Herzinger and Hannes Stein agree with Diner's observations and focus their study on the current political-ideological debate in Germany following unification: "Anti-Americanism, they write, is a *Weltanschauung* deeply rooted in European cultural history. . . . America is the universal image of horror, a metaphor for a tremendous and inconceivable threat. All fears of loss of orientation, self-alienation and self-dissolution are projected toward "Americanism." . . . America is the symbol for a departure to the unknown."[4]

Under the headline "Who is afraid of America?" the authors describe the controversy between anti-Americans and their foes as just another dimension of an overlapping confrontation of ideologically divided camps—the one opposing western values and the "open society," the other supporting and defending these values.

In Herzinger and Stein's view, the conflicting attitudes toward America reflect a much deeper antagonism between liberal and antiliberal forces in German society today. Importantly, they argue, the antiliberal forces are not confined to the conservative and reactionary circles but are also found on the left of the political spectrum: Right and left—conclude the authors—unite in the rejection of the "open society" and the country that symbolizes this open society more than any other.

Both Diner and Herzinger/Stein give impressive accounts of the intellectual debates in Germany. Importantly, these debates are hardly representative of the attitudes of the general public. I am surprised that neither mentions this limited scope of their studies, disregarding the available empirical data: For—in spite of the great quantities of anti-American "literature" produced by academicians, other intellectuals, political fringe groups, and their spokespersons over the years in the German language—all empirical evidence shows that the majority of Germans have a basically positive attitude toward America and what it symbolizes.

German Attitudes Toward America

Modern methods of opinion polling make it possible to determine empirically what the public or sectors of the public think about the United States. (West) German public opinion vis-à-vis the United States is well documented for the time following World War II.

Although Germany started and lost two horrendous World Wars in which the United States was on the victorious side, the enmity of the past has not left deep scars in the collective conscience of the German public. A majority of West Germans view the end of World War II not so much as a catastrophic military defeat but as a moment of liberation, and they see the occupying forces from the West (and prominently the U.S. forces) as liberators.

Regarding the early postwar years, several accounts refer not to anti-American sentiments in the population but, on the contrary, to widespread pro-Americanism: "In the early years of the Federal Republic of Germany, the popularity of the USA was overwhelming. The United States virtually became an *Ersatzvaterland*. Powerful sentiments of relief, of gratefulness explain this effusive enthusiasm for America in the fifties."[5] Hans Eberhard Richter defines these sympathies for the United States in West Germany at that time as "a psychological Americanization reaching the under-conscience."[6]

Some examples for the popularity of the Americans may suffice: Surveys show that "three out of four Germans did not have any objections to German women dating U.S. soldiers." Likewise, two out of three Germans perceived American aid as a genuine contribution toward democratization and not as a concealed effort to "Americanize" the Germans."[7]

Major "cracks" in this harmonious picture of a generally pro-American West German public first become visible in the seventies, in the context of the Vietnam War. Numerous German politicians, journalists, and academicians voiced their opposition against the U.S. military operations in Southeast Asia, setting off a heated ideological debate, in which those leaning to the left strongly criticized the Americans; those on the right and in the center defended the United States.

Negative attitudes toward the United States in West Germany reached a previously unseen level in the early eighties in connection with the debate regarding the installation of U.S. medium-range missiles on German territory. Many West Germans opposed the deployment of these missiles. For the first time after World War II, a considerable group of West Germans perceived their country's national interests in conflict with the strategic interests of the Western Alliance and the North Atlantic Treaty Organization (NATO)—headed by the United States.

The "peace movement's" argument that the missile deployment threatened the very existence of Germany gained support in large parts of the population: "In view of this supposed threat emanating from the American ally, the leftist opponents of nuclear arms considered the divergence between the democratic Federal Republic and the totalitarian German Democratic Republic as negligible. . . ."[8]—and openly questioned the alliance, one should add.

Importantly, voices favoring disengagement from the West and the United States were also raised in parts of the ruling Social Democratic Party (SPD). Some left-leaning politicians in that party argued that Bonn should even consider moving away from the western "community of values" (*Wertegemeinschaft*). In the wake of the assumed "structural inability of the West to reach peace," West Germany should opt for a "German-German Community of Responsibility" (*Deutsch-Deutsche Verantwortungsgemeinschaft*).[9]

It should be noted that the nationalistic argument according to which West Germany's subordination under NATO (and U.S. political control) is detrimental to pursuing national unification (or antiunification, to use a wording from the Korean debate) was not popular in the West in the early eighties. The "peace movement" was spearheaded by political forces leaning to the left, who openly opposed national reunification. Speaking out for national unification in West Germany in those days was considered "politically incorrect" and restricted to political circles on the right fringe. A majority of the West German population did not consider unification to be a realistic option at that time. Therefore the issue whether the presence of U.S. troops in Germany or membership in NATO could be seen as hindering unification was not raised. Interestingly, to my knowledge, the question was also not included in surveys of public opinion in the seventies and eighties.

German unification in 1990 not only changed the world, it also had major implications for United States–German relations. While there was considerable reluctance to support Germany's unification in that country's immediate neighborhood, the government in Washington from a very early stage actively supported the union in the heart of Europe.

Nevertheless, the end of the Cold War in Europe sparked debates in Germany over whether time was ripe for a fundamental shift in political orientation. One school of thought argued that with the unification of the country (and the inclusion of the East) Germany had become "more German"—or less western. There was also talk of a "new German identity"—and even the old concept of Germany's *Mittellage* (central location, as opposed to the western integration), was revived.[10]

But again, in my eyes, these debates were confined to academic and intellectual circles and their forums. They were not reflected in surveys of the public opinion, let alone in the actual foreign policy of the federal government of the united Germany. Berlin left little doubt that it was politically, economically, and culturally rooted in the western alliance and an expanding European Union.

More recently, U.S.-German relations have experienced new strains. These are due mainly—but not exclusively—to differing opinions on both sides of the Atlantic of how best the international community should deal with Iraq. In this context, Henry Kissinger ascertained a "crisis" in the bilateral relations, for which he makes German Chancellor Gerhard Schröder responsible, on the basis of his handling of the issue in the electoral campaign leading up to the general elections for the Bundestag on September 2, 2002.[11]

Numerous U.S. commentators have attributed the narrow election victory of Schröder and his coalition government to their stand against German participation in any American attack on Iraq. Interestingly, a parallel has been drawn between the role the United States played in the parliamentary elections in Germany and the presidential elections in South Korea some months later. According to the commentator of the *Washington Post*: "For the second time in four months, anti-Americanism has helped propel a leader to power in a country that for decades has depended on a close security alliance with the United States. South Korea's President-Elect Roh Moo Hyun may be less cynical and opportunistic than Germany's Gerhard Schröder, but he has a few things in common with him: a grounding in domestic populism, unfamiliarity with English and the United States, and a gut desire to shift the balance of power in his country's relationship with Washington."[12]

Traditionally, elections in Germany are won or lost on domestic issues. Also, in the recent campaign, the economic situation was the focal point of most debates. Still, analysts agree that Gerhard Schröder's unambiguous statement against any German military participation in a war against Iraq may have been decisive. They cite three reasons:

1. At a crucial time of the campaign, the Iraq issue diverted public attention away from the unfavorable economic record of the incumbent government.
2. The issue helped mobilize the core members of the Social Democrat and Green parties, many of whom by tradition tend to be pacifists.
3. Most significantly, Schröder profited from public opinion, as a clear majority of Germans adamantly opposed an attack on Iraq—and even more so possible involvement of the German military.

During the peak of the campaign, when Schröder made his "anti-American" statement, 81 percent of the German public opposed a German role in a military attack against Iraq.[13]

The widespread disapproval of a military role for Germany in the Middle East is one expression of a more general and evolving skepticism of the German public toward the role of the United States in international affairs. According to survey data published in *Der Spiegel,* the number of Germans who consider the United States to be the guarantor of peace and security in the world has been on the decrease. While in 1993 some 62 percent believed this is to be the case, in 2002 this figure declined to 48 percent. Furthermore, two-thirds of Germans share the view that the United States is intervening in international crises in pursuance of its own narrow national interests. Ten years earlier, merely 58 percent of respondents shared this view. All but favorable is the average German's perception of President George W. Bush: In early 2002, only 19 percent had a positive view of the chief executive, while 50 percent had a negative view.[14]

German commentators have explained the changes in German public opinion toward the United States as a general aversion against American foreign policy behavior: "American omnipotence and mainly America's unilateral use of power to promote her national interests seem to have contributed to a more negative image of the USA. . . . The Iraq issue is thus an expression of a deep-rooted alienation in terms of foreign policy, an expression of differing foreign policy priorities and differing perceptions of threat."[15]

In spite of the widespread public aversion against U.S. policy choices in the world, a majority of Germans continue to entertain positive basic attitudes toward America.

The available data indicate that rejection of U.S. policies in a given historic situation should not be equated with anti-Americanism. Ten years ago the number of self-proclaimed German pro-Americans reached 72 percent. In spite of all the negative reporting, today 68 percent of Germans still consider themselves to be basically pro-American.

Like the figures published in *Der Spiegel*, the Pew Global Attitudes Project has recently stated that 61 percent of Germans have a favorable opinion of the United States (the related figure for South Korea from the 2002 survey is 53 percent).

Nevertheless, the same report on a more cautious note mentions that "strongly positive feelings toward the U.S. and favorable opinion have diminished among major U.S. allies in western Europe."[16]

This shows that there is in Germany what may be called a sneaking decline of sympathy for the sole superpower. Whether this is indicative of a major sociological and demographic trend or merely a short-lived public reaction to what are seen by many as misconceived U.S. policies, only the future will show.

Attitudes Toward America: Comparative Remarks Regarding West Germany and South Korea

One can think of several commonalities between Germany and Korea, and probably even more between South Korea and West Germany before unification. But a closer than superficial look will reveal more differences than similarities—also pertaining to the respective relations with and attitudes toward the United States.

Let me begin with the commonalities: First and foremost one must mention national division, which in both countries came about as the result of international war and has been conserved for decades as a result of the global confrontation between East and West. In this confrontation, Korea, like Germany, became a military front, with the United States assuming the role of the guarantor power over West Germany and South Korea.

The United States invested heavily in both countries, assisting in economic development and deploying tens of thousands of U.S. forces, with the explicit objective of defending its allies against a possible military aggression and "communization."

In both countries, the dynamics of demographics have led to a dwindling of the generation that witnessed and profited at first hand from U.S. assistance and protection at the height of the Cold War. This age group is making place for a younger generation "who do not remember the liberation of Korea, the Korean War, and the American economic assistance that saved (South) Korea in its aftermath."[17] Likewise in Germany—to quote former Chancellor Helmut Kohl—"memories of the United States' generous help for us Germans have faded. Many have no memories of the Marshall Plan, the Berlin airlift, the help and support during the Cold War and reunification."[18]

Ironically, in South Korea today many members of the new generation not only disregard the American contributions to their country's political and economic development, in some cases they even accuse their trans-Pacific partner of being responsible for national division and other difficulties. Blaming Washington for the rift and calling it an obstacle on the path toward unification has at no time been a proposition held by a sizable group of people in West Germany: As explained earlier, there, only a small minority blamed the United States for the division of the two Germanies.

Comparing the empirical data and taking into consideration my highly subjective personal observations in both countries, I would argue that anti-American sentiments (or attitudes highly critical of U.S. policies) are more pronounced in South Korea today than they were at any given time in West Germany prior to unification.

I would suggest that this divergence is due to differing intensities of nationalism in the two countries.

Korean nationalism, I would argue, is today stronger than German nationalism. In view of the crimes committed in the name of the German nation by the fascist dictators (and following an effective U.S.-inspired reeducation campaign), a sound majority of Germans today are basically antinationalistic. Nationalism in Germany to this very day has a negative connotation. For historical reasons, nationalism in Korea has a different, I would argue, positive flavor: Korea has not led aggressive wars and has not attacked its neighbors. To the contrary, the Koreans have been attacked and colonized and nevertheless succeeded in defending their national identity.

In our context, the diverging intensity of national feelings is relevant, as this has implications regarding the attitudes toward unification and national unity—and indirectly toward the United States, which in both Germany and in Korea has been perceived as a major player in the national affairs.

While the overwhelming majority of West Germans prior to unification never believed they would live to see unity and were rather indifferent to the idea (thus any accusation that the United States was blocking unification was a nonstarter), national unification for a majority of South Koreans continues to be a serious concern and a strong desire.

Here, too, continuous North Korean propaganda that the Americans (and their military presence in the South) stand in the way of national reunification has fallen on fruitful ground with many. On the other side, various East German efforts to promote the "neutralization" of Germany as a stepping-stone to unification never had a serious impact on public opinion in West Germany for the stated reason.

One final explanation for the diverging intensity in anti-American sentiments is of a more structural nature:

While the U.S.-West German relations have all along been embedded in the multilateral framework of NATO, U.S.-South Korean relations have from the very beginning been more or less confined to the bilateral level. Therefore, in the case of Germany, most decisions of strategic relevance were taken in a multilateral setting, with Germany as a partner and the United States acting—in the best of all cases—as primus inter pares. In the Korean strategic setting, important policy decisions are clearly identified and identifiable as solely U.S.-inspired. Structurally, bilateralism here has opened the door to the accusation of unilateralism.

Although I have highlighted the differences between Germany and South Korea, I would like to end by stressing important similarities that are relevant in this context: both countries may be called middle powers, both are democratic republics, and both have experienced national division and catastrophic wars.

All these political factors have affected the way Koreans and Germans think and what they believe. More recently, it has become clear that the democratically elected governments of both nations are keen on participating actively in all decisions that they believe affect their people directly or indirectly. Only if the sole superpower takes this paradigm shift into account in its decision-making process can the growing threat of anti-American opinion be halted.

Notes

1. Gesine Schwan, *Antikommunismus und Antiamerikanismus in Deutschland. Kontinuität und Wandel nach 1945* (Baden-Baden: Nomos Verlagsgesellschaft, 1999), p. 19.

2. Dan Diner, *Feindbild Amerika. Über die Beständigkeit eines Ressentiments* (Munich: Propyläen Verlag, 2002), pp. 8, 25.

3. Ibid., pp. 9, 25.

4. Richard Herzinger and Hannes Stein, *Endzeit-Propheten oder Die Offensive der Antiwestler. Fundamentalismus, Antiamerikanimus und Neue Rechte* (Hamburg: Rowohlt, 1995), p. 23.

5. Arnulf Baring, *Unser neuer Grössenwahn. Deutschland zwischen Ost und West* (Stuttgart: Deutsche Verlags-Anstalt, 1988), p. 122.

6. Quoted in Schwan, *Antikommunismus und Antiamerikanismus*, p. 28.

7. Ibid., p. 217.

8. Herzinger and Stein, *Endzeit-Propheten*, p. 50.

9. Ibid.

10. Ibid., p. 44

11. "German-U.S. Relations Thrown into Crisis," *Korea Times*, October 23, 2002.

12. Quoted in "Roh and Bush." *International Herald Tribune*, December 23, 2002.

13. For a first analysis on the elections to the Bundestag, see Dieter Roth and Matthias Jung, "Ablösung der Regierung vertagt. Eine Analyse der Bundestagswahl 2002," *Aus Politik und Zeitgeschichte*, December 9, 2002 (B 49–50), pp. 3–17.

14. *Der Spiegel*, May 18, 2002, pp. 26–31.

15. Peter Rudolf, "Deutschland und die USA—eine Beziehungskrise?" *Aus Politik und Zeitgschichte*, December 2, 2002 (B 48), pp. 16–23, quote on p. 17.

16. The Pew Research Center for the People and the Press, *What the World Thinks in 2002. The Pew Global Attitudes Project* (Washington DC: Pew Research Center, 2002), pp. 53–71, quote on p. 53.

17. David Steinberg, "Rising Anti-American Sentiment in Korea," *Korea Times*, August 28, 2002.

18. *International Herald Tribune*, November 18, 2002. "In the long term, Kohl says, anti-Americanism will not succeed."

Part II

Structural and Strategic Phenomena

7

The Structural Basis of "Anti-Americanism" in the Republic of Korea

Bruce Cumings

Like the currents flowing

away under the frozen surface

of the stream

       they have gone,

but like the water's force

even now they return, pounding

voices that will not let me be.

Kim Chi Ha[1]

What is a "structure," students often ask. It might be the division of a country, which establishes for nearly six decades a black-and-white logic directing all attention to one side, and little if any to the other. It might be an archipelago of foreign bases in South Korea, beginning with the massive Yongsan facility in the middle of Seoul. It might be a peculiar form of international relations, in which a foreign commander retains operational control of a country's military forces. It might be a raft of unexamined assumptions that floats on the surface of a relationship, masquerading as a series of truths—received wisdom—but ultimately designed to warn inquiring people away from probing more deeply. It might be a submerged history: fleeting, disappearing, and then lost moments, which retain unanswerable force and truth the minute they are recalled or uttered. It might be the imperceptible way in which racism still tinges white American attitudes toward nonwhites, in spite of decades in which racist is the worst thing you can call someone. In this chapter (not to be quoted or cited without the author's permission), I use structure in all those meanings.

It might be useful to make some distinctions regarding the South Korean phenomenon that the media call "anti-Americanism." The first would answer the question: Is the Republic of Korea (ROK) different than any other country today? Except for the weeks after September 11, a continuous distaste for American power and policy in one country after another has marked the Bush administration. The baselines here are the denunciation of the Kyoto Treaty, the International Court of Justice, and the 1972 Anti-Ballistic Missile Treaty, a general tendency toward bluff and stark threats, an inveterate unilateralism, and of course, the months-long buildup toward war with Iraq, which has generated unprecedented tensions with European allies. A January 2003 *New York Times* article reported that relations between the United States and "two of its most crucial allies—Germany and France—are at their lowest point since the end of the Cold War." Other observers would say, the lowest point since World War II, because Europeans have a widespread sense that the United States is at odds with its traditional allies not just over Iraq but over the usefulness of the world system that Americans did so much to build since 1945. Whether the emergent strains over American policy are healed or not, a senior European diplomat said, "will be the defining moment on whether the United States decides to stay within the international system."[2]

Another distinction would address the term *anti-American* itself: it assumes a uniform opposition to Americans as such instead of distaste for American policies; it also assumes a uniform America, as if all citizens should equally and patriotically feel abused by foreign criticism. In fact, Americans are as conflicted today as they were back in the 1960s, or perhaps more so, with voters split down the middle in their partisan preferences. President Bush, after all, only got into office through a split decision, five to four, on the Supreme Court; and lost the popular vote by more than half a million. I was one of those in the 500,000-plus majority, and I do not see the values and interests that this majority represented connected in any way with the policies of this administration. Does that make people like me anti-American?

A third distinction is to ask whether Koreans today are more critical of Americans than they were in the 1980s or whether they are simply more free to express their views in the raucous, bumptious atmosphere of a democracy that also subjects its own leaders to withering criticism. (Kim Dae Jung always seems to be honored more outside his own country than within it; not long after he won the Nobel Peace Prize in 2000, his popularity ratings were at the lowest of his five-year term.) Until the decades of military dictatorship ended, you could go straight to jail for publicly advocating the withdrawal of U.S. troops; but now all kinds of chickens are coming home to roost from an unfortunate and repressed past. So it might be that, as Americans, we are merely experiencing what Korean presidents, chaebŏl leaders, university administrators, and the dictatorial generals themselves have experienced in the past decade.

One thing is clear, though: Koreans do not call for the United States to return to an international system of its own making, as do Europeans. In Europe that system was always multilateral, beginning with the four-power allied occupation of Germany at the end of the war. In East Asia, however, ever since General Douglas MacArthur's arrival in Tokyo in September 1945, unilateralism has been the name of the game. MacArthur paid no attention to Allied opinion in running the occupations of Japan and (at a distance) South Korea; instead he was the hero of the expansionist, Asia-first wing of the Republican Party (which is the original, if distant source of Bush's unilateralism). Furthermore, the onset of the Cold War led the United States to revive Japan as a regional engine of the world economy, shorn of its political and military clout, and then to reinvolve it in its former colonial economies; it was in that context that Secretary of State George Marshall and Undersecretary of State Dean Acheson moved in early 1947 toward the creation of a separate state in southern Korea and toward an American security guarantee of that same state.[3] Many Koreans now believe that Japan—the just-defeated enemy—bulked much larger in American policy than did concern for Korea's division or for the authoritarianism of the successive governments that the United States supported in Korea. Since taking office, the Bush administration has had three crises in East Asia, one each with Japan and China and a continuous one with North Korea; it is hard to say that any of them have been handled effectively. A few weeks after the inauguration, the captain of the *U.S.S. Greeneville* took his ship out for maneuvers off Waikiki Beach. Why? Because several wealthy civilian contributors to the U.S. Navy were in town hoping for a submarine ride, courtesy of the U.S. taxpayer.[4] As these guests milled around and play-acted at the controls, the captain ordered his nuclear attack submarine to leap to the surface, which it did—just in time to capsize the *Ehime Maru* and kill nine Japanese tourists, four of them high school students. It took weeks for the Bush administration finally to make a proper apology for this reckless incident.

On April Fool's Day, an EC-3 reconnaissance plane was spying off the southern coast of China when it apparently got clipped by a Chinese fighter jet and was forced to land on Hainan Island. A Chinese pilot died and the Chinese leadership chose to keep the crew and the plane for a while, in order to ask the crew some questions and examine the plane. This detonated Bush's first China crisis, with a predictable media din about how awful it was that the Chinese should force down an American plane that just happened to be flying along 7,000 miles away from its base. (During the Cold War, we sent spy planes along Soviet coasts and they sent theirs along ours, governed by an elaborate protocol of mutually accepted rules of the game. China, however, possesses no such capability.)

As the crisis unfolded, China did everything it could to treat the crew well and, after it was satisfied that it had gotten what it wanted from them by way of explanations, sent the crew home.[5] Later, the EC-3 came home as well, albeit in boxes, after the Chinese demanded that it first be dismantled. After some initial false starts, the Bush administration settled down to a patient negotiation that resolved this tempest, aided by interaction between George W. Bush and his father. Less noticed in the successful resolution of this crisis was the arrogance implied in retaining and utilizing an enormously expensive surveillance capability long after the Cold War had ended and the Soviet Union disappeared, and when we face no comparable aerial spying from China.[6]

In between these two events, ROK President Kim Dae Jung showed up as the first foreign leader to meet with President Bush in the Oval Office. In the run-up to his visit, Secretary of State Colin Powell told reporters that the president would pick up where the Clinton administration left off in working toward a deal that would engage North Korea and shut down its missile program. Kim Dae Jung, fresh from winning the Nobel Peace Prize, was expecting to welcome the North Korean leader to Seoul in the spring, this meeting being the follow-on to the summit in June 2000 in Pyongyang, where the leaders of the two Koreas shook hands for the first time since the country was divided. Soon both Powell and Kim had to backtrack, caught up short by the President's own hard line—a meeting that was a diplomatic disaster by any standard. Kim returned home with his advisers publicly calling the meeting embarrassing and privately cursing President Bush.[7] Powell backed and filled and right-wing Republicans lambasted him for "appeasement," while President Kim's upcoming summit and his "Sunshine Policy" were suddenly plunged into deep trouble, with Pyongyang abruptly canceling a cabinet-level meeting that had been scheduled in Seoul. Kim Jong Il has yet to reciprocate by showing up in Seoul.

In June 2002, two teenage girls on their way home from school were crushed by an American armored vehicle on a narrow country road south of Seoul. The two soldiers in the vehicle were subsequently acquitted by a U.S. military court of all charges, including negligent homicide and unintentional manslaughter. This incident was the proximate cause of demonstrations against U.S. policy in Seoul, with the key demand being a direct apology from President Bush. Six months after the event, prompted by the largest such demonstration on December 14, 2002, and the impending presidential election, President Bush finally put in a direct call to President Kim and apologized. There may have been a good investigative article in the leading American newspapers that scrutinized this June incident, but if so, I missed it. Koreans often call attention to the enormity of these events in Korea and the paucity of coverage—or seeming concern—in the United States. It is not as though this were a new story, either; accidents of this sort and crimes by American soldiers, including many murders and rapes, go back decades, but there is much less press interest in such stories than there is for similar events involving American troops in Europe or Japan.

Another "Crisis" with North Korea

It would not be stretching things to say that the Bush administration botched its early relations with all three East Asian countries. However, on the Korean Peninsula, it now has two difficult relationships to manage: the one with the Republic of Korea and a crisis with North Korea that began in October 2002. In August 2001, I attended a conference at Yonsei University that overlapped with the annual independence day celebrations, some of which I observed. I was struck by the violence of emotion directed not at Americans but at the Bush administration; the president, rather than the American flag, was burned in effigy. A relative lull in U.S.-Korean relations ensued thereafter, punctuated by Pyongyang's unprecedented official condolences published within twenty-four hours of the September 11 attacks, and President Bush's State of the Union address in January 2002, where the North found itself part of a new "axis of evil."

Many commentators have pointed out that no "axis" existed between the Democratic People's Republic of Korea (DPRK), Iraq, and Iran; the North has had close relations with Teheran since the revolution in 1979 and has exported SCUD missiles to it. However it has no relationship with Iraq, and Iraq and Iran hate each other as a result of the devastating war they fought in the 1980s. Some believe that North Korea was thrown into this "axis" to provide a non-Muslim country for Americans to hate. The phrase also resonated with Ronald Reagan's "evil empire" rhetoric. But this ended up as another mess created by the Bush administration; a year later, the president had completely dropped any reference to this "axis." But the media continued to do his work for him; in early 2003, *Newsweek* ran a cover story on Kim Jong Il—"Dr. Evil" (see below).

For Mr. Bush, "evil" has a clear meaning: some people (or regimes) are so beyond the pale that there can be no relationship with them; they should just go to hell, and the sooner the better. Koreans, however, lack a comparable concept of evil. In an interesting, iconoclastic book, C. Fred Alford has argued that "Koreans do not believe in evil." Evil is not a moral category for them but an intellectual one, "the result of erroneous dualistic thinking."[8] In Korean civilization, human beings create relationships among one another, and the closer such relationships are, the more the separation and division implied by good versus evil cannot be allowed to appear. In an increasingly globalized world, Alford argues, a neoliberal "theoretical order" subjects the world "to a single analytic framework," creating lines and divisions between liberal beliefs that Americans take to be "self-evident." As Americans also have the power to impose this framework on others, the rest of the world can easily turn itself into an enemy by rejecting these same ideas and principles. In this light, North Korea becomes "evil" merely by sticking to the essential nature it created for itself after 1948, a top-to-bottom alternative to western capitalist and American values.

Nonetheless, the evidence suggests that the North was still willing to work with the Bush administration for months after the "axis of evil" speech and in spite of Bush's references to Kim Jong Il as untrustworthy and "a pygmy." While Bush's advisers continued to argue over whether to confront or to engage Pyongyang, Kim Dae Jung's leading adviser on the North, Lim Dong Won, reopened high-level contacts in April 2002.[9] The North responded with energetic diplomatic activity for the next several months, renewing high-level talks with the South, concluding a number of agreements on relinking railways and establishing new free export zones in the North, and culminating in Kim Jong Il's August 2002 meeting with President Putin and the unprecedented visit by Japanese Prime Minster Junichiro Koizumi to Pyongyang in September. In that same month came the release of a new preemptive attack doctrine from the U.S. National Security Council and the October visit to Pyongyang by James A. Kelly, where he resolved the administration's internal disputes over engagement versus confrontation by producing both—hinting at a new package of "engagement" goodies—while accusing the North of having a new, second-track nuclear weapons program, this time using enriched uranium. A codicil to the preemptive doctrine appeared in December, which called for a mix of deterrence, interdiction, and preemption to be used against "the world's most dangerous regimes and terrorists" that "threaten us with the world's most destructive weapons."[10]

The combination of this new Bush doctrine (deeply unsettling to the North) and the unfortunate Kelly visit pushed the North over the edge. Soon Pyongyang began to rerun the script of the crisis in 1993–94, this time on fast-forward (expelling inspectors, withdrawing from the Non-Proliferation Treaty (NPT), and restarting its Yongbyun reactor). The rerun began when Kelly presented evidence that the North had imported enriched uranium from Pakistan. According to him, the North Koreans at first denied it and then admitted it, not without a certain belligerent satisfaction. Some time in 1998, Bush administration leaks say, the North Koreans made a deal with America's long-time ally in Islamabad to trade their missiles for Pakistan's uranium enrichment technology. Some time last summer, the same sources say, evidence that the North was manufacturing enriched uranium came to light. It is a very slow process, but if they maximize their efforts, using 1,000 centrifuges that they may or may not have, they could manufacture one or two very large and unwieldy atomic bombs every year, on the model of Pakistan's nuclear program.[11] Shortly after Kelly's return to Washington, a high American official told reporters that the 1994 Framework Agreement that froze the North's Yongbyon reactor was null and void, a self-fulfilling prophecy, since President Bush's advisers had declared it a dead letter soon after coming to power. (There is nothing in the agreement prohibiting uranium enrichment, Bush spokesmen to the contrary, but the North certainly violated the spirit of the agreement.)

Since then, the "crisis" sequel quickly emerged, with the North Koreans pushing hard, knowing that the president was preoccupied with Iraq and the Bush administration was changing its tune almost every day. Washington will not negotiate with the North Koreans, which would reward "nuclear blackmail." Wait a minute; we better talk to them or they'll soon become a nuclear power—but we can't "reward" them, so we will "talk" but not "negotiate." Hold on! The DPRK is getting out of line again: we better take the problem to the UN Security Council. Whoa; no, we can't, because China won't go along. Let's send a low-level or back-channel envoy to Pyongyang. Nothing doing, Pyongyang wants to talk with someone who actually makes decisions. We can't do that, though, because that would be like recognizing this regime or yielding to "blackmail," which Washington has consistently refused to do since Kim Il Sung came to effective power in the North—way back in February 1946.

In the middle of this business, a joint operation between the United States and Spain interdicted a North Korean freighter carrying SCUD missiles to Yemen; it looked like the United States would take over the ship. In the event, however, Washington had to let the ship proceed, since there is no international law against missile sales between sovereign governments, and the United States is the world's leading seller of missiles. Just as a decade ago, obsessive concentration on the problem at hand in Pyongyang is met by inattention and confusion in Washington, and North Korea keeps winning. As Leon Sigal (one of the very few reliable American experts on this problem) put it to me, "You don't want to get into a pissing match when the other guy has a full bladder."

Push came to shove and finally Washington enunciated its presumed bottom line. William Perry, who had been President Clinton's defense secretary, put it this way back in 1994: "We do not want war and will not provoke a war over this or any other issue in Korea"; but if UN sanctions "provoke the North Koreans into unleashing a war . . . that is a risk that we're taking."[12] Back then, though, President Clinton could not stomach that risk with a determining congressional election just four months away, because his commander in Korea, General Gary Luck, had told him a new Korean War would last six months and he would need to be prepared with 100,000 body bags. Perry reiterated this stance, almost word for word, in an important editorial in the *New York Times* on January 19, 2003: the United States must "make clear our determination to remove the nuclear threat even if it risks war."

In 2003, President Bush repeated over and over again that the United States had no intention of "invading" the DPRK, while hard-liners in the Pentagon revived Clinton's plans for a "surgical strike" against Yongbyon. Diplomats say that Washington is ready to talk to Pyongyang but will not negotiate or reward "nuclear blackmail," and they all lament Kim Jong Il's multiple interruptions of Bush's march toward war against Iraq. But the extended dilation of the Iraq problem—due to Bush's decision in September 2002 to put the problem of Iraq's "weapons of mass destruction" (WMD) in the hands of the UN Security Council and the International Atomic Energy Agency (IAEA)—was clearly the occasion for North Korea to fast-forward the current crisis. Bush had serial plans for "the axis of evil": first Saddam Hussein, then North Korea, and then Iran. Kim Jong Il, however, was understandably a man in a hurry.

This sequel has the same solution as the original: direct negotiations that will get North Korea's nuclear program frozen and eventually dismantled (as called for in the 1994 agreement) and its medium- and long-range missiles decommissioned by buying them out, at the price of American recognition of the DPRK, written promises not to target the North with nuclear weapons or attack it, and indirect compensation in the form of aid and investment (i.e., the quid pro quo). Indeed, William Perry was the point man for getting both jobs done in 1998–2000 as Clinton's roving ambassador, moving toward mutual diplomatic recognition and a full buyout of Kim Jong Il's missiles *in spite of* intelligence evidence that in 1998 North Korea had begun to import aluminum centrifuge tubes and other technology relevant to a separate nuclear program to enrich uranium. But President Bush cannot yet star in the new sequel because of the new foreign policy commitments (preemption, preventive war) he has made.

"Anti-Americanism" Is Anti-Bushism

Many Korean protesters see American policy as standing in the way of South–North reconciliation; if some Americans see that as a harsh judgment, it is hard to conclude from the above account of recent events that the North is solely to blame for the new crisis now besetting the peninsula. The North clearly sought diplomatic engagement with Washington from Bush's inauguration until the October 2002 meeting with Kelly, and our allies in Seoul and Tokyo as well as our partners in Moscow and Beijing reciprocated and engaged with the North; only Washington did not. Pyongyang then found itself declared "evil" and under a new threat of preemptive attack. As if to underline this dangerous new departure in U.S. policy, the Pentagon periodically leaks plans to use nuclear strikes against hardened underground bunkers in Iraq and North Korea, either preemptively or early in a conventional conflict, and carries out war games using such scenarios with dummy nuclear weapons.[13] Any general sitting in Pyongyang would thus take careful notice of the new "Bush Doctrine" or be fired for dereliction of duty.

In 2003 Bush was forced to repeat many times that "we have no intention of invading North Korea," while backing off an any number of presumed commitments and "red lines" that might lead to confrontation with North Korea.[14] Relations with Seoul also became very rocky, as both Kim Dae Jung and the new president, Roh Moo Hyun, cling to a doctrine of engagement. Again, it is not clear that the distress is directed at Americans generally; instead, it is directed at the Bush administration's derelict, conflicted, and ham-handed Korea policy over the past two years.[15]

So it appears that the incessant use in the media of the term *anti-American* to describe the discontent in Seoul is flawed and inappropriate. It would be closer to the truth to say that the Bush administration is as responsible as any other party for the upsurge in protest. Of course, it is possible to find restaurants in Seoul that post signs saying "Americans not welcome" and posters that denounce Americans in general terms. You can find the Korean term *pan-Mi* ("anti-American") on buttons and posters. When I observed demonstrations in August 2001 and December 2002, I was prepared to tell people, if they asked, that I was from New Zealand. But no one bothered me in the slightest. Many Americans and westerners have participated in the massive, dignified, and impressive candlelight vigils held in Seoul on Saturday nights in the past several months. Furthermore the term *pan-Mi* is a typically terse protester's usage and has long been a ubiquitous symbol for any number of causes expressing some sort of dissatisfaction with American policies, but usually not Americans or the United States as such. My first book was banned by the Chun Doo Hwan dictatorship (thus enhancing sales of the pirated translation) and denounced by regime scribes as *pan-Han*, *pan-Mi,* and *ch'in-Buk* ("anti-Korean, anti-American, and pro-North"), all at the same time. Considering the source, I was proud to be the target of this terse invective.

A recent Korea Gallup Poll showed an increase in those who "dislike the United States" from 15 percent in 1994 to 53 percent in 2003. News reports on this poll did not give the actual questions posed to respondents, but when asked the opposite question —"Do you like the United States?"—the response was 64 percent in 1994 and 37 percent in 2003.[16] Putting these results another way, 36 percent of people surveyed in 1994 said they disliked the United States—not a particularly comforting figure. More to the point, there is little to indicate one way or the other whether such poll results stem primarily from the Bush administration's policies and the acquittal of the two soldiers or from a growing "anti-Americanism." But one poll for the *Sisa Journal* in 2002 found that 62 percent of the respondents thought that President Bush's policies toward North Korea had not been helpful.[17]

Furthermore, the entire tenor of the recent demonstrations differs from the actual high point of opposition to U.S. policy, in the mid-1980s. On December 14, 2002, a few days before the presidential election, I witnessed what was probably the largest of the "anti-American" demonstrations—both from a high floor of a downtown hotel in Seoul and by mingling with the demonstrators. I participated in massive antiwar demonstrations in New York and Washington in the 1960s and observed many student demonstrations in Korea from the 1960s forward, but I have never seen such an impressive political statement. Tens of thousands of young people, families with little children, painted protesters festooned with slogans, and a sprinkling of middle-aged and elderly people held candles protected from the wind, moving slowly under billowing white banners and calling on the United States to support North–South reconciliation, reform the Status of Forces Agreement (SOFA) agreement, move military bases outside of Seoul, and bring real justice to the soldiers who killed the two teenage girls. It was serious and yet amiable, moving and dignified, and very well organized (both by the protesters and the forces of order).

"Anti-Americanism" in the Past

In the mid-1980s, Seoul was an armed camp. Chun Doo Hwan undertook a vast expansion of paramilitary riot police, numbering around 150,000 by the mid-1980s. They bore the main brunt of demonstrations, wearing a strange protective armor: black helmets; tight screens over their faces; leather scabbards protecting the backs of their necks; padded clothing; thick elbow, knee, and shin guards; heavy combat boots; long metal shields in their left hands and riot batons in the right; and wire-mesh masks, helmets, body padding, and long batons to ward off Molotov cocktails. On any given day they could be seen sitting in buses with grated windows all over downtown Seoul, awaiting their next encounter. These were the Darth Vader–like figures that showed up frequently in photos in the *New York Times*, often with no accompanying article (for none was needed). During this period Han Yun-jo, the woman who owned Samyang Chemicals and wangled an exclusive contract to supply tear gas to the state, frequently paid the highest annual taxes of any businessperson in Korea ($3.4 million tax on a gross income of $7.3 million in one year).[18]

Kim Dae Jung returned home in February 1985, and I was fortunate to be part of an American delegation that accompanied him back to Seoul from exile in the United States, in hopes that our presence would prevent another airport murder like that which had cut down Benigno Aquino on the Manila tarmac two years earlier. The Chun regime was smarter than to do that but still stupid enough to cause a huge fracas at Kimp'o Airport; a phalanx of Korean Central Intelligence Agency thugs in brown windbreakers pummeled and threw prominent Americans to the floor (two congressmen were on the delegation), while roughly snatching Kim and his wife into a waiting car and subsequent years of "house arrest" (riot police surrounded Kim's neighborhood and occupied the homes of his next-door neighbors, surveilling his every movement and refusing to allow him to speak publicly). When we got to the bus that would take us into Seoul, hundreds of Cholla people in tattered winter clothing milled around us, exclaiming that Kim was their "great leader." On the left side of the road leading into Seoul were thousands of riot police. On the right side of the road were enormous numbers of Seoul's common people—workers in denims, students in black uniforms, mothers in long skirts, little kids wrapped tightly against the wind, old men and women in traditional dress—with placards hailing Kim's return. It seemed as though the whole population had been divided between the riot police and the demonstrators.

The touchstone of protests in the 1980s, of course, was the Kwangju Rebellion. It is not a stretch to say that an entire generation of young people was raised in the shadow of Kwangju, just as students in the 1960s lived with Vietnam and the civil rights movement. American officials often saw the students' protests in a narrow empirical light: the students claimed U.S. involvement in Chun's two coups (in December 1979 and May–June 1980) and especially in supporting Chun's crackdown at Kwangju. The American Embassy would respond that there was no such involvement, which as a matter of high policy in Washington may have been true, but which could not have been true in the dailiness of American-Korean relations. The United States maintained operational control of the ROK Army; Chun was head of the powerful Defense Security Command; he grossly violated the agreements of the joint command twice, in December 1979 and May 1980: Why did the United States not act against those violations? With his service in the Vietnam War and his positions in military intelligence, Chun had to have a thick network of ties with American counterparts: had they stayed his hand, or did they even try? Above all, why did President Reagan invite this person to the White House and spend the early 1980s providing him with so many visible signs of support?

There was no good answer to most of these questions, and especially not the last one. The first of many anti-American acts was the arson of the Kwangju United States Information Service office in December 1980; by the mid-1980s, such acts were commonplace, with many young people committing suicide for their beliefs. To make this long and unfortunate story short, Korean-American relations are light years better today than they were two decades ago. Furthermore, few Americans seem to understand that the 1980s gave birth to a huge variety of protest groups, labor unions, and civic organizations that made a huge contribution to Korean democratization and bequeathed to that country the strong civil society that it has today.[19]

Before the turmoil of the 1980s, Korean feelings toward Americans were mixed, with supporters of the alliance giving voice to their pro-American attitudes and detractors finding that their views could hardly be expressed publicly. Any Americans who have ever spent time on the streets of Seoul quickly learn that plenty of Koreans do not like them. When I lived in a Korean home in the late 1960s, little kids in the neighborhood would tag along behind me sing-songing *mmmooooonkeeeee* ("monkey") and shouting out various Korean epithets that took me a while to learn. One day I was strolling in a back street with a Korean friend and a man heaved out of a bar, spied me, and spit full in my face—to the overwhelming mortification of my friend, who later patiently explained that not all Koreans liked Americans. (Or, as a colleague once suggested, maybe it was just me they didn't like.)

James Wade, an American expatriate who lived in Korea for decades, wrote a book (*One Man's Korea*) in the 1960s that perfectly captures the atmosphere of Korean-American relations in the period 1945–80. He has every vignette right—every encounter in the streets, every visit to the U.S. military bases, to the Embassy, to the Seoul Civilian Club, or the many other places where Koreans and Americans came into contact. Wade renders all these with accuracy and empathy. The period during and after the Korean War was the worst, of course, because that was the "American century" at its height and Korea at a depth it had never plumbed before. Wade records American soldiers complaining in the mid-1950s about "sensitivity" manuals that said Koreans were "proud and dignified." "All the people we've seen so far have been filthy beggars, or farmers living in huts worse than animals. They're not even civilized, let alone dignified or proud." Wade captures the argot of an American Army captain in 1966, hulking over Koreans as if they were all his coolies: one of them had run an American flag up a pole, improperly: "'God damn it!' he bellowed. 'Look at that mucking flag. They've got it all bass-ackwards.' Glaring wildly about, he continued shouting: 'Hey! Where's Skoshi? Where's Boy-san? Somebody get over here on the double, hubba-hubba.'"[20]

I had many similar experiences as a Peace Corps volunteer, when I would sneak into the Embassy cafeteria or a snack bar on the Yongsan base or the Civilian Club in search of a good cheeseburger. Koreans did all the hard labor in the Embassy and military compounds. A Korean would be scurrying around while a soldier waited: "Bolly-bolly, Mr. Park, time's a-wasting" (i.e., *ppalli-ppalli*, "hurry up!"). That was in 1968. Recently an American reporter noted that often "the first thing passengers may see" as they disembark at the "dazzling new" Inchon airport is "American sergeants in combat fatigues barking orders to arriving American service members."[21]

I have never quite gotten over my first encounters with the American official presence in Seoul. These Americans ranged from gruff military officers to nervous Embassy officials to members of the AID (Agency for International Development) mission; they included hard-nosed anticommunists always warning of a North Korean attack as well as civilian liberals who deplored the authoritarianism of the Park regime. But all of them lived in compounds in Yongsan or nearby Itaewon, and they all—including the liberals—expressed attitudes toward Koreans that ranged from querulous condescension to crude racism to outright shock that people like me lived with Koreans and ate their food. Hardly any of them ventured out into "the economy"—and when they did they took an official car, or a "kimchi cab" (Korean taxicab), the driver of which would have to show identification at the gate before being allowed in to pick them up.

Many Americans experienced in Korean affairs will say this was one of the few countries that never said "Yankee go home," but it is also difficult to find, among the millions of Yankees who have served or worked in Korea since 1945, many who took the time to learn about Korea's long history and deep culture or to pick up the language. A remarkable Maryknoll priest who labored for decades among the poor in Pusan, Aloysius Schwartz, noted in his 1966 book (*The Starved and the Silent*) that most Americans lived behind compound walls, with swimming pools and large numbers of servants—and so did many American missionaries, with western-style homes in Seoul, beach houses on the coast, and speedboats for summer recreation. And how could any eye miss the "Yankee princesses" (*yang kongju*), who numbered in the tens of thousands? One priest said more than 6,000 prostitutes lived in his parish alone.[22]

I returned from Seoul to attend graduate school at Columbia University, and my first encounter with a professor was in a meeting with Michel Oksenberg, who later became one of my advisers. "What's it like in Seoul," he asked. "Well, to tell the truth," I said, "it's like an occupied city and a garrisoned country. American military bases are all over the place, surrounded by a nauseating scene of prostitution and poverty." Mike's eyes grew cold, and he changed the subject. A few years ago, shortly before his untimely and tragic death from cancer, he told me that his son, now a military officer, had been based in Seoul and Mike had visited him. "That city's like an armed camp!" Mike exclaimed. "It's really still got an American occupation going on." He then related that his son had been one of the officers in charge of a weeks-long orientation for new U.S. troops and had been appalled that only twenty-four hours of the instruction time was devoted to Korean history, culture, and language. He recommended that it be doubled to forty-eight hours. He was turned down.

In 1894 the Japanese Army established its main base at Yongsan on the outskirts of old Seoul; now it is a gigantic complex covering 630 acres smack in the middle of an enormous, sprawling, bustling city. Whenever trouble develops, American commanders retreat to an old fortified underground bunker—just as Japanese commanders did. I can't think of another capital city quite like it, where you turn a corner and suddenly see a mammoth swath of land given over to a foreign army. U.S. troops first occupied it in 1945, and the commander of the occupation established his residence in the executive mansion of the former Japanese governor-general, later known as the "Blue House." The military government operated out of the old government-general headquarters (*sotokofu*), built in 1915 in a Beaux Arts style, but shaped so it would look like the first character of Nippon from the air, and placed so as to disrupt the geomancy (feng-shui or *p'ungsu* in Korean) of the old royal palaces. Other high officers billeted at the Bando (Peninsula) Hotel, long the main lodging place for Japanese officials and wealthy tourists visiting Seoul. In the 1960s the Bando sat across the street from the U.S. Embassy (in a building formerly occupied by the Mitsui Corporation), but later it was destroyed and the Embassy moved to a spot catty-corner from the old government-general building. In the 1990s President Kim Young Sam finally tore down both the old Blue House and the colonial government-headquarters. Koreans know these things, but Americans are usually blithely unaware of the historical physiognomy and symbolism of their presence in this venerable city, the capital since 1392.

The American Responses to the Recent Protests

The recent problems between the United States and the ROK have occasioned a petulance that seems surprising, coming from Americans who have long experience in Korea and presumably possessing eyes to see the same problems James Wade and many others discerned long ago. Richard Allen, who was a paid lobbyist of the ROK during the dictatorships and often registered as an agent of the ROK by the U.S. Justice Department,[23] recently wrote that Roh Moo Hyun's election made for "a troubling shift" in U.S. relations with the ROK. Now here was the first democratic election since 1971 involving two major candidates in which the winner got near a majority, when Park Chung Hee barely eked out a victory over Kim Dae Jung's 46 percent of the vote. For Allen, however, Korean leaders seemed now to have "stepped into the neutral zone" and had even gone so far as to suggest, in the current nuclear standoff, that Washington and Pyongyang should both make concessions: "the cynicism of this act constitutes a serious breach of faith." Maybe American troops should be withdrawn, Allen suggested, "now that the harm can come from two directions—North Korea and violent South Korean protesters."[24]

In Allen's opinion, the U.S. "is responsible for much of Seoul's present security and prosperity"; the implication being that Koreans are biting the hand that feeds them. Other Americans wonder how Koreans can criticize the United States, when "North Korea is rattling a nuclear sword." A Pentagon official argued that "it's like teaching a child to ride a bike. We've been running alongside South Korea, holding on to its handlebars for 50 years. At some point you have to let go."[25] Another American military official in Seoul said of Roh's election, "There is a real sense of mourning here."[26] Meanwhile American business interests stated that troop withdrawals would cause investors to "seriously reconsider . . . their plans here.[27] This remarkable combination of petulant irritability and grating condescension somehow seems unremarkable both to the people who say such things and sometimes to the reporters who quote them.

Allen also complained that some Koreans "still blame America for the division of Korea" in 1945. An index of the gulf separating American and Korean knowledge of this history is a reporter's article in our paper of record, saying that "Many young South Koreans sincerely believe what North Korea has taught for decades: that American troops arrived here in 1950 and split the nation in two. In reality, the Communist North attacked first."[28] He seemed unaware that American combat divisions landed in early September 1945, a few weeks after John J. McCoy directed Dean Rusk and a colleague to an adjoining room to find a place to divide Korea that would keep Seoul in the American zone.[29] Americans consulted no allies, let alone any Koreans, in coming to this fateful (and unilateral) decision, which was followed by the three-year U.S. military occupation government that created the Republic of Korea. In 2002

Hyundae heir Chung Mong Jun, whose presidential candidacy gave way to Roh Moo Hyun's, remarked to an American reporter that "For Koreans, it is very ironic that we were divided by World War II, and Japan, your defeated enemy, was not."[30] It is a perfectly reasonable and understandable judgment about an errant and unjust division of a country that had well-recognized boundaries and integrity for more than a millennium. But few Americans are even aware of this fact, let alone feel any responsibility or remorse for it. Nor do most Americans understand that U.S. troops have now been based in Korea for nearly six decades; but is it unreasonable—or "anti-American"—for some Koreans to ask if they ever plan to go home? How would Americans feel if the situation were reversed, and foreign troops had been resident on our soil for more than half a century?

A decade ago President Roh Moo Hyun called for the withdrawal of American troops from Korea. During his presidential campaign, attacks by his opponents led him to say he had long before repudiated that position. Meanwhile successive administrations in Washington have treated such demands as heresy and plan to keep American troops on the peninsula—forever? The "Nye Report" in 1995 projected at least another fifteen years for the existing bases and troops, in spite of the end of the Cold War and the collapse of the Soviet Union. Three years later Secretary of Defense William Cohen stated publicly that the United States would keep its troops in Korea "even after unification." A blueprint for the Bush administration's policy toward East Asia, done under the leadership of Richard Armitage (now Colin Powell's deputy in the State Department), also called for an indefinite retention of troops in Korea and Japan.

Yet troop withdrawal has been a subject of internal and external debate in Washington going all the way back to the Kennedy administration, when Averell Harriman, undersecretary for East Asia, first began planning for such a withdrawal.[31] Richard Nixon was the only president successfully to do so, however, taking out the Seventh Infantry Division, or about 20,000 troops. Amid a Beltway debate in the mid-1970s that ranged from outright calls for full withdrawal on the left and the (libertarian) right to maintaining or reinforcing the status quo, Jimmy Carter campaigned on a platform to get the troops out. When he became president, however, he found that the forces of inertia in the government organs responsible for national security were immovable on this issue; bureaucrats presented him with evidence of a big expansion of the North Korean Army, and soon the withdrawal was dead. Subsequently Carter wrote that "I have always suspected that the facts were doctored by DIA [Defense Intelligence Agency] and others, but it was beyond the capability even of a president to prove this."[32]

Were Harriman, Nixon, and Carter unwitting dupes of the North Koreans? All sorts of studies in the 1970s showed that U.S. troops were not necessary to defend the ROK, and that they were either hostages to a new Korean war, no matter how it might start, or a "tripwire" guaranteeing U.S. involvement—regardless of Congress's constitutional responsibility to declare war.[33] Often missed in these debates, however, is a structural condition growing out of the Korean civil war: The troops are there to block a North Korean invasion, but also to restrain the South. Because of the revolutionary challenge presented by the new North Korean government and the volatility of the Syngman Rhee government, with its frequent threats to march north, in early 1950 Secretary of State Dean Acheson fashioned a civil war deterrent: we would contain the North and constrain the South. This is the essence of what he meant to say in his famous "Press Club" speech in January 1950 and is clearly presented in internal documentation.[34] The United States has not departed from that civil war deterrent to this day, and it is a key reason for the continued presence of U.S. troops in Korea; we do not trust the Koreas to be alone together. I would guess that American planners are even more loath to leave the two Koreas to their own devices, now that Roh Moo Hyun has been elected.

Racism in Korean-American Relations

Many Koreans believe that racism pervades American attitudes toward Korea and Koreans and coverage of their affairs. Mostly unbeknownst to our mainstream media, time and again they have protested biased treatment of Koreans, whether it is the recent James Bond film *Die Another Day*, where Bond desecrates a Buddhist temple with his amorous adventures while caricaturing the North as a hellhole[35]; *Newsweek* cover stories (see below); the presumed "black-Korean" conflict in the 1992 Los Angeles disturbances[36]; American coverage of the 1988 Olympics, which ranged from the blatant racism of P. J. O'Rourke in *Rolling Stone* to the more subtle aversions and aspersions of Ian Buruma in the *New York Review of Books*[37]; or the ease with which Americans blamed Koreans for the Koreagate scandals instead of blaming the congressmen who were happy to pocket the Korean ambassador's wads of cash.

What is racism? Consider these statements:

- from the American Commander in Korea, John Wickham: "Lemming-like, the people are kind of lining up behind [Chun Doo Hwan] in all walks of life."
- A sentiment deemed "characteristic of many near the top of [the U.S.] government": "These [North] Koreans are wild people."[38]
- Korean authoritarianism goes back to the Confucian tradition.
- Koreans are "the Irish of the Orient—highly emotional, very nationalistic."
- Koreans are "about as subtle as *kimchi* . . . and as timid as a *tae kwon do* chop."[39]
- "Koreans could not strike the first blow in their own defense."
- "Koreans are not ready for self-government."
- "Unlike the Philippines, Koreans are not yet ready for democracy."[40]

None of these statements is overtly racist; they do not call names or use what the U.S. Supreme Court calls "hate speech." Yet if we substitute *Americans* or *blacks* for *Koreans* and imagine foreigners of great influence giving voice to these views, we sense that these are biased judgments. Every statement beginning "Koreans are . . ." violates the extraordinary diversity found in Korea or among Koreans abroad. Furthermore, such statements ignore the context in which Korea, a unitary nation going back to antiquity, was first colonized for nearly half a century, then divided for an even longer period, and experiencing a devastating civil war along with the most acute Cold War tensions felt by any country in the world.

Americans of Korean descent now inhabit all professional walks of life and contribute in a wide variety of ways to American culture, and their growing prominence negates any holistic construction that begins, "Koreans are. . . ." To take just one example, a hugely talented artist who was murdered on the streets of New York at the age of twenty-nine, Theresa Hak Kyung Cha: she once painted an American flag marked only with the word *AMER*—meaning "bitter" in French. Her various works of art dwelt on Korea's twentieth-century history of colonization and division, yet without "falling prey to the lure of racial exceptionalism," and thus they "exceed their own specificity to situate themselves within the global conflict of North and South, of the West and the Rest, or of darker and lighter races. No history (of any single nation) without (the) histories (of other nations). Each society has its own politics of truth; each oppressed people, their own story of special horrors and inflicted sufferings."[41]

David Theo Goldberg locates contemporary racism, after the end of formal racist institutions like slavery or segregation, in an Anglo-Saxon liberalism that is "self-conscious in its idealization of acceptable social conditions" (truths that are self-evident, norms of democracy, civil society, and the rule of law), leading to a denial of the possibility of "Otherness" (who can possibly disagree with these ideals, or reject democracy and the market), or at best, a mere tolerance of the Other (who has yet to learn the self-evident truths). Accusations of racism by people of color are thus seen as "irrational appeals to irrelevant categories," because they implicitly delimit liberal universalism, and invalidate its claims of plurality and openness. Power shows itself in the dual liberal practice of *naming* ("all Koreans are . . .") and *evaluating* (the degree to which Koreans fall short of idealized liberal categories). Liberalism will then "furnish the grounds of the Other's modification and modernization, establishing what will launch the other from the long dark night of its prehistory into civilized time."[42] (Note that this formulation is similar to C. Fred Alford's, about the western concept of evil.)

When Attorney General John Ashcroft recently spoke at the annual gathering of global elites in Davos, Switzerland, he reacted to accusations of racial profiling of Muslims in his Justice Department by saying that he does not distinguish people according to their race, but according to their values.[43] It is a perfect illustration of Goldberg's point: I am not a racist, I accept all people *who value the same things I do.* I am incapable of discrimination *unless we are talking about people who do not value modern liberalism.*

This difficult, complex, and subtle phenomenon, about which many readers will disagree, came to a head in Korea in the financial crisis in 1997–98. Overnight, Koreans found their treasury bankrupt, their currency worth half what it had been, their livelihoods in deep jeopardy, and their economic model—long the presumed source of "the Korean miracle"—lambasted as "crony capitalism." What the economy needed was not more state-led growth but market transparency and accountability, the rule of law, a $70-billion bailout, and the fickle fingers of International Monetary Fund (IMF) and U.S. Treasury officials trifling with the best-laid plans of Korea's renowned economic czars—all in the interest of a complete reform of the Korean model. Most shocking to Koreans, however, was the instant, invidious re-*naming* and re-*evaluating* of their most prized modern achievement, their own unique path to industrialization. Most galling, top American officials like Secretary of the Treasury Robert Rubin and Federal Reserve Chairman Alan Greenspan were at the center of this overnight inversion of values.[44] Long applauded for the illiberalism of their political economy (industrial policy, "getting prices wrong," etc.), Koreans were now required to get with the liberal program (which, in its neoliberal phase, would incidentally bring huge American banks, accounting firms, and other multinational corporations into the Korean market and undercut Korean comparative advantages). If this crisis seems now forgotten, it had a critical role in generating the attitudes now dubbed "anti-Americanism." In my opinion, Korean leaders generally reacted to all this unwanted, hypocritical and ill-thought criticism with gracious dignity, while getting their noses back to the grindstone and securing a return to rapid economic growth by 1999.

We have been talking about South Korea. Prominent Americans lose any sense of embarrassment or self-consciousness about the intricate and knotty problems of racial difference and Otherness when it comes to North Korea and its leaders. Recently Greta van Susteren introduced a Fox TV News segment on Kim Jong Il as follows: "Is he insane or simply diabolical?"[45] This trope merges the Beltway discourse of the 1990s, when Kim came to power and was widely said to be crazy, with media efforts to do Bush's work regarding the "axis of evil." *Newsweek* likewise did the administration's work with a January 2003 cover story on "Dr. Evil," just as it covered Kim Il Sung's death in July 1994 with a racist cover story entitled "The Headless Beast." During the previous crisis over the Yongbyon nuclear facility, ABC's *Nightline* correspondent Chris Bury described Kim Jong Il as "a 51-year-old son about whom little is known other than his fondness for fast cars and state terrorism."

Presumed East Asian experts reinforced this imagery. On the same *Nightline* segment, Richard Solomon, once a scholar of China and later a Nixon/Bush National Security Council official, said this: "Not a bad way to look at it is to think of the Waco, Texas crisis, where you have a small ideological, highly armed and isolated community. . . ."[46] Mad dog Kim Il Sung becomes David Koresh in this rendering, and it was perfectly believable: If you are dealing with insanity, anything is possible. North Korea is an American tabula rasa, and anything written upon it has currency—so long as the words are negative. It thus ends up thrice cursed, a Rorschach inkblot absorbing anticommunist, Orientalist, diabolical, and rogue-state imagery. But then that was its original image, both in American strategy (Truman called his 1950 intervention a "police action" to catch North Korean criminals) and in Hollywood (in films like *The Manchurian Candidate*). Perhaps the real mark of our time is the deafening absence of any contrary argument in the mainstream American media; everyone wishes Kim Jong Il's socialism-in-one-family would just go away, the sooner the better. Unfortunately, he is not acting according to script.

Another widespread trope is that "we don't know anything about North Korea," and therefore it's the scariest place on earth, or the nuttiest, or the most dangerous. Helen Louise Hunter was for two decades "a Far East specialist" in the Central Intelligence Agency, which is where her 1999 book first appeared as a long internal memorandum. When he was a congressman, Stephen Solarz read her "brilliant and breathtaking" study and concluded that is for North Korea ("a country about which we knew virtually nothing") "what the Rosetta stone was to ancient Egypt." So rare and privileged was Ms. Hunter's knowledge that it took Solarz a decade to get the Central Intelligence Agency (CIA) to declassify it. I had to read to page 68 of this book before I learned anything new, which is that Kim Il Sung University has a baseball team (the Japanese introduced this venerable American game to Korea, and, given its popularity in the South, I had wondered if any remnant of that interest survived in the North).[47]

In fact, we know as much or more about the origins of the DPRK as any communist state because of two captured archives: the one MacArthur got in Japan and the one he got in North Korea (the good general did not come back empty-handed from his march to the Yalu). Decades ago, scholars like Dae-sook Suh and Chong-sik Lee utilized original Japanese police and military records to trace the rise of Korean communism from 1918 onward, Kim Il Sung's guerrilla background in the 1930s, and the origins and nature of the DPRK where those same guerrillas formed the core of the regime for the next fifty years. More recently, excellent scholarship has come from those who can read the North Korean materials, like Haruki Wada of Tokyo University, who produced an excellent book (available only in Japanese and Korean) arguing that North Korea emerged as a "guerrilla state," anticolonial (and thus anti-Japanese) to its core, yielding a thoroughgoing, recalcitrant foreign posture that also reproduced some of the ancien régime's "hermit kingdom" tendencies and that successfully kept both the Soviet Union and China at arm's length. Charles K. Armstrong of Columbia University also published an important book using the same archive, *The North Korean Revolution, 1945–1950.*[48]

The Return of History

It takes only a few days in the archives of the U.S. Military Government or the State Department to realize that the Korean critique of Americans for their country's division, the Military Government's suppression of alternative political forces, U.S. support for a succession of dictatorships, and American complicity in political massacres (Yosu in 1948, Cheju in 1948–49, the Chiri-san guerrillas, many others like Nogun-ri during the war, and Kwangju in 1980) is echoed time and time again in classified reports. In 1949 David Mark, a State Department official, undertook a full review of American policy toward Korea, which echoed many subsequent findings by scholars: Yŏ Un-hyŏng's "People's Republic" and the local committees that it spawned could have been utilized by the United States, because the local organizations were in every county and only came to be dominated by leftists and communists *after* the American command came out against them in December 1945. This is now history, Mark wrote; "nevertheless it has set the pattern for political power development in South Korea."[49] The late 1940s were indeed the crucible of Korean politics thereafter.

The fledgling CIA's first biographical study of a foreign leader was done on Syngman Rhee, as were some of its earliest political analyses on foreign governments. South Korean political life, a 1947 report stated, was "dominated by a rivalry between Rightists and the remnants of the Left Wing People's Committees," described as a "grass-roots independence movement which found expression in the establishment of the People's Committees throughout Korea in August 1945." As for the ruling political groups,

> The leadership of the Right [sic] . . . is provided by that numerically small class which virtually monopolizes the native wealth and education of the country. Since it fears that an equalitarian distribution of the vested Japanese assets [i.e., colonial capital] would serve as a precedent for the confiscation of concentrated Korean-owned wealth, it has been brought into basic opposition with the Left. Since this class could not have acquired and maintained its favored position under Japanese rule without a certain minimum of "collaboration," it has experienced difficulty in finding acceptable candidates for political office and has been forced to support imported expatriate politicians such as Rhee Syngman and Kim Koo. These, while they have no pro-Japanese taint, are essentially demagogues bent on autocratic rule.

The result was that " extreme Rightists control the overt political structure in the U.S. zone," mainly through the agency of the Japanese-built National Police, which had been "ruthlessly brutal in suppressing disorder." The structure of the southern bureaucracy was "substantially the old Japanese machinery," with the Home Affairs Ministry exercising "a high degree of control over virtually all phases of the life of the people."[50]

For the next fifty years, the acceptable political spectrum consisted of the ruling forces and parties of Rhee, Park, Chun, Roh, and Kim Young Sam, and an opposition deriving from the Korean Democratic Party founded in September 1945, led by figures like Kim Song-su, Cho Pyong-ok, and Chang Myun. The ROK did not have a real transition to the opposition until Kim Dae Jung's election in 1998, and it did not have a president until February 2003 who was not part of the political divide (and political system) going back to the U.S. occupation. (Kim Dae Jung got his political start in the self-governing committees that sprouted near the southwestern port of Mokp'o; the right always used that against him to claim that he was a Communist or pro-North, but in fact he made his peace with the existing system in the late 1940s and was an establishment politician thereafter; "the three Kims" were dominant figures from the 1960s onward, however much he was hounded by the militarists.)

Ever since this early and determining point, however, South Korean politics has had a suppressed "third force," with strong roots in the southwest but a presence all over the country. If we locate these forces on the "left," we reduce them to the polarized and caricatured constructions of the Cold War, in which any kind of mayhem committed by the right is insufficient truly to distance them from American support, so long as they remain firmly anticommunist, and anything on "the left" is to be avoided at all costs. For decades these political and social forces resided of necessity in the long memories of participants in the local committees, labor and peasant unions, and rebellions of the late 1940s, harboring many personal and local truths that could not be voiced. Suppressed memory, though, is history's way of preserving and sheltering a past that possesses immanent energy in the present; the minute conditions change, that suppressed history pours forth. Thus, in the past fifteen years, Koreans have produced hundreds of investigations, histories, memoirs, oral accounts, documentaries, and novels that trace back to the years immediately after liberation.

We now have a remarkable variety of personal memoirs of the local committees, the Yosu-Sunch'on Rebellion, the insurgency on Cheju and its draconian extermination, and an extensive record of massacres before and during the Korean War, perpetrated by the Rhee regime and sometimes by Americans.[51] Very little of this has gotten into English and is generally unknown in the United States except of course for the July 1950 massacre at Nogun-ri. That massacre hit the front pages of American newspapers in late September 1999,[52] as if no one had ever imagined that such things could have happened during the Korean War. In this curious American lexicon, civilian massacres—about which one could read in *Life Magazine* or *Collier's* in the summer of 1950—disappear into oblivion because of a false construction of the nature of the Korean War, never to be mentioned again. They are lost for a sufficiently long time, such that that when they reappear, they counterpoint everything about the received wisdom on this "forgotten war."

Koreans have been experiencing a cathartic politics in the past decade, where many suppressed and unpalatable truths have come forth with enormous political force. President Roh Moo Hyun is the first of the ROK's leaders not to have a recognizable lineage back to the 1940s. His lineage is more recent, to the extraordinary turmoil of the 1980s, when he put his career and his life in danger to defend labor leaders and human rights activists; through marriage he is also connected to a family blacklisted politically for events going back decades. His electoral victory is inexplicable, however, apart from the amazing political catharsis and turning point that came in 1995–96, in the "Campaign to Rectify the Authoritarian Past" that brought Chun Doo Hwan and Roh Tae Woo into the docket, where they were successfully prosecuted for high treason and monumental corruption. An admirably thorough and honest investigation of the Kwangju rebellion began, Chun's foul dictatorship was completely discredited, and he found himself with a death sentence hanging over his head until President-elect Kim Dae Jung magnanimously pardoned him.

A sophisticated social science analysis by Professor Doh Shin demonstrated deep and widespread support for the cashiering of Generals Chun and Roh: their arrest and prosecution both for their role in squashing the Kwangju rebellion and their coup d'état and for taking nearly $1 billion in political contributions merited "strong support" from more than 65 percent of respondents in a scientific poll, and over 15 percent said they "somewhat support" these actions. By contrast, there was much more tepid support for punishing the conglomerate leaders who provided the political slush funds.[53]

With little notice in the United States, Koreans have been going through an admirable process of reckoning with their history, analogous to South Africa's Truth and Reconciliation Commission. This commission defined that vexing term *truth* in four ways: factual or forensic truth, personal or narrative truth, social or "dialogue" truth, and healing or restorative truth. The Korean tide of suppressed memory and contemporary reckoning with the past has established all those meanings of truth for courageous people who, after the dictatorships ended, have pressed their case against all odds for years. For Americans, these Korean truths establish official lies at all levels, perpetrated for half a century, but also (in the commission's words) "reduce the number of lies that can be circulated unchallenged in public discourse."

For scholars, the strong democracy and civil society that emerged from the bottom up in the South, in the teeth of astonishing repression and with very little support from agencies of government in the United States, validates a method of going back to the beginning and taking no received wisdom for granted. I remember how, as a young man working in the U.S. archives, I came across vast internal records of the suppression of peasant rebels in South Cholla in the fall of 1946, the breaking of strong labor unions in the cities, the American-directed suppression of the Cheju and Yosu rebellions and the many guerrillas that operated out of Chiri-san in the period 1948–55 (finally extinguished in the joint U.S.–ROK counterinsurgent program known as "Operation Rat-Killer"). I wondered how all this could have disappeared without any apparent trace. Then one day I read Kim Chi Ha's poem, *Chiri-san* (Chiri Mountain),[54] and came to believe that I did not know the half of it:

> *A cry*
>> *a banner*
>
> *Before burning eyes, the glare of the white*
> *uniforms has vanished.*
> *The rusted scythes, ages-long poverty,*
> *the weeping embrace and the fleeting promise to return:*
> *all are gone,*
> *yet still cry out in my heart.*

Notes

1. Kim Chi Ha, "Chiri Mountain," trans. David R. McCann, in *The Middle Hour: Selected Poems of Kim Chi Ha* (Stanfordville, NY: Human Rights Publishing Group, 1980), p. 51.

2. David Sanger, "To Some in Europe, the Major Problem Is Bush the Cowboy," *New York Times*, January 24, 2003, pp. A1, A10.

3. This is well known to diplomatic historians but rarely seeps into public commentary about Korea policy. Relevant documents include Marshall's note to Acheson that said, "Please have plan drafted of policy to organize a definite government of So. Korea and *connect up* [sic] its economy with that of Japan" (740.0019/Control [Korea] file, box 3827, Marshall to Acheson, January 29, 1947); and Acheson's declassified testimony in executive session before the Senate Foreign Relations Committee in March 1947 to the effect that Korea is a place "where the line has been clearly drawn between the Russians and ourselves," which sent the nonplussed senators into the historical oblivion of discussions "off the record" (forever). U.S. Senate, Committee on Foreign Relations, Historical Series, *Legislative Origins of the Truman Doctrine* (Washington: U.S. Government Printing Office, 1973), p. 22.

4. Reporting subsequent to the event showed that the ship was not on routine maneuvers but went out only because the Navy did not want to disappoint the civilians.

5. My colleague Professor Guy Alitto was an interpreter for the crew, and in October 2001 lectured at the University of Chicago about the crew's experience on Hainan.

6. The EC-3s are based at the innocuously named Whidbey Naval Air Station; some 60,000 people are directly employed by or indirectly benefit from the presence of this facility on Whidbey Island, in the Puget Sound near Seattle.

7. An unnamed adviser said it was "embarrassing" in *Korea Herald*, March 13, 2001; I spoke with a Korean member of the National Assembly at a conference on Korea on March 13 who talked about Kim's advisers cursing Bush for his ham-handed tactics.

8. C. Fred Alford, *Think No Evil: Korean Values in the Age of Globalization* (Ithaca, NY: Cornell University Press, 1999), p. 2. Korean Christians believe in evil, of course, but they have imported the same doctrine of good and evil that President Bush believes in.

9. Subsequently, Lim said he had had taken a "very long and detailed letter" from President Kim to DPRK leader Kim Jong Il. In the letter, President Kim emphasized that since the September 11 attacks, "the global strategy of the United States has fundamentally changed," and that the United States "is prepared to resort to military means of counter-proliferation," so Kim Jong Il must "clearly understand that North Korea itself is also included in the possible targets." Reuters News Service, Martin Nesirky quoting a speech by Lim Dong Won in Cheju City, April 12, 2002.

10. National Security Council, "National Strategy to Combat Weapons of Mass Destruction," December 2002.

11. I draw on *New York Times* and *Wall Street Journal* articles on this issue, October 18–22, 2002. The best information on this subject is in Seymour Hersh's article in the *New Yorker*, "The Cold Test," January 27, 2003, pp. 42–47. Hersh presented considerable evidence (gotten mostly from the CIA) that Pakistan had helped the DPRK with blueprints, models, and "cold tests" of simulated nuclear explosions, using the enriched uranium processes that produced Pakistan's atomic bombs. Hersh noted, however, that the Clinton administration had been aware of these imports but went ahead with engaging Pyongyang anyway, in hopes of buying out both their nuclear program and their missiles.

12. Quoted in the *Chicago Tribune*, April 4, 1994. In a memorandum to the UN dated April 10, 1996, the DPRK stated that "a second Korean War would have broken out had the United Nations chosen to repeat its past by unilaterally imposing 'sanctions' against the DPRK." Press Release, April 10, 1996, DPRK Mission to the UN, New York.

13. Hans M. Kristensen, "Preemptive Posturing," *Bulletin of the Atomic Scientists* 58, no. 5 (September/October 2002): 54–59. Kristensen describes such a nuclear war game carried out in 1998, based on declassified documents.

14. David Sanger, "Bush Welcomes Slower Approach to North Korea," *New York Times*, January 7, 2003, pp. A1, A10; see also Sanger, "Nuclear Mediators Resort to Political Mind Reading," *New York Times*, January 12, 2003, p. A13.

15. White House reporters say the Bush administration has been and remains deeply split over policy toward North Korea: "'You step out of a meeting on this,' a senior foreign policy official said, 'and you realize that you've heard 12 ideas and no consensus.'" David Sanger and Julia Preston, "U.S. Assails Move by North Koreans to Reject Treaty," New York Times, January 11, 2003, p. A1.

16. "Anti-U.S. Sentiment Deepens in South Korea," Washington Post, January 9, 2003, pp. A1, A18.

17. Howard W. French with Don Kirk, "American Policies and Presence Are Under Fire in South Korea, Straining an Alliance," New York Times, December 8, 2002, p. A10.

18. George E. Ogle, South Korea: Dissent within the Economic Miracle (Atlantic Highlands, NJ: Zed Books, 1990), p. 99.

19. See Bruce Cumings, "Pikyojŏk simin sahoe wa minjujuŭi" (Civil society and democracy: a comparative inquiry), Ch'angjak kwa Pip'yŏng (Creation and criticism), (Seoul, May 1996).

20. James Wade, One Man's Korea (Seoul: Hollym, 1967), pp. 105–7.

21. Howard W. French with Don Kirk, "American Policies and Presence Are Under Fire in South Korea, Straining an Alliance," New York Times, December 8, 2002, p. A10.

22. Aloysius Schwartz, The Starved and the Silent (New York: Doubleday, 1966), pp. 63–64, 75.

23. See Bruce Cumings, "South Korea's Academic Lobby," JPRI Occasional Paper No. 7 (May 1996).

24. Richard V. Allen, "Seoul's Choice: The U.S. or the North," New York Times, January 16, 2003, Op-Ed page.

25. James Dao, "Why Keep U.S. Troops?" New York Times, January 5, 2003, News of the Week in Review, p. 5.

26. Howard W. French, "Bush and New Korean Leader to Take Up Thorny Diplomatic Issues," New York Times, December 21, 2003, p. A5.

27. Tami Overby, an employee of the American Chamber of Commerce in Seoul, as quoted in James Brooke, "G.I.'s in South Korea Encounter Increased Hostility," New York Times, January 8, 2003, p. A10.

28. James Brooke, "G.I.'s in South Korea Encounter Increased Hostility," New York Times, January 8, 2003, p. A10.

29. Foreign Relations of the United States, 1945 (Washington, DC: U.S. Government Printing Office), v. 6, p. 1039.

30. Howard W. French with Don Kirk, "American Policies and Presence Are Under Fire," p. A10.

31. Max Holland was kind enough to show me Harriman's 1963 memorandum from the Harriman Papers.

32. See Don Oberdorfer's full discussion in The Two Koreas: A Contemporary History (New York: Addison-Wesley, 1997), pp. 84–108.

33. The Center for Defense Information put out several papers arguing this point of view in the 1970s; one of the best sources is Doug Bandow, Tripwire: Korea and U.S. Foreign Policy in a Changed World (Washington, DC: Cato Institute, 1996). For an insider's account of the fate of the Carter troop withdrawal program, see Robert G. Rich, "U.S. Ground Force Withdrawal from Korea: A Case Study in National Security Decision Making," Executive Seminar in National and International Affairs, 24th Session (1981–82), Foreign Service Institute, U.S. Department of State.

34. As U.S. Ambassador to Korea John Muccio put it in November 1949, the problem was in getting sufficient military assistance "to enable the Koreans to defend this area and at the same time keep them from getting over-eager on moving North." Later he remarked bluntly, "We were in a very difficult position, a very subtle position, because if we gave Rhee and his cohorts what they wanted, they could have started to move north the same as the North started

to move south. And the onus would have been on us. . . ." State Department 895.00 file, box 946, Muccio to Butterworth, November 1, 1949; Truman Library, Muccio oral history interview no. 177, December 27, 1973. On several occasions before June 1950, Acheson also spoke directly to the problem of giving offensive weaponry like tanks and an air force to the South.

35. "Koreans United in Hatred of New Bond Flick," Reuters News Service, January 7, 2003.

36. A careful, sensitive treatment of this episode is available in Nancy Ablemann and John Lie, *Blue Dreams: Korean Americans and the Los Angeles Riots* (Cambridge, MA: Harvard University Press, 1995).

37. O'Rourke did a sort of racist potpourri/travelogue in *Rolling Stone*, October 1988, dwelling on Korean facial features that he found outlandish (for example). Buruma compared the 1988 games to those Hitler sponsored in 1936; after visiting Korea's Independence Hall, he asked if his "revulsion" against Korean nationalism was "a sign of decadence," or is there something "to the idea of the rise and fall of national, even racial vigor?" See Ian Buruma, "Jingo Olympics," *New York Review of Books*, November 10, 1988

38. Wickham's comment and the widespread "sentiment" are both found in Oberdorfer, *The Two Koreas*, pp. 79, 132.

39. Oberdorfer, *The Two Koreas*, p. 8.

40. These last three statements encapsulate American diplomacy at the time of the Japanese annexation in 1910 (the United States was the first major power to remove its legation from Seoul), at the end of the colonial period in 1945 (when this idea was reflected in Roosevelt's trusteeship policy), and in 1995 (when Secretary of State George Shultz infuriated Koreans with words to this effect). The other statements I have heard many times; they often appear in the American press, and, to my chagrin, are things I have sometimes said myself over the years.

41. Trinh T. Minh-Ha, "White Spring," in *The Dream of the Audience: Theresa Hak Kyung Cha (1951–1982)*, ed. Constance M. Llewallen (Berkeley: University of California Press, 2001), pp. 38, 105.

42. David Theo Goldberg, *Racist Culture: Philosophy and the Politics of Meaning* (Cambridge, MA: Blackwell, 1993), pp. 6–7, 150–51.

43. Alan Cowell, "Ashcroft Soaks Up a World of Complaints," *New York Times* (January 25, 2003), p. A8.

44. See Bruce Cumings, "The Asian Crisis, Democracy, and the End of 'Late' Development," in *The Politics of the Asian Economic Crisis*, ed. T.J. Pempel (Cornell University Press, 1999), pp. 17–44.

45. Fox News, January 15, 2003, 10:08 p.m.

46. *ABC Nightline*, November 16, 1993, transcript #3257. Solomon was the first official in the first Bush administration to highlight North Korea as "the number one threat to Asian security," in a speech on October 11, 1990, that got wide media coverage.

47. Helen-Louise Hunter, *Kim Il-song's North Korea*, foreword by Stephen J. Solarz (Westport, CT: Praeger, 1999). Hunter's book is not without value. It has some excellent information on arcane and difficult to research subjects like North Korean wage and price structures, the self-sufficient neighborhood living practice that mostly eliminated the long lines for goods that characterized Soviet-style communism, and the decade of his young life that almost every North Korean male is required to devote to military service in this "garrison state" (an apt term, that one). She points out many achievements of the North Korean system, in ways that would get anyone outside the CIA labeled a sympathizer—compassionate care for war orphans in particular and children in general (pp. 45, 101), "radical change" in the position of women (p. 95), genuinely free housing (p. 195), preventive medicine on a national scale accomplished to a comparatively high standard (pp. 221–22), infant mortality rates comparable to those of the most advanced countries until the recent famine (p. 227), and the author's frequent acknowledgment that the vast majority of Koreans did in fact revere Kim Il Sung, even the defectors from the system, whose information forms the core evidence for this book.

48. Charles K. Armstrong, *The North Korean Revolution, 1945–1950* (Ithaca, NY: Cornell University Press, 2003). See also Dae-sook Suh, *The Korean Communist Movement, 1918–48*, 2 vols. (Princeton, NJ: Princeton University Press, 1968); Robert Scalapino and Chong-sik Lee, *Communism in Korea*, 2 vols. (Berkeley: University of California Press, 1972).

49. David E. Mark's study of Korea since liberation, included in Muccio to State, 740.0019/ Control (Korea); the study is undated, but the covering letter was stamped May 23, 1949.

50. Central Intelligence Agency, "Korea," SR-2, summer 1947, and "The Current Situation in Korea," ORE 15–48, March 18, 1948.

51. Among many other new sources on Cheju, see Yoksa munje yon'guso, eds., *Cheju 4.3 Yon'gu* (Study of the April 3rd Cheju [rebellion]) (Seoul: Yoksa pip'yong-sa, 1999). On Yosu, see *Yo-Sun Sakon* (The Yosu-Sunch'on incident) (2 vols.), Yosu chiyok sahoe yon'guso (Yosu: Yosu Community Research Institute, 1998); an international symposium on the Yosu Rebellion was held in October 2002 at Yosu University, attended by some 200 delegates from the ROK, Japan, Taiwan, and Okinawa (some of them refugees who fled after the rebellion). A "Truth Commission on Civilian Massacres during the Korean War" was founded in September 2000, including more than fifteen "victims' groups" throughout the country. A number of historians from Cheju have been conducting research in the U.S. National Archives in recent years, preparing a multivolume history of the rebellion.

52. On September 30, 1999, a woman named Chon Chun-ja appeared on the front page of the *New York Times*, pointing to a hill where, she said, "American soldiers machine-gunned hundreds of helpless civilians under a railroad bridge"; she was 12 at the time, surviving under a pile of dead bodies to later recall American soldiers "play[ing] with our lives like boys playing with flies." The best English source on Nogun-ri is Charles Hanley, Sang-hun Choe, and Martha Mendoza, *The Bridge at No gun Ri* (New York: Holt, 2001); there are, again, many Korean-language accounts and memoirs of this massacre.

53. Doh C. Shin, *Mass Politics and Culture in Democratizing Korea* (New York: Cambridge University Press, 1999), pp. 203–8.

54. Kim Chi Ha, *The Middle Hour: Selected Poems of Kim Chi Ha,* p. 51.

8

Anti-Americanism and the U.S. Role in Inter-Korean Relations

Victor D. Cha

Introduction: The Train Wreck

The discussion in Korea and the United States on anti-Americanism is akin to a train wreck in slow motion. This is because each side is completely missing the point made by the other. In November and December 2002, when CNN broadcast the images of young South Koreans demonstrating against the U.S. alliance, burning American flags, hanging effigies of President Bush, and throwing Molotov cocktails into U.S. military bases, Americans became both perplexed and upset. Why, they asked, are South Koreans demonstrating against the alliance at a time when the North Korean nuclear threat appears to be rising? Many attributed this either to South Korean "free-riding" off the security guarantees offered by the alliance or simple allied ungratefulness. Moreover, the images of flag burning struck a very deep negative chord among Americans in a post–September 11 environment.

By contrast, in Korea, the thousands who participated in demonstrations did not see them as anti-American per se but as the expression of a new Korean identity. Building on the momentum of the World Cup and South Korea's unexpectedly strong showing, young Koreans finally felt as though their voices were being heard. They were a new, young generation that for the most part were educated, affluent, and free to speak their minds without fear of persecution. The twenty-somethings crowd constituted a post–Korean War generation that had very different images of the United States than their elders. Rather than viewing the United States as a savior from North Korean aggression, many saw—and were taught to see—the Americans as backers of past authoritarian regimes in Korea. Moreover, these Koreans believed that they were being very American-like in their expression of differences with the Bush administration's policy toward North Korea. What they are in fact expressing is a difference of opinion on policy with the Americans, and Americans should not interpret this as anti-Americanism. When confronted with the question of why the demonstrations do such violent things as burn American flags or torch U.S. installations, Koreans respond that such activities do not express the main message of the demonstrations.

Rather, they reflect the views of a small radical fringe, but not the main thrust of this new Korean identity.

Hence the train wreck in slow motion. What Americans view as a very real aspect of the demonstrations (i.e., flag burnings), the South Koreans discount as marginal and not of central import. This lack of communication and mutual understanding has thus given rise to the conservative as well as mainstream backlash against Korea in early 2003, with angry members of Congress as well as opinion makers calling for a withdrawal of U.S. forces from Korea.

What is so interesting about the events of 2002–3 is that, in many ways, they represent an unprecedented change in the role played by the United States in inter-Korean relations. For nearly fifty years, since the formation of the alliance, the role of the United States in inter-Korean relations was relatively uncontroversial. The animosity in Seoul–Pyongyang relations and the Cold War structure of regional security dictated one basic principle: The United States guaranteed deterrence against a North Korean attack of the South; moreover, U.S.-South Korean unity on a policy of diplomatic isolation and nondialogue toward the North was indisputable. But since the loosening of the diplomatic deadlock on the peninsula,[1] this basic logarithm has been called into question. Despite arguments to the contrary from policy elites, the U.S. role in inter-Korean relations has become a contested one, with the spectrum of views ranging from supporters of the Cold War template to dissenters who see the United States fundamentally as an obstacle to improvement in inter-Korean relations. The contested nature of the U.S. role became increasingly evident in the aftermath of the June 2000 North–South Korea summit's relaxation of peninsular tensions in South Korean eyes, followed by the Bush administration's designation of North Korea as part of an "axis of evil." Moreover, as the South Korean presidential elections of 2002 showed, for the general public, the distinction between the United States as security guarantor and ally against the North and as a spoiler of inter-Korean reconciliation has become muddled at best and destroyed at worst.

This chapter looks at the different roles played by the United States in inter-Korean relations. These roles could be described roughly as uncontested and contested. In the former vein, the United States played a dual role as "co-container." Inter-Korean dialogue was for all intents and purposes nonexistent, because the only mode of interaction on the peninsula occurred between adversarial sides. In this context, the U.S. role remained primarily one of deterrence and defense of the peninsula's security; in inter-Korean relations, its role was limited to Washington's support of South Korea's containment and isolation of the North. The second role played by the United States is as a "facilitator." Here, the basic dynamic referred to American efforts, through dialogue with the North and through entreaties to the South, to create greater interaction between the two Koreas. This was ostensibly for the purpose of reducing tensions on the peninsula. But it often emerged from alliance management needs, when an anxious South Korea did not want dialogue between the United States and the Democratic People's Republic of Korea (DPRK) to move too far afield from North–South talks for fear that such progress would undercut South Korean leverage.

The third role played by the United States is arguably as an "impeder" of North–South relations (these are contested notions). In this view, the United States is seen as the primary obstacle to improvements in inter-Korean relations. Although this view has been held by the radical fringe in Korea for some time (as well as in North Korea), I focus on this role only as it applies to mainstream public opinion in South Korea recently.

Rather than go through a historical description of these three U.S. roles, this chapter attempts to identify the variables at play that might explain the changes in the perceived U.S. role between the two Koreas over time. This analysis is not meant to make a monocausal argument, which insists dogmatically that there is one and only one variable to explain every degree of change in the U.S. role. Instead, I seek an interpretive explanation that is empirical, inductive, and what some might argue analytically "eclectic."[2] The explanations roughly include four different factors: structural and relative capabilities-based explanations; alliance management explanations; domestic-politics explanations; and perceptual explanations. Some of these could be seen as competing explanations, others as complementary. But the idea is to provide in this fashion a comprehensive rendering of the important factors in understanding how and under what conditions changes occur in the U.S. role in inter-Korean relations. Future research can draw out from this interpretation any worthwhile testable hypotheses. In the next section, I look historically at each of the variations in the U.S. role, with a discussion of alternative explanations. I conclude with a discussion questioning the purported permanency of the current view of the American "impeder" role that became fashionable after the 2002 presidential election in South Korea.

America as Co-container

The time periods for the U.S. role as co-container, facilitator, and impeder roughly correspond to major breakpoints in twentieth-century international relations.

United States Role in Inter-Korean Relations (IKR):
Strategic Environment

U.S. role in IKR	Cold War	Post–Cold War	Post-Summit
	Co-container	Facilitator	Impeder

As one might expect, the containment phase coincided with the Cold War when North–South tensions were at their height and there was little dispute over what the desired and actual role of the United States was between the two Koreas. There were brief periods during which inter-Korean relations saw some warming of relations (i.e., July 1972 North–South joint communique; 1984–85 exchanges), but these were short-lived and did not amount to much change.[3] The predominant relationship was adversarial. The South Koreans had virtually no interest in improving relations with the North. And because of this, the United States role in inter-Korean relations was by definition limited to support of the ally's position. On the rare occasions, when Washington did pursue small gestures probing the possibility of a thaw on the peninsula (i.e., in the role of facilitator), the South Koreans reacted in a strongly negative way, raising acute fears of allied abandonment in Seoul. During the détente period, for example, even while the South had managed the 1972 North–South joint communique, they were extremely critical and suspicious of any inkling of détente spreading to the U.S.–DPRK relationship. In March 1972, Seoul immediately contested U.S. intimations that it might lift travel restrictions on North Korea. In July 1972, Foreign Minister Kim Yong-sik filed strong protests over Secretary of State Rogers's use of the formal designation *DPRK* in referring to the North. Both acts by the United States were seen as departures from past practice and were harshly criticized as the first steps toward U.S. recognition of the regime.[4]

The question arises as to why the South Koreans were so strongly opposed to the slightest deviation from the co-container role played by the United States. Part of the answer lies in a capabilities-based argument in which successive South Korean governments from Syngman Rhee to Park Chung Hee to Chun Doo Hwan experienced insecurity as a result of relative parity of power with their northern adversaries. CIA estimates put the North Korean economy, measured in per capita terms, on par with that of South Korea or higher through the 1970s. The North was endowed with more mineral resources and the industrial legacy left by the Japanese. And while the South experienced political instability, coups, and the death of its chief executives, the North experienced a fairly stable leadership under Kim Il Sung. Moreover, while the North had the staunch support of Beijing and Moscow, the South faced the prospect of the U.S. troop withdrawals contemplated during the Johnson, Nixon, and Carter administrations. This may have given rise to a zero-sum co-containment expectation by the insecure South of its ally in the United States as the only acceptable role in inter-Korean relations.

Such a capabilities-based explanation, however, does not account for the fact that by the 1980s and 1990s the South was beginning to far outpace the North in material terms. Yet there continued to be strict adherence to the view of the United States as co-container and strong resistance in the 1990s, in particular to the new American role as facilitator in inter-Korean relations. As discussed in the section on the United States as facilitator, this suggests that the causal variables extend beyond relative power to perceptual biases.

The "Restraint" Rationale

Before looking at the U.S. role in inter-Korean relations in the 1980s and 1990s, however, it is useful at this point to note an additional role played by the United States on the Korean Peninsula in the early Cold War years. In addition to the explicit co-container function, Washington also played an implicit role of restraint on its ally's ambitions on the peninsula. Both the Syngman Rhee (1948–60) and Park Chung Hee governments were never shy about their desires for unification, which raised serious concerns in the U.S. government about avoiding entrapment in a second Korean conflict. In this sense, the U.S. role in inter-Korean relations was arguably as co-container, seeking to restrain both sides while allying strongly with one. In other words, in accordance with the American security commitment to its South Korean ally, the U.S. role in inter-Korean relations was explicit and uncontested. However, there was also an implicit role that the United States played with regard not only to containing North Korea but also to *restraining its South Korean ally.*

Particularly in the early Cold War years, South Korean governments made no secret of their desire for unification by force (*pukch'in t'ongil* or *songong t'ongil*). This ambition was manifest not only in the well-known stories of Syngman Rhee refusing to sign the armistice treaty and deliberately trying to sabotage the negotiations during the Korean war because he wanted to prosecute the war with U.S. support to the end. It was also evident during Park Chung Hee's rule. Despite Park's renunciation of Rhee's unification-by-force principle and acceptance of a unification-by-peace principle (laid out in the July 4 North–South joint communique), the South Korean leader clearly considered North Korean provocations, such as the failed North Korean commando raid on the Republic of Korea (ROK) presidential Blue House in 1968, as the opportunity to retaliate against the North militarily.

The United States saw absolutely no use in inflaming a second conflagration in Asia (given the war in Vietnam) and therefore was hypersensitive to becoming potentially entrapped into a conflict by its ally's overzealous actions. Successive American administrations therefore viewed the alliance relationship with South Korea in dual terms: not merely as containment of the North but also as binding or restraining the South. This restraining rationale was evident in very specific messages sent by the Lyndon Johnson administration during the 1968 crises (e.g., the Vance mission, in which Cyrus Vance was dispatched as a special envoy to tell Park that the United States would not tolerate any unilateral military retaliation by the South Koreans for the Blue House raid).

American archival records, moreover, reveal the extent to which this preoccupation with restraining the ally was interwoven with arguments for the United States holding operational command authority within the alliance.[5] The traditional rationale for the United States holding operational command authority was not just for enhanced defensive fighting efficiency but also to keep a leash on unilateral offensive acts by the South Koreans.[6] As far back as the establishment of USFK (United States Forces Korea) during the Eisenhower years, U.S. officials worried about ROK entreaties for command authority. It was standing policy that any unilateral ROK military actions would prompt Washington to the severest of actions, including the immediate cessation of economic and military aid, disassociation of the UN Command from support of ROK actions, and even the use of U.S. forces to impose martial law. NSC 5817 ("Statement of U.S. Policy Toward Korea," August 11, 1958) stated that if the ROK unilaterally initiated military operations against Chinese or North Korean forces in or north of the Demilitarized Zone (DMZ), then: (1) UN Command ground, sea, and air forces would not support such operations directly or indirectly;

(2) the United States would not furnish any military or logistic support for such operations; (3) all U.S. economic aid to Korea would cease immediately; and (4) the UN commander would take any action necessary to prevent his forces' becoming involved in the renewal of hostilities and to provide for their security.[7] In White House deliberations on the issue in the late 1950s, President Eisenhower went so far as to say that the United States would covertly support new leadership, forcibly remove Rhee, or even threaten abrogating the alliance.[8] A Memorandum of Discussion stated that Eisenhower argued, ". . . if we became aware that President Rhee was moving north to attack North Korea, we would simply have to remove Rhee and his government. . . . Such a move would simply have to be stopped." Again Secretary Herter agreed with the president but asked how we proposed to keep the Communists from counterattacking and seizing South Korea. The president stated with emphasis that "everything possible must be done to stop a unilateral South Korean move on North Korea before it started, including deposing Rhee. Thereafter, if South Korea wanted to go on to commit suicide, we would say go ahead and do it. . . . If ever this attack on North Korea occurred, the President said that the military alliance between the U.S. and the Republic of Korea would be broken at that moment."[9] Retaining operational control of ROK forces therefore was arguably as much a tool of alliance restraint as it was of deterrence and war fighting.[10] Admittedly, the U.S. concern about a South Korean preemptive attack has abated considerably over the years (particularly after democratization in 1987) and the United States transferred peacetime authority to the South in 1994. But the point remains that the U.S. role in inter-Korean relations during the Cold War was a dual one that featured not only containment of the North but also restraint of the South.

America as Facilitator

The second role played by the United States in inter-Korean relations was as a "facilitator." Here, the basic dynamic referred to American efforts, through dialogue with the North and through entreaties to the South, to create greater interaction between the two Koreas. This was ostensibly for the purpose of reducing tensions on the peninsula. But it often emerged from alliance management needs, when an anxious South Korea did not want U.S.–DPRK dialogue to move too far afield from North–South talks for fear that such progress would undercut South Korean leverage. The strongest form of this was when the United States would make inter-Korean dialogue a precondition for improvements in U.S.–DPRK relations.

The United States as a facilitator of inter-Korean relations became most relevant in the immediate post–Cold War years. The height of this phase was probably 1993–96 during the (first) North Korea nuclear crisis and the negotiations and implementation of the Agreed Framework. The official U.S. position has been that it has always supported tension reduction between the two Koreas. This may be true. This "theology" of American efforts at improving inter-Korean relations, however, has in practice been greatly informed by the alliance management exigencies that come with American pursuit of nonproliferation objectives on the peninsula. In other words, U.S. desires to facilitate North–South dialogue stemmed not just from benign and ideal desires to see Korean reconciliation but also from complaints by the allies in Seoul that the United States was pressing too fast in its own bilateral contacts with Pyongyang in a manner that excluded Seoul. The primary reason for U.S. interest in bilaterals with North Korea, in turn, largely derived from U.S. nonproliferation concerns. Hence, the United States was "facilitating" inter-Korean relations for nonproliferation reasons: In order to enable U.S.–DPRK nonproliferation negotiations, Washington needed Seoul's backing and therefore pressed for its allies' desires not to be excluded from negotiations on the peninsula.

This dynamic was especially evident during the Kim Young Sam administration. Seoul opposed any moves forward in U.S.–DPRK relations without corresponding improvements in North–South dialogue. From the ROK's perspective, this asymmetry raised fears of abandonment in the context of the alliance.[11] The concern was that the United States, by moving too fast with the North, was (1) undercutting Seoul's own efforts at inter-Korean dialogue; (2) giving the North the impression, by not consulting with Seoul, that the alliance was not strong; and (3) potentially being lulled into a situation where it might sacrifice South Korean security interests for some quick and easy deal with the North. For this reason, the South Koreans have always been hypersensitive to any asymmetry—real or perceived—in the two tracks. During the Agreed Framework negotiations, for example, American negotiators were acutely sensitive to avoiding any actions or discussions with the North that might be seen as alienating the South. The United States, on a daily basis, debriefed its ally about negotiations with the North and held fast to a clause in the 1994 agreement that required the North to improve North–South relations as a condition of the agreement, despite eleventh-hour threats by the North Koreans to trash the entire agreement if the United States did not expunge this condition. U.S. officials made deliberate efforts to consult Seoul and urge Pyongyang to engage in dialogue with the South, but very clearly the perception in Seoul was that the inordinate pace of U.S.–DPRK relations undermined North–South dialogue. Gong Ro-myong's first enunciation of "balance and parallel" (*Choul kwa pyongheang*) came on the heels of replacing foreign minister Han Sung-joo, who was held responsible for allowing the ROK to be "excluded" from talks with North Korea). With the exception of President Kim Young-sam's first few months in office, when he tried to encourage his own "Sunshine Policy," this was the case for much of his administration.

Three effects of this asymmetry in dialogues (U.S.–DPRK leading inter-Korean dialogues) therefore obtained: (1) The South sought de facto veto rights over the pace of U.S.–DPRK dialogue (2) the leverage Seoul employed was the alliance, and in particular the U.S. obligation to alleviate allied abandonment fears in order to shore up the alliance; and (3) the result was a feeding of latent anti-Americanism at perceived high-handedness and disregard on the part of Washington, which arguably rooted the groundswell of anti-Americanism evident at the end of 2002. The irony of this dynamic was that U.S.–DPRK bilateral talks leading to the Agreed Framework arguably were a necessary condition for the greatly improved North–South dialogue that culminated in the June 2000 summit, but even before this, in the scheduled 1994 summit between Kim Young Sam and Kim Il Sung (prior to his death in July of 1994).

As noted earlier, the source of the South Korean opposition to the United States as "facilitator" cannot be explained purely by power variables. By virtually every measure, the South by the 1980s and 1990s dwarfed the North, yet Seoul continued to pine for the American co-container role in inter-Korean relations. If anything, power asymmetries should tell us that the wider the gap grows, as it did in the post–Cold War era, the less concerned the South should have been about America's facilitating role. In the end, these anxieties had little to do with power, nor was the United States somehow "selling out" its ally's interests (how this would happen was never explained). It had much more to do with, as Sam Kim has said, the zero-sum mentality and politics of competitive legitimation on the peninsula.[12] Under such conditions, any North Korean diplomatic gain was by definition an ROK loss; thus, any forward movement in U.S.–DPRK dialogue, however minimal, was necessarily a victory for the North over the South that was deemed intolerable. The ROK (particularly during the Kim Young Sam administration) basically wanted all dialogue channels to Pyongyang to come through Seoul. During the Kim Young Sam years, South Korea wanted American and Japanese humanitarian food aid not to go directly to Pyongyang but to be provided through Seoul after the North first came to Seoul to request help. During Roh Tae Woo's regime, there was also apprehension after Kanemaru Shin's mission to Pyongyang that the Japan track was progressing without forcing the North to talk with the South.

Seoul's Attribution Errors

While Seoul's complaints about Washington as a facilitator were made with reference to specific issues (e.g., food aid, ballistic missiles, electricity, etc.), I argue that at the core the problem is a cognitive or perceptual one. Both sides (but Seoul more so) suffer from fundamental attribution errors in their evaluation of the problem. Referred to as "correspondent inference theory," this body of theory derived from social psychology observes that individuals often distinguish unconsciously between situational and dispositional factors in understanding behavior. The most common attribution error occurs when a person overestimates dispositional factors in explaining another's behavior.[13] Individuals not only place greater weight on dispositional interpretations of an actor's behavior but also greatly discount situational factors or constraints as variables in explaining the same behavior.[14] Thus, when I make a major donation, I am viewed as a generous person (when the real reason could be that I felt peer pressure to make that contribution at that time).[15] For example, if I were late for a meeting, I might say that it was because my schedule made me late. Contrarily, if another person were late, I might consider her to have been irresponsible.

Robert Jervis and Jonathan Mercer have applied these social psychology findings to international relations generally and to alliance theory specifically.[16] Building on attribution error dynamics and the actor-observer bias, Mercer has argued that *between allies, we tend to interpret undesirable behavior by the other as dispositional, and desirable behavior by the other as situational.* The reason, as Mercer argues, has largely to do with the cognitive constraints we face in distinguishing between what motivates our actions versus what motivates the other's actions:

> By taking credit ourselves for desirable behavior, we do not credit the other for his desirable behavior. And yet, we are quick to place blame on the other when his behavior is undesirable. . . . This tendency is compounded by an egocentric bias that leads us to exaggerate our influence when we get what we want and to minimize the influence of third parties or other situational forces. We do this in part because we know more about our efforts than the efforts of others, and in part to gratify our ego (p. 62).

I argue that these attribution errors are relevant to U.S.–ROK alliance interaction over North Korea. In particular, complaints by Seoul about how the United States is forging ahead with Pyongyang at the expense of the alliance are being met by Washington's utmost efforts to respond to the ally's complaints and fears of abandonment. But these responses are subject to acute attribution errors. For example, if the ally responds positively to the complaints—that is, the desirable behavior—this action is seen as not motivated by a genuine value assigned to the alliance (dispositional) but by immediate and more pragmatic situational factors (e.g., "they were forced to respond the way we wanted, not that they wanted to"). In other words, the positive behavior is assigned little value, because the belief is that if the situational factors were not compelling, then the ally would have responded negatively rather than positively.

Conversely, if the ally does not respond to the ally's complaints—that is, undesirable behavior—this behavior is seen as representing the true disposition of the ally (assigns no value to the alliance) rather than as motivated by the situation. The result is mutual frustration, as neither side feels that the ally is responding in a genuine fashion.

Arguably, this attribution error occurs more consistently on the South Korean than the American side. This is a function of power disparities (the power disparities here are within the alliance, not between the two Koreas). In general, it is more difficult to placate the abandonment fears of a smaller ally than a larger one. Smaller allies are much more likely to become subject to a spiral of insecurity stemming from the fundamental attribution error. If the greater ally does not address the smaller ally's concerns, this validates fears of abandonment. On the other hand, if the greater ally does offer reassurance, the smaller ally is still unsatisfied—it sees these reassurances not as dispositionally motivated (i.e., an earnest attempt by the ally to reassure), but as situationally determined (i.e., the ally reassured not because it wanted to but because the situation dictated it).

Attribution errors abound in the history of the U.S.–Korea alliance. As early as 1972, for example, South Korean president Park Chung Hee protested strongly over American intimations of a slight thaw in relations with North Korea (pursuant to the atmosphere of détente created by Nixon's visit to China, Secretary of State Rogers made reference to North Korea by its official title—DPRK—for the first time).[17] In response to Seoul's complaints, the United States stopped any further initiatives to the North. Rather than taking comfort in the U.S. response, however, Seoul interpreted the American response as situational—that is, Washington discontinued the probes with Pyongyang largely because they realized the dialogue was fruitless, not because of Seoul's complaints. The Park government did not interpret the American response as dispositional—that is, a genuine understanding of allied abandonment concerns.

Attribution errors were evident in the Clinton administration as well. During the U.S.–DPRK negotiations on the Agreed Framework, for example, the Kim Young Sam government complained vigorously about how the United States was pressing forward with dialogue with the DPRK and leaving Seoul behind. National Assembly members screamed about how the Americans were pursuing their own narrow non-proliferation interests on the peninsula at the expense of relations with their South Korean ally.[18]

Interviews with U.S. government officials intimately involved in the negotiations found that the United States heard the South Korean concerns very clearly and responded by going to extraordinary lengths to consult with its ROK counterparts on a daily if not hourly basis on the status of negotiations. American negotiators engaged in daily debriefings and regular consultations to the point where they quipped that they were not certain which was the harder negotiation, that with the North or the ally in the South. Objectively speaking, the American response might be interpreted as earnest attempts to placate the ally. But in Seoul, the South Korean reaction was to view such "desirable behavior" on the part of Washington as motivated more by the situation than by disposition. In other words, the reason the United States chose to consult with the ROK was because it realized, as the negotiations progressed with the North, that Seoul would emerge as the only feasible source of funding for the Agreed Framework's provision of alternate nuclear power reactors to the North. By contrast, the United States viewed its extraordinary actions to inform Seoul as deriving from the value Washington assigned to the ROK as an alliance partner and to trilateral policy coordination.

Finally, attribution errors plague U.S.–ROK alliance relations in the Bush administration. In his 2002 State of the Union address, President Bush's reference to North Korea as part of the "axis of evil" raised concerns in Seoul at a time that Washington was contemplating phase two of the war against terrorism on the Korean peninsula. In light of the June 2000 summit, which was popularly perceived in the ROK as a watershed event in reducing tensions on the peninsula, Bush's reference again prompted complaints that the 2002 State of the Union speech was pursuing its own interests with a punitive solution and discounting allied accomplishments and interests. However, when President Bush arrived in South Korea for summit talks in February 2002 and stated clearly that the United States was not contemplating preemptive action against the North, the South Korean interpretation was not positive.[19] The popular response was not to view Bush's statements as backtracking from his earlier "axis of evil" message, in deference to allied concerns, but as situationally motivated. In short, the United States could not prosecute another war while still militarily engaged in Afghanistan. It could not calculate the Chinese response. Moreover, even if the United States were contemplating a preemptive attack against the North, skeptics argued, it would be strategically appropriate to announce otherwise while Bush was in Seoul.

By contrast, interviews with officials involved in the Bush visit found that the president did not appreciate the full impact of his "axis of evil" statements until he was on the ground in Seoul. Embassy briefings impressed on the president how concerned the South Koreans were about the direction of U.S. policy. Hence, Bush's subsequent statements during the summit with Kim Dae Jung, denying a preemptive attack, were motivated by a genuine desire to placate allied concerns and right a wrong impression. But in the end, the South Koreans were still not comforted by the president's statements. At the same time, the Americans felt that they did the right thing but got no credit for it from their ally.

America as Impeder

The third role played by the United States on the peninsula is as an "impeder" of North–South relations (these are contested notions). In this view, the United States is seen as the primary obstacle to improvements in inter-Korean relations. Although this view has been held by the radical fringe in Korea in *minjung* ideology for some time (as well as in North Korea), I focus on this role only as it applies to recent mainstream public opinion in South Korea. The strong form of this occurs when spokespersons for the United States makes statements or take actions on the peninsula that are seen not only as impeding relations but also as unnecessarily inflaming tensions on the peninsula.

The role of the United States as impeder became salient from mid-2000, after the June inter-Korean summit. It arguably became more salient after January 2001. There is no denying the existence of such sentiment among radicals, but I date the impeder role in terms of its mainstream relevance and the product of a confluence of two critical factors. First, Kim Dae Jung's Sunshine Policy, based firmly in an ideology of unconditional engagement with the North, facilitated the June 2000 meeting, which at the time far exceeded anyone's expectations. The summit's joint declaration, family reunions, joint infrastructure projects, and ministerial meetings propelled North–South relations forward by leaps and bounds. What distinguished the policy was its explicit non-zero-sum view of interaction with the North. The South not only eschewed any pretense of making engagement conditional but also denied any need for dialogue channels to come through Seoul only. The Sunshine Policy had no objection to all forms of world engagement with the reclusive regime. This was a far cry from the fixation of previous South Korean administrations on the relative pace of North–South dialogue.

The Sunshine Policy had the unintended consequence of creating nationwide perceptions of the United States as an impediment to inter-Korean relations. As noted earlier, this view began to solidify with the first summit between Bush and Kim in March 2001. Kim tried to lecture the newly inaugurated Bush administration on the policy's wisdom; but this effort was spectacularly unsuccessful. Bush then called a "time out" on Clinton's engagement with the North and undertook a policy review in June 2001 that stated an unconditional offer to meet with the North Koreans. But President Bush's January 2002 "axis of evil" speech reduced the chances for dialogue (even though the North had announced earlier that it was not interested in meeting with the United States because of its high-handed attitude).

What emerged from the Sunshine Policy was therefore a dual dynamic reinforcing the U.S. role as impeder. On the one hand, the success of the policy created an impression among many South Koreans that the overbearing military presence of the United States on the Korean peninsula was no longer necessary. Indeed, during the summer of 2000, in the aftermath of the summit, numerous demonstrations sprouted up at U.S. military facilities protesting the American presence. In addition, the memories of the U.S. role as savior during the Korean War were explicitly extinguished on what was then to be its fiftieth anniversary (the ROK government explicitly ordered a toning down of the celebrations because of the new-found détente with the North). On the other hand, however, when the Sunshine Policy proved to be less successful than initially believed in terms of eliciting North Korean reciprocity, the popular response was to look for scapegoats—making the U.S. presence and Bush's statements prime targets.

A second critical factor contributing to the view of the United States as impeder was a "decoupling" dynamic in the alliance. In short, United States and ROK security interests on the peninsula had always been dissimilar. The ROK's first priority was peninsular defense, whereas for the United States, the key concern, particularly in the post–Cold War era, was the nuclear proliferation threat posed by the North. After September 11, 2001, the concern about this threat was transformed into a homeland security issue. This is not to argue that the two sides do not share similar security interests in deterring a second North Korean invasion of the peninsula. But while this contingency has been effectively deterred, the gaps in the two allies' views on proliferation have become more clear. The South Koreans' view of the U.S. hard-line policy toward the North is not seen as justified, in large part because the Sunshine Policy, in their eyes, reduced the primary threat posed to the South (i.e., another conventional invasion) even though it may not have appeased all American concerns about the longer-range threats still posed by the North. This decoupling of U.S. nonproliferation concerns from those of South Korea contributes to Seoul's view of the United States as unduly "spoiling" the inter-Korean party after the June 2000 summit.

The change in the roles played by the United States on the peninsula is therefore in good part a function of the current state of combined interests at the time. Whether the United States is a facilitator or impeder at the core is determined by disparate perceptions of what interests are at stake at the given moment. During the containment role, there is little difference in interests. But in the facilitation phase, the United States is often seen in the South as delinking its proliferation interests from South

Korea's. And in the impediment phase, South Korea is seen as delinking its peninsular interests from those of U.S. homeland security on the peninsula.

American as the Permanent Obstacle?

Is this perception of the United States as an impediment to North–South reconciliation a permanent one in Korea? As noted at the outset of this chapter, a snapshot of the political scene at the end of 2002 and beginning of 2003 might lead one to believe so. Political maverick and former labor activist lawyer Roh Moo Hyun was elected upon a clear wave of anti-Americanism, and his campaign rhetoric, very critical of Bush's "axis of evil" speech, appeared to resonate with a broad-based constituency in South Korea. Perhaps for the first time in South Korean political history, it appeared to many, particularly young Koreans, that the Americans were more threatening to the country than the communists from across the DMZ. December 2002 polls showed that South Koreans harbored more negative images of the United States than they did of North Korea (Table 8.1).

On New Year's Eve, 23,000 Koreans gathered in Seoul in the vicinity of the American Embassy in a candlelight demonstration demanding the Bush administration's apology for the deaths and revision of the Status of Forces Agreement (SOFA). Nowhere was this view more clearly demonstrated than in the *Sixty Minutes* story that caught a group of young Koreans self-righteously responding, to a loaded question, that President Bush was more scary to them than Kim Jong-il.[20] Public opinion polls a fortnight after the election of Roh painted the picture of a changing demographic in which a younger "post–Korean War" generation informed with a less grateful, more critical view of the United States had risen to political significance.[21] While 26 percent of middle-aged South Koreans held negative images of the United States, an astounding 76 percent of youth in their twenties and 67 percent of those in their thirties responded in a similar fashion (Table 8.2). Moreover, 51 percent of South Koreans polled believed that North Korea's nuclear intransigence at the end of 2002 and beginning of 2003 was the result of the Bush administration's hard-line policy (only 24.6 percent attributed the problem to North Korean actions and intentions).[22] Implicit in these numbers, some might argue, is the counterfactual argument that North–South reconciliation after the June 2000 summit would be entirely conceivable if not for the overbearing American preoccupation with the proliferation issue. Or, as one conservative commentator characterized the radical position: "There is no task more urgent than the reunification of the Korean nation, and the greatest obstacles to unification are the United States and its politics of strength."[23]

Not Yet

A deeper and nuanced analysis of the situation, however, would look beyond the heat of the presidential election campaign at the end of 2002 and look in particular for

Table 8.1

Images of the United States and North Korea

	United States	North Korea
Positive	37.2	47.4
Negative	53.7	37.0
Don't Know	9.1	15.6

Source: Gallup Korea Survey (1,054 sample size), December 2002.

Table 8.2

Negative Attitudes Toward the United States by Age Distribution

Age	United States	North Korea
20s	76	32
30s	67	29
40s	53	39
50s +	26	47

Source: Gallup Korea Survey, December 2002.

longer-term trends that either confirm or disconfirm what had transpired. Here I would argue that the situation may not be as bleak as is commonly believed.

For the U.S. role as impeder in North–South relations to be permanent, one would expect to observe two continuing trends. At the "street" or general public level, a growing and unconditional dissatisfaction with the U.S. military presence in Korea should be ever-present, because this would represent the embodiment of the American impeder role as viewed by the post–Korean War generation. And at the elite level, a widening gap in policy toward North Korea between Washington and Seoul should be evident as Roh pursues engagement in defiance of a harder-line position taken by the Bush administration.

Neither of these trends is indisputably evident, contrary to the popular perception. First, at the street level, there is no denying the groundswell of dissatisfaction at the U.S. military presence, expressed through flag burnings, effigies of George Bush, and the demonstrations in downtown Seoul. The proximate event fueling this movement was the acquittal by a U.S. military trial of two servicemen for the accidental vehicular death of two South Korean schoolgirls in November 2002. The popular outrage over this outcome, fueled by the heat of presidential campaign rhetoric, turned one dimension of the election into a choice between the "pro-American" Lee Hoi Chang and "anti-American" Roh Moo Hyun.[24]

What is most interesting, however, about the public anger and demonstrations at Yongsan at the end of 2002 is that they were soon followed by counterdemonstrations by other South Korean nongovernmental groups expressing support for the American presence in Korea and calling for continuation of the long-standing alliance. These demonstrations, organized by Korean War veterans' and religious groups numbering in the tens of thousands, wanted to make clear that the protest activities seen by the world at the end of 2002 did not represent all of Korean public opinion, and that a "silent majority" of Koreans still strongly supported the United States. On January 8, 2003, some 1,000 Koreans rallied outside the U.S. military base at Osan, burning a North Korean flag and waving pro-U.S. banners. On January 11, a rally of 30,000-strong Christians gathered in the vicinity of the U.S. embassy in a show of "pro-Americanism." The following week, the largest pro-U.S. rally ever, of nearly 100,000 (according to organizers) gathered in Seoul, supporting the U.S military presence in Korea, referring to Americans as "blood brothers," and equating support for the alliance with peace in Korea (rather than the association with war, as anti-American demonstrations had done). And on the weekend after the presidential inauguration in February, civic groups planned a rally of nearly 1 million in Seoul, including former prime ministers, university presidents, democracy civic groups, and veterans' affairs associations in favor of the United States.[25]

Two key observations are worth noting from these events. First, anti-Americanism is a much more contested and far less one-dimensional notion than popular perception gives it credit for. And, second, Korean views of the United States are far from zero-sum. Nowhere was this more apparent than in April 2003, when civic groups organized another anti–North Korean, pro-U.S. rally in front of Seoul's city hall; and only a few blocks away, another demonstration (near the Kyobo building in Gwanghwamun) another group protested the South Korean dispatch of troops to the Iraq War.[26] The point is that the reality of the situation in South Korea is that, as the "pro-American" demonstrations showed, one can strongly support the United States and its presence in Korea in spite of disagreeing with its policy toward North Korea. And as the "anti-American" demonstrations showed, one can oppose inequities in the alliance and demand revision of SOFA, but at the same time support the alliance. Civic group leaders who organized the demonstrations in December 2002 noted exactly this point. Indeed, polls at the height of anti-American sentiment in that month still showed a clear majority of respondents (55 percent) supporting a U.S. troop presence (Table 8.3).[27]

If the U.S. role as impeder to Korean peace were truly permanent, then neither of these observations should be pertinent. In other words, one would expect that anti-Americanism would be an uncontested "truth" rather than a contested proposition. And views on the U.S. presence and alliance would be zero-sum and one-sided.

Katharine Moon has referred to this as the distinction between *banmi* anti-Americanism and *bimi* anti-Americanism.[28] The former term refers to a deeper ideological and hegemonic view of the United States. Had this been what was represented in Korea, then the U.S. role as impeder would be permanent. The term *bimi* refers less to an ideological opposition to the United States and more to a critical yet supportive view. Arguably, not only is this latter view less severe, but it is actually healthy for the

Table 8.3

Attitudes on the Withdrawal of U.S. Forces from Korea

Age	In favor of withdrawal	Opposed to withdrawal	Don't know/not applicable
20s	47.2	42.4	10.4
50+	13.4	67.6	19.1
All	31.7	54.8	13.6

Source: Gallup Korea Survey, December 2002.

alliance. *Bimi* anti-Americanism is arguably a product of the development and democratization of South Korea. It reflects the emergence of a young, affluent generation that is educated and views quality-of-life issues—such as the environment, labor, and rule of law—as critical to the national agenda. Sometimes referred to as part of the 3–8–6 generation (thirty-somethings, who went to college in the 1980s and were born in the 1960s), this generation's views will naturally tend to bump up against some of the more anachronistic aspects of a Cold War alliance that puts a major foreign military presence in the heart of the host nation's capital city. In this sense, South Korean complaints represent growing pains within the alliance as the junior partner matures rather than a permanent fissure in the relationship.

The backpedaling in the South Korean viewpoint on U.S. troops, evident particularly from March 2003 onward, offers another lesson about how deep and zero-sum anti-American views may run. A number of prominent conservative American commentators filled the pages of major newspapers with op-ed columns criticizing the South Koreans as ungrateful allies and calling for the pullout of U.S. troops after the anti-American demonstrations at the end of 2002.[29] This was followed by explicit references in early March 2003 by Secretary of Defense Donald Rumsfeld that "adjustments" in the U.S. presence on Korea were being considered, and that there was a movement within the Pentagon and State Department bureaucracy toward serious study and plans for changing the U.S. presence on the peninsula.[30]

If the United States were viewed as a true impediment to inter-Korean relations, one would expect the popular response to be somewhat welcoming of these steps. On the contrary, South Koreans from all walks of life expressed vehement opposition to these U.S. plans. In an unusual public plea, ROK prime minister Koh Kun, on behalf of the new Roh government, asked Ambassador Hubbard on March 6 that the United States not withdraw forces from Korea. Newly elected President Roh, who during the campaign called for a more equal relationship with the United States and pointedly asked the top ROK military brass whether they had prepared for self-reliant defense, called for an end to anti-U.S. vigils in Seoul. As one observer noted, "The anti-American demonstrations here have suddenly gone poof. U.S. soldiers are walking the streets of Seoul again without looking over their shoulders. The official line from the South Korean government is: Yankees stay here."[31] If anything, a permanent U.S. impeder view should have given rise at least to conditional welcoming of the U.S. plans, but not to the sort of unadulterated opposition that was evident.

Second, a permanent U.S. impeder role would suggest greater gaps in the Roh government's policies toward North Korea and that of the Bush administration. Most certainly, the campaign rhetoric gave the impression that the gaps would be quite wide, but in actuality, since Roh has taken office, the gaps have closed, with a distinct moderating tendency in the Roh government's attitudes toward both the North Korea issue and, as alluded to above, the relationship with the United States. Just after the December elections, Roh met with anti-American civic groups and called for moderation. Despite campaign statements that he would not meet with Americans purely for photo opportunities, Roh did just that on January 15, 2003, stating that in spite of his past position, as a human rights lawyer, supporting a U.S. troop pullout, he acknowledges that "U.S. troops are necessary at the present for peace and stability on the Korean peninsula and will be in the future as well."[32] After North Korea's three cruise missile tests in February–March 2003, the ROK president criticized such actions and stated that the prospect of a nuclear North Korea is unacceptable. In terms of critical foreign policy advisers, the president chose experience over ideology and individuals with substantial understanding and interaction with the United States.[33] He supported publicly the U.S. war in Iraq and, in a controversial decision, agreed to dispatch a contingent of noncombatant forces to that country. Despite explicit pledges to maintain a primary role for the South Koreans in "mediating" talks between the North and the United States, Roh not only acceded to being excluded from the U.S.–North Korea–China talks in Beijing (April 23–24, 2003) but also defended the format by saying that substance was more important than form. And in an extraordinary public admission, in an interview with the *New York Times* during his first summit trip to the United States, Roh admitted that his signing of a declaration in his past activist days calling for the removal of U.S. forces from the Korean peninsula was a "mistake."[34]

Granted, at the time of this writing, we are still early in the Roh government and things could change rapidly. But there is no denying that, since December 2002, there has been a substantial moderating tendency in the position of the Roh leadership. Indeed, expectations of shortcomings in U.S.–South Korea relations in December 2002 have been replaced in April 2003 by new confidence in the relationship. When this author wrote an op-ed piece in the *Washington Post* the day after the South Korean election, predicting such a moderation in policy of the new ROK government, few if any believed it.[35]

If the impeder role for the United States in inter-Korean relations were permanent, one would not expect this sort of outcome, particularly given the current government's ideological beliefs. Again, this assessment is greatly handicapped by the fact that the Roh government is only in its infancy and U.S.–ROK relations have yet to be fully tested by the North Korean crisis and bilateral meetings; but the question naturally arises as to why the moderation in Roh's position thus far has been so marked and contrary to what many experts had predicted.

A variety of factors could explain this moderation. These range from the differentiation between campaign promises made by candidates and their actual policies to the "politics meets reality" argument, which holds that new leaders taking office for the first time often find that the policies they may have criticized are the way they are for a reason. But there are also three longer-term factors that deserve deeper consideration.

First, and perhaps most important as a facilitating condition, is the fact that South Korea is a vibrant democracy. Roh Moo Hyun, as chief executive, contends with a very different support base than he did during the election campaign. In the most parsimonious terms, his policies need to represent the majority of the country rather than a more narrow local constituency. This basic dynamic is common to most liberal democracies and resonates with recent Korean political history. Many were deeply concerned in 1998, when Kim Dae-jung took office, that his past views and beliefs would lead to extremely difficult policies with the United States. But Kim, as Roh has done, made appointments across the political aisle, moved more to the center, and ended his presidency as perhaps the most pro-American president in South Korea's modern political history. In this sense, the moderation of political maverick Roh is as much a function of the moderating impulses of the democratic system as it is the result of a political cycle.

Second, although political leaders change in South Korea, geography does not. Korea, whether divided or united, will remain a relatively smaller country in a region of great powers all contending for influence on the peninsula. Historically, Korea has contended with this geostrategic environment with one of two grand strategies. One has been a policy of isolation or neutrality (hence the "hermit kingdom"), trying to remove itself from the region's power politics. This proved relatively unsuccessful (and arguably is still practiced in North Korea today). The other strategy has been to become allied with one of the great powers. This strategy was fairly successful vis-à-vis China before the twentieth century, and it was clearly a successful strategy in the postwar era, turning the South into the most vibrant liberal democracy in Asia and the third-largest economy in the region, eleventh largest in the world. In the future, it behooves Korea's interests to continue placing its "bets" on a relationship with a great power with regional interests that is the furthest away and shares the same political and market values and regime type as the United States. Detractors might argue for a different strategic choice, but this is largely a reactionary view that does not take account of the powerful, almost indisputable logic of the alliance with the United States. This geostrategic logic inclines toward moderation in President Roh's view on the alliance when compared with his past views. Nowhere was this more evident than in his admission, in May 2003, that his past opposition to the alliance was misconceived.[36]

Third, Roh's moderation is intimately tied to economic development imperatives, particularly with regard to policies toward North Korea. At the beginning of 2003, it was clear that the crisis over North Korea was having a vastly negative effect on the South Korean economy. Roh's desires to continue South Korea's slow but steady recovery from the financial crisis of 1997–98 is perhaps his most important domestic objective (indeed, voter exit polls pointed to this as the highest-priority issue). Arguably, South Korea has made the most serious internationally recognized effort at reforming its economy, yet much of the international confidence in this effort was being undermined by North Korean agitation.

On February 11, Moody's Investor Service downgraded South Korea's national outlook for the first time, after repeated positive assessments since the financial crisis of some five years ago. The following week, Standard and Poor's did not increase Korea's foreign currency and local corporation credit rating; it cut back the expected growth outlook from 5.7 to 5 percent. What makes this fairly innocuous judgment significant is that Standard and Poor's (S&P) had upgraded Korea's credit rating in the year prior (to A–) and its general national outlook to stable, leading many experts to bank on further upgrades, given improvements in South Korean credit fundamentals in the public and private sectors and progress in corporate restructuring.

What is the primary reason for these sober assessments? S&P Director Takahira Ogawa could not have been more direct, stating: "There is a risk from the North, which constrains the sovereign rating of South Korea." Those who think that an eternally optimistic South Korean government, committed to the peaceful status quo and engagement with North Korea, will be able to muddle through are sorely mistaken. All it took was one short-range missile test by Pyongyang into the Sea of Japan for the Korean Composite Stock Market Price Index (KOSPI) to tumble almost 4 percent (24 points) in one day, despite a litany of parallel confidence-inducing events, including Roh Moo Hyun's inauguration, the U.S. announcement of the resumption of food aid to the North, and Secretary of State Colin Powell's statements in Seoul that the United States would eventually seek to dialogue with North Korea.

After North Korea's second short-range missile test, the Korean stock market dropped to its lowest level in 16 months; the Japanese Nikkei closed at its lowest level in 20 years, and the Korean won depreciated to a four-month low. Wall Street investment houses, including J.P. Morgan, Merrill Lynch, Goldman Sachs, and ABN AMRO, all issued reports in the first quarter of 2003 advising investors to shed Korean shares (despite acknowledging that these shares were undervalued).[37] Investment from the United States tumbled 72 percent during the January–March 2003 quarter and the Korean stock market dropped 18.3 percent.[38] South Korean economic growth estimates are predicted to shrink to 1.4 from 6.2 percent in 2002.

The economics of the North Korean threat therefore suggest that gaps between the United States and South Korea may narrow. As has been frequently noted, Seoul and Washington may not share identical interests with regard to North Korean proliferation, but this does not rule out the possibility that they could care about the same thing for different reasons. Roh's presidency is five years, according to the Korean constitution, but his immediate tenure is one year before the next general election in 2004. And the primary issue for voters is continuing the slow but steady recovery of the economy since the 1997–98 financial crisis (according to voter exit polls at the presidential elections in December 2002). If North Korea continues to agitate in ways that hurt international investor confidence in South Korea and South Korea's growth, then there is a limit to how far the South Korean public and elite can continue to blame the United States, and not North Korea, for the problems. Some might contend that these imperatives would push South Korea in the direction of appeasing the North to avert further destabilizing actions. But the opposite appears to be taking place. During Roh's May 2003 visit to the United States, he admitted that he was not naive about North Korea's record of ignoring agreements and that he "doesn't trust North Korea that much."[39] The point is not that this is the assured direction in which U.S.–ROK relations are likely to go. Far from it. The point is that there is a strong counterargument, laid out above, for why the elite gaps between the United States and the ROK on North Korea may narrow. And initial evidence at the start of the Roh presidency offers some confirming evidence. The narrowing of such gaps lends credence to the view that the U.S. role as impeder between the two Koreas may be less permanent than many of the younger generation are led to believe.

Notes

1. This is loosely defined as the shift toward greater fluidity in dialogue around the peninsula that started with Soviet and Chinese recognition of the South in 1990 and 1992; the beginnings of Japan and U.S. dialogue with the North, and, of course, North–South dialogue culminating with the 2000 summit.

2. Peter Katzenstein and Nobuo Okawara, "Japan, Asia-Pacific Security, and the Case for Analytical Eclecticism," *International Security* 26, no. 3 (Winter 2001/02): 153–85.

3. For the history of these periods, see Victor Cha, "National Unification: The Long and Winding Road," *In Depth* 4.2 (Spring 1994), 89–123.

4. For further discussions, see Victor Cha, *Alignment Despite Antagonism: The United States-Korea-Japan Security Triangle* (Stanford, CA: Stanford University Press, 1999), Ch. 4. Also see *Far Eastern Economic Review,* 1 July 1974 ("America in Asia 1974," Kim Sam-o "Credibility Gap"); and *Korea Herald* 12 March 1972 ("Travel Ban Easing on North Korea Favored").

5. This section is based on American archival documents declassified from the Eisenhower administration. Although these archives have been available for some time, I believe this is the first analysis of the "restraint" aspect of the U.S.–ROK alliance that utilizes these materials about U.S. contingency plans on South Korean governments.

6. Operational command authority dates back to the outset of the Korean War, when Syngman Rhee (July 14, 1950) transferred authority over Korean forces to the commander in chief of UN forces. In the aftermath of a mutual defense treaty (October 1953), the two governments signed a memorandum of understanding giving operational control authority over ROK forces to the UN Command (November 1954). In 1961, this understanding was revised to pertain only to control authority over forces to defend against an external communist invasion. In the late 1970s, the Combined Forces Command (CFC) was created (November 7, 1978) to provide a structure in which the United States could gradually transfer authority over to the Koreans (Ralph Cossa, "The Role of US Forces in a Unified Korea," *International Journal of Korean Studies* 5, no. 2 [fall/winter 2001], p. 120). Operational control authority was put in the hands of the CFC commander and the United Nations Command (UNC) body's duties extended only to maintaining the terms of the armistice. Pursuant to the goals of creating the CFC, in October 1994, peacetime operational control of Korean forces was transferred to Korea, giving the deputy CFC commander (a Korean) peacetime authority over a range of activi-

ties including unit management, movements, precautionary actions, patrols, combined tactical training, and troop readiness. Even under these conditions, however, the authority of the peacetime commander is greatly curtailed not only in wartime but also at peacetime readiness levels beyond defcon 3 (Lee Soo Hyong, "Restructuring the U.S.-Korea Alliance," *Korea Focus*, March–April 2001).

7. NSC 5817, "Statement of U.S. Policy Toward Korea," August 11, 1958, in *Foreign Relations of the United States* (FRUS), 1958–60, vol. XVIII, document 237, p. 485.

8. The provision regarding covert support of alternative leadership to Rhee (in the event he planned unilateral action) was first contained in a president-approved revision of a 1953 NSC policy document on Korea (NSC 170/1 Annex A). See NSC 170/1, "U.S. Objectives and Courses of Action in Korea," November 20, 1953, in FRUS 1952–54, pp. 1620–24. The revision stated: "To select and encourage covertly the development of new South Korean leadership prepared to cooperate in maintaining the armistice, and if Rhee initiates or is about to initiate unilateral action, assist such new leadership to assume power, by means not involving overt U.S. participation until and unless U.S. overt support is necessary and promises to be decisive in firmly establishing such new leadership." This provision was considered extremely sensitive and circulated only to the secretaries of State and Defense, chairman of the Joint Chiefs of Staff, and director of the Central Intelligence Agency. Subsequent NSC policy reviews on Korea made reference to the annex (later known as annex F) as regular practice, but the actual contents were kept separate. The internal instructions noted, "This revision is being disseminated only to [selected] addressees . . . , and it is requested that special security precautions be observed in the handling of this memorandum and that access to it be very strictly limited on an absolute need-to-know basis." ("Memorandum from the Acting Executive Secretary of the National Security Council [Gleason] to the Secretary of State, February 18, 1955," in FRUS, 1955–57, vol. XXII, document 21, pp. 37–38). The provision about U.S. unilateral abrogation of the treaty took place in the context of deliberations a couple of years later on revising NSC 5817, which was then standing policy on Korea (revised as NSC 5907). See NSC 5907, July 1, 1959, "Statement of U.S. Policy Toward Korea," FRUS, 1958–60, document 279, pp. 571–79. Also see superseding policy document NSC 6018, November 28, 1960, which carried the same provisions (FRUS, 1958–60, vol. 18, document 334, pp. 699–707).

9. Memorandum of Discussion at the 411th Meeting of the National Security Council, Washington June 25, 1959 (FRUS, 1958–60, vol. 18, document 277, p. 569).

10. One State Department–Joint Chiefs of Staff (JCS) meeting on Korea in 1958 highlighted the criticality of command authority in this context: " . . . we retain operational control of the Republic of Korea armed forces so as to preclude any possibility of unilateral action on the part of the Republic of Korea Government in attacking North Korea." Memorandum on the Substance of Discussion at a Department of State–Joint Chiefs of Staff Meeting, Washington, February 28, 1958. Secret. In FRUS, 1958–50, vol. 18, document 216, p. 443.

11. Abandonment is the fear that the ally may not provide support in contingencies where support is expected. See Glenn Snyder, *Alliance Politics* (Ithaca, NY: Cornell University Press, 1997). For applications of the concept to Asia, see Cha, *Alignment Despite Antagonism*.

12. On these two aspects of North-South competition, see Samuel Kim, "North Korea in 1999: Bringing the Grand Chollima March Back In," *Asian Survey* (January/February 2000): 1401–13; and "North Korean Informal Politics," in *Informal Politics in East Asia*, ed. Lowell Dittmer, Haruhiro Fukui, and Peter N.S. Lee (New York: Cambridge University Press, 2000), pp. 237–68.

13. Fritz Heider, *The Psychology of Interpersonal Relations* (London: Erlbaum, 1958). Jones and Davis referred to this as correspondent inference theory. See Edward E. Jones and Keith E. Davis, "From Acts to Dispositions: The Attribution Process in Person Perception," *Advances in Experimental Social Psychology 2*, ed. L. Berkowitz (New York: Academic Press, 1965), pp. 219–66. Also see Edward E. Jones and Victor A. Harris, "The Attributes of Atti-

tudes," *Journal of Experimental Psychology* 3 (January 1967): 1–24. For an indispensible and digestible overview of this body of literature, see Jonathan Mercer, *Reputation and International Politics* (Ithaca, NY: Cornell University Press, 1996), pp. 48–53.

14. Lee Ross, "The Intuitive Psychologist and His Shortcomings: Distortions in the Attribution Process," *Advances in Experimental Psychology 10*, ed. L. Berkowitz (New York: Academic Press, 1977), pp. 173–220; and Edward Jones, "The Rocky Road from Acts to Dispositions," *American Psychologist* 34, no. 2 (1979): 107–17.

15. Follow-on work found that actor-observer perspectives also biased strongly whether situational or dispositional factors matter more. When one viewed other's actions, these were interpreted as dispositional, but when one viewed one's own actions, these were interpreted as situational. E.E. Jones and R.E. Nisbett, *The Actor and the Observer: Divergent Perceptions of the Causes of Behavior* (Morristown, NJ: General Learning Press, 1971); and George Quattrone, "Overattribution and Unit Formation: When Behavior Engulfs the Person," *Journal of Personality and Social Psychology* 42, no. 4 (1982): 593–607.

16. Robert Jervis, *Perception and Misperception in International Politics* (Princeton, NJ: Princeton University Press, 1976); and Mercer, *Reputation and International Politics*, pp. 59–65.

17. For the history, see Cha, *Alignment Despite Antagonism*; and Don Oberdorfer, *The Two Koreas* (New York: Addison-Wesley, 2001).

18. Leon Sigal, *Disarming Strangers* (Princeton, NJ: Princeton University Press, 1998).

19. See "Text of Bush-Kim Press Conference," February 20, 2002, www.washingpost.com/wp-dyn/articles/A38110–2002Feb20.html.

20. *Sixty Minutes*, aired February 8, 2003.

21. For example, according to polls in early 2003, some 58.7 percent of Koreans in their twenties and thirties viewed the Korean war as a proxy war between the United States and Soviet Union (versus a national average of 44.5 percent) rather than as the result of an illegitimate armed invasion by the North (24.2 percent versus a national average of 31.2 percent). See Chosun Ilbo-Gallup Korea polls, published January 1, 2003 at www.gallup.co.kr/News/2003/release004.html.

22. See MBC-Korea Research Center polls, aired January 1, 2003.

23. Cited in Choong Nam Kim, "Changing Korean Perceptions of the Post–Cold War Era and the U.S.-ROK Alliance," *East-West Center Analysis*, no. 67 (April 2003), p.5.

24. This was, of course, neither the only dimension of the 2002 presidential campaign nor of the demonstrations in Seoul at the time. In the case of the campaign, for voters the main priority affecting voter choice (according to exit polls) was not the United States or policy toward North Korea, but economic recovery from the financial crisis (followed by rooting corruption out of the government and society). The demonstrations also were more than an embodiment of anti-Americanism, as popularly portrayed in the media. Instead, they were seen by many scholars and public commentators in Asia as an expression of a new youthful Korean identity. The catalyst for this, arguably, was not the death of two Korean schoolgirls but rather the World Cup and the Korean national team's unexpected success. The outpouring of nationalism that accompanied this event became hard to differentiate from the "peace demonstrations" that soon followed the World Cup rallies in downtown Seoul. See Han Sang Jin and Koo Hagen papers presented at the Korean Centennial Conference, East-West Center, Hawaii, January 2003.

25. Kyung-Ho Kim, "Conservatives Push to Keep U.S. Troops," *Korea Herald*, February 26, 2003; Jong-Heon Lee, "Anti-U.S. Sentiment Cooling in South Korea," United Press International, January 20, 2003; Sang-Hun Choe, "Tens of Thousands of South Korean Christians Rally to Support U.S. Military, Condemn North Korea," Associated Press, January 11, 2003; Jae-Hwan Kim, "Pro-U.S. Demonstrators Burn North Korean Flag Outside American Air Base," Agence France Presse, January 8, 2003.

26. "South Korean Groups Hold Rallies Against North Korea, U.S. War in Iraq," BBC, aired April 19, 2003.

27. "NYT Editorial on U.S. Troop Pullout Sparks Controversy," *Hankook Ilbo*, December 28, 2002; and "55% of South Koreans Want U.S. Troops to Stay," December 24, 2002.

28. Katharine Moon (Department of Political Science, Wellesley College), "Political Sociology of USFK-Korea Relations," unpublished paper presented at the Ilmin Institute, Korea University, November 7, 2002.

29. Richard Allen, "Seoul's Choice: The U.S. or the North," *New York Times*, January 16, 2003; William Safire, "Three-Ring Circus," *New York Times*, January 2, 2003; *Buchanan and Press*, MSNBC, aired January 3, 2003, 2 p.m. EST; *Meet the Press*, NBC, aired January 5, 2003, 10 a.m. EST.

30. Robert Marquand, "Rethinking U.S. Troops in South Korea," *Christian Science Monitor*, March 10, 2003.

31. Doug Struck, "Anti-U.S. Sentiment Abates in South Korea; Change Follows Rumsfeld Suggestion of Troop Cut," *Washington Post*, March 14, 2003; James Brooke, "Musing on an Exodus of G.I.s, South Korea Hails U.S. Presence," *New York Times*, March 7, 2003. Granted, part of this new-found opposition was due to fears that the United States might preemptively attack North Korea. But this argument made little sense. First, U.S. statements intimated a repositioning rather than withdrawal of U.S. forces, in which case they would still be vulnerable to North Korean counterattack. Second, a repositioning of some 17,000 U.S. troops away from the DMZ would not remove the deterrent to a U.S. preemptive attack as the entire American expatriate community (numbering some 20,000), not to mention South Koreans, would still be acutely vulnerable to North Korean artillery.

32. Kwanwoo Jun, "South Korean President-Elect Roh Softens Anti-U.S. Image," Agence France Presse, January 15, 2003.

33. The appointment of Sung-Joo Han as ambassador to the United States offers a small example of the change in thinking. At the time of then-president-elect Roh's special envoy delegation's trip to Washington, members of the delegation scoffed at the idea that someone identified as a more conservative, establishment-type might be chosen for this post, and yet only a few months later, this was exactly the president's choice.

34. David Sanger, "South Korean Leader Wants U.S. Troops to Stay, for Now," *New York Times*, May 13, 2003.

35. Victor D. Cha, "Stay Calm on Korea," *Washington Post*, December 20, 2002.

36. David Sanger, "South Korean Leader Wants U.S. Troops to Stay, for Now," *New York Times*, May 13, 2003.

37. Na Ji-hong, "Global Securities Firms Pessimistic on Korean Shares," *Chosun Ilbo*, March 18, 2003.

38. "Foreign Investment in South Korea Falls," Associated Press (April 4, 2003).

39. David Sanger, "South Korean Leader Wants U.S. Troops to Stay, for Now," *New York Times*, May 13, 2003.

9

Between *Banmi* (Anti-Americanism) and *Sungmi* (Worship of the United States)

Dynamics of Changing U.S. Images in South Korea

Chung-in Moon

On the golden jubilee of the Republic of Korea (ROK)–U.S. alliance, Seoul and Washington experienced unprecedented strains in their relationship. The tragic death of Hyosun and Misun, two Korean middle-school girls, and subsequent widespread anti-American sentiments in South Korea overshadowed the joy and celebration of a fifty-year relationship. Cries of "Abandon the United States" are on the rise in South Korea; these sentiments have, in turn, precipitated in-kind responses from some conservative elements in the United States, who call for the United States to "Abandon South Korea." Conflicting views between the two allies on how to handle the North Korean nuclear problem have further complicated and even worsened Seoul–Washington ties. Although President Roh Moo Hyun's visit to the United States and his conciliatory gesture have contributed to defusing the negative spiral of "mutual abandonment," the inertia of uneasy bilateral relations still remains.

Central to this development is the *banmi* (anti-American) attitude prevalent in South Korea. But there is nothing new about *banmi*, since it has recently become ubiquitous throughout the world.[1] Anti-American sentiments or attitudes from South Korea have persisted since the days of the first encounter with the United States in the second half of the nineteenth century, and they are likely to continue in the future. Their scope and depth are not fixed but vary over time, depending upon Zeitgeist, actors, and issues.[2] Thus, it seems grossly misleading to identify *banmi* as the dominant, fixed national mood in South Korea. *Banmi* is only one aspect of South Korea's national psyche with regard to the United States, as there are, in fact, a variety of Korean positions toward the United States, ranging from *sungmi* (worship) to *hyommi* (loathing).

This chapter aims at understanding the complex nature of anti-Americanism in South Korea. The first section elucidates the diverse images of the United States in the minds of South Koreans involving *yonmi* (associate with America), *chinmi* (pro-American), *sungmi* (worship America), *banmi* (anti-America), and *hyommi* (loathe America). The second examines how anti-Americanism has been misunderstood at home and abroad not only by looking into the ambivalent nature of Koreans' perception of the United States but also by disaggregating the anti-American phenomenon. The third section explores the causes of anti-Americanism over time. Finally, the concluding section suggests options to overcome the anti-American phenomenon and to improve the Korean-U.S. relationship.

Many Images of the United States in Korea

Korean perception of the United States has been neither fixed nor monolithic. Rather, it has changed over time, depending on the overall context of Korea's global, regional, and bilateral relations. At the time of port opening in the late nineteenth century, the image of America in Korea was extremely polarized between reformists and conservatives.[3] While reformists had a very favorable image of the United States, conservatives portrayed it as a barbarian nation.

Korean reformists in the late Yi dynasty were greatly influenced by Hwang Jun-hon, a late-nineteenth-century Chinese diplomat who wrote *Chosun Ch'aengnyak* (Chosun's strategy). Hwang was the first person to suggest the importance of *yonmi* in Korea's survival strategy. Acutely sensing imminent threats arising from Russian expansion, he advised Koreans to "become friendly with China (*chinjoong*), tie with Japan (*gyolil*), and associate with the United States." Hwang believed that "Korea could get help and avoid disasters were it to turn the United States into a friend," because the United States was rich and strong, civilized, fair, and righteous in deterring the strong while supporting the weak. Moreover, since the United States was geographically far away from Korea, it was less prone to interfere with Korea's domestic affairs.[4]

Several Korean reformists of the time echoed a similar sentiment. Hong Young-shik, who visited the United States as the first Korean delegate in 1883, and Park Jung-yang, who opened the first Korean mission in the United States in 1898, submitted positive reports on the United States to King Ko Jong. Their reports, along with the *Hansung Sunbo*, a leading reformist newspaper of the time, contributed to the favorable portrayal of the United States. For them, the United States was a country of tolerance and righteousness. The United States was rich because its per capita income rose from $230 in 1840 to $990 in 1880, six times faster than that of the United Kingdom. It was also considered a strong nation, with an enormous military potential. The United States was a trustworthy and brotherly country, not only because of its willingness to help Korea in case of intervention by foreign powers but also because it received Korean delegations warmly.[5]

This positive image notwithstanding, there were some skeptics among the reformists. Yoo Gil-joon is a case in point. Yoo went to the United States as a member of the first Korean delegation in 1883 and remained in the United States for 2 ½ years. Upon his return, he published an influential book entitled *Seoyu Gyunmun* (Travel journal of the west) in 1895. Although he made positive remarks about the United States with regard to its material abundance and civilization, Yoo was critical of the American republican political system, favoring a monarchy instead. He also differed from Hwang Jun-hon regarding its strategic importance. He believed that Korea could benefit from the United States as a trading partner, not as a military and political ally, because of its isolationist policy and geographic distance. Yoon Chi-ho represented another example of the mixed opinions regarding the United States. Yoon was the first Korean student to spend five years in the United States (1888–93). He argued that there was a lot to learn from the United States in terms of humanism, civilization, morality, and freedom, but its racial prejudice prevented him from strongly endorsing the United States. In fact, Yoon was haunted by the specter of racial discrimination after he returned to Korea, making him an extreme anti-American during the Japanese colonial period.[6]

Meanwhile, conservatives' perception of the United States was outright hostile. As with earlier seclusionists, they likened Americans to beasts and western barbarians who did not appreciate basic courtesy and morality.[7] It seems well worth citing Lee Manson's Ten Thousand People's Petition to the King (*Manminso*). In his petition, Lee maintained that American Christian missionary works must be rejected because they were bound to erode Confucian ethical codes. He also refuted Hwang's idea of associating with the United States. According to him, the Americans were no different from Russians, because they were barbarians, and there was no need to ally with one barbarian, the United States, to fight against another, Russia.[8] Conservatives took a fierce anti-American stance not only because of anticipated backlash effects on the tradition and power base of Confucianism that buttressed the Yi dynasty but also because of the imprudent and provocative American behavior shown through the *General Sherman* warship incident in 1866, in which sailors engaged in the killing of innocent citizens and ransacking of properties in Pyongyang.

During the Japanese colonial period, Korean perception of the United States was also rather mixed. Despite the fact that the United States lent its support to national fighters for independence, such as Syngman Rhee, Ahn Chang-ho, and Phillip Suh, anti-American sentiment was pronounced among the elite as well as the masses. The Taft-Katsura Agreement in 1905, in which the United States tacitly approved Japan's influence over the Korean peninsula, accelerating its annexation of Korea, obviously triggered anti-American sentiment among Koreans. Three incidents further damaged Korean perceptions of the United States. The first was related to Woodrow Wilson's doctrine of self-determination for weak states, which inspired Koreans under Japanese colonial rule to seek self-determination and independence. This precipitated the March 1 Movement in 1919. Nevertheless, Korean delegates attending the Paris Peace Conference in 1919 received no support from the United States. Another was the Washington Naval Disarmament Conference in 1921–22, which made Japanese colonial rule over Korea a fait accompli through the Quadruple Agreement between the United States, the United Kingdom, France, and Japan, leaving Koreans all the more disillusioned with the United States. Last, penetration of socialist influence into colonized Korea in the 1920s, coupled with the advent of the "Yellow Peril," led Koreans to regard the United States as an economic imperial power.[9]

However, since 1945, the Korean image of America has been radically altered. *Chinmi* became widely shared among Koreans. During this period, the United States was perceived as a liberator of Korea from Japanese colonial rule. At the same time, the United States was the principal sponsor for the founding of the Republic of Korea in 1948, after a three-year trusteeship. More importantly, it was felt to have saved the South Koreans from North Korean military invasion, thus assuring their security through the patronage of military alliance. Most Koreans believed that with the U.S.–ROK alliance, the forward presence of American troops, and the provision of military assistance (providing South Korea with a credible security umbrella), and with American economic assistance and guidance to an export-led economic growth strategy, the foundation for Korea's economic miracle had been laid. It was in this context that *chinmi* (a pro-American stance) began to dominate the national psyche.

Proximity to the United States through missionary connections, American education, and/or the mastery of English was the surest way to achieve social upward mobility.[10] Some South Koreans even worshipped the United States (*sungmi*). They regarded American ideas, values, and power as the deus ex machina. Their love of America was almost blind, as special treatment of American forces in South Korea was virtually taken for granted, often allowing them to enjoy special status above the rule of law. Regardless of the ruling and opposition parties, Korean politicians were desperate to get American endorsement and blessing. They went to Washington to take part in photo sessions with American politicians because their American connection was an important electoral asset back home in Korea. The American ambassador in Seoul was powerful enough to be the only counterpart to the president of South Korea. While American-educated scholars dominated South Korean educational institutions, proximity to American military officers was vital to the promotion of South Korea's military personnel.[11] South Korea was the only country in the world where the slogan of "Yankee, Go Home!" could not be heard. The United States, which took the place that China had once held, became the center of the universe for South Koreans in the second half of the twentieth century. *Chinmi* and *sungmi* emerged as new norms and beliefs for many Koreans.[12]

However, consolidation of *chinmi* and *sungmi* did not bring about the demise of anti-American sentiment. Progressive forces continued to blame the United States for national division, systematic suppression of leftist groups, and the artificial implantation of pro-American conservative forces, economic dependence through the aid economy, and persistent support of authoritarian regimes. But the first overt signal of anti-American sentiment (*banmi*) surfaced in the early 1970s. The American decision to pull out its seventh division in 1971 as part of the Nixon Doctrine, the increasing American critique of the Yushin regime and human rights violations in the South, Carter's plan to withdraw American forces in 1977, and Washington's efforts to abort Seoul's nuclear weapons plan precipitated anti-American sentiments among Park Chung Hee and his conservative followers. Nevertheless, the anti-American sentiments of the Yushin establishment did not win a great deal of popular support. On the contrary, those in the movement formed a subtle coalition with liberal forces in the United States in fighting the Yushin dictatorship.

However, authentic and massive anti-American sentiments erupted in the wake of the Kwangju Uprising in 1981. American failure to deter deployment of Korean combat forces under its operational control to the Kwangju area and the subsequent large number of civilian casualties from combat forces sent by Chun Doo Hwan precipitated extensive anti-American sentiment among South Koreans. Such sentiments were further intensified because of the Reagan administration's expedient endorsement of the Chun Doo Hwan regime. The image of the United States as guardian of an authoritarian regime continued to tarnish its image, implanting *banmi* in the national psyche of South Koreans.

Trade conflicts between Seoul and Washington in the late 1980s were another source of anti-Americanism. Having experienced record trade deficits with South Korea, the United States not only exerted enormous pressure for the opening of markets in the agricultural and service sectors but also employed a variety of measures—involving antidumping decisions, the imposition of countervailing duties, and quantitative restrictions—to correct South Korea's unfair trade practices. The American trade offensive enraged South Koreans. According to a survey conducted in 1988, some 46.6 percent of 1,000 respondents identified trade pressures, especially on the opening of the agricultural market, as the largest source of anti-Americanism, followed by the Kwangju incident (27.4 percent), unruly behavior of American athletes during the opening ceremony of the Seoul Olympics (8.4 percent), and the presence of American forces (3.9 percent).[13]

In late 1980s, *banmi* even devolved into *hyommi* (loathing of the United States), which became manifest through a mass media campaign against "ugly Americans." The primary target was American soldiers stationed in South Korea. Their misbehavior was disproportionately and exaggeratedly portrayed by Korean mass media. The secondary target was Korean Americans, whom South Koreans at home had previously envied. Humiliating caricatures of Korean Americans in South Korea's TV dramas were the most vivid testimonial to the trend. Finally, Korean mass media were assertive in undermining the American myth by portraying the United States as a declining hegemony as well as a country rife with drug addiction, crime, racial discrimination, and AIDS. America was no longer seen as a powerful, abundant, and benevolent patron but rather as a loathsome, ugly, and greedy competitor.[14]

As such, images of the United States in South Korea have not been monolithic but have varied over time in diverse forms. Starting with *yonmi*, Korean perception of the United States has shown a devolutionary dynamic from *chinmi* and *sungmi* to *banmi* and *hyommi*.

Anti-Americanism Misunderstood

Judging by the above discussion, it is undeniable that anti-Americanism has become increasingly widespread in South Korea since the mid-1980s. Nevertheless, the nature of anti-Americanism has been grossly misunderstood and the term has often been abused and misused by many for political purposes. Although Korean perception of the United States has shown a pattern of devolutionary dynamics from *yonmi* and *chinmi* into *banmi* and *hyommi*, such attitudes cannot be separated into distinctive categories. They constitute an overlapping structural whole whose disaggregation becomes virtually impossible. Ambivalence seems to be the correct word to describe the nature of anti-American phenomenon.[15] Like and dislike, respect and disrespect, love and hatred, and worship and contempt coexist in South Koreans' perception of the United States.

Such ambivalent attitudes were most eloquently demonstrated by Yoon Chi-Ho, one of the first Koreans to study in the United States, for five years (1888–93) at Vanderbilt and Emory universities. Yoon urged Korea to benchmark the United States for social advancement through missionary works and education. For him, the United States was the symbol of abundance and civilization. Yet, after he returned to Korea, he became extremely anti-American. He even suggested that Korea join Japan in forming a "Yellow coalition" to combat American racism, endorsing Japan's Manchurian invasion as well as the Pacific war by defining them as racial wars. It was the racial discrimination he experienced during his stay in the United States that drove him to be anti-American. The following passage from his diary provides us with an important clue to the understanding of his ambivalent attitude toward the United States: "I heard a young man saying that he would sooner pull down his church than to admit a colored member to the aggregation [congregation]. How is this prejudice compatible with the boasted civilization, philanthropy, religion of this people?"[16] The two opposing attitudes of *banmi* and *chinmi* were deeply ingrained in the internal world of Yoon Chi-ho.

The same can be said of many contemporary South Koreans. Let us take an example of conservative newspapers in South Korea. They strongly support the continuation of the ROK–U.S. alliance and are critical of anti-American sentiments. Yet they have not only taken initiatives in calling for the amendment of the Status of Forces Agreement (SOFA) but have also been aggressive in making biased reports on the United States and its soldiers stationed in South Korea. Mass media's ambivalent reporting can be seen as one of the primary sources of the distorted image of the United States.

It is equally intriguing to note another manifestation of this ambivalence in that many South Koreans show a very strong pro-American attitude in person, but in public or in a group tend to switch to an anti-American tone. An interview with a forty-two-year-old housewife who participated in the candlelight protest over the death of two middle-school girls underscores the essence of ambivalence embedded in contemporary anti-Americanism, "Although I attended the candlelight protest, I do not consider myself anti-American. . . . My greatest concern is how to improve English proficiency of my son, 9th grade student, and my daughter, 6th grade. If possible, I wish I can send them to the U.S. for early education. I believe other housewives would have the same wish."[17] It is truly surreal to witness so many South Koreans making a long line in front of the American Embassy in Seoul to get entry visas into the United States amid the combat police force deployed to protect the embassy from anti-American demonstrations. A similarly ambivalent attitude can also be found among intellectuals. Some liberal intellectuals in South Korea openly criticize the United States, but many are *gireogi appa* ("seasonal birds fathers") who left their families in the United States so that their children might have a better education.

It is this ambivalent attitude that makes the anti-American phenomenon all the more difficult to understand. *Chinmi* and *banmi* appear to be two sides of the same coin, which cannot be separated analytically or empirically. The personal and national psyche of South Koreans constantly oscillates ambivalently between these two extreme poles.

Apart from the issue of ambivalence, the *banmi* phenomenon should not be treated as if it were a monolithic one. It should be disaggregated into at least three dimensions. The first is anti-Americanism as an ideology. Radical 3–8–6 students (those who are in their thirties, entered college in the 1980s, and were born in the 1960s) in the 1980s were armed with the anti-American ideology that activated massive student movements.[18] The National Liberation (NL) group took the initiative in the ideological campaign against the United States. They attributed to the United States all the miseries of South Korea, such as the rise of authoritarian regimes, structural inequality, national division, and the Korean conflict. They believed that American occupation of the Korean peninsula, implantation of a peripheral capitalist economy, and systematic exclusion of the popular sector by the United States were responsible for the uneven and dependent development of Korea based on an authoritarian regime. To the followers of the NL group, termination of American influence was integral to the eradication of all South Korean tragedies.[19] It was with this ideological orientation that the 3–8–6 generation engaged in violent anti-American movements, as manifest by attacks on the Pusan offices of the U.S. Information Agency (USIA) in March 1982, the Taegu USIA office in May 1983, occupation of the Seoul USIA office in May 1985, and moves against several other American facilities.[20] The anti-American phenomenon as an ideology played an important role in the process of democratic transition, since it helped to unify the *minjung* sector. But the democratic transition and consolidation since 1987, the relative weakness of student movements, and the increasing critique of violent action severely undercut the ideological thrust of the 3–8–6 generation's anti-Americanism. It no longer drew public appeal.

The second dimension of anti-American sentiment is that it fluctuates along with events and changing circumstances. These changes in sentiment can be differentiated from the anti-American ideology in the sense that the former is spontaneous, unorganized, and hyperbolic while the latter is contrived, organized, and systematic. Anti-American sentiments are mostly influenced by events and the prevailing national mood. Thus, mob psychology as dictated by the mass media tends to characterize this sort of anti-American phenomenon. Unfair trade pressures from the 3–8–6 generation in the mid-1980s, unruly behavior shown by American athletes during the opening ceremony of the 1988 Seoul Olympics, the 2002 Salt Lake City Winter Olympics' Short Track incident, and cultural and legal insensitivity of U.S. Forces in South Korea (as shown in the events surrounding the accidental deaths of two middle-school girls) have all been responsible for affecting the ups and downs of anti-American national sentiments.[21] They come and go but do not disappear for good because they constitute an inseparable part of the Korean national psyche, based on the difference between "us" and "others." I would argue that the anti-Americanism shared by the majority of South Koreans falls into this category.

The third dimension is anti-Americanism as an expression of democratic maturity in South Korea. American exemptionalism used to be a common practice under past authoritarian regimes, which placed the utmost policy priority on national security. Since American forces came all the way to South Korea in order to assure its national security, it was thought natural for the South Korean government to exempt American forces from the application of South Korean law. However, since the democratic transition in 1987, overall domestic political parameters began to change. While the implementation of local autonomy empowered local governments, the expansion of civil society fostered the proliferation of nongovernmental organizations (NGOs). It is in this context that the special legal status of American forces stationed in South Korea began to encounter major challenges.

National security could no longer justify American forces' privileged position in Korean society. Citizen groups argue that they should also be subject to the rule of law. Local governments in the American military base areas have also joined civic groups in fighting for the preservation of their citizens' rights, which they believed to have been sacrificed in the name of national security.[22] Calls for the amendment of the SOFA, protests over environmental pollution, public attention to human rights violations by American soldiers at and around American military bases, and a demand for the termination of the bombing range in the Maehyang-ri underscore this trend. The candlelight protests over the death of two middle-school girls were also a result of public grievances over the American military court's questionable legal handling of the case, rather than opposition to the ROK–U.S. alliance per se and presence of American forces in South Korea. Thus, the third variety of anti-Americanism is more concerned about the correction of negative legacies of the past authoritarian regimes in the process of democratic consolidation rather than an expression of outright anti-Americanism based on nationalist sentiments. However, such citizen efforts still pose a major dilemma for the ROK–U.S. alliance.

Finally, current anti-Americanism should be differentiated from negative sentiments toward President George W. Bush.[23] South Koreans as a whole strongly endorse and emulate the universal values embodied in American culture and civilization.[24] The quest for liberty, human rights, and democracy, the rush to the United States for education, and the dominance of American intellectual paradigms in South Korean academic circles, all indicate Korea's willingness to learn about and accommodate to American values and aspirations. Although Koreans welcome the United States as a body of culture and civilization, they often oppose the United States as a political entity wrapped in partisan ideology and interests. Recent anti-American sentiments and movements are targeted not at the United States and its people per se but at the

Bush administration. Its moral absolutism, unilateralism, and offensive realism—as manifest in the doctrine of preemptive attacks and the potential use of tactical nuclear weapons as well as increased military spending—have become sources of grievances against the United States among the Korean public. Thus, equating "anti-Bushism" with anti-Americanism is tantamount to committing the fallacy of misplaced concreteness. A change of administration or American foreign policy might significantly ameliorate the anti-American stance in South Korea.

Causes of Anti-Americanism: Evolutionary Dynamics

The anti-American phenomenon in South Korea has been by and large misunderstood. Anti-Americanism as an ideological phenomenon has visibly dwindled, whereas anti-American sentiments have come and gone. But democratic maturity and civic alertness to American exeptionalism are likely to continue and could easily escalate into anti-American movements.

What makes the situation worrisome is that South Koreans' perception of the United States has been sliding in a negative direction over time. According to a survey by the USIA in 1965, some 68 percent of 500 respondents answered that the United States was the most preferred country.[25] A *Donga Ilbo* survey conducted in November 1981 revealed that 60.6 percent of 1,504 respondents identified the United States as the most preferred country, followed by Switzerland (9.4 percent) and Israel (7.7 percent). Meanwhile North Korea was the most disliked country (59.4 percent).[26] Since 1984, however, South Korean preference of the United States has continued to deteriorate. According to a *Joongang Ilbo* survey in 1984, only 37.3 percent of 1,500 respondents replied that the United States was the most preferred country, and the figure declined to 19.5 percent in 1990.[27] In the most recent survey conducted by Gallup Korea on February 26, 2002, only 13.2 percent of 1,032 respondents replied that the United States was the most preferred country.[28]

A more striking aspect is the generational difference. While the older generation favors the United States, the younger generation shows a tendency to dislike it. According to the same Gallup Korea survey, half of all those aged fifty or older revealed that they like the United States, but 70.3 percent of the age group in their twenties and 74 percent of those in their thirties responded that they disliked the United States. Another opinion survey of high school and college students revealed a much more shocking result: 41.5 percent of 200 student respondents answered that China was their most preferred country, followed by North Korea (31.5 percent). Only 8.5 percent identified the United States as the most preferred country.[29]

What factors account for the downward spiral? Causes of anti-Americanism have varied over time, depending on national ambience. As discussed above, during the opening of the Yi dynasty and the Japanese colonial period, anti-American perception was shaped by the interplay of several factors. First, the China-centered worldview widely held by the elite and masses of the Yi dynasty led them to portray Americans as a western barbarian people because the United States was located outside of the

Chinese cultural sphere. Its tacit alliance with Japan was another factor. The Taft-Katsura Agreement, a lukewarm American attitude during the 1919 Paris Peace Conference, the Washington naval conference, and recognition of Japanese rule over Korea all bred a feeling of betrayal among Koreans. And in the 1930s, the United States was also criticized for its imperial behavior. The socialists' critique of the United States underscores such attitude. Moreover, racial discrimination and arrogance, manifested through the "Yellow Peril," evoked a hostile attitude toward the United States.

In the postindependence period, anti-American sentiments were cultivated by revisionist historical interpretations. For revisionist intellectuals, the United States is neither the savior of the Korean nation nor a benevolent patron. On the contrary, they argue that the United States was not only responsible for national division but also instrumental in the outbreak of the Korean War through Dean Acheson's declaration excluding South Korea from its defense perimeter. Moreover, the United States is also blamed for Korea's distorted political and economic development by not only patronizing authoritarian regimes but also systematically excluding the popular sector through coercive means. Some scholars have even attributed the outbreak of the Korean War to the United States, arguing that it was an extension of the war of national liberation. In the 1980s, the Kwangju Uprising, pressures for trade liberalization, and cultural clashes played an equally important role in fostering anti-American feelings.[30]

These factors still remain as background conditions in shaping contemporary Korean perceptions of the United States. There are additional variables that have factored in the formation of the most recent anti-American phenomenon in South Korea. First is the growing cognitive incongruence between power and status. Since the 1990s, South Koreans, especially youths, tend to believe that South Korea is a powerful country. In their eyes, South Korea is no longer weak and dependent. It is the twelfth-largest economy in the world. More importantly, South Korea's entry into the final four of World Cup Soccer profoundly elevated Korea's national pride. They want a corresponding recognition of their international status from the United States. Nevertheless, Korean youths perceive that South Korea has not gotten such treatment from the United States. For them, the SOFA, unfair legal treatment of the tragic death of the two schoolgirls, occasional violation of Koreans' human rights at American military bases, and acquisition of American military equipment (e.g., the F-15 fighter plane) are convincing testimony of the unequal relationship with the United States. American insensitivity to South Korea's quest for status comparable to its power can be seen as one of the critical causal factors of recent anti-American sentiment.

Second, recent anti-American sentiment appears to be related to the power shift in South Korea's domestic politics. The 3–8–6 generation and those who are close to the Roh Moo Hyun government understand that pro-American forces have been dominant in every aspect of Korean society and that the pro-American establishment has monopolized material and positional values in that society. For them, an anti-American stance is equivalent to a rejection of the establishment, which might lead to a more even distribution of material and positional values. Two telling examples can be found in the composition of the presidential staff of Roh Moo Hyun. One is that most of key presidential staff belong to the 3–8–6 generation, which used to participate actively in the anti-American movements of the 1980s. Another example is that the National Security Council in the office of the president is mostly staffed with those who were trained in South Korea and Europe, whereas American influences are rarely found.

Third, President Bush's foreign policy has also served to aggravate negative feelings toward the United States. Most Koreans have shown their utmost sympathy to the victims of the September 11 attack and have strongly denunciated al-Qaeda and other terrorists. Nevertheless, they have been critical of American unilateralism, such as the invasion of Iraq without the endorsement of the United Nations. In a similar vein, the advent of the Bush doctrine and its aggressive stance toward North Korea has had a profound effect. The accusation that North Korea is a rogue state and part of the axis of evil, rejection of the "Sunshine Policy," and the strategic doctrine of preemptive attack and increased possibility of military conflict on the Korean Peninsula have all contributed to the spread of anti-American sentiments in South Korea. Such feelings have been especially widespread among Korean youths in that they regard America as an obstacle to the building of peace on the Korean peninsula.

Fourth, every society, in coping with domestic or external hardship, has a tendency to look for a scapegoat. Such a trend has been most pronounced in South Korea. South Koreans tend to blame others rather than themselves in the face of major incidents. National division, the Korean War, the military coup in 1961, the Kwangju incident, and the International Monetary Fund crisis are all believed to have been caused by the United States. The inertia of scapegoating and unfounded conspiracy theories has amplified anti-American sentiments in South Korea, masterminded by progressive intellectuals and NGOs. The role of the Jongyojo (the National Teachers' Union) deserves careful attention in this regard. This union's members have championed progressive ideas in teaching, and its members have implanted anti-American sentiments in the minds of Korean youths.

Finally, lack of knowledge of the United States also matters. South Koreans tend to treat the United States as a unitary actor while ignoring its pluralistic nature. As noted before, President Bush is equated with America. Most Koreans fail to take account of liberal forces in the United States who oppose the Bush positions. Failure to appreciate the dynamic and pluralistic nature of American politics and society has contributed to the rise and proliferation of ill-informed perception in South Korea. What makes the situation worse is the silence of those Korean intellectuals who have a more realistic knowledge of the United States. Their opportunistic behavior has compounded the anti-American phenomenon.

Conclusion: What Should Be Done?

The images of the United States in South Korea are not fixed. They show a wide spectrum ranging from *yonmi* to *hyommi*. Thus, *banmi* cannot be seen as the dominant national phenomenon in South Korea. In most cases, *banmi* and *chinmi* coexist, producing an ambivalent personal and national psyche. Nevertheless, anti-American sentiments have been on the rise. Korean youths' perception of the United States seems particularly troublesome, clouding the future of the ROK–U.S. relationship. What should be done? There are no easy solutions. But we can think about some concrete steps.

First, we need to start with the humble assumption that we cannot get rid of anti-American attitudes, since they are an inseparable part of Koreans' personal and national psyche. We should live with them. The more we try to remove them artificially, the more enduring they are likely to become. But we can minimize them while maximizing pro-American or "know-America" attitudes. In other words, we should not be oversensitive to anti-American sentiments. We should consider them part of a normal process in a country that is undergoing a great social, political, and ideological transformation.

Second, we should avoid politicizing the anti-American phenomenon. As can be seen in the recent negative entanglement of "abandon the United States" and "abandon South Korea" campaigns, the sensationalized politicization of anti-American sentiments in South Korea and the United States is bound to result in a negative outcome and to undermine the mutual interests of these two nations. In this regard, the role of mass media in both countries seems critical. Sensationalized anti-Americanism by the mass media has worsened rather than ameliorated the situation.

Third, more efforts need to be made in order to enhance intersubjective understanding. South Koreans should neither oversimplify nor distort their perceptions of the United States. They should enhance their knowledge of America and Americans in a more objective manner. Studying in the United States does not necessarily require expertise in American studies, but more systematic efforts to improve the popular understanding of America would nevertheless be useful. In this regard, America studies should be encouraged. Most of the universities and colleges in South Korea have research institutes on Japanese, Chinese, and Russian studies, but very few have research institutes solely devoted to American studies. Systematic promotion of American studies would not only facilitate the dissemination of objective knowledge on the United States but also prevent purposeful distortion of the United States by anti-American forces.

Given the asymmetry of power and attention, it might be inconceivable for the United States to render similar efforts in understanding South Korea. Nevertheless, the United States can be more prudent in dealing with South Korea. It should avoid leaving South Koreans with an impression of its unilateralism by engaging in more consultation and consensus-building with South Korea in managing alliance affairs. A greater sensitivity to the Korean culture and people seems essential in order to improve Korean perceptions of the United States.

Finally, despite the 100-year history of ROK–U.S. relations, a few powerful elites monopolize the channels of communication and interaction between the two. More diversified channels of communication should be institutionalized and developed, ranging from the power elite and opinion leaders to civic groups. In particular, bilateral networks among civic groups in the two countries are of critical importance.[31]

Likewise, a more systematic and institutionalized approach to bilateral understanding and cooperation between the ROK and the United States will greatly improve Korean perceptions of the United States.

Notes

1. See Clyde Prestowitz, *Rogue Nation* (New York: Basic Books, 2003).

2. For a historical overview of Korean perception of the United States, see Young-ick Lew et al., *Hankukinui Daemiinsik* (Korean perception of the United States) (Seoul: Mineumsa, 1994); Pyong-choon Hahm, "The Korean Perception of the Untied States," in *Korea and the United States: A Century of Cooperation*, ed. Youngnok Koo and Dae-sook Suh (Honolulu: University of Hawaii Press, 1984); Special Issue on the United States, *Quarterly Sasang* (Winter 2000).

3. Byong-gi Song, "Soikukgiui Daemi Insik" (Perception of the United States during the period of closure), in Lew et al., *Hankukinui Daemiinsik*, pp. 11–54; Young-ick Lew, "Gaehwagiui Daemin Insik" (Perception of the United States during the opening period) in Lew et al., *Hankukinui Daemiinsik*, pp. 55–142.

4. Jun-hon Hwang, *Chosun Ch'aengnyak* (Strategy for Korea), translated by Il-mun Cho, (Seoul: Konkuk University Press, 1977), pp. 13–14.

5. Lew, "Gaehwagiui Daemin Insik," pp. 66–71.

6. Kuksa Pyonchan Wiwonhoe, *Yoon Chi-ho Ilgi* (The Diary of Yoon Chi-Ho) (Seoul: Tamgudang, 1973). Also see Lew, "Gaehwagiui Daemin Insik," pp. 103–4.

7. Song, "Soikukgiui Daemi Insik," pp. 11–54.

8. Lew, "Gaehwagiui Daemin Insik," pp. 117–19.

9. Ho-min Yang, "Iljesidaeui Daemiinsik" (Perception of the United States during the Japanese colonial rule), in Lew et al., *Hankukinui Daemiinsik*, pp. 143–224.

10. Hee-sup Im, "Haebanghuui Daemininsik" (Perception of the United States in the post-liberation era) in Lew et al., *Hankukinui Daemiinsik*, pp. 225–78.

11. See Chi-won Kang, "Mikukeun Uriaege Muoetinga" (What is the U.S. for us?) (Seoul: Baegui, 2000); Young-ye Jang, "Daehakgyoyukae Bburinaeryn *Sungmi* Sadaejuui" (*Sungmi* sadaejuui embedded in college education), in Sangyoung Rhyu et al., *Hanmi Gwangyeui Jaeinsik 1* (Rethinking Korean-U.S. relations) (Seoul: Doori, 1990), pp. 299–322.

12. See Chung-in Moon, "21segi Hanmi Gwangyeui Saeroun Jipyongul Uihayeo" (Toward the new horizon of Korean-U.S. relations in the 21st century), *Shindonga*, January 1996, pp. 38–45.

13. Chung-in Moon et al., *Hankuk Minjokjuui Yongu: Insikjok Bunsok* (The anatomy of Korean nationalism: A perception analysis) (Seoul: Institute of International Peace Studies, Kyunghee University, 1988), p. 134.

14. See Donga Ilbosa, ed., *Mikuk, Chogangdaekukui Bitgwa Geuneul* (America: Light and shadow of superpower) (Seoul: Donga Ilbosa, 1996), A special supplement to *Shindonga*, special issue, January 1996.

15. On the issue of ambivalence, refer to Lew Young-ick's excellent discussion "Tongsijokeuro bon Daemiinsik" (Perception of the United States over time), in Lew et al., *Hankukinui Daemiinsik*, p. 281. Lew argues that while Koreans had a well-defined perception of China as the supreme authority for respect and worship and Japan as an island barbarian, their perception of the United States was uncertain.

16. Kuksa Pyonchan Wiwonhoe, *Yoon Chi-ho Ilgi*, pp. 407–8, December 8–9, 1889. Requoted from Lew, "Tongsijokeuro," p. 103.

17. *Donga Ilbo*, March 4, 2003.

18. These 3–8–6 students were the major driving force of democratic change in the mid-1980s.

19. Sung-bo Kim, "80nyondai *Banmi* Jajuhwaundongui Jongyegwajong" (Process of anti-American self-reliant movement in the 1980s), in *Hanmi Gwangyesa* (Korean-American history), ed. Young-ho Park and Gwangsik Kim (Seoul: Silchonmunhaksa, 1990), pp. 394–432.

20. For a full list of these attacks, see Sang-gi Nam, "Hankukinui Daemin Insikgwa Banmiundongui Jonmang" (Koreans' perception of the United States and prospects for anti-American movements), in Sang-hwan Jang et al., *Hanmigwangteui Jaeinsik 2* (Rethinking Korea–U.S. relations 2) (Seoul: Doori, 1991), pp. 360–63.

21. South Koreans felt insulted when the American delegates showed a disorderly attitude during the opening ceremony of the 1988 Seoul Olympics, and a South Korean short track athlete lost a gold medal to an American player because of an Australian referee's misjudgment. But most South Koreans attributed the mishap to American influence. Finally, most Koreans believe that a proper expression of condolence to family members of the victims and the appreciation of Korean legal culture by American Forces in South Korea could have prevented the escalation of anti-American sentiments in the aftermath of the tragic death of two middle-school girls.

22. For an excellent handling of this issue, see Katharine H.S. Moon, "Nationalism, Anti-Americanism, and Consolidation," in *Korea's Democratization*, ed. Samuel Kim (Cambridge: Cambridge University Press, 2003), pp. 135–58.

23. See chapter 7 in this volume.

24. Chaibong Hahm, "Sadaewa *Banmi* Saiaeseo: (Between worshiping the great and Anti-Americanism), *Quarterly Sasang* (Winter 2000): 52–68.

25. USIA, *Hankuk Yeoronae Natanan Mikuk* Pyongga (Assessment of the United States reflected in Korean public opinion) (Seoul: USIA, 1966), p. 1.

26. Quoted from Ho- Gi Kim, "Ije Mikukuen Upda?" (Now, no America?), *Shindonga* 46, no. 1 (January 2003): 362.

27. The Ioongang Ilbosa, Bureau of Data Bank, "A National Opinion Survey on the Occasion of the 26th Anniversary of the Joongang Ilbo" (Seoul: Joongang Ilbo, 1991).

28. Gallup Korea DB, http://gallup.chol.com/svcdb, accessed July 25, 2003.

29. Hon-ok Park, "Chungsonyonui *Banmi* Gamjung-Siltaewa Daechaek (Anti-American sentiments of Korean youths—present status and counter-measures), *Oigyo* (Diplomacy) 62 (July 2002): 136.

30. Hee-sup Im, "Haebanghuui Daemiinsik" pp. 253–66; Sang-sop Park, "Daehagsaengui *Banmi* Uisik (Anti-American consciousness of college students)," in *Mikukeu Uriaegye Mueot Inga* (What is the U.S. to us?), ed. HankukBangsong Saupdan (Seoul: Korea Broadcasting System, 1989), pp. 300–319; Rhyu, *Hanmi Gwangyeui Jaeinsik 1*; Jang, *Hanmigwangteui Jaeinsik 2.*

31. Hyun-jin Lim, "Simhwadoineun Hanmigaldeung, Siminsahoi Netwokeuro Pulja" (Let's resolve worsening Korean-American conflict through networks of civil society), *Shindonga* (June 2003), pp. 268–80.

Part III

Alliance Perspectives

10

Revamping the Korean-American Alliance

New Political Forces, Paradigms, and Roles and Missions

Chung Min Lee

Roh's Victory and South Korea's Changing Security Consensus

The election of Roh Moo Hyun as South Korea's new president in December 2002 marked a major turning point in South Korean politics, the future of the Republic of Korea (ROK)–U.S. alliance, and the strategic makeup of a unified Korea. In sharp contrast to his campaign rhetoric during the campaign, President Roh has toned down his views on a range of foreign policy and national security issues, particularly with respect to the future of the Korean-American alliance. During his visit to the ROK–U.S. Combined Forces Command (CFC) a few weeks after his victory, Roh reaffirmed the importance of the alliance not only in the evolving context but, more importantly, even after unification. Although foreign policy and South–North relations did not really emerge as crucial campaign issues in South Korea's presidential elections since the restoration of democracy in 1987, the December 2002 poll was starkly different. In the midst of the second North Korean nuclear crisis that erupted in mid-October, when Pyongyang revealed that it was working on a uranium-enriched nuclear weapons program, candidate Roh Moo Hyun of the ruling Millennium Democratic Party (MDP) and Lee Hoi Chang of the opposition Grand National Party (GNP) clashed over Seoul's overall policy toward North Korea. Roh argued during the final stretch of the campaign that a hard-line posture vis-à-vis Pyongyang would not convince North Korea to discard its nuclear option. He also stressed that if Lee won the election, the chances of a conflict could increase based on Lee's more conservative strategy toward the North.

As a long-time supporter of outgoing President Kim Dae Jung's "Sunshine Policy" or comprehensive engagement with the North, President Roh has reaffirmed that he would continue to abide by the basic contours and tenets of the

Sunshine Policy. At the same time, Roh has also stressed that the Korean-American alliance must be more balanced, given the rise of new strategic and political forces. As the *Washington Post* reported the day after the election, "Roh Moo Hyun campaigned on a vow to draw at least symbolic distance between Washington and Seoul. South Korea has traditionally been one of the United States' most fiercely loyal allies."[1] During the heated debate between Roh and Lee in the weeks preceding the election, Roh stressed that he would not "kowtow" to the United States and also called for the "maturation and advancement" of the bilateral alliance. While Roh's views on the United States, the 37,000 U.S. forces stationed in South Korea, and U.S. policy toward North Korea, have gone through various iterations during his career as a member of the National Assembly, a presidential candidate, and finally president, supporters claim that Roh never really espoused anti-Americanism—only that he has consistently called for a more balanced alliance. Indeed, Roh's supporters claim that there is nothing wrong with his call for a more balanced relationship with the United States, given that he was merely articulating South Korea's growing desire for a more equal partnership with the United States based on enhanced nationalism, the call for more autonomy in the all-important security alliance with Washington, and the need for South Korea to take the lead in shaping overall policy toward North Korea.

President Roh's key security and related political challenges are principally three-fold. First, he has to draft and implement a viable North Korean policy road map that satisfies three interrelated conditions: convincing North Korea to give up its nuclear weapons program, forging a policy consensus with the United States and Japan, and building and sustaining a bipartisan consensus within South Korea. Second, Roh has to articulate his vision for a revamped Korean-American alliance that takes into account the core strategic interests of Korea and the United States while continuing to pursue inter-Korean détente. And third, he has to articulate more precisely his vision for a unified Korea, including the type of security arrangements that would enhance Korea's critical security and economic interests while retaining key ties with the United States. Or, as the *New York Times* noted, "Mr. Roh's challenge now is to reconcile the dual yearnings of South Korea's sophisticated and increasingly affluent younger generations for more autonomy from the United States and reduced tensions with continued reliance on American security."[2]

How Roh will be able to reengineer South Korea's long-standing alliance with the United States may depend critically on forces that are, for the moment, beyond his immediate control; for example, North Korean leader Kim Jong Il's long-term game plan and key policy initiatives toward the North in the aftermath of the Six Party Talks. At the same time, despite Roh's populist inclinations (particularly on socioeconomic issues) and his express wish to make the Seoul–Washington relationship more equal and mature, sustained friction in the alliance and corresponding changes in U.S. defense policy toward South Korea (including the status of U.S. forces) could result.

Since his victory, however, Roh has reaffirmed the need to maintain South Korea's alliance with the United States and, for its part, the Bush administration has also toned down its hard-line rhetoric toward North Korea. Beginning with Secretary of State Colin Powell's remarks in late December 2002, Washington has emphasized that notwithstanding the serious nature of North Korea's violation of the 1994 Agreed Framework, the United States government does not perceive the North Korean nuclear standoff as a "crisis" and that it stands ready to talk. As Powell stated, "It [the North Korean nuclear problem] is not a crisis, but it is a matter of great concern, and that's why we have spent so much time working with our friends and allies to apply pressure on North Korea and why we are talking to the United Nations."[3] President Bush has also repeatedly emphasized that the United States has no intention of using military force against North Korea, although he has not absolutely precluded other options.

> I view the North Korean situation as one that can be resolved peacefully, through diplomacy. The international community—particularly those countries close to North Korea—understand the stakes involved. . . . There is strong consensus, not only amongst the nations in the neighborhood and our friends, but also with international organizations, such as the IAEA [International Atomic Energy Agency], that North Korea ought to comply with international regulations. *I believe this can be done peacefully, through diplomacy, and we will continue to work that way. I take—all options, of course, are always on the table for any President, but by working with these countries we can resolve this.*[4] (Emphasis added.)

A number of options have been aired recently including the "tailored containment" and a "bold approach" toward North Korea that would include some type of a security guarantee to the Pyongyang regime. That said, the key question is whether North Korea's core security can realistically be guaranteed by the United States in the face of worsening structural decay. At the same time, the Bush administration is unlikely to consider a bold approach that provides North Korea with key incentives in the absence of verifying North Korea's dismantling of its nuclear weapons capabilities.

A more troubling dimension of the ongoing second North Korean nuclear crisis is how the Roh government will ultimately cope with North Korea if Pyongyang persists in pursuing a nuclear weapons program. While Roh has repeatedly stated that a nuclearized North Korea is unacceptable, he has also stated that only peaceful means should be considered in convincing North Korea to give up its nuclear or other weapons of mass destruction (WMD) assets. Such a view assumes that given the right mix of incentives, such as a de facto security guarantee from the United States, the North will bargain away its nuclear option. However, if North Korea were indeed serious about negotiating its WMD assets, it could have done so when Kim Dae Jung and Bill Clinton were both in office—arguably the most engagement-prone leaders in South Korea and the United States. One of the most vexing aspects of South Korea's changing security consensus—particularly in public sentiments about the North Korean military threat, including its nuclear weapons program—is the increasingly popular belief that even if North Korea succeeds in acquiring nuclear weapons capability, such a turn of events may not necessarily be harmful to South Korea's security interests. For example, many South Koreans believe that North Korea would not actually use nuclear weapons or other WMD assets against the ROK, given their common ethnic heritage and nationality. Alternatively, a not insignificant portion of South Koreans argue that one of the major reasons why a North Korea with nuclear weapons is not necessarily a threat is because they have been developed primarily for bargaining purposes and in response to growing North Korean vulnerability. Indeed, such a view was echoed by the incumbent minister of unification, who stipulated that one should not overstate the threat from North Korea's ballistic missiles, since they were being developed primarily for bargaining purposes and that at any rate, North Korea would not use them against South Korea. Although he was roundly criticized for his remarks, the important point is that his views are actually shared by a growing segment of the public. The core elements of this "new security school" can be summarized as follows.

Key Elements of South Korea's "New" Security School

- North Korea's WMD assets, including its nuclear weapons program, can be negotiated on the basis of a security guarantee from the United States and matching economic/political incentives from the United States, South Korea, and Japan.
- Even if North Korea possesses nuclear weapons, Pyongyang is highly unlikely to use them in any real sense against South Korea.
- If North Korea refuses to cooperate with either the IAEA or the UN Security Council, South Korea should still pursue a policy of engagement, since containment will push North Korea further over the edge. Internationalizing the issue (e.g., taking it to the UN Security Council or pursuing such policies as the Proliferation Strategy Initiative) could compel North Korea to cross the "red line" and emerge as a declared nuclear weapons state, such as India and Pakistan.
- Notwithstanding the importance of the ROK–U.S. alliance, South Korea's longer-term security can be best guaranteed by greater autonomy and decreasing its security dependence on the United States.
- A "Grand National Arrangement" is the best guarantee for South Korean security, including the adoption of more progressive and self-reliant foreign policy postures.

To be sure, such views are not shared by a majority of South Koreans, but it is important to keep in mind that a growing number of South Koreans subscribe to the concept of greater autonomy and the need to accelerate South–North reconciliation. What is missing in the current security debate is not an agreement on whether the alliance should be "modernized" or "revamped" owing to new political and strategic developments but rather the taking into account of *alternative security* arrangements and corresponding costs. Some of the key costs associated with South Korea's more autonomous security arrangements could be summarized as follows.

Potential Costs of an Autonomous Security Posture

- A significant reduction in the composition of the U.S. Forces Korea (USFK) or a total withdrawal of the USFK would mean a major increase in South Korea's defense budget (from a current 2.7 percent of GDP to at least 5 to 6 percent of GDP).
- The lack of strategic intelligence provided by the United States could be critical to South Korea's longer-term defense and security needs. For the foreseeable future, it is highly unlikely that South Korea would be able to operationalize strategic intelligence platforms.
- If South Korea pursues a security policy strategy that does not include the CFC as a central pillar, and assuming further that Washington could choose to withdraw its forces from South Korea, Japan would likely emerge as the key "front state" in Northeast Asia.
- Absent a U.S. security umbrella, South Korea would have no choice but to cope directly with a potentially more aggressive China, particularly as it goes into the "unification tunnel."
- The *economic impact* of a U.S. troop withdrawal would be detrimental to South Korea's economic well-being, given that foreign direct investment (FDI) in South Korea and foreign private sector lending to South Korea could dip significantly.
- South Korea's foreign policy anchor would have to be shifted owing to a diluted relationship with the United States, but alternative arrangements could be highly problematic (e.g., the consequences of a more robust security relationship with China).

In essence, as South Korea ponders alternative security arrangements or at the very least a revamped ROK–U.S. alliance, the cumulative consequences have not yet been thoroughly reviewed. Proponents of a radical reengineering of the alliance, including the total and immediate withdrawal of the USFK, are still a small minority in South Korea, but a growing sector of Korean society probably subscribes to the desirability of the eventual withdrawal of U.S. forces. Notwithstanding the positive aspects of "Koreanizing" Korean defense and security, it is crucial to bear in mind that in order for defense autonomy to work, it must be backed up by significantly higher defense budgets, strategic intelligence platforms and related assets, and a restructured military force.

As noted above, the inauguration of Roh Moo Hyun symbolizes a new page in Korean politics, foreign policies, and national security strategies. But President Roh came into office at a time of unparalleled security discord not only within South Korea but also with respect to the Korean-American alliance. Recent revelations that up to several hundred million dollars was transferred to North Korea through the Hyundai corporation a few weeks prior to the June 2000 summit constitute but one example of the excesses of the Sunshine Policy as practiced by the former Kim Dae Jung government. In the process, however, South Korea's intelligence gathering and assessment capabilities vis-à-vis the North have also been unduly politicized—a development that has already had major consequences. There is every reason to applaud an alliance that seeks to modernize itself in the aftermath of new geostrategic, economic, or political changes. That said, such efforts should be fostered on the basis of a common security paradigm, and to the extent possible, there should be a joint road map on key (though by no means all) security issues. National sentiments, however strong, should not be misconstrued or misperceived as national interests, nor should they serve as critical guidelines in the shaping of South Korea's twenty-first-century security strategy.

The ROK–U.S. Alliance in Transition

As the Roh administration puts into place key policies that will shape South Korea's foreign, national security, and unification policies, Seoul's version of cohabitation may result in increasing political burdens; namely, the parallel pursuit of a fundamental breakthrough in South–North relations while at the same time implementing potentially far-reaching change in the ROK–U.S. alliance. The administration's goal of realizing an enduring "peace system" on the Korean Peninsula rests on four key platforms: (1) the maintenance of ROK–U.S. security cooperation and a more self-reliant foreign policy; (2) institutionalization of South–North summits and South–North reconciliation and cooperation mechanisms; (3) the fostering of peace and a denuclearized Korean Peninsula by convincing North Korea to abandon its WMD arsenals in exchange for a comprehensive aid package; and (4) the enunciation of a peace declaration by the leaders of South and North Korea and the pursuit of an inter-Korean peace treaty.[5]

Although prospects for a total withdrawal of U.S. forces from South Korea remain slim, there is an outside possibility that ground forces could be pared down significantly over the next five years. To be sure, senior officials in Washington and Seoul continue to emphasize that the bilateral relationship has improved since the outbreak of unprecedented anti-American demonstrations and protests in 2002.[6] As an example, the commander of the USFK, General Leon J. LaPorte, stated before the U.S. Senate Armed Services Committee that the "Republic of Korea–United States alliance has weathered challenges for over 50 years, and this partnership will continue to endure." Despite LaPorte's assurances, however, he also noted that the two allies have begun the process of "redefining" the alliance, including future roles, missions, functions, structures, and the stationing of troops.[7]

If recent developments can serve as a guide, the possibility remains high that major adjustments will be made in the structure of the USFK during President Roh's five-year term (2003–8), including, at a minimum, the repositioning of the 2nd Infantry Division from near the Demilitarized Zone (DMZ) to south of the Han River. As a case in point, recent discussions between ROK and U.S. officials resulted in an agreement to consider the relocation of the USFK while not "weakening the combined deterrent effect against North Korea." Deputy Minister of Defense Cha Young Koo and Deputy Assistant Secretary of Defense Richard Lawless announced on April 9, 2003, during the first meeting of the "Future of the Alliance's Policy Initiative," that both sides discussed the need for realignment while not advancing to the stage of considering a redeployment schedule. The two officials also stressed that no discussions had taken place on reducing the current force structure of the USFK.[8]

The advent of the Roh administration has resulted in the rise of a new generation of political leaders and key policy makers with little if any direct recollection of the Korean conflict and the virtually uncontested acceptance of the Korean-American alliance by the political elites as well as the public. As the most liberal government to be voted into office since the ROK's inception in 1948, the Roh administration's overall *weltanschauung* and corresponding policy preferences could be summarized as follows. First, as noted above, a concerted effort to push a comprehensive "post–Cold War mindset" or moving away from conventional notions of threat and net assessments and, in particular, to place greater emphasis on North Korean vulnerabilities as it seeks to balance regime survival with its brand of reforms.[9] Second, notwithstanding the need to maintain a robust ROK–U.S. alliance, the Roh administration advocates a parallel need to foster a more equal partnership with the United States. Throughout his race for the presidency in 2002, Roh portrayed himself as a leader who would be able to send a strong message to Washington that "business as usual" would no longer be considered the norm in the ROK–U.S. relationship, even as he valued the continuing role of the alliance.[10] After he became president, however, Roh stressed that "we will foster and develop this cherished alliance. We will see to it that the alliance matures into a more reciprocal and equitable relationship."[11] Such contrasting signals were evident even as President Roh entered the Blue House (the official presidential residence). After a North Korean combat aircraft tracked a U.S. RC-135S reconnaissance aircraft in international air space for twenty-two hours in early March 2003, President Roh mentioned in an interview that "it was a very predictable chain of events" and urged the Bush administration "not to go too far."[12] Thus, the constant pull between a yearning for greater autonomy in South Korea's alliance with the United States, even as it understands the critical utility of sustaining the alliance, has come to illustrate the Roh administration's complex attitude toward the United States—a phenomenon that began with the inauguration of the Kim Dae Jung administration in 1998. As an example, despite tensions between the Kim Dae Jung administration and the Bush administration over Seoul's comprehensive engagement with the North, President Bush reaffirmed Korea's strategic importance during his February 2002 visit to Seoul. In part, Bush stated that "I understand how important this relationship is to our country, and the United States is strongly committed to the security of South Korea. . . . No one should ever doubt that this is a vital commitment for our nation."[13] After the September 11 terrorist attacks, U.S. Undersecretary for Political Affairs Marc Grossman stated, in a speech given in October 2001, that "our alliance with South Korea is forged in blood. More than 33,000 Americans and 225,000 Koreans died during the Korean War. Our mutual defense treaty with South Korea has promoted democratic and free market ideals for over half a century. It is no surprise South Korea stands shoulder to shoulder with us now to face the current crisis."[14]

Further, as the former commander of U.S. Forces in Korea General Thomas Schwartz testified before the Senate Armed Services Committee in March 2002, "Our alliance continues to be one of the greatest enjoyed by the U.S., and remains essential to the peace and security of Northeast Asia. This great alliance is effectively deterring North Korean aggression today, and if called upon, will successfully defeat a North Korean attack."[15] For its part, the ROK continues to maintain that the ROK–U.S. alliance serves as the heart of its national security strategy, even into the postunification era. As one Ministry of National Defense report recently noted, "the ROK–U.S. alliance has to be emphasized even more strongly in consideration of such factors as uncertain threat perceptions in the post-unification era, fluctuating major power dynamics, and disparate interests between maritime and continental powers."[16] Thus, at least from the perspective of political leaders, senior military officials, and policy elites, the ROK–U.S. alliance stands out as one of the cornerstones of postwar U.S. engagement in the Asia-Pacific region and a key success story in postwar U.S. foreign policy.

Despite significant shifts in global and regional security dynamics—such as the global end of the Cold War,[17] the dissolution of the Soviet Union, China's more pragmatic strategy toward the two Koreas, and incremental progress in inter-Korean relations, such as the June 2000 South–North summit—the principal objectives of the ROK–U.S. alliance have remained remarkably consistent since its inception more than half a century ago. First and foremost, the alliance remains committed to deterring aggression on the Korean Peninsula, and if deterrence fails, to defending the territorial and political integrity of the ROK. Since the late 1980s, the threat of a major conventional war akin to the 1950 North Korean invasion has declined, perhaps even significantly, owing to a combination of factors—such as North Korea's virtual economic collapse, the rising conventional defense capabilities of the ROK armed forces, and both Chinese and Russian opposition to any outbreak of major war on the Korean Peninsula. That said, the ROK continues to emphasize the potential for major war as illustrated by its defense objectives outlined in the 2000 Defense White Paper:

> First, "defending the nation from external military threats and invasion" means protecting it from any possible external military threat as well as those immediate threats from North Korea, which, as the nation's *main enemy*, could endanger our survival. Second, "upholding peaceful unification" means that the nation helps to unify the divided Korea by deterring war on the peninsula, defusing military tension, and maintaining peace and stability. Third, "contributing to regional stability and world peace" demonstrates our willingness to contribute to and enhance a cooperative military relationship with neighboring countries based on our national status and security capabilities.[18] (Emphasis added.)

Second, the alliance continues to play a critical role in preserving the U.S. strategic presence in Northeast Asia, not only as the only forward base for U.S. forces on the Asian continent but also as a crucial front line vis-à-vis the U.S.–Japan alliance. For example, the *Defense of Japan 2001* White Paper noted that "maintaining peace and stability on the Korean Peninsula is an essential part of the peace and stability of the East Asian region as a whole, including Japan."[19] As a RAND study noted in 2001, it is imperative for the United States to pursue an integrated regional strategy in order to "preclude in Asia the growth of rivalries, suspicions, and insecurities that could lead to war" and, further, to focus on three related subordinate goals: (1) preventing the rise of a regional hegemon; (2) maintaining regional stability; and (3) managing Asia's multiple transformations.[20] Implicitly, the report suggests that an increasingly powerful China could have major repercussions for U.S. strategy and military posture in the Asia-Pacific region, noting that: "One of the most important changes is the emergence of China as a rising power, its military modernization program, and its enhanced role in the East Asian region. For the U.S. military, this highlights the *near-term* question of how to respond to a possible Chinese use of force against Taiwan. In the *longer-term*, China's increased power will entail substantial implications for the region and for U.S. strategy and its military—particularly if China pursues a policy of regional hegemony."[21]

Third, the alliance serves as one of the key pillars for a *de facto multifaceted* Pacific Alliance including the U.S.–Japan, U.S.–Australia, and U.S.–Thailand alliances. Beyond their military rationales, these alliances have matured significantly since their inception to become de facto political alliances. While outstanding political, historical, and security legacies significantly curtail the possibility of a collective security mechanism such as the North Atlantic Treaty Organization (NATO), they serve as the primary building blocks for the creation of a more institutionalized multilateral security grouping.

In essence, the ROK–U.S. alliance by almost every measure has shown remarkable resilience over the past five decades. As the alliance ponders the future, however, there are a number of challenges that may have profound implications for the alliance. While domestic political support for the alliance remains relatively high, democratization in South Korea has resulted in the rise of more diverse security perceptions, national security postures, greater autonomy in the context of the ROK–U.S. alliance, and a rise in NGOs and Netizens who advocate the withdrawal of U.S. forces and termination of the ROK–U.S. defense treaty.[22] Extreme anti-Americanism continues to be rejected by the majority of South Koreans, but there is no denying that a highly vocal, networked, and aggressive anti-American movement persists within South Korea.

Interestingly, while North Korea has never publicly stated that U.S. forces from South Korea should not be withdrawn, former President Kim Dae Jung and other high-ranking officials have insisted, since the June 2000 summit, that North Korean leader Kim Jong Il actually supports the role of U.S. forces. In an interview given on August 6, 2001, President Kim stated that the reason why the joint statement released after Kim Jong Il's meeting with Russian President Putin called for the withdrawal of U.S. forces from South Korea was to "signal a desire on the part of North Korea to improve ties with the United States" and further, that "Chairman Kim Jong Il told me that 'I agree with the notion that the U.S. forces are necessary' and that he repeated his statement to visiting Secretary of State Madeleine Albright and South Korean newspaper publishers when they visited the North."[23] At the same time, President Kim and other high-ranking ROK officials have repeatedly emphasized the need for U.S. forces in Korea even after unification. For example, former Minister of Foreign Affairs and Trade Han Seung-Soo remarked in June 2001 that "even after Korea is unified or the threat of military invasion is removed, U.S. forces in Korea are needed to maintain regional stability." Minister Han also noted that "Koreans consider the United States as a country that does not harbor territorial ambitions in Northeast Asia and continue to support the traditional partnership between Korea and the United States."[24] During a meeting with President Bush in February, President Kim stated that "Korea and the U.S. are strong allies, and I believe that this is important and vital for the national interest of both our countries. And so that's our top priority."[25]

Despite official and institutional support for the alliance, however, differences have surfaced between the United States and South Korea over their respective North Korean policies, particularly since the advent of the Bush administration. Although the Kim Dae Jung administration and the Clinton administration shared similar perceptions vis-à-vis North Korea—for example, that comprehensive engagement offered the best hope for a sustained reduction in tension between the two Koreas as well as the United States and North Korea—the Bush administration has been unwilling to jump-start talks with the North, given its perception of North Korea as one of the critical sources of global and regional instability. On June 6, 2001, the Bush administration announced its North Korean policy guidelines, after a six-month review that included three key agendas: (1) improved implementation of the Agreed Framework relating to North Korea's nuclear activities; (2) verifiable constraints on North Korea's missile programs and a ban on its missile exports; and (3) a less threatening conventional military posture.[26] While South Korea reacted positively to the Bush policy review by attaching significance to Bush's promise to expand assistance to the North Korean people, ease sanctions, and take other political steps, Seoul basically chose to downplay Bush's reminder that the United States was willing to do so "if North Korea responds affirmatively and takes appropriate action." Indeed, then South Korean Minister of Foreign Affairs Han Seung-Soo remarked that "Bush's decision will help for a favorable atmosphere for the holding of a second inter-Korean summit."[27] While hopes were rising in Seoul that Washington–Pyongyang talks would trigger an impasse in South–North relations (including a return summit), one U.S. weekly argued that prospects for any breakthrough between the United States and North Korea were ill founded one month after the policy review announcement.

> Yet even before the applause has died down, disillusionment is setting in among those hoping for a breakthrough. That's because the Administration's decision to renew contacts with Pyongyang is far from a softening of its hard-line stance. . . . Bush wants North Korea to halt missile exports to places like Syria and Iraq and

demonstrate conclusively that it is not making nuclear weapons. These were Clinton's goals as well. But Bush also is insisting that Pyongyang pull back troops and artillery from the border area. . . . A year has gone by since the unprecedented summit between the two Kims in Pyongyang. That was a moment of euphoria. Now it seems the process of building relations will be, at best, a long, hard slog for Pyongyang, Seoul, and Washington.[28]

While the Kim Dae Jung administration continued to press Washington to jump start its talks with Pyongyang right after the conclusion of the North Korean policy review by the Bush administration in the summer of 2001, the Bush administration refused to negotiate at length with North Korea until such time that Pyongyang illustrated a willingness to give up its nuclear weapons program. In his State of the Union Address in January 2002, President Bush referred to North Korea, Iraq, and Iran as being part of an "axis of evil." While Bush's speech also generated significant debate in the United States and elsewhere (such as Europe and the Middle East), Bush's "realistic" assessment of North Korea as a "regime arming with missiles and weapons of mass destruction, while starving its citizens" hit a raw nerve in the Kim Dae Jung government. Indeed, although Seoul did not directly or officially criticize the Bush administration or President Bush, given that Bush was planning to visit Seoul in February 2002, officials seethed privately that Bush's hard-line rhetoric would force North Korea into a corner. The Kim–Bush summit in February 2002 ended on a relatively high note, given that Bush did not directly refer to North Korea in Seoul as a member of the axis of evil and supported Kim Dae Jung's Sunshine Policy. Nevertheless, while the summit may have resulted in damage control, it did not really alleviate the perception gap between Kim Dae Jung and George W. Bush. As a South Korean newspaper editorial noted the day after Bush's departure, "to many people's relief, U.S. President George W. Bush left here yesterday without wreaking havoc with the fledgling inter-Korean rapprochement. . . . For South Korea's part, diplomatic damage control seems to have been done, though it will take some time to know for sure."[29]

New Rationales, Roles, and Missions

Beyond the issue of contrasting approaches toward North Korea, the ROK–U.S. alliance confronts two major strategic challenges. To begin with, the threat spectrum has changed significantly since the alliance was first initiated, which requires more expanded and tailored roles and missions for the alliance. Although the possibility of a major war cannot be discounted, North Korea's ability to wage a full-scale conventional conflict has ebbed considerably since the 1980s, owing to a confluence of factors such as North Korea's economic decay, South Korea's force improvement plans, termination of the Russian-North Korean defense treaty, and failure on the part of North Korea to decouple South Korea from the United States. Although the specter of a major conventional conflict has decreased, North Korea's robust WMD program, the potential for an outbreak of a range of low-intensity conflicts (LIC), and even a

North Korean collapse have all contributed to the rise in nonlinear scenarios on the Korean Peninsula. While the ROK–U.S. Combined Forces Command continues to train and prepare for a wide range of conflict spectrums, off-line scenarios—including variations of WMD threats concomitant with collapse scenarios—could pose significant challenges to the ROK–U.S. political and military leaderships.

The ROK's prevailing threat perceptions until the early 1970s were dominated by three major concerns: the possibility of another North Korean invasion; North Korean–sponsored terrorism, incursions, and probes; and South Korea's gradual but increasingly costly participation in the Vietnamese conflict from the mid-1960s; and (4) very heavy military dependence on the United States including strategic intelligence on and around the Korean Peninsula.

Even until South Korea became deeply involved in the U.S.-led war effort in South Vietnam—the ROK deployed three full infantry divisions at the height of its presence in Vietnam—the alliance was parochial in its strategic focus and marked by the ROK's security and economic dependence on the United States. It was not until the late 1970s that the ROK began to perceive security in more autonomous terms (propelled in part by Jimmy Carter's initial moves to withdraw U.S. ground troops from South Korea), although still within the confines of the alliance. As a case in point, President Park Chung Hee embarked on an ambitious defense modernization program from the early 1970s (the Yulgok Program) in an effort to incrementally increase South Korea's indigenous weapons development capabilities, including Seoul's modest but autonomous ballistic missile program.[30] By the late 1980s and into the mid-1990s, the alliance would undergo profound changes owing to the collapse of communism in Eastern Europe; German unification; political, economic, and strategic convulsions in North Korea (such as the death of Kim Il Sung in 1994, sustained economic decline from the late 1980s onward, and Pyongyang's self-engineered nuclear crisis of 1993–94). Although the threat of major war continued to decline in the 1980s and into the 1990s, the alliance would grapple with three emerging threats: (1) North Korea's WMD arsenal, including a formidable ballistic missile inventory (which currently numbers over 500); (2) the possibility of a regime, state, or structural collapse, with corresponding repercussions for Korean, American, and Japanese security; and (3) nonlinear scenarios going into the "unification tunnel" that could be highly disruptive, volatile, violent, and problematic (such as limited Chinese military intervention in support of an interim North Korean regime after the downfall or ouster of Kim Jong Il).

The alliance was also being transformed from a parochial to a broader-framed alliance with an increasingly ambitious security agenda. While South Korea "does not participate extensively in global military roles and missions, including combined operations, elsewhere in the region and beyond,"[31] this may change, perhaps even significantly, after September 11. Beyond relatively light UN Peacekeeping tasks in East Timor, the Western Sahara, and the India/Pakistan border, South Korea may be asked by the United States to assume more direct military operations in support of the war against terrorism, as illustrated by the Bush administration's formal request to the ROK to commit combat forces to the Iraqi theater. As of early October 2003, the Roh administration was continuing to grapple with this issue, given the lack of popular support for sending combat personnel into the Iraqi theater. Nevertheless, if the UN Security Council passes a new resolution in support of postwar peacekeeping operations, the Roh administration would be hard pressed not to commit combat troops to Iraq.

By the late 1990s, the alliance was confronting a seemingly contradictory goal: providing different levels of assurance to North Korea in order to foster positive behavioral change, particularly with regard to WMD and ballistic missiles, while at the same time, preparing for a range of off-line scenarios, including violent collapse that could have major repercussions for the ROK and the United States. By the 1990s, the alliance was becoming increasingly alarmed at the prospects for protracted crises on the peninsula despite an incrementally decreasing threat of major conventional war. North Korea's increased emphasis on asymmetrical forces, including WMD and ballistic missiles (even while it continued to deploy the world's fifth largest conventional armed forces) was posing new demands on the alliance. In the coming years, that is, by 2020 or so, the ROK is likely to confront a very different strategic picture, especially if the peninsula is unified under its auspices. As noted below, a unified Korea would likely be confronted by very different dynamics, including the possibility of a more nationalistic national security paradigm with matching force modernization programs. But the strategic dispositions of a unified Korea would also be affected significantly by the actions and strategies of its more powerful neighbors, notably China and Japan, but particularly in the context of Beijing's longer-term regional strategic ambitions.

While the list invariably can be expanded to include extremely remote scenarios (such as a military coup in North Korea followed by immediate peace negotiations with the South and rapid dissolution of the North Korean state), the biggest challenge would arise from major political disruptions such as a renewal of the nuclear crisis based either on incontrovertible evidence that despite the Agreed Framework, Pyongyang succeeds in building nuclear weapons, North Korea walks out of the agreement as its obligations become increasingly intrusive, Pyongyang chooses to discontinue its moratorium on long-range missile tests and also fails to abide by IAEA inspections. Other crises could erupt, such as breakdown in the North Korean command structure in the aftermath of some form of a violent political transition, leading to a partial failure in the center's control over regional military units. Moreover, sustained economic hardship could result in increased demonstrations and even sporadic armed revolt, which could lead to major challenges to the regime's authority.

Beyond North Korea-centric scenarios, disruptions or even conflict could break out in East Asia, with significant repercussions for South Korean security and the ROK–U.S. alliance. The rise of China and potential strategic discord with the United States could significantly increase regional tensions. If the Taiwan Straits issue turns into even a limited military exchange between Beijing and Taiwan, Washington (and perhaps even Tokyo under certain circumstances) could be drawn into a highly volatile conflict in the Taiwan Straits. Moreover, as excerpts from the "Nuclear Posture Review" report note, "due to the combination of China's still developing strategic objectives and its ongoing modernization of its nuclear and nonnuclear forces, China is a country that could be involved in an immediate or potential contingency."[32] The Chinese media reported in mid-March of 2002 that Beijing's vice foreign minister told the U.S. ambassador that "China wants to make it very clear that China will never yield to foreign threats, including nuclear blackmail," and Chinese officials also attacked the United States for covering up its support for Taiwan through the "Nuclear Posture Review."[33]

But all of these scenarios are based on internal disruptions in North Korea, which would significantly curtail South Korean and U.S. policy responses. To be sure, in the event of substantial disarray in the North with a breakdown in central political authority, Seoul and Washington have to be very careful about the types of signals they would send to Pyongyang. However, in the absence of real-time and highly accurate all-source and single-source intelligence (particularly in a rapidly evolving political and military situation within North Korea),[34] it would be difficult to take an active position until such time as central political authority were restored. Nevertheless, despite the difficulties imposed by political turmoil in North Korea, the ROK National Command Authority and adjacent organizations must be prepared for such a contingency. To be sure, countermeasures are most probably in place, although they cannot be publicized for obvious operational reasons. Nevertheless, CPXs games, scenario planning, and interagency contingency planning (not to mention high-level attention) are crucial to ensure that the ROK can effectively manage the political, military, economic, and social fallout from a range of potential developments.

Nevertheless, efforts designed to influence a "soft landing" for North Korea are unlikely to result in positive outcomes. The point here is not to denigrate policies that have been implemented thus far in Seoul and Washington but to emphasize that even under the most optimistic of scenarios, North Korea's fundamental behavior to the ROK is unlikely to be significantly altered on the basis of inducements and broader engagement. Moreover, given the increasing probability of some form of collapse in the North, the key political and policy challenge lies in drafting and updating appropriate measures to enhance damage limitation and ensure that the political integrity of the ROK does not suffer undue damages in crisis situations. Being prepared for a full-scale invasion is something the ROK cannot ignore. At the same time, however, preparing for crises or lesser conflicts short of all-out war warrants increasing attention as North Korea enters into a "twilight zone." To do otherwise would be not only militarily self-defeating but also politically inexcusable. In a similar way, North Korea could opt to conduct war to achieve limited strategic aims, such as the capitulation of the South Korean government following Seoul's collapse. If the North Koreans made it very clear that their objective was *not* to engage in a protracted war with U.S. forces, political pressure could mount in Washington to accept the terms of a North Korean peace treaty. Moreover, if an extremely weakened South Korean government or an interim government emerged that was willing to accept North Korean conditions of a truce—for fear that a sustained U.S. effort to recapture Seoul could only materialize by ironically destroying Seoul—Pyongyang's hand would be significantly strengthened.

It is also important to emphasize that the geostrategic environment in which the ROK–U.S. alliance was formed more than fifty years ago has either been transformed significantly or no longer exists. Indeed, the dissolution of the Soviet Union, Moscow's termination of its military alliance with North Korea, China's pragmatic strategy toward the two Koreas, an expanded, more complex threat spectrum on the Korean Peninsula, and South Korea's transformation into the world's twelfth-largest economy (followed by greater defense autonomy), among other factors, have all combined to reorient the strategic identity of the alliance. Already, the alliance is shifting from being predominantly an alliance focused on the North Korean threat to a more flexible alliance that is taking into account the possibility of a very different strategic equation on the peninsula over the next ten to twenty years. The political consensus for maintaining the alliance remains fairly strong, but a new strategic raison d'être must be formulated in order to preserve and strengthen the alliance beyond the scope of a North Korean threat-centric alliance. While the context is different, the April 1996 U.S.–Japan Joint Declaration on Security: Alliance for the 21st Century paved the way for a number of significant developments in postwar Japanese security policy. Equally important, the Joint Declaration laid the foundation for sustaining the alliance even in the aftermath of the dissolution of the former Soviet Union.[35] As South Korea and the United States celebrated their fiftieth anniversary in October 2003, it is fitting to consider a Korean-American version of the 1996 U.S.–Japan Joint Declaration. Or, as one authoritative study on the future of the alliance noted in 1995:

> Depending on the end states that the two countries deem most beneficial to their respective long-term interests, the U.S.-ROK alliance could encompass new forms of cooperation or the countries could become far less interdependent in the future. . . . The need to plan for a very different future—even under conditions of continued North Korean threat—is incontestable. The events in Europe in the late 1980s and early 1990s offer a sobering reminder of the potential for rapid and unanticipated change. In Korea, it is impossible to know when major change—including unification—might occur. But should such change ensue, the peninsular and regional security environment would undergo a major transformation.[36]

Future roles and missions of the ROK–U.S. alliance, if indeed the two countries continue to perceive a need for preserving the alliance well into the first half of the twenty-first century, can only be properly defined on the basis of new strategic guidelines for the alliance. Although the top political leaderships continue to emphasize the importance of sustaining the alliance even after Korean unification, neither Seoul nor Washington has paid enough attention to building a new strategic framework. In part, this absence stems from the persistence of the North Korean threat—albeit in more varied forms than before; but it would be a mistake to assume that the alliance can be sustained without paying greater attention to articulating a new and more credible strategic framework. In light of the sea change in U.S. defense planning and foreign policy priorities after September 11—notably the "Nuclear Posture Review" and the shift to preemptive deterrence—there is a distinct possibility that the ROK may be called upon to assume its "fair share" in the ongoing war against terrorism into the foreseeable future, including more robust commitments for coalition warfare in out-of-area contingencies. Although enlargement of the North Atlantic Treaty Organization has resulted in positive dividends for the transatlantic alliance, it is also noteworthy that the United States has assumed the overwhelming majority of the military load, dating back to the Gulf War, the Bosnian and Kosovo campaigns, and more recently the war against terrorism in Afghanistan. Or as one French defense analyst commented, "without major reform, NATO risks becoming a two-tiered alliance in which the United States does the fighting and the Europeans pick up the garbage."[37]

Reinventing the ROK–U.S. Alliance by Choice

For more than fifty years, stability has been maintained in Northeast Asia by a confluence of factors, but one of the most important elements was the leading security role of the United States. With the economic emergence of the region and the cumulative acquisition of diverse national capabilities, most of the regional actors are in the process of revamping their national security strategies. While China is still in the process of redefining and articulating a comprehensive strategy, it confronts a spectrum of domestic challenges that are unlikely to be easily resolved. But China is in the process of developing a more sophisticated national security strategy. At the same time, while Japan excelled in economic development and technological innovations, strategic thinking was largely confined to the boundaries set forth by the U.S.–Japan security alliance. In the case of South Korea, its principal strategic concern has always been focused on meeting a range of political and military challenges from the North.

As these and other East Asian countries ponder their respective national security strategies over the next two to three decades, the geopolitical, socioeconomic, and technological foundations on which they have to formulate their strategies will differ significantly from the earlier era. With the ending of the Cold War, strategies can no longer be characterized as global, regional, and local. The amalgamation of cooperation and conflict strategems will increasingly complicate, if not obfuscate, traditional state diplomacy. The need to respond to a security threat environment that is increasingly complex, unconventional, and invisible may also accelerate in East Asia, although this is true of other regions as well.

Thus, just as NATO has reengineered itself following the end of the Cold War, the U.S.–ROK alliance will also have to be reconfigured in the postunification era. It is important to define the terms and conditions of unification, given the cumulative implications of a Korea that is unified under the auspices or leadership of South Korea or North Korea. Assuming that Korea is going to be unified under the leadership of the ROK, the process by which unification occurs—through a negotiated political settlement, gradual integration, collapse and absorption, or in the worst-case scenario, through conflict—the political makeup of a unified government and the strategic choices that a unified Korea undertakes are likely to emerge as the principal benchmarks of a unified Korea. From the post–Korean War period until today, however, China did not really factor into South Korea's strategic equation in the absence of official relations, limited economic exchange, the central role of the U.S.–ROK alliance and, for good measure, China's own rigid alliance with North Korea. The collapse of the Soviet Union, China's four modernizations, North Korea's accelerating structural problems, and South Korea's democratization, among other factors, have all combined to bolster the China element within the spectrum of South Korea's looming strategic choices. Historically, Korea had little choice but to pursue a Sinocentric-continental national security strategy; but to everyone's surprise (most of all, to Koreans themselves), Korea successfully adopted an essentially maritime national security strategy principally through its postwar alliance with the United States and strategic alliances with other like-minded states such as Japan and Australia.

To be sure, it could be argued that South Korea's conclusion of a mutual defense treaty with the United States was made more by default than design. But President Syngmann Rhee's decision to actively seek a bilateral defense pact with the United States and thereby place South Korea firmly in the "western" security camp had significant intended and unintended consequences. For the first time in its history, the shaping of Korea's security culture was to be determined in large part by a power other than China, Russia, or Japan. Although North Korea formed alliances with the Soviet Union and China, the American equation forever transformed South Korea's strategic options. A confluence of factors resulted in South Korea's rise from poverty to the world's twelfth-largest trading power and as Asia's third most powerful economy but one of the most important factors was South Korea's adoption of a broad maritime strategy built on the foundations of the U.S.–ROK alliance. While South Korea's alliance with the United States is unlikely to be altered well into the foreseeable future, it is also equally true that South Korea has to begin to think about longer-term foundations for the alliance, particularly if unification occurs rapidly. The contemplation of postunification paths, including possible security arrangements, must be given serious treatment within the broader security community in South Korea, such as redefining a strategic raison d'être for maintaining the U.S.–ROK alliance well into the postunification era while taking into due consideration new geopolitical realities such as China's mid- to long-term calculus vis-à-vis the Korean Peninsula.

How South Korea contemplates its future security options will be determined to a large extent by four main factors: (1) the process by which unification occurs—through a negotiated settlement, by North Korea's collapse and unification by absorption, or variations of the status quo followed by the absorption scenario; (2) the need to formulate a new strategic basis to sustain its alliance with the United States as well as its de facto alliance with Japan in an era of South–North reconciliation, a significant diminution in the North Korean threat, or in the postunification era; (3) defining Korea's longer-term strategic requirements, including key power projection capabilities and desirable force structures; and (4) constructing a new domestic security consensus in light of expected transformations in and around the Korean Peninsula, including generational shifts in Korean politics and the emergence of new security elites.

The reconfiguration of South Korea's longer-term strategic options is emerging as a critical national security and foreign policy task despite the current focus on reengineering South–North relations. Although the debate on the contours of a unified Korea emerges from differing political perspectives, the net consequences are going to reverberate throughout Northeast Asia. At a minimum, a unified Korea must assume a nonnuclear posture, a robust deterrent capability but not one that threatens the regional balance, a free-market system that maintains critical ties with the global economy, and a democratic regime that espouses, guarantees, and promotes universal values. Various options are already being articulated ranging from maintaining the U.S.–ROK alliance, sustaining the transpacific alliance but with a greater emphasis on political rather than military linkages, a multilateral security enclave, or even de facto neutralism. Forging domestic political support for sustaining the U.S.–ROK alliance in the midst of shifting domestic politics, fragile South–North relations, and reconfiguration of great-power strategies toward the Korean Peninsula in the post–Cold War era portends formidable challenges for the ROK in the early years of the twenty-first century. History, however, should not be repeated, since the cumulative consequences of Korea's strategic choice a hundred years ago resulted in dynastic collapse, colonization by Japan, partition, and devastating conflict. Ensuring South Korea's sound strategic choice in the early part of the twenty-first century is the single most important task for all Koreans regardless of their political persuasions.

How other states acted under the shadow of much stronger powers or volatile geopolitical environments—such as Finland, Israel, or even Taiwan—could provide insights into possible strategic paths for Korea. Nevertheless, none of these states, or even others, face Korea's enduring geopolitical challenge: ensuring security, autonomy, prosperity, and stability right in the middle of the convergence of the globe's four most powerful countries. This basic geopolitical structure remains unchanged one hundred years after the collapse of the East Asian world order at the end of the nineteenth century. Sustaining the benefits flowing from a "maritime strategic culture," even as it contends with the rebirth of a continental giant, is likely to foster incrementally greater strategic ambiguity. Should China evolve into a "large Taiwan," China may not pose an insurmountable security dilemma to Korea—that is, in deflecting potential external pressures from China while continuing to retain its central security linkages with the United States. But even a fully democratized and free China cannot but seek to bring the Korean Peninsula once again into its strategic fold. Thus, the new challenge confronting Korea differs profoundly from the security dilemma that unfolded a century ago: preserving Korea's identity and security within the Chinese strategic orbit. Henceforth, the primary question is how Korea can retain relative strategic autonomy without being pulled into a new Chinese strategic orbit. Overcoming geography is impossible in Korea's case, but crafting a nonexclusionary buffer zone is something that Korean strategists have to grapple with, perhaps with greater urgency than at any other time since the collapse of the East Asian international order a century ago.

Seen from this perspective, South Korean defense planners and its political leadership have to take a long look at South Korea's longer-term security options in the early part of the twenty-first century. For the past fifty years, outstanding geopolitical factors placed a premium on maintaining the status quo in the ROK–U.S. alliance. As a result, while decision makers in Seoul and Washington virtually perfected the art of maintaining the alliance, both sides neglected shifting undercurrents that, over time, resulted in inertia rather than "new thinking." To be sure, this is not to downgrade the importance of maintaining the ROK–U.S. alliance; only that the emergence of new political or geostrategic forces dictates the need to fundamentally review all of the core tenets of the alliance. U.S. Secretary of State Colin Powell alluded to such a move after his first meeting with President Roh on February 25, 2003.

> I reaffirmed to him [Roh] the security commitment of the United States to South Korea, a commitment that has been intact for 50 years, and will remain intact, as long as that is needed, and we expect it will be for some time into the future. *But I also said that there is no reason why we shouldn't constantly review, with our South Korean friends, in the closest coordination and full cooperation and transparency, how we could be better guests here in South Korea and what kind of footprint we should have in the country.* But our commitment to the defense of South Korea, and our commitment to maintaining a strong presence in this part of the world, is unchanged and unshakeable, and I believe he was reassured by that.[38] (Emphasis added.)

Although it may be tempting for South Korea to contemplate seriously a strategic future that includes a significantly reduced security dependence on the United States, such a move would entail major costs for the ROK or even a unified Korea under the auspices of the ROK. Beyond the financial, technical, and intelligence burdens that would be placed on South Korea if it chose to downgrade—however incrementally— its alliance with the United States, the most important cost would lie in foreclosing the critical support the United States would most likely play in fostering Korean unification. As the case of the former West Germany aptly illustrated in the period leading up to unification in 1990, it was Bonn's critical alliance with Washington that crystallized and finalized German unification, rather than West Germany's *Ostpolitik* or its growing ties with the former Soviet Union. Notwithstanding South Korea's burgeoning economic relationship with China or the latent promises of Seoul's Sunshine Policy, it is critical for South Korea to remember that the search for greater autonomy must be balanced by a strong dose of realism as it earnestly begins to enter into the unification tunnel. Seen from this perspective, the maintenance of a robust alliance—albeit modernized and more in tune with new political forces—with the United States still remains as the best security guarantee for South Korea in an era of unprecedented domestic and external transformations.

The strategic contours of a unified Korea are likely to be defined significantly by environmental factors (the dissolution of the North Korean threat and the potential rise in major power competition), the degree of coinciding security interests between a unified Korea and the United States (as well as other key U.S. allies in the region), capabilities-based security and defense-planning dynamics of a unified Korea, and the political aspirations of a unified Korea. Other factors will also come into play, such as formidable unification costs, particularly in the advent of a North Korean collapse followed by absorption and the handling of North Korea's robust WMD assets. While all possible permutations of a unified Korea simply cannot be tabulated at this time, five basic security alternatives can be posited in the postunification era: (1) reconfigured ROK–U.S. alliance; (2) strategic autonomy and dissolution of the ROK–U.S. alliance; (3) a new bilateral security arrangement between a unified Korea and regional power other than the United States; (4) neutrality; and (5) a multilateral security arrangement or collective security pact. Other permutations could be considered, but for the most part, a unified Korea would confront five basic security alternatives. Depending on the political makeup of a unified Korea and the process by which unification takes place, the ROK–U.S. alliance could be reconfigured significantly. Domestic political currents in Korea as well as the United States would emerge as critical factors, given that the U.S. Congress may call for an early withdrawal of U.S. forces (particularly ground forces) in the event of a South Korea–led unification process. Table 10.1 illustrates some of the possible alternative security arrangements for a unified Korea.

Assuming that a unified Korea emerges in the throes of a South Korea–led initiative and is supported by the major powers, the most likely security arrangement is a reconfigured U.S.–ROK alliance. If unification occurs through a negotiated political settlement, it is hard to imagine the continued maintenance of the ROK–U.S. alliance, much less any deployment of U.S. forces. A new alliance is a theoretical possibility that could be heightened if the two Koreas are unified through a negotiated settlement. China probably stands out as the most likely candidate that could forge a new alliance with a unified Korea while alliances with the Russian Federation or Japan are probably unlikely. A strictly neutral Korea guaranteed by a four-power agreement could also be considered, although—given the history of Korea at the core of Northeast Asia's strategic interests—it is difficult to imagine a unified Korea that is neutral. A strategically independent Korea that remains unaligned remains an outside possibility, given that new nationalistic sentiments following unification may result in a domestic political consensus that rejects a military or even a close political alliance with a major power. Finally, a unified Korea that remains significantly attached to a multilateral security accord or institution is another possible outcome, assuming that a Northeast Asian security mechanism emerges over time that is able to function along the lines of the OSCE (Organization for Security and Cooperation in Europe).

All of these possible postunification security arrangements entail risks and costs for Korea. A strategically independent Korea may harbor offensive strategic ambitions, such as an independent nuclear arsenal with matching offensive platforms including long-range ballistic missiles, a virtual blue-water navy, and robust air and space platforms. But a unified Korea that pursues the nuclear option will most likely result in a termination of the U.S.–ROK alliance, Japan's nuclear armament, and intense Chinese and Russian suspicions of a nuclear-armed Korea. Combined with the tremendous financial constraints that are likely to confront a unified Korea, a strategi-

Table 10.1

Alternative Security Arrangements for a Unified Korea

ROK–U.S.	Autonomy	New alliance	Neutrality	Multilateral
Robust alliance	Autonomy	ROK–China	Political neutrality	Abrogate bilateral alliance
Reconfigured alliance	Weak autonomy	ROK–Russia	No foreign forces	Maintain bilateral/ multilateral ties
Regional alliance	Strong autonomy	ROK–Japan	Multilateral security linkages	Maintain strictly multilateral ties
				(Reconfigured ARF or new grouping)
Political alliance	Total strategic independence	ROK–major powers	Strict neutrality	Minimal military linkages (PKO)

Source: Adapted from Jonathan D. Pollack and Young Koo Cha, *A New Alliance for the Next Century* (Santa Monica, CA: National Defense Research Institute, RAND, 1995), p. 50.

cally autonomous Korea with WMD ambitions is the worst possible security alternative. Seen from these perspectives, South Korea's current and emerging strategic interests would be best served by "tailoring" the ROK–U.S. alliance to better meet a spectrum of over-the-horizon challenges. Enhanced autonomy, in the final analysis, should be pursued within the context of modernizing the alliance; not discarding the very foundation that has enabled South Korea to emerge as the world's twelfth-largest trading power.

In summary, the rise to the fore of anti-American sentiments in South Korea preceding the December 2002 presidential election should be seen as a major wakeup call for Seoul and Washington. Although the Roh and Bush administrations have taken a number of damage-limitation steps, coupled with more forward-looking management alternatives, the fact remains that mutual confidence had been eroded significantly over the preceding twelve months. From a South Korean perspective, it could be argued that expressions of anti-Americanism should be seen in the context of parallel developments, such as rising South Korean confidence, growing nationalism, and a concomitant desire to minimize fallout from the vestiges of great-power politics. But the critical point here is that South Korea should not tolerate a national security discourse that downgrades or minimizes the very real contribution to stability and prosperity that was possible through the underpinnings of the ROK–U.S. alliance. Expressions of nationalism and growing self-awareness are to be expected of an emerging middle power; but unlike other middle powers, South Korea continues to confront a spectrum of strategic and economic challenges that necessitates robust security ties with the United States and close partnership with Japan.

Whatever the longer-term lessons one can gain from ongoing difficulties and changes in the Korean-American partnership, a fundamental lesson should not be ignored; namely, that there will be strategic consequences if South Korea continues to pursue a more autonomous and exclusionary national security strategy at the expense of its core security relationship with the United States. At the same time, the prevailing conventional wisdom in South Korea that the United States continues to be actively engaged on the Korean Peninsula for its own intrinsic strategic interests may be partially correct, but if a majority of South Koreans no longer welcomes the presence of U.S. forces, there is no doubt that Washington may very well opt to disengage itself formally from South Korea and the Korean Peninsula. Such a turn of events is not very likely, but neither should it be discounted. As the ROK and the United States celebrate the fiftieth anniversary of their unnatural alliance in October 2003, it is fitting to imagine just how the ROK could have evolved in the absence of a security anchor with the United States. Transforming this unnatural alliance into an alliance by choice remains as the most critical task confronting a new generation of Koreans and Americans.

Notes

1. Doug Struck, "Anti-U.S. Mood Lifts South Korean," *Washington Post*, December 20, 2002, p. A1.
2. Howard W. French, "Seoul May Loosen Its Ties to the U.S." *New York Times*, December 20, 2002.
3. Colin L. Powell, Interview on NBC's *Meet the Press with Tim Russert*, December 29, 2002, www.state.gov/secretary/rm/2002/16240pf.htm.
4. "President Discusses Iraq and North Korea with Reporters," December 31, 2001, Office of the Press Secretary, the White House, www.whitehouse.gov/news/releases/2002/12/print/20021231–1.html.
5. "10 Point National Agenda of the Roh Administration," *Joongang Ilbo*, January 5, 2003.
6. The main cause of the outbreak of anti-American demonstrations and candlelight vigils in the fall of 2002 was the accidental death of two South Korean middle-school students by a USFK vehicle during military exercises. In particular, the acquittal of the two soldiers involved in the accident prompted mass protests by a number of NGOs, civic groups, and the media.
7. "U.S.-South Korea Alliance Will Endure, U.S. Commander Says," U.S. Department of State, International Information Program, usinfo.state/regional/ea/easec/laporte0315.htm.
8. In a ten-point statement released by Cha and Lawless, the two sides agreed to recognize South Korea's increasingly robust capabilities, the need to adapt the alliance to changing strategic realities, enhancing cooperation on key facets of South Korea's force modernization programs, expanding the role of the ROK armed forces for defense of the peninsula and beyond, and to relocate the main headquarters of the USFK from central Seoul. See "GIs to Be Realigned, Not Removed," *Korea Herald* (April 10, 2003).
9. Foreign Minister Yoon Young Kwan, as he assumed his position on February 28, 2003, emphasized the primary importance of a "post–Cold War mindset," since such a perception was essential to bringing to closure the status of the Korean Peninsula as the last remaining Cold War frontier. Despite the increasing use of the phrase "post–Cold War mindset or mentality," it continues to be ill defined. For the most part, however, advocates of a "post–Cold War mindset" usually refer to the need to perceive inter-Korean relations, in particular the nature of

the North Korean military threat, in a holistic sense rather than through the lenses of *Realpolitik*. Since the late 1990s, the phrase has been widely used in the media and the academic and policy-making communities as a code word for the hard-line postures toward North Korea advocated by conservatives and "right wing" figures and organizations.

10. Throughout the heated 2002 campaign, then-candidate Roh Moo Hyun of the ruling party and Lee Hoi Chang of the opposition party staked out contending positions on South–North relations. Roh accused Lee of pursuing confrontational tactics with the North and argued that the election was about choosing the path to war or peace. He asserted that if Lee won the presidency, war tensions would rise on the Korean Peninsula, followed by inevitable economic repercussions such as the flight of capital ("Selected Speeches by President Roh Moo Hyun Before the Inauguration, January 12, 2002," www.president.go.kr/app/pre_speech). Subsequently, the then-president-elect began to stress a more balanced view on key developments on the Korean Peninsula. In a speech delivered a few days before his inauguration, Roh stated in part that "we don't want war nor a North Korean collapse. However, North Korea must also realize that there is no alternative but to undertake reforms and openness." He went on to note that "there are some who are voicing their concerns about the ROK-U.S. alliance, including a misunderstanding that our people are against the deployment of U.S. forces [in South Korea]. But this is not true ("Selected Speeches by President Roh Moo Hyun Before the Inauguration, January 20, 2002," www.president.go.kr/app/pre_speech).

11. "Roh Moo Hyun's Inauguration Speech, February 25, 2003," www.bbc.com.

12. "'Don't Go Too Far,' South Korea Leader Tells Bush," www.timesonline.co.uk/article/20030305.

13. "Bush Says U.S. Committed to Peace, South Korea's Security," *U.S. Department of State International Information Programs*, February 20, 2002, www.usinfo.state.gov/regional/ea/easec/rokpg.htm.

14. Marc Grossman, "Enduring Alliances in the Face of New Threats," Speech at the DACOR Annual Meeting, Washington, DC, October 12, 2001, www.state.gov/p/6583.htm.

15. Statement of General Thomas A. Schwartz, Commander in Chief United Nations Command/Combined Forces Command and Commander, United States Forces in Korea Before the 107th Congress Senate Armed Services Committee, March 5, 2002, http://usinfo.state.gov/regional/ea/easec/schartwz0306.htm.

16. *Han Mi Dongmeng gwa Ju Han Mi Goon* (The Korean-American Alliance and the U.S. Forces in Korea) (Seoul: Ministry of National Defense, April 2002), p. 46. Lately, the term *main enemy* (or *jujeok* in Korean) has generated vigorous debate within South Korea. The Ministry of National Defense (MND) since the late 1980s has referred to North Korea as the ROK's "main enemy," and North Korea has maintained that unless South Korea stops referring to the North as their main enemy, progress in inter-Korean talks can only be stymied. After rancorous debate within South Korea, the MND stated in March that it will postpone the publication of the annual *Defense White Paper* until the changeover in government in February 2003. Supporters of Kim Dae Jung's "Sunshine Policy" have argued, in the main, that referring to North Korea as the main enemy only hardens North Korea's position, while proponents of a hard-line posture toward North Korea continue to argue that unless North Korea also rejects its stated aim of communizing the South, there is no reason for South Korea to stop referring to the North as the main enemy.

17. While the broader East–West conflict and the U.S.–Soviet conflict in particular ended more than a decade ago, the Cold War between the two Koreas persists in the absence of a formal peace treaty that would bring formal closure to the Korean War (1950–53). Thus, while the global Cold War has been terminated, the Cold War remains very much alive on the Korean Peninsula.

18. *2000 Defense White Paper* (Seoul: Ministry of National Defense, 2000); available at www.mnd.go.kr/mnden/emainindex.html.

19. *2001 Defense of Japan* (Tokyo: Urban Connections with permission from Self-Defense Agency, 2001), p. 29.

20. Zalmay Khalilzad et al., *The United States and Asia: Toward a New U.S. Strategy and Force Posture* (Santa Monica, CA: Project Air Force, RAND, MR-1315–AF, 2001), p. xiii.

21. Khalilzad et al., *The United States and Asia*, p. xii.

22. There are virtually hundreds of Web sites dedicated to the promotion of various levels of anti-Americanism and the withdrawal of U.S. forces from South Korea. Netizen groups such as the "Movement for the Eradication of Crimes Committed by U.S. Forces in South Korea" and many others publicly call for the immediate withdrawal of U.S. forces and abrogation of the ROK–U.S. defense treaty. While Internet polls are highly unreliable, one online poll, conducted by a citizen's group called Song-al, noted in a November 11, 2001, posting that out of 111 primary, junior high school, and high school students who were asked the question "Who do you think is the worst after the U.S. terrorist attacks?" respondents answered as follows: (1) Osama bin Laden (57 respondents, 51%), (2) the United States (33 respondents, 29%), (3) film directors who make violent movies (9 respondents, 8%), (4) Afghanistan (8 respondents, 7%), and (5) Israel (4 respondents, 3%). Key issues that drive anti-Americanism in South Korea include such factors as the presence of U.S. forces, the Status of Forces Agreement (SOFA) as a major impediment toward South–North reconciliation and unification, and overall economic, military, technological, and even cultural dependency, and so on.

23. *Joong-ang Ilbo*, August 6, 2001, http://service.joins.com. August 8, 2001.

24. *Joong-ang Ilbo*, June 12, 2001, http://service.joins.com. June 12, 2001.

25. "President Bush and President Kim Dae Jung Meet in Seoul," Office of the Press Secretary, the White House, February 20, 2002, www.whitehouse.gov/news/releases/2002/02/print/2000220–1html.

26. "Statement by the President," Office of the Press Secretary, the White House, June 13, 2001, www.whitehouse.gov/news/releases/2001/06/20010611–4.html.

27. "U.S. to Restart Talks with N. Korea Soon Without Any Preconditions," *Korea Herald*, June 10, 2002.

28. Moon Ihlwhan and Stan Crock, "Don't Expect a Breakthrough Between Washington and North Korea," *Businessweek online*, July 2, 2001, www.businessweek.com/magazine/content/01_27/c3739171.htm.

29. "Above Anti-Americanism," *Korea Herald*, February 22, 2002.

30. For additional details, see Chung Min Lee, "North Korea's Missiles: Strategic Implications and Policy Responses," *Pacific Review* 14, no. 1 (2001): 104–7.

31. Donald H. Rumsfeld, *Report on Allied Contributions to the Common Defense* (Washington, DC: U.S. Department of Defense, March 2001), p. II-9.

32. Donald H. Rumsfeld, "Nuclear Posture Review" (excerpts), submitted to the U.S. Congress on December 31, 2001, www.globalsecurity.org/wmd/library/policy/dod/npr.htm.

33. "China Bluntly Rebukes U.S. Over Nuclear Policy Review," *New York Times* (March 17, 2002), www.nytimes.com/2002/03/17/international/asia/17CHIN.html.

34. An intelligence source from one intelligence discipline is referred to as "single-source intelligence" and SOF-related examples of intelligence discipline includes HUMINT, SIGINT, COMINT, ELINT, FISINT, IMINT, and TECHINT. For additional details, see Headquarters, Department of the Army, *FM 34–36 Special Operations Forces Intelligence and Electronic Warfare Operations* (Washington, DC: Department of the Army, September 30, 1991), pp. 1–5, 1–6.

35. The April 17, 1996 U.S.–Japan joint declaration announced, in part, that "the President and the Prime Minister reiterated the significant value of the Alliance between Japan and the United States. They reaffirmed that the U.S.-Japan security relationship, based on the *Treaty of Mutual Cooperation and Security the United States of America and Japan*, remains the cornerstone for achieving common security objectives, and for maintaining a stable and prosperous environment for the Asia-Pacific region as we enter the twenty-first century." For the full text, see www.mofa.go.jp/region/n-america/us/security/security.html. While this particular segment reaffirmed the long-standing position of the two governments, the declaration created a frame-

work from which the United States and Japan were able to extricate key strategic dividends. For the United States, it continued to anchor Japan firmly into the U.S. security framework at a time when Japan's growing defense capabilities could result in greater security autonomy. Japan's close security partnership with the United States also enables Tokyo to play a critical role as a central buffer between the United States and an increasingly self-confident and potentially aggressive China. Conversely, Japan also gains from revamping the alliance into one with de facto global underpinnings while enabling it to assume a more robust security role without damaging the prevailing regional strategic balance.

36. Jonathan D. Pollack and Cha Young Koo, *A New Alliance for the Next Century* (Santa Monica, CA: NDRI-RAND, 1995), p. 28.

37. Comment by Julian Lindley-French, quoted in Peter Finn, "Military Gap Grows Between U.S., NATO Allies," *Washington Post*, May 19, 2002, p. A22.

38. "Press Conference by Secretary Colin L. Powell, Seoul, Korea, February 25, 2003," www.state.gov/secretary/rm/2003/17933pf.htm. See also "Powell Reaffirms U.S. Commitment to S. Korea's Security," March 28, 2003, www.usembassy.state.gov/seoul/wwwh41a5.html.

11

Brothers versus Friends

Inter-Korean Reconciliation and Emerging Anti-Americanism in South Korea

Kim Sung-han

Brothers versus Friends

During the Cold War, South Korea and the United States maintained a staunch alliance against North Korea's communist regime. Owing to the very nature of North Korea, neither ally had any reason to doubt the resolve of the other. However, the demise of the Cold War era enabled North Korea and the United States to explore a new relationship very different from the one that had previously existed. In the early 1990s, a new environment emerged, in which South Korea–U.S. and inter-Korean relations were affected by the changing diplomacy between Pyongyang and Washington. A delicate "triangular relationship" thus emerged between North Korea, South Korea, and the United States as Washington began to involve deeply itself in the North Korean nuclear question as part of its post–Cold War global strategy.

The U.S.–North Korea Agreed Framework, concluded in Geneva on October 21, 1994, was designed to reduce the Cold War structure on the Korean peninsula. One assumption was that if the accord helped ease tensions drastically, then the value of the Korea–U.S. alliance might be lost. But this assumption was too simple to be persuasive, because there could be various factors compelling the two countries to prolong their alliance even if the nuclear issue were resolved. In addition, the June 2000 inter-Korean summit meeting created a controversy on whether tension reduction on the Korean Peninsula would be compatible with the existence of the Republic of Korea (ROK)–U.S. alliance. South Koreans began to think of the relationship between inter-Korean relations and ROK–U.S. relations. This means that they have begun to think of the relationship between "brothers" and "friends."

A variety of questions were raised: (1) Does the United States welcome inter-Korean reconciliation and cooperation or want North Korea to remain a rogue state? (2) is there any need for South Korea and the United States to continue to rely on each other even after the threat from North Korea disappears? and (3) why do the two allies not replace their existing relations with new ones to meet the new requirements of international relations?

In July–October 2002 the Pew Research Center and *International Herald Tribune* conducted a survey of more than 38,000 people in 44 countries called "What the World Thinks in 2002."[1] The survey found that since 2000, favorable ratings for the United States had fallen in 20 of the 27 countries for which the previous data were available. What caught our eyes was that favorable ratings for the United States among the U.S. allies—the United Kingdom, Germany, Japan, and South Korea—had also fallen by 8 percent (from 83 to 75 percent), 17 percent (from 78 to 61 percent), 5 percent (from 77 to 72 percent), and 5 percent (from 58 to 53 percent), respectively, than in the year 2000, or two years earlier. It was notable that South Korea showed the lowest favorable ratings among the U.S. allies.

According to a poll conducted by Gallup Korea in December 2002, however, the majority (54.8 percent) of South Koreans (1,054 individuals) surveyed answered that they did not want U.S. troops to leave, while 31.7 percent agreed.[2] The remaining 13.5 percent did not reply. A problem is that the rate of support for the American military presence has dropped significantly from ten years ago. In a survey conducted by the same organization, the percentage of those in favor of the withdrawal of U.S. troops rose by some 10 points, from 21.3 to 31.7 percent, while the percentage of those who wanted U.S. soldiers to stay decreased by some 8 points, from 62.2 to 54.8 percent. This phone survey was conducted on December 14, when anti-U.S. sentiment peaked as tens of thousands of citizens joined candlelight vigils across the country to protest the way the U.S. was dealing with an incident in June 2002, when two fourteen-year-old Korean schoolgirls were fatally run over by a U.S. armored vehicle.

On the other hand, many South Korean people tend to believe that North Korea's nuclear weapons, if any, will be aiming at Americans or Japanese, not its southern "brethren." At the inter-Korean cabinet-level talks in Seoul on January 22 to 23, 2003, North Korea's chief delegate Kim Young-Song said, "At this moment, all inter-Korean projects face grave obstacles posed by outside forces which do not like us to join our hands. . . . the North and South should uphold the great cause of national independence and crush attempts by outside forces seeking to meddle in intra-national affairs and forge ahead, without interruption, with all issues including economic projects which have been agreed upon by the two sides."[3] This was a prime example of North Korea's propaganda strategy to drive a wedge between Seoul and Washington.

Can we say, then, that the South Korean people are facing a dilemma in which they do not know which to choose and how to deal with their brothers in the North, who share their blood, and their friends across the Pacific, who shed blood together during the Korean and Vietnam Wars?

Inter-Korean Summit and ROK–U.S.–DPRK Triangle

Inter-Korean Summit

The inter-Korean summit meeting in June 2000 provided the two Koreas with a hope of resolving the Korean question by themselves and of overcoming the "abnormal" circumstances in which the United States and North Korea were involved in the discussions concerning the Korean question. In particular, the first article of the North–South Joint Declaration of June 2000 created an atmosphere for North–South dialogue and reconciliation by declaring the importance of the "independent" resolution of the unification issue.

Korean peninsular issues can be categorized into two areas: inter-Korean issues and international issues. North–South reconciliation, the separated families issue, and economic cooperation belong to the first category, while the weapons of mass destruction (WMD) issue, establishment of a peaceful regime on the peninsula, and the future status of U.S. armed forces in Korea belong to the second. The United States has always been involved in Korea-related international issues. The United States and North Korea issued a joint statement on October 12, 2000, heralding the opening of a new chapter in relations between the two countries. The two sides agreed to exert every effort to put an end to their decades-old hostility and establish a new bilateral relationship. Following this significant step toward improving U.S.-North Korean relations, North Korean leader Kim Jong Il announced that North Korea would not carry out further ballistic missile testing.

The delicate "triangular relationship" among the two Koreas and the United States thus became more complicated. To adapt to the new circumstances, it was necessary to develop fresh ways of thinking.

Perceptions of the Triangular Relationship

How did the United States, or the Clinton administration, perceive North–South relations? Right after the inter-Korean summit, the United States probably thought that the North Korea–U.S. axis had been replaced by the inter-Korean axis for the Korean question and that it could lose its leadership role in dealing with the Korean issue. in a situation where the United States tried to resolve the North Korean issue on the basis of its own policy priority, or "nonproliferation," South Korea–U.S. relations could have come under stress if South Korea and the United States competed in fostering relations with North Korea.

Then how did South Koreans perceive North Korea–U.S. relations? It was quite a relief that North Korea, which had not spared any effort to alienate South Korea for so many years, now recognized the importance of South Korean participation in efforts to solve outstanding inter-Korean issues. South Korea saw North Korea's economic problems as unsolvable without an improvement in overall North–South relations. South Korea, however, also found it difficult to engage with the North if North Korea–U.S. relations remain stagnant due to a deadlock in North Korea's WMD-related negotiations with the United States.

Last, North Korea's perception of South Korea–U.S. relations was complex. North Korea, which had branded trilateral South Korea–U.S.–Japan cooperation on North Korea policy a collaboration of foreign powers, was defensive about South Korea–U.S. cooperation aimed at stopping the North's development of WMD. North Korea would focus efforts on improving relations with the United States for the time being and hoped that the South would be instrumental in blocking U.S. pressure that might arise during North Korea–U.S. negotiations. North Korea thought that it did not have to raise its voice against U.S. forces stationed in South Korea, which might help South Korea and the United States reaffirm the necessity of the South Korea–U.S. alliance. It would be to the North's advantage to have an increasing number of "anti-American activists" in South Korea speak on its behalf.

Triangular Game After the Summit

Before the inter-Korean summit meeting in June of 2000, the two Koreas appeared to be competing against each other to form a coalition with the United States. The United States (the Clinton administration), on the other hand, was tempted to form coalitions with both North and South Korea. South Korea's Kim Young Sam administration (1993–98) thus made it clear that progress in North Korea–U.S. relations should not hinder South Korea–U.S. relations in any way. This was an effort to deter the creation of a "double coalition" by the United States with the two Koreas.

The Kim Dae Jung administration, in contrast, signaled its intention of playing a leading role in dealing with inter-Korean issues. President Kim Dae Jung noted that the "abnormal" aspects of North Korea–U.S. relations, which created problems such as the WMD issue, had a negative impact on South Korea–U.S. relations as well, and that the normalization of U.S.–North Korean relations was thus essential. Strange as it may seem, North Korea agreed to the summit talks because of South Korea's efforts to normalize inter-Korean relations.

However, the triangular relationship began to take a new shape after the summit meeting. South Korea and the United States started to "compete" to reach North Korea. The Clinton administration, which had appeared to be worried about losing its leadership role after the inter-Korean summit meeting, invited a North Korean special envoy to Washington, where the U.S.–North Korea joint communiqué was adopted. President Clinton even tried but failed—because U.S. presidential elections became controversial in November 2000—to visit Pyongyang for a historic summit with the North Korean leader Kim Jong Il.

The South Korea–U.S. relationship could have been under stress, however, if South Korea and the United States further competed to maintain the leadership role in resolving the Korean question. Accelerated progress either in inter-Korean relations or in U.S.–North Korean relations might have become a burden on South Korea–U.S. relations unless they were mutually harmonized.

Thus, the three players in this triangular game had to achieve "Pareto optimality" by searching for ways to ensure that bilateral relations within the larger triangular game would not be harmed. Whether such bilateral relationships can progress without damaging each other would depend on North Korea. Since the North did not "change," however, domestic support for relations with North Korea both in South Korea and in the United States waned.

The "comprehensive and integrated approach" (or the "Perry process") toward the North aimed at gradually reaching a win-win solution through concessions from each party: North Korea ceases to engage in the WMD program by being assured of its system's survival, while the United States lifts sanctions and normalizes its relationship with North Korea. In addition, South Korea takes the initiative for cooperation with the North, which would lead to peaceful coexistence, not absorption. The problem was that North Korea did not have any intention of forgoing its nuclear development programs.[4] But many the South Korean people and probably their political leadership believed, at the end of 2000, that President Clinton would have to go to Pyongyang for a "grand bargain," and they later contrasted President George W. Bush with his predecessor, who seemed to have understood the Korean situation better.

The Bush Administration and the Emergence of a New Game

"American Internationalism" After September 11

"Offensive Realism"

The presidential victory of the Republican Party, which had branded Clinton's North Korea policy as "crazy," was a disaster from North Korea's point of view and that of the school of engagement in South Korea. The Bush administration called for peace through strength and took a unilateralist position on international issues under the leitmotif "American internationalism." It focused on multilateral cooperation (through the United Nations or regional organizations) only as a way of complementing its unilateralism. This was labeled "unimultilateralism," in which the United States pays attention to multilateralism only when U.S. unilateralism is unworkable. However, the Bush administration believed that while cooperation via multilateral organizations was a good way to build the groundwork for antiterror activities, it tended to slow things down and thus would necessarily place limits on Washington's multilateral cooperation efforts.[5]

It seems that the United States is ready to "act alone" when multilateral efforts have failed. Richard Perle, president of the Defense Policy Advisory Board, has made it clear that the United States is prepared to act alone to protect itself from terrorist attack. Earlier, U.S. Deputy Defense Secretary Paul Wolfowitz said there could be no single all-embracing coalition. He said what was needed were different alliances suited to different missions. Some allies might join with the United States publicly, while others might choose quieter, more discreet forms of cooperation.[6] Anyhow, the September 11 terror attacks exposed the vulnerability of the United States to the outside world, while at the same time showing the real nature of the U.S. military power through the Afghan war.

In this light, the United States has shifted from the "offensive liberalism" of the Clinton era to "offensive realism" under the Bush administration (see Table 11.1). Former President Clinton seemed to believe in a liberal grand strategy, thereby taking an interest in U.S. initiatives for resolving humanitarian crises. It was offensive liber-

Table 11.1

Two Types of Realism and Liberalism

	Peace through strength (skepticism re the UN)	Willingness to intervene in humanitarian crises	Unilateralism (U.S. ready to act alone)
Defensive realism	3	2	2
Offensive realism	4	1	4
Defensive liberalism	1	3	1
Offensive liberalism	2	4	3

Key: Range of commitment from 4 (highest) to 1 (lowest).

alism in the sense that it was aimed to nurture and disseminate "democratic peace" around the world, even through military means, as was done in stopping the humanitarian crisis in Kosovo. A typical defensive liberalism usually favors multilateral and/or regional organizations and tends to avoid largely unilateral military action such as that which was taken in Iraq.

On the other hand, after the September 11 terror attacks, President Bush seemed to be taking a stance of offensive realism, which is different from the defensive realism of previous Republican administrations. Defensive realism, which is frequently referred to as "structural realism," came on the scene in the late 1970s with the appearance of Waltz's theory of international politics. Waltz assumes that states aim merely to survive and that they seek security above all else. Nevertheless, he maintains that the structure of the international system forces great powers to pay careful attention to the balance of power, because power is the best means for survival. The anarchic nature of international relations encourages states to behave defensively and to maintain rather than upset the balance of power.[7]

The Bush administration was trying to change the direction of U.S. foreign policy from offensive liberalism to defensive realism by criticizing the Clinton administration's foreign policy for having been too "interventionist" without having geopolitical priorities—for instance, in Somalia, Bosnia, Kosovo, Iraq, and so on. The Bush administration seems to believe that Clinton's "liberal strategy" would have turned out to be unsuccessful due to the absence of geopolitical priorities.

However, the war against terrorism after September 11 has been pushing the United States to take a stance of offensive realism. For defensive realists, the international structure gives states little incentive to seek additional increments of power; instead, it pushes them to maintain the existing balance of power. Offensive realists, on the other hand, believe that status quo powers are rarely found in world politics; they look for opportunities to gain power at the expense of rivals and to take advantage of those situations where the benefits are likely to outweigh the costs. They believe that the international system forces great powers to maximize their relative power because that is the best way to maximize their security.

The United States may have realized that it needed to maximize its power relative to that of the other great powers. It withdrew from the Anti-Ballistic Missile (ABM) Treaty in June 2002; confirmed its more aggressive nuclear posture in the "Nuclear Posture Review" report; and is poised to launch a full-scale attack on Iraq despite the criticisms from the international community.

In this light, it was practically impossible to expect the majority of the South Korean people to understand what had made the offensive realist policy of the United States possible. On the contrary, they began to suspect that the United States might be using North Korea to justify a missile defense system or its counterproliferation policies.

"Preemptive Attack" and North Korea

The September 11 terror attacks incurred a large number of casualties despite the fact that they were carried out without advanced technology but by conventional means. In this light, the attacks further heightened concern that, should terrorists launch an attack using WMD such as chemical and/or biological weapons, the world could suffer a catastrophe that incurs casualties hundreds of times or more greater than those of September 11.[8]

An open society like the United States is particularly vulnerable to WMD terrorism. Information on nuclear, chemical, and biological weapons is readily available on the Internet and in many "how-to" books. There is increasing evidence of illegal trafficking in nuclear materials. Above all, a number of countries hostile to the United States are known to be developing WMD and missile capabilities, and some are suspected of supporting terrorist groups.[9]

Should these countries lose control over terrorist groups after providing them with WMD material or technology, or should support countries themselves become embroiled in a civil war or political confusion, the danger of catastrophic terrorism will increase. Seen through this prism, the rationale for pursuing a missile defense system to counter WMD-loaded ballistic missile attacks against the U.S. homeland, U.S. forces stationed overseas, and U.S. allies has been strengthened. The second stage of the U.S. war against terrorism after the Afghan war is thus focused on preventing terrorism using weapons of mass destruction—nuclear, chemical, or biological.

Against this backdrop, President Bush gave an address at West Point on June 1, 2002, that should have received more attention than it did. Marking a dramatic break with doctrines that have governed more than a half-century of U.S. foreign and military policy, he declared that new threats require the United States to adopt a new policy of "preemptive action."

"Deterrence—the promise of massive retaliation against nations—means nothing against shadowy terrorist networks with no nation or citizens to defend," he said. "Containment is not possible when unbalanced dictators with weapons of mass destruction can deliver those weapons on missiles or secretly provide them to terrorist allies," he argued. In line with this new Bush doctrine, the White House has drawn up a new national security strategy that will enable the United States to launch preemptive military strikes against groups or countries that pose a threat to America and its allies.[10]

More than fifty years ago, at the beginning of the Cold War, the National Security Council explicitly rejected the notion of "preventive" or "preemptive" war, calling it "repugnant" to American values and principles. That policy stood the United States in good stead for decades and played a crucial role in preventing the Cold War from turning into a hot war.[11]

If the doctrine of deterrence was sufficient to defeat the former Soviet Union, why would it not work against Iraq or North Korea? U.S. officials argue that terrorist groups and rogue states are not like the former Soviet Union, governed by predictable and logical principles of self-preservation. Precisely because the usual calculus of self-interest is meaningless to them, the United States cannot afford to wait for an actual incursion before it acts. The best defense here is a good offense.[12]

The argument is persuasive, but only in special circumstances and only if the new security doctrine is applied with great caution and circumspection. It should not be interpreted to give the United States carte blanche authority to intervene wherever it pleases without clear evidence.

But, the problem is that President Bush's new security doctrine and its rather "negative" repercussions in the international community have put North Korea in the position of an underdog who, from the perspective of many South Koreans, might be less evil than the United States. It was very difficult for the South Korean people to understand that the United States is at war against terrorists who do not believe in "deterrence." On the contrary, South Koreans gave credit to North Korea's argument that the United States violated the Geneva Agreed Framework (Article 3, clause 1) by discarding negative security assurance (NSA) to North Korea.

Highly Enriched Uranium Nuke Problem: Confessional Diplomacy Blocked?

In early October 2002, U.S. Assistant Secretary of State James A. Kelly visited Pyongyang to begin talks on a wide range of issues, including the reduction of North Korea's nuclear, missile, and conventional armaments. During those talks, Kelly and his delegation revealed recently acquired information indicating that North Korea had been running a program for several years to enrich uranium for nuclear weapons, in violation of the U.S–North Korea Agreed Framework and other agreements. Surprisingly, however, North Korean officials acknowledged that they did indeed have a nuclear development program and considered the Agreed Framework nullified.

Before this occurrence, the Bush administration had been demanding that North Korea comply with the International Atomic Energy Agency (IAEA) safeguards agreement and accept "special inspection" by the end of this year at the latest. The Agreed Framework provides that North Korea must come into full compliance with its safeguards agreement with the IAEA when a significant portion of the light water reactor (LWR) project is completed but before delivery of key nuclear components. As for major milestones in the LWR project, completion of the significant portion of the first LWR is expected in the first half of 2005.

The KEDO (Korean Peninsula Energy Development Organization) construction schedule assumes a couple of months or so between the completion of a significant portion and the shipment of the components, but it is likely to be a significantly longer time, which could be very disruptive for the whole process. The best compliance review took two years in South Africa, while unofficial IAEA estimates are as high as three to four years for North Korea. In the case of South Africa, it actually took three years from the time inspections were agreed to under the Non-Proliferation Treaty (NPT) until the process was completed. The North thus had to be convinced to start the compliance process soon to avoid the schedule delay. North Korea refused, however.

To make matters worse, North Korea's clandestine highly enriched uranium (HEU) nuclear development program has been disclosed. North Korea now has the additional burden of dismantling the nuclear program to enrich uranium for nuclear weapons in a prompt and verifiable manner. President Bush, President Kim Dae Jung, and Prime Minister Junichiro Koizumi in their trilateral summit meeting on October 27, 2002, called on North Korea to dismantle the program and come into full compliance with all its international commitments, including the Agreed Framework, the NPT, North Korea's IAEA safeguards agreement, and the South–North Joint Declaration on Denuclearization of the Korean Peninsula.

But what had motivated North Korea to acknowledge the existence of a secret nuclear weapons program was still somewhat unclear. There must be a particular reason for North Korea to take the risk of setting the rest of the world against it, especially at a time when it was becoming more dependent on outside help for food and energy.

Some say that it was related to North Korea's trend toward "confessional diplomacy." Their point was that Pyongyang's acknowledgment of the secret nuclear program appeared to have been intended to convey the message that Kim Jong Il was now a new kind of leader who no longer resorts to secrecy. The same approach was already tried in September, when Kim Jong Il, faced with Japanese demands for an explanation for the disappearance of eleven Japanese citizens in the late 1970s, apologized for what he acknowledged were official kidnappings. But, it is hard to say that North Korea tried the same approach or repeated the same mistake to the United States while the confession to Japan was producing a lot of criticisms among the Japanese public against the North Korean regime.

The most plausible explanation is that Pyongyang reached the conclusion that securing nuclear weapons was necessary not only to ensure the survival of its regime but also as an indispensable bargaining chip in dealing with the United States. With the time approaching under the Geneva Agreed Framework to comply with the IAEA safeguards agreement and to lay bare North Korea's past nuclear activities, which presumably included the clandestine production of plutonium, Pyongyang must have felt that it needed another nuclear weapons program in order to be taken seriously by the United States.

In addition, Pyongyang did not necessarily choose the timing of its admission or confession. Presented with irrefutable evidence by visiting U.S. special envoy James Kelly, North Korea must have decided to take the gamble of trying to turn adversity into advantage. Pyongyang must have concluded that, if it could no longer hide its new nuclear program, it would use it instead to draw the United States into talks and make a big deal.

The United States has maintained a very firm position by saying that it will not resume a dialogue with North Korea until the North dismantles its nuclear program. But the "progressive" forces in South Korea tend to believe that the Bush administration, without providing a "smoking gun" for HEU, has blocked North Korea's sincere diplomacy of confession for its own strategic purposes—that is, to make North Korea remain a "rogue state," which would thus serve to justify the U.S. drive for a missile defense system.

Triangular Structure

The triangular diplomatic structure was thus changed after the Bush administration came in. To grasp the nature of these triangular relations, it is important to understand the interrelationship between two sides of the triangle, namely U.S.-North Korean and inter-Korean relations; and to review changes and tasks in U.S.-South Korean relations.

Policy Structure of Inter-Korean Relations

As seen in Table 11.2, North Korea's top priority in its policy toward South Korea is regime survival, which would prevent the deepening economic deterioration from developing into a political threat to the Kim Jong Il regime. In order to achieve this goal, the North Korean regime has set as its objective the overcoming of its own economic difficulties.

The policy means available to North Korea include North Korea's reconciliation with South Korea and Kim Jong Il's "improved" image, through which North Korea tries to maximize economic assistance from South Korea as well as the international community. North Korea assumes that the most effective tool is the U.S.-North Korean relationship. North Korea's discussion with the United States, regardless of its pace of development, can be regarded as an important means for North Korea, mainly because United States recognizes North Korea as a negotiating partner in various kinds of talks at the global, regional, and peninsular levels.

On the other hand, South Korea's goal in its North Korea policy is to achieve peaceful coexistence of the two Koreas, thereby ultimately reaching peaceful reunification of the peninsula. Thus, the South Korean objective of its North Korea policy comprises the dismantling of the Cold War structure on the peninsula.

The policy means available to South Korea include its economic capability, even if reduced by its financial crisis, to assist its northern brethren, because South Korea can still provide economic and humanitarian assistance to North Korea. South Korea's

Table 11.2

Inter-Korean Policy Structure

	North Korea's Policy toward the South	South Korea's Policy toward the North
Goal	Regime survival	Peaceful coexistence
Objective	Overcoming economic hardship	Dismantling Cold War structure
Means	Inter-Korean reconciliation Kim Jong Il's new image U.S.–North Korea relations	Economic superiority Diplomatic relations with four powers ROK–U.S. alliance

willingness to improve inter-Korean relations and its diplomatic relationship with all of the four surrounding powers can be regarded as another means. And the South Korea–U.S. alliance itself may be the most powerful means that South Korea has, because North Korea feels the alliance as a big political burden it has to overcome, particularly in negotiating with the United States.

Policy Structure of U.S.–North Korea Relations

North Korea's nuclear development program and ballistic missile threat stand out as the most serious proliferation challenges in the era of terror. The U.S. policy toward the Korean Peninsula in general and North Korea in particular is part of a larger framework of global and Korean strategic interests. At the global level, the United States must prevent the spread of WMD among the nations that do not already possess them. At the level of the Korean Peninsula, the United States must reduce the tension between the two Koreas in order to prevent the outbreak of a civil war.

In contrast with geopolitical interests of the United States, the primary task facing North Korea is to maintain its state system and regime survival. Concrete policies must be implemented to maintain the North Korean socialist system. Thus, the North Korean authorities are seeking normalization of its relations with the United States in order to make the Kim Jong Il regime durable by removing security threats from the United States and resolving its current economic difficulties.

In dealing with the nuclear and missile issues, the United States found it necessary to engage North Korea in the international community, insisting that North Korea observe international norms and become more interdependent with other countries. If North Korea resists this process, however, the Bush administration seems to believe that a "soft collapse" of North Korea is a viable option.

As shown in Table 11.3, the United States has various means of achieving its goals. Among others, providing food assistance to North Korea is regarded as a meaningful one, since North Korea is suffering from a serious food shortage. In addition, the United States can lift economic sanctions against North Korea, which would indicate

Table 11.3

U.S.–North Korea Policy Structure

	U.S. policy toward North Korea	North Korean Policy toward the United States
Goal	WMD nonproliferation and Northeast Asian order	Regime survival
Objective	Engaging North Korea ("soft collapse"?)	Normalizing NK–U.S. relations
Means	Food assistance Lifting economic sanctions Eliminating North Korea from list of terrorism sponsors Preemptive strikes	WMD "card" and WMD Geneva Agreement Inter-Korean talks ("independent resolution") Threatening South Korea

the removal of North Korea from the list of terrorism-sponsoring countries. "Preemptive strike" can also be added as a new security doctrine of the United States.

For North Korea, on the other hand, the primary means available is to utilize the WMD "card" and/or WMD themselves. In addition, North Korea could threaten South Korea or explore "independent" resolution of the Korean question with South Korea when its negotiation with the United States reaches a stalemate.

Policy Structure of ROK–U.S. Relations

As seen in Table 11.4, the strategic interests of South Korea and the United States in the post–Cold War era converge mostly over the issue of establishing a new order in Northeast Asia. South Korea and the United States both desire a stable power balance in the region. It is against this backdrop that the United States describes its participation in bilateral or multilateral security cooperation in Northeast Asia as a "stabilizing force." This may well be akin to the United States performing the role of a "balancer" between China and Japan. South Korea does not want another hegemon in addition to the United States to emerge in Northeast Asia.

The interests of the United States as a superpower are in line with those of South Korea as a semideveloped country, seeking to prevent North Korea from remaining a threat to the region and thus to engage North Korea as a responsible member of the world community.

Policy means available to the United States include military and economic capability, while South Korea is seen to have geopolitical importance because it is located between China and the United States. In addition, if anti-American sentiment is exacerbated in South Korea, it could become a political burden to the United States, since South Korea is a "proud" example of a nation that has achieved democracy and economic development under the security umbrella of the United States. Last, if the United States leaves South Korea, it will have an impact on the Japan–U.S. alliance, since Japan will remain the only Asian country hosting U.S. forces.

Table 11.4

ROK-U.S. Policy Structure

	U.S. Policy toward South Korea	South Korean Policy toward the United States
Goal	Maintaining Northeast Asian order	Maintaining balance of power in Northeast Asia
Objective	Maintaining ROK–U.S. alliance	Maintaining (more equal) ROK–U.S. alliance
Means	Diplomatic network Military capability Economic capability	Success of democratization Link with Japan–U.S. alliance China "card"

Korean Peace Building versus ROK–U.S. Alliance

Assuming North Korea's cooperation, the overall scenario for terminating the Cold War structure on the Korean Peninsula will proceed as shown in Table 11.5. But Table 11.5 represents "wishful thinking," since the goal cannot be achieved without genuine cooperation from North Korea.[13] In order to realize each step, inter-Korean relations must continue to improve, while negotiations between the U.S.–Japan and North Korea progress. As of late 2003, however, the road map process of dismantling the Cold War structure on the Korean Peninsula has not come to the end of even its first stage.

If the process of creating a peace system reaches the final stage, as seen in Table 11.5, the issue of U.S. forces in Korea is likely to be critical in inter-Korean negotiations. The first step North Korea is expected to take is to argue that once a peace treaty is concluded, U.S. forces stationed in Korea would no longer be necessary, since peace on the peninsula would have been assured.

The "normalization" process of the triangular relationship between North and South Korea and the United States will mean the establishment of a peace regime on the Korean peninsula. The issue of the status of U.S. forces will be ripe for discussion when the Armistice Agreement is transformed into a peace treaty between the two Koreas on the basis of mutual trust.

However, this issue will also be affected by the U.S. viewpoint. The U.S. military presence in South Korea is closely associated with the American security strategy for Northeast Asia. Even after the realization of peaceful coexistence of the two Koreas and eventual national unification, the United States will likely want to continue to maintain military forces on the Korean peninsula as a deterrent to regional hegemony on the part of China or Japan and as an apparatus for encouraging cooperative efforts to resolve regional issues. This will certainly benefit Korea.

If Washington believes its Northeast Asia strategy is challenged by the peace regime–building process on the Korean peninsula, the United States might approach the third stage of this process with strong skepticism. This, in turn, would provoke Korean

Table 11.5

Road Map for Building Peace on the Korean Peninsula

First stage: Maintaining the armistice system	Observance of the 1953 Korean Armistice Agreement; South–North/U.S.–North Korea/Japan–North Korea talks; four-party peace talks
Second stage: Fulfillment of the South-North Basic Agreement	Operating subcommittees and commissions under the 1992 Basic Agreement; implementing confidence-building measures between the two Koreas; nuclear verification; comprehensive assistance to the North (including North Korea's entry in international financial institutions); solution of the missile problem; lifting U.S. sanctions against the North; accelerating U.S.–North Korea/Japan–North Korea normalization talks
Third stage: Turning the armistice system into a permanent peace system	Consolidation of inter-Korean confidence; North Korea joins the Chemical Weapons Convention (CWC); achieving conventional arms control on the Korean Peninsula; signing the peace agreement between the two Koreas endorsed by the international community; normalization of U.S./Japan–North Korea relations; realization of the North east Asia Security Dialogue (NEASED); and redefining the status of U.S. Forces Korea (USFK)

nationalism, which could result in a negative synergistic effect on the ROK–U.S. relationship. Therefore both South Korea and the United States should be prepared to act prudently on the dual issues of establishing a peace regime on the Korean Peninsula and determining the future status of U.S. forces in Korea.

Thus, the United States will have to readjust and redefine the strategic role of U.S. forces in Korea not only from the viewpoint of the Korean Peninsula but also in terms of a broader framework linked to the maintenance of geopolitical equilibrium, or balance of power, in Northeast Asia.[14] To adjust the ROK–U.S. alliance to a regional strategic approach means that even if the threat from North Korea dissipates, the ROK–U.S. alliance can continue to contribute to regional stability.[15]

Conclusion

In light of the above analysis, the most recent origin of the anti-American sentiment in South Korea dates back to June 2000, right after the inter-Korean summit meeting was held. The summit gave many South Koreans hope that the two Koreas would be able to tackle their problems "independently." This nationalistic feeling provided the basis on which U.S. Forces Korea (USFK)-related incidents received worse reactions from the South Korean population than expected. A series of events afterward related USFK relegated the United States to the role of observer, rather than an active player or supporter, of the Korean question.

The "inequity" of the Status of Forces Agreement (SOFA), camptown politics near the U.S. military bases in Korea,[16] the alleged No Gun Ri massacre by U.S. troops during the Korean War, Washington's refusal to close down or relocate its bombing range at Maehyang-ri, and environmental pollution by the USFK have all worked to fuel anti-American sentiment. The recent turn of events—post–September 11 international controversies on the "causes" of terrorism, President Bush's "axis of evil" speech, the "Kim Dong-sung incident" at the 2002 Winter Olympic Games, the FX fighter selection process, and the incident of the accidental death of two middle-school students, and so on—appears to have exacerbated growing anti-American sentiment in South Korea.[17]

In the meantime, the United States has reacted sensitively to the rising tide of anti-American sentiment in South Korea and is concerned that this development could lead to demands for the withdrawal of U.S. troops from the peninsula. But, the United States believes that a continued South Korea–U.S. alliance will actually help South Korea deal with the North, as this pushes the North to deal with the United States through South Korea while preventing China from intervening in inter-Korean affairs.

In essence, the U.S. view is that the South Korea–U.S. alliance faces two major challenges, one stemming from North Korea's efforts to drive a wedge between Seoul and Washington and the other from South Korea's growing anti-American sentiment and potential demands for the withdrawal of U.S. troops. The United States also maintains that the current alliance should continue even after the resolution of North Korean problems, in order to counter the possible threat to regional security created by conflicting interests among the major powers in Northeast Asia. In this respect, the United States recognizes that South Korea–U.S. relations should focus on how to manage the "success" rather than failure of any rapprochement in inter-Korean relations.

Notes

1. *International Herald Tribune*, December 5, 2002.

2. *Korea Times*, December 23, 2002.

3. *New York Times*, January 23, 2003.

4. The Bush Administration saw that North Korea embarked upon a secret HEU (highly enriched uranium) nuclear development program around 1999.

5. For example, the United States prefers to utilize its domestic legal institutions rather than resorting to the International Criminal Court in order to bring terrorists to justice.

6. Perle said, "I can promise you that if we have to choose between protecting ourselves against terrorism or a long list of friends and allies, we will protect ourselves against terrorism." Perle told an international security conference in Germany that America's top priority was not necessarily to build an international coalition but rather self-defense. BBC, March 2: Quoted in *MARPAC's Asia-Pacific Intelligence Brief*, March 3, 2002.

7. John J. Mearsheimer, *The Tragedy of Great Power Politics* (New York: Norton, 2001), pp. 19–20. Mearsheimer coined the words "offensive" versus "defensive" realism, but I have elaborated those concepts by distinguishing them from "offensive" versus "defensive" liberalism, as shown in Table 11.1.

8. Livermore Study Group, "A National Strategy against Terrorism Using Weapons of Mass Destruction," www.llnl.gov/str/Imbro.html.

9. No non–state organization has the capability of weaponizing chemical and biological (CB) material thus far. Terrorists' mere possession of CB material, however, can rouse extreme public anxiety, and their seizure of state-possessed CB weapons will cause a more serious problem.

10. The White House, "The National Security Strategy of the United States," 2002; available at whitehouse.gov/nsc/nss.html.

11. During the 1962 Cuban missile crisis, for example, it enabled President John F. Kennedy to resist the counsel of some of his advisers that he carry out a preemptive attack to destroy Soviet missiles being deployed on the island, thus avoiding an all-out nuclear war between the two superpowers.

12. A secret Pentagon plan for the next five years directs the military to focus more of its spending to combat Afghanistan-style threats and weapons of mass destruction. The "Defense Planning Guidance" for 2004 to 2009 puts into action the Pentagon's plan to replace a Cold War–era strategy of being able to fight two major theater wars at the same time with a more complex approach aimed at dominating air and space on several fronts. See William M. Arkin's analysis in the *Los Angeles Times*, July 14, 2002.

13. As to the potential roles of USFK when North Korea collapses, see William O. Odom, "The U.S. Military in Unified Korea," *Korean Journal of Defense Analysis* XII, no. 1 (Summer 2000): 7–28.

14. Many are warning against a possible arms race, including nuclear weapons, when the U.S. troops leave the region: Larry M. Wortzel, "Planning for the Future: The Role of U.S. Forces in Northeast Asian Security," *Heritage Foundation Backgrounder*, July 26, 2000. Concerning the dynamic structure of the U.S.–China–Japan relationship, see Neil E. Silver, "The United States, Japan, and China," *A Council on Foreign Relations Paper* (New York: CFR, 2000).

15. As to the argument that U.S. troops should remain to deal with unconventional security threats in this region, see Robert Dujarric, *Korean Unification and After: The Challenge for U.S. Strategy* (Indianapolis, IN: Hudson Institute, 2000).

16. See Katharine Moon, *Sex Among Allies: Military Prostitution in U.S.-ROK Relations* (New York: Columbia University Press, 1997).

17. A recent unofficial survey shows that issues cited as being behind anti-American sentiment in Korea include USFK (55 percent), the Bush administration's hard-line policy to North Korea (13 percent), and U.S.-led globalization (12 percent). In addition, while almost 26 percent of survey respondents recognized a continued need for the U.S. military presence, 59 percent expressed indifference and more than 15 percent saw no need for U.S. troops in South Korea. At the moment, there seem to be three kinds of anti-Americanism in South Korea: (1) ideological anti-Americanism, among those who are ideology-bound, including radical student organizations, leftist scholars, and journalists; (2) pragmatic anti-Americanism, among moderate NGOs and those who look to specific issues such as SOFA, the environment, and wartime operational control, and so on, rather than denying the United States itself; and (3) popular anti-Americanism, which tends to be episodic and exists among those who respond to events in an emotional manner. The current problem is that ideological anti-Americanism, though not widespread, fosters efforts by its adherents to form coalitions with the second group, so that they will become more influential with the third group.

12

The U.S.–Korean Status of Forces Agreement as a Source of Continuing Korean Anti-American Attitudes

James V. Feinerman

Among the irritants in the bilateral relationship between the United States of America and the Republic of Korea, the United States–Republic of Korea Status of Forces Agreement (SOFA) has both periodically and recently loomed large. Ever since the end of the Korean War, this arrangement has provided a basis for stationing a fairly large contingent of U.S. military personnel on bases in South Korea, both along the 38th parallel and elsewhere, to preserve the uneasy peace between North and South Korea and to serve large American strategic interests on the Korean Peninsula and in the larger Northeast Asian security sphere.

While the objections to the agreement have not remained uniform over time, nor has the level of discontent been continuously at the same fever pitch as in recent years, the lingering unhappiness, repeated calls for revision (some of which have led to periodic changes) and the scope that the large American military presence provides for friction with the Korean population make the agreement highly problematic. Yet, from a U.S. perspective, the vociferous calls either for wholesale revision of this agreement or total withdrawal of U.S. forces from South Korea is both puzzling and vexing. While most reasonable Americans would acknowledge that we have stationed our troops in Korea on the basis of military and strategic logic that serves U.S. interests, they would also expect that even greater advantages accrue to the population of South Korea as the immediate beneficiaries of the U.S. military's presence in the face of an implacable enemy with a huge, unpredictable military force deployed only miles away from their national capital, which not only fought them to a draw in a bitter civil war but has also demonstrated again and again that it is an outlier at international law willing to employ terror and assassination to work its unfathomable will.

On the other hand, the Korean unhappiness with U.S. troops on their soil should hardly come as a surprise. Numerous incidents over the years where members of the military have committed crimes in Korea but been tried in U.S. military courts obviously create a basis for resentment. The end of the Cold War, which de-escalated the global threat of Communism, caused some pressure (even in the United States) to scale back the deployment of U.S. forces on the front lines. President Kim Dae-jung's "Sunshine Policy" may have further emboldened at least some South Koreans to believe that the danger of renewed war from the north was now over, making the continued presence of foreign soldiers in their territory more unbearable. Further insult came when the new Bush administration not only threw cold water on the very idea of the Sunshine Policy but also labeled North Korea as a key component of the "Axis of Evil." Whatever hopes of a rapprochement, along with a potential for withdrawal of U.S. troops in its aftermath, appeared to be quite affirmatively dashed.

In the rest of this chapter, I will attempt to place the U.S.–Korea Status of Forces Agreement in some comparative context as a matter of both U.S. military and international law. Then, the chapter will consider some of the events that have recently militated in favor of revision of the Status of Forces Agreement and finally assess the prospects for success of recent revisions and proposals for further future change and the possible consequences.

Status of Forces Agreements: In General

Military forces serving in the territory of other nations subject to international law and with the consent of the host country is not a new phenomenon, although since the mid-twentieth century the frequency and extent of such stationing has grown considerably. At the end of World War II, following the surrender of Germany and Japan, Allied Forces remained in those vanquished nations for the better part of a decade, pursuant to the relevant peace treaties concluding the conflict. A series of agreements creating the framework for the North Atlantic Treaty Organization (NATO) required increasing international cooperation of member nations' armed forces over the latter half of the twentieth century.[1] The implementation and further development of military partnerships have convinced participant nations of the absolute necessity to enunciate clear legal arrangements for the military and civilian personnel of foreign military forces who are stationed in a receiving state. International and national legal requirements must be observed, but at the same time there are practical and theoretical questions that must be addressed in crafting such arrangements.[2]

Thus, nations are constrained in developing rules for visiting military forces by evolving international legal standards and customary international law. National law also cannot be ignored if the implementation of agreements governing the stationing of visiting forces is to be smooth and well received by the local populace. The balance must be struck between the need for some limited immunity of foreign forces located on foreign territory so that they may carry out the essential functions for which they were invited into the host nation and the need for the receiving country to maintain its territorial sovereignty to exercise the will of the population governed, whose continuing consent is ultimately necessary for acceptance of the visiting forces. As shall be seen below, setting and maintaining this balance in Korea has proven problematic, particularly in recent years.

All modern status of forces agreements begin with a starting principle that limited immunity must be provided by the host country to the visiting foreign armed forces. There is a firm basis in international law and most nations' domestic law for this principle. In the United States, an early and famous case, *The Schooner Exchange,*[3] in an opinion authored by Chief Justice John Marshall, dismissed an action by American shipowners whose vessel was seized by a French warship and forcibly assigned to the French navy at a time when the United States and France were not at war and maintained friendly relations. Noting that sovereigns had the right to allow "foreign princes" to pass through their territory, Justice Marshall continued:

> The grant of a free passage, therefore, implies a waiver of all jurisdiction over the troops during their passage and permits the foreign general to use that discipline and to inflict those punishments that the government of his army may require.[4]

Over the centuries, a more restrictive notion of sovereign immunity has been adopted by most nations, including the United States. As a result, immunity will usually only be granted for those actions that can be carried out only by a sovereign state (*jure imperii*) but not for those actions that a state may take that are not limited to state actors, such as commercial transactions, contracts and employment and personal injury or damage to property (*jure gestionis*). Thus, only acts necessary to official duties and reserved to a sovereign power enjoy immunity.[5] Moreover, the codified law of the United States with regard to sovereign immunity explicitly permits the United States to waive sovereign immunity pursuant to international agreements such as treaties concluded with foreign nations.[6]

As various international legal experts have noted, certain standards for allowing a sending state to exercise criminal jurisdiction through its own military authorities within the territory of receiving states have entered into an evolving customary international law in this realm.[7] In post–World War II international law, this emanates from Article VII of the NATO SOFA, which have enjoyed wide acceptance beyond the NATO member countries (and were even followed during the Cold War by the states that were parties to the Warsaw Pact!). Yet, the very nature and contemporary evolution of customary international law means that such conceptions are not static. On the contrary, as competing concerns begin to vie for attention and rise or fall in public esteem, they can displace even long-established rules of customary law and refashion them. Thus, as popular consciousness about environmental damage, noise pollution and other hazards attendant to stationing foreign military forces on a nation's territory has developed, customary international law has incorporated such concerns in its ambit. Eroding faith in the omniscience of the executive, along with diminution of executive powers, may give other governmental and nongovernmental centers of power in a nation a larger voice in shaping international legal commitments. In addition, the convergence of national legal regimes in more general ways may affect the evolution of international law.

The relationship between international law and the law of the receiving state can also affect the general international law with regard to foreign military forces. For example, national law can determine the contours of authorization for foreign armed forces to enter a nation's territory, including limitations on the purpose, size, and length of stay of the foreign forces; coordination of the governments of the sending and receiving states and parliamentary oversight by the receiving state may also be mandated. Legislative control of military forces, as opposed to untrammeled executive prerogative, is a developing trend among the world's democracies, although still in its nascent phase in the United States.

Finally, there must also be some accounting for the necessary evolution of any long-term SOFA in the light of particular circumstances. In the case of the United States–Republic of Korea SOFA, which relates to a military presence of United States forces on Korean territory that has lasted over half a century, it would be absurd to expect that the relationship would remain unchanged over such a long period. During such a span of time, both national and international law are not static; more importantly, the underlying circumstances that may have induced the initial placement of forces will likely also have undergone considerable change. As the rationale for authorizing the presence of foreign military forces on another state's territory evolves, a concomitant alteration of its legal underpinnings—whether by domestic legislation or amendment of treaties—should be expected.

Status of Forces Agreement Where the United States Is a Party

It is impossible to consider both the present form and the calls for revision of the U.S.–Korean Status of Forces Agreement in isolation. As the world's sole remaining superpower, and after maintaining U.S. military bases around the globe ever since the end of World War II, the United States has developed a long history of negotiating and implementing Status of Forces Agreements in almost every corner of the world. To some extent, the basic terms and formal outline of these agreements are universal and identical; in a few important instances, however, they can differ substantially. Overarching any consideration of them also must be some understanding that the deployment of a global power's military in foreign territory, regardless of the consent of the host nation, international legality, and other exigent circumstances is likely to lead to resentment and problems of implementation. Some of these are generic and predictable:

Overwhelming military power (even when wielded circumspectly) can engender envy and worse; young recruits, stationed far from home with few outlets for their predictable impulses, can often behave very badly; and most human endeavors—but especially anything as fraught with danger as projecting military might, even in peacetime—statistically produce a certain inevitable percentage of accidents.

In United States practice, especially outside the North Atlantic region (perhaps betraying a certain Eurocentrism), there has also been a history of jealously guarding U.S. prerogatives. This has led to an insistence in any bilateral Status of Forces Agreement that American interests, including all the legal rights of individual U.S. service members, be fully protected. With regard to non-common-law legal orders, this may include requiring trial of criminal offenses in U.S. military courts to preserve rights guaranteed in the United States Constitution to every U.S. citizen. These would include, but are not limited to: trial by jury; an absolute right to silence during interrogation so as to avoid self-incrimination; immediate access to a defense attorney, and so on. Such insistence may offend both international law and custom, which generally makes criminal jurisdiction territorial and ensures the right of any nation to prosecute criminal violations that occur within its borders in its own courts, under its own laws. Nevertheless, those negotiating Status of Forces Agreements have continued to press for such protections out of not only a residual American or common law xenophobia (that other legal regimes are inadequate to protect fully the inalienable legal rights of U.S. citizens) but also a position of power that allows them to make such provisions a sine qua non for extending the U.S. military umbrella. Nations that desire to avail themselves of the advantages of this protection are coerced into accepting the terms. Obviously, such scenarios give rise to future difficulties.

As recent scandals involving the United States occupation forces in Iraq bear out, there are other problems not always anticipated by the traditional approaches to Status of Forces Agreements. One major irritant, which has become a burgeoning scandal during the Iraq occupation, is the status of civilians, such as contractors, who are nationals of the same countries as the visiting forces. U.S. civilians can be tried only by U.S. courts-martial during a declared war. U.S. military practice holds contractor employees not subject to military law under the Uniform Code of Military Justice (UCMJ) when accompanying U.S. forces, except during a declared war. Maintaining discipline of contractor employees is the responsibility of the contractor's management, not the military chain of command.

Contractors may be prosecuted under U.S. law in certain circumstances, depending on the offense. Military contractors who are U.S. nationals could be prosecuted by a U.S. federal court under the U.S. War Crimes Act.[8] The act defines a war crime as any grave breach of the 1949 Geneva Conventions (such as torture or inhuman treatment) or any violation of common article 3 of the Geneva Conventions (which not only includes torture, but also "outrages upon personal dignity" and "humiliating and degrading treatment"). Penalties include fines or imprisonment for life or any term of years, and the death penalty if death results to the victim. Contractors might also be prosecuted under the Military Extraterritorial Jurisdiction Act of 2000, known as MEJA.[9] This law permits the prosecution in federal court of U.S. civilians who, while employed by or accompanying U.S. forces abroad, commit certain crimes.

Generally, the crimes covered are any federal criminal offense punishable by imprisonment for more than one year. MEJA authorizes Defense Department law enforcement personnel to arrest suspected offenders and specifies procedures for the transfer of accused individuals to the United States. Prosecutions under the Military Extraterritorial Jurisdiction Act would be handled by federal civilian authorities. The MEJA law appears to be untested to date. It was enacted primarily to protect U.S. soldiers and their dependents living abroad. One problem facing the U.S. military at its foreign bases was that military contractors could commit crimes with virtual impunity since local authorities would have little interest in prosecuting a U.S. citizen committing a crime against another U.S. citizen on a U.S. military base.

Status of Forces Agreements: General Provisions

One of the objections to the U.S.–Korea Status of Forces Agreement is the lack of reciprocity. For example, the NATO Status of Force Agreement[10] is a "reciprocal" agreement, covering the forces of each member country in the territory of any of the other member countries. In general, the United States usually enters into Status of Forces Agreements that are not "reciprocal"; that is, they cover United States forces in host countries but not those countries' forces in the United States. This emanates largely from a belief that the dispatch of troops is almost always a one-way proposition, from the United States to other countries. In practice, this would mean that a visiting Korean military official who struck and injured a U.S. citizen while driving drunk in the United States would be subject to trial in a U.S. court, an American counterpart who committed the same offense in Korea would be tried by a U.S. court martial not a local Korean court.

Some Koreans have claimed this is inequitable in the light of different provisions, to take two examples, in the supplementary agreement with respect to Germany under the NATO Status of Forces Agreement[11] and the U.S.–Japan Status of Forces Agreement.[12] Any discrepancy between the arrangements for treatment of U.S. forces in other agreements creates the supposition that preferential treatment is accorded American forces under the U.S.–Korean agreement, slighting Korean sovereignty.

Any perception of more favorable treatment for Japan and Germany gives rise to particular offense in Korea due to the fact that while Japan and Germany were defeated enemies in World War II, which had committed heinous war crimes, Korea fought on the side of the allies and then further contributed to world peace and security by holding down the "Eastern front" of the Cold War. Even the different circumstances today, including the fact that the 38th parallel remains a virtual war zone despite the 1953 cease-fire and the potential for conflict with Kim Jong Il's regime, do not to the mind of most Koreans justify less generous treatment.

Under the Status of Forces Agreement between Japan and the United States—the so-called U.S.–Japan SOFA, which dictates service members' legal rights in Japan—those charged with a criminal offense are protected from incarceration by the Japanese until they are indicted. The United States has always seen this action as overly harsh, but after a twelve-year-old schoolgirl was raped by three servicemen in 1995, the United States bent its objections and promised to consider handing over suspects of heinous crimes.[13] Okinawa has been transformed by the 1995 attack, when rage against the presence of U.S. forces overflowed into the streets. Over every incident, big and small that has followed, politicians pelted the U.S. military with demands that it impose curfews, change treaties, and shut down bases. The three men are serving seven-year sentences in a special Japanese prison ward for U.S. servicemen south of Tokyo.

After serving their sentence, the men will receive dishonorable discharges and be returned to the United States.

The relevant facts with regard to the Okinawa case are not dissimilar to dozens of attacks by U.S. military personnel on Korean citizens, which have resulted in the same levels of outrage. On September 4, 1995, three U.S. servicemen stationed in Okinawa, two of whom were Marines, allegedly forced an elementary-school girl into a car and raped her. Despite this being an obvious crime that was committed outside of any U.S. military installation, the United States Forces, Japan (USFJ), which took the suspects into custody, refused to allow the Japanese authorities to carry out the arrest warrant, and indicated that they would turn the suspects over only after charges were filed. Since that time, at least three other high-profile rape cases have occurred on Okinawa, galvanizing public opinion against the presence of U.S. forces on that island.[14] Each case involved a violent sexual assault and pressure from local Japanese authorities for the U.S. military on Okinawa to turn over the suspect for prosecution. These cases and a series of other incidents—mostly drunken brawls and traffic accidents (at least resulting in a death)—led Okinawan Governor Inamine to set out on what he called a "pilgrimage" to the thirteen other Japanese prefectures that hosted U.S. military facilities. Inamine sought to convince the governors of these prefectures to support his campaign to force the central government to revise the U.S.–Japan SOFA. Every one of the governors agreed, including the right-wing governor of Tokyo, Shintaro Ishihara.[15]

It should be noted that Status of Forces Agreements do not deal solely, or even primarily, with questions of jurisdiction for criminal offenses committed by foreign military personnel. Among their many provisions, these treaties must create a regime governing the use of facilities and geographic areas, customs and duties for any imported equipment and goods, taxation, labor regulations, military postal and other communications facilities, civil claims, health and sanitation and environmental concerns. In almost every agreement, the trend has been for more permissive and expansive regimes of several decades ago to yield to greater restriction and protection of local interests. Particularly in areas such as the environment, where basic consciousness had barely developed three or four decades previously, rapid development of scientific knowledge, technical capability, domestic legislation, and vocal nongovernmental groups with specific concerns has completely transformed the landscape and required major, extensive revisions.

The U.S.–ROK SOFA

The basis for stationing U.S. forces in South Korea is a series of agreements closely related to the termination of hostilities fifty years ago on the Korean peninsula. The underlying legal basis for their presence is the "ROK–US Mutual Defense Treaty of 1953" (MDT).[16] The ongoing status, rights, and duties of U.S. forces stationed in Korea are regulated by the "Status of Forces Agreement between the Republic of Korea and the United States" (SOFA).[17] In addition, a further basis for United States intervention in the Korean conflict and continued presence in Korea was the right of self-defense in its collective form, under both customary international law and Article 51 of the United Nations Charter. Article 2 of the MDT provides that the United States and ROK will develop "appropriate means with which to deter external armed attack and to take suitable measures in consultation and agreement to implement" this treaty and its purpose. Under Article 4 of the MDT, the ROK grants the United States rights to deploy land, air, and sea forces in and about the territory of the ROK as determined by mutual agreement.

The SOFA further regulates the status of U.S. forces stationed in Korea pursuant to the MDT. The original SOFA comprised a Main Agreement (a Preamble and 21 articles), as well as 3 annexes (Agreed Minutes, Agreed Understandings, and Exchange of Notes). In 1991, the Agreed Understandings and Exchange of Notes were eliminated, and "New Understandings" were adopted.[18] Between 1995 and 2000, repeated talks were held to revise further the SOFA, based upon concerns that changing conditions in Korea, as well as rising anti-Americanism blamed on resentments of Korean citizens stemming from crimes committed by U.S. servicemen against Koreans, required changes. The overall charge not only of Korean nongovernmental organizations (NGOs) organized to protest the presence of United States forces in Korea but also of both ordinary citizens and knowledgeable academic commentators is that the SOFA is riddled with unequal, inequitable, and otherwise unreasonable provisions.[19]

On December 28, 2000, the Republic of Korea (ROK) and the U.S. governments completed negotiations to revise the SOFA. ROK chief delegate Song Min-soon, Director General for North American Affairs of the Ministry of Foreign Affairs and Trade, and his U.S. counterpart, Deputy Assistant Secretary of Defense for Asia–Pacific Affairs, Frederick Smith, agreed upon and initialed the revised Agreement. Both governments agreed that this SOFA revision reflected the will of President Kim Dae Jung and President Clinton and the people of both nations to enhance U.S.–ROK security cooperation in a mature and balanced manner. They expressed the mutual understanding that this SOFA revision reflected both nations' interests in a wide range of fields, including criminal jurisdiction, environment, labor, quarantine regulations, facilities and areas, non-appropriated fund facilities, and civil proceedings. The revision was hoped, in the long term, to contribute to maintaining a stable environment for U.S. troops stationed in the ROK and to further enhancing the alliance between the ROK and the United States.

The major contents of this revision included the following:

1. On major crimes, both sides shall advance the timing of transferring the accused SOFA personnel to Korean authorities from the then current "upon completion of all judicial proceedings" to "at the time of indictment." If the Korean police arrest someone for an egregious crime, such as murder or rape, the Korean police will have the right to maintain custody. The Korean government agreed to the protection of the rights of the accused SOFA personnel, a key concern of U.S. military lawyers not only in Korea but in any non-common-law jurisdiction.

2. A provision on environmental protection was included in the SOFA revision, stating that the U.S. Armed Forces stationed in Korea will respect Korean environmental laws and regulations, and Korea will consider the safety of SOFA personnel. Based on this provision, both sides were to sign a memorandum of special understandings that would include cooperative measures for environmental protection.

3. Both sides promised to shorten the cooling-off period of labor disputes by Koreans employed by U.S. Forces Korea, enhance regulations governing stable employment, and allow qualified SOFA dependents to work in the ROK.

Despite this relatively recent revision in the SOFA, there continue to be calls for yet another round of changes, for reasons that may be made clearer below.

Criminal Jurisdiction

The most recent downturn in relations between South Korea and the United States began after the accidental deaths of two South Korean teenagers in the summer of 2002. A U.S. armored vehicle traveling on a winding road during a military maneuver hit the two girls. The two American personnel involved were on duty at the time of the accident, meaning that under the existing SOFA they were tried in a closed hearing by a U.S. military court. Under Korean pressure, the soldiers were charged with negligent homicide and court-martialed. The Korean government, reacting to increasing public pressure, demanded that the Americans be tried in a Korean court, where their chances of a fair trial ranged from questionable to impossible. In the U.S. court martial, both defendants were acquitted; no superior officers were tried or otherwise held accountable. Several months later, President Bush sent a letter to the South Korean people expressing regret, but that belated and impersonal gesture seems to have done little to assuage a growing anger among the South Korean people, media, and government. Over the past decade, this resentment has been whipped up to a fever pitch by a handful of activists and organizations that have made the termination of U.S. military presence in Korea their goal, spearheaded by educated individuals and the Internet-savvy nongovernmental organizations and civic action groups they have created.[20]

More importantly, from the Korean perspective, the U.S. side has rejected a waiver of criminal jurisdiction, refusing to allow the South Korean judiciary to try the U.S. soldiers because the two GIs had been charged with "negligent homicide" under the U.S. Uniform Code of Military Justice. This incident triggered a wave of nationwide protests involving people from different quarters including school children, student-youth, writers, journalists, clergy and religious activists, women, trade unions, peace proponents, and politicians. A variety of protest actions were launched throughout South Korea—demonstrations, mass rallies, signature-collecting and fund-raising, memorial events, and so on. Nationwide meetings were held on five occasions within a matter of five weeks after the tragedy occurred, and even primary school children came to join in protest. Leading Korean mass media, which had generally refrained from reporting on GIs' crimes and troubles between the U.S. Forces Korea (USFK) and residents of localities, now pay far more attention to new developments. Floods of e-mails came into the media, government organs, and NGO Web sites. The public was virtually unanimous in demanding that the GIs be brought to justice in a South Korean court.

One example reported in the Korean and foreign press is instructive as to the range and depth of Korean resentment. On the afternoon of July 20, 2002, some five hundred citizens gathered at the square in front of Uijeongbu Station to mark the "Day of Action for Citizens of Uijeongbu, Tongduchon and Yangju." They were from areas that host U.S. bases. Mok Yong Dae, representative of a "Measure Committee of Northern Kyonggi-do" organized to protest the GIs' killing of the two Korean teenagers, shouted: "This is a place we can never forget in which Ms. Yun Kum I was murdered by GIs in 1992 [referring to an incident a decade earlier]. We must change Uijeongbu and Tongduchon into 'Towns of Hope' that shall not be called 'U.S. camp village' any longer, into towns free from GIs' crimes for ever!" This speech drew enthusiastic applause. In the evening, the participants held a procession, carrying candles in hand, to organize a human chain around the 2nd Infantry Division base.

Historically, few cases alleging crimes committed by GIs have been decided by Korean courts because of the SOFA between South Korea and the United States. The criminal charges against GIs with respect to Koreans, which have included murder, robbery, sexual harassment and violence, arson, violation of traffic regulations, and so forth, have usually been left to U.S. courts-martial. The claim of South Korean activists is that this is the result of the South Korea–U.S. SOFA being more discriminatory and unfavorable to South Koreans than the similar agreements the United States has concluded with NATO nations and Japan.

Even in Japan, however, the change has been slow to come and unsatisfying to local residents. As the discussion above of the rape case from September 1995, Okinawa demonstrates, the United States was reluctant to turn the suspects over until after charges were filed in Japan. According to the September 20, 1994, *Asahi Shimbun,* from the 1972 return of Okinawa to Japanese jurisdiction until the mid-1990s, there had been a number of serious crimes by U.S. servicemen against local citizens—a dozen homicides and over 500 other incidents including arson, robbery, and rape.[21] The Japanese government at the highest levels did not share the public enthusiasm for wholesale revision and sought instead to use the opportunity created by this incident to pursue other goals in the U.S.–Japan military relationship.

U.S. Forces' spokesmen in Korea complained of "inaccurate" news media reports "that have created false impressions in the Korean public" concerning the command's response to the June 2002 accident that killed the two teenage Korean girls. In their statement the spokesmen complained that the reports called into question "the genuineness of our sorrow and the actions we have taken since the accident."[22] The statement went on to say, "Members of the USFK community have been deeply saddened by the tragic accident. Each of us in USFK wishes there was something we could do to change the events of that tragic day. We again apologize, and accept full responsibility for what happened."[23] Media reports continued to suggest that no statements of remorse or official apologies were made or they were late in being presented. However, the command noted that Lt. Gen. Daniel Zanini, 8th Army commander, expressed condolences immediately after the accident occurred. Senior officials also visited the girls' families the day of the accident to express condolences.

The next day, U.S. military officials "presented an initial solatium payment of 1 million won (about $800) to each family to help provide for their immediate needs." Such a payment was made to express condolences but did not admit guilt in an accident. After those initial expressions of remorse, official apologies were made by Gen. Leon LaPorte, the USFK commander, Maj. Gen. Russel Honoré, commander at the time of the accident, Assistant Secretary of State for East Asian and Pacific Affairs James Kelly, and U.S. Ambassador to Seoul Thomas Hubbard. Some of those officials issued apologies several times. Yet the opponents of any U.S. military presence on the Korean peninsula were not about to let things rest and needed to paint the U.S. forces and other U.S. government representatives as unrepentant, insufficiently contrite, and callously indifferent to Korean lives in order to advance their cause.

USFK accepted responsibility for the accident and consulted with Korean government officials on compensation to be paid to the families. Under terms of the Status of Forces Agreement that governs the U.S. military presence in the country, 75 percent of the compensation decided on was to be paid by USFK, with the Korean government paying the remaining 25 percent. Soldiers from the unit involved also donated more than $22,000 to the two families to express their deep sorrow for the accident. A fund was established to create a memorial to the two girls near the site of the accident.

Another misperception created by media reports concerns the issue of jurisdiction over the two soldiers. Jurisdiction was presented in Korean press reports as an example of an inequity in the Status of Forces Agreement. Under the SOFA, the U.S. military had jurisdiction since the soldiers were on duty at the time of the accident. Yet, as the U.S. command pointed out, the South Korean military has exclusive jurisdiction over its own soldiers under Article 2 of the Korean Military Court Act. Korean soldiers who commit crimes on or off duty are never tried in Korea's civilian courts. Thus, as U.S. military experts on Korean have privately noted, Korean forces that had caused the same sort of fatality would not have been subject to the legal process—despite being Korean nationals—that those opposed to the U.S. military presence in Korea sought to impose on the U.S. servicemen.

The accident itself, in which Shim Mi-Son and Shin Hyo-sun were killed, though tragic, is of a type all too common in Korea. One Korean news report states that approximately eighty-two children are killed or injured in traffic accidents every day in Korea and 70 percent of those accidents involve children walking on or along a road. An editorial in the *Joongang Ilbo* published shortly after this accident described the road as very dangerous, especially to pedestrians, and commented that it was amazing that more accidents did not happen. Yet, in the light of these facts, and despite all efforts at apology, the U.S. military was not able to placate outrage over this accident. In part, the United States was incompetent in dealing with this situation because of the efforts of increasingly well-organized anti-U.S. NGOs seeking to turn this accident into a political incident. In addition, electioneering politicians of all parties attempted to use this issue to show their independence against the United States by condemning the United States and calling for the prosecution and punishment of the two soldiers primarily involved in the accident in Korea's domestic legal system. Current President Roh, in fact, probably owes his victory in the presidential election to his adroit management of anti-U.S. sentiment as a campaign tool.

In South Korea with tight control over dissent even after democratization, particularly involving North–South issues under the National Security Law, many dissidents have found work in NGOs and have used environmental and human rights issues to attack the U.S. presence in South Korea. Under Kim Dae-jung's administration, the number of these NGOs and their prestige increased. Most activities by Korean anti-American NGOs have the aim of undermining the ability of U.S. troops to maintain trained troops in Korea. Mistakes made by the U.S. military are exaggerated far beyond similar mistakes made by the Korean military or industry.

At the same time, soldiers turned over to Korea for trial would lose many of the rights taken for granted by U.S. citizens. They lose the right to a trial by a jury of their peers. They lose the right to a lawyer during questioning. They may be detained over a period of days without being charged. Indeed, the treatment of ordinary citizens by their own government under Korean criminal process falls far short in actual practice of basic human rights protections for the accused in a criminal case. After the recent accident, South Korea's government calls for prosecution of the two soldiers were purely political. From a U.S. perspective, what SOFA protections remain are designed to protect soldiers who are already risking their physical safety for the protection of South Korea from having to sacrifice their rights and freedom for the political satisfaction of activists. The legal circumstances surrounding this accident provide a textbook example of what the SOFA was intended to provide for U.S. service personnel stationed abroad, particularly in the face of a hostile environment of politicized opposition to the presence of U.S. forces.

The United States State Department warns all U.S. citizens visiting or living in Korea on its Web site for the Seoul Embassy that there remain very real differences between the Korean and U.S. legal systems.[24] While a reading of the Korean Constitution may lead one to conclude that the Korean and U.S. legal systems are virtually the same, the State Department advises U.S. citizens that there are a number of very significant differences. The main point is that an American in Korea (i.e., non-military personnel not covered by the SOFA) is subject to Korean laws, not American laws. The most significant ways in which Korean law differs from that of the United States and other Western countries involve access to counsel; post-arrest communication; double jeopardy; and bail. On each of these issues, Korean law diverges greatly from what a U.S. citizen might reasonably expect, not only under U.S. law but under the legal system of most developed democracies.

An American, used to having his lawyer present at every step of legal proceedings, may be disconcerted to find that under Korean law an attorney need not be present during questioning of a suspect by the public prosecutor's office. Police and public prosecutors may also question a suspect without an attorney present.[25] Americans accustomed to their "one phone call" may be taken aback when Korean authorities do not allow them that privilege. Under the U.S.–ROK Consular Convention, Korean police officials must notify the Embassy as soon as an American is arrested. The police may make this notification in writing, however, and it will often be a week or more before the Embassy is apprised of an arrest. The most marked difference between the two legal systems is the possibility of double jeopardy in Korea. Having been found innocent of a crime is no protection against being tried again for the same offense. Not only defendants but also prosecutors who feel a verdict is incorrect may appeal that verdict; as a result, an already-acquitted individual may be re-tried and subsequently convicted of the same crime. Moreover, a prosecutor who is unhappy with a sentence may appeal and request a harsher one. Finally, although bail is legally possible under Korean statutes, it frequently is not granted and may not be as readily available as in the United States.

Ironically, the nationwide June Struggle of 1987, which led to the collapse of Korea's authoritarian regime and opened a road toward democratization, began a process of reform of Korean criminal justice. Under the authoritarian regime, "crime control" values dominated over "due process" values with regard to criminal procedure. The Korean Constitution's Bill of Rights was merely nominal, and criminal law and procedure were no more than instruments for maintaining the regime and suppressing dissidents. It was not a coincidence that the June Struggle was sparked by the death of a dissident student tortured during police interrogation.[26]

Thus, it is hardly surprising that representatives of the United States government have fought to avoid the application of local jurisdiction to U.S. citizens who, under the SOFA, enjoy far greater due process protections.

Environmental Concerns

Along with the important concerns about evasion of local criminal justice that have long dogged U.S.–Korean relations, the most significant new irritant in relations may be the rising environmental consciousness of Korean citizens and a new focus on the environmental hazards resulting from the long-term operation of U.S. bases on Korean territory. Typical is this statement by one Korean activist:

> There are currently 36,000 U.S. troops based at 95 bases in South Korea, which cover a total area of 60,700 acres. The effects of those troops are not limited to the facilities and bases alone; they extend into the communities surrounding the bases. During the time from the posting of U.S. troops in 1945 to the present, environmental pollution has been constant, and the military has neglected to be concerned about the impact. Not only the water, soil and noise pollution produced on and near bases is of concern, but also the physical and mental health impairments of Korean citizens and the destruction of pre-existing community lifestyles brought about by the U.S. military actions that must be considered.[27]

Those living near bases have long experienced the negative effects of the polluting activities caused by U.S. military forces and their bases. During the past half-century, in a divided nation strongly preoccupied with resisting North Korean Communism, the strategic tensions made difficult efforts to improve conditions and to criticize the environmental depredation of Korean-based U.S. forces. In fact, in earlier years, with a repressive, authoritarian regime closely allied with the United States, raising such questions was in itself difficult. With the advent of democratization and lessening of tensions with North Korea, many in South Korea are now making efforts to improve the conditions near U.S. military installations. In October 1996, the environmental action group "The Green Union" joined together with eleven regional groups to assess the environmental damage caused by thirty U.S. military bases in South Korea, the first such research conducted since the establishment of these bases in 1945.[28]

When the SOFA was signed in 1967, before the rise of environmental consciousness in either the United States or Korea, it did not stipulate environment-related requirements. Furthermore, the stated legal position of the United States with regard to all SOFAs was clearly shown in the language in the original SOFA Article 4, "Facilities and Areas—Return of Facilities":

> The Government of the United States is not obliged, when it returns facilities and areas to the Government of the Republic of Korea on the expiration of this Agreement or at an earlier date, to restore the facilities and areas to the condition in which they were at the time they became available to the United States armed forces, or to compensate the Government of the Republic of Korea in lieu of such restorations.

In the light of this language, no responsibility rests upon the United States to remediate environmental harms caused by the bases established on Korean soil. Yet, modern understanding of environmental protection had led to calls in Korea that U.S. military authorities be held responsible if and when they are unable to return the environment on and around military bases to their original nonpolluted condition. In order to realize this, the Korean government feels it must now make greater demands of U.S. military authorities to provide greater stipulations regarding the environment in any revision of the SOFA.

In Japan, too, there have been serious concerns raised about the environmental hazards resulting from U.S. military operations in that country. In 2000, about 100 tons of PCB-contaminated waste produced by the U.S. forces stationed in Japan (USFJ) were returned to Japan after being rejected by other countries.[29] The waste, collected from the U.S. bases across Japan, had been stored in the USFJ's Sagamihara depot in Kanagawa Prefecture. The waste originally was headed for Canada for disposal. But failing to obtain permission there, the ship with the cargo then left for the United States. U.S. port authorities, however, refused permission to unload the cargo, citing domestic law that prohibits bringing in PCBs produced outside the country.[30] The USFJ indicated that it would reship the waste out of Japan within one month, but no specifics have been revealed. The Japanese government took the stance of waiting to see what will happen next. Frustratingly, the Japanese government is not allowed to intervene in the disposal of wastes produced by the U.S. military.[31] Importing and exporting hazardous wastes are strictly controlled under Japanese domestic law related to the Basel Convention, an international treaty regulating transboundary movements of environmentally hazardous wastes and their disposal. However, according to the Japan–U.S. Status of Forces Agreement, U.S. military cargoes are exempted from the set of procedures required by the Basel Convention or Japan's domestic Foreign Exchange Law. The SOFA also blocked disclosure of information of hazardous substances that might exist on U.S. bases. Everything about PCBs stored in Sagamihara—how toxic they are, how much there is in total, or how long they have been stored—has been kept secret from the local government and citizens. Thus, although the Korean side may be unhappy with environmental protection under the SOFA, it differs little from the situation under the Japan–U.S. SOFA or environmental terms in other SOFA agreements (with rare exceptions) to which the United States is a party.

Land Use—"Facilities and Areas"

The U.S.–ROK SOFA regulates the maintenance, administration, and return of facilities used by U.S. forces in Korea.[32] Under the SOFA, U.S. forces are not required to make any payment or compensation to Korea for the use of "facilities and areas" granted to the United States; on the other hand, the Korean government is required to make appropriate payments to the owners and suppliers of facilities and areas on behalf of the United States.[33] Moreover, there is no specific period or term for the grant of facilities and areas to the United States under the SOFA. This has led to numerous resentments on the part of individuals and groups in Korea, who feel understandably that facilities and areas no longer needed for military purposes should be returned to Korea. In addition, there is strong feeling that certain sites, now surrounded by densely populated areas, should be returned to civilian uses.

Under the revised U.S.–ROK SOFA, a new Land Partnership Plan (LPP) has been developed to deal with these issues. The goal is to provide a comprehensive plan for more efficient use of land and stationing of U.S. forces in Korea. It is also planned to rationalize the placement of U.S. military bases in Korea, which have been scattered across forty-one troop installations and an additional fifty-four small camps and support sites. This reflects the fact that a conflict has arisen between the security and defense needs of Korean and U.S. forces and the burgeoning population of Korea. Rapid economic growth and urban development have increased the demand for prime land and have heightened tensions over encroachments of military encampments on civilian populations, leading to friction.

The LPP was negotiated to reduce the forty-one installations to twenty-three, consolidating the bases on which U.S. forces are located. Cost-sharing arrangements between the United States and the Republic of Korea have been established, with the general idea that the United States will pay the costs of relocating units from camps it wishes to close, while the Korean side will pay the costs of relocating units from camps it has asked to be closed.[34]

The rationale from the United States perspective, and its relationship to the congeries of issues complicating U.S.–ROK relations, was made clear by the United States ambassador to Korea:

> Among these challenges is the environment of increasing urbanization in which our forces operate. This has caused us to examine how to maintain deterrence while minimizing the impact our forces have on the land and people of Korea. One answer is to reduce the number of bases we maintain in Korea, consolidating them for greater efficiency. To do this, we are implementing the jointly developed and agreed upon Land Partnership Plan; this will return to the Korean Government nearly half of all the land which U.S. bases now use.[35]

Other Issues: Anti-Americanism and Military Deployment— Be Careful What You Wish For

As an astute former United States ambassador to South Korea, Donald Gregg, has noted:

> Anti-Americanism and the "Sunshine policy" have a complex relationship that surfaces unexpectedly. While Koreans criticize President Kim severely for being too generous in implementing his policy toward North Korea, they take a very dim view of President Bush's hard line toward Pyongyang. A February poll taken in Seoul had six out of ten Koreans believing that the "axis of evil" statement linking North Korea to Iraq and Iran was "inappropriate." It is as though the South Koreans believe that it is okay for them to criticize the Sunshine policy, but not for foreigners to do so, particularly the U.S., which many Koreans blame for the original division of Korea in 1945.[36]

Most Americans, particularly those of a certain age and life experience, have been surprised by sporadic outbreaks of anti-Americanism. This is particularly dismaying to Americans who remember that we saved South Korea twice during the past century, shedding American blood and expending American treasure first to liberate Korea from Japanese occupation and then to spare South Korea from Communist domination by waging the Korean War. Quite rightly, most Americans expect that all Koreans are, or should be, deeply grateful to us. But these sacrifices were completed over half a century ago, a long time in any estimation. Probably, the majority of Koreans over sixty are still grateful, but younger Koreans have quite a different point of view. For them, the Korean War is history; they can barely keep track of what has happened in the past six months.

So, instead they remain incensed over a speed-skating decision at Salt Lake City that they believe "robbed" Korea's Mr. Kim of a gold medal, and awarded it to a (Japanese) American named Ohno. Fortunately, when the United States met Korea in a soccer match, as Korea co-hosted the FIFA World Cup last summer, the United States managed only to tie South Korea, and Korea went on to greater glory in subsequent rounds, preventing a further aggravation of anti-American sentiments.

While Koreans criticize President Kim severely for being too generous in implementing his policy toward North Korea, they have taken a very dim view of President Bush's hard line toward Pyongyang. A February 2002 poll taken in Seoul had six out of ten Koreans believing that President Bush's 2002 State of the Union "axis of evil" statement linking North Korea to Iraq and Iran was "inappropriate." South Koreans seem to feel that only they can criticize the Sunshine Policy, but not foreigners, particularly Americans, which many Koreans in an exercise of collective historical amnesia blame for the original division of Korea in 1945.

As Richard Halloran, a long-time observer of the region and U.S.–Korea relations has recently noted:

> Anti-Americanism is clearly on the rise in Korea and appears to be undergoing a fundamental change. Before, it was more anti-baseism, with the Koreans demanding that the 37,000 American troops posted in their country go home. Now, that has ballooned into a demand that Seoul's alliance with the United States be dismantled. On the American side is a basic change in attitude that began with the terrorist assault of Sept. 11. It is still in its formative stage, but Americans seem to have become less tolerant in dealing with other nations, a mood that might best be expressed: "If you are not with us, you are against us."[37]

Yet Halloran went on to quote David Steinberg, director of Asian Studies at the School for Foreign Service at Georgetown University in Washington, D.C., as saying that—as far as Koreans are concerned—on issue after issue, "When in doubt, it is the Americans who are wrong." Halloran also noted the deep-rooted causes of present-day Korean anti-Americanism. Many Korean nativists will recite a long list of alleged misdeeds of the United States. They reach back to the treaty of 1882 that helped to open the "Hermit Kingdom," a 1905 agreement between the United States and Japan that Koreans contend led directly to the brutal Japanese occupation that lasted until 1945, and a U.S. conspiracy to divide Korea after World War II. American support for Korean dictators, from Syngman Rhee to Park Chung Hee to Chun Doo Whan, is easily recalled. Chun's responsibility for what happened in the South Korean city of Kwangju—uprisings in the 1980s and a subsequent massacre, with alleged connivance of U.S. forces—deepened anti-American sentiments among Koreans. More recently, especially with the ascendancy of the Bush administration, in Korean eyes, the United States has prevented reconciliation with North Korea.

Halloran finished his essay with a speculative consideration of possibilities for the next steps in U.S.–ROK relations. He outlined five scenarios:

1. One would be to mount an intense, high-level diplomatic campaign intended to reverse the Korean mind-set.
2. A second would be to move the bloated U.S. military headquarters out of Seoul and consolidate it with other American forces in a less visible location. The United States has offered to do so if Korea will find a new site and pay for the move. So far, the Koreans have refused.

3. A third possibility would be to muddle through, allowing the sore to fester and treating it with Band-Aids.
4. Fourth, the United States could withdraw its military forces from Korea, which would have an incalculable strategic effect from the Russian Far East to Singapore.
5. Last, if worse comes to worst, the United States could abrogate its security treaty and let the Koreans fend for themselves.

The temptations to pursue the last few alternatives will only grow over time, unless serious attention is given to both U.S. and South Korean security concerns and the best means for addressing them over the long term. Ironically, despite Secretary of Defense Rumsfeld's views that the all-volunteer military has already achieved peak performance, the solution may lie in greater professionalization of the U.S. military. As one commentator has noted:

> Since the advent of the all-volunteer military in 1973, the enlisted ranks have been a place for young people with limited prospects; those looking to escape bad neighborhoods, bad families, and bad job markets.

A 1993 survey of new recruits found that they come from homes where 78.4 percent of fathers and 84.5 percent of mothers did not have college degrees. They come from the ranks of the unemployed, working in dead-end jobs as cashiers, in factories, at fast-food franchises. A 1994 RAND study on Army recruiting trends listed the youth unemployment rate, which has risen almost 27 percent since 1989, as by far the most significant factor affecting the army's ability to attract high quality recruits. These are young men and women who are shipped to countries they know little about and have little interest in, who are disconnected from their culture and their families and arrive overseas with a misguided sense of superiority because of their role as a protecting force. Yet they find themselves ghettoized in GI camptowns, on the bottom rung of society economically, denied entrance to clubs, bypassed by taxis, protested against, regarded on the street with wariness or utterly ignored—second-class citizens in their own country, they are sent overseas to be treated like second-class citizens in other people's countries.[38]

In the long run, either greater professionalization of the U.S. forces resident in Korea, minimizing the incidents that give rise to current anti-American fervor or greater "Koreanization" of the U.S. military's backup on the peninsula may be the only alternative to total withdrawal.

At the same time, there is no shortage of bad information, which exacerbates tensions on both sides, with regard to the SOFA and other matters affecting bilateral relations. Even "experts" are not immune. Take, for example, this recent statement with regard to the deaths of the two teenage Korean girls discussed above:

> Furthermore, anti-American sentiment was fueled by the handling of a tragic accident in which a U.S. army truck had crushed and killed two teen-aged Korean girls walking on the road. Under the SOFA [Status of Forces Agreement] between the

United States and South Korea, U.S. soldiers who violated the law in South Korea were tried only in the U.S. military court in South Korea, not in the South Korean courts. When the trial took place, the two soldiers involved in the incident were judged not guilty, but the news sparked a series of demonstrations outside the U.S. Embassy protesting not only the decision but the SOFA agreement which robbed South Korea of its right as a sovereign state to control matters of justice in its own courts. *This SOFA agreement was nothing but a vestige of the consular jurisdiction clause of the infamous unequal treaties that the Western powers had imposed on Korea and other Asian states in the nineteenth century. Such arrangements had no place in a U.S./South Korean relationship that was supposed to be based on equality and reciprocity.* (Emphasis added)[39]

As should be abundantly clear, the SOFA agreement with Korea, like those with NATO, Japan, and numerous other countries, has nothing to do with "unequal treaties," except in the perfervid imaginations of those who passionately oppose the stationing of United States forces abroad and have little or no understanding of international law and history. Though these agreements and their implementation remain problematic, they are the product of negotiation (and renegotiation) by sovereign states and other entities that enjoy genuine legal equality. Their very evolution over decades of practice and implementation, including future revisions now in contemplation of the parties, demonstrates this significant reality.

Conclusion

A rethinking of the U.S. military presence, not only resulting from anti-American pressures emanating from South Korea, is now already under way. In the words of one recent analyst: "The U.S. alliance with the Republic of Korea has been America's most consistently dangerous commitment since the end of World War II."[40] Bandow went on to note that America's relations with South Korea have been complicated by Washington's unnatural military presence on the Korean Peninsula, and that no solution would be likely until that unnatural presence was removed. The 37,000 U.S. troops in the South are viewed by many, on both sides of the Pacific, as a Cold War artifact; some would even go further and call for a complete reconsideration of the U.S.–ROK alliance, no longer considering it as valuable as was once thought.

Certainly, there has been value, for both the United States and Korea, in this decades-long relationship and the military cooperation. For the United States, it brought stability to a volatile region, containing Communist expansion in Northeast Asia and creating a peaceful environment for the Asian economic miracle that transformed South Korea, Japan, and their neighbors. For Korea, U.S. protection allowed South Korea to concentrate on its economic and social development, while the North emphasized military expansion at the expense of its people and society.

Bandow argues that the American "tripwire" has discouraged South Korea from investing more heavily in its own defense, citing one estimate that recreating the U.S. defense capabilities would cost $30 billion to replicate, twice South Korea's present annual defense budget.[41] This view echoes the attitudes of many who feel that treating a South Korean ally that is now a rich, developed country according to terms established when it was a poor, devastated nation weakened by civil war makes no sense. What is more immediately relevant is a concern that the U.S. military shield provided by troops stationed under the SOFA is either taken for granted or even viewed with hostility by those who have benefited so greatly from it.

Former South Korean President Kim Dae Jung proclaimed, more than a bit prematurely, that, "The danger of war on the Korea peninsula has disappeared," before turning over his government to his successor, Roh Moo Hyun.[42] As the architect of his Sunshine Policy, seeking rapprochement with the North, it is not surprising that Kim would have advocated such a point of view; but even when he said them, his words sounded quite naive.[43] In hindsight, knowing that North Korea had already resumed its nuclear development program, the world now understands just how badly misguided Kim was.[44] President Roh campaigned for office on a largely anti-American platform (not unlike that of his German counterpart, Gerhard Schroeder, in whose country American forces have also been stationed pursuant to SOFA agreements for over half a century). Roh argued that his nation could "mediate" in any war between America and the North and calling for "concessions from both sides." Indeed, he even stated that "we should proudly say we will not side with North Korea or the United States."[45] A former labor lawyer riding a tide of public resentment toward the United States, Roh won election to be president of South Korea, campaigning on a vow to create greater distance between Washington and Seoul. That pledge foreshadowed strains in the relations between the two allies. But analysts predicted it would not result in a fundamental change in America's military presence or the political bonds between the two nations.

Anti-American sentiment seems to have tracked closely the South's improving relations with Pyongyang. Immediately after the 2000 summit between Kim Dae Jung and Kim Jong Il, thousands of students took to the streets demanding that U.S. troops go home. The fiftieth anniversary of the outbreak of the Korean War on June 25, 2000, provided another opportunity to demand that Washington withdraw.[46] The large U.S. military presence in South Korea creates tinder for the next spark—whether a traffic mishap or violent crime—provided by individual service personnel. Doug Bandow cites Aidan Foster-Carter's thumbnail analysis of the dilemma for the United States: "The U.S. is resented as a bully, just as Japan is forever a war criminal. Conversely, China—despite repressing North Korean refugees—is seen as a benign protector; and North Korea is indulged as a wayward sibling."[47] Thus, there is now greater willingness to reconsider deployment of U.S. military forces in South Korea.

The ongoing conflict in postwar Iraq has led to a new determination to shift forces currently in South Korea to other theaters of U.S. military operations. A May 17, 2004, report in the *New York Times* said: "In what would be the first move of American troops from South Korea to Iraq, the shift would involve about 4,000 troops from the U.S. Army's 2nd Infantry Division, according to a senior Pentagon official in Washington."[48] The argument is succinctly expressed by a scholar from the Hoover Institution:

South Korea's 600,000 troops ought to assume the primary role in defending their own country, relieving U.S. troops for security operations in liberated Iraq or for swift-response roles in the campaign against terror, for example. American forces are stretched thin around the globe in the Balkans, Afghanistan, Japan, Germany, and now the Philippines and Kyrgyzstan. A rebalancing of American power should have taken place after the collapse of the Soviet Union, when the world enjoyed a brief respite from major threats.[49]

There is a justifiable feeling that the United States should no longer feel obliged, due to its commitment to defend South Korea, to act as a whipping boy for that country's awakened nationalism and longstanding unhappiness with its history of subservient relationships to a series of foreign overlords.

By the middle of 2004, the United States had announced its plan to withdraw a third of its 37,000 troops stationed in South Korea by the end of 2005. The announcement came amid lingering uncertainty over the unresolved standoff over North Korea's nuclear arms development program and rising anxiety about the U.S.–South Korean military alliance.[50] A withdrawal on such a scale would be the first major troop reduction on the Korean Peninsula since 1992.

While these troop withdrawals will certainly have an impact on South Korea, there are different assessments as to what it might be. Some conservatives fear that North Korea might be tempted to exploit the military vacuum left by departing U.S. troops; anti-U.S. radicals and peace activists worry that by reducing its exposure of its troops to North Korean attack, the United States might take a more aggressive stance toward the North. About 7,000 U.S. forces and their families would also move from the Yongsan Base in Seoul to an expanded facility south of the capital by 2006. The proposed changes, along with anti-American sentiment among many young South Koreans, have triggered concern in some quarters that President Roh Moo Hyun, may be endangering the U.S.–South Korean alliance by advocating a greater role for his country in its defense.

In the end, the converging realities—that the United States now requires its forces to be more flexibly deployed around the globe and that South Korean political realities make it untenable for a large number of American troops to be stationed permanently there—must change the circumstances on the ground on the Korean Peninsula. Inevitably, this will lead to yet another re-negotiation of the SOFA to reflect those changes. While that event will permit the other concerns outlined above to be revisited and possibly lead to major alterations of the terms of the United States–Republic of Korea SOFA, it may be that nothing short of total withdrawal of foreign forces will satisfy the demands of certain organized groups in South Korea. Only the aftermath of such a decision can decide the practical wisdom of such a course. In the interim, parallel developments in the law affecting SOFAs around the world will determine the space for negotiation allowed the United States and the Republic of Korea as long as forces remain on Korean soil.

Notes

1. Lord Robertson (Secretary General of NATO), "Preface," in *The Handbook of the Law of Visiting Forces*, ed. Dieter Fleck (Oxford: Oxford University Press 2001).

2. See, for example, R.J. Erickson, "Status of Forces Agreements: A Sharing of Sovereign Prerogative," *Air Force Law Review*, vol. 37 (1994), pp. 137–53.

3. *The Schooner Exchange v. McFadden and Others*, 7 Cranch 116, 3 L.Ed. 287 (1812).

4. Ibid., 7 Cranch at 136.

5. See "Section 451. Immunity of Foreign State from Jurisdiction to Adjudicate: The Basic Rule," especially "Comment a. Restrictive theory of immunity," *Restatement of Foreign Relations Law of the United States*, at 396 (Washington, DC: American Law Institute 3d ed., 1986).

6. Foreign Sovereign Immunities Act, 28 United States Code Sections 1604, 1605(a), 1607, 1609, 1610(a), 1610(b), and 1610(d) (1976).

7. Dieter Fleck, "Introduction," in *The Handbook of the Law of Visiting Forces,* ed. Dieter Fleck, pp. 6–7 (Oxford: Oxford University Press 2001) (citing R.R. Baxter in his foreword to S. Lazareff, *Status of Military Forces under Current International Law* (Leyden, 1971)).

8. United States War Crimes Act of 1996, 18 U.S.C. 2441 (1996).

9. Military Extraterritorial Jurisdiction Act of 2000 (Public Law 106–778) (hereafter "MEJA").

10. Agreement between the Parties to the North Atlantic Treaty regarding the Status of Forces, June 19, 1951, 4 U.S.T. 1792, T.I.A.S. NO. 2846, 199 U.N.T.S. 67.

11. Agreement to Supplement the Agreement between the Parties to the North Atlantic Treaty regarding the Status of their Forces with Respect to Foreign Forces stationed in the Federal Republic of Germany, with Protocol of Signature, August 3, 1959, 14 U.S.T. 531, T.I.A.S. No. 5351, 481 U.N.T.S. 262.

12. Agreement under Article VI of the Treaty of Mutual Cooperation and Security between the United States and Japan, Regarding Facilities and Area and the Status of United States Armed Forces in Japan, signed in Washington, DC, on January 19, 1960, and entered into force on June 23, 1960. 11 U.S.T. 1652, T.I.A.S. 4510.

13. See A.B. Norman, "The Rape Controversy: Is a Revision of the Status of Forces Agreement with Japan Necessary?" *Indiana International and Comparative Law Review*, vol. 6 (1996), pp. 717–40.

14. See Chalmers Johnson, "Three Rapes: The Status of Forces Agreement and Okinawa," JPRI Working Paper No. 97, January 2004, www.jpri.org/publications/workingpapers/wp97.html.

15. Article, "Governor Inamine's Nationwide Pilgrimage to Form Alliance to Force Central Government to Move on Revision of the Japan–U.S. Status of Forces Agreement," *Asahi Shimbun*, June 14, 2003, p. 33.

16. Mutual Defense Treaty between the Republic of Korea and the United States of America, signed in Washington, DC, on October 1, 1953, entered into force on November 18, 1954.

17. Agreement under Article 4 of the Mutual Defense Treaty between the Republic of Korea and the United States of America, Regarding Facilities and Area and the Status of United States Armed Forces in the Republic of Korea, signed at Seoul on July 9, 1966, entered into force on February 9, 1967, 17 U.S.T. 1677, T.I.A.S. 163.

18. Understandings on Implementation of the Agreement under Article 4 of the Mutual Defense Treaty between the Republic of Korea and the United States of America, Regarding Facilities and Area and Status of United States Armed Forces in the Republic of Korea, and Related Agreed Minutes, signed in Seoul on February 1, 1991, and entered into force on February 1, 1991.

19. Seung-Hwan Choi, "Policy Provisions for the Revision of the ROK-US Status of Forces

Agreement," *Journal of East Asian Affairs*, vol. 14, no. 2, pp. 241–77, at 247 (Fall/Winter 2000).

20. See Victor Cha and Michael E. O'Hanlon, "A Clumsy U.S. Risks Ties to Seoul," *Los Angeles Times*, December 11, 2002.

21. Not turning over offenders was based on Article 7, Paragraph 3, Item 5(C) of the Status of Forces Agreement (SOFA) under the U.S.–Japan Security Treaty (i.e., "Agreement on Facilities and Zones, and on the Status of United States Forces in Japan," which is based on Article VI of the Treaty of Mutual Cooperation and Security Between Japan and the United States of America; Treaty No. 7 of 1960). In response, vociferous protests spread throughout Japan, demanding the immediate turnover of the suspects, severe punishment for U.S. servicemen who commit crimes, and the prevention of their repetition, as well as a review of the SOFA. But here the Japanese government attempted to deal with the incident through the implementation of the SOFA, and at the same time use this as an opportunity to work with the U.S. government in expanding the U.S.–Japan military alliance into a global institution while calling that undertaking a "redefinition" of the U.S.–Japan Security Treaty.

22. Jim Lea, "U.S. Forces Korea rebuts 'inaccurate' reports on girls' deaths," *Stars and Stripes*, Pacific ed., Sunday, July 28, 2002.

23. Ibid.

24. http://usembassy.state.gov/seoul/wwwh3421.html (accessed May 12, 2004).

25. However, the suspect may refuse to answer questions during police and public prosecutors' interrogation. In such cases, the authorities will usually allow counsel to attend. Korean attorneys are currently lobbying for greater access to their clients.

26. Kuk Cho, "The Unfinished 'Criminal Procedure Revolution' of Post-Democratization South Korea," *Denver Journal of International Law and Policy*, vol. 30, no. 3 (2002), pp. 101–20. Professor Cho goes on to observe:

> [A] number of problems still remain which disturb the change in the Constitution and overshadow the constitutional procedural rights. Police practices of avoiding the warrant requirements for arrest and search-and-seizure have continued. Guarantees of procedural rights for criminal suspects in policy interrogation still remain incomplete and fragile. Investigators enjoy their dominant role in the criminal procedure scheme, while citizens are often treated merely as an object of the investigation. The judiciary is reluctant to exclude illegally obtained confessions and physical evidence in trials. (Ibid.)

27. Dongshim Kim, "South Korea," in *Country Reports*, www.foreignpolicy-infocus.org/basecleanup/countryreports.pdf. Kim is also secretary of the National Campaign for the Eradication of Crime by U.S. Troops in Korea.

28. Ibid.

29. Editorial, "PCB-contaminated waste stored at U.S. base needs to be disposed of quickly," *Asahi Shimbun*, April 20, 2000, p. 2. See also Article, "PCB industrial waste: Legal barricade stands against disposal in U.S.; Federal law prohibits imports; Shipment's destination remains pending," *Daily Yomiuri*, April 20, 2000, p. 38.

30. The United States Environmental Protection Agency subsequently amended its rules in order to clarify that PCB waste in U.S. territories and possessions outside the customs territory of the United States may be moved to the United States for proper disposal. This rule interprets the prohibition on the manufacture of PCBs in Toxic Substances Control Act to allow the movement of most PCB waste for the purpose of disposal because such movement is not considered "import" for purposes of the definition of "manufacture" as that term is used in the Act. This allows disposal of PCB waste in the mainland of the United States where facilities are available that can properly dispose of PCB waste. Federal Register, Vol. 66, pp. 17467–78, March 30, 2001.

31. It did not help matters that the Japanese government learned that in Germany the U.S. government had borne expenses for restoring to their original states a number of similar sites (Ibid.)

32. Articles 2–5.

33. Article 5.

34. Article, *Korea Update*, vol. 15, no. 1 (January 16, 2004) p. 8.

35. Ambassador Thomas C. Hubbard, "U.S.-Korea Relations in Transition," Remarks to the Korean Military Academy Alumni Association War Memorial Museum Hall, Seoul Republic of Korea, March 25, 2003, www.state.gov/p/eap/rls/rm/2003/19195.htm.

36. Donald Gregg, "Anti-Americanism and Sunshine Policy," Speech, 2002.

37. Richard Halloran, "The Rising East," *Honolulu Star-Bulletin*, July 21, 2002.

38. Kevin Heldman, "On the Town with the U.S. Military in Korea," www.zmag.org/zmag/articles/feb97army.html.

39. James B. Palais, The Partnership between Korea and the United States," in East-West Center, *Papers: James B. Palais and Victor D. Cha: U.S.-Korea Relations*, January 9, 2003, posted January 8, 2003, www.eastwestcenter.org//events.

40. Doug Bandow, "Bring the Troops Home: Ending the Obsolete Korean Commitment," Policy Analysis, no. 474, May 7, 2003, p. 1 (Washington, DC: Cato Institute).

41. Ibid., p. 3 (citing "U.S. Troops Pull-Out to Cost $30 Billion," *Korea Times*, October 1, 2002).

42. Calvin Sims, "A Cease-Fire Takes Hold in Korean Propaganda War," *New York Times*, June 17, 2000, p. A3.

43. Even at the time, a more sceptical *Far Eastern Economic Review* queried, "What Thaw in North Korea?" *Far Eastern Economic Review*, June 29, 2000, p. 6.

44. Assistant Secretary of State James Kelly's visit to Pyongyang in October, 2002, led to an admission by North Korea that it was actively processing nuclear material. Kelly charged the North with cheating on the "Agreed Framework," negotiated by the Clinton administration, which in 1994 froze North Korea's nuclear activities in exchange for construction of two light-water reactors and regular shipments of oil.

45. Bandow, supra note 40, at 2. See also Demick, "South Korean Candidate Loses Ally; Presidential hopeful's purported anti-U.S. remark alienates him from Hyundai scion," *Los Angeles Times*, December 19, 2002, p. 3. A key player, Chung Mong Jun, a World Cup organizer and former presidential contender himself, withdrew his endorsement of Roh Moo Hyun just hours before the polls opened, prompted by anti-American remarks made by Roh, saying that the United States might start a war with North Korea and that the South would have to intervene.

46. See generally, Eric V. Larson, Norman D. Levin, Seonhae Baik, and Bogdan Savych, *Ambivalent Allies? A Study of South Korean Attitudes Toward the U.S.*, Rand Report TR-141–SRF, March 2004.

47. Bandow, supra note 40, p. 8 (citing Carter, "Spleen versus Sense in Seoul," *Far Eastern Economic Review*, December 19, 2002, p. 25).

48. James Brooke and Thom Shanker, "U.S. to Shift 4,000 GIs to Iraq from South Korea," *New York Times*, May 17, 2004.

49. Thomas Henriksen, "The Two Koreas: Time to Leave South Korea" *Hoover Digest*, no. 3 (Summer 2003), www-hoover.stanford.edu/publications/digest/033/henriksen.html.

50. Article, "South Korea: U.S. Wants to Pull Out One-third of Troops," *USA Today*, June 7, 2004.

13

Anti-Americanism, Korean Style

Hahm Chaibong

August 15, 2003, marked the fifty-eighth anniversary of Korea's liberation from Japanese colonial rule. Liberation Day has always provided the backdrop for marches and rallies celebrating liberation, denouncing Japan for not coming clean of its past, and otherwise reaffirming national identity and cohesion. However, instead of providing an occasion for another show of unity, last year's celebrations revealed for all to see the deep ideological fault line running through South Korean politics. The occasion was presaged by a dramatic protest staged by members of the radical student organization, *Hanchongnyon*. On August 7, thirteen college students draped in South Korean flags stormed an American base, climbing atop an armored personnel carrier, calling for an end to "United States war mongering on the Korean peninsula" and burning an American flag. Even though the protest lasted only ten minutes before all the participants were arrested, it dramatically transformed the character of the Liberation Day celebrations that followed a week later.

On Liberation Day itself, massive rallies were held by those who, in support of the radical students, called for an end to the "American threat to peace on the Korean peninsula" and the withdrawal of the American forces from South Korea. Simultaneously, massive rallies were organized by veterans of the Korean War, among others, who carried a giant Stars and Stripes alongside South Korea's national flag of equal size. The participants in these marches called for continued close ties between South Korea and the United States and the punishment of "pro-North leftists."

As the Liberation Day marches dramatically illustrate, South Koreans are deeply divided when it comes to the United States. In this country, which used to be one of the staunchest American allies and a bastion of anti-communism, a growing segment of the population is turning "anti-American" and "pro-North Korean." Although perhaps a bit more nuanced, the current South Korean government's behavior seems to betray a similar attitude. When it comes to North Korea, South Korea increasingly parts ways with the United States. If in the past it was South Korea that almost always took the harder line vis-à-vis the North with the United States playing the moderating role, in recent years the roles have reversed. Now it is the United States that tries to pressure, sanction, and punish the North for its "roguish" behavior while South Korea tries to "engage" or "appease" the North.

Americans, policy makers and public alike, are baffled by what they see as a rather sudden and recent surge of anti-Americanism in South Korea. Some are indignant at the "ungrateful" South Koreans. For their part, "pro-American" South Koreans argue that it is, after all, only a small minority, a radical fringe that is anti-American. Others say that it is a protest against the "unilateralism" of the current Bush administration, not against the United States in general. Still others say that it is only a manifestation of an effort on the part of South Koreans to steer a more independent course in foreign policy vis-à-vis the United States, a sign of the country's maturity and democracy.

Whatever one may think of the reason, the irony is lost on few. The United States–South Korea alliance, undergirded by a mutual defense treaty of fifty years' standing, has served as the foundation for security and prosperity in the region. It was forged in a bitter war fought against a common enemy, North Korea. It oversaw the transformation of South Korea from one of the world's poorest nations to one of its most dynamic economies. It also oversaw South Korea's transition from authoritarianism to democracy. All throughout, the military alliance defended South Korea from its belligerent and erratic neighbor to its north. It stands as a shining example of how such a partnership can contribute to nation-building as well as regional security.

However, the end of the Cold War, the economic collapse of North Korea, and the economic development and democratization of South Korea, all of which should have been cause for celebration, have instead become the backdrop for the expression of anti-American sentiment among a growing segment of the South Korean public. Why is this the case? How is it that in the wake of such resounding success the alliance, which made it all possible, seems to be in trouble as never before? Why are South Koreans, who seem to have benefited the most from the bilateral relations, so critical of it?

In the following I elaborate on the short-, mid-, and long-term causes of the current surge of anti-American sentiment in South Korea. By way of putting things into perspective, however, I start by elaborating factors that can and will serve the alliance in the long run, despite recent difficulties. These are long-term forces that have been building over the past decades and have been bringing increasing convergence between the institutions and values of the two countries. Any discussion of anti-Americanism must be premised on an understanding of such long-term trends and factors.

American Values in South Korea

In 2002, South Korea sent 49,046 students to American colleges and universities.[1] There were only two other countries that sent more, India and China, which sent 66,836 and 63,211 respectively.[2] Given the size of South Korea's population (45 million) relative to those of India (1 billion) and China (1.3 billion), this is an astonishing figure. Japan, which ranked fourth, with 46,810, has a population three times that of South Korea. Koreans coming to the United States to study are not only college and university students. According to South Korea's Ministry of Education and Human

Resources, 5,925 elementary, middle, and high school students came to the United States to study in 2001.[3] This was an increase of 100 percent over the year before.[4] Indeed, since 1998, there has been a twofold increase in the number of elementary and middle school children abandoning the local school system to come to the United States. Although figures are scarce, it is no secret that boarding schools in the United States have been inundated with applicants from South Korea in recent years.

Interestingly enough, South Korea's Ministry of Education says that more than 90 percent of the elementary and middle school students are studying in the United States "illegally." Because South Korean law does not allow elementary and middle school children to go abroad to study unless they are accompanied by their parents, whose job postings take them to foreign countries, many who send their children anyway are in effect breaking the law (as of 2001, it has become legal for high school students to go abroad to study). An ever-increasing number of South Korean parents are breaking the law to have their children receive an American education.

One of the consequences of the increasing number of school-aged children coming to the United States is the "lonely goose husband/wife" phenomenon. This term refers to those Korean parents who work and live alone in South Korea while their spouses and children reside in the United States for the sake of the children's education. This has become a major social issue, arousing debates on everything from educational reform to the meaning and role of family and parenthood. The financial consequences have been dire as well. According to the Bank of Korea, South Koreans sent more than U.S. $635 million overseas in the first half of 2002 alone, most of it to the United States, to pay for tuition and related expenses.[5]

Another aspect of the South Korean society with important implications for the future of the South Korea–U.S. relationship is the rise of Christianity. More than 35 percent of South Koreans who profess to have a religion are Protestant Christians, while another 7 percent are Roman Catholics. Given that Christianity was introduced only a century ago, its spread is astonishing. In terms of political and economic influence, Christianity far outweighs Buddhism and Confucianism, religions that have been around for a millennium and half a millennium, respectively. Leading universities such as Yonsei, with the oldest western-style medical school in Korea, as well as Ewha Women's University, the largest women's university in the world with some 40,000 students, were both founded by Christian missionaries. There are innumerable other colleges, high schools, middle schools, and elementary schools that were founded either by missionaries or by Korean Christians with the explicit purpose of providing "Christian education."

The vast majority of the Christian missionaries were Americans, and the links between Korean and American Christian churches and organizations are innumerable. Indeed, the very success of Christianity in South Korea—in stark contrast to its fate in other East Asian countries—is due in large part to its close association with the United States. The first Koreans to convert to Christianity, such as Yoon Chi-ho (1865–1945), Yi Sangjae (1850–1927), Suh Jaepil (Phillip Jaehison, 1864–1951), and Rhee Syngman (1875–1965), did so because they thought of it as an "American" religion.[6]

That many American missionaries worked and sacrificed for the cause of Korean independence during Japanese occupation also left a lasting impression. It is no accident that many of the "pro-American" rallies in recent months were organized by Christians and church-related groups. The close association between Christianity and America in the minds of Koreans continues to this day.

South Korea and the United States are growing closer than ever before also in terms of political and economic institutions and the values that support them. South Korea made a successful transition to democracy in 1987. Since then, its democracy has been consolidated through numerous reforms and three consecutive open, fair, and hotly contested presidential elections. In 1992, Kim Young Sam was the first civilian in thirty years to be elected president. In 1997, the opposition candidate, Kim Dae-jung, won the election. In 2000, President Kim won the Nobel Peace Prize in recognition of his struggle for human rights and democracy during the long years of authoritarian rule in South Korea. He has championed "universal values," or human rights and democracy, in debates against other Asian leaders such as Lee Kuan-yew of Singapore and Mahathir Mohamad of Malaysia, who argued for "Asian values." In late 2002, Roh Moo Hyun, who became his party's presidential candidate through the first-ever American-style primaries, was elected. Today, South Korea has one of the most vibrant and consolidated democracies in the world, let alone in East Asia. It has come farther and faster in terms of accepting and transplanting American-style liberal democracy than almost anyone else outside the mature democracies of the West.

In recent years, South Korea's economic system has also been undergoing reforms to more closely approximate the free-market economy of the United States. Until 1997, the South Korean economy was the best example of the "East Asian economic model." However, after the Asian financial crisis hit, South Korea undertook a quick and fundamental reform of its economy along free-market principles. As a result, the South Korean economy is now one of the most "open" economies in East Asia, surpassing those of Japan and Taiwan in terms of the thoroughness of its pro-market reforms. Succeeding democratically elected governments have undertaken drastic measures against the conglomerates, or *chaebol*, that were guaranteed privileged access to credit and government protection under the old system. The governments have also been battling the powerful labor unions to guarantee a more flexible labor market. Thus, there seems to be a national consensus on reforming the economy along free-market lines.

All these facts underscore the extent to which South Koreans and Americans increasingly share fundamental values and institutions. South Koreans think that the American-style education is the best there is. There is a vast store of goodwill toward Protestant Christianity, the "American religion," which is also the fastest growing religion in South Korea. If one were to ask the average South Korean about the ideal political values and institutions, more often than not he or she will say "human rights" and "liberal democracy," which are recognizably American priorities. There is a clear consensus on the part of the government and the public that in order for it to continue to grow, South Korea's economy must be reformed to conform more closely to the American-style free-market economy. Why then, are we currently witnessing an alarming rise in "anti-American" sentiment in South Korea? What are the factors that lead South Koreans to become anti-American despite the overwhelmingly "pro-American" direction in which their society seems to be heading?

Short-Term Causes: The Festivities and Deaths

In 1995, South Korea's per capita income topped US $10,000. It was a moment for celebration. Given that only thirty years ago South Korea was one of the poorest nations on earth, with a per capita gross national product (GNP) of US $81 (1964), there was just cause for celebration. Indeed, South Korea had beaten the odds. To achieve such prosperity, it had to overcome the legacies of colonialism, a devastating war with North Korea, two coups d'état, and dictatorship in addition to fundamental shifts in the international political and economic order, such as the Cold War, the oil crisis, the end of the Cold War, and globalization. However, the celebration was short-lived. Scarcely two years into the vaunted *manbul shidae* ("era of 10,000 dollars"), South Korea was hit with a financial crisis that brought the nation to the brink of bankruptcy. When foreign investors—alarmed by the economic crisis that first hit Thailand and then swept through Malaysia and Indonesia in quick succession—lost confidence in the South Korean economy and decided to pull their investments, South Korea suddenly faced the very real possibility of default. Humiliated, South Korea turned to the International Monetary Fund (IMF) for an emergency bridge loan that came with a steep price tag, "IMF conditionality." South Koreans called this a "Day of National Humiliation," a reference to the day back in 1910 when Korea lost its independence to Imperial Japan. Indeed, for the next three years, South Korea lost its economic independence, as its economic policy had to be approved by the IMF.

However, true to form, South Koreans rallied behind President Kim Dae-jung, who assumed office in 1998, at the depth of the economic crisis, to rebuild the economy in an astonishingly short time. In 1999, the South Korean economy grew at 11 percent. By 2002, South Korea had the fourth-largest foreign reserves in the world and had paid back the IMF loan years ahead of schedule. By the time of the June 2002 World Cup, co-hosted by South Korea and Japan, South Koreans were celebrating once again. When the national team reached the quarter finals, after having beaten in succession all the "great powers" in soccer—Portugal, Spain, and Italy—Korea's improbable success provided the occasion for an outburst of national pride and solidarity never before witnessed. It was the first time in anyone's memory that Koreans came together not to oppose someone or something, be it a dictator, the communists, or insensitive remarks made by right wing Japanese politicians, but simply to celebrate Korea and being Korean. The rallying cry for this festive occasion was *Tae-han-minkuk,* the official name of the country otherwise known as South Korea. This was something new and exhilarating.

The youths who jammed all the major plazas and thoroughfares of all Korea's major cities to root for the national team seemed uninhibited by the memory of sub-jugation by foreign powers, authoritarianism, poverty, and war, which weighed so heavily on their parents' and grandparents' shoulders. These rambunctious, carefree, and loud young men and women had grown up amid increasing affluence; they were well traveled, Internet-savvy, and proud. How long had it been, in recent memory, that Koreans could feel so proud of their identity without effort, intellectual or emotional? In the "Red Devils," the hordes of cheering fans all wearing identical red shirts, South Korea had finally come of age. Or so it seemed in the summer of 2002.

Even at the height of the soccer festivities, however, news began to trickle out that two fourteen-year-old middle-school girls were killed when an American armored personnel carrier on exercise ran over them as they were coming home from school. In fact, the accident occurred on the very day of the South Korean soccer team's greatest triumph, the day it beat Italy. It was also quickly reported that under what was called the Status of Forces Agreement (SOFA) between the United States Forces Korea (USFK) and South Korea, the Korean prosecutor's office and police had no jurisdiction whatsoever over the soldiers or any facet of the case.

When the U.S. Military Tribunal acquitted the soldiers of all charges, the Korean public was outraged. The same crowd that came out to celebrate being Korean now came out to express anger, frustration, and a sense of utter helplessness. It turned out that being Korean really did not amount to much after all. When two innocent young girls lost their lives and no one took responsibility for it, the reason being that the Korean justice system had no say over the conduct of American soldiers stationed in Korea, it brought back to everyone, including those of the new generation, the old sense of futility and helplessness that Koreans had become so accustomed to but believed they had recently overcome. Many, including both Koreans and Americans, tried to explain the fine points of the American legal system, which emphasized the intent rather than the result; it was also pointed out that South Korean troops serving in Afghanistan and Tajikistan, as part of peacekeeping operations, served under SOFA agreements very similar to the one signed between South Korea and the United States. But none of this seemed to help. President George W. Bush took a while to "apologize" for the incident, first saying that it was not customary for U.S. presidents to make public apologies when, in fact, no crime had been committed by Americans. Then, when he reconsidered, his apologies were conveyed only indirectly through the U.S. ambassador to Korea. This did not help matters either. When the apology did finally come, it was already too late to make much difference.

Midterm Causes: The Fall of Communism and Democratization

South Korea was founded upon the twin ideologies of nationalism and anticommunism. After suffering thirty-five years of harsh colonial rule under the Japanese, nationalism became second nature to Koreans. At the same time, the national division that immediately followed liberation and the ensuing ideological standoff between the two Koreas instilled in South Koreans a strong sense of anticommunism. The

Korean War cemented South Korea's anticommunist ideology, as it demonstrated the brutality of the North Korean communist regime, which would not hesitate to wage a bloody war against fellow Koreans. The problem was that the two ideologies pulled the nation in two very different directions. While nationalism made Koreans deeply suspicious of any foreign intervention in their affairs, anticommunism made it necessary for South Koreans to maintain a close relationship with the United States.

The tension inherent between the two ideologies soon became apparent. In the immediate aftermath of independence, there was a widespread call for the punishment of those who collaborated with the Japanese and had prospered under the colonial rule. However, as was the case in postwar Germany, the American occupying forces and the conservative right-wing government established in 1948 employed the services of many of the pro-Japanese collaborators in the fight against communist and leftist elements within South Korea. To the chagrin and anger of many, many of those who were trained by the Japanese police and military were rehabilitated, and drafted in the war against communism.[7] The failure to punish the "pro-Japanese collaborators" has haunted the South Korean political and historical conscience ever since.

The anticommunist ideology also justified the normalization of relations between South Korea and Japan, much sooner than most Koreans had anticipated. The Cold War and the Korean War gave South Koreans a new and more threatening enemy in North Korean communists, while Japan, its former colonial master, became a major partner in the struggle against communism. Under the U.S. umbrella, both nuclear and ideological, South Korea had to quickly make amends with Japan as the two countries became the bulwark against communism in East Asia. With pressure from the United States and pressed by the urgent need for economic aid, President Park Chung Hee restored full diplomatic relations with Japan in 1965, only twenty years after Korea was freed from Japan's colonial yoke. There were massive demonstrations against what many saw as a sellout. To be sure, South Korea never signed a formal alliance treaty with Japan, reflecting its unease with the seemingly unrepentant former colonial power. However, the threat of communism and North Korea bound South Korea and Japan in a most unlikely "virtual alliance."[8]

Under this arrangement South Korea prospered. Even while at times forced to devote up to a quarter of the national budget to national defense, South Korea was able to achieve stunning economic growth. It also made a successful transition to democracy. None of this would have been possible in the absence of the security arrangements and economic cooperation with the United States and Japan.

However, with the end of the Cold War and the overwhelming economic and political success of the South, anti-communism began to lose its force. In its stead, the discourse of nationalism began to reclaim its primacy. With the transition to democracy and liberalization, views that were banned as threats to national security began to be debated publicly. These included ultranationalistic interpretations of Korea's modern history, which cast South Korea's path to political and economic development as well as its close relationships with the United States and Japan in an extremely negative light. According to such arguments, the Korean people of both the South and the North were victims of superpower confrontation. Korea suffered national division because the superpowers used them as pawns in their own strategic games, with little or no consideration for the interests of the Korean people. The Korean War was not a war between communists and those who tried to defend freedom. Rather, it was a nationalistic war to rid the nation of foreign influence, namely the United States, and a puppet regime in the South supported by it. Kim Il-sung, the North Korean dictator, was not a war criminal who started a fratricidal war with the help of the Soviet Union and Communist China but a leader of the Korean nation who tried to liberate his southern brethren from the imperialists. The reunification of the peninsula was thwarted by the intervention of American imperialists who saw Korea as the linchpin of their strategy to dominate the Asia-Pacific region.

Furthermore, as North Koreans and ultranationalists in the South argue, the North does not have foreign troops on its soil, as the South does. The North did not capitulate to the Japanese by hurriedly normalizing relations with the former colonial aggressors, the way the South did back in 1965. Despite its poverty, the North has been able to maintain its sense of national pride and independence, while the South sold its soul to capitalism and American imperialists, even though it came to enjoy a modicum of economic prosperity by doing so. And once nationalism became the sole criterion by which to measure legitimacy, the close security and economic alliance forged between Korea, the United States, and Japan suddenly took on a sinister tone. The United States military presence in South Korea was no longer a tripwire to deter communist aggression but a barrier to reunification. The close economic tie between South Korea and Japan was perpetuating Korea's dependence on Japan.

Such arguments originally found acceptance among radical students and leftist intellectuals of the South in the 1980s. In their opposition to military-backed regimes, which, they thought, were in turn backed by the United States, they began to turn to a virulent form of nationalism to criticize both the dictatorship and its "patron." Such arguments are, however, finding increasing acceptance among a wider public in the postauthoritarian and post–Cold War South Korea. With the collapse of the Soviet block and the ensuing collapse of the North Korean economy, neither communist ideology nor the North Korean regime seems to be a serious threat anymore. The United States is no longer seen as the "guarantor" of South Korea's security. Instead, the occasional crimes committed by American soldiers stationed in South Korea are receiving unprecedented attention as South Koreans become increasingly conscious of their rights, individual and national. The huge U.S. base in the heart of Seoul, the capital city, is no longer seen as a symbol of American commitment to South Korean security but as one of injured national pride.

Long-Term Causes: National Identity versus Civilization

The past century has been a period of major and multiple "clashes of civilizations" for Koreans. Until the late nineteenth century, Koreans were part of a stable and largely peaceful world order. The Chŏson dynasty (1392–1910) voluntarily and enthusiastically became a part of the regional order, with China at its center. By actively learning and absorbing the neo-Confucian civilization emanating from China, Chŏson built a civilization with proud intellectual and cultural achievements.[9] However, with the advent of the West, it was forced to come to terms with a civilization very different from the one it had adopted 600 years earlier. After a failed effort to defend the "orthodoxy," Koreans changed their minds and tried to adopt the western way. Their efforts proved futile, however, as Japan, which was quicker to adopt the ways of the West, annexed Korea as part of its growing empire.[10]

Under Japanese colonial rule, Koreans were forced to adopt a modern civilization as interpreted by the Japanese. From 1910 to 1945, Koreans lived under Japanese political, economic, social, educational, and cultural institutions. All Koreans had to learn the Japanese language while the brightest students went to Japanese universities. Shintoism, the Japanese state religion, was forced upon Koreans. Seoul became a miniature Tokyo. Starting in the late 1930s, the teaching of Korean language and history was altogether banned, while Koreans were forced to exchange their names, both first and last, for Japanese ones. It looked as though Korea was going to be fully absorbed into the Japanese empire without a trace.

Then, with the defeat of Japan in World War II, yet another civilization was imposed on Koreans. The Japanese surrender of 1945 brought independence and what Koreans thought would be a chance for them to chart their own destiny. However, in the ensuing Cold War, the North became a Soviet "satellite," adopting a Soviet-style communist system while the South came under U.S. military rule from 1945 to 1948. The next half-century saw the two Koreas trying their best to adopt the political, economic, social, educational, and cultural institutions and values of their respective "senior partners." The North's effort to emulate the Soviet model failed utterly for both internal and external reasons. The fall of the Soviet Union and the eastern bloc removed whatever sources of external support communist North Korea had enjoyed. The failure to adopt reform measures to overhaul its decrepit system has resulted in a state failure of disastrous proportions. In stark contrast, the South succeeded, despite fits and starts, in its efforts to adopt liberal democracy and a capitalist economy. Today, South Koreans continue to pursue avidly the values and institutions of democracy and a free-market economy.

Regardless of the successes and failures, the process of such fundamental and total civilizational transitions left deep psychological scars on the collective Korean psyche. The most difficult thing, of course, was to try to hold onto a sense of "Koreanness" as the nation moved from the Chinese to Japanese to American spheres of influence. These efforts have resulted in a time-honored tradition of antiforeign sentiment. The advent of the West at the end of the nineteenth century produced an "antiwestern" reaction that lasted much longer in Korea than in either China or Japan. The modernizers of this period, for their part, expressed a virulent form of anti-Chinese and anti-Confucian sentiment. They regarded China and Confucianism, so long intrinsic to their identity, as the major obstacles to modernization. When the Japanese intention of annexing Korea became obvious, a powerful anti-Japanese movement and senti-ment was mobilized. During the Japanese occupation, even while absorbing and in some cases even prospering under the modern civilization that was imposed on them, Koreans continuously stoked the fire of anti-Japanese nationalism.

Given the enormity of the challenges, it must be said that, on the whole, Koreans, at least those in the South, succeeded admirably in adapting themselves to shifting "global standards," whether they were Chinese, Japanese, or American. However, during each and every period of civilizational transition, there were those who tried to uphold the "tradition" or "orthodoxy" against the encroachment of an alien civiliza-tion, inevitably regarded as "barbaric" and "heterodox." Even though Koreans had ultimately to give up their tradition in the face of the more powerful new civilizations, it took much adjusting, psychological and intellectual as well as physical, to adapt to the new realities and identities.

Anti-Americanism then is an expression of a deep-seated sense of anxiety regard-ing Korean identity. It is a reaction to yet another chapter in their history where Kore-ans are forced to adapt to a new civilization. It is not so much America per se that is the object of nationalist sentiment. America just happens to be the hegemon of the time and the possessor of the "global standard" that Koreans are forced to adopt. Nationalism needs imperialist aggressors. Japan, the former colonial master that con-tinues to be an overwhelming economic presence and the United States, which main-tains ground troops on South Korean soil, are the imperialists of choice.

Conclusion: Back to the Future

In the short run, anti-American sentiment in South Korea was born of a confluence of factors: the euphoric mood in South Korea due to successful economic recovery and World Cup success, suddenly soured by the news of accidental deaths of schoolgirls killed during an American military exercise. The midterm cause that exacerbated what could have been a passing incident was the revisionist and ultranationalist dis-course that began to receive public articulation and attention in the aftermath of the Cold War, economic development, and democratic transition. Born of the success of the United States–South Korea alliance, they have now become its most severe critic. From the long-term perspective, the current surge of anti-American sentiment in South Korea is a part of an effort to articulate a sense of national and cultural identity on the part of Koreans, who have had to go through major civilizational shifts. Anti-Ameri-canism as currently expressed in South Korea is part of the process of more fully accepting the "global standard" and an effort to find the right balance between being "Korean" and being "global."

Of course, what may be most important are the short- and midterm causes, be-cause, as John Maynard Keynes so famously quipped, "in the long-run we are all dead." However, even in the short and medium term, there are more reasons for hope than for despair regarding the future of the South Korea–U.S. relationship. As we look to the future, we see more and more South Koreans flocking to the United

States to be educated, imbibing American values and learning about American institutions, the knowledge of which they plan to take back to their homeland to put into practice. The already closely conforming political and economic institutions of the two countries are growing closer still, while the network of personal connections between Koreans and Americans established in the elementary, middle, and high schools, as well as the colleges and universities, will prove to be a great reservoir of goodwill, mutual understanding, and appreciation that will serve the bilateral relationships well into the future.

As South Korea continues to pursue its dream of building a prosperous nation with strong democratic institutions, the United States will continue to provide the standard as well as the example. At the same time, South Koreans will insist on articulating and retaining their sense of cultural identity even while absorbing the global/American standard. There will be times when they will see the need to bring in more universal standards and values. At other times they will emphasize their cultural difference and particularities. The important thing will be to strike the right balance each time, so that xenophobic nationalism cannot hold sway and undermine what has been one of the most fruitful and successful bilateral relationships in history.

Notes

1. Institute of International Education, www.opendoors.iienetwork.org/.
2. Ibid.
3. *Chosun Ilbo*, September 12, 2002.
4. Ibid.
5. Ibid.
6. For an account of the history of the role of Protestant Christianity in Korea, see Kenneth M. Wells, *New God, New Nation: Protestants and Self-Reconstruction Nationalism in Korea, 1896–1937* (Honolulu: University of Hawaii Press, 1991).
7. See, for example, Bruce Cumings, *Korea's Place in the Sun: A Modern History* (New York: Norton, 1997), especially "Chapter 4: The Passions, 1945–1948."
8. See, for example, Victor Cha, *Alliance Despite Antagonism: The United States-Korea-Japan Security Triangle* (Stanford: Stanford University Press, 2000).
9. For an account of the transmission of neo-Confucianism from China to Korea, see Hahm Chaibong, "Family Versus the Individual: The Politics of Marriage Laws in Korea," in *Confucianism for the Modern World,* ed. Daniel A. Bell and Hahm Chaibong (Cambridge: Cambridge University Press, 2003,) pp. 334–59.
10. For an account of the Korean response to the changing world order in the late nineteenth–early twentieth centuries, see, Hahm Chaibong, "Civilization, Race or Nation? Korean Visions of the Regional Order in the Late 19th Century," in *Northeast Asia Between Regionalism and Globalization: Korea at the Center,* ed. Charles Armstrong, Gilbert Rozman, and Samuel Kim (Armonk, NY: M.E. Sharpe, forthcoming 2005).

Part IV

Civil Society Perspectives

14

Citizen Power in
Korean-American Relations

Katharine H.S. Moon

Until recent years, "anti-Americanism"[1] in South Korea seemed like an oxymoron to many observers both within and outside the country. After all, for about half a century, Koreans shared ties of blood through the loss of Korean and American lives in the Korean War, a common enemy, and a moral and military commitment to the defense and prosperity of South Korea. For most of those fifty years, Koreans have been known to "love" Americans, welcoming them with open hearts in gratitude and friendship for American military and economic aid during their struggling years and admiring many aspects of American political and cultural life. Korea was one of the few places in the world where "Yankee go home" was not supposed to be uttered.

Since the explosion of civic activism and candlelight vigil protests on the streets of Korea in the winter of 2002–3, American policy makers, observers, and the media have tended to shake their heads at the unthinkable development, scratch their heads in consternation at this "new phenomenon," or respond with a sense of hurt and anger at the "ingratitude" of the Korean public. Korean elites and American observers have been regarding anti-Americanism as a weapon of the Korean masses, something dangerous and unpredictable, a "critical wild card" in the future of the bilateral relationship.[2]

But anti-Americanism is neither a new phenomenon in Korea nor a dangerous weapon. How much it serves as a wild card depends significantly on how policy elites in Korea and the United States understand and manage the public's assertion of their interests in the foreign-policy and security arena. To do that, we need to place anti-American activism in the larger context of social movements and political developments in Korea's fast-growing democracy. Last, we need to acknowledge that anti-Americanism is not solely a Korea-made problem; Americans, through actions and inactions and transnational activism in the East Asia region, have helped create this dynamic of contention.

Accumulated Grievances

Koreans did not all of a sudden discover grievances and publicize complaints against the United States, particularly against the troops stationed in Korea. Historian Max

Hastings recounts an incident during the Korean War that would resonate today, in the aftermath of the deaths of the two teenage girls who were run over by a U.S. armored vehicle in June 2002. In the summer of 1951, he writes, the "Eighth Army was forced to issue a forceful order" for soldiers to cease "to take a perverse delight in frightening civilians" and attempting to "drive the Koreans off roads and into ditches." The order concluded with the following words: "We are not in this country as conquerors. We are here as friends."[3] Here the implication is that the soldiers were deliberately abusive, whereas the deaths of the two girls were declared accidental by both governments. But whatever may be recorded as historical record in American books and documents, such incidents are not lost on those Koreans who have lived near U.S. bases for decades and whose lives have been physically, psychologically, and economically touched by the troop presence, particularly since the permanent basing of troops in the mid-1950s.

Ironically, it was the powerless and most despised in Korean society who periodically voiced their grievances in camptowns prior to democratization in the late 1980s. In the 1960s and 1970s, camptown women who worked as providers of sex to the U.S. troops publicly demonstrated against sexual violence and demanded accountability from the U.S. military and local Korean authorities for the murder of their peers, allegedly by U.S. personnel. For example, in 1969, more than 300 prostitutes staged a protest in front of the 8057 American Unit in Bupyong, demanding justice for a peer, Lee Unja, who allegedly had died at the hands of a U.S. serviceman. The *Korea Times* (May 15, 1969) reported, "The hearse, carrying the girls in white mourning dress, stopped in front of the unit's front door en route to a burial site and shouted: 'Come out Teni [Tenney]. Let him appear before us.' They also attempted to enter the unit compound and were stopped by about 50 American military police and 30 Korean police." Two years later, approximately 200 camptown prostitutes "carrying sticks" staged a similar protest outside Camp Ames to demand the immediate arrest of another alleged GI murderer.[4] Even under the authoritarian rule of Park Chung Hee, the Korean media periodically covered local residents' complaints and frustrations toward the U.S. military. On August 7, 1968, *Dong-a Ilbo* charged U.S. military police at Bupyong with "unlawfully confining people, searching houses and assaulting local residents" and cited various incidents of violence and mistreatment toward Koreans.[5] And the U.S. military monitored such tensions as well: One U.S. Forces Korea (USFK) civilian observer of community relations stated in a memorandum in 1968: "It is easily conceivable that the large number of assaults by U.S. personnel against Korean national females, no matter what provocation might have been given for these assaults, could be made into a major article condemning American brutality."[6]

With Washington's unilateral withdrawal of the 7th Infantry Division from Korea in 1970–71 and the ensuing reconfiguration of remaining troops came social chaos, tension, and violence as new groups of soldiers encountered one another and the local Korean residents. For example, from July 13 to August 9, 1971, the majority of villagers in Anjong-ri near Camp Humphreys took to protests against the command's imposition of off-limits decrees, following racial violence a few days earlier, on local bars and restaurants. During a series of protests, the crowd hurled stones at U.S. military personnel, overturned the Pyongtaek County Police superintendent's car, demanded to meet the commander of Korea Support Command (KORSCOM), and stated in a formal letter to the commander that the crowd outside was holding a total of six U.S. soldiers hostage. The U.S. base authorities and local Korean National Police initially responded to the protests with blockades, gas grenades, and increased police presence. More than $54,000 of damage was reported by the Korean side alone. The candlelight vigils in the winter of 2002–3 were by comparison peaceful and orderly, although tens of thousands across the country were involved.

As in the past, today's anti-Americanism is often expressed in emotional utterances and hyperbolic rhetoric, but there are many real and legitimate personal grievances at the root of public criticism. And many of the grievances, past and present, sound strikingly similar: sexual crimes/abuse of women; negative impact of base decisions on local economies; lack of information exchange and consultation with local residents about U.S. military activities; arrogance toward Koreans and ignorance of Korean customs and ways. Although policy elites in both countries may not consider the loss of W5,000 (US $4) cab fare a serious matter, such is not the case for the taxi driver who was not paid his fare by a GI, a common and recurring complaint over the decades. There are other variations on this theme—for example, elderly peddlers and store owners in camptowns expressing resentment and resignation at the recurring petty theft allegedly committed by GIs over the years, and other forms of daily humiliation.[7] Moreover, given Koreans' tendency toward collective identity and historical memory, one cab driver's or storekeeper's experience gets added to and conflated with the numerous other accounts of such incidents across time.

This type of collectivized psychology and narrative of a specific event tends to baffle if not outright annoy Americans, but here it is important to keep in mind that whether individual or communal, criticism and resentment toward Americans' behavior are not new. Along with memories of American heroism, the memory of past misunderstandings, slights, excesses, or abuses by U.S. troops and/or command—whether alleged, accidental, intentional, or otherwise—remains alive. Older generations have passed on to their kin their experiences of American racism and arrogance, along with their genuine admiration and gratitude, since the days of the Korean War. Some accounts may have been diluted and depoliticized as family history and survivor stories, but others have been passed down as stories of victimization and wrongs that should be righted. Villagers in Maehyang-ri, for example, have knitted together stories of past suffering with accounts of new ones (regarding noise pollution and property damage from the Koon-ni strafing range), together with the frustration that no one, neither Koreans nor Americans, wanted to hear about such grievances for decades. Such frustrations and humiliations become a source of collective *han* (accumulated frustration; unfulfilled hope).

For most of the half-century of hosting U.S. troops, local grievances have gone suppressed or ignored by Korean government officials and Korean society at large. The areas housing U.S. bases still remain, though to a lesser degree than ten or more years ago, "pariah towns," shunned by "normal," "regular" Korean society. Camptowns have been synonymous with prostitution, drugs, violence, gangsters, and moral decadence, and they served as "buffer areas" that would absorb and block the spread of negative foreign influence in Korean society. Their economies became dependent on the spending of U.S. service personnel, while citizens' grievances and demands were stifled by local police and government officials. In general, the local governments avoided conflicts that might jeopardize relations with the nearby U.S. command, and under the authoritarian Park and Chun regimes, the local officials' political mandate had come from Seoul, not local residents. Lacking political autonomy, it was in the interest of local officials to keep camptown problems suppressed and out of the political limelight.

Accumulated grievances, once repressed, suppressed, and/or neglected by either Korean or American authorities, form one strand of the twofold lineage of current anti-Americanism. The other strand is the accumulated rhetoric, protest culture, and mobilizational power of the democracy movement, past and present.

Democratization and Social Movements

Since the late 1990s, anti-Americanism as a nationwide phenomenon has been made possible by what I call the "activist establishment" in contemporary Korea. This includes, on the one hand, the individuals who had fought in the 1970s and 1980s against the military regimes and authoritarian politics. For many, their political awareness and experience came of age during years of repressive crackdowns, surveillance, and imprisonment by the Park, Chun, and Roh regimes. These activists earned their colors in a context where political engagement was tantamount to physical and rhetorical confrontation, self-sacrifice, zero-sum outcomes, the maintenance of strict loyalties, and mistrust of political elites. They helped shape a political environment in which *t'ujaeng* (struggle/fight) was the one reliable resource and method of influence, and energy was focused on challenging and resisting "big power" (e.g., military regime, *chaebol*, Japan, the United States).

In particular, through their exposure to the Kwangju era and self-identification as victims of it, and their related experimentation with leftist anti-American ideology and study groups, hard-core activists became sensitized to American actions and inactions in the context of Korean-American relations. Jae-kyoung Lee notes that by the mid-1980s, "virtually all efforts of the student movement would concentrate on the struggle against the United States."[8] These traditional activists also became accustomed to vying with the central government and the *chaebol* for recognition and legitimacy as "keepers of the national conscience." Here, the legacy of anti-Americanism in the 1980s—when dissidents believed that they represented the "real" Korean nation, in contrast to the "puppet regime" of Chun Doo Hwan (with the Reagan administration serving as puppeteer)—still resonates. As in the past, the contemporary turn toward anti-American nationalism can be read as a rallying cry for the formation and recognition of the Korean *nation* under *their* moral and political leadership.

Some members of Hanch'ongnyon, Chon'kuk Yonhap, and One Korea, would belong to this "people's movement" (*minjung*) category of social activism.[9] Despite this ancestry, today's anti-Americanism is mainstream and moderate, due to the leadership and influence of civil society organizations that are part of the new wave of democratization in the 1990s[10]: the "citizens' movements," nongovernmental organizations (NGOs), and professional organizations such as the Citizens Coalition for Economic Justice (Kyongsillyon), Korea Federation of Environmental Movements (KFEM), Green Korea United (GKU), Korea House for International Solidarity (KHIS, Kukje yondae), and Lawyers for Democratic Society (Minbyon). "Emphasizing that they would lead a new generation of social movements, the citizens' groups rejected the class-based and confrontational strategies of the past in favor of a nonviolent, peaceful, and lawful movement style and specific policy alternatives."[11] In contrast to the anti-American movement of the 1980s, which tended to be violent, heavy on rhetoric (nationalist and anti-imperialist), and light on empirical research and analysis, the current movement emphasizes expert investigation of problems, comparative analysis with other countries, and institutional measures for redress (i.e., through the National Assembly and the courts). Their conscious aim is to advance citizens' rights and welfare through democratic channels of expression.

In this active milieu of civil society activism, local camptown grievances and interests have gained national attention and political weight through the network of the established citizens' movement and people's movement NGOs, most of which are based in Seoul, and through the Internet. The head of the National Campaign for the Eradication of Crimes against Korean Civilians by U.S. Troops, the main watchdog group monitoring U.S. troop behavior, has emphasized that local grievances and complaints prompt the mobilization of activists and organizations and give legitimacy to the larger social movement that criticizes U.S. policies and behaviors.[12] This bridging of Seoul and the regions, the activist elite and local villagers is a new development made possible through democratization and the growth of civil society. Complaints toward U.S. bases serve as the magnet for both types to come together.

In addition, many local governments in the areas housing U.S. installations have joined citizen-activists to call for changes in base-community relations. In May 2000, the Inchon City Council coordinated efforts with NGOs to form the first "Citizens' Congress for the return of land used by the USFK in Bupyong."[13] They aimed to reclaim land that the U.S. military was using as a junkyard. Bupyong is one example among others where officials, merchants and residents viewed the U.S. base as an obstacle to economic progress and city planning. Having been dependent on the bases when alternative sources of income were not readily available, camptowns have increasingly grown ambitious to pursue more cutting-edge modes of income generation. Moreover, they seek to slough off the cast of pariah town and transform their economic and social image.

Through the U.S. base issue and the anti-American movement, local governments also have been seeking to transform their political power vis-à-vis the capital. Officials of the fourteen local governments that house U.S. bases met for the first time in

Taegu on May 24, 2000, to establish a "nationwide consultative body" of local governments. They "outlined the present situation of U.S. military bases in their respective areas. They also explained the status of relationships between U.S. military bases and local governments, the impact of U.S. military bases on regional development and the size of revenue losses caused by the presence of U.S. bases, as well as how the revenue losses were calculated."[14]

The consultative body submitted legislation to the National Assembly, calling for increased central government grants and aid to local governments and the establishment of local development committees at central and local levels; they also called on the national government to make thorough environmental impact assessments around U.S. base areas. They claimed that local governments and residents bore a disproportionate and undue share of the burden of maintaining the U.S. troop presence.[15] In a sense, these local governments were challenging the central government's near-monopoly of power over policies regarding U.S. bases and were asserting their own conceptualization of national security as needing to incorporate and balance the needs of local residents and governments.

Studies on decentralization emphasize that power struggles between the central government and the lower-level administrative units are an inevitable part of the political process of democratization.[16] Moreover, the struggles concern both policy options and social movements. Indeed, new laws that allowed for the establishment of local assemblies in 1991 and the popular election of local government officials in 1995, thereby restoring local self-rule after more than thirty years, have facilitated the new political consciousness and activism among citizens and local officials. In particular, local leaders require the votes and support of everyday residents, not solely the central government. Jong Soo Lee notes that with decentralization, local Korean governments generally have focused on social policies more than other issues.[17] Many of the anti-American issues publicly aired since the mid-1990s fall into this category: environmental and noise pollution, waste disposal, damage to personal property, transportation and infrastructural development, and the safety of women and girls.

Yet, the meaning of democracy and the process of democratization would be empty if all local governments and residents held uniform views and advocated the same policy measures regarding the U.S. bases. And regrettably, the U.S. media by and large have portrayed citizen activism in Korea since the late 1990s in such a manner. But that is not the case. Even the local areas housing U.S. installations are not of one voice; rather, differences of interest and opinion exist. In Kunsan, when activists critical of the U.S. base presence and the Status of Forces Agreement demonstrated publicly in the late 1990s, some local store owners catering to the U.S. military community asked the activists to tone down their protests in regard for their livelihoods.[18]

Pyongtaek, which houses the U.S. Air Force Base (Osan), is the most obvious outlier. It was the meeting ground for the first pro-U.S. rally among camptowns amid the heavy anti-American protests around the country in the winter of 2002 and 2003. In mid-January, pro-U.S. demonstrators denounced the candlelight vigil-goers as radical leftists and thanked the U.S. military for its continued presence.[19] The local

Pyongtaek Simin Sinmun (Pyongtaek Times) pointed out that not only Pyongtaek residents but also about 300 people from Seoul, Inchon, Suwon, and other areas had come together to form a crowd of 900 in support of the U.S. military and the patriotic defense of the South against the communist North.[20]

More recently, with the talk of moving the U.S. 8th Army Headquarters from Seoul to Pyongtaek, the differences of political opinion and economic interests have become more apparent. Many local business interests are gearing up to enlarge their pocketbooks through the prospective increase in the U.S. presence.[21] At the same time, it is clear that anti-base activists, some of whom had opposed the first proposed plan to move U.S. troops from Seoul to Pyongtaek in the early 1990s, have geared up for another fight. They had a public confrontation with officials of the Kyonggi Provincial Council in mid–late March 2003. They challenged the representational legitimacy of the council's passing of a resolution in support of the transfer of U.S. troops from Seoul to Pyongtaek. The local Labor Party and other progressive parties joined forces with the local chapter of the Korean Confederation of Labor Unions, the Pyongtaek Farmers' Association, and other NGOs, such as the Pyongtaek Committee to Oppose the Expansion of U.S. Bases, to release a public statement and promise citizen activism to oppose the "antidemocratic" procedures of the provincial council and the repositioning of U.S. forces from Yongsan.[22]

To understand the characteristics and dynamics of organized anti-Americanism requires an acknowledgment of what it is not. It is not a monolithic movement or about ideological determination. It is not equivalent to nationalism or tantamount to generational amnesia about the Korean War and communism. It is not just *anti*-something but *for* something: to exercise newly developed democratic muscles and to express grievances and assert interests in a freer political environment.

Viewed from the lens of social movements, anti-Americanism is a form of collective action through coalition politics, encompassing a wide spectrum of political orientations, interests, and degrees of commitment. The constituent groups and individual participants include religious activists, law professionals, environmentalists, academics, radical students, peace activists, both the progressive Korean Confederation of Trade Unions (KCTU) and the conservative Federation of Korean Trade Unions (FKTU), leaders of mainstream NGOs, reunification activists, local government officials, common villagers, National Assembly members, and the media. The combination and intensity of commitment to issues and activism among these participants is not of a fixed nature. Organized anti-Americanism is characterized by peaks and valleys; there is quiet and lull through time, then intensified attention and activism when something happens, such as Nogun-ri, Maehyang-ri, the revision of the the Status of Forces Agreement (SOFA), oil seepage from U.S. bases, FX fighter plane sales, President George W. Bush's "axis of evil" remark, and, more recently, the crushing death of two teenage girls who were run over by a U.S. armored vehicle.[23]

This loose coalition style of activism allows disparate groups to pool human, financial, and political resources as well as expertise, enabling a larger impact on society than one or two organizations alone might muster. On the other hand, it is difficult for these groups to sustain momentum and effort on any one particular issue because each member organization has its own set of concerns and agendas that may have nothing to do with the anti-American issue at hand. Additionally, each member organization has to weigh the costs and benefits of particular political and social activities to ensure that their core interests and constituencies are kept intact. As each issue arises, goals, methods, and responsibilities need to be negotiated and coordinated anew with old and new participant groups. And even though media coverage tends to overgeneralize, there is heated debate within the coalition movement over differences of opinion and competition over political interpretation and policy prescriptions regarding the Korea–U.S. relationship.[24] This mode of coalition activism is a salient form of civic participation in postauthoritarian Korean society, and civic groups and individual leaders are very adept at networking and pooling resources case by case.

Made in Korea? Making Transnational Connections

Anti-Americanism in Korea–U.S. relations is not made in Korea or by Koreans alone. The national anti-American movement must be understood in the context of regional and international anti-base activism. Korean and Okinawan activists have been exchanging information, agendas, and "personnel" since the late 1980s. In particular, since the 1995 gang rape of an Okinawan teenage girl by U.S. marines in Okinawa, the anti-base activism on the island has broadened and intensified within and stretched outward toward Korea. For example, in 1997, Okinawans visited Seoul to participate in the weekly Friday demonstration in front of Yongsan Garrison (organized by the National Campaign in Seoul). In 1998, Okinawans formed the *Han-Oki minjung yondae* (people's solidarity) with the purpose of educating themselves about U.S. military-related problems affecting Koreans in particular and of networking with peace activists in Taiwan, Philippines, and Puerto Rico. The Han-Oki members were reported to be learning eagerly the Korean language.[25]

Korean activists also extended their solidarity and network to Okinawa. In August 1996, Kim Yonghan, a Pyongtaek resident-turned-anti-base activist, visited Japan at the invitation of Japanese peace activists. He participated in activities commemorating the fifty-first year of the bombing of Hiroshima, learned about the particularities of the U.S. presence in Japan, the nature of the anti-base movement in Okinawa, and enlisted Okinawans' help in the Korean return-of-land movement he helped lead in the mid- to late 1990s. The transnational women's movement against militarism and violence against women particularly has served as a key network for information exchange, coalition building, and a broader audience. Activists from the United States and Okinawa/Japan have helped lead the transnational movement through regular conferences and people-to-people exchanges, in addition to personal communication.

On the other side of the Pacific Rim, activists from Vieques, Puerto Rico, have built bridges of cooperation and solidarity with Koreans, especially those protesting the use of the Koon-ni range for bombing practice. Ismael Guadalupe Ortiz, a leader of the anti-base movement in Vieques, visited Maehyang-ri in July 1999 and expressed alarm at how much worse the situation is for the Korean villagers, given that they live much closer to the strafing area than their Vieques counterparts.[26] Such words of empathy were highlighted by the Korean media and NGO groups in their newsletters and periodicals. More recently, Guadalupe sent a message of "solidarity with the people of Korea" condemning and protesting the U.S. troops' role in the deaths of the two teenage girls: "This is one more abuse added to those crimes perpetrated by the U.S. military against the Korean people since the Korean War. These crimes committed by the U.S. are awaiting the repudiation of the world community. . . ."[27] This message was delivered not only to Koreans but also made available to "netizens" (Internet citizens) around the world by various Web sites.

In return for the Vieques support, Korean activists have visited the island to learn about the nature of the problems the residents face and the organization and activities of the Puerto Rican movement. Both groups have staged marathon campouts, teach-ins, and sit-ins near U.S. installations in their respective lands. (The Vieques protests have been more severe in that participants broke into the military area and staged a sit-in for over a year.) And each side has publicly expressed moral support for the other's cause as part of a larger solidarity movement critical of U.S. military power.

The 1990s allowed for citizens not only in Korea but elsewhere in the world to claim access to and participation in international relations. Not only new actors but also new issues entered the political arena, many of which had been deemed personal or private or simply "national" in nature and therefore not legitimate as international policy concerns during most of the Cold War era. But the 1990s became the decade of NGOism around the world and this transformed previously "soft" issues like migration, the environment, and gender-based war crimes into major issues on national and international agendas. In Korea also, the 1990s were the foundational years for the NGOism and civil society activism nationally and internationally. Hyuk-Rae Kim observes that democratization in Korea is linked to "both an unprecedented growth of the NGO sector in general and the emergence of environmental and citizens' movements specifically." For example, 62 percent of NGOs advocating for citizens' rights, 51.4 percent for the environment, 48.9 percent for youth, and 44.8 percent for human rights were established between 1993 and 1996. With respect to international relations, he comments, "Improving the quality of life, overshadowed over the years as a result of the country's growth-first strategy, was now to be an important part of the government's mission. Multiple dimensions of national security from economic and ecological security . . . to communal and societal security . . . were also emphasized as forming a new and more comprehensive foreign and security policy agenda for South Korea."[28]

Related to these structural changes are new interpretations of old practices, so tha grievances that once were not considered political matters or policy issues are no viewed by Koreans and many Korea watchers around the world in a different lig' Prostitution is a good example. It was the murder of a prostituted woman, Yun Ku ̧ ̣, that breathed life into what has become the organized anti-American moveme of the 1990s and 2000s. For the first time in Korea–U.S. relations, widespread publicity and protest against the United States ensued after the death of a prostitute and the public became sensitized to the SOFA. For certain, Yun's murder at the hands of a U.S. serviceman was not the first. For example, murder cases surfaced as early as the1960s and 1970s, and some were as egregious as the one involving Yun twenty years later. But hardly any Korean, even among progressive activists in the 1970s and 1980s, had considered such women's lives to have any value or moral legitimacy, or at least enough to be taken up through activism. It was only through international activism around the issue of women's human rights, the unearthing of the history, and the politics of the "comfort women" (*chongsindae*), the new policy agenda against human trafficking (highlighted by the Clinton administration), as well as the new democratic opening in Korea that contemporary Korean prostitution and violence against women by a foreign military came to be seen as a national sovereignty and human rights problem.

Murders and other forms of violence against any civilian, prostitute or not, should have been a legitimate legal and public concern twenty or thirty years ago. For Koreans and Americans, the actual human suffering and losses, as well as calls for redress, should not be overlooked or dismissed because of their recent politicization by activists into anti-American rhetoric.

Public expressions of anti-American sentiments and activism have been an ongoing part of the work environment for U.S. officials in South Korea since the early 1980s. Although anti-Americanism in that decade was limited to small groups of radical students and contained by a repressive Korean regime, its substance was much more ideological, violent, and condemning than its later version. The point is that anti-Americanism as a policy matter is not new; it has been around for at least two decades in the Korea–U.S. relationship. Moreover, prompted by the Iran hostage crisis and acts of terrorism in the 1980s, anti-Americanism as a foreign policy issue was salient in U.S. policy and academic circles in the late 1970s and 1980s, but neither American academics nor policy elites paid substantive and/or consistent attention to the issue or tried to understand it, address it, or adapt to it.[29] Lessons were lost, and analyses and responses were piecemeal and reactive. With respect to Korea after the Kwangju period of the 1980s, American policy managers began to take stock of Korean anti-Americanism only in the past few years and the public only in the past year.

No one should be surprised that critical sentiments have popped up in Korea. The problem is partly an oversight and neglect on the part of Americans. There has been a consistent stream of contentious events in the 1990s and a deterioration of civil-military relations and public diplomacy in the lower reaches of U.S.–Korea relations. In part, policy managers on both sides, and especially in the U.S. military, have not been able to keep up with the rapid political and social changes in Korea. In part, public relations and the nurturing of civil-military ties are not the strong suit of most military establishments, and the United States is no exception. But these are urgent tasks that the U.S. military and other authorities must take responsibility to address constructively, creatively, and consistently. Regardless of their length of stay in Korea, U.S.

forces are suffering from a crisis of "institutional presence." James Burk, sociologist and former editor of *Armed Forces and Society*, defines this as the social significance of an institution in society, encompassing material and moral dimensions.[30] On both counts, the military has become weak: In most of the camptowns, the USFK's economic importance has decreased and is viewed by residents as a deterrent to local development; its role as a provider of social services and humanitarian aid has significantly declined since the 1950s and 1960s; its isolation and estrangement from Korean social and cultural life is increasingly evident. On the one hand, Koreans increasingly view the U.S. military as a "predatory institution,"[31] questioning its moral legitimacy in Korean society, and on the other, USFK efforts at community outreach tend to focus on the past rather than the present and future generations of Koreans.

Specifically, the tendency has been to maintain regular contacts with already publicly known pro-U.S. groups in Korea, like veterans' associations, and to eschew interactions with critical or outright anti-American groups. Of course, the more radical Korean activists also avoid any substantive engagement with USFK personnel; therefore a cycle of mistrust, mutual suspicion, and hostility is in place. Engaging activist critics is a difficult task, both in terms of form and content, but ignoring and avoiding them ensures further alienation and the loss of moral legitimacy in Korean society. Again, recognition of the diversity of activists and issues is a necessary first step at constructive engagement. Recent interviews with some members of the USFK, including civilian officials, reveal a tendency to lump together activists as "dissidents." The very term *dissident* itself reflects the very social and political distance between USFK members and Korean civil society. There are very few "dissidents" in today's Korean democracy, but there are many critics. Most of these critics are intent on conducting their political activity within the rule of law, and the larger society reinforces this tendency: the vast majority of respondents in annual surveys by the Sejong Institute is opposed to unlawful protests and political behavior.[32]

Many U.S. officials in Korea understand that Korea has been changing dramatically throughout the 1990s and that some of the criticism and vigilance by watchdog groups are an inevitable part of democratization and changing expectations regarding division and reunification. Others, especially those who had been in Korea in the turbulent 1980s or posted to truly more hostile or dangerous environments in other countries, view the Korean version of anti-Americanism as mild and not serious. Others still, especially in the military, for whom the Korean War and the 1960s remain a living memory of and metaphor for U.S.–Korea relations, have seemed stumped and/or hurt by the turn toward public anti-Americanism among Koreans.[33] And many if not most American officials distinguish between public sentiments and personal relationships; they speak of the warmth, generosity, and friendship they share with Koreans. It is understandably difficult to square away these conflicting and sometimes confusing perceptions and experiences. Formulating a common perception of anti-Americanism as a serious policy matter may be just as challenging as coming up with appropriate responses.

Criticisms and complaints about U.S. military bases have accompanied troops in

Germany, France, Italy, the United Kingdom, Okinawa, and the Philippines. Such criticism in Korea should be understood in a historical, regional, and international context. Particularly in Asia, the anti-base movement cannot be viewed as a bilateral problem. Policies, actions, and inactions on the part of the United States toward the Philippines and Okinawa affect perceptions in South Korea and vice versa. Moreover, anti-base movements are not simply national social movements. Their audience, rhetoric, methods of protest are borrowed and shared across borders. A recent report by the Center for Strategic and International Studies (CSIS) indeed refers to public sentiment in South Korea as the "wildcard" in the future of the U.S.–Korea alliance and the role of the United States in East Asia.[34] To what extent public sentiment remains a wildcard depends partly on the maturation of democratic politics in Korea and partly on the ability of policy managers on both sides of the Pacific to conduct sophisticated and multilevel analysis and construct creative and fair responses to public protest and interests. There is no short-term miracle or resolution on the horizon, but given that democratic deepening takes a long time, pressing ahead with better policy management is the most immediate option.

To that end, an historically and culturally informed microlevel understanding of anti-Americanism will serve as a necessary guide for analysis and response. Awareness of the evolution of Korean civil society, the organizational logic, linkages, and conflicts among different civil society organizations, the tensions inherent in political decentralization, and the institutional habits and standard operating procedures of various Korean and U.S. government bureaucracies are essential. In that endeavor, it is necessary for Korean and American policy elites to recognize the differences among actors and their interactions, interests, and methods among the various critics of the United States and the Korea–U.S. relationship in order to (1) discern real and legitimate grievances in the local communities; (2) address them sincerely and constructively at the local levels before they become politicized bilateral policy issues; (3) assess the possibilities for improved communication and consultation on specific issues by the two governments and NGOs; and (4) related to the last point, develop democratic space within Korea through institutional channels for foreign and security policy concerns among citizens.

There is no doubt that in the end, elites manage, control, implement, and are accountable for foreign policy decisions and actions. Foreign policy by definition and nature require a "managed democracy." The challenge is to practice democratic management of foreign policy concerns among the populace. To date, segments of civil society have become hyperactive on Korea–U.S. issues, sometimes throwing their weight around without adequate information or a wide range of interpretive schemes, while political elites and institutions have tended to ignore or reluctantly engage citizens on a piecemeal basis. To be sure, there is a lack of trust, information sharing, and dialogue between representatives of civil society and those of the state on matters of foreign policy and national security. Finding ways to bridge the gaps and to build social capital among the disparate actors and interests will improve foreign policy management and the further maturation of democracy in South Korea.

Notes

1. In this chapter, *anti-Americanism* refers to various forms of public criticism regarding Korea–U.S. relations, U.S. policies toward the Korean Peninsula, and the role and conduct of U.S. troops. The term is a misnomer; in most cases, the focus is on criticism (*pi-mi*), not opposition to, hatred or ill will toward the United States and its people (*pan-mi*).

2. Center for Strategic and International Studies, *A Blueprint for U.S. Policy Toward a Unified Korea: A Working Group Report of the CSIS International Security Program* (Washington, DC: CSIS, 2000), p. 26.

3. Max Hastings, *The Korean War* (New York: Simon and Schuster, 1987), p. 241.

4. *Pacific Stars and Stripes*, July 28, 1971.

5. Eighth U.S. Army translation. See Katharine H.S. Moon, *Sex Among Allies: Military Prostitution in U.S.-Korea Relations* (New York: Columbia University Press, 1997), p. 185, fn 69.

6. John B. McReynolds, USFK, Memorandum, "Community Relations Advisory Council (CRAC), Bupyong (ASCOM)," November 1, 1968.

7. People's Solidarity for Participatory Democracy, *Ch'amyo sahoe* (Participatory society) (April 2002), pp. 28–29.

8. Jae-Kyoung Lee, "Anti-Americanism in South Korea: The Media and the Politics of Signification," unpublished Ph.D. dissertation, University of Iowa, 1993, p. 131.

9. Sunhyuk Kim, "State and Civil Society in South Korea's Democratic Consolidation: Is the Battle Really Over?" *Asian Survey* 37, no. 12 (December 1997).

10. According to Hyuk-Rae Kim, the vast majority of NGOs in Korea were established between 1987 and 1996. "The State and Civil Society in Transition: The Role of Non-Governmental Organizations in South Korea," *Pacific Review* 13, no. 4 (Winter 2000): p. 603.

11. Ibid., p. 1142.

12. Personal interview, Seoul, March 27, 2002.

13. *Munhwa Ilbo*, May 30, 2000.

14. *Daehan Maeil Sinmun*, May 24, 2000 (U.S. Information Service, Korea, translation).

15. Republic of Korea National Assembly, Bill #16102, *Migun kongyo chiyok chiwon mit chumin kwon'ikpoho e kwanhan pomlyulan* (Legislative bill on support to the USFK regions and protection of the rights and interests of residents) www.assembly.go.kr (Access date: March 27, 2003).

16. Ilpyong J. Kim and Eun Sung Chung, "Establishing Democratic Rule in South Korea: Local Autonomy and Democracy," *In Depth* 3, no. 1 (1993); Kyoung-Ryun Seong, "Delayed Decentralization and Incomplete Democratic Consolidation," in *Institutional Reform and Democratic Consolidation in Korea*, ed. Larry Diamond and Doh Chull Shin (Stanford, CA: Hoover Institution Press, 2000); Desmond King and Gerry Stoker, eds., *Rethinking Local Democracy* (London: Macmillan, 1996), chapters 1 and 2.

17. Jong Soo Lee, "The Politics of Decentralization in Korea," *Local Government Studies* 22, no. 3 (Autumn 1996): p. 68.

18. Personal interview, Iksan, Korea, May 2002.

19. *Joong-ang Ilbo*, January 14, 2003.

20. January 15, 2003. www.pttimes.com (Access date March 27, 2003).

21. *Pacific Stars and Stripes*, June 19, 2003.

22. Ohmynews, March 18, 2003, http://news.naver.com/new_print.php?office= ohmynews&article_id=27184 (Accessed April 29, 2003); Pyongtaek NGO, April 18, 2003, www.ptngo.org/plus/d_board.php3?table=admin&query=view&1=101... (Access date: April 29, 2003).

23. Personal interview, Iksan, Korea, May 2002.

24. Personal interviews with activists, Seoul, Iksan, Ilsan, Osan, spring 2002. Also see

Yujin Chong, "'Minjok'ui irum uro sunkyolhaejin ddaldeul" (Daughters who have become pure in the name of the "nation"), *Tangdae Pip'yong* 11 (2000): pp. 219–45 and *"P'yonghwarul mandun danun kot"* (To make peace). In *Ilsang ui ogapkwa sosuja ui inkwon* (Daily oppression and the human rights of minorities) (Seoul: Saram Saenggak, 2000), pp. 89–114.

25. *Hankyore sinmun*, August 2, 2000, www.hani.co.kr/section-00300. . . / 00300401 1200008022127001.htm (Access date: March 4, 2002).

26. Korea House for International Solidarity, *Saram i saram ege* (People to people) (October/ November 2000): p. 25.

27. Base21, www.base21.org/show/show/php?p_cd=0&p_dv=0&p_docnbr=21475 (Access date: October 2, 2002).

28. Hyuk-Rae Kim, "The State and Civil Society in Transition," p. 603.

29. Until recently, social science and policy literature on anti-Americanism was sparse. For a sampling of earlier writings, see Alvin Z. Rubenstein and Donald E. Smith, eds., *Anti-Americanism in the Third World: Implications for U.S. Foreign Policy* (New York: Praeger, 1985); Stephen Haseler, *The Varieties of Anti-Americanism: Reflex and Response* (Washington, DC: Ethics and Public Policy Center, 1985); Thomas Perry Thornton, ed., *Anti-Americanism: Origin and Context*, Annals of the Academy of Political and Social Studies (May 1988).

30. James Burk, "The Military's Presence in American Society," in *Soldiers and Civilians: The Civil-Military Gap and American National Security*, ed. Peter D. Feaver and Richard H. Kohn (Cambridge, MA: MIT Press, 2001).

31. Ibid., p. 251.

32. Sook-Jong Lee, "Trust and Civic Participation in Korea," *International Studies Review* 3, no. 2 (December 2000), p. 71.

33. Edward Olsen writes that what stands out among the liberals and conservatives who have openly "questioned the value of keeping U.S. forces in Korea to protect what they see as South Korean ingrates . . . " is their " emotionally bitter tone," *Far Eastern Economic Review*, February 20, 2003, p. 22.

15

Perception of American People, Society, and Influence

Psychological, Social, and Cultural Analysis of Anti-American Sentiments in South Korea

Uichol Kim and Young-Shin Park

Although Korea has a long history, voluntary contacts and exchange with other countries were largely limited to China for some 2,000 years. From China, Korea adopted its political, social, religious, and artistic traditions. When the Korean Peninsula was unified by the Shilla Kingdom in A.D. 676, Buddhism became the dominant religion, and remarkable achievements in architecture, sculpture, painting, and philosophy were made during this era. Confucianism was introduced in the sixth century, influencing the governmental and educational systems. When the Koryo dynasty was founded in 918, Buddhism became the national religion. With the founding of Yi dynasty in 1392, Confucianism was adopted as the major guideline, not only for official and political functioning but also for the private life of the people.

Although Korea benefited from the voluntary contact with China, her experience with other nations has been largely negative. During the Shilla dynasty, numerous invasions weakened the kingdom and led to its eventual collapse. During the Koryo dynasty, the Mongol invasion and subjugation exacted a heavy toll. During the Yi dynasty, the country was ravaged by a series of invasions by the Japanese and by Manchus. Following these incidents, Korea retreated into a stringent isolationism and became known as the "Hermit Kingdom." The isolationist policy was further buttressed by the cultural chauvinism of the ruling class, to whom it was inconceivable that anything of value could be learned from any foreign country other than China. In the nineteenth century, xenophobic and chauvinistic isolationism became the law of the land and contacts with other nations were strictly forbidden. This policy was carried out so thoroughly that, even when China and Japan had been forced to open their country to the western nations, Korea was virtually unknown abroad. During an era when the world was progressing at a rapid pace, Korean economic, social, military, and political structure remained virtually unchanged.

Korea was forced to open her ports to Japan in 1876 and to western nations in 1882. Korea found herself a battleground among foreign powers (i.e., Japan, China, Russia, and the United States). The Sino-Japanese (1894–95) and Russo-Japanese (1904–5) Wars were fought over Korea, with Japan emerging as the victor. An informal agreement was reached between the United States and Japan (the Taft-Katsura Agreement) in which the United States would maintain control of the Philippines and Japan would annex Korea. Korea was annexed by Japan in 1910.

During its occupation, the Japanese government endeavored to enlarge the Japanese Empire by forcefully eradicating the Korean language, culture, and identity. All Koreans were ordered to exchange their names for Japanese ones and to use the Japanese language in school. They were punished if they used the Korean language. Koreans were forced to denounce their religion and to adopt Shintoism (the national religion of Japan). However, Koreans tenaciously clung to their traditions, and very few remnants of Japanese imperialism remained after Japan's defeat. What remained was a deep resentment and anti-Japanese feeling that persisted for half a century.

With the defeat of Japan in 1945, Koreans were ecstatic over their newly acquired freedom. But to their despair, the country was partitioned along the thirty-eighth parallel. Although Korea was not an aggressor in World War II, it became the victim of Cold War politics. Both Americans (in the south) and the Soviet Union (to the north) established military rule in their respective territories. For the first time in nearly 2,000 years, a nation that had prided itself on unity and independence was divided by external forces. The border of the thirty-eighth parallel was eventually reestablished after the Korean War, and the division of the two Koreas is still a political reality.

American Influence in Korea: Dual Track, Dual Influence

The initial contact with the West, whereby Christianity was brought to Korea, was voluntary, and it helped to modernize and transform Korean society. The spread of Christianity in Korea is a phenomenon in itself. Christianity was not imposed as a form of colonialism, as has been experienced in other countries. It was adopted and indigenized, blossoming to become one of Korea's major religions, as Buddhism had done centuries before. Since its introduction some 200 years ago, it has become the fastest-growing religion in Korea. It claims over 12 million followers (around one-quarter of the population), with more than 30,000 churches throughout South Korea.

Christianity was introduced to Korea through documents brought back from China by diplomatic travelers in the seventeenth century. Peter Lee, the first priest, was ordained in China and became the first Christian to be martyred in Korea. Later, Catholic priests were invited to come to Korea in disguise to promote the officially "forbidden" religion. Despite the existence of an official policy banning Christianity, there were about 20,000 followers by 1853. Persecutions had been sporadic before that time, but in a last desperate gesture of antiforeignism, thousands of Christians were martyred in the last part of the nineteenth century.

A diplomatic treaty with the United States was signed in 1882, which provided protection for missionaries, various medical personnel, and educators. Unlike the missionaries in China and Japan, who remained aloof and distant, missionaries in Korea actively integrated into the Korean communities, learning the language, adopting the customs, and living like other Koreans. They became integrated to become an essential part of changing Korean society. As a first step, American missionaries translated the Bible and hymns into *hangul* (the Korean writing system) and went around the countryside first teaching *hangul* and then, through *hangul,* teaching the Bible to everyone, including women and peasants.

Beyond the religious needs, missionaries were active in establishing tuberculosis sanitariums, leper colonies, hospitals, schools, and universities. Among the institutions founded by American missionaries are major hospitals (e.g., Severance Hospital, established in 1885), schools (Baejae High School, found in 1885, and Kyongshin, in 1886), and universities (Yonsei University and Ewha Women's University in 1886 and Sungshill University in 1887). These missionaries met a deeply felt need among Koreans for modern education as a tool leading to personal advancement and social reform. They quickly became identified with progressive movements and introduced the ideals of democracy and human rights. After the Japanese annexation, American missionaries encouraged the resistance movements against the Japanese colonization and sent protests to their own government demanding American intervention. However, such protests were met with chagrin since the American government supported the Japanese annexation and colonization of Korea.

Christianity had a major effect on all strata of Korean society. For example, the first Christians who learned the Protestant system of church government became leaders of Korea. In the first National Assembly set up in 1948, some 42 percent of the elected assemblymen were Christians, whereas only 4 percent of the population was Christian. In addition, the first two presidents of the Republic of Korea (Syngman Rhee and Yun Bo Sun) and the last two presidents (Kim Yong Sam and Kim Dae Jung) are Christians. Unlike China and Japan, where Christianity penetrated mainly the urban areas, it penetrated all strata in Korea.

The contact with the West has been a mixed blessing for Korea. At the social level, missionaries provided the necessary tools to transform a conservative, hierarchical, nepotistic, and chauvinistic society. American missionaries played a key role in transforming Korea by introducing modern education, health care, and democracy. Even after a century, the third generation of the missionary families (such as Underwood and Linton) still live and work in South Korea, championing the cause of a better Korea.

After the Korean War, American universities provided opportunities to obtain higher education for many aspiring Koreans. And, with the special favorable status given to Korea, many Korean students were able to complete their graduate studies in the United States. Some were able to obtain scholarships (e.g., Fulbright fellowships, East-West Center fellowships, and university scholarships) to pursue their studies. The vast majority of Korean scholars, politicians, and businessmen with foreign degrees obtained them from schools in the United States.

At the political level, however, the United States was a key player in undermining Korean sovereignty and aspiration for realizing modern democracy. At the turn of the nineteenth century, the United States played a key role in forcing Korea to open its doors, and it allowed Japan to annex Korea in 1910. In 1945, the United States divided Korea and placed it at the center of Cold War politics. Even though Japan was the defeated enemy, it was not divided like Germany. Instead, the American government helped to rebuild Japan, and divided Korea with the Soviet Union as a spoil of World War II. Even after the Korean War, the United States government focused its attention on controlling the spread of communism rather than meeting the aspirations of the Korean people for modernization and democracy.

For the five years after the liberation, the Korean Peninsula became the battlefront for ideological supremacy, leading to the Korean War in 1950. The Korean War lasted for three years, during which more than 3 million people lost their lives and 10 million were dislocated and separated from their families. With the tentative armistice agreement signed in 1953, the Korean Peninsula continued the legacy of Cold War politics. After the Korean War, the size of the Korean army quadrupled to 600,000, and police were given expanded powers. Rhee's government received 70 percent of its total budget from the United States and was totally dependent on the United States.

According to Choi (1993), although the United States publicly supported the democratization of South Korea, the institutionalization of liberal democracy was relatively low on its priority list. The U.S. military government placed anticommunism as its top priority and the creation of a market economy as its second priority. In 1948, it supported the authoritarian rule of Syngman Rhee as the first president of South Korea and enacted the National Security Law to control the rise and proliferation of left-wing groups. The National Security Law gave the U.S. military and South Korean government the right to use coercive force against Koreans citizens who challenged their authority or demanded their civil rights. The goal was to suppress all dissent and eliminate all opposition, all the way from the socialist left to the conservative right.

Modern South Korea

On April 19, 1960, students protested against the rigged March 15 election and government corruption. Rhee declared martial law and the police were mobilized to suppress the student demonstration. When the troops refused to take action against the demonstrators, Rhee was forced to resign on April 26. In August, the National Assembly elected Yun Bo-sun as Rhee's successor.

On May 16, 1961, General Park Chung Hee led a coup d'état and declared martial law. In March 1962, Yun Bo Sun was forced to resign and Park appointed himself acting president. In October 1963, upon taking office as the newly elected president, Park criticized American democracy and supported a "guided democracy" that would limit freedom of speech for the greater good of society. Park pointed out that a strong leadership was essential in transforming a backward South Korea and supported the idea of "Korean democracy."

Rather than focusing on the development of a civil society, Park emphasized national security interests as the top priority and economic progress as the basis of the development of a strong state. Park felt that the United States was using liberal democracy and human rights as a way of controlling and protecting its own interests while keeping South Korea economically, socially, and politically backward. Park rejected the dependency created by the United States and lashed out against the neocolonialist and expansionist policy of the United States. From the beginning, the United States did not support Park and his policies. The United States attempted to block his coup d'état in 1961 and rejected Park's Five Year Plan.

Park believed that reliance on the United States and on light industries would not transform the South Korean economy. He pushed for the development of heavy industries, such as car manufacturing, the steel industry, shipbuilding, and construction. Since the United States was unwilling to support these initiatives and provide the necessary technological and financial assistance, Park turned to Japan. On December 18, 1965, Park signed a treaty normalizing diplomatic relations with Japan. As a compensation for their thirty-five years of colonial occupation, the Japanese government paid the South Korean government $200 million plus $300 million in investment loans (Federation of Korean Industries 1991; Sakong 1993). The South Korean public was outraged when they learned about the paltry settlement and also about not obtaining a formal apology from the Japanese government. Even with the fierce opposition, Park went ahead with his Five Year Plan and used the money obtained from the Japanese government to invest in the heavy industries that, he hoped, would transform the South Korean economy.

For Park, the Japanese society and economy provided an ideal model for South Korea. As early as 1963, Park stated that "the case of the Meiji imperial restoration will be of great help to the performance of our own revolution," and "my interest in this direction remains strong and constant" (Amsden 1989, p. 52). South Korea adopted tested Japanese technologies and followed the example and direction laid out by Japan. Japan became South Korea's most important trading partner after 1965. Thousands of managers, engineers, skilled workers, bureaucrats, and company executives went to Japan to learn about modern Japanese technology and the Japanese management style. In terms of technology transfer payments for importing foreign technology from 1962 to 1976, Japan was ranked first, with 56.1 percent of the total, followed by the United States with 29.7 percent (Sakong 1993). The foreign direct investment from Japan increased tenfold after 1965. For the total direct foreign investment from 1962 to 1991, 43.4 percent came from Japan; the United States was a distant second, with 27.6 percent (Sakong 1993).

At the beginning of the 1960s, South Korea had all the problems of a resource-poor, low-income, underdeveloped nation. The vast majority of people were dependent on agricultural products produced on scarce farmland. The literacy rate and educational level was one of the lowest in the world. South Korea's per capita gross national product (GNP) in 1961 stood at a meagre $82, and South Korea was considered one of the poorest nations in the world. From 1965, however, South Korea experienced a phenomenal transformation in the economic, educational, and social sectors. The economy grew at an average annual rate of over 8 percent, to become one of the fastest growing economies in the world. The per capita GNP increased to $1,640 in 1981; by 2002, it had increased to $10,000.

Although Park's policies did not allow for any dissent in the political sphere, his economic policy transformed South Korea into the most rapidly developing economy in the modern world. Park's strong leadership was a double-edged sword. Under his strong leadership, large-scale corruption, incompetence, nepotism, and American interference—which had plagued the previous governments—were controlled. The guided development he had initiated supported the *chaebols* (large conglomerates) on a contingency-based model. In other words, a few select companies (e.g., Daewoo, Hyundai, Lucky-Goldstar [LG], and Samsung) received heavy government subsidies and a monopoly of the domestic market on condition that they used their capital to become competitive in the international market. At the same time, his strong leadership was absolutist and did not allow for any dissent or opposition, as from Kim Yong Sam and Kim Dae Jung.

The Political Sphere

Park Chung Hee made national security and economic development his highest priorities. Park used the threat from North Korea to justify his dictatorship and ruled with an iron fist. Under the National Security Law, political dissidents such as Kim Dae Jung and Kim Yong Sam were arrested, harassed, and tortured. This law was used to deny South Korean citizens basic human rights. Park ruled South Korea for nearly twenty years (1961–79), until he was assassinated on October 26, 1979.

With the political crisis, martial law was declared and Choe Kyu Ha was named acting president. On December 12, 1979, General Chun Doo Hwan initiated a bloody military coup d'état and took over military control. In April 1980, when students demonstrated against the government, Chun declared martial law and brutally crushed the demonstration in Kwangju. Some thirty political leaders were put under house arrest, the National Assembly was dissolved, and all political activity was banned. On August 16, Choe Kyu Ha was forced to resign and Chun appointed himself president on September 1. As soon as Chun took office, he replaced the National Assembly with 81 appointees; he also dismissed 937 editors and journalists and forced newspapers, and radio, and TV stations to consolidate under the government's control.

Prior to Chun's coup d'état, the students believed that the United States supported the democratization of South Korea. During the April 19, 1960, demonstration, many missionaries and Korean Christians were key players in bringing down Rhee's government. However, student activists were alarmed to learn that the American government did not intervene to stop the Kwangju Massacre. They realized that United States government actually supported Chun's regime or at least tolerated it as they had done with President Park. With this realization, anti-American sentiments began to spread among the university students. In 1982, students took over the American Cultural Center at Busan; in Kwangju in 1985, they denounced American imperialism and dominance.

Chun appointed general Roh Tae Woo, who had assisted him in the 1979 takeover, as his presidential successor in June 1987. Over a million people demonstrated in cities across the country to protest the continued dictatorial rule, nepotism, and corruption. During this time, with the ousting of Ferdinand Marcos in the Philippines by a popular uprising, the U.S. government made it clear to Roh that it would not support the imposition of martial law. On June 29, 1987, Roh was forced to accept political reforms, direct presidential elections, and the restoration of civil rights. The argument that the American government actually supported the dictatorial rule of Park, Chun, and Roh was thus confirmed and verified. It was only when the American government refused to support Roh's government that he was forced to accept the wishes of the South Korean public in allowing direct presidential elections and the restoration of civil rights. The activist students saw the American government as a supporter of dictatorship and a barrier to democracy and human rights.

With the breakdown of the coalition between opposition leaders Kim Yong Sam and Kim Dae Jung, Roh was elected president on February 25, 1988. This represented the first peaceful transfer of power in modern South Korea. Before the 1993 election, Kim Yong Sam joined Roh's government and was elected as the first civilian president. When Kim Dae Jung was elected in 1997, for the first time political power was peacefully transferred to an opposition leader.

When Kim Dae Jung took over the country, the economy contracted by more than 30 percent. He led the country from economic collapse to recovery. South Korea received assistance from the International Monetary Fund (IMF) and had to accept painful economic remedies. During this time, many South Koreans became resentful of the United States for forcing Korean companies to accept the bitter pill and sell Korean companies at bargain prices. The drastic fiscal and monetary IMF policy created social turmoil and economic hardship for many Koreans. Although the South Korean economy did recover from the crisis and paid off the IMF loans, the resentment against the United States as the controlling agent of the IMF spread and simmered in the minds of South Koreans. During his presidency, Kim Dae Jung introduced his "Sunshine Policy," which represented a shift in the policy of isolating North Korea toward promoting positive engagement through dialogue, cooperation, and family reunions. It received national support and international attention. He traveled to Pyongyang on June 15, 2000, for a historic summit meeting with Kim Jong Il. Later that year, he received international recognition when he was awarded the Rafto Prize for Human Rights and the Nobel Peace Prize for promoting peace and dialogue with North Korea. The Sunshine Policy is an indigenous Korean model that is based on the long-term relationship and sharing that many Koreans could identify with and support (Kim 2001). The policy was seen as reducing tensions between the two Koreas and helping to bring about eventual reconciliation (as evidenced by the family reunions, tours of Mt. Kumkang, and the joining of the railway line).

The Sunshine Policy, however, was placed into jeopardy when U.S. President George W. Bush was elected. He questioned the viability of the policy and labeled North Korea part of the "axis of evil." Most recently, President Bush announced the policy of "tailored containment" toward North Korea without prior consultation with the South Korean government. Many South Koreans became alarmed by this outside interference, which, in effect, had the American government dictating the foreign policy of South Korea and undermining the initiative of the South Korean government. In addition, Korean media had been reporting that numerous crimes were being committed by American soldiers and that American military bases were polluting the environment—all of which deeds continue to go unpunished because of the Status of Forces Agreement (SOFA). Military governments have previously banned these reports. Many Koreans have become alarmed by the total disregard of American military personnel and officials stationed in South Korea. With the deaths of two Korean girls who were run over by a military vehicle in June 2002, in which the drivers were found not guilty, the emotional outcry against the United States coalesced at the national level. The anti-American sentiment became especially potent among the younger generation and influenced the election of Roh Moo Hyun as the president of South Korea in 2002.

The purpose of this chapter is to examine the psychological, social, and cultural basis of anti-American sentiments in South Korea. Although many national studies have been conducted to examine various facets of such anti-American sentiments, they are mainly opinion polls and surveys that fail to examine the psychological and cultural dynamics (Kim et al. 1997). Our intention is to provide an indigenous psychological analysis (Kim 2000; Kim et al. 1999, 2000) of anti-American sentiments in South Korea, using both qualitative and quantitative methodologies.

Method

An open-ended questionnaire was developed by the present researchers to examine Korean students' and adults' perception of American society and people and its impact on South Korea, the Korean Peninsula, and the world. A total of 270 middle school students and their parents (270 mothers and 270 fathers) and 140 senior high students and their parents (140 mothers and 140 fathers) completed an open-ended survey developed by the present researchers. In sum, 1,230 participants were asked to write their responses to the following questions:

1. What is your perception of the following aspect of the United States: (a) society, (b) people, (c) companies, (d) government, (e) culture, (f) values, and (g) soldiers stationed in South Korea.
2. What is your perception of American influence on following the aspect of South Korea: (a) society, (b) economy, (c) companies, (d) people, (e) culture, (f) politics, (g) relationship between North and South Korea, and (h) unification.
3. What is your perception of American influence in the world: (a) politics, (b) economy, (c) security, and (d) culture.

Based on the results of this open-ended questionnaire, a structured questionnaire was developed that tapped into the following five areas: (1) perception of American society,

(2) perception of American people, (3) perception of American influence on South Korea, (4) perception of American influence on the Korean Peninsula, and (5) perception of American influence in the world. In addition, respondents were asked about their knowledge of American society and trust in American people and institutions.

The items in the structured questionnaire were translated into English, attempting to capture the psychological meaning of the Korean phrases. The items used in the structured questionnaire were based on the concepts of phrases provided by the respondents in the open-ended questionnaire. In the questionnaire, respondents were asked to evaluate 62 statements about American society, 67 statements about the American people, 31 statements about the American influence on South Korea, 29 statements about the American influence on the Korean Peninsula, and 41 statements about the American influence in the world. A five-point scale used was as follows: 1 = definitely false, 2 = somewhat false, 3 = in between, 4 = somewhat true, and 5 = very true. In addition, respondents were asked to rate their knowledge of 12 aspects of American society, again using a five-point scale: 1 = not at all, 2 = very little, 3 = know somewhat, 4 = know well, and 5 = know very well. Respondents were also asked the degree to which they trusted American people and institutions on a five-point scale: 1= completely distrust, 2 = distrust somewhat, 3 = in between, 4 = trust somewhat, and 5 = trust very much. Finally, various demographic and background information was obtained. Data were collected in December 2002, just before the presidential election.

Results

Sample Characteristics

A total of 171 middle school students, 250 university students, and 171 mothers, and 171 fathers of the middle school students living in Seoul and Gyeonggi province completed the structured survey developed by the present researchers.

Factor Analyses

Factor analyses were conducted on the following five aspects of the United States: (1) perception of American society, (2) perception of American people, (3) perception of American influence on South Korea, (4) perception of American influence on the Korean Peninsula, and (5) perception of American influence in the world. Based on the factor analyses, dimensions were extracted and scales constructed. Correlational analyses with the background information and the scales were conducted.

Perception of American Society

For perception of American society, six factors or dimensions were found. The first three dimensions are positive and the next three dimensions are negative. The six dimensions and examples of representative items are presented below:

Figure 15.1   **Perception of American Society**

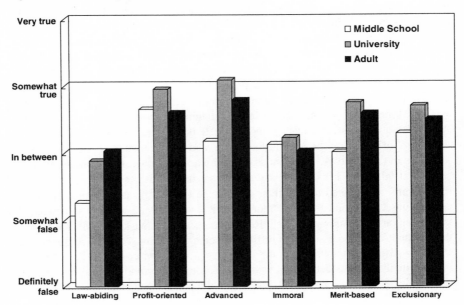

1. *Law-abiding:* Orderly, law-abiding, just, trustworthy, promotes diversity, and equality is upheld.
2. *Advanced:* World leader, advanced, wealthy, competitive, and efficient.
3. *Merit-based:* Individual achievement is recognized, rewarded for performance, individualistic, and free.
4. *Profit-oriented:* Motivated by profit, controlling, aggressive, arrogant, materialistic, and commercial.
5. *Immoral:* Hedonistic, depraved, sexually immoral, and vulgar.
6. *Exclusionary:* Ethnocentric, authoritarian, racist, exclusionary, and conservative.

Figure 15.1 provides the mean score of the six dimensions for middle school students, university students, and adults. The results indicate that Korean respondents have a mixed view of American society. They are likely to see it as being advanced and merit-based but also as profit-oriented and exclusionary. They are not likely to perceive American society as being law-abiding.

University students are most likely to view American society as being advanced and merit-based but at the same time profit-oriented and exclusionary. The university students have a mixed view of the United States, admiring it on the one hand and disliking it on the other. The middle school students have the most negative view of American society; they are least likely to see its positive aspects. They are least likely to see American society as law-abiding, merit-based, and advanced. Overall, adults have a positive view of American society and are least likely to have a negative view.

Figure 15.2   **Perception of American People**

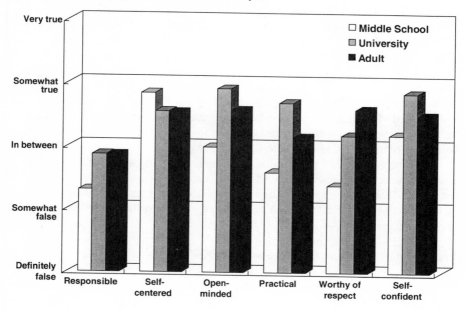

When the correlations between the six dimensions and background information are examined, those individuals with greater knowledge of and contact with the United States have more positive views of American society. Those who are not satisfied with the political functioning in Korea had the most negative view of American society.

Perception of American People

For perception of American people, six factors or dimensions were found. The six dimensions and examples of representative items are presented below:

1. *Responsible:* Civic-minded, responsible, honest, family-oriented, trustworthy, hard-working, and ethical.
2. *Self-centered:* Selfish, vulgar, arrogant, cruel, immoral, racist, and dislikable.
3. *Open-minded:* Open-minded, independent, proactive, optimistic, and enjoy life.
4. *Practical:* Individualistic, practical, honest, and progressive.
5. *Worthy of respect:* Live in a rich country and speak English well.
6. *Self-confident:* Patriotic, high self-esteem, and proud of their culture.

Figure 15.2 provides the mean score of the six dimensions for middle school students, university students, and adults. As in the case of their perception of American society, Korean respondents have a mixed view of the American people. They are likely to view Americans as being open-minded and self-confident as well as self-centered. They are not likely to view Americans as being responsible.

The middle school students had the most negative view of American people. They were most likely to see them as self-centered and least likely to see them as being responsible, open-minded, practical, worthy of respect, and self-confident. In contrast, the adults had the most positive view of American people. They were more likely to view American people as being open-minded, worthy of respect, and self-confident and least likely to view them as being self-centered. University students had a mixed view of American people. They were most likely to see them as open-minded, practical, and self-confident. At the same time, they viewed Americans as being self-centered and not likely to be responsible.

When the correlations between the six dimensions and background information were examined, those respondents who had greater knowledge of and contact with the United States had a more positive view of it. Those respondents who were not satisfied with the political functioning in Korea were most likely to view American people negatively.

Perception of American Influence in South Korea

For perception of American influence in South Korea, four factors or dimensions were found. The four dimensions and examples of representative items are presented below:

1. *Dominant:* Oppression, dominance, economic dependence, colonial, and pressured.
2. *Subservient:* Follow, imitate, envy, assimilate, and accept things American.
3. *Progressive:* Protectorate, progress, technological assistance, modernize, and support.
4. *Destructive:* Destroy Korean culture, promote American popular culture and influence.

Figure 15.3 provides the mean score of the six dimensions for middle school students, university students, and adults. All three groups viewed American influence as being negative in terms of dominance, subservience, and destruction. The university students were most likely to see the negative impact, viewing American influence as being dominant, promoting of subservience, and destructive. The middle school students also had a negative view of American influence and were least likely to see its influence in terms of progress. The adults had the least negative views of American influence in South Korea.

When the correlations between the four dimensions and background information were examined, those respondents who had greater knowledge of and contact with the United States had a more positive view of American influence in South Korea. Those respondents who were not satisfied with the political functioning in Korea were most likely to view American influence in South Korea negatively.

Figure 15.3   **American Influence in South Korea**

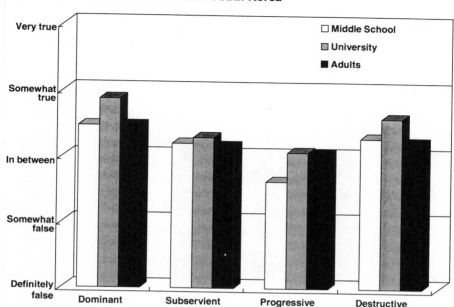

Perception of American Influence on the Korean Peninsula

For the perception of American influence on the Korean Peninsula, five factors or dimensions were found. The five dimensions and examples of representative items are presented below:

1. *Blocks unification:* Interferes, blocks, oppose unification and supports the division.
2. *Interferes excessively:* Interferes and threatens North Korea, controls and dominates South Korea.
3. *Has limited impact:* North Korea resists, rejects American influence, the United States cannot control or influence North Korea.
4. *Has broad influence:* Excessive influence on North and South Korea.
5. *Is helpful:* Helpful, necessary and essential for unification.

Figure 15.4 provides the mean score of the six dimensions for middle school students, university students, and adults. Although some university students and adults viewed American influence on the Korean Peninsula as being helpful, most respondents reported a negative view. All three groups agreed that American influence was blocking unification of the two Koreas, interfering excessively on the Korean Peninsula, that it had a limited impact on North Korea, and that it was attempting to broaden

Figure 15.4   **American Influence in the Korean Peninusula**

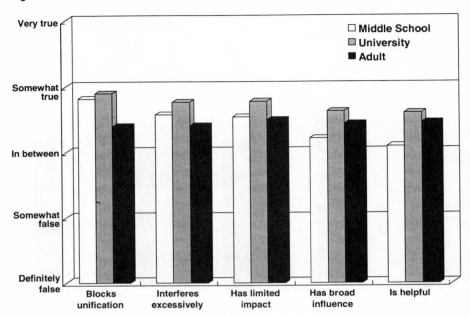

its influence. The university students held the most negative view and adults held the least negative view.

When the correlations between the five dimensions and background information were examined, those individuals with greater knowledge of the United States and greater contact with it had a more positive view of American influence on the Korean Peninsula. Those who were not satisfied with the political functioning in Korea had the most negative view of the American influence in the Korean Peninsula.

Perception of American Influence in the World

For the perception of American influence in the world, four factors or dimensions were found. The four dimensions and examples of representative items are presented below:

1. *Is imperialistic:* Colonial, monopolistic, exploitive, threatening, controlling, inciting war, interfering, and arrogant.
2. *Behaves as a superpower:* World leader, influential, powerful, and controls world economy.
3. *Promotes justice:* Promotes justice and world peace, represents democracy, and center of power.
4. *Promotes Americanization:* Spreads commercialism, materialism, and popular American culture.

Figure 15.5   **American Influence in the World**

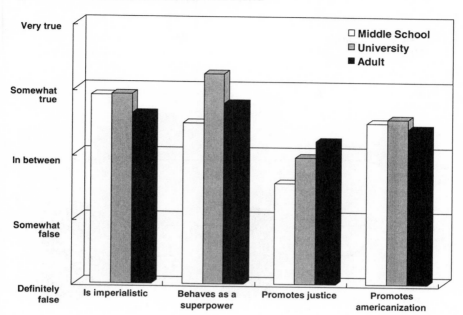

Figure 15.5 provides the mean score of the four dimensions for middle school students, university students, and adults. All three groups agree that the United States is a superpower. Except for some adults, who view the United States as promoting justice, most Koreans view American influence in the world negatively. They are likely to view American influence as imperialistic and promoting Americanization. The university students and the middle school students had the most negative view of American influence

When the correlations between the four dimensions and background information were examined, those individuals with greater knowledge of and contact with the United States had more positive views of American influence in the world. Those individuals who were not satisfied with the political functioning in Korea had the most negative view of American influence.

Trust of American People and Institutions

Trust of the American people includes the following seven items: people, politicians, teachers/professors, workers, police, business executives, and President Bush. Trust of American institutions included the following items: Congress, media, school/ university, public institutions, military, large companies, and legal system. The overall means for the three groups are presented in Figure 15.6.

Overall, the trust of American people and institutions is very low. The middle

Figure 15.6 **Trust of American People and Institutions**

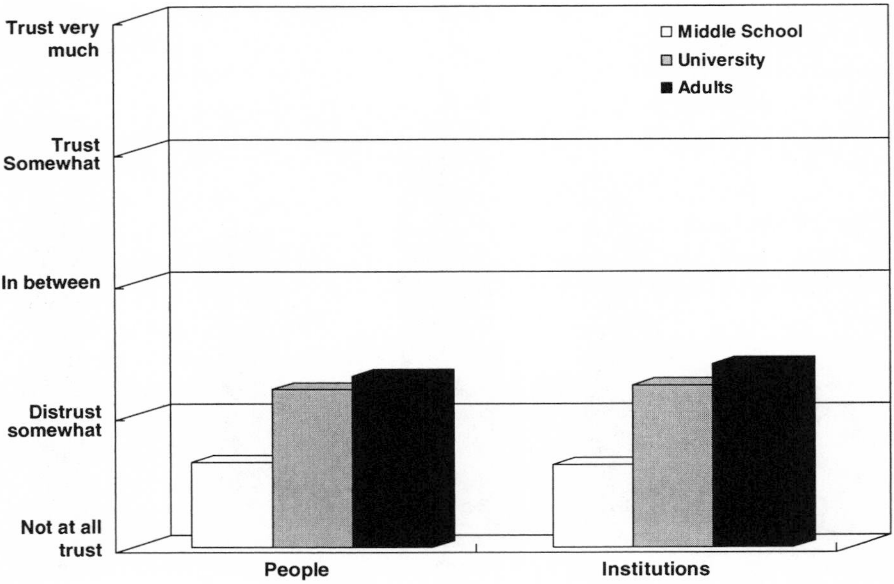

school students had the lowest score and adults had the highest score. Within the sample, those respondents who had greater knowledge of and contact with the United States had higher levels of trust for both people and institutions.

For trust of American people, Koreans are least likely to trust the American police, followed by President Bush and other politicians. The highest level of trust was found for American teachers/professors. For trust of American institutions, Koreans are least likely to trust the American Congress, followed by the military and legal systems. The highest level of trust was found for American schools/universities. The results suggest that Koreans are least likely to trust American politicians and the political system. They are most likely to trust educators and educational institutions.

Discussion

The present researchers provide an exploratory analysis of Korean respondents' perceptions of American people and society and their influence on Korea and the world. The results indicate largely negative views. The most negative view was held by the youngest generation, the middle school students, and the most positive view by the adult generation, the parents of the middle school students. University students had a very mixed view of the United States.

The current results challenge the commonly held assumption that the younger generation will have a positive view of the United States and emulate its values and norms. The results clearly indicate a generational change in which the younger generation does not perceive a positive influence from the United States, only a negative influence, which is very different from their parents' views. This may be due to several factors. The older generation grew up during the social and economic crises and some experienced the Korean War firsthand. They therefore recognize the positive influence of the United States in protecting and building South Korea.

The younger generation grew up after the 1980 Kwangju Massacre, and since then most of the media coverage of the United States has been negative. From 1980, the relationship with the United States was portrayed in a negative light, including reports of unfair trade negotiations with the United States, a series of crimes committed by American soldiers going unpunished, and even sports events in which biased refereeing and outcomes were perceived. The younger generation grew up being exposed to this negative media coverage, which was not balanced by positive information. Although the United States may bring accusations of biased media coverage, such coverage can also be attributed to the unequal relationship and outcome that Koreans had to accept for fifty years (e.g., the SOFA). In addition, the American government and businesses did not put much effort into providing positive information and contact. It could be said that the American government took the relationship for granted and felt that Koreans would be forever grateful.

On the flip side, the young generation grew up during a time of economic growth and affluence. The adult generation grew up during the times of poverty and social turmoil, when "Made in USA" was associated with quality and was admired. The young generation grew up during a period in which Korea became a world leader in many areas: Samsung is now the world leader in memory chip development and production, Hyundai is a world leader in shipbuilding and the automotive industry, Pohang Steel is a world leader in the steel industry, and Korean companies are world leaders in TFD-LCD display panels. Korean products are considered to be equal to or have surpassed the quality of products made in the United States. The adult generation grew up listening to American pop music, while the younger generation is listening to Korean hip-hop and rap. They are less likely to listen to American pop music or to consider it better. Even when Michael Jackson visited Korea, he did not attract as much attention as the national pop stars. The young generation is self-confident and optimistic about the future. They feel that they can create a better nation for themselves and for their country.

The phenomenal success of the Korean soccer team in the 2002 World Cup helped to build collective confidence in the young generation and in their country. Millions of people gathered in city halls, university campuses, or parks to cheer for the Korean team. The "Red Devil" logo and T-shirts were developed by the soccer fans, who were once considered to be delinquent teenagers. Everyone wore the T-shirts and cheered with them for the victory of the Korean team. The very success of the Korean soccer team increased the collective efficacy of the young generation.

The election of President Roh Moo Hyun and the growing anti-American sentiments represent a desire of the younger generation to be self-determining in their own lives and in their own country. Korea, in the minds of young people, is no longer "a shrimp amid the battle of whales" but an emerging contributor and partner in the global village. Korea has not reached its full economic or political stature in the global arena, but its ability to do so has become a reality in the minds of the young Koreans. The young people have confidence in themselves and are demanding that they become the self-determining agents of their own country, including the relationship with North Korea and the United States.

Those respondents with greater contact with the United States and knowledge of it had more balanced and positive views of the American people and society and their influence in Korea and in the world. Overall, the vast majority of respondents had had no contact with American people and society. The university student sample had relatively greater contact through watching TV programs or learning English from foreigners. The results indicate that the best way to reduce anti-American sentiments is to provide accurate information about the United States and promote direct contact with the American society and people.

The results suggest that although anti-American sentiments are strong, they are not based on direct personal contact and experience. It is likely that Korean respondents have developed anti-American sentiments largely from the media and through informal contacts. Subsequent interviews conducted with middle and high school students indicate that they obtain and share negative views of the United States through the Internet. The results also suggest that the strong anti-American sentiments are susceptible to change if the people holding them obtain more information or develop personal contacts. Since there are no agencies that promote American studies, culture, or tourism for Koreans, it is unlikely that anti-American sentiments will decline. The American government and business have failed in promoting themselves to Koreans.

For Koreans it is very difficult to obtain visas to travel to the United States and study there. It is much easier to travel and study in other English-speaking countries, such as Australia, Canada, England, and New Zealand. More and more people are deciding to travel to these countries rather than the United States. The United States is the only country among the above five English-speaking nations that requires a visa to travel there. While obtaining the visa, Korean applicants have experienced a humiliating interview process, which treats them like potential criminals. Japanese, on the other hand, are given a nonvisa exemption status, and Koreans feel as though they are being treated as second-class people. Japan attacked the United States and bombed Pearl Harbor, but it is Koreans who are treated like former enemies.

Since Koreans are more likely to be exposed to negative news about the United States and positive influence or contact with the United States is likely to be minimal, the anti-American sentiments have coalesced and will likely increase. Since people are likely to process and assimilate information that is consistent with their view and to reject information that is inconsistent, anti-American sentiments will likely increase. In other words, based on the current trend, anti-American sentiments will increase, especially since the young generation holds much more negative views than the adults do.

Finally, the anti-American sentiment in other parts of the world has been ideologically driven, with left-leaning activists being most critical of American policy or traditional religious groups; an example is that of those Muslim clerics who are critical of American influence. The anti-American sentiment in South Korea is driven by neither ideology nor tradition. It reflects the growing confidence of the younger generation in itself and in its nation. The American government is unaware of the changing tide and sentiments of the young generation, has ignored it, and is unprepared for it.

Korea has always accepted its subjugated role in relation to China and recently to the United States. However, the educational and economic success in South Korea is producing a new generation of Koreans who are confident of their personal and collective ability to be active players and contributors in the international arena. They do not shy away from speaking English or from international competition. They are well versed in modern technology. They want to participate in the international arena as equals.

References

Amsden, A.H. 1989. *Asia's Next Giant: South Korea and Late Industrialization*. New York: Oxford University Press.

Choi, J.J. 1993. "Political Cleavages in South Korea." In *State and Society in Contemporary Korea*, ed. H. Koo. Ithaca, NY: Cornell University Press.

Federation of Korean Industries. 1991. "The 30 Year History of the Federation of Korean Industries (*Chungkyungrun 30 ryunsa*). Seoul: Federation of Korean Industries.

Kim, U. 2001. "Analysis of Democracy and Human Rights in Cultural Context: Psychological and Comparative Perspectives. In *Democracy, Human Rights, and Peace in Korea: Psychological, Political, and Cultural Perspectives*, ed. H.S. Aasen, U. Kim, and G. Helgesen, pp. 53–94. Seoul: Kyoyook Kwahasa.

———. 2000. "Indigenous, Cultural, and Cross-Cultural Psychology: Theoretical, Philosophical, and Epistemological Analysis." *Asian Journal of Social Psychology* 3: 265–87.

Kim, U., H. Harajiri, and U.C. Cho. 1997. "The Perception of Japanese People and Culture: The Case of Korean Nationals and Korean Sojourners." In *Progress in Asian Social Psychologies*, ed. K. Leung, U. Kim, S. Yamaguchi, and Y. Kashima. Singapore: John Wiley & Sons.

Kim, U., Y.S. Park, and D.H. Park. 2000. "The Challenge of Cross-Cultural Psychology: The Role of Indigenous Psychologies. *Journal of Cross-Cultural Psychology* 31, no. 1: 63–75.

———. 1999. "The Korean Indigenous Psychology Approach: Theoretical Considerations and Empirical Applications. *Applied Psychology: An International Review* 45: 55–73.

Sakong, I. 1993. *Korea in the World Economy*. Washington, DC: Institute for International Economics.

16

Changing Perceptions in U.S.-Korean Relations and the Rise of Anti-Americanism

William Watts

Roh Moo Hyun, the newly elected president of the Republic of Korea (ROK), has faced a major problem that he surely neither wants nor needs: a rising tide of anti-Americanism that has assumed proportions previously unseen on the Korean Peninsula. In the December 2002 elections, Roh, the candidate of the ruling Millennium Democratic Party (MDP), handily defeated Lee Hoe Chang, candidate of the Grand National Party (GNP), the opposition leader who had narrowly lost to outgoing President Kim Dae-Jung in the 1996 presidential face-off.

Roh has vowed to continue Kim's "Sunshine Policy" of pursuing an opening with North Korea. He has also expressed concern over the dominant role of the United States in South Korean life, at one point calling for the withdrawal of U.S. forces from the country. And late in his presidential campaign, he expressed reservations about remaining tied to the U.S. alliance in the event of U.S.-North Korean hostilities. (This statement caused the rupture of his short-lived political coalition with Chung Moon Joon, scion of the Hyundai industrial empire and briefly a presidential challenger.)

All this may complicate Roh's relations with Washington. President George W. Bush is known for his desire to "bond" with foreign leaders, à la his ties with Great Britain's Prime Minister Tony Blair and Russia's President Vladimir Putin. That may not be easy with Roh. At the same time, the realities of dealing with the unpredictability of North Korean leader Kim Jong Il will introduce sobering considerations of national interests and national security into any bilateral dialogue. Roh's May 2002 visit to the United States and his summit meeting with Bush were, by most accounts, a considerable success. The two leaders appeared to establish comfortable working ties, giving the bilateral relationship a welcome and much-needed boost. But tough sledding lies ahead, and the alliance is sure to come under continued testing.

Sources

This chapter examines several recent surveys of public and elite/leadership opinion in the Republic of Korea, covering the changing shape of views that Koreans hold of the United States, the American people, and U.S. policies. Also included, for purposes of comparison and reference, are findings that pertain to other countries in the region and various regional issues. Finally, we cite some American views that may help to put the bilateral views into a larger context and focus.

Along with studies by Potomac Associates (in cooperation with Opinion Dynamics Corporation), the Gallup and Roper Organizations, and Korean sources, we will draw in particular upon three recent efforts that provide a wealth of information on various themes related to U.S.–Korea relations:

A Potomac Associates study of the views of "next-generation leaders" in the Republic of Korea (hereinafter referred to as "Potomac"): We organized this effort with the cooperation and support of Dr. James Przystup of the National Defense University. During a three-week period in November and December 2001, Gallup Korea interviewed fifty-one Korean citizens, thirty to forty-nine years of age, who showed promise of assuming positions of leadership in the years ahead. Telephone and in-person interviews were carried out almost entirely in the greater Seoul metropolitan area. The limited size of the sample precludes rigorous statistical comparisons and discussions of margins of error. Our findings in this unique exercise should, therefore, be viewed as indicative and impressionistic.

The final list of persons interviewed was drawn from several sources: the Asia Foundation, the American Embassy in Seoul, Korea stock exchange listings, National Assembly members, various newspaper and Web site listings, Gallup Korea's own extensive database, and personal contacts. The sample was broken down as follows: political figures (eight, evenly divided between members of the Grand National Party and the New Millennium Democratic Party), government and other public officials (eight), government and other public officials (eight), members of the business community (nine), individuals from the academic community (eight), media and press figures (eight), representatives of nongovernmental organizations (NGOs) (six), and the military (four).

A global study was undertaken by the Pew Research Center for the People and the Press (hereinafter "Pew"). Most fieldwork was conducted by local research organizations in forty-four countries, under the direction of Princeton Survey Research Associates, between July and August 2002. This massive undertaking included samples of varying sizes of adults eighteen years of age and older, with those of particular significance to this report as follows: United States, 1,501; Republic of Korea, 719; Japan, 702; China, 3,000 in six cities; and Russia, 1,002.

The latest Chicago Council on Foreign Relations quadrennial examination of general public and elite views was conducted for the first time in cooperation with the German Marshall Fund of the United States (hereinafter CCFR/GMF). Telephone interviews with 2,862 men and women, eighteen years of age and older, plus 400 in-home interviews of persons in the same age group, were carried out by Harris Interactive between June 1 and 30, 2002. In addition, telephone interviews were conducted between May 17 and July 15, 2002, with 397 national opinion leaders drawn from government, business and labor, the media, religious institutions, special-interest groups, and private foreign policy organizations. (Fieldwork in prior Chicago Council efforts was conducted by Gallup.)

Korean Views of the United States, U.S. Policy, and the American People

Overall Attitudes Toward the United States and Others

Positive/Negative

"Next-generation leaders" in the Potomac study ranked the United States first in expressions of positive, as opposed to negative, personal feelings (although with reservations), followed closely by China. Japan and especially Russia lagged far behind. Thus:

"At a personal level, how would you describe your feelings about [country]?"

	Japan	China	Russia	United States
Very positive	—	4%	2%	12%
Somewhat positive	25%	49	10	47
Neither positive nor negative	51	43	70	31
Somewhat negative	22	4	18	10
Very negative	2	—	—	—

Japan. The clouds of history hang heavily over Korean perceptions of Japan, as the Potomac survey makes clear. Personal feelings toward Japan followed a classic bell curve, with a bare majority opting for a neutral "neither positive nor negative." Those on the positive and negative sides split fairly evenly, although nobody expressed "very positive" views. Media representatives were a bit more positive than the norm. Overall, Japan was particularly faulted on two counts: failure to atone adequately for its past behavior and its potential reemergence as a military power/threat.

China. With 53 percent of the Potomac sample viewing China positively, it ranked second only to the United States, trailing by just 6 percentage points. None of the respondents held "very negative" feelings about China, while a substantial segment held a neutral, open-minded position. Depending on the course of future events, the views of that large uncommitted group could move in either direction. As we shall see below, many hope that greater warmth will prevail. In comparative terms, China was seen overwhelmingly as "primarily a market and economic opportunity" rather than a "potential military threat, with expansionist interests toward Korea."

Russia. Russia drew the largest bloc saying "neither positive nor negative," perhaps indicating uncertainty and a sense that Russia is not all that important in the thinking of most respondents. Those taking one side or the other fell a bit more on the negative side. In general terms, politicians were the most favorably inclined toward Russia, while businesspeople and NGO figures were most critical. It is worth noting that the academics were unanimous in their neutrality. While a majority saw Russia as "primarily a market and economic opportunity" rather than a "potential military threat, with expansionist interests toward Korea," a substantial minority registered concern about Russia's threat potential.

It is important to note that the relatively positive views of the United States, recorded in late 2001, underwent a veritable sea change in succeeding months. Here are subsequent opinion findings about the United States and the American people, recorded in Korea, Japan, and Russia in the global Pew study; also a more recent survey by Gallup Korea for the *Chosun Ilbo,* a leading Korean daily:

Favorable/Unfavorable Views of United States

	Very favorable	Somewhat favorable	Somewhat unfavorable	Very unfavorable	Don't know
Japan	13%	59%	23%	3%	2%
South Korea	**4**	**49**	**37**	**7**	**3**
Russia	8	53	27	6	6

Favorable/Unfavorable Views of Americans

	Very favorable	Somewhat favorable	Somewhat unfavorable	Very unfavorable	Don't know
Japan	10%	63%	22%	2%	3%
Russia	9	58	21	3	9
South Korea	**4**	**57**	**30**	**5**	**4**

Like/Dislike the United States

	(1) Like very much	(2) Like some-what	(1+2)	(3) Dislike some-what	(4) Dislike very much	(3+4)	Don't know
Total	6%	31%	37%	34%	20%	54%	9%
Male	7	31	38	32	24	56	6
Female	5	31	36	35	17	52	12
20s	2	20	22	45	31	76	6

30s	2	25	27	40	27	67	6
40s	2	40	42	32	18	50	8
50s+	17	39	56	19	8	27	18

Comparative clustered positive/negative views about the U.S. show the following:

	Positive	Negative	Don't know
Gallup Korea (12/02)	37%	54%	9%
Pew (7–8/02)	53	44	3
Potomac (12/01)	59	41	—

This represents an impressive, steady, and substantially negative shift in popular sentiment. The causes, manifold and complex, and are discussed further on.

Levels of Trust

Trust in the United States, as recorded in the Potomac study, was relatively strong, again followed by China, Japan, and Russia. More recent data specifically citing the trust issue are not available. Common sense would indicate that these earlier numbers have followed the negative trend just seen in like/dislike measurements.

"And how much do you trust [country]?"

	Japan	China	Russia	United States
A great deal	2%	—	—	9%
Somewhat	31	55%	10%	63
Not too much	65	43	88	26
Not at all	2	—	2	2
No opinion	—	2	—	—

United States. Levels of trust of the United States appeared a bit stronger than those accorded to warmth of personal feelings. Academics were most trusting, with unanimity in the positive column. Politicians, on the other hand, were the least trusting, with a majority on the negative side.

Japan. This amounted to a two-thirds/one-third negative balance in levels of trust. The real divide was between those who trust Japan "somewhat" and those who said "not too much." The business community and NGO members were slightly more negative. Members of academia registered the highest level of trust, possibly attributable to growing levels of academic exchange between the two countries.

China. For China, the picture was considerably brighter: a small majority trusted China "somewhat," offsetting a minority that said "not too much." Politicians, academics, and women were a bit more positive, while government and public officials and the military were less so.

Russia. Russia did particularly poorly on this measure. Only politicians trusted Russia "somewhat" above the very low norm. A large majority expressed "not too much" trust in Russia, with unanimous negative ratings among the business community, media and the press, the NGO community, military, and women. The younger age group was not far behind.

In its later global study, Pew introduced a significant caveat on a trust-related issue: "Do you think the world would be a safer place or a more dangerous place if there was another country that was equal in military power equal to the United States?"

	Safer	More dangerous	Don't know
Japan	6%	88%	6%
South Korea	**36**	**56**	**8**
Russia	25	53	22

Here, despite many misgivings about the United States, a majority of Koreans expressed tolerance of the U.S. role as the sole superpower. More than one in three, however, felt that the world would be a safer place if the United States faced a superpower competitor—presumably as a check against problems that many Koreans see in current bilateral relations. (This theme is developed further on.) Whatever the reasons, this is a significant proportion, larger than that found in regard to Russia.

Future Importance of Selected Countries

In one of the most significant findings in the Potomac study, a majority expected that links with China over the next ten years would assume greater importance for Korea than those with the United States:

	China	Japan	Russia
Korea's ties more important with	53%	24%	8%
Korea's ties more important with the United States	41	75	92

The United States vis-à-vis China. Majorities of almost all survey categories ranked future ties with China as more important than those with the United States, with the highest numbers being seen among NGO representatives and women. Two groups stood out in putting the United States first: members of academia, many of whom have exceptionally close ties with their counterparts in the United States; and members of the military, who have unique bonds with their American colleagues.

Reasons given by those who gave China preeminence over the United States included the following:

- Geographic propinquity
- China's rising economic strength; potential superpower
- China potentially a larger market
- Stronger cultural links
- Development of a Northeast Asia bloc
- China potentially easier to deal with than the United States; possible bargaining chip
- Greater potential to play a role in China's development
- Potential long-term decline of U.S. influence in Far East, matched by rise of China

Implicit in some of these comments is a sense that, for many Koreans, China is increasingly a country with which Korea feels comfortable. Travel to China is now possible, and visitors often feel a sense of kinship. China is also a country that can and does say "no" to the United States. That ability and strength can appeal to the Koreans' widespread sense of annoyance in dealings with the United States, which is discussed more fully below. Frustration with U.S. policy toward North Korea, for example, seen by many South Koreans as heightening South–North tensions, can play into China's hands.

Those who looked to the United States as the key partner mentioned:

- The existence of a Pax Americana
- The importance of the ROK–U.S. military alliance
- The overriding national interest in maintaining close ties with the United States
- The United States has been and will continue to be Korea's closest ally
- China is a potentially threatening neighbor
- China has an uncertain future; inherent instability of its national system

These are powerful reasons favoring a continuing, close relationship between the Republic of Korea and the United States. While the growing fascination with China should not be underestimated, neither should it be too quickly interpreted as ensuring some kind of basic new future realignment. Indeed, links between Korea and China on one hand and Korea and the United States on the other do not have to be seen as some kind of zero-sum game. Stability in Northeast Asia would be enhanced, not weakened, by solid ties both ways. For the foreseeable future, Korea may have the luxury of not having to choose between China and the United States, all the more so if China continues to be seen by Washington policy makers as playing a constructive and supportive role in the "war on terrorism."

The United States vis-à-vis Japan. By a three-to-one margin, respondents believed that future ties with the United States will be more important to Korea than those with Japan. That was the unanimous view of the military, a view also held well above the norm by government and public officials and the older age cohort. NGO officials and women were the only groups that put Korea's future ties with Japan ahead of those with the United States.

Those who stressed ties with Japan cited a number of factors:

- Geography (mentioned frequently)
- Development of a Northeast Asian and/or Asian bloc (also mentioned frequently)
- Growing emergence of China (again, frequently)

Bilateral U.S.–ROK Ties

Assessments of Current Ties with United States

"How do you rate the strength of relations between the Republic of Korea and the United States?"

- Very strong   16%
- Somewhat strong   61
- Not too strong   23

The assessment of ties between the United States and the Republic of Korea mirrored quite closely the levels of trust in the United States, with a 77 to 23 percent "strong–not too strong" balance here, and a 72 to 28 percent positive-negative balance on trust. This linkage is surely closely tied, as we now see, to what our sample saw as the chief benefits to Korea of bilateral ties—security.

Principal Benefits to the Republic of Korea

Respondents were also asked to choose, from among four alternatives, the first and second most important benefits to the Republic of Korea of bilateral ties:

	Security ties	Economic ties	Growth of democratization ties and human rights	Cultural	Other*
Most important benefit	70	22	6	—	2
Second most important	20	68	2	6	4
[1st and 2nd] combined	90	90	8	6	6]

* "Presenting obvious goals and objectives as leading country" and "pioneering and scientific-technical mind," both volunteered

The picture is crystal-clear: security first, economics second, and everything else trails far behind. Security was particularly important to members of the media; the third item, democratization and human rights, drew special notice from academics. The relatively high levels of trust that we noted for the United States—easily surpassing those recorded for China, Japan, and Russia, in that order—can be linked to the primary importance of the bilateral security relationship, a relationship that has endured for over half a century but now finds itself under severe strains.

Major Beneficiary in the U.S.–ROK Relationship

"Who do you think benefits most from the relationship, the United States or the Republic of Korea?"

- United States   59%
- Republic of Korea   37
- Hard to measure, but unequal   2
- Don't know   2

A clear majority were of the view that the United States benefits most from the bilateral ties, a view held unanimously by the military respondents and more heavily than the norm by media persons. NGOs, women, and—interestingly—politicians felt that Korea was the principal beneficiary. This sense of an unequal relationship found clear expression in naming problems in bilateral ties.

Major Problems in the Relationship

In the Potomac study, when respondents were asked to pinpoint, in their own words, what they thought were the most important problems in relations between Korea and the United States, we found frequent concurrence on a number of telling items:

- U.S. "hegemonism"
- Excessive Korean dependency on the United States
- Impact of the U.S. military presence
- American unilateralism, egoism, and attitude of superiority
- U.S. interventionism in Korea's internal affairs
- Unfair U.S. trade conditions and unequal economic status
- Discrimination against Koreans
- "Flunkeyism" of Korean government toward the United States
- Generalized anti-Americanism
- Aggressive U.S. policies that heighten South–North tensions
- United States putting Japan ahead of Korea
- Korea just a member of the Pax Americana
- Cultural differences; American cultural insensitivity
- Visa problems

This is a powerful list of grievances. For anyone who has been involved in U.S.-Korean affairs over the years, these expressions of concern and thinly disguised resentment will come as no surprise. The enormous American presence in the Republic of Korea and the impact that U.S. policy can have in and on Korean life touch raw nerves among the Korean citizenry. Such a catalogue of complaints and even indictments represents a warning signal and call for attention that should not be lightly dismissed. The very fact that this catalogue has endured over time makes it all the more disturbing.

Some of the policy-related complaints were underscored in the 2002 Pew report. Thus, by a margin of 53 to 41 percent, Korean respondents placed "different policies" above "different values" as the principal cause of difficulties between the two countries. (By way of comparison, Japan cited values above policies by 61 to 34 percent.) And when Pew asked individuals how they assessed the impact of American influence in their country, looking at a number of specific policy and/or value areas, Korean respondents gave highest ratings to such things as democracy; ways of doing business; movies, TV, and music; and scientific/technological prowess, while faulting foreign policy approaches and the spread of U.S. customs and ideas, thus expressing further uneasiness with the huge American presence in Korea.

A summary listing of the Pew findings follows, listed in order of most favorable Korean views:

Overall positive:	ROK (%)	Japan (%)	China (%)
1. U.S. technological/scientific advances: **admire/don't**	81/16	89/7	87/5
2. Opinion of Americans: **favorable/unfavorable**	61/35	73/24	n/a
3. American ways of doing business: **like/dislike**	59/32	40/40	36/24
4. American ideas about democracy: **like/dislike**	58/37	62/27	n/a
5. American music, movies, and TV: **like/dislike**	53/38	74/18	55/36
6. Opinion of the United States: **favorable/ unfavorable**	53/44	72/26	n/a

Overall negative:

	ROK (%)	Japan (%)	China (%)
7. The United States does: **too much/right amount/ too little** to solve world problems	39/30/19	53/32/7	n/a
8. Spread of American ideas/customs: **good/bad**	30/62	49/35	n/a
9. U.S. policies: **increase/lessen/no effect** gap between rich and poor	67/12/13	69/4/17	n/a
10. U.S.-led efforts to fight terrorism: **favor/oppose**	24/72	61/32	n/a
11. U.S. foreign policy considers others: **yes/no**	23/73	36/59	n/a

n/a = question not allowed in China

The breakdown on the last item is worth spelling out. Respondents in each country were asked:

"In making international policy decisions, to what extent do you think the United States takes into account the interests of [country]?"

	(1) Great Deal	(2) Fair amount	(1+2)	(3) Not too much	(4) Not at all	(3+4)	Don't know
Korea	5%	18%	(23%)	54%	19%	(73%)	4%
Japan	4	32	(36)	49	10	(59)	5
Russia	3	18	(21)	45	25	(70)	9

Korean views are the most negative, with almost three respondents in four holding the view that the United States takes Korean concerns into account either "not too much" or "not at all." That negative/cynical view, outstripping perceptions of both Japan and Russia, is in line with what we noted earlier: the extent to which Koreans believe the world would be a safer place if there was another superpower to challenge U.S. dominance.

Security Ties

Given the importance Korean respondents in the Potomac study placed on the security relationship, it is not surprising that any idea of a rapid removal of U.S. forces from Korea has not gained widespread support; just one in four were of that view in late 2001.

Level of U.S. Forces: "When Korea is unified, do you think the level of U.S. military forces should":

- Remain the same   12%
- Be reduced gradually   63
- Be reduced quickly   11
- Be eliminated altogether quickly   14

More recently, the December 2002 Gallup Korea study for *Chosun Ilbo*, previously cited, found the following in response to a question about calling for the removal of U.S. military personnel:

	Favor	Oppose	Don't know
Total	32%	55%	13%
Male	30	61	9
Female	34	48	18
20s	47	43	10

30s	42	47	11
40s	26	61	13
50s +	13	68	19

As might be expected, age plays a major role: most supportive of U.S. troop withdrawal are Koreans in their twenties and, to a lesser degree, in their thirties; that is, individuals who have no firsthand memory of the Korean War and U.S. involvement in helping the Republic of Korea to survive the attack from the North. In the same survey, Korea Gallup recorded a view of the roots of the Korean War that many American observers would find hard to accept. When asked to choose between several alternatives as "closest to your thought" about the roots of the war, responses came out as follows:

- Proxy war of the superpowers, the U.S. and USSR   45%
- Illegal invasion by North Korea   31
- War of national liberation for unification of Korea   12
- Invasion by South Korea for unification by going north   3
- Other/don't know   9

Missile Defense and the War on Terror. In the Potomac survey, a two-to-one majority voiced opposition to the deployment of U.S. antimissile defense facilities on Korean soil. Mirroring this reserve, three in four favored only limited support to the Bush administration's war on terror, specifically not to include military involvement. As noted above, the Pew report found a balance of 72 to 24 percent saying they "oppose the U.S.-led efforts to fight terrorism." (In Japan, 61 to 32 percent "favor" these efforts; in Russia, the balance was 73 to 16 percent "in favor." This question was not permitted in China.)

Anti-Americanism

In discussing this topic, it is important to be clear about what one means by "anti-Americanism." This is a catch-all phrase that can cover a multitude of sins. The fact that young Koreans can, at one and the same time, burn American flags and apply for an American visa to go to university or college in the United States says something important. "Anti-Americanism" is often directed not at America as an ideal or Americans as individuals. Rather, the focus is often an artifact of U.S. policy and the role of the United States in Korean life—major sources of concern and resentment discussed earlier. While not belittling the problem involved, it is crucial to remember the nuances of distinction in what it represents.

A near-majority in the Potomac study believed anti-Americanism was "growing" (49 percent, with 43 percent "staying about the same" and 8 percent "declining"). At the same time, a considerably larger majority did not see it as overly threatening to Korea–U.S. ties. These are ranges of views that have likely been influenced by subsequent events.

Reasons for the surge of anti-Americanism in South Korea are manifold:

- Bush's "axis of evil" formulation, engendering widespread anger over its perceived impact on South–North talks.
- A broad sense that U.S. policy impedes progress in those talks and lessens any chance of finding accommodation with the regime of Kim Jong-il.
- Disqualification of the ROK speed skater at the 2002 Winter Olympics in Salt Lake City, with the gold medal awarded to an American.
- Jay Leno's unfortunate attempt at humor, on his late-night talk show, to the effect that the Korean was so angry at his disqualification that "he kicked his dog in anger when he got home—and then ate it."
- Imposition of steel tariffs, characterized by former Ambassador to the United States Kim Kyung-won as follows: "the U.S. government's decision to increase import taxes on steel contradicts the country's assertions about free trade. When the U.S. does not follow a regulation that it has created, it is hard to expect other countries to accept the regulation as well."
- A flood of anti-American comments in ROK media (extensively reported in an overnight review of the Korean press).
- A campaign for the boycott of American goods, pressed on the Internet.

Aside from these specifics, there are a number of larger issues of perception that play a role:

- Growing nationalism in Korea, especially among younger Koreans.
- A view of the roots of the Korean War, noted above, that places greater responsibility on the United States than on North Korea.
- A powerful sense of Korea's emergence as a regional economic and political power, too long under the American shadow. Also as noted above, this spawns resentment against what many Koreans see as American arrogance, U.S. intrusion into Korean affairs, and excessive domination in Korean life.

Finally, of course, there is the growing negative fallout from what is widely seen as improper, often criminal behavior of individual members of the U.S. Armed Forces stationed in Korea. This has been sharply dramatized by the killing in June 2002 of two Korean schoolgirls, run over by a U.S. military vehicle during military maneuvers. The responsible soldiers were subsequently acquitted by an American military court martial.

Formal apologies tendered by President Bush and other senior American officials did little to stem the subsequent tide of anguish and anger. The episode generated massive anti-American street demonstrations and protests, along with renewed calls for revision of the Status of Forces Agreement (SOFA), which has largely exempted American military personnel from local legal proceedings while in the performance of active duty. On December 17, 2002, the Korean Foreign Ministry announced that a special task force would be convened to "make joint efforts to improve the operation of the SOFA and to prevent accidents involving U.S. military drills," according to a Foreign Ministry spokesman. The task force includes officials from the Foreign Ministry, the Defense Ministry, the U.S. Embassy, and United States Forces Korea.

While the level of street demonstrations and other forms of overt protest has eased, the issue of anti-Americanism is not about to disappear. It has been a constant in the bilateral relationship almost from the beginning. Its focus is not necessarily focused on Americans per se but on grievances related to policy issues and perceived slights, discussed above. It is probably also fed by what is seen as lack of American interest in, and knowledge about, Korea and its people.

Only the future will tell how deep and how lasting this continuing problem will prove to be. In this regard, a knowledgeable American observer, just returned from Seoul, struck a worrisome note at a recent meeting in Washington. He reported his surprise and concern over openly critical attacks on U.S. policy, made to him by senior individuals who have been consistent over the years in their support of the bilateral link. Their endorsement of the views of individuals who are generally seen as part of a more radical element impressed this thoughtful witness as new—and ominous.

Overall Assessment

Taken together, these various survey findings represent a cautious, pragmatic—and sobering—evaluation by Koreans of the current state of affairs on the Korean Peninsula and of major issues that face policy makers in Seoul and Washington. It is clear that change is in the air, with many pressures pushing ties in new and possibly divergent directions.

Most Koreans do see a number of things that provide hope and encouragement for the future. They also find a lot lacking both on the home front and in relations with their key ally, the United States. Attitudes toward Japan remain heavily clouded by the heavy hand of history, although passage of time has eased that burden. Such negativism stands in sharp contrast to the positive and, for the longer term, hopeful look they cast toward China, their giant and increasingly important/influential neighbor. Overall, one senses a widespread feeling of domestic unease, a feeling that is aggravated by a concern (just noted) of being taken for granted and of being relegated to second-class status, where they find themselves subject to whims of a Pax Americana, playing second fiddle to Japan, and exposed to political and economic subordination.

This weighs heavily on a proud, intensely nationalistic people, encouraging anti-American sentiments. With such feelings, a "China card" gains in value. Not all the criticisms are ipso facto valid. But in a relationship as important and intense as the one between the United States and the Republic of Korea, it is incumbent on both partners to give these expressions of concern appropriate attention. While there are many positive building blocks already in place and ready to be expanded upon, there are also a number of anxieties and warning signals that need to be addressed.

17

The Tipping Point

Kwangju, May 1980

William M. Drennan

The concept of the "tipping point," popularized by Malcolm Gladwell in his book of the same name,[1] is drawn from epidemiology and holds that "small changes will have little or no effect on a system until a critical mass is reached. Then a further small change 'tips' the system and a large effect is observed."[2] Gladwell applies this idea to the social realm, holding that the "'tipping point' is that magic moment when ideas, trends, and social behaviors cross a critical threshold and 'take,' causing a tidal wave of far-reaching effect." Such a moment occurred in the Republic of Korea (ROK) twenty-three years ago. The central act in this Korean drama, and the tipping point for the anti-Americanism now so prominently on display in South Korea, was the brutal suppression of a popular uprising in the southwestern city of Kwangju in May 1980. The virulent strain of anti-Americanism that infected South Korea as a result of Kwangju has become an epidemic that now threatens the half-century-old U.S.–ROK security relationship.

An examination of the historical record shows clearly that the erosion of popular support among Koreans for the United States had its genesis in the events of 1979–81, beginning with the assassination of President Park Chung Hee, the seizure of power within the ROK military by a group of army officers led by Major General Chun Doo Hwan, the consolidation of political power by the Chun clique following the Kwangju uprising, and the assignment of blame for the violence to the United States.

The purpose of this chapter is to examine the 1979–81 period, using the Kwangju uprising as the centerpiece of the analysis, and to provide an assessment of the uprising's enduring impact, for it is the author's contention that it is impossible to understand the deterioration of the U.S.–Korean relationship without an understanding of the Kwangju uprising and its aftermath.

Americans, to the extent that they are aware of contemporary Korea at all, have

---

The views expressed in this chapter are solely those of the author writing in a private capacity.

seen periodic news reports—usually accompanied by graphic footage of firebomb-throwing students and tear gas-firing riot police—of the raucous domestic political scene in South Korea. Until recently the occasional burning of the American flag captured on video or displayed in the newspapers seemed relatively minor when compared to anti-American protests, riots, hostage taking, and assassinations in other parts of the world. Americans who follow events in Korea have in the past generally accepted the assurances of the Republic of Korea government that anti-Americanism is resident in only a small minority of Koreans and that the vast majority of Koreans are staunchly pro-American. Both President Kim Dae Jung and his successor, Roh Moo Hyun, repeated this mantra in early 2003 following months of the largest, most prolonged anti-American protests in the history of the alliance; this against a backdrop of polling data that show a steady decline in the image of America among Koreans, especially younger Koreans.

ROK politics has long been dominated by political leaders whose parties are oriented to personality rather than to issues or ideology.[3] Until the 1997 election of Kim Dae Jung, the successful parties and leaders differed little in their philosophies or in their single-minded quest for power. Political leaders in Korea still tend to view politics as a zero-sum, winner-take-all affair. The major actors in the Korean political drama under examination in this chapter certainly fit this mold. Park Chung Hee, Chun Doo Hwan, Roh Tae Woo, Kim Young Sam, Kim Dae Jung, and Kim Jong Pil dominated the ROK political scene for years beginning in the early 1960s; all but Kim Jong Pil would eventually serve as president and all are protagonists in the events of 1979–81. Park and Chun, in particular, are central to the story.

The Rise of Park Chung Hee

Park Chung Hee was born in 1917 in the southeastern Kyongsang region, the youngest of seven children of a poor farming couple. Korea was under Japanese colonial rule, having lost its sovereignty in 1910. Quickly tiring of his first job as a primary school teacher, Park joined the Imperial Japanese Army in 1940. Trained at the military academies in Manchukuo and Tokyo, he served as a second lieutenant for the last year of the Imperial Army's existence. Following Japan's surrender, Park was selected to attend the second class of the newly established Korean Military Academy (KMA) in September 1946, graduating three months later as a captain.[4]

Arrested in 1948 on suspicions of being associated with communists in the South Korean military, he survived a death sentence by informing on others.[5] He was reinstated in the army in 1950, emerged from the Korean War as a brigadier general, and was promoted to major general in 1958. Park was unusual for a senior Korean military officer in that he eschewed social functions and shunned close ties with American officers.[6] Among Korean officers, he earned a reputation for honesty by refusing to help rig elections for the corrupt regime of President Syngman Rhee (1948–60), winning a loyal following among younger KMA graduates.[7]

The corruption of the Rhee regime motivated Park and a small group of disgruntled officers drawn primarily from KMA's eighth class to conspire to overthrow the government in 1960. They were preempted, however, by student-led antigovernment demonstrations in April 1960. When the Korean military refused to intervene, the Rhee regime was toppled, replaced by a weak parliamentary government headed by former premier Chang Myon. However, when senior officers who had thrived under Rhee were allowed to remain in place, Park and his co-conspirators decided to act. In May 1961 they staged a military coup d'état and established a Military Revolutionary Committee headed by Park to rule the country.[8] He was elected president in 1963 under a new constitution and won reelection for what should have been a final term in 1967. Park, however, had no intention of allowing the constitution to stand in the way of his retaining power.

In 1969 Park succeeded in amending the constitution so that he could run for a third term, and in 1971 he defeated opposition leader Kim Dae Jung, but by a surprisingly small margin. Increasingly autocratic, Park was determined to remain president for life and to never again allow the opposition to mount such a serious challenge. In 1972 he instituted the "Yushin" (revitalizing) Constitution, which established, among other things, a six-year presidential term, no limit on the number of terms, election of the president by an electoral college rather than by popular vote, and the authority of the president to appoint one-third of the members of the National Assembly. The Yushin Constitution in essence created one-man rule, with Park firmly in control of all three branches of government.[9]

The 1970s were a period of increasing pressure on Park, both at home and abroad. Domestic opposition to his dictatorship grew steadily and was met by increasingly harsh repression. Hopeful signs in 1971–72 of improved relations with North Korea had quickly evaporated. By the second half of the decade, the Korean economic machine, the foundation of Park's claim to legitimacy,[10] was running out of steam. Relations with the United States, South Korea's essential ally, were at an all-time low as a result of the Nixon Doctrine, the 1973 kidnapping and near murder of Kim Dae Jung by agents of the Korean Central Intelligence Agency (KCIA), the U.S. withdrawal from Vietnam and the subsequent victory of North Vietnam over the South, President Carter's emphasis on human rights, and his initiative to withdraw U.S. troops from Korea.[11] If the alliance with the United States was strained by these events, it was nearly broken as a result of the "Koreagate" scandal (the attempt by the Park regime to buy influence in the U.S. Congress), prompting a senior U.S. official to observe that "1977–78 was as difficult a period between treaty allies as could be imagined."[12] For Park, it would be nothing compared to the next year.

The political opposition, never completely suppressed and apparently sensing Park's vulnerability, increased its pressure on the regime in 1979. Kim Young Sam, a longtime opponent of Park who had been silenced for a time by the president's repressive measures, returned to the leadership of the opposition New Democratic Party (NDP) in May, backed by Kim Dae Jung and vowing to confront Park "both inside and outside parliament to force Park's resignation."[13]

In August, riot police stormed NDP headquarters, an action that resulted in the death of one person and the hospitalization of over thirty, including two members of the National Assembly.[14] In early September, the Korean Supreme Court, at Park's bidding, ordered Kim's suspension from the presidency of the NDP. Kim replied by calling for the overthrow of the government, "with the implication that this should be by force if necessary."[15]

Park reacted swiftly to Kim Young Sam's call for his ouster. In an unprecedented move, Park had Kim expelled from the National Assembly in early October, prompting the United States, in an equally unprecedented move, to recall its ambassador for consultations on the deteriorating political situation in South Korea.[16]

Events quickly spun out of control. On October 13, the entire opposition quit the National Assembly in protest over Kim's expulsion. Two days later, riots broke out in Masan and the neighboring city of Pusan, Kim's hometown and political base; martial law was declared in Pusan the next night.[17] Initially, soldiers from Pusan patrolled the streets, but in a move with ominous implications for the future, they were soon augmented by paratroopers from other parts of the country.[18]

At the time of the Pusan-Masan riots, U.S. Secretary of Defense Harold Brown was in South Korea for the annual ROK–U.S. Security Consultative Meeting, and while Park no doubt was embarrassed by having to declare martial law during Brown's visit, he must have welcomed the secretary's assurance that the United States would not, in effect, use the presence of its forces as a means to pressure Park to institute the democratic reforms demanded by the opposition and championed previously by President Carter.[19] Brown made it clear that the U.S. interest in regional and peninsular stability now transcended the administration's earlier focus on human rights.[20]

Whatever comfort Brown's visit may have provided the South Korean president proved to be ephemeral. On October 26, Park was assassinated by the head of the KCIA, an old friend and KMA classmate, who, under severe criticism for his supposedly ineffective handling of the Pusan-Masan riots, reportedly feared for his job.[21]

Park's death created a political vacuum. The National Assembly had long been rendered impotent, political parties had been neutralized, the military were split along generational and regional lines, and many opposition politicians and dissidents were in jail. The prime minister had no independent political base, the head of presidential security had been killed with Park, and the KCIA chief was under arrest for Park's murder.[22] There was no clear succession plan, no heir apparent, and no one with sufficient political standing to assume leadership. More importantly, there was no solid institutional foundation upon which to construct a successor administration.[23] The ROK was not facing a revolution, however. While power was up for grabs, the contenders were all from within the Park Chung Hee establishment, "dominated by individuals with military and security experience."[24]

In the immediate aftermath of Park's assassination, Prime Minister Choi Kyu Hah was named acting president and martial law was declared nationwide with the exception of Cheju Island, thereby enabling the civilian government to continue to function by having the martial law command report to the cabinet rather than directly to Acting President Choi.[25] And, in a move that would prove to have historic implications, the head of the Defense Security Command, Major General Chun Doo Hwan, was ordered to conduct the investigation into the death of President Park.[26]

The Emergence of Chun Doo Hwan

Chun Doo Hwan's military career was influenced by Park Chung Hee from the beginning. Like Park, Chun was from a peasant family from North Kyongsang province, and Park had supported Chun's application to the KMA. The popular Chun graduated in the lowest third of Class 11, the celebrated class of 1955, the first to be trained under a rigorous four-year curriculum modeled after West Point, a class noted for the solidarity of its members.[27] Chun solidified both his position as the unofficial leader of Class 11 and as a Park loyalist by organizing a parade of KMA graduates in support of Park's coup in 1961.[28] Shortly thereafter, Chun, along with Roh Tae Woo and five other young officers, formed the secretive Hana Hoe (One Association).[29] All were Taegu natives, all were graduates of KMA Class 11, and all were "reinforced by a sense of elitism that placed them apart from the ragtag officer corps trained at Chinese or Japanese army schools in the pre-war colonial period." An exception to the disdain these junior officers felt for their seniors was General Park, who is reported to have viewed them with pride.[30]

Park also understood the need to control them. He assigned a major general as their nominal patron and posted the members to positions important to his regime (Chun, for example, was a battalion commander in the presidential security service in the mid-1960s).[31] "They were born to the purple," said one knowledgeable observer. "They enjoyed all the perks of prestige and money at a time when people didn't have much."[32]

Although Park ordered the organization disbanded in 1973, Hana Hoe survived and continued to recruit the most promising KMA graduates to its ranks for several more years.[33] By the 1970s, Hana Hoe members occupied key billets throughout the ROK Army structure, and "[a]t the head of this cabal, whose existence was carefully shielded from the public gaze ... stood Chun Doo Hwan."[34] The bonds forged among its members endured, as Chun and friends would demonstrate in the weeks following Park Chung Hee's assassination.

Park had succeeded during his long rule in keeping the armed forces under control, but with his death there was nothing to prevent the reemergence of the factionalism and bitter rivalries that lay just below the surface.[35] Chun, having lost his patron Park Chung Hee, nevertheless found himself in a powerful position in his dual role as head of the Joint Investigation Headquarters of the Martial Law Command and as commander of the Defense Security Command. He moved quickly to weaken the power of the KCIA, and in the process emerged as a powerful actor within South Korea's security apparatus.[36] Exactly why he used that power to seize control of the army is not entirely clear, but two possibilities (or a combination of the two) are likely explanations.

One is that General Chung Seung Hwa, martial law commander and army chief of staff, was about to banish Chun to the remote East Coast Defense Command and sack Roh Tae Woo as commander of the 9th Infantry Division, compelling Chun, with the help of Roh and the rest of the leadership of Hana Hoe, to strike first.[37] Another explanation is that Chun and other Park loyalists were unwilling to allow power to pass to the hands of civilian politicians, whom they deeply distrusted.[38]

In any case, on the night of December 12, 1979, Chun, with the help of a regiment from Roh's division[39] had General Chung arrested, on suspicion of complicity in the assassination of Park, and seized the Ministry of National Defense after a brief firefight.[40] In short order the Chun forces purged the top ranks of the ROK military and installed their own people. Within days, Chun, still wearing the two stars of a major general, had replaced the four-star generals holding the positions of chairman of the joint chiefs of staff, chief and vice chief of staff of the army, deputy commander of the ROK–U.S. Combined Forces Command, and commanders of the First and Third ROK Field Armies, as well as the commanders of the units comprising the Capital Garrison Command in Seoul. He also installed a new home minister (the official in control of the national police), and minister of national defense.[41]

The "coup within the army" was complete, presenting Acting President Choi and U.S. officials in Seoul and Washington with a fait accompli.[42] There were now, in the words of the U.S. ambassador, "dual authority structures—the formal one headed by the president and the effective one headed by General Chun."[43]

Chun attempted to reassure senior American interlocutors that what has become known as the "12–12" incident was strictly a military matter designed to cleanse the defense establishment of a corrupt senior leadership grown stale.[44] And there is little evidence that those clamoring for democratic reform in the wake of Park's death and the lifting of Emergency Decree Number 9 (which had banned all criticism of the Yushin system) adequately perceived Chun's coup as the threat to liberalization that it would prove to be.[45] Choi Kyu Hah heightened expectations that democracy would soon take root in Korea when he pledged in his presidential inaugural address nine days after the 12–12 incident, that a new constitution, approved by the people, would be adopted within a year, to be followed shortly thereafter by a general election.[46] And although the nation remained under martial law, with the Chun-dominated military poised in the background and the lengthy constitutional revision process causing skeptics to question the viability of Choi's promised reforms, there were some hopeful signs during the first months of 1980.

The Crisis Builds

The government began releasing student activists detained under the harsh provisions of Park Chung Hee's Emergency Decree Number 9. People were free to speak out. Kim Dae Jung was released from house arrest. Expectations ran high for the direct election of the next president.[47] The opposition began to believe that the political tide was running in its favor.

Perhaps the high point of what has been called the "Seoul spring" came in late

February and early March, when Kim Dae Jung and hundreds of other dissidents had their civil rights restored and the universities, closed since Park's assassination, were reopened.[48] What looked so promising in March, however, began to unravel in April.

Students were back on campus, and their leaders, many of whom had recently been released from prison, were once again on the scene. April marked the twentieth anniversary of the student uprising that had driven Syngman Rhee from office, and the students were reportedly concerned that the 1980 drive for democracy was well under way without their having played a part—an intolerable situation to students in a land that for centuries has viewed students as the conscience of society.[49] "[T]his time a whole liberalization [sic] movement had been under way for six months without them being involved. They had to show at least that they were still a progressive force." It was not long before they were back on the streets demanding the lifting of martial law and an acceleration of the pace of political reform.[50]

In mid-April, Chun Doo Hwan had himself promoted to lieutenant general and assumed the duties of acting chief of the KCIA.[51] Already the most powerful man in South Korea as the de facto head of the military following the 12–12 coup, Chun was now personally in charge of the two most powerful organs of the state security apparatus —the Defense Security Command and the KCIA.

A confrontation between the students and the military was now almost inevitable, for if the students saw themselves as "the political conscience of the Korean nation . . . the military officers regard[ed] themselves as the guardians of the state."[52] The students added Chun's ouster to their list of shouted demands and took to the streets in increasing numbers, watched by a military uneasy with both the students and the increasingly raucous competition between Kim Young Sam and Kim Dae Jung for political supremacy within the opposition camp.[53]

Tensions continued to escalate through the first two weeks of May. In a rare interview with western reporters, Chun stated his concerns clearly. "I feel strongly that our political trend is headed in a worrisome direction. The problems are complex: guaranteeing our national security, realizing our modernization and prosperity, and preventing any element from dividing our nation. I feel as though we are being forced to drift aimlessly, gripped by wrong ideas and totally disregarding the realities."[54]

When student leaders presented the Choi government with an ultimatum to lift martial law by May 14 or face massive demonstrations, the crisis reached the boiling point. On May 15, following two days of increasingly violent clashes, 50,000 demonstrators gathered in front of the Seoul railway station and attempted to march to the city center. They were blocked by a huge force of riot police backed by army troops. The two sides fought for over two hours, resulting in the death of one police officer. Concerned that the military was about to intervene, student leaders the next day called off demonstrations, repairing to Ehwa University to plan their next move.[55] They never got the chance.

The specter of Seoul being paralyzed by tens of thousands of demonstrators, and the prospect of an opposition leader winning a free election, were more than Chun and his colleagues could take.[56] Their fate under a Kim Dae Jung or a Kim Young

Sam regime was predictable. The young generals were faced with either acquiescing to the rise to power of civilian politicians, whose commitment to stability and national security the generals viewed with suspicion,[57] or taking the final step in the bid for power begun on the night of December 12. They chose the latter.

On May 17, the hapless president, Choi Kyu Hah, under pressure from Chun, extended martial law to Cheju Island, thereby encompassing all of the Republic of Korea. This technical adjustment to the martial law declared the previous October removed the cabinet from the military chain of command, sweeping away the fiction of civilian control of the military that had existed since the 12–12 incident. Martial Law Decree Number 10 was issued, closing colleges and universities, prohibiting political gatherings, imposing press censorship, and banning criticism of present and past presidents. Student leaders were rounded up and jailed. Kim Young Sam was placed under house arrest, and Kim Dae Jung, Kim Jong Pil, and other politicians were imprisoned.[58]

With President Choi now thoroughly emasculated, Chun and his band were in control of the entire country, or so it seemed on the morning of May 18. Within hours, student-led demonstrations in the southwestern city of Kwangju would prove them temporarily wrong and change the course of South Korean history.

Kwangju Erupts

Kwangju, population 750,000 at the time of the uprising, is the capital of South Cholla province, which, along with North Cholla, constitutes a region long known for its unique character. Cholla residents and the rest of Korea have shared a mutual antipathy for centuries, with Cholla natives viewed with suspicion and hostility by the rest of Korea—enmities that they pay back in equal measure. Regionalism, which one western observer has called Korea's substitute for racial and religious intolerance, is nowhere stronger than between the two southwestern Cholla provinces on the one hand and the two southeastern Kyongsang provinces on the other.[59]

Kim Dae Jung's arrest by the army cabal of Park loyalists from the hated Kyongsang provinces enraged Cholla residents. Kim was not only Park's nemesis but also the Cholla region's favorite son. Demanding Kim's release, Chun's arrest, and the lifting of martial law, student protesters surged onto the streets of Kwangju in the early afternoon of May 18, and when the police and local army units proved unable or unwilling to contain them, Special Warfare paratroopers, who had been deployed to the city to guard against civil unrest, moved in.

According to an American Peace Corps eyewitness, at about 3:00 p.m. on May 18, special warfare troops wielding batons and bayonet-tipped rifles charged the demonstrators gathered in the vicinity of the provincial capital building, violently dispersing the crowd. The next day demonstrators stoned the Catholic Center on Kwangju's main street, where the martial law command had set up a command post. Paratroopers again moved on the crowd and then fanned out, beating any young men they could find, apparently in an attempt to intimidate the population.[60]

Another Peace Corps volunteer recorded the following on May 19: "This [military crackdown, beatings] is seen as a conspiracy against Cholla-do . . . the soldiers are from Kyongsang-do . . . reportedly they are on speed. They are brutal, and have been foul of mouth—and singing the praises of the late great [President Park Chung Hee]. I have also been [asked]—Why doesn't the U.S. do something? Why don't [American] troops step in and stop this craziness?"[61]

Five people were reported killed on May 19, the first fatalities of the growing confrontation. Reporters told of indiscriminate beatings and shootings. One American observer is quoted in *Time* magazine as follows: "Anybody in the soldiers' way was beaten unmercifully. When they saw the injured lying in the street, the soldiers beat them again. The American saw paratroopers shoot and kill a mother and her five-year-old child. When he shouted in protest, Why are you doing this? a soldier yelled back, This is Korea, not America."[62]

An angry crowd burned the local government-controlled television station to the ground for broadcasting government reports denying any casualties.[63]

The violence continued to escalate the next day, with casualties on both sides. The paratroopers, lacking shields to protect themselves from rocks thrown by angry townspeople, reportedly became enraged. "Seeing my fellow soldiers being killed or injured, I could feel the animal stirring inside me," one soldier said.[64]

On the afternoon of May 20, demonstrators attempted to breach the barricade around the provincial capital building with a captured armored personnel carrier. A demonstrator killed or injured 7 of the 300 soldiers deployed around the building when he drove another vehicle into their ranks. Whether the first shots were fired before or after this assault is not clear, but soon "scores of Kwangju citizens lay dead on the street as panicky soldiers shot their way clear of the crowd." Angry mobs stormed police stations, seizing weapons and ammunition; others took dynamite from a local coal mine; still others drove off with new armored personnel carriers, jeeps, and trucks from the local Asia Motor Company plant. Firefights continued through the remainder of the day.[65]

By Wednesday May 21, the city was in revolt. More than 200,000 people took to the streets. Gunfights erupted throughout the day, "with the special forces probably inflicting the heaviest casualties when they shot their way out of the city centre [sic]."[66] Tired, outnumbered, and now outgunned, the troops withdrew to the outskirts of the city, where additional army units established a cordon, cutting Kwangju off from the outside world.[67] Unrest spread to other towns and villages throughout South Cholla.[68]

For the next five days the people of Kwangju controlled the city. They established a committee of civic leaders to negotiate with martial law commanders. "Among their demands: the removal of all troops, release of hundreds of people arrested during the riots, compensation for the families of the dead and wounded and no government retaliation."[69] But, as happens so often in Korea, compromise among the groups comprising the committee proved to be impossible.

The "Committee of Citizens and Students of the May 18 Uprising" soon split into two irreconcilable factions. A more moderate group of older citizens wanted to avoid further bloodshed. Younger militants, however, seized control of the committee and demanded a fight to the finish unless the government agreed to a further list of political demands amounting to the turnover of the government to dissidents, including Kim Dae Jung, and the arrest and trial for murder of Chun Doo Hwan.[70] The militants, led by Yun Sang Won, a twenty-nine-year-old labor organizer, wanted to make Kwangju a "symbol and rallying point for other revolutionaries." Yun and other rebel leaders were determined to "present Chun and his followers with a dilemma: If you do not have the guts to kill more people, you surrender. And if you do have enough guts, then you prove yourself a barbarian."[71]

The militants' ascendance made a negotiated settlement impossible, and the government soon warned that "this state of lawlessness in the Kwangju area cannot be tolerated indefinitely."[72] The military, with a reported 10,000 troops in the area, including elements of the 20th Infantry Division, a Seoul-based unit normally under the ROK–U.S. Combined Forces Command, began moving back into the city as it finalized plans to retake Kwangju by force. A cynical last-minute appeal by Yun that the U.S. ambassador mediate with the Martial Law Command[73] was rejected on the grounds that "such a role was inappropriate for the U.S. ambassador and would not be accepted by the ROK authorities."[74]

In the predawn hours of May 27, the army launched Operation *Chungjong* (Loyal Heart). Special Warfare troops "wearing regular army uniforms to disguise their identity" quickly overran the last pockets of rebel resistance, including the provincial capital building.[75] In contrast to the indiscriminate violence that enraged the citizens of Kwangju and ignited the insurrection, the final assault was evidently tightly controlled.[76] According to an eyewitness, "It was quick and relatively clean. They didn't seem to shoot anyone except people with guns."[77] According to western journalists on the scene, seventeen rebels, including Yun Sang Won, the leader, were killed and an unknown number wounded at the capital building.[78] Prisoners were treated harshly. An ABC cameraman reported seeing soldiers tie prisoners up with wire and kick them in the head.[79]

The most serious domestic uprising in South Korea since the Korean War was over. Precise casualty figures have never been established—according to government figures, 164 civilians and 23 soldiers and policemen died[80]; the opposition claims that as many as 2,000 died, although no proof has ever been offered to support this higher number.[81]

With Kwangju subdued, Chun moved quickly to consolidate his grip on power. In a move reminiscent of Park Chung Hee in 1961, Chun established a twenty-five-member Special Committee for National Security Measures, ostensibly headed by President Choi but in reality controlled by Chun through his position as head of the full committee's Select Standing Committee, whose membership consisted of thirty generals loyal to Chun.[82] In August, Chun promoted himself to four-star general, retired from the army, forced the resignation of President Choi, and, on August 29, assumed the presidency.[83] In October his proposed new constitution was overwhelmingly approved by voters evidently weary of turmoil and instability.[84] Chun—backed by the military, the bureaucracy, and "a new generation of elites whose ascendance has been accelerated by the actions of the military"—was the master of the South Korean political scene.[85]

In early February 1981, a series of moves were carefully choreographed by Ronald Reagan's national security adviser Richard V. Allen designed, to spare Kim Dae Jung's life (he had been condemned by a martial law court on trumped up charges that he had fomented the Kwangju uprising). Following this, Chun was allowed to visit the newly inaugurated President Reagan at the White House.[86] Chun returned triumphant from his trip to the United States and, at the end of the month, was elected president for a seven-year term under the provisions of the new constitution.

Four years of strained relations between Seoul and Washington came to an end as the Carter administration's emphasis on human rights gave way to the Reagan administration's focus on the Soviet (and North Korean) threat. If there were any doubts that the new administration would overturn the perception that the Carter administration accommodated America's foes while pressuring her friends and allies, they were dispelled by the reception given Chun in exchange for the life of Kim Dae Jung. But as official U.S.–ROK ties were being strengthened, the positive image of America in the eyes of the average Korean began to erode—a trend that has continued ever since.

The Image of the United States

For years, the United States was viewed by many Koreans as the "beautiful nation," the country that had saved Korea from communist conquest and that continued to provide indispensable protection after the armistice. During the eighteen years of Parks one-man rule, the United States was viewed as a supporter by both the regime and its opponents. On the one hand, the regime—its seizure of power by military force notwithstanding—gained an aura of respectability as a result of the U.S. government's willingness to work with it in the absence of any viable alternative. In addition, the U.S. military presence helped to ensure the stability necessary for economic growth, which was the foundation of Park's domestic program and his only real claim to legitimacy. On the other hand, Park's opponents—consisting principally of dissident politicians, intellectuals, and university students—viewed the United States as the exemplar of freedom, democracy, and human rights.[87]

Opposition leaders routinely invoked American democratic ideals in their criticism of the regime and occasionally sought safe haven in the United States from the repression and intimidation meted out by Park's draconian internal security forces, which were largely successful in suppressing the weak and divided opposition.[88] The U.S. refusal to heed calls for American intervention on behalf of one faction or another seemed not to dampen the dissidents' basically friendly disposition toward the United States. The opposition was essentially moderate and reformist, its goal the establishment of a liberal democracy patterned after the United States.[89]

Throughout Park's years in power, the United States remained delicately poised between the two groups, a position that grew increasingly perilous as the regime became more repressive and the opposition grew more strident and emboldened. Encouraged by the Carter administration's early emphasis on human rights, the opposition increased its pressure on Park, assuming that they had U.S. support.[90] It was inevitable that, given the uncompromising, zero-sum nature of Korean politics, the United States would eventually be trapped between the authorities and their opponents.

The Kwangju uprising proved to be the trap. Within months, the myth of U.S. responsibility for the bloodshed in Kwangju began to take root.[91] The ground had been well prepared by Chun and his followers, eager to create the impression of strong U.S. backing for their coup.[92] They orchestrated a disinformation campaign beginning at the height of the Kwangju crisis and continuing through the summer of 1980 as they consolidated their grip on power. Public statements by senior U.S. officials, including the president of the United States, were taken out of context and distorted in such a way as to make calls for restraint and the return of civilian control of the government appear to be declarations of support for Chun's actions. The campaign of distortion was effective, particularly among intellectuals and students, who turned their anger and frustration on the United States, the perceived "wire puller" behind the coup.[93]

Contributing to the impression of U.S. complicity in the events of May 1980 was the belief that Chun could not have ordered Korean troops into action in Kwangju without the approval of the American four-star general in Seoul, whom many people mistakenly believe was in command of the ROK armed forces. The basis for this belief dates to the summer of 1950, when ROK President Syngman Rhee placed the ROK military under the "operational command" of General Douglas MacArthur, the commander in chief of UN forces, shortly after the North Korean invasion. Due primarily to the fact that the fighting stopped in 1953 under a temporary armistice rather than a permanent political settlement, this military arrangement remained unchanged until the creation of the ROK–U.S. Combined Forces Command (CFC) in November 1978. The commander in chief of the Combined Forces Command (CINCCFC)[94] assumed responsibility for deterring aggression and, should deterrence fail, for defending the Republic of Korea. To enable CINCCFC to fulfill his peacetime mission of deterrence, the ROK government placed some—but not all—ROK armed forces under his operational control.

Military Command Arrangements

The "Terms of Reference for the Military Committee and ROK–U.S. Combined Forces Command," dated July 27, 1978, established the "mission, organization, functions and command relationships under which the Republic of Korea and the United States control military forces in Korea."[95] In accordance with this agreement, the CINC is tasked to "exercise *operational control* over all forces *assigned or attached* to the command in the prosecution of assigned missions."[96] Under the Terms of Reference, the ROK government can remove any of its forces from CFC operational control merely by informing the CINC of its intent to do so. All the CINC can do in the event of notification is to inform ROK officials of the impact of their decision on his ability to perform his missions of deterrence and defense.[97]

The distinction between command and operational control is fundamental to understanding the basic error in the accusation of U.S. responsibility for the suppression of the Kwangju uprising. Unfortunately, "[t]he concept of operational control . . . is almost universally misunderstood outside the security community. It is not the same as command . . . ."[98] "Command denotes complete responsibility for a military unit, including training, equipment, logistics, and personnel welfare. Operational control refers to the authority to control the tactical operations of a unit committed to a particular battle."[99]

A fact sheet issued by the Public Affairs Office of the Combined Forces Command explains the difference between command and operational control in Korea:

"Command authority of ROK Armed Forces always remains with the ROK Government as a function of national sovereignty. However, operational control (OPCON) of ROK Armed Forces by the ROK–U.S. Combined Forces Command (CFC) is a specific delegation of control over ROK forces for purposes of meeting missions entrusted to CFC by both governments."[100]

The Special Warfare Command is one element of the ROK military that has never come under the operational control of CFC. The troops whose violent suppression of civilian demonstrators in Kwangju triggered the insurrection in May 1980 were from the Special Warfare Command. No American officer has ever exercised operational control over them, because they have never been assigned or attached to CFC.[101] In that regard General John Wickham, CINCCFC at the time, has written that "the ROK officer corps was well aware that the CFC CINC only had operational control over those ROK forces designated by the Korean government and absolutely no authority over national forces." He has said, "Essentially, I was powerless to prevent a military coup."[102] In fact, according to South Korean military officials, the special warfare troops were sent into Kwangju precisely because they were "free of the constraints of the U.S.-controlled Combined Forces Command . . . ."[103]

The issue of the 20th Infantry Division, sent to help restore order and reestablish government control in Kwangju, needs to be addressed for several reasons: prior to Park's assassination the division had been under CFC OPCON; its removal for martial law duty illuminates the procedures under which units are placed under and removed from CFC OPCON; the division's participation in Operation Chungjong has been cited to buttress the arguments of those who assert U.S. responsibility for Kwangju. In the aftermath of Park's assassination, ROK authorities, after proper notification, withdrew the 20th Division from CFC OPCON for martial law duty. Subsequently, only one of the division's three regiments—the 60th—was returned to CFC OPCON, and on May 16, ROK authorities notified CFC that they were once again removing the 60th Regiment for martial law duty in Seoul. General Wickham, CINCCFC, was in the United States on that date, and the Deputy CINC, Baek Sok Chu, a Korean four-star general, acknowledged the notification by ROK military authorities.[104] "Acknowledged" is the operative word, since, under the provisions of CFC, each nation retains the right to remove its units from CFC OPCON upon notification.[105] In the event of such notification, the CINC "can neither approve nor disapprove, but can only point out the effect such removal might have on the CFC's mission of external defense. Once forces are removed from CFC OPCON, the CFC Commander no longer has authority over them."[106] The ROK government has the sovereign right to remove elements of its armed forces from CFC OPCON. If it exercises that right, "[a]lthough the CINCCFC is obligated by the nature of his responsibilities to inform the ROK Government [ROKG] on all matters affecting external defense readiness, there is no provision in the binational agreement that would allow him to refuse to comply with the ROKG's decision."[107]

The consolidation of the 20th Division under ROK military command and control in May 1980 is an example of the proper procedures being followed, and differs in that regard from the manner in which units of Major General Roh Tae Woo's 9th Division were moved in support of the 12–12 intraarmy coup. Forces from the 9th were removed from their positions between Seoul and the Demilitarized Zone without notifying CFC. This violation of the Terms of Reference infuriated American officers and illustrates the central dilemma of CFC from an American point of view: the United States "has responsibility without authority."[108] As one veteran observer put it, there is "no way for the U.S. commander leading the CFC to forestall a politically ambitious South Korean general from pulling out his CFC troops to stage a coup."[109]

In addition to the disinformation campaign waged by the Chun clique, three other factors contributed to the widespread erroneous impression that CINCCFC bore ultimate responsibility for the military action against the citizens of Kwangju. First, most people have no detailed knowledge of the command arrangements in Korea. It is likely that in 1980, most civilians had never even heard of CFC (at the time of the Kwangju uprising, the command had been in existence for only eighteen months.) The average Korean, to the extent that he or she knew anything about command arrangements, likely remembered only that an American had been the top officer in the United Nations Command since MacArthur.

Second, explanations of the realities of the CFC command structure fail to convince many Koreans, who find it incredible that the United States would participate in a command structure that leaves it all but powerless to prevent abuses by renegade Korean generals. The fact that no significant changes were made to the structure following the December 12, 1979, intraarmy coup and the subsequent Kwangju uprising buttresses this view.[110]

Third and most important, many Koreans, including some who understand the intricacies of CFC command arrangements, consider the details of the command structure to be mere technicalities. They emphasize instead the putative moral responsibility of the United States for Korea's well-being, a responsibility that extends, in their eyes, beyond protecting the country from external aggression to encompass shielding Korean citizens from the excesses of their own government and armed forces.[111]

And, one hastens to add, protecting them from their own excesses as well. William Gleysteen, the U.S. ambassador at the time, has observed that the Carter administration's "high human rights profile emboldened opposition and dissident elements in Korea, encouraging them to climb out on a limb from which we could not rescue them. These groups sought U.S. help, sometimes for the crudest kind of intervention in Korean domestic affairs, to compensate for their political weakness."[112]

The Myth of U.S. Responsibility

Military command arrangements in Korea are complex, but they are not impossible to understand. Unfortunately for the image of the United States, too many people, Americans as well as Koreans, who have a responsibility to master the details clearly have not done so. Statements made over the years by Ambassador Gleysteen suggest that he understood neither the command relationships in Korea nor his own lack of military authority. Several years after the Kwangju uprising, Gleysteen wrote: "In making contingency arrangements to reassert government authority in Kwangju if negotiations failed, Korean military authorities *requested permission* to move the 20th Infantry Division from the Seoul area to Kwangju. . . . The U.S. Commander [General Wickham] *concurred after checking with me* (and I reported *our* decision to Washington). . . ."[113]

Gleysteen's imprecise language on this and other occasions only added to the confusion surrounding military relations in Korea and damaged the very case he was attempting to make—that the United States was not responsible for Kwangju.[114] Other examples of confusion about command relations in Korea abound in the media as well as the scholarly literature.[115]

The U.S. government, in its 1989 statement on the Kwangju uprising, attempted to finesse the misstatements of Gleysteen and others: "In . . . publications and interviews Ambassador Gleysteen has stated that the U.S. 'approved' the movement of the 20th Division, and a U.S. Department of Defense spokesman on May 23, 1980 stated that the U.S. had 'agreed' to release from OPCON of the troops sent to Kwangju. Irrespective of the terminology, under the rights of national sovereignty the ROKG had the authority to deploy the 20th Division as it saw fit, once it had OPCON, regardless of the views of the U.S. Government."[116]

But the report, issued in response to a 1988 request from the ROK National Assembly, was years too late to have any widespread influence in getting the facts before the public. The myth of U.S. responsibility had long since become conventional wisdom in South Korea and among some American critics, who, at best, dismiss efforts to correct the record as little more than special pleading and, at worst, simply ignore inconvenient facts long available in order to perpetuate the myth.[117]

If government officials and expert observers have difficulty coping with ROK–U.S. command arrangements, it is hardly surprising that the average Korean would lack a comprehensive understanding of them. This fact, coupled with the expectation on the part of at least some Kwangju citizens that the U.S. military would intervene to save them from the brutality of their own armed forces, convinced many Koreans that the United States was in league with the Chun cabal. For many Koreans after the bloody events in Kwangju, it was an easy step from being antigovernment to being anti-American.[118]

During the Cold War the United States was faced with the dilemma of balancing the need for security and stability in a dangerous world with the desire to promote democracy and human rights. American officials seldom faced a stark either-or choice, but in those instances when they did—Hungary in 1956 and Czechoslovakia in 1968 are examples—the United States, taking the world as it was rather than how it should be, put security and stability considerations ahead of human rights concerns. President Carter's secretary of defense implied as much during his visit to Seoul days before Park's assassination and again shortly after the events of May 1980. Following Kwangju, the United States "decided not to threaten disruption of the ROK-U.S. security relationship . . . because of the North Korean military threat."[119] General Wickham has noted that "The American mission was over a barrel, because our basic objective was to protect the ROK from invasion. That left us obliged to accept the realities of the Korean political apparatus, with all of its warts, and to work with it as best we could. Our leverage was limited because of our security commitment, and because the Koreans, particularly the military, were increasingly intolerant of U.S. intervention in their domestic affairs."[120]

The Reagan administration made it clear during both the 1980 presidential campaign and after taking office that by "enhancing the security relations between the two countries, the administration not only would be serving America's strategic interests but would be in a better position to have some influence over the South Korean government in human rights matters."[121] Events in South Korea since 1987 would seem to bear out the soundness of this approach.

In Korea, however, realpolitik often collides with Confucian expectations of responsibility, loyalty, and protection. "To the Westerners, international relations are simply a means of pursuing self-interest. But to East Asians, international relations are an extension of the five relationships that Confucius expounded."[122] Many Koreans felt betrayed when the United States, cast in the role of the elder brother, did not meet their expectations.[123] This clash of cultures, together with a lack of understanding of the essential but complex aspects of the ROK–U.S. military relationship and the distortions perpetrated by the Chun regime, have poisoned U.S.-Korean relations to a degree unimaginable before 1980.

Should the United States have done more to prevent Chun from seizing power? Understandably, that question has been pondered by senior officials, both in Seoul and Washington. In retrospect, most if not all have reluctantly concluded that there was little the United States could have done. At a press conference in August 1980, President Carter expressed his frustration: "We are deeply concerned about Chun and some of the policies he's put forward. Under the new leaders in Korea our influence is limited, and we've got the option of expressing our extreme displeasure by withdrawing our forces, which might destabilize that whole region of Asia, or accepting some political development of which we disapprove. We would like to have a complete democracy with full and open debate, free press and elected leaders. The Koreans are not ready for that, according to their own judgment, and I don't know how to explain it any better."[124]

By late 1980, the Iranian revolution, the Soviet invasion of Afghanistan, and the situation in Korea had ameliorated to some degree Carter's emphasis on human rights as the locus of U.S. national security and foreign policy. The same cannot be said of some critics of U.S. action (or inaction) in Korea in the period from 1979 to 1981. Seemingly oblivious to the larger context in which Korea policy was playing out and dismissive of the threat posed by North Korea to the South and to U.S. interests, a few persistent American critics continue to hold the United States responsible for the rise of Chun Doo Hwan and the suppression of Kwangju; indeed, they have become arguably more strident in their condemnations than are the victims themselves.[125]

With no experience in making official decisions (where less-than-perfect information is the norm) or formulating and implementing policy (often in a chaotic environment), these critics are quick to condemn, in the most strident language, those who have done these things.[126] In their conspiratorial, black-and-white world, the routine classification and limited distribution of cables between U.S. officials in Washington and Seoul are seen as proof of a cover-up, and the performance of official duties such as engaging members of the ROK government and military as evidence of a conspiracy. Anything less than a massive U.S. intervention in South Korean domestic affairs in 1979–81, to include the use of the U.S. military to oppose the armed forces of the host nation, is labeled a criminal abrogation of America's responsibility to the "Korean people," for whom they purport to speak.[127] The critics' orientation is revealed in the following passage: "There is no evidence that the United States approved, or had control over, the vicious attack on Kwangju by the Korean Special Forces. But you don't have to pull the trigger to be responsible for a crime."[128]

The Legacy of Kwangju

Kwangju was an ideological watershed for Korea, especially on university campuses. Anti-Americanism, to that point a minority view having more to do with traditional xenophobia than with a genuine distrust or hatred toward the United States per se, burst upon the scene within months of the Kwangju uprising. Many students, intellectuals, clergy, and members of the rapidly expanding middle class now subscribe to a revisionist history that holds the United States responsible for most if not all of the problems besetting South Korea. The United States has never made a secret of the fact that it maintains relations with South Korea, including a mutual defense treaty—to further its own interests; indeed, true to the western tradition of international relations, it takes such an orientation as a given. The discovery of this orientation by opponents of the Korean government, however, led to a fundamental reinterpretation of the history of U.S.-Korean relations, including the

Korean War, which cost the lives of more than 33,000 Americans. [In a Confucian culture where "the pursuit of self-interest is despised, an activity attributed to enemies, not friends," U.S. involvement in the war is now dismissed by many (especially younger Koreans) "as just another example of the American pursuit of self-interest in its fight against communism."[129]]

Student leaders opposed to the Chun regime clandestinely launched a "conscientization movement" on college campuses beginning in late 1980, imbuing activists with a neo-Marxist ideology calling for, among other things, the complete restructuring of society, rejection of the United States for dividing the country and supporting military governments, and reunification with North Korea.[130] The first evidence of this trend toward radicalization and anti-Americanism occurred when students firebombed the American Cultural Center in Kwangju in December 1980. Sixteen months later, students from Koryo Theological Seminary set fire to the American Cultural Center in Pusan, killing one Korean and injuring three others studying in the library.[131] Korean and American officials dismissed the attack as an aberration, the work of a few extremists among the student population.[132]

The officials were wrong. Attacks against American targets escalated throughout the 1980s. The student movement, which had previously lacked an intellectual foundation save for a romantic attachment to democracy,[133] began to coalesce around Minjung ideology, an eclectic blend of Marxism and nationalism heavily influenced by Third World anticolonial, antiwar, antinuclear thinking as well as by liberation theology and the western European peace movement.[134] Minjung ideology's deficiencies—in terms of intellectual rigor, internal consistency, and historical accuracy— were more than offset by its strong visceral appeal to students looking for an emotionally satisfying, psychologically reassuring belief system that projected blame onto an outside power.

The adoption of Minjung ideology transformed the student movement. Whereas their predecessors in the 1960s and 1970s struggled against military dictatorship, the radicals in the 1980s identified the United States as the real enemy—the power behind illegitimate military regimes and the barrier to democracy and reunification.[135] Anti-Americanism, previously a situation-specific phenomenon that would resubmerge once the passions associated with a discrete problem had cooled, became the principal element in a radical ideology that quickly spread throughout Korean campuses nationwide and, over time, from there into Korean society.

The passage of time has shown that it is unrealistic to expect that the facts of the 1979–81 period will have any meaningful impact on the anti-Americanism of Koreans, any more than it has had on their sympathizers in the United States. The 3–8–6 generation,[136] the veterans of the radicalized campuses of the 1980s, and successor generations constitute the new majority in South Korea, as demonstrated by the result of the 2002 presidential election. Raised in the affluence made possible by the U.S. security screen, they do not look upon North Korea as a serious threat; rather, they see the presence of U.S. forces as an impediment to improved relations with the North. And, in overwhelming numbers, they dislike or hate the United States, according to recent opinion polls, feelings on full display in large anti-American demonstrations in 2002 and early 2003, laying siege to the U.S. Embassy, calling for the boycott of U.S. goods, and verbally and physically assaulting U.S. troops and other Americans on the streets of Seoul.

Conclusion

Anti-Americanism has entered the mainstream in South Korean society (the periodic, ritualistic assurances of Korean governments to the contrary notwithstanding) and its genesis was the Kwangju uprising. In the eyes of many Koreans today, the United States was the "wire puller" behind Kwangju and therefore bears ultimate responsibility.

Kwangju, though, was not caused by U.S. manipulation. In one sense, it was not "caused" at all; it "happened." In the aftermath of Park Chung Hee's assassination, Korean factionalism, authoritarianism, emotionalism, routine brutality, regional hatreds, the propensity to go to extremes and to view compromise as treasonous were compressed in time and space until they reached a critical mass and simply exploded. The Kwangju uprising began as another in a seemingly endless series of student demonstrations, in and of itself an unremarkable event given the raucous nature of Korean politics and student activism. The combination of Cholla students being confronted by elite troops from outside Cholla, troops trained for the toughest wartime missions, proved deadly. The Special Forces commander "blamed the violence on what he called 'excessive protests and the fact that his soldiers—all trained in behind-the-lines guerrilla warfare—'didn't know how to retreat.'"[137] And the demonstrators evidently did not know how to stop. Surveying the destruction during the height of the fighting, a horrified Kwangju student said, "This is something we never intended."[138]

Koreans have never conducted a full, impartial investigation into the events of Kwangju in May 1980. Powerful forces work against it. Following the 1988 National Assembly hearings into the Kwangju uprising: "U.S. officials privately assert[ed] that it suited the purposes of all parties to make the U.S. part of the Kwangju dogma—the government because it had a cynical interest in undermining U.S. criticism of domestic policies and ensuring that Washington shared the burden of guilt, and the opposition because the Americans were an easier target to snipe at than a repressive military regime."[139]

While the 1996 "trial of the century" of Chun Doo Hwan, Roh Tae Woo, and the other leaders of Hana Hoe did reveal additional details, the trial was in reality a cynical (and successful) effort by President Kim Young Sam to divert attention from allegations of massive fraud in his 1992 presidential campaign; it was not a genuine attempt to illuminate fully the facts behind the uprising and its suppression. In helping to form the Democratic Liberal Party in 1990, Kim, the former dissident politician who had long opposed military governments, cast his lot with the leaders of the 1961 and 1979–80 military coups to enhance his chances of winning the presidency in 1992.

From the beginning of his administration in February 1993 until November 1995, Kim Young Sam, in blocking all attempts to hold Chun and Roh accountable for the

December 1979 intraarmy coup and the May 1980 Kwangju uprising, urged Koreans not to "dig up the murky past or to mete out punishments against specific persons," and to "let history determine the full truth" of the suppression of the Kwangju uprising. Only in the face of demands that he reveal the extent to which Roh's huge slush fund might have been used to finance his 1992 presidential campaign did Kim, desperate to change the subject, turn on his two immediate predecessors, declaring a need to "fulfill this historic task" of "rectifying wrongs of the past." Kim had Chun, Roh, and their key lieutenants arrested, tried, and convicted under an extraconstitutional "special law to punish." Both Chun and Roh were convicted in 1996, served a short time in prison, and were then pardoned in time to join Kim Young Sam on the rostrum during Kim Dae Jung's inauguration in February 1998.[140]

In making security and stability, rather than democratization and human rights, the foundation of its South Korea policy, the United States was guilty of nothing more than prioritizing among equally important but—at least in the short run—incompatible goals, given political conditions on the peninsula. To have reversed the order, as some critics in both Korea and the United States advocated, would have risked achieving neither.[141] While America's critics would never admit it, in fulfilling its treaty obligations and guaranteeing the security of South Korea, the United States helped give the South Korean people time to reach a working political consensus. For all its power, the United States did not have the ability or desire to do for Koreans what Koreans in the past had been unwilling or unable to do for themselves—seize control of their own political destiny. The dramatic events of 1987 and the continuation of democratization since then show that South Koreans have finally done just that.

And yet, despite that progress, the central fact regarding the tragic events of May 1980 remains that "[w]hat the South Koreans have never been able to face is that Kwangju was about Koreans killing Koreans."[142] Unless and until they do face that unpleasant fact, the United States will remain the scapegoat, the ROK–U.S. alliance will remain hobbled, and the ghosts of May 1980 will continue to haunt Korean society.

Notes

1. Malcolm Gladwell, *The Tipping Point: How Little Things Can Make a Big Difference* (New York: Little, Brown, 2000).

2. www.wordspy.com/words/tippingpoint.asp.

3. Gregory Henderson, *Korea: The Politics of the Vortex* (Cambridge, MA: Harvard University Press, 1968) pp. 5, 266; David I. Steinberg, "U.S. Public Perceptions of Korea," *Korea–U.S. Relations: The Politics of Trade and Security*, ed. Robert A. Scalapino and Kongkoo Lee (Berkeley: University of California Press, 1988), p. 223.

4. John K.C. Oh, *Korea: Democracy on Trial* (Ithaca, NY: Cornell University Press, 1968) pp. 128–30; Ron Richardson, "Obituary: Park Chung Hee, 1917–1979," *Far Eastern Economic Review*, November 9, 1979, p. 12.

5. John K.C. Oh, *Korean Politics* (Ithaca, NY: Cornell University Press, 1999) pp. 36, 49–50. See also the detailed account serialized in the *Chosun Ilbo*, beginning in October 1997, "Cho Gap-je Spit on My Grave: The Life and Death of a President," http://english.chosun.com/servlet/english.ArtListMan?code=n3_&page=1&year=&mon=.

6. Oh, *Korea: Democracy on Trial*, pp. 130–32.

7. Sohn Hak-Kyu, *Authoritarianism and Opposition in South Korea* (London: Routledge, 1989) p. 19.

8. Oh, *Korea: Democracy on Trial*, pp. 97–106; "Cho Spit on My Grave."

9. Sohn, *Authoritarianism and Opposition in South Korea*, pp. 46–47. The results of the 1978 presidential election illustrate the effectiveness of Park's Yushin system. Of 2,578 electoral votes cast, Park received all but one (p. 143); "Cho Spit on My Grave."

10. Park Han Sik, "Two Ideologies in One Culture: The Prospect for National Integration in Korea," in *Korean Reunification: New Perspectives and Approaches*, ed. Tae-Hwan Kwak, Chonghan Kim, and Hong Nack Kim (Seoul: The Institute for Far Eastern Studies, Kyungnam University, 1984), p. 138.

11. On Carter's troop withdrawal effort, see Don Oberdorfer, *The Two Koreas: A Contemporary History* (Reading, MA: Addison-Wesley, 1997), pp. 84–94, 101–8; William H. Gleysteen, Jr., *Massive Entanglement, Marginal Influence: Carter and Korea in Crisis* (Washington, DC: Brookings Institution Press, 1999), pp. 20–30.

12. Assistant Secretary of State for East Asian and Pacific Affairs Richard Holbrooke, quoted in Ron Richardson, "As Difficult an Allied Period as Can Be Imagined," *Far Eastern Economic Review*, May 14, 1979, p. 46. On Koreagate, see Robert B. Boettcher, *Gifts of Deceit: Sun Myong Moon, Tongsun Park and the Korea Scandal* (New York: Holt Rinehart & Winston, 1982).

13. Ron Richardson, "The Opposition Gets Tough," *Far Eastern Economic Review*, June 8, 1979, p. 12; Gleysteen, *Massive Entanglement, Marginal Influence*, pp. 51–52.

14. Ron Richardson, "Dissent, But Not in the Streets," *Far Eastern Economic Review*, August 29, 1979, p. 12; Gleysteen, *Massive Entanglement, Marginal Influence*, pp. 51–52.

15. Ron Richardson, "New Fire for the Cauldron," *Far Eastern Economic Review*, September 21, 1979, p. 15.

16. Ron Richardson, "Anatomy of a Crisis," *Far Eastern Economic Review*, October 19, 1979, p. 26; Gleysteen, *Massive Entanglement, Marginal Influence*, pp. 51–52.

17. Gleysteen, *Massive Entanglement, Marginal Influence*, p. 52.

18. Ron Richardson, "Troubled Nights for Park," *Far Eastern Economic Review*, November 1, 1979, p. 24.

19. Ibid., p. 26.

20. Stephen Barber, "Nothing But a Personal Affair," *Far Eastern Economic Review*, November 9, 1979, p. 14.

21. Richardson, "Anatomy of a Failed Coup," p. 16; Gleysteen, *Massive Entanglement, Marginal Influence*, pp. 53–76; John A. Wickham, *Korea on the Brink: From the 12–12 Incident to the Kwangju Uprising, 1979–1980* (Washington, DC: National Defense University Press, 1999), pp. 3–26; "Cho Spit on My Grave."

22. Lee Chong Sik, "South Korea in 1980: The Emergence of a New Authoritarian Order," *Asian Survey* 21, no. 1 (1981): 25.

23. Ron Richardson, "Legacy of The Strongman," *Far Eastern Economic Review*, November 9, 1979, pp. 10–13.

24. Gleysteen, *Massive Entanglement, Marginal Influence*, p. 4.

25. Richardson, "Legacy of The Strongman," p. 11; Wickham, *Korea on the Brink*, p. 18.

26. The mission of the Defense Security Command is to monitor ROK military units for any hint of disloyalty. The DSC commander reports directly to the president.

27. David Kim, *Profiles of Korean Leaders* (New York: The Asia Society, 1988), p. 29; Suh Dae-Sook, "South Korea in 1981: The First Year of the Fifth Republic," *Asian Survey* 22, no. 1 (1982): 108; Wickham, *Korea on the Brink*, pp. 20, 38.

28. John McBeth, "The Classmates' Coup," *Far Eastern Economic Review*, January 12, 1989, p. 25; "Cho Spit on My Grave."

29. For information on Hana Hoe and its predecessor organization, the Taegu Seven Stars,

see Oh, *Korean Politics*, pp. 76–78; Wickham, *Korea on the Brink*, pp. 20, 127; "Cho Spit on My Grave." On the purge of Hana Hoe members from the military by President Kim Young Sam in 1993, see Oh, *Korean Politics*, pp. 133–34.

30. Shim Jae Hoon, "Cabal in Eclipse," *Far Eastern Economic Review*, March 14, 1991, p. 30.

31. For details on the rise and fall of Major General Yun Pil-yoon, whom Park had placed in control of Hana Hoe, see Oh, *Korean Politics*, pp. 77–78; "Cho Spit on My Grave."

32. Quoted in McBeth "The Classmates' Coup," p. 25.

33. Oh, *Korean Politics*, p. 77. See also Shim, "Cabal in Eclipse," p. 30; McBeth, "The Classmates' Coup," p. 25.

34. Shim, "Cabal in Eclipse," p. 30.

35. Donald N. Clark, ed., *The Kwangju Uprising: Shadows Over the Regime in South Korea* (Boulder, CO: Westview Press, 1988), p. 1; McBeth, "The Classmates' Coup," p. 26.

36. Sohn, *Authoritarianism and Opposition in South Korea*, p. 167.

37. Wickham, *Korea on the Brink*, pp. 32, 38; McBeth, "The Classmates' Coup," p. 26.

38. Ron Richardson, "Young Generals, New Loyalties," *Far Eastern Economic Review*, December 28, 1979, p. 13.

39. John McBeth, "The Sure Successor," *Far Eastern Economic Review*, June 4, 1987, p. 16; Wickham, *Korea on the Brink*, p. 59. Major General Roh was the commander of the 9th Infantry Division, deployed between Seoul and the Demilitarized Zone.

40. Wickham, *Korea on the Brink*, p. 63.

41. Richardson, "Young Generals, New Loyalties," p. 14.

42. For detailed accounts of the 12–12 Incident see Wickham, *Korea on the Brink*, pp. 53–76; Gleysteen, *Massive Entanglement, Marginal Influence*, pp. 77–98; Oh, *Korean Politics*, pp. 74–97.

43. William H. Gleysteen, Jr., "Korea: A Special Target of American Concern," in *The Diplomacy of Human Rights*, ed. David D. Newsom (Lanham, MD: University Press of America, 1986), p. 94. See also Oh, *Korean Politics*, p. 78; Wickham, *Korea on the Brink*, p. 38.

44. Wickham, *Korea on the Brink*, pp. 69–76; Gleysteen, *Massive Entanglement, Marginal Influence*, p. 85; Mark Peterson, "Americans and the Kwangju Incident: Problems in the Writing of History," in *The Kwangju Uprising: Shadows Over the Regime in South Korea*, ed. Donald N. Clark (Boulder, CO: Westview Press, 1988), p. 58.

45. Gleysteen, "Korea: A Special Target of American Concern," p. 94.

46. Lee, "South Korea in 1980," p. 126; Shim Jae Hoon, "Democracy Under the Microscope," *Far Eastern Economic Review*, January 18, 1980, p. 28.

47. Ron Richardson and Shim Jae Hoon, "A Promise That Must Be Honored," *Far Eastern Economic Review*, February 22, 1980, p. 15.

48. Ibid.

49. "The Pain of Enduring Political Puberty," *Far Eastern Economic Review*, May 30, 1980, p. 42. Probably nowhere else in the world is there so ancient and continuous a tradition of student demonstration, memorializing, and active participation in national politics as in Korea. Henderson, *Korea: The Politics of the Vortex*, p. 201.

50. Ron Richardson, "Barricades on the Road to Democracy," *Far Eastern Economic Review*, May 23, 1980, p. 8.

51. Shim Jae Hoon, "Parachuting Into Power," *Far Eastern Economic Review*, April 25, 1980, p. 24; Wickham, *Korea on the Brink*, pp. 119, 121–22.

52. David I. Steinberg, *The Republic of Korea: Economic Transformation and Social Change* (Boulder, CO: Westview, 1989) p. 16.

53. Shim Jae Hoon, "The End of a Fight for Freedom," *Far Eastern Economic Review*, March 14, 1980, pp. 30–31.

54. "Chun: A Shadowy Strongman," *Time*, May 26, 1980, p. 32.

55. Richardson, "Barricades on the Road to Democracy," p. 9; Peterson "Americans and the Kwangju Incident," p. 53.

56. Richardson, "Barricades on the Road to Democracy," p. 9.

57. Wickham, *Korea on the Brink*, p. 51.

58. Shim Jae Hoon, "The Dragnet's Odd Man Out," *Far Eastern Economic Review*, May 23, 1980, p. 10.

59. Michael Shapiro, *The Shadow in the Sun: A Korean Year of Love and Sorrow* (New York: Atlantic Monthly Press, 1990), p. 168.

60. Tim Warnberg, "The Kwangju Uprising: An Inside View," *Korean Studies* 11 (1987): 50.

61. Linda Lewis, "The Kwangju Incident Observed: An Anthropological Perspective on Civil Uprisings," in *The Kwangju Uprising: Shadows Over the Regime in South Korea*, ed. Donald N. Clark (Boulder, CO: Westview Press, 1988), pp. 15–16. Brackets in original.

62. "Ten Days That Shook Kwangju," *Time*, June 9, 1980, p. 41.

63. Henry Scott-Stokes, "Cabinet Resigns in South Korea as Riots Grow," *New York Times*, May 21, 1980, p. A1.

64. Quoted in John McBeth, "A Festering Wound," *Far Eastern Economic Review*, January 12, 1989, p. 25.

65. Shim Jae Hoon, "Gunfire Ends the Insurrection," *Far Eastern Economic Review*, May 30, 1980, p. 9.

66. McBeth, "A Festering Wound," p. 25.

67. Warnberg, "The Kwangju Uprising," p. 42; Shim, "Gunfire Ends the Insurrection," p. 10.

68. Shim Jae Hoon, "Protesters Control South Korean City; At Least 32 Killed," *New York Times*, May 22, 1980, p. A1.

69. John Nielsen with Andrew Nagorski, "Insurrection in South Korea," *Newsweek,* June 2, 1980, p. 42.

70. Shim, "Gunfire Ends the Insurrection," pp. 9–10; Wickham, *Korea on the Brink*, p. 141.

71. Bradley Martin, "Kwangju Revisited," *Far Eastern Economic Review*, May 26, 1994, p. 46; Bradley Martin, "Yun Sang Won: The Knowledge in Those Eyes," in *The Kwangju Uprising: Eyewitness Press Accounts of Korea's Tiananmen*, ed. Henry Scott-Stokes and Lee Jai-eui (Armonk, NY: M.E. Sharpe, 2000), pp. 87–105. See also Lee Jai-eui, "Operation Fascinating Vacations," in *The Kwangju Uprising*, ed. Scott-Stokes and Lee, pp. 19–40.

72. Quoted in "30,000 in South Korea Continuing Kwangju Protest Despite Warning," *New York Times*, May 25, 1980, p. A1. See also Wickham, *Korea on the Brink*, pp. 133–34, 141–43.

73. Surviving leaders have stated that they neither expected nor wanted American intervention; rather, their purpose in calling for the United States to step in "was to give people outside the inner circle the courage to stay the course." Martin, "Kwangju Revisited," pp. 44, 46.

74. Henry Kamm, "South Korean Troops Recapture Kwangju in Predawn Strike," *New York Times*, May 27, 1980, p. A1; United States, Department of State, *United States Government Statement on the Events in Kwangju, Republic of Korea, in May 1980 and Appendix* (Washington, DC, June 19, 1989), p. 21; Gleysteen, *Massive Entanglement, Marginal Influence*, p. 140.

75. *United States Government Statement on the Events in Kwangju*, p. 22; Wickham, *Korea on the Brink*, pp. 144–45; Martin, "Kwangju Revisited," p. 46; Martin, "Yun Sang Won," p. 103.

76. Henry Scott-Stokes, "As Tanks Rumble Off, a Korean City Springs Back to Life," *New York Times*, June 1, 1980, p. A3. See also Wickham, *Korea on the Brink*, pp. 144–45, 183.

77. Quoted in John Nielsen et al., "Koreas Day of the Generals," *Newsweek*, June 9, 1980, p. 52.

78. Terry Anderson, "Remembering Kwangju," in *The Kwangju Uprising: Eyewitness Press Accounts of Korea's Tiananmen*, ed. Henry Scott-Stokes and Lee Jae-eui (Armonk, NY: M.E. Sharpe, 2000), p. 51.

79. Warnberg, "The Kwangju Uprising," p. 46.

80. Yoon Sung-min, "Report on the Kwangju Incident to the National Assembly National Defense Committee, June 7, 1985," in *The Kwangju Uprising: Shadows Over the Regime in South Korea*, ed. Donald N. Clark (Boulder, CO: Westview Press, 1988), p. 91.

81. "1994 Kwangju City government statistics break down the official victims into 154 dead, 47 official missing, 2,710 injured, and 505 questioned/detained/convicted. Other groups calculate that the number is higher for example, that there are 107 unofficial missing and the Injured Peoples Association claims higher numbers of injuries. In addition, there are the 120 wounded who have died since 1980." Linda S. Lewis, *Laying Claim to the Memory of May: A Look Back at the 1980 Kwangju Uprising* (Honolulu: University of Hawaii Press, 2002), p. 173, n. 22.

82. Henry Kamm, " 'Security' Panel, Heavily Military, Created by Seoul," *New York Times*, May 31, 1980, p. A1; Ron Richardson, "The Chon [sic] Brigade Takes Over," *Far Eastern Economic Review*, June 6, 1980, p. 12.

83. Steinberg, *The Republic of Korea*, p. 60.

84. Shim Jae Hoon, "Voters Get Chuns Message," *Far Eastern Economic Review*, October 31, 1980, pp. 27–28; Han Sung-Joo, "Korean Domestic Politics and Korea-U.S. Relations," *Korea-U.S. Relations: The Politics of Trade and Security*, ed. Robert A. Scalapino and Kongkoo Lee (Berkeley: University of California Press, 1988), p. 159.

85. Shim Jae Hoon, "Chun Banks on Young Blood," *Far Eastern Economic Review*, December 12, 1980, p. 22; Peterson, "Americans and the Kwangju Incident." p. 60; Han Sung-Joo, "The Emerging Political Process in Korea," *Asian Affairs* 8, no. 2 (1980): 87; Lee "South Korea in 1980," p. 143.

86. See Richard Holbrooke and Michael Armacost, "A Future Leaders Moment of Truth," *New York Times*, December 24, 1997, p. A17, and Richard V. Allen, "On the Korea Tightrope, 1980," *New York Times*, January 21, 1998, A17. For a detailed account of the effort to save Kim Dae Jung's life, see Gleysteen, *Massive Entanglement, Marginal Influence*, pp. 171–89. See also Gleysteen, "Korea: A Special Target of American Concern," p. 98.

87. Tim Shorrock, "The Struggle for Democracy in South Korea in the 1980s and the Rise of Anti-Americanism," *Third World Quarterly* 8, no. 4 (1986): 1198.

88. John K.C. Oh, "South Korea 1975: A Permanent Emergency," *Asian Survey* 16, no. 1 (1976): 41.

89. Vincent S.R. Brandt, "South Korean Society," in *Korea Briefing, 1990*, ed. Lee Chong-Sik (Boulder, CO: Westview Press, 1991), p. 92.

90. Gleysteen, "Korea: A Special Target of American Concern," p. 93.

91. Ibid., p. 96.

92. Nielsen, "Koreas Day of the Generals," p. 53.

93. Gleysteen, "Korea: A Special Target of American Concern," p. 96; James F. Larson, "Quiet Diplomacy in a Television Era: The Media and U.S. Policy Toward the Republic of Korea," *Political Communication and Persuasion* 7 (1990): 90; Robert A. Kinney, "Students, Intellectuals, and the Churches: Their Roles in Korean Politics," *Asian Affairs* 8, no. 3 (1981): 90; Wickham, *Korea on the Brink*, pp. 154–59; Gleysteen, *Massive Entanglement, Marginal Influence*, pp. 138, 141–42; Oh, *Korean Politics*, pp. 85–86; Jay-kyong Lee, "Anti-Americanism in South Korea: The Media and the Politics of Signification," Ph.D. diss., University of Iowa, 1993, pp. 100–104, 127.

94. CINCUNC and CINCCFC are the same person, a U.S. Army four star general (who has several other "hats" in addition to these two). The United Nations Command remains responsible for armistice matters.

95. CFC Fact Sheet, "ROK Units Under Operational Control of the Combined Forces Command," *The Kwangju Uprising: Shadows Over the Regime in South Korea*, ed. Donald N. Clark (Boulder, CO: Westview Press, 1988), p. 93.

96. Quoted in Cha Young Koo, *Northeast Asia Security: A Korean Perspective* (Washington, DC: Center for Strategic and International Studies, 1988), p. 37, emphasis added.

97. Wickham, *Korea on the Brink*, p. 30.

98. Robert Martin, "Security Relations: A U.S. View," in *Korea-U.S. Relations: The Politics of Trade and Security*, ed. Robert A. Scalapino and Kongkoo Lee (Berkeley: University of California Press, 1988), p. 192.

99. Park Tong Whan, "From Extended Deterrence to Global Interdependence: The Future of U.S.-South Korean Security Relations," in *Korea 1991: The Road to Peace*, ed. Michael J. Mazarr, et al. (Boulder, CO: Westview Press, 1991), p. 152.

100. CFC Fact Sheet, "ROK Units Under Operational Control of the Combined Forces Command," *The Kwangju Uprising: Shadows Over the Regime in South Korea*, ed. Donald N. Clark (Boulder, CO: Westview Press, 1988), p. 93.

101. Wickham, *Korea on the Brink*, p. 43. "Contrary to the belief held even today by many Koreans, neither the Special Forces brigades nor the Capital Security Command had ever been under CFC operational control. Both units were considered to have overriding national missions to protect the central government and vital installations in Seoul and, therefore, had never been committed by the ROK Government to CFC peacetime control." Wickham, *Korea on the Brink*, p. 60.

102. Wickham, *Korea on the Brink*, p. 179.

103. McBeth, "A Festering Wound," p. 24.

104. John McBeth, "Taking the Rap," *Far Eastern Economic Review*, January 12, 1989, p. 26; *United States Government Statement on the Events in Kwangju*, p. 13; Wickham, *Korea on the Brink*, p. 125.

105. Wickham, *Korea on the Brink*, p. 30.

106. *United States Government Statement on the Events in Kwangju*, p. 5.

107. CFC Fact Sheet "ROK Units Under Operational Control of the Combined Forces Command," p. 94.

108. Steinberg, "U.S. Public Perceptions of Korea," p. 219.

109. Shim Jae Hoon, "Without Influence," *Far Eastern Economic Review*, July 6, 1989, p. 25.

110. Douglas G. Bond, "Anti-Americanism and U.S-ROK Relations: An Assessment of Korean Students Views," *Asian Perspective* 12, no. 1 (1988): 166 n.

111. Park Kwon-sang, "Korean Perceptions of America," in *Reflections on a Century of United States-Korean Relations*, Conference Papers, June 1982, Academy of Korean Studies and the Wilson Center (Lanham, MD: University Press of American, 1983), p. 137.

112. Gleysteen, "Korea: A Special Target of American Concern," p. 90.

113. Ibid. p. 96, emphasis added. In his memoirs, published in 1999, Gleysteen correctly noted that "[a U.S. army four-star general] headed the U.S.-Korea Combined Forces Command and, in this capacity, had *operational control* over all South Korea forces *assigned* to defend against North Korea. At the normal state of defense alert, this excluded two units important to domestic security: the Capital Security Command in Seoul and the highly mobile brigades of Special Warfare Forces." Gleysteen, *Massive Entanglement, Marginal Influence*, p. 21, emphasis added.

114. The following comment from a Korean writer is representative of the way Gleysteen's early misstatements prejudiced the truth: "Given [the] repeated acknowledgment by Gleysteen of the U.S. officials' approval to move the 20th Division, the recent Korean government explanation [during National Assembly hearings in 1988] that . . . the U.S. was in no way involved in moving the unit to Kwangju in 1980 is hardly believable." Lee Samsung, "Kwangju and America in Perspective," *Asian Perspective* 12, no. 2 (1988): 73.

115. Some examples: "Kwangju. . . whose suppression by force was ordered by U.S. commander Gen. John Wickham. . . ." Shim Jae Hoon, "Guarded friendship," *Far Eastern Economic Review* December 26, 1985, pp. 13–4. "Under an agreement between Seoul and Washington, all South Korean forces are under the command of an American." John Burgess, S. Koreans Hold U.S. Library, *Washington Post*, May 24, 1985, p. A1. "[A] U.S. general was supreme commander of both American and Korean troops and his permission was necessary for the Korean troops to be released [for duty in Kwangju]." Larson, "Quiet Diplomacy in a Television Era," p. 86. "[The U.S.] commander-in-chief in Korea commands the South Korean as well as the American forces there." Leon V. Sigal, *Disarming Strangers: Nuclear Diplomacy with North Korea* (Princeton, NJ: Princeton University Press, 1998), p. 44.

116. *United States Government Statement on the Events in Kwangju*, p. 18.

117. See, for example, Bruce Cumings, introduction to Lee Jae-eui, *Kwangju Diary: Beyond Death, Beyond the Darkness of the Age*, trans. Kap Su Seol and Nick Mamatas (UCLA Asian Pacific Monograph Series, 1999). "Americans trained [the ROK army], bankrolled it, and since a wartime compact in 1950, have *commanded* it . . ." (p. 190). "[T]he armys Ninth Division (commanded by Roh [Tae Woo]), *Seouls capital garrison, and various special forces* [were] all *nominally under American operational control* . . ." (p. 23). "General John A. Wickham release[d] the 20th Division of the ROK Army. . . .Once again *U.S.-commanded* troops had been released for domestic repression . . ." p. 24), emphasis added.

118. Lee Manwoo, "Anti-Americanism and South Korea's Changing Perception of America," in *Alliance Under Tension: The Evolution of South Korean-U.S. Relations*, ed. Manwoo Lee, Ronald D. McLaurin, and Chung-in Moon (Boulder, CO: Westview Press, 1988), p. 12; Nayan Chanda, "Big Brother Watches," *Far Eastern Economic Review*, December 26, 1985, p. 12; Kim Jin-Hyun, "Vortex of Misunderstanding: Changing Korean Perceptions," in *Korea-U.S. Relations: The Politics of Trade and Security*, ed. Robert A. Scalapino and Kongkoo Lee (Berkeley: University of California Press, 1988), p. 234.

119. *United States Government Statement on the Events in Kwangju*, p. 22.

120. Wickham, *Korea on the Brink*, p. 147. See also Gleysteen, *Massive Entanglement, Marginal Influence*, pp. 5, 33.

121. A. Glenn Mower, Jr., *Human Rights and American Foreign Policy: The Carter and Reagan Experiences* (New York: Glenwood Press, 1987), pp. 144–45.

122. Lee Chong-Sik, "Commentary: Kwangju and the Korean People," in *The Kwangju Uprising: Shadows Over the Regime in South Korea*, ed. Donald N. Clark (Boulder, CO: Westview Press, 1988), p. 80.

123. Kim Jinwung, "Recent Anti-Americanism in South Korea: The Causes," *Asian Survey* 29, no. 8 (1989): 751–52.

124. Quoted in Wickham, *Korea on the Brink*, p. 163.

125. Lewis, *Laying Claim to the Memory of May*, pp. 88–89.

126. See Tim Shorrock, "Kwangju Diary: The View from Washington," in *Kwangju Diary: Beyond Death, Beyond the Darkness of the Age*, ed. Lee Jae-eui, trans. Kap Su Seol and Nick Mamatas (Los Angeles, CA: UCLA Asian Pacific Monograph Series, 1999), pp. 151–72. Congressional testimony by the deputy secretary of state is "at best evasive, and, at worst, perjury" (p. 169). The 1982 deployment of ROK special warfare troops is erroneously ascribed to the U.S. military, then labeled as "moral turpitude" (p. 171). The 1989 U.S. government "White Paper" on Kwangju is "at best a whitewash and at worst a grotesque lie" (p. 171). U.S. officials in Washington and Seoul who served during Kwangju need to be "brought to account for their crimes and misdeeds" (p. 172).

127. See Tim Shorrock, "Ex-Leaders Go on Trial in Seoul," *Journal of Commerce*, February 27, 1996, p. 1A; Tim Shorrock, "Debacle in Kwangju," *Nation*, December 9, 1996, pp. 19–22; "The U.S. Role in Korea in 1979 and 1980: A Special Report" by Tim Shorrock, www.kimsoft.com/korea/kwangju3.htm; Cumings, introduction to *Kwangju Diary*, pp. 17–35; Shorrock, "Kwangju Diary," pp. 151–72.

128. Shorrock, "Debacle in Kwangju," p. 20.

129. Michael C. Kalton, "Korean Modernity: Change and Continuity," in *Korea Briefing, 1990*, ed. Lee Chong-Sik (Boulder, CO: Westview Press, 1991), pp. 124–25. See also Park Han Sik, "Two Ideologies in One Culture," p. 146.

130. Vincent S.R. Brandt, "South Korean Society," p. 92; Dong Wonmo, "University Students in South Korean Politics: Patterns of Radicalization in the 1980s," *Journal of International Affairs* 40, no. 2 (1987): 237, 254–55.

131. Suh Dae-Sook, "South Korea in 1982: A Centennial Year," *Asian Survey* 23, no. 1 (1983): 95–96; Dong, "University Students in South Korean Politics." p. 238.

132. Suh, "South Korea in 1982," p. 95.

133. Hyun Chong-Min et al., "The Benevolent Leader and Democratic Institutions: A Study of Korean Childrens' View of Politics," *Journal of Northeast Asian Studies* 6, no. 4 (1987–88): 50; Lee Manwoo, Ronald D. McLaurin, and Chung-in Moon, *The Odyssey of Korean Democracy: Korean Politics, 1987–1990* (New York: Praeger, 1990), p. 16.

134. Kim Jin-Hyun, "Vortex of Misunderstanding: Changing Korean Perceptions," in *Korea-U.S. Relations: The Politics of Trade and Security*, ed. Robert A. Scalapino and Kongkoo Lee (Berkeley: University of California, 1988), p. 231. *Minjung* ideology rests on two central tenets. The first is that Korea's problems stem from the division of the country by the United States in 1945, resulting in Korea's political, military, and cultural dependence on the United States. The second, flowing from that dependency, is that the U.S.-backed regimes that have ruled Korea since the founding of the Republic have been against the people (*minjung*), the nation (*minjok*), and democracy (*minju*). Lee Manwoo, Ronald D. McLaurin, and Chung-in Moon, *Alliance Under Tension: The Evolution of South Korean-U.S. Relations* (Boulder, CO: Westview Press, 1988), p. 15; Lee, McLaurin, and Moon *The Odyssey of Korean Democracy*, pp. 7–8; Dong, "University Students in South Korean Politics," pp. 239, 244 n.

135. Shorrock, "The Struggle for Democracy in South Korea in the 1980s and the Rise of Anti-Americanism," p. 1206; Kim Jinwung, "Recent Anti-Americanism in South Korea: The Causes," *Asian Survey* 29, no. 8 (1989): 762.

136. Koreans in their thirties, educated in the 1980s, and born in the 1960s.

137. McBeth, "A Festering Wound," p. 25.

138. Quoted in "Season of Spleen," *Time*, June 2, 1980, p. 38.

139. John McBeth, "Taking the Rap," *Far Eastern Economic Review*, January 12, 1989, p. 26.

140. On the trial, see Oh, *Korean Politics*, pp. 172–81; Wickham, *Korea on the Brink*, pp. 185–91. On Kim Young Sam's actions, see President Kim Young Sam, address, "Kwangju's Sacrifices Uphold Civilian Democracy, May 13, 1993," in *Korea's Quest for Reform & Globalization: Selected Speeches of President Kim Young Sam* (The Presidential Secretariat, 1995), pp. 32–36; Andrew Pollack, "Seoul Bars Prosecution of Presidents," *New York Times*, October 30, 1994, p. 4; Lee Sung-yul, "Reinvestigation Opens into 1979 Coup; Ex-Presidents Chun, Roh May Face Insurrection Charge," *Korea Herald* (Internet edition), November 28, 1995; "President Kim Pledges to Punish Two Former Presidents," *Korea Herald* (Internet edition), December 2, 1995; Shim Jae Hoon, "Beating the Heat," *Far Eastern Economic Review*, December 7, 1995, p. 18.

141. For a scathing critique of the consequences of getting priorities wrong, see Gleysteen, "Korea: A Special Target of American Concern," pp. 85–99.

142. Quoted in McBeth, "Taking the Rap," p. 26.

18

Anti-Americanism or "Anti-Baseism"

U.S.–South Korean Relations through Changing Generations

Brent (Won-ki) Choi

To Koreans, the public square of Gwanghawmun and City Hall in Seoul is something more than just a plaza in which to while away weekend afternoons. It holds special political significance as the focal point of the people's struggle against the military regime of the 1980s. This is where people gathered to defy the iron-fisted regime of President Chun Doo Hwan; that defiance gradually led to the democratization of the country. The site took on new meaning in 2002. As many as a million Koreans gathered at the heart of their capital to cheer on their national soccer heroes in the World Cup, tens of thousands converged on the square with lighted candles to cherish the memory of two schoolgirls who were killed last summer by a U.S. military vehicle in a road accident, and tens of thousands more celebrated the election of a new president, Roh Moo Hyun. Though all three gatherings were unprecedented in South Korea in scale, the most troubling was the series of candlelight protests of the deaths of the two girls. It is easy to label these protests anti-American. Look and you realize that the protesters are not displaying anti-Americanism but what we might call anti-baseism, which is an anger not toward America itself but toward the U.S. military bases on the peninsula. It is an expression of the Koreans' wounded pride and perhaps reflects an inevitable stage in South Korea–U.S. relations for the new century.

One might not notice, at first, the connection between the World Cup, the death of the schoolgirls, and Roh Moo Hyun's victory, but it is there. South Korea's postwar generation is fully emerging now and is asserting itself in society. The new generation already makes up more than three-quarters of the population and has been demanding a new social order in politics, economics, and Seoul's relationships with its neighbor to the north and the outside world, particularly with the United States. October 2003 marked the fiftieth anniversary of the South Korea–U.S. mutual defense alliance, and Seoul and Washington are divided as never before over policy toward North Korea. The strain on their ties is clear and indicates that it is time the two nations moved away from their long-standing policy of blockading the North in favor of a new strategy—sinification—aimed at getting Pyongyang to open its doors.

This chapter will focuses on the following three questions regarding South Korea's postwar generation and the Gwanghwamun protests:

- In what context should we address the protests? If there is an anti-U.S. sentiment within South Korean society, exactly how widespread and deep is it?
- How does the generation shift affect the Seoul–Washington alliance?
- How are we going to align Seoul–Washington relations from here?

Anti-Americanism or Anti-Baseism?

For a journalist, finding the right context for a story is never an easy task. Take a look at how differently Americans and Arabs viewed the September 11 terrorist attacks in New York and Washington and you'll see how important context can be. This also applies to the deaths of the two South Korean schoolgirls. Protests followed immediately upon the deaths last June, but they did not gain much intensity until months later, from October to December. Major U.S. media like the *New York Times* and some South Korean media defined the rallies as "anti-U.S." If I presume right, the term was used not because of how well it reflects the reality but because it sounded simple and easy. I would call the protests "anti-base" and a symptom of seriously wounded national pride. The year 2002 was a time of great pride for South Koreans in general and especially the postwar generation middle-class South Koreans. The financial crisis that plagued them during1997–98 was finally behind them, and to add to their self-confidence, they watched as their boys of summer marched proudly into the semifinals of the World Cup. About a million South Koreans came out to Gwanghwamun and its city hall to cheer for the national team while watching the game on jumbo television screens in the square. Their wild chants of "*DAE-HAN-MIN-GUK*" were broadcast around the globe by CNN and other worldwide media. There was never a time when the average Korean felt prouder simply to be Korean.

The accident that claimed the lives of the two girls ended that euphoria in an instant. The girls' deaths brought sorrow, and the old feelings of loss and incompetence crept back. It was a harsh reminder of how powerless South Korean courts are under the Status of Forces Agreement (SOFA). Sorrow quickly gave way to rage. The courts-martial in October, which found the driver and commander of the vehicle not guilty, left an already brokenhearted nation very angry. In this digital age, the postwar generation first voiced their outrage online; those Internet chats eventually led to the candlelight protests.

The situation might be likened to the African-American community's reaction to the rulings in the Rodney King case over a decade ago in Los Angeles. A massive riot broke out when blacks in Los Angeles protested the acquittals of the white policemen who were caught on videotape beating Rodney King after a traffic stop. The reaction of South Koreans to the acquittals of the GIs was similar, though much milder in nature. After the Rodney King verdict, 55 people were killed, 2,200 injured, and 10,000 arrested; in addition, nearly $1 billion in property damage was done. Some South Koreans, after the courts-martial, clashed with riot police, but most who protested just marched through downtown Seoul with candles in their hands.

A few lessons became clear to me after observing the major events of 2002 at the Gwanghwamun plaza. First, anti-baseism among South Koreans may be widespread, but it does not run deep. Most of the protesters raised their voices against the United States for looking down on Koreans and refusing to revise the SOFA. Hardly any, however, demanded the withdrawal of U.S. troops, nor did they demand an end to the mutual defense treaty; even fewer had any clear ideas on how to fix the SOFA.

Second, South Koreans are passionate about their dislike of the way they are treated by the U.S. military stationed on their land. If you had joined one of the rallies, you would have seen how acutely people felt sorry, not only that the girls died but also that they were unable to have any say in how the case was handled. Not long ago I wrote an article that basically said the Americans did all they could to compensate the families for the accident. I was attacked by enraged "netizens" who claimed that I wouldn't be so easygoing if those two girls had been my sisters. When I said "passionate," I also meant lacking in logic. If American servicemen deserved to be tried by South Korean courts for a traffic accident that occurred while they were doing their job, would that mean we would allow our own servicemen serving in East Timor to be tried in local courts if they were involved in a similar accident there? I asked that of one of the protesters but received no answer.

Third, there's not much chance of South Koreans' anti-baseism developing into full blown anti-Americanism. As I recall, most of the protesters gathered at the plaza were armed not with Molotov cocktails; rather, they were wearing Nike shoes, Levi's jeans, and winter coats with the logos of various U.S. companies embroidered on them. But none of them seemed to give that fact a second thought. In fact, when South Koreans gathered at Gwanghwamun in late December to welcome Roh Moo Hyun, their sixteenth president, they were dancing in the plaza to the Tony Orlando classic "Tie a Yellow Ribbon." (The word for *yellow* in Korean is *norang*, which sounds like a little like *Roh*.)

Most of the people there insisted that they were not anti-American. One man in his forties who attended the rally with his children said he was there purely to remember the girls, who died so tragically. Lee Jeong-hyeon, a South Korean pop singer who joined the crowd too, said she has no hard feelings against the United States.[1]

Still, I won't deny the presence of radicals in the crowd. Yes, there were those who tried to take advantage of the anti-baseism, the crowd, and the wounded national pride. Looking at the newspaper photos from a few days earlier, one might note pickets signs reading, "U.S. Army Go Home" mixed in among the 100,000 or so candles. There have even been reports of groups of thugs attacking American servicemen. But these do not reflect the mainstream sentiment.

To rate degrees of anti-American sentiment on a scale of 1 to 7, with the insanity of an Osama bin Laden rating a 7, South Korea currently gets a rating of 1. So far, this event, which brought out 100,000 people peacefully waving candles, has been the biggest outpouring of anti-U.S. feeling in fifty years.

Generational Change and Its Effect on Seoul–Washington Ties

The true core of the problem lies not in anti-baseism but in the emergence of a new generation in Korean society. Looking back, the accident that killed the girls was not the first tragic event of its kind. According to one research study, some 200 to 300 crimes have been committed by U.S. servicemen against Korean civilians every year since 1953.[2] Some cases were far more horrifying to Koreans than the accident involving the two schoolgirls. Why were there no protests about those? Why were there protests now? The answer involves the long-shared interests of the two allies. Seoul and Washington had a common enemy, common strategy, and common vision. The Korean War (1950–53), as tragic as it was, tightened this bond both politically and militarily. For decades, any notion of anti-U.S. feeling was simply unthinkable to Koreans. In the mid-1970s, when former U.S. President Jimmy Carter tried to withdraw American troops from South Korea, faulting President Park Chung Hee's administration for being a dictatorship, President Park was joined by opposition politicians in protesting the plan. As for common strategy, South Korea also served as a fortress of anticommunism, keeping the North Koreans, and indirectly the Russians and Chinese, in their box. Seoul served as a shining example of what could be achieved by adopting an American-style market economy in Asia. South Koreans were almost blindly devoted to the United States from the 1950s to the 1980s. North Korea and Japan were the targets of their hatred. Pro-U.S. sentiment began to slowly decline in the 1980s. The results of three surveys illustrate the point well. A U.S. Information Service survey conducted in South Korea in 1965 asked people to name their favorite country; 68 percent chose America. Less than 1 percent said they did not like the United States.[3]

That was the war generation. Those born after the Korean War began to have their own ideas. Having no personal memories of the war, their most striking memory is of the Gwangju massacre, when government troops brutally suppressed a protest there against the dictatorial regime of President Chun Doo Hwan. Not only the protesters but innocent passersby—even pregnant women—suffered the dictator's wrath. Most people who came of age at that time—the South Koreans now in their thirties and forties—believe that the United States silently backed the brutal regime. While the older generation views the United States through a single prism—the blood pledge of the Korean War—younger South Koreans reflect more deeply on their ties to America. They consider the Gwangju movement, the influence of Hollywood, McDonald's, the deaths of the schoolgirls, and a host of other positive and negative factors.

The generation gap is clearest in looking at North Korea. The postwar generation is more sympathetic to the North Koreans, seeing them as poor, starving compatriots rather than enemies. South Korean movies prove that point quite well. In the 1960s, hit movies like *Marine of No Return* (1963) and *Red Muffler* (1964) featured soldiers who fought bravely and died in the Korean War. The 1970s featured all kinds of anticommunist movies. *Nambugun* (1990), however, serves as a carefully built bridge between the themes of the movies of the old and young generations by focusing on the emptiness of ideological fights. Films like *Swiri* (1998) and *Joint Security Area* (2000) express how many young people these days feel about their nation's divided status. Both movies deal with personal relationships between North and South Koreans. They practically scream, "We couldn't care less about communism versus capitalism. Either way, Koreans lose their lives. It's human life that matters most."

But even the postwar generation is divided. They differ largely in three areas. Some of them, let's call them generation A, remember the Gwangju massacre and a vague fantasy about North Korea. During the 1970s and 1980s, there was even a pro–North Korea club on university campuses in Seoul. The other half of the postwar generation, generation B, feels sorry for the North Koreans. Generation A lacks focus in their policy. Sure, they managed to send some representatives to the National Assembly, but so far they have failed to differentiate themselves from the old-line politicians. Generation B, on the other hand, is younger—the first generation in Korea to grow up with the Internet at its fingertips. While generation A was limited in its opportunities to expand, the newer generation revels in the privilege of the World Wide Web, which links hundreds of thousands of people through the Internet and mobile phones. Their most notable political victory was not the election of a few marginal assembly members but their influence in propelling a man seen as one of their own into the Blue House, the center of South Korean political power.

December 19 was more than a political struggle, it was a clash between the war generation and the postwar generation. Roh's rival, Lee Hoi Chang, who is sixty-eight, represented the old generation. He graduated from the most prestigious high school and university in Korea, served as a Supreme Court justice, and symbolized anticommunist and pro-U.S. values. On a visit to Washington last January, Lee was greeted by several high-level U.S. officials, including Vice President Dick Cheney and Secretary of State Colin Powell. Those meetings only intensified the younger generation's view of him as a representative of the status quo.

Roh, who is just fifty-seven, symbolized the postwar generation. He was not even considered a contender for the Millennium Democratic Party's presidential nomination. He is a self-educated man. His only power base outside the party was No-sa-mo, his Internet fan club, which promoted him to the online masses. He had never visited the United States, and that was part of his appeal. He won the hearts of young voters by promising that he would not kowtow to Washington.[4]

New Alignment and New Issues for South Korea and the United States

The emergence of the younger members of the postwar generation in South Korea, however, is not likely to affect the existing Korea–U.S. relations in any fundamental way. The postwar generation grew up watching Hollywood films and eating Big Macs. When I was young, for example, we likened the sound of a gunshot to "ppang-ppang" and expressed bewilderment by saying, "Ai-goo!" Koreans in their twenties are more likely to choose "bang-bang" and blurt out "Oh, my God!" Another factor is the number of middle-class people who pour all their energy into sending their children off to the best schools in the United States. That exposure to American society and values makes it nearly impossible for South Korea to become truly anti-U.S., in view of how tightly its interests are entangled with those of America. Furthermore, even though the older generation may have lost this election, it is far too early to rule them out as a powerful force in society.

But one thing is sure: Roh's victory makes it clear that we can never go back to the unconditional admiration South Koreans once had for America. There is a Korean saying that many drops eventually become a downpour. Although anti-baseism is now just low-level frustration with the relationship between Korea and the U.S. troops stationed there, the trend should not be completely played down. It could grown into something even nastier for the two Koreas. This danger requires some adjustments to the style and alignment of the U.S.–South Korea relationship. The two countries should revise their common goals, common policy, and division of roles when it comes to North Korea and the presence of U.S. troops on the Korean Peninsula.

North Korea: From the Brink of Collapse to Sinification

For fifty years Seoul and Washington strove toward the common goal of preventing a recurrence of the Korean War by maintaining U.S. troops on the Korean Peninsula as a deterrent. That common enemy kept the alliance strong, through good times and bad. But North Korea's new reality is weakening the old ties, which were centered on maintaining status quo and inducing the Stalinist regime to change.

In 1989, South Koreans watched as a divided Germany reunited. In the years that followed, they saw the inequity and social strife that sudden reunification brought, and they came to hope for a more gradual melding of North and South, so as to lessen the shock. Many saw inducing the North to open its doors as the best option for economic unity, followed by peaceful coexistence. South Koreans came to believe the best way for the peninsula to unify would be to help the North take practical economic and social steps similar to those that had been taken by China.

Bringing Chinese-style reform to North Korea is well worth considering, now that the reclusive regime has proved itself a total failure by starving to death upward of 1 million of its people since the mid-1990s. If the South's old reunification plan, which includes the destruction of the North Korean regime, is carried out, South Korea will face astronomical economic, political, and social costs. According to estimates by Goldman Sachs, a sudden reunification like that of Germany would cost South Korea $3.55 trillion.[5] That is no small sum for any nation. Fortunately, Pyongyang has itself been showing some keen interest in opening its doors. A decade ago the North opened its first free-trade zone in the Rajin-Sonbong, which has failed, probably because of a lack of true resolve on the part of North Korean authorities to make it "free." But recently they have announced plans for a host of future-oriented attempts at the same concept. The plan to name Chinese-Dutch tycoon Yang Bin to head the Sinuiju special administrative region, aimed at making the place a second Hong Kong, was especially eye-catching. The North also seems enthusiastic about the linking of inter-Korean railroads, and—in the more distant future—roads and seaways. However slowly and despite frequent stops and starts, the North is changing. It is time the United States and South Korea sat down and mapped out a plan to open up the North, on the model of China, while at the same time keeping Pyongyang's arms in check.[6]

Return of the Perry Process

The United States has so far offered three basic North Korea policies: (1) a Cold War–era military deterrence policy, (2) a Clintonian engagement policy, and (3) the moderate policy known as the Perry process. In contrast, South Korea is in a transitional stage from the hard-line confrontational policy to President Kim Dae-jung's "Sunshine Policy." Political conflict is unavoidable if this continues, which is precisely why a return to the Perry process is needed. The plan, named for the man who hatched it, former U.S. Secretary of Defense William Perry, was endorsed by both Republicans and Democrats in 1998. It is also important that South Korea sit in the driver's seat, with the United States right beside it, in developing the principles of this new North Korea policy.

The Issue of U.S. Forces Korea (USFK)

U.S. authorities have been careful not to mix the issue of U.S. troops on the Korean Peninsula with their North Korea policy. They have insisted that the arrangements be worked out strictly between the two allies. While this makes sense legally, it does not work that way in actual practice. It is about time that we seriously reviewed the mid- to long-term goals and functions of the American troop presence on the peninsula based on changes in inter-Korean relations and the possible reduction of the North Korean threat. Why cannot South Korea and the United States offer to reduce the number of American troops and pull back some of those stationed along the Demilitarized Zone (DMZ) if North Korea will do the same and also give up its weapons of mass destruction? That could significantly reduce anti-U.S. sentiment in the South as well as improve cooperation among the two allies. The two nations might also consider turning over command of their combined forces to the South Korean military.

Reducing Anti-Baseism

The first step is for Seoul and the USFK to get on with rearranging the roughly 100 U.S. installations scattered throughout the peninsula to allow Korean city planners to use land that is no longer needed by the military. The two sides should recheck, from both a political and strategic standpoint, whether it is wise to maintain the U.S. 8th Army's Yongsan Garrison in Seoul. Yongsan is significant for several reasons. From an emotional point of view, many Koreans remember that Japan's military also used the area as a base when it colonized Korea. Also, it has become too open and too known to outsiders. The area was on the outskirts of Seoul when the 8th Army set up there. It is now part of the busy downtown of one of the world's largest capitals. Moving the USFK headquarters out of Seoul would be an important symbolic gesture. To top it off, Yongsan is also within range of North Korea's field guns.

There is also a problem of communication between the USFK and the Korean public. As a journalist, one thing I noted during the recent protests was an almost complete lack of communication between the U.S. military and the public, coupled with a lot of bad timing. Unlike the U.S. Embassy in Seoul, the military there, after half a century of operating in the country, still lacks effective channels for promoting and disseminating its version of events. That leads to a widespread feeling that the U.S. military in Korea is indifferent to how its presence affects the Korean people. I have experienced this personally. For the past several years I have formally and repeatedly requested an interview with the commander of the USFK. I am still waiting for a reply.

Success Story: Jeffrey D. Jones

Things may not be as bad as they seem. Once Americans try to understand the working of the Korean mind, these problems could melt away faster than imagined. The change in Korean perceptions of the American Chamber of Commerce (AMCHAM) in Korea is a wonderful example. For decades, AMCHAM was widely perceived as an unofficial Washington envoy sent to put economic and diplomatic pressure on Seoul. It symbolized U.S. power and arrogance, and it was not unusual to hear of Molotov cocktails being thrown through its windows. The arrival of Jeffrey D. Jones, the new president of the chamber, in 1998 almost completely erased that negative image in about three years. Mr. Jones's secret was his understanding of how Koreans think and his fluency in Korean, thanks to his earlier experience as a Mormon missionary in Korea.[7]

His other strength was his constant interaction with the South Korean media. He was the face and voice of AMCHAM, hosting seminars, appearing on television, and making numerous contributions to newspaper columns. His appearances on local television talk shows especially helped narrow the emotional gap. He also offered his advice on a range of issues. He lent his opinions to the Ministry of Commerce, Industry and Energy on a policy for small and midsize companies and a number of investment policies. AMCHAM is now seen as a friendly foreign partner, despite the hard fact that little has changed in its actual function. The case offers much to reflect upon. It is really a shame that after fifty years of partnership, we have failed to produce a Jeffrey Jones to bridge the gaps between South Koreans and U.S. troops.

Conclusion

So the big question is: "How to define the alliance?" I believe there are few differences in relationships between nations and relationships between people. Allies could be defined simply as friends, and that is what South Korea and the United States have been. Friendship is not perfect. Friends do not always get along, and the relationship is not one-sided either. Friends might agree 80 percent of the time but disagree the other 20 percent. But they are still friends.

The friendship between South Korea and the United States, unfortunately, has not been a normal one. South Koreans have been free from the outset to support the United States, but they were rarely allowed to criticize it. While that was the choice made by South Korean leaders, not Americans, it is still part of the relationship. With that in mind, perhaps the protests we've seen lately were an inevitable step for South Korea to make its friendship with the United States normal. The new generation in South Korea does not want to be protected, it wants a friend with whom it can walk side by side.

There is a Korean saying that the earth hardens after a rain. Consider the candlelight protests a rain. And now the earth, the basis of our relationship, can be solidified.

Notes

1. Lee Jong-Hyun, "Anti-Americanism?" *Ilgan Sports*, December 3, 2002.
2. Park Young Ho, *Han Mi Gwan Ke Sa* (Seoul: Sil Chun Mun Hak, 1980), p. 393.
3. Kim Ho Ki, "Yi Je Mi Kukeun Upda," *Sindonga*, January 2003.
4. Nomuhyun, "Minjudang," *Dae Han Mae Il*, December 12, 2002.
5. Staff reporter, "Tong Il Bi Yong," *Kuk Min Ilbo*, April 21, 2000.
6. Lee Hong-Ku, personal interview, December 7, 2002.
7. Jeffrey Jones, "Hankuk Gwa Mikuk," *Joongang Daily*, October 11, 1998.

19

Industry and National Identity

Globalizing Korean Auto Manufacture

Dennis L. McNamara

Expanding economic ties have distinguished the U.S.–Republic of Korea (ROK) alliance over the past decade. Friction was apparent in earlier transitions from Korea's aid dependence, to rapid economic growth, and then to interdependence. The changes continue today, with no consensus as yet in South Korea on the benefits of the new global economic partnership with the United States. Indeed, efforts to reorient the Korean economy from a highly nationalistic state-business alliance to the Anglo-Saxon model of a more liberal, open economy draw fierce opposition, prompting strong anti-American sentiments. The fact that foreigners hold 36 percent of publicly traded stocks in South Korea causes widespread concern.[1] Foreign domination of the Korean liquor market and the impending sale of the venerable Jinro Liquor firm to foreign interests have been widely publicized.

Fanning the flames, Crest Securities has quietly emerged with the largest block of publicly traded shares of the beleaguered SK Corporation, prompting widespread fears of foreign domination of Korea's third-largest chaebol. Professor Kang Hee-joon of Indiana University wrote recently of the dilemma: "That Crest Securities is owned by a foreign entity should not, however emotionally important it is to Korean investors, be an important factor. If an active participation in the management is to be blocked simply because the suitor is a foreign entity, Korea will have a harder time attracting foreign investment."[2] But others would argue that "the Korean economy has lost direction" with the influx of foreign ownership and reforms toward an Anglo-Saxon model.[3]

It is in this context that General Motors has taken on the daunting challenge of operating a Korean auto firm, GM Daewoo Auto and Technology Company (GMDAT). Six months after the purchase, the firm has struggled to maintain last year's sales. One industry expert noted no new image of the firm has emerged since the sale, and questioned whether the necessary "harmonization" is possible between Korean and U.S. management.[4] This chapter looks to attitudes in the economic partnership by examining the underlying structures of market and association that give shape to the economic alliance. I argue that a middle ground must be found in the tension between globalization or market liberalization and localization or promotion of locally owned and managed enterprise.

Borders

Borders give identities. Globalization undermines existing borders but also stimulates emergence of new boundaries. If the fading of former borders seems evident in the Korean political economy, what is emerging is less clear. The ambiguity can be unsettling, for narrative constructions about borders such as the "nation-state," the "national economy" or "national industries," and indeed of "national society," remain at the foundation of national identities. Little stands in the way of the relentless integration of industries worldwide, "global sourcing," and global convergence of markets and consumer tastes. Local rebordering or "demarcation" might best be considered a way of channeling or regulating the transition rather than halting or reversing the process. Korean industry is perhaps most closely identified with the auto industry but also with steel, shipbuilding, and now computer chips. What changes can we expect in Korean borders of "national industry," given the recent foreign acquisitions of Daewoo Motor and Samsung Motor?[5]

A focus on *trust* draws attention to the architecture of solidarity among groups, and especially in markets where higher levels of trust in exchange relationships permit lower transaction costs. *Social capital* might be thought of as the foundation for trust in society, and networks as the necessary structure.[6] Social capital results in cohesion but can also lead to exclusivity. The "closure" of network structure, that is, the extent to which all actors are interrelated, may facilitate effective norms and discourage "free rider" behavior, but it may also close off the networks to new channels of information. Some highlight the more cohesive or "sticky" character of tight networks as a barrier to the flexibility demanded in global markets today. A number of scholars have singled out Korea's business networks, and particularly the distinctive nexus of business and state, as one key to rapid economic development. Structural adjustment demands some flexibility in this network, yet not the kind of fluidity that would erode efforts at collective action.

My topic then is Korean social capital in a rapidly changing automobile industry, and my focus "demarcation" or the new borders spurred by the entry of GM Daewoo into the industry. I look first to the changes, then to the networks, and finally to trust and transitions in the conclusion. My premise is that new networks will affect existing forms of interest exchange among state, capital, and labor, although at this point I can only identify the structural changes and initial indications of transformations. The rebordering of the industry is significant not only for the future of the Korean industry in global competition but also for the directions of globalization on the peninsula. The transformation of Korean identities, whether as producer or consumer, with the influx of foreign ownership into a tightly held local industry, provides a prism on shifting attitudes toward its market partners.

Korea's Auto Industry

The South Korean auto industry churned out 3.1 million units in 2003, ranking fifth worldwide in auto production, just behind China.[7] South Korea had already gained fifth place among the world's largest auto producers by the mid-1990s, and it weathered the financial crisis to recover earlier production levels by 2000. Unlike most national auto industries, the South Korean industry was organized initially to serve foreign rather than local markets; grew rapidly with exports; particularly to the United States; and developed a local market only in the past decade, almost exclusively with local products.

Korea has followed the model of Japan, the United States, and major European makers with a commitment to a "full-set" industry, vertically integrated with multiple tiers of suppliers and subassemblers serving chaebol-dominated assemblers. The term *chaebol* refers to family-controlled, diversified conglomerates, similar to the prewar Japanese *zaibatsu*. But Korea has never been able to develop the sophistication and scope of products in its auto-parts industry to meet the demand of the auto manufacturers and thus remains dependent on foreign auto-parts firms for critical components.[8] This leads to a further feature of dominant local ownership, despite the fact that the industry could develop only with the technology and even capital investment of leading foreign automakers. Mitsubishi Motors and its partners retain only a 5 percent share in Hyundai Motors, although Mitsubishi provided much of the initial technology in the firm's development. Daewoo Motor was originally a joint venture with General Motors, buying out its partner in 1992. As recently as the early 1990s, the Samsung Group called upon Nissan Motors of Japan to develop its auto-manufacturing arm. In retrospect, the Korean automobile industry was remarkably international from the outset with respect to ambitions, markets, and technology, yet remarkably local in its ownership.

Perhaps the most striking feature of the auto industry on the peninsula has been early state support and direction, continuing state oversight, and remarkable crisis intervention by the state.[9] Automobiles have been a priority in state economic planning from the 1960s. State roles of broker and at times director have been central to the restructuring of the industry across four decades, including the consolidation following the recent Asian financial crisis. The state has also been prominent on both the production and consumption sides of the industry. State labor controls permitted development of low-cost mass production on the peninsula and were the target of the successful labor organization mobilization of 1987.[10] Hagen Koo has written recently of the image of "industrial warriors" in Korea's heavy industries as an "image created by the state in order to exhort workers to hard work, discipline themselves, and sacrifice for the nation."[11] The state played a major role not only in worker identity but also in consumer identity. Consumer practices provided a forum for discussion of national identity, with the powerful coalition of state and firms urging local austerity on behalf of national development through the early 1980s but then shifting to local consumption to build domestic demand. Nelson defined "consumer nationalism" as "making consumer choices in the best interest of the nation."[12] In a chapter titled "Driving Consumption: South Korean Cars," she wrote of "cars as the most significant markers of South Korea's arrival at a sophisticated stage of industrial and economic development."[13] Given the prominence of the auto industry in national economic priorities often presented as critical for the nation's survival in development of worker identity and labor organization and in consumer identity, what happens now with the sudden entrance of foreign ownership into what had been a locally owned and managed industry?

GM Daewoo

General Motors of the United States has long been involved with the Korean auto industry. GM and Shinjin established GM Korea in 1972 as a 50/50 joint venture. Financial difficulties forced Shinjin to sell its share in the venture to Daewoo in 1978. GM and Daewoo agreed to rename the venture "Daewoo Motor" in 1983. Management differences forced GM to sell off its share to Daewoo in 1992, although GM technology remained at the core of Daewoo production. GM returned to the peninsula to purchase major parts of Daewoo Motor in April 2002, including its most modern plants in Gunsan and Changweon, Korea, and in Hanoi, Vietnam, as well as nine sales subsidiaries in western Europe and Puerto Rico. What they did not purchase is a further thirteen plants worldwide—including in Poland, Uzbekistan, and Egypt—and the older Daewoo plant in Bupyeong, Korea. Autonomy is one major difference between GM's earlier effort on the peninsula and the new investment. GM, in effect, has no local production partner. The state-owned Korea Development Bank retains 33 percent of the shares only to guarantee financing and oversee disposal of debt assumed from Daewoo Motor on behalf of Korean banks in the private sector. GM holds 42.1 percent of the total shares, its Chinese partner, Shanghai Automotive Industry Corporation (SAIC) holds 10 percent, and its Japanese affiliate Suzuki Motors holds 14.9 percent. The partnership with Asian affiliates in GM Daewoo highlights GM's new position in Asia as a major regional producer, far different from its earlier partnership with Daewoo. They expect GM Daewoo to play a major role in the local industry, where Daewoo Motors produced 900,000 units as late as 2000 and enjoyed a 20 percent share of the local market.[14]

Apart from the influx of foreign automakers into manufacture on the peninsula, their suppliers have likewise moved in among local first-tier suppliers.[15] That specter led the president of the government's Korean International Economics Institute (KIET) to lament, already in 1999, "sale of Daewoo Motors to foreigners will result in the death of auto-parts suppliers and weakening of Korea's automobile research and development strategy."[16] The strong demand for more advanced technology in Korea's auto-parts industry has attracted a number of major foreign parts firms, including Delphi and Visteon of the United States and Denso of Japan. One industry observer estimated that about 200 Korean joint ventures with foreign firms now operated in the auto-parts industry.[17] Denso-PS (Poongsung) serves as a major supplier for Kia, although the locally owned Hyundai Mobis supplies for Hyundai Motors worldwide and remains the largest local parts firm.

GM itself stands atop an extensive supply chain of machinery and electronics firms producing parts for the auto assemblers. GM's supply chain in the region will deeply affect the "supporting industries" for car makers on the peninsula. If GM departed South Korea in 1992, Delphi did not. Established in 1989 as a subsidiary of GM Korea, Delphi Automotive Systems Korea (DASK) had developed six local joint ventures by 2002, with total annual sales of $1.1 billion.[18] Collaboration with another GM affiliate on the peninsula, Delco Electronics, permitted a wide variety of high-techcomponents for the automobile industry. Delphi Korea (DASK) remains closely associated with Daewoo Motor, supplying up to 20 percent of their parts through 2001.[19]

The Society of Industry

How will foreign ownership in local auto manufacturing networks affect solidarity and, more generally, producer and consumer identities? Fligstein's emphasis on "markets as politics" sheds lights on the societal character of what is sometimes portrayed as simply "impersonal" market exchange.[20] He examines social structures that mitigate cutthroat competition in order to stabilize property rights, rules of exchange, and, indeed, market share. His model best describes stable markets and established conceptions of market control, particularly by the organized interests of large firms. The South Korean auto industry, however, suggests a new struggle for control in which the simultaneous effects of global competition, inward foreign investment, market liberalization, and regionalization of the industry have undermined earlier efforts by the state to "rationalize" the industry, and challenged efforts of dominant chaebols to sustain stable market monopolies. Hyundai and its recently acquired Kia Motors now enjoy a remarkable 75 percent share of local auto sales. But the battle will soon be joined to carve up the expanding Korean auto market, now Asia's second largest, among new global firms with extensive manufacturing facilities in place on the peninsula. What role might the foreign firms play in reshaping conceptions of control, including state policy and state controls, environmental restrictions, access to local financing, sharing of information on government industrial, finance, and trade policy, car safety legislation, and so on?

Other scholars have highlighted the relative competitiveness of the social organization of automobile industries in different nations. Biggert and Guillen identified, for instance, distinctive "organizing logics" of the industry in South Korea, in contrast to Taiwan, Argentina, and Spain. They argued that alignment of entrepreneurial "practices" with local institutional patterns is a necessary condition of effective adoption. "Social endowments" of some nations permit rapid adoption of production, distribution, and financial institutions to changes in demand on the consumption side and in technology on the production side. Among these endowments, they contrasted "organizing logics" in some nations favoring vertical integration among larger firms versus horizontal cooperation among small and midsize firms, as well as nations linked to the global economy by local ownership versus foreign ownership of production facilities. What they did not consider was the shift in a nation like South Korea from local to foreign ownership and management in auto production and, indeed, in the pyramid of suppliers. I am particularly intrigued by state-business and interfirm institutional arrangements and precedents in South Korea's auto industry and how these might be adapted to the new blend of local and foreign ownership.

Biggert and Guillen faulted the Korean institutional logic, largely state policy, for not fostering development of related small and medium-size industries and for commodity production no longer responsive to improvements demanded in international automobile markets.[21] Among students of Korea's development trajectory, an earlier emphasis on the primary role of the state has given way to a new appreciation for a state nested or "embedded" with the business community, with state incentives to overcome tendencies toward closure and exclusiveness.[22] Some would argue that webs of personal ties through school, hometown, or family provide the solidarity necessary for enterprise in turbulent Korean markets, but that solidarity across the society or "public trust" is relatively weak.[23] I have maintained that state and major textile firms bartered, argued, and ultimately succeeded with industry policies because of multiple, mutually reinforcing channels, whether clientelist, corporatist, or simply market contracts.[24] Multiple channels of information and resource flow permitted effective mutual surveillance precluding monopolization of subsidies or export quotas and other rent-seeking behavior. The state has played a far more extensive, directive role, however, in the nurturing of the auto industry from its birth. Remarkable concentration in the major chaebols has been another feature, though in close collaboration with state agencies. How will the introduction of foreign ownership affect these embedded modes of policy formation, industry-state ties, or labor relations in the auto industry?

Industry Networks

Conventional foreign-invested "assembly" industries such as garments and footwear or home electronics do not demand the extensive transfer of capital, plant, and technology necessary for automobile manufacture. Localization of a supply line is a further condition for profitable production in autos, particularly for the "just in time," lean inventory patterns popular in the contemporary global auto industry. The long supply line of multiple first-, second-, and third-tier suppliers in the Korean auto industry has long faced problems of capital and technology, in part due to adversarial ties to the assembly firms and their in-house first-tier supply firms.[25] The growing number of foreign-invested joint ventures in auto parts production and the influx of global first suppliers into the local industry may turn the supply line from basically a locally owned to more international set of firms but also from a bilateral supplier for their main assembler and its export market to a more regional supplier with contracts with more than one assembler.

Identities of local suppliers are indeed in transition, as are identities of industry associations at the top. Not only the Korean Automobile Manufacturers Association and the Korea Auto Industries Cooperative Association but also the peak Korean Federation of Industries must adjust their policies and national identity to fit an industry blending foreign and locally owned firms. What has gained far more media attention in South Korea is the adjustment in the labor sector. Financing on the part of the government and Daewoo creditors, and labor opposition to "restructuring" of the firm, were cited as the major reasons on the Korean side for the painfully slow GM acquisition. GM apparently finally acceded to labor demands for maintaining production at the older Bupyeong plant, with a compromise that provides for GM Daewoo purchase of plant production for six years without any commitment to purchase the plant itself. Earlier images of "industrial warriors," or more recent models of industrious workers committed to development of the firm and nation, will be challenged in the context of U.S.-style labor relations at a foreign-owned industrial plant.

Transitions in identity among suppliers, industry associations, and labor may pale in the face of transitions among consumers. Korean automakers sold 1.3 million cars at home, and exported a further 1.8 million in 2003. Imports of cars from abroad in 2002 amounted to only 30,491 units.[26] Already by 1999 the nation had achieved the plateau of one vehicle for every four people in a population of 46.8 million people. Registrations in 2003 reached 14.5 million in 2003 amounting to one vehicle for nearly every three people in the nation. The meager import figures offer one indication of local identification with the industry and opposition to foreign imports. The size of the local market and difficulties of promoting imports makes the market all the more attractive to foreign investors. South Korea's rapid development process has not permitted the more gradual transition from producer-nation to consumer-nation apparent in neighboring Japan or advanced industrialized nations of the West. A cohesive, state-promoted asceticism on behalf of national development provided a focus for work commitments and a rationale for constrained consumption through the mid-1980s. The need to spur local consumption in order to absorb excess production of export-oriented chaebols led to an abrupt reversal and a new campaign for consumption, though again constrained in the financial crisis of 1998. Now a local population with expanding demand for automobiles may well make the transition not only from production to consumption, but to consumption of products from a foreign-owned firm in Korea.

Regionalization of the industry adds a further complication to the transition. GM, Delphi, and Renault all have extensive production and marketing facilities in China and Japan. Integration of production among affiliates, and particularly of parts networks, would reshape GM Daewoo and Renault-Samsung. Daewoo autos might be sold through SAIC in Shanghai, for instance, together with GM's Buick sedan, and Suzuki Motors in Japan might develop a common platform for a minicar with Daewoo for sales in the region. GM Daewoo has already entered discussion with Yantai, a Chinese auto manufacturer in Shangdong Province with long ties to Daewoo, about expanding manufacturing cooperation. There are plans to ship unfinished GM Daewoo cars to China and Thailand for final assembly.[27] No one has yet suggested bringing

SAIC Buicks to the peninsula, or Suzuki products, but regional networks may well, in time, include both production and consumption. Regional networks owned and managed by foreign firms give quite a different identity to auto plants on Korean territory, as distinct from long precedents of locally owned and managed firms simply exporting to the United States and Europe.

Discussion

I began with borders and identity, trust and social capital. Transitions in Korean auto manufacturing provide a window on the reconstitution of social capital, specifically the reorganizing of critical networks of production and consumption in the industry. The study comes to a focus in solidarity and flexibility, testing the borders of closure to permit flexibility yet solidarity and identity. For instance, reordering the Korean state in the local auto industry poses considerable risks for the effective operation of its industry oversight offices and ultimately for the identity of the state.

The state must protect Daewoo creditors, suppliers, and preclude oligopoly by any one assembler in the sector. A state financial institution, the Korea Development Bank (KDB), is the major local investor in the foreign-owned and managed GM Daewoo and holds three seats on the firm's board of directors. The KDB has the dual task of supporting the firm's applications for local credits, and supervising payment of the remaining debts from Daewoo Motor. Participation on the board of directors ensures KDB and state oversight but also indicates commitment to the success of the enterprise. Only a successful enterprise will be able to continue operation of massive plants in Gunsan and Changweon and possibly Bupyeong over the long term, operations critical for a long supply line within the country, and for the nation's continued export growth. Although the Busan plant of Renault-Samsung is relatively new, successful operation is also important for the survival and continued growth of the local assembly and parts industries. The state has consistently worked to avoid the monopoly of a single assembler in the auto industry but confronts today the dominance of the Hyundai-Kia group in domestic sales and exports. Assuming that the state continues to nurture the industry and to intervene at times of crisis and threatened collapse, it must now redefine a national interest in a local industry with multinational investment.

Trade associations and suppliers within the industry will likewise need to adjust their goals. Trade associations must now press the government for auto industry policies that align with industry rather than directly national interests. An industry of multinationally invested firms, with strong links to auto markets and manufacture in neighboring China and Japan, may well develop quite different priorities on trade, environmental controls, support for research and technology, and so on, than were prominent in a locally invested industry. Trade associations confront the possibility of irrelevance if they cannot find ways to meld the new diversity of firm interests into coherent policy priorities. Suppliers too must redefine their place, confronting the dual challenge of upgrading production to gain a place in "global sourcing" and specializing their engineering to gain a place in the "cooperative associations" of the assemblers on the peninsula. A first- or second-tier supplier can diversify its customer base but usually still must rely on major "design-in" contracts with a single firm to maintain economies of scale and technological expertise. Some firms, which in the past could serve local commodity auto assemblers, may now have the opportunity to serve the more diverse product lines of the foreign-invested firms, though some will no doubt lose their links to Daewoo Motor due to the multinational's ability to source from affiliates elsewhere in Asia.

The rebordering of consumer and labor identities may well prove the most profound change spurred by multinational investment in the auto industry. Particularly in South Korea, with the very small number of foreign-made autos, the advent of foreign-invested autos in the booming local market for cars may prompt a redefinition among consumers of the link between industry and nation or may result in simple rejection of the products of a foreign-invested firm in favor of cars from the locally owned Hyundai. State-supported campaigns to direct market behavior on behalf of national goals will probably persist, particularly in times of crisis, and continue to affect consumer choices. Organized labor in the auto industry will likewise face changes in patterns of industrial relations. The regional dynamic will become more important with GM Daewoo and Renault-Samsung coordinating production among sites in Northeast Asia according to cost advantages, depriving local labor of the job security possible in a firm committed to continue production on the peninsula. A changing state role in the local industry may also affect labor's relations with state agencies concerned with labor policy.

Recommendations

What have we learned about the new U.S.–ROK economic partnership, with U.S. direct investment in a critical South Korean industry? What steps might be taken to ease the shift in attitudes to support the new partnership? Certainly harmonization of management strategies and procedures at the local level is critical for the future of the joint venture. Leslie Sklair wrote recently of the tension between national economic interests and the transnational's interest in shareholder profit: "Major globalizing corporations of today rarely connect making profits with national goals. They identify with the developmental goals of the places where they and their subsidiaries are doing business rather than their states of origin."[28] General Motors Asia will need to harmonize their strategies to align with national goals in the auto industry. Hyundai and Kia will remain largely local firms with global ambitions. GM Daewoo must carve out a niche as a global firm with local commitments.

Other foreign firms in South Korea face similar challenges. Foreign firms with a strong global structure need to balance local interests carefully, convincing local society of the firm's global advantages as well as their contribution to local employment and consumption. The fact that largely foreign-owned transnationals bring a strong regional network to the peninsula should likewise be highlighted. If South Korea is indeed committed to developing as a regional hub of trade and investment, foreign firms with strong Asian networks, particularly with bases in China and Japan, can play a major role in creating manufacturing and market links with South Korea.

Local industry associations and labor federations need to adjust their goals to balance the interests of foreign firms. The Korea Automobile Manufacturers Association represents the interests of their five members—Hyundai, Kia, GM Daewoo, Ssangyong, and Renault Samsung Motors. Kim Dong-jin, the president of Hyundai Motor Company, chairs the association and must somehow redirect the group to reflect the regional and global interests of their two foreign-owned member firms. The task will be particularly difficult on issues of clear national interest, such as labor relations on the one hand, or, on the other, technology-related issues such as automobile pollution legislation, where foreign firms may have advantages in providing more sophisticated controls. Local labor must strengthen its regional and international ties with counterpart organizations in Japan and China especially, as well as with labor in the United States, to learn of effective strategies for negotiating with GM Daewoo or other transnationals. The Korean state remains a major player in labor organizations, particularly evident in the Tripartite Commission's efforts to develop a corporatist strategy of labor-management relations.

Perhaps the biggest challenge for the foreign firms will be adjusting to negotiations with organized labor in South Korea. In the long term, stable labor relations will be a key for successful foreign investment, demanding commitments from the firms as well as labor organizations. Foreign firms need to collaborate with other auto firms to craft industry-wide standards for employment security, wages and benefits, training, and so on.

Finally, the state needs to play an active role in promoting direct foreign investment on the one hand and finding ways to integrate the strengths of foreign firms into coherent national economic policies on the other. Korea's role as hub within the Northeast Asia region is one example. The Roh administration appears committed to shifting from more narrow goals of locally owned and managed firms on behalf of "national industries" into a wider national interest in local, regional, and global market growth, which promote local manufacture and services, employment, and consumption. The shift would support the expanding Korea–U.S. economic partnership, in line with an Anglo-Saxon model of a more liberal economy. But local interests cannot be ignored nor national interest surrendered. Thus, I believe state policy makers must recognize continuing local concern for national ownership of local firms and national economic priorities. This, then, is the compromise that must be struck between globalization or market liberalization on the one hand and localization or promotion of locally owned and managed enterprise on the other.

Conclusion

Society in South Korea has proved remarkably resilient not only in successful pursuit of local industrial growth and wider economic development but also in confronting and successfully navigating through profound economic and political crises. The resurgence following the financial crisis is only the latest example. Four decades of an emerging organizational "logic" in South Korea's automobile industry suggests remarkable flux, whether in rapid expansion or production, export growth, multiple crises, or dramatic state intervention. Each crisis has resulted in new borders among firms, between industry and state, and between local and international markets. Changing borders have resulted in changing definitions of a "national industry," a "Korean firm," "patriotic consumer," or "industrial warrior." Multinational investment in the industry today is again pushing out old borders and pressing for new identities. A lag is apparent between structural and attitudinal changes regarding foreign investment. Addressing this discrepancy, particularly the antiforeign and anti-American sentiment, is the responsibility of both the foreign investor and the local state and society.

Notes

1. Chang-sup Lee, "Korea's Pain in Transition to Anglo-Saxon Economic Model," *Korea Times*, April 17, 2003, p. 7. Performance of foreign firms also draws attention. The Korea International Trade Association tracks the performance of non-Korean firms (i.e., firms with more than half their shares held by foreign investors). They reported that foreign firms accounted for 8.3 percent of exports in 2002, or $12.3 billion, down from 9.7 percent in 2000. Export leaders among foreign-invested firms included Amkor Technology (U.S.), Nokia TMC (Finland), GM Daewoo, Song Korea, BaSF Korea (Germany), and Fairchild Korea (U.S.). "Foreign Firms Here Account for 8.3% of Exports Last Year," *Korea Times*, January 29, 2003, p. 10.

2. Hee-joon Kang, "Foreign Investors Watch South Korea-Crest Feud," *Korea Times*, April 17, 2003, p. 10

3. Lee, "Korea's Pain in Transition to Anglo-Saxon Economic Model," p. 7.

4. "GM Daeucha chulbeom 6 gaeweol myeongam" (Six months since the launching of GM Daewoo Auto), *Kyeonghyang Sinmun*, April 18, 2003, http://kari2.hmc.co.kr:8080/autosmweb.nsf/b5edc5fb8a4e334e49356.

5. The literature on multinational business management provides some directions for firms such as General Motors or Renault in their adjustment to their new Asian networks. The specific questions of how GM Daewoo or Renault-Samsung will integrate local and global management styles remains to be answered. General Motors broke off their twenty-year joint venture with Daewoo in 1992, apparently unable to find common ground with Daewoo management. Will majority GM ownership in the new venture permit a more successful adjustment of two management styles?

6. Bourdieu defined *social capital* as "the aggregate of the actual or potential resources which are linked to possession of a durable network of more or less institutionalized relationships of mutual acquaintance or recognition." See Pierre Bourdieu, "The Forms of Capital," in *Handbook of Theory and Research for the Sociology of Education*, ed. J.G. Richardson (Westport, CT: Greenwood Press, 1985), pp. 241–58. See also Paul S. Adler and Seok-Woo Kwon, "Social Capital: Prospects for A New Concept," *Academy of Management Review* 27, no. 1 (2002): 22.

7. "China Overtakes S K in Auto Production," *Korea Times*, February 2, 2003, p. 12.

8. South Korea imported $1.2 billion of auto parts in 2000 and $1.1 billion in 2001, with roughly half that amount originating in Japan each year. "South Korea Imports, 8708 Parts and Accessories for Motor Vehicle, January to December." *World Trade Atlas* (New York: Global Trade Information Services, 2003).

9. Andrew E. Green, "South Korea's Automobile Industry," *Asian Survey* 32 (1992): 411–28; Seok-jin Lee, "Bringing Capital Back In: A Case Study of South Korean Automobile In-

dustrialization," Ph.D. dissertation, Yale University, 1992; Tae-wan Han, "A Comparison of Industrial Policies in Japan and Korea: MITI and the Economic Planning Board in Heavy and Auto Industries Promotion," Ph.D. dissertation, University of Hawaii, 1998.

10. Ronald A. Rodgers, "Industrial Relations in the Korean Auto Industry: The Implications of Industrial Sector Requirements and Societal Effects for International Competitiveness," in *Social Reconstructions of the World Automobile Industry: Competition, Power and Industrial Flexibility*, ed. Frederic C. Deyo (New York: St. Martin's Press, 1996), pp. 87–135.

11. Hagen Koo, *Korean Workers: The Culture and Politics of Class Formation* (Ithaca, NY: Cornell University Press, 2002), p. 209.

12. Laura C. Nelson, *Measured Excess: Status, Gender, and Consumer Nationalism in South Korea* (New York: Columbia University Press, 2000), p. 25.

13. Ibid., p. 101.

14. Equally significant is the entry of Renault into the Korean auto industry with the acquisition of Samsung Motors in 2000. Renault-Samsung enjoys today an established sales network of about 100 sales outlets on the peninsula. Renault acquired Samsung's Busan factory with a capacity of 240,000 units annually, and with technology under license from Nissan, Renault's Japanese partner. Like GM Daewoo, Renault-Samsung has plans for export to China and other areas in the region. Renault cannot match the scale of GM worldwide, but its very effective integration with Nissan, Japan's second-largest automaker, may give Renault an immediate advantage over GM in regional sales and production.

15. The Korean Automobile Manufacturers Association listed a total of 79,544 firms in the transport industry in 1998, including 27,419 (34 percent) auto industry–related firms with 714,538 workers. Han'guk Jadongcha Gongeop Hyeophoe (Korea Automobile Manufacturers' Association, KAMA), *Han'guk ui jadongcha saneop 2000* (Korea's automobile industry, 2000) (Seoul: KAMA, June 2000), pp. 6–7.

16. See BBC News, "Daewoo," http://news.bbc.co.uk/1/hi/business/566014.stm. December 15, 1999.

17. Interview May 24, 2001, with Mr. Kim San, senior manager, Planning & Research Team, Korea Auto Industries Coop. Association. For a list of Japanese joint-ventures in Korean auto parts, see Brown and Co., Ltd., and Yano Research Institute, compil., *Japan Auto Parts Industry, 2001* (Tokyo: Brown and Co., 2001), pp. 676–78.

18. Joint ventures include Daewoo Automotive Components (general products), Ltd., Shinsung Packard (connectors and wire harnesses) Co., Ltd., Daesung Electric (automotive switches) Co., Ltd., Korea Door Systems (door latches) Co., Ltd., Delkor Corporation (batteries), and Sungwoo (airbags and seat belts) Corporation. Chon, Choon Taek, president of Delphi Automotive Systems Korea, "Delphi: World's Leading Auto Parts Supplier—Interview with Korea Biweekly," October 30, 2002, www.kisc.org/weekly/vol_25/insight/main.htm. For corporate data on Delphi worldwide, see www.delphi.com.

19. "Delphi Korea Holds Parts as Daewoo suspends Operations at Three Plants; Other Suppliers Also Threatening," *Wall Street Journal*, August 29, 2002, then excerpted in *Automotive Digest*, www.automotivedigest.com/ view_are.asp?articlesID=6995. GM's major auto parts supplier, Delphi, was spun off only recently as an independent firm and continues today as the world's largest auto parts manufacturer. Delphi had sales of $26.1 billion in 2001 with 192,000 employees worldwide at 179 manufacturing sites. See www.delphi.com.

20. Neil Fligstein, "Markets as Politics: A Political-Cultural Approach to Market Institutions," *American Sociological Review* 61 (August 1996), 656–73.

21. Nicole Woolsey Biggart and Mauro F. Guillén, "Developing Difference: Social Organization and the Rise of the Auto Industries of South Korea, Taiwan, Spain, and Argentina," *American Sociological Review* 64 (October 1999): 722–47; Eun Mee Kim, "The Development of Producer-Driven Commodity Chains in the Automobile Industry in Korea: Relations to Japan and the United States," *International Studies Review* (Seoul) 3, no. 1 (June 2000): 59–84; Naeyoung Lee and Jeffrey Cason, "Automobile Commodity Chains in the NICS: a Com-

parison of South Korea, Mexico, and Brazil," in *Commodity Chains and Global Capitalism*, ed. Gary Gereffi and Miguel Korzeniewicz (Westport, CT: Greenwood Press, 1994), pp. 223–44; Hyung Kook Kim and Su-Hoon Lee, "Commodity Chains and the Korean Automobile Industry," in *Commodity Chains and Global Capitalism*, ed. Gary Gereffi and Miguel Korzeniewicz (Westport, CT: Greenwood Press, 1994), pp. 281–96.

22. David Kang has recently argued that mutual interdependence between state and capital in the Third and Fourth Republics constrained corruption. See David C. Kang, *Crony Capitalism: Corruption and Development in South Korea and the Philippines* (New York: Cambridge University Press, 2002). Some segments of the economy remain plan-rational, others market-rational with the state role limited to regulation. Eun Mee Kim, "Contradictions and Limits of a Developmental State: With Illustrations from the South Korean Case," *Social Problems* 40, no. 2 (May 1993): 228–49. Chung-in Moon, "The Demise of a Developmentalist State? Neoconservative Reforms and Political Consequences in South Korea," in *Politics and Policy in the New Korean State: From Roh Tae-Woo to Kim Young Sam*, ed. James Cotton (New York: St. Martin's Press, 1995), pp. 67–84. For a broader comparative view of ties between business and state, see Taehoon Moon, "The Relationship between Business and Government in Three Policy Areas in Korea: Economy, Environment, and Technology," Ph.D. dissertation, State University of New York at Albany, 1992; Meredith Jung-en Woo-Cumings, "Introduction: Chalmers Johnson and the Politics of Nationalism and Development," in *The Developmental State*, ed. Meredith Woo-Cumings (Ithaca, NY: Cornell University Press, 1999), pp. 1–31; James Cotton, "The Asian Crisis and the Perils of Enterprise Association: Explaining the Different Outcomes in Singapore, Taiwan and Korea," in *Politics and Markets in the Wake of the Asian Crisis*, ed. Richard Robison, Mark Beeson, Kanishka Jayasuriya, and Hyuk-Rae Kim (London: Routledge, 2000), pp. 151–68.

23. Yong-hak Kim and Son Jae-suk, "Trust, Cooperation and Social Risk: A Cross-cultural Comparison," *Korea Journal* 38, 1 (Spring 1998): 131–53. They cited the argument of Korea as a nation with high private trust but low public trust. Sanctioning systems are then needed to induce noncooperators to cooperate whether in the United States, Japan, or Korea, but most dramatically in Korea.

24. Dennis L. McNamara, *Market and Society in Korea—Interest, Institution and the Textile Industry* (London: Routledge Press, 2002).

25. Haeran Lim, "Trust and Economic Development: Comparison of Sub-contracting Relations among Korea, Japan, and Taiwan," *Korean Journal of Policy Studies* 15, no. 1 (2000): 57–75. Byeong-ho Gong, "Cooperative Relationship between Assemblers and Suppliers in the Automobile Industry: A Comparative Study of Japan and Korea," International Economic Conflict Discussion Paper, no. 65 (Nagoya, Japan: Economic Research Center, School of Economics, Nagoya University, 1993). Korea Institute for Industrial Economics and Trade KIET, *Subcontract System in the Korean Automobile Industry and Suggestions for Improvement* (Seoul: KIET, 1997).

26. Han'guk Jadongcha Gongeop Hyeophoe (Korea Automobile Manufacturers' Association [KAMA], www.kama.or.kr. Seoul: KAMA, February 8, 2004.

27. David E. Zoia, "Signs of Life at GM Daewoo," WardsAuto.com, March 19, 2003.

28. Leslie Sklair, *The Transnational Class* (Malden, MA: Blackwell, 2001), p. 53.

20

Conclusion

Anti-American Sentiment in Korea and Its Importance—A Guide for the Perplexed?

David I. Steinberg

It is perhaps presumptuous for any single individual to draw conclusions from a conference and its papers that were intended to approach the issue from a broad spectrum of approaches rather than from a single lens. From the first, conference objectives were not designed to reach a singular conclusion but rather to air an issue many regarded as important, even vital, to the continuing, effective role of the United States in Northeast Asia. The meeting operated with an unstated title but a clear theme— Anti-American sentiment in Korea. The conclusions drawn from all these disparate papers, now chapters of this book, and their discussions must for the most part be subjective both to the writer and to the individual reader who will glean from these chapters those aspects of the problem most germane to his or her interests. Each of the chapters reaches conclusions that illuminate aspects of the question but provide no overarching analysis or approach; that was inherent in the nature of conference. Yet the various points emerging from the conference cry to be drawn into a conceptual web that will assist those concerned with the problem, which all would agree is important to some unquantifiable degree, and to offer some suggestions for ameliorating some of the most egregious aspects of the tensions that clearly have been created over time. Thus the ultimate but inchoate objective was to make policy recommendations that would improve or send into remission what some would regard as a cancerous sore affecting areas and issues far beyond those that are peninsula-bound.

An essay such as this must then be an idiosyncratic response to the meeting itself and this book—which grew out of it—and to the problem as this writer has observed it develop in various forms and through its diverse incarnations over the four decades of his engagement with the Korean Republic. Although he believes that a close association with the Republic of Korea is in the national interests of both states for their individual overlapping but not coterminous reasons, others in both countries might disagree. Yet this was one rationale for the conference and this volume (see "Introduction"), and the discussions reflected to a considerable degree the need for a closer relationship. Whether formalized by a defense treaty or involving U.S. forces on the peninsula, and whatever their force composition, number, and location, these are essentially peripheral questions to the major focus on the strength of the bilateral relationship within the context of a volatile Northeast Asia and U.S. global and regional priorities.

It would be simplistic to assign primary blame for the tensions apparent in contemporary U.S.-Korean involvement to one side or another. There has been sufficient evidence of a mutuality of responsibility and a long history over more than a century, in which both governments over many administrations have concentrated on shorter-term objectives, thus exacerbating the problems over extended periods. This has resulted in an apparent increase in anti-American sentiment that has mushroomed over time, most importantly, more rapidly in the recent past. There are historical roots for such reactions that cannot be ignored. This sentiment, according to polls, is widespread to some degree among every demographic, regional, or other segment of this population, although differing significantly among them, where once it was concentrated in small, demographically specific groups, as in a minority radicalized student population.

Yet this phenomenon cannot be characterized as a sweeping condemnation of the American relationship, experience, actions, or ideals. Even though in the past the American imprimatur was important for political legitimacy and was so sought by aspirants to or holders of power, this is no longer as significant. Thus, although such opinions can and have affected policies and have influenced at least one recent national presidential Korean election (that of 2002), they are not an "ism" in the sense of a cohesive hatred of the total American experience except perhaps among a small minority of Koreans (see Chapter 5). Thus, although we may use the term *anti-Americanism*, it is shorthand for a less comprehensive set of attitudes than linguistically would be the case. As a sentiment, it is real and pervasive; as a holistic posture, it exists only at the periphery of South Korean society.[1]

It seems evident that since 1945 there have grown contradictory Korean reactions to the United States' overweening presence and role on the peninsula and in Korean-American relations. The positive response has been the obvious pride in Korean accomplishments—a place in the international sun that few foreigners and Koreans could have predicted, where, as a twelfth largest economy in the world and a member of the OECD (Organization for Economic Cooperation and Development) the value of the total annual exports of Korea around 1961 was about the value of eight hours of exports in 2003, and where incomes have risen from perhaps $50 annually in the mid-1950s to more than $10,000 in 2003. Had one attempted to anticipate or predict Korea's chances for economic or political success in the mid-1950s, the prognostications would have been universally negative. All the factors of production at that time—land, labor, and capital—were going against Korea's achievements. The movement from authoritarian rule to a vibrant procedural democracy, from a suppressed civil society to one that presents a vigorous set of alternative centers of influence, and where the military has quietly and without incident retired to the barracks, all these are remarkable accomplishments on any international scale. At a visceral level, this pride was apparent in the virtually unanimous and enthusiastic Korean response to their remarkable performance in the 2002 World Cup; this unanimity of pride has been continuously mentioned by Koreans of all political persuasions and ages. Korean pride is thus the converse of antipathy or concern toward aspects of American policy or society.

With that set of impressive accomplishments and pride goes the parallel and contradictory emotion of vulnerability and fear of abandonment. The American security umbrella and the American image (often mixed, but at the same time both are still regarded as important) have been present for so long, reinforced by the U.S. role in liberation from the Japanese colonial conquest and in saving the South from the northern invasion, compounded by the economic assistance that the United States has provided for some three decades. The importance of the U.S. market for the burgeoning Korean manufacturing sector and the growing numbers of Koreans who have studied in, visited, or now reside in the United States have contributed to this relationship. All these have created what in Confucian parlance might be called the "elder brother" syndrome. In such hierarchical relationships, the United States has been perceived as the elder brother, which presumes responsibilities for both the elder and younger siblings: protection on the part of the elder toward the younger and support on the part of the younger for the older. In a strongly hierarchical society such as Korea, and where Confucian vestiges remain significant in spite of the pervasive modernization that has taken place, this is not surprising. Indeed, some Koreans continue to use the term in reference to contemporary U.S.-Korean relations even as it is denied in international diplomatic usage. In the minds of many, the relationship between the United States and South Korea is reminiscent of the historic relationship between China and Korea. The Korean attitude toward China was characterized by Koreans as *sadaejuui*, the "ism" of serving the great. This was regarded as positive in the imperial period, as a sign of Korea's cultural debt to China. Today that phrase has been applied to relations with the United States, but the connotation has shifted dramatically and negatively; it is now often translated as "flunkyism."

The threat of abandonment, whether through troop withdrawals (Nixon, Carter, and second Bush administrations) and disagreements over what the Koreans regard as critical and emotional issues, especially how to deal with North Korea, and conflicting statements by various members of the Congress, which in the pluralistic United States are taken for granted but which sometimes cause consternation overseas, result in considerable anguish in some Korean circles, especially among the mature elements of the population, those who have held power for so long.[2] The December 2002 presidential election, in which anti-American sentiment played an important role, has demonstrated that the American imprimatur is no longer needed for political legitimacy; indeed, the reverse may now be the case, with a younger population that approached the relationship from a distinctly different and more negative vantage point than that of their elders. The generational gap may be interpreted by the fact that as Korean youth feel more pride than vulnerability, the older generation may feel just the opposite.

Yet if too great a reliance on the United States has become a political sin in the South, too little consideration raises security concerns and a feeling of vulnerability.

As the United States negotiated bilaterally with North Korea in the early 1990s, leading to the Agreed Framework with the North in 1994, many influential South Koreans erroneously (and unrealistically from an American perspective) believed that the United States would take on Pyongyang as a "trophy wife," abandoning its faithful spouse South Korea, who was with the United States during difficult periods.[3] The Kwangju incident of 1980 (see Chapter 17) is illustrative of both aspects of the relationship. The government misrepresented the American position as supporting repression to give the state's actions political legitimacy, while the population of Kwangju waited for deliverance by the "elder brother." The Kwangju incident remains the single most critical event that sparked specific anti-American actions, such as attacks on official U.S. buildings.

Many of the contributors to this volume believe that the policies of the Bush administration beginning in 2000 have exacerbated negative opinions in Korea about the United States and its policies and generated fear for the security not only of the South Korean people but also those of the North. In a Confucian mode, although many, perhaps most, Koreans regard the United States as a friend, they regard North Koreans as "brothers" because of history, ethnic singularity, and cultural cohesiveness (see Chapter 11). This is in part due to the end of the Cold War and the belief among Korean youth that North Korea presents no danger to them. The division of Korea remains the most emotional issue on the peninsula. As a multicultural society, and in spite of the unipolarity of the United States as the world power, the United States may have difficulty in understanding, emotionally, the cultural unipolarity of the peninsula and its political implications.

At the same time, there have been apparent insensitivities to the changing Korean scene by various American administrations and departments within each administration. There is no denying that in spite of the image of the cold, poverty, destruction, and desolation as a result of the Korean War, there were vested U.S. interests in keeping a major presence in Korea on the part of the U.S. military, for command in Korea was a plum assignment often leading to advancement, but it was also a favored place by some civilian groups as well.[4] For years Korea was an unrecognized but nevertheless important post, which few wanted to abandon. With that commitment to Korea, which was founded on a mixture of genuine concern for Korea under the threat from the North and the "communist bloc" together with the protection of Japan that had become the U.S. linchpin in its Northeast Asia policy, it was also a place for advancement within the American military establishment and later in the American business community.

As a corollary to some internal bureaucratic and self-serving interests within the U.S. establishment, both public and private, Koreans charge that the United States has acted in South Korea in terms of its own national and individual interests. This cannot be denied, but many Koreans fail to understand that there is, or can be, a mutuality of interests that can combine the altruism that Koreans were led to expect by the propaganda of their own authoritarian regimes and the self-interests of national, institutional, and individual Americans, and the U.S. national interests as well.

In some sense, the early propagandistic "Pollyanna" approach to the Korean-American relationship, which served the mutual interests of both parties at that time and was officially promulgated, has led to later and unnecessary disillusionment on the part of many Koreans.

Some of the tensions associated with the relationship have resulted because of the intensity of the bilateral association between the two states, which might have been mitigated by some regional and overarching organizational entity that was unfortunately lacking in Northeast Asia. Where the U.S. relationships with some other states were in a sense brokered through multilateral channels, especially on sensitive issues, mutual problems could be diffused to a broader multilateral forum, thus alleviating collisions between the two countries. This seems to have been the case in Germany, where the North Atlantic Treaty Organization could be invoked in German-American problems, and such may in the future be the case in Korea where the World Trade Organization becomes the international forum for bilateral trade disputes between the two countries. In Southeast Asia, for example, the U.S. concern for terrorism and the approach to combating it has been couched in resolutions of the ten member states of the Association of Southeast Asian Nations, thus making such actions by individual states more palatable than would have been the case of direct, unilateral American pressure.

The United States has often held Korea up as an example of a successful American foreign economic assistance program and the inculcation of American democratic political values. This ethnocentrism has been used to justify the total U.S. foreign aid program to the Congress; it lacks, however, both nuance and demonstrable causation. Although most would agree that U.S. economic aid was essential to the survival of the Korean state, some would argue that it was often of the wrong type or was misused by governments with different objectives. To most Koreans, according to the surveys cited in this volume, the correlation of U.S. with Korean democratic values is not made. The reverse is rather the case; Koreans charge with considerable validity that the United States has supported authoritarian regimes for its own security interests. As Katherine Moon has noted, "Anti-Americanism in South Korea is in part an effort to confront the history and legacy of authoritarianism and the nationalism that was framed and imposed by dictators to justify their rule."[5] Ironically, the anti-American movement has given civil society groups a means through which to strengthen their own roles in Korean society. "In this context [of democratic consolidation], anti-Americanism serves as a 'big tent' under which disparate groups and interests can share organizing methods, moderate radical tendencies, bridge differences, coordinate action, draw a following, and achieve greater public impact both within and outside South Korea."[6] Anti-American sentiments and action in a real sense contribute to democratic deepening and community efficacy over the longer term even as it multiplies distance between the official positions of both governments. As Samuel Kim has also noted, "Anti-Americanism helps build social capital at the local level, acts as a force-multiplier in foreign and security policy, and provides a common national purpose for cooperative action among diverse groups."[7] As Katherine Moon has stated (Chapter 14), the inclusion of local autonomy in the revision of the Korean constitution of 1997 and its gradual implementation (which still has a considerable distance to travel) has given local political forces a democratic voice in affecting Korean-American relations.

The implications for both the United States and Korea, separately and in their relations, are important. Although there are those, including highly placed Korean government officials, who downplay the importance of anti-American sentiments and who anxiously await a cooling-off period from the individual incidents that prompt demonstrations in the streets and condemnation in the press, there is every likelihood that this neglect, in no way benign, in analyzing and then treating the fundamental causes of such feelings will simply prompt further sores to erupt and exacerbate the cumulative infectious bacteria of such incidents. Anti-American sentiment is likely to continue, and even if quiescent for a period, "[i]t may only mean that the feelings are lying dormant until either another event triggers a further round of protests on the fundamental issues or concerns are addressed."[8] Seung-Hwan Kim also comments," Looking ahead, anti-Americanism in South Korea is unlikely to disappear. It has been accumulating over the protracted period of the bilateral relationship, and its causes are too complex to be resolved overnight."[9] Another conference reached related conclusions:

> Participants [of a July 10–12, 2003, conference] all agreed that the problem of anti-Americanism has not been resolved. Indeed, the reality is that anti-Americanism may always exist, although it may temporarily subside and be driven underground. But it will rise again when triggered by a catalyzing event. As a Korean participant noted, the future attitude of Koreans will be affected by several factors: (1) political forces, fueled by election cycles—the next national elections in April 2004 will be important, and a resurgence of anti-American sentiments is likely; (2) the future of North Korea and its behavior will also make a difference; (3) the role of China—if China continues to grow in economic strength but pursues benevolent policies, then South Korea may grow closer to China and away from the United States; and (4) future U.S. policies will greatly affect Korean attitudes. If the United States continues to be perceived as a "unilateral, vengeful superpower," or if a military conflict breaks out on the Korean peninsula that is not coordinated with South Korea, there will be a devastating effect on U.S.-Korean relations.[10]

Professor Kim Uichol (Chapter 16) notes that such attitudes are more prevalent among middle school students than among those at college level.[11]

Lee comments that "The rise and the uncontainable expansion of anti-American sentiments in South Korea translate, at least to a certain extent, into a failure of U.S. public diplomacy, which is designed to promote an overseas, pro-U.S. climate of opinion."[12] Writing in 1993, he attributes this at least in part to the censorship of the Korean media during the Kwangju period, and the movement away from human rights in the early Reagan administration in an effort to reestablish closer links to the Korean government—links that had been frayed during the Carter period because of Carter's predilection to withdraw all U.S. forces from Korea and his concerns over human rights in the South. Yet if this failure were true in an era of censorship, what must we make of the situation since 1987, when the press was far less intimidated by any Korean administration? Clearly, then, if there were a failure of U.S. public diplomacy in the 1980s and before, in the contemporary period that failure has become more acute and thus more dangerous for the continuance of the alliance.

Why has this happened? Historical events cannot be renegotiated, although they may be reinterpreted. Although Americans tend to forget them, if indeed they know of them at all, in Korea the Taft-Katsura Agreement of 1905, in which the United States gave Japan a free hand in Korea in return for a similar response in the Philippines is well known. The March 1, 1919, independence movement was spurred by a naive interpretation of President Woodrow Wilson's Fourteen Points and his "self-determination of nations." The division of Korea in which Koreans played no role, and other incidents lost in history to most Americans are still vibrant in the Korean community because they are taught in the school system. Revisionist history is not the answer. These factors must be accepted.

History is not the only issue. Contemporary insensitivities exacerbate problems. When large numbers of troops are placed in areas of high civilian populations, incidents are bound to occur. Yet the need to consider how such problems are to be addressed, and their cumulative effects, seems to have escaped attention. The courts-martial of two servicemen in the accidental deaths of the two middle-school girls in 2002, for example, need not to have taken place just prior to a Korean presidential election, whatever might have been the verdict. That no American in the chain of command was held responsible in some moral if not legal sense offends Korean custom and sensitivities.

Many Koreans smart under the assumptions, often justified, that the United States pays more attention to Japan than to Korea and that the dice are loaded in terms of the U.S.–Japan bilateral relationship, with invidious comparisons (justified or not—see Chapter 12), especially about the Status of Forces Agreement (SOFA). This volume demonstrates (Chapters 2 and 3) that indeed the Japanese relationship has been paramount. Because Korea has vastly improved its formal ties to Japan, that the Korean administrative structure and legal code evolve from the Japanese model, and youth in Korea either consciously or unconsciously mimic much of Japanese popular culture, the Japan comparison has been, and continues to be, important to Korea.[13]

The SOFA is perhaps the contemporary focal point for anger. It was reluctantly renegotiated only several years ago, but its initial premise of the United States in 1965 was that the Korean legal system could not be trusted. Its salience today stems not only from incidents where it is invoked or maligned by one side or the other but also from the fact that it is a document—a defined agreement that could be renegotiated—in contrast to the more abstruse causes of anti-American sentiment.

Lee considers that "Anti-Americanism is conceived as a product of an ongoing symbolic struggle over how to define and redefine the United States in South Korea. The struggle over defining the United States constitutes part of the larger struggle waged between the authoritarian regime [Chun Doo Hwan] and civic forces over general politics and the history of South Korea."[14] Redefining the U.S. role is only part of the issue. In some sense, the U.S. Department of Defense in 2003 was attempting to redefine the military and security role of the United States by withdrawing the 2nd Infantry Division from the Demilitarized Zone and reconstituting the composition of the U.S. forces on the peninsula.[15] The wisdom of this move in terms of relations with North Korea is a matter separate from this essay, but the manner in which it has been discussed points out that the problem is not only redefining the U.S. role in Korea but, equally important, the manner in which that redefinition takes place or is negotiated and how that role is to be played, as well as the relationship of that role to the South Koreans. In part the alliance, once held in place by a common perception of an external threat, has atrophied because such dangers are no longer perceived to be credible by a significant portion of the Korean people and, indeed, to some degree by part of the American populace.

Many Koreans have commented on the unilateralism, or at least the perceived unilateralism, of the United States in dealing with the South. Influential Koreans have complained that Koreans are informed, but not consulted.[16] Even if such actions are not reported in the Korean media, they aggravate official ties and compound the impression of U.S. arrogance (a factor that is continuously invoked in any discussion of anti-American sentiment in Korea) and reinforce Korean vulnerability. This unilateralism may be understandable to Americans when issues of security are paramount, as there are differences in priorities between the global reach of the United States and the peninsular and regional interests of South Korea, but they do not sit well in South Korea.

Unilateralism is sometimes interpreted not simply as a difference in security objectives but rather in discriminatory terms—that elements of ethnic or racial discrimination continue to play a role, however residual, in the relationship between the two states. This is obviously a sensitive subject and not one that lends itself to easy policy changes, largely because it may even be unconscious. Korea wishes to be perceived by the external world as a modern society "on a par with other developed nations [and this] has made its public extremely sensitive to perceived discrimination by America or what it believed are insults to its dignity."[17] Too often this sentiment is ignored or forgotten when decisions are reached.

The totality of anti-American sentiment is a result of a complex, interacting set of factors that range over time and act not as discrete elements but have cumulative effects that create a gestalt greater than the sum of its parts. On the Korean side, there is the rise of Korean nationalism and pride in Korea's accomplishments, Korean vulnerability, and a set of cultural differences that affect the relationship. These range from Confucian residuals, such as the "elder-brother" syndrome, previously discussed, to differences in the cultural context of the need for apologies, for differences in the legal tradition, and for explicit recognition of responsibility. There is the Korean media factor, exacerbating existential problems (see Introduction). Historical errors on both sides continue to reverberate through the press and through the school system, reinforcing the myopic vision whereby the relationship is viewed. For the United States, past and residual racial prejudices, arrogance, policy differences in trade and investment, the importance of Japan to U.S. interests in the region, unipolarity, but most importantly policy toward North Korea all exacerbate these issues, added to which is the presence, prevalence, and location of U.S. forces and the problems that they inevitably bring. These factors will not disappear, but they may be prevented from growing.

As Chung-min Lee wrote (Chapter 10):

> In summary, the rise to the fore of anti-American sentiments in South Korea preceding the December 2002 presidential election should be seen as a major wakeup call for Seoul and Washington. Although the Roh and Bush administrations have taken a number of damage-limitation steps, coupled with more forward-looking management alternatives, the fact remains that mutual confidence had been eroded significantly over the preceding twelve months. From a South Korean perspective, it could be argued that expressions of anti-Americanism should be seen in the context of parallel developments, such as rising South Korean confidence, growing nationalism, and a concomitant desire to minimize fallout from the vestiges of great-power politics. But the critical point here is that South Korea should not tolerate a national security discourse that downgrades or minimizes the very real contribution to stability and prosperity that was possible through the underpinnings of the ROK–U.S. alliance. Expressions of nationalism and growing self-awareness are to be expected of an emerging middle power; but unlike other middle powers, South Korea continues to confront a spectrum of strategic and economic challenges that necessitates robust security ties with the United States and close partnership with Japan.

What, then, might be done to alleviate the issues between the two states that give rise to anti-American sentiment? The conference considered a number of such issues, including the external and internal changes that have occurred on the peninsula. In a sense, the glue that has held the alliance together has melted. The end of the Cold War and the growing incapacity of North Korea to threaten the South as a result of its economic incapacities (the nuclear issue is now only reemerging and, to many Koreans, North Korean bellicosity is directed against the United States and Japan, not fellow Koreans in the South), which is possible only in extremis, has meant there has to be a new conceptual basis for the stationing of U.S. forces on the peninsula, not simply defending a weak South against a militarized North. Such a close relationship if it is to continue, as Victor Cha and others have pointed out, should be based on a shared set of values rather than the exigencies of an immediate or incipient emergency. Some of those values are articulated by Professor Hahm (Chapter 13). This must be articulated by the leadership of both states and has yet to be done. The relationship must also be "brokered" through the deepening of institutional relationships between both countries, not only at the official level. There are opportunities for such strengthening through the increased number of Korean Americans, and through exchanges that penetrate both societies. Korean civil society, with the exception of a number of religious-related institutions, has been isolated from similar organizations in the United States and Europe, and some have advocated a concerted effort to assist in establishing such links.

Others have pointed out that the Korea that Americans once knew has changed. The vertical structure of Korean society, to which the Americans had become accustomed, has become more horizontal. Although this may make policy formulation and agreement more difficult, conceptually this is more in keeping with the American egalitarian ideal, of which president Roh Moo Hyun is in fact an exemplar. Koreans have advised Americans that they should diversify contacts and no longer rely on the administrative and intellectual hierarchy to which they have become habituated and with which they have been relatively comfortable.

Since the policies of both states have diverged in dealing with the most sensitive issue in South Korea—that of relations with the North—and have resulted in a spurt of anti-American sentiment in which South Koreans accuse the United States of being against or even preventing unification with the North, this issue requires the greatest sensitivity of Americans. Understandably, given the diverse national interests of both parties, this is likely to continue to be a matter of contention, but it can be moderated by the leadership on both sides. The responsibility of the Americans in this instance is paramount, as they have the greatest power and are viewed in the North as the greatest threat.

Some have suggested that the informal or semiformal contacts between Americans and Koreans on policy issues be expanded. Although there seems to be a proliferation of international forums on such issues, many of which are funded by Korean sources, more track II diplomacy seems to be required to educate elites in both states about the complexity of the relationship and the issues to be confronted. Such programs, however, must expand beyond the attendance of the "usual suspects"—those who are already sensitive to the issues and attend such forums.

The visual elements of the purported arrogance of Americans in Korea, as exemplified through the occupation of such bases as Yongsan in downtown Seoul, need to be modified. Recently, after some years of negotiations, plans seem under way to move the headquarters of the U.S. and UN command from what had been the headquarters of the Imperial Japanese military command during the colonial period. This is long overdue.[18]

On the Korean side, strangely, in spite of what seems a myriad of Koreans who have studied and are studying in the United States (see Chapter 13), there are few institutions within Korea that study U.S. society, its institutions, and its arcane decision-making processes, and such institutions could help to elucidate the complexities of the American decision-making process for Koreans. If, indeed, the Korean media contribute to exacerbating tensions between the two states, is there some means by which the press can police itself (without government intervention) to report accurately and without bias on issues in the relationship between the two countries? Such institutions have existed in the past, within the press itself, in the nongovernmental community that monitors the media, and in the diverse schools and departments of journalism and media in a wide range of universities in Korea.[19]

The conference and this volume explore a wide spectrum of issues—from the psychological to the institutional, from the strategic to the alliance. It does this in the context of the changes in Korean society and in comparative focus. The conclusion, then, of this effort to examine a phenomenon of critical import to both nations, is perhaps mundane—that more sensitivity and knowledge is needed on the part of both administrations and peoples, and that the leadership of each state has a responsibility to engage each other and their respective peoples in such dialogues. As quotidian as such conclusions might be, the need is no less acute if the interests of both peoples and states are to be served. But a cancerous sore should never go undiagnosed and untreated, and this volume is a first step in that healing process.

Notes

1. See "Introduction." The Korean public's negative response to the violent August 1996 radical student demonstrations at Yonsei University, which may be described as anti-Americanism in action and as a philosophy, was evidence of how limited this appeal was.

2. Peripheral events sometimes assume salience on both sides of the alliance. Where Koreans regarded the burning of a few American flags by youthful demonstrators as a fringe event, Americans reacted strongly to those images. When some American writers called for the removal of U.S. troops from Korea because of these incidents, the Koreans were considerably agitated, while most Americans felt that these opinions were not in the mainstream.

3. See "On Politics and Old and New Wives," in David I. Steinberg, *Stone Mirror: Reflections on Contemporary Korea* (Norwalk, CT: EastBridge Press, 2003), pp. 232–44.

4. If this were true, perhaps the replacement of the Korean command by that in the Middle East and the Gulf as avenues of senior military mobility may make it easier to renegotiate the U.S. military presence in Korea.

5. Katherine Moon, "Korean Nationalism, Anti-Americanism, and Democratic Consolidation," in *Korea's Democratization*, ed. Samuel Kim (Cambridge: Cambridge University Press, 2003), p. 141.

6. Ibid., p. 137.

7. Samuel Kim, "Korea's Democratization in the Global-Local Nexus," in *Korea's Democratization*, ed. Samuel Kim (Cambridge: Cambridge University Press, 2003), p. 28.

8. Mark Manyin, "South Korean Politics and Rising 'Anti-Americanism': Implications for U.S. Policy Toward North Korea" (Washington, DC: Congressional Research Service (RL 319060), May 6, 2003.

9. Seung-Hwan Kim, "Anti-Americanism in Korea," *Washington Quarterly* (Winter 2002–3).

10. U.S.-Korea Relations, Opinion Leaders Seminar Report, July 10–12, 2003, Washington, DC. Co-sponsored by the Korea Institute for International Economic Policy, the Korea Economic Institute, and the Korean-American Association, pp. 7–8.

11. Some Korean observers credit this to the radical, anti-American views of many in the teachers' union and their methods and materials in teaching about Korean history and current events.

12. Jae-Kyoung Lee, "Anti-Americanism in South Korea: The Media and the Politics of Signification," unpublished Ph.D. dissertation, University of Iowa, 1993, pp. 197–98.

13. During the Vietnam War, Korean officials said that as Japan profited economically from the Korean War, Korea would do the same from the Vietnam War. Koreans also commented that as Japan came onto the world stage through the Tokyo Olympics of 1964, so would Korea through the Seoul Olympics of 1988. Both statements proved to be accurate.

14. Lee, "Anti-Americanism in South Korea," p. 209.

15. Had the relocation of these forces been discussed a decade or so ago, the United States most likely would have asked for some quid pro quo from the North Koreans. This is not now the case.

16. Personal interviews, Washington, DC and Seoul, 2002–3. This approach is not new. In the early years of the U.S. economic assistance program to Korea, anecdotes abound of how U.S. officials would present economic aid projects to the Korean government on the last day of the U.S. fiscal year, projects that higher officials had not seen, and demanded immediate approval that minute or that Korea would lose the funds for that year—a position obviously unacceptable to a state in dire need of support.

17. Stephen W. Linton, "Impact of Anti-American Sentiments in the ROK on the ROK-U.S. Security Alliance." Conference on the 2002 Presidential Elections in the Republic of Korea: Implications and Impacts. Asia-Pacific Center for Security Studies, Honolulu, April 2003.

18. In 1965 in a public address this writer called for the removal of U.S. forces from this site, and he was roundly castigated by the U.S. military.

19. In June 2003, a Korean reporter published an interview with an American on U.S. force reductions, but the interview never took place, causing great consternation in American official circles.

About the Editor and Contributors

Kent E. Calder's most recent book, *Pacific Defense: Arms, Energy, and America's Future in Asia*, received the 1997 Mainichi Asia-Pacific Grand Prix for its analysis of how economic change is transforming the U.S.-East Asian security equation. He is also the author of *Strategic Capitalism* and of *Crisis and Compensation*, which was awarded the 1990 Ohira Prize for its account of how domestic politics have shaped Japanese public policy processes, and coauthor of *The Eastasia Edge*. He has served as special adviser to the U.S. ambassador in Tokyo, taught at Harvard University, and held staff positions with the U.S. Congress and the Federal Trade Commission.

Victor D. Cha (Ph.D. Columbia, B.A./M.A. Oxford) is associate professor of government and D.S Song-Korea Foundation Chair in Asian Studies in the Edmund Walsh School of Foreign Service, Georgetown University. He is the award-winning author of *Alignment Despite Antagonism: The United States-Korea-Japan Security Triangle* (winner of the 2000 Ohira Book Prize) and has written articles on international relations and East Asia in many journals. Professor Cha is a former John M. Olin National Security Fellow at Harvard University, two-time Fulbright Scholar, and Hoover National Fellow and CISAC Fellow at Stanford. He serves as an independent consultant to the U.S. Department of Defense (Office of the Secretary of Defense), Booz Allen, SAIC, and CENTRA Technology, and has testified before Congress on Asian security issues. He has been a guest analyst for various media. He serves on the editorial boards of *Asian Security*; the *Journal of Comparative Governance*; and the *Korean Journal of International Relations*. Professor Cha is currently director of the American Alliances in Asia Project at Georgetown University.

Brent (won-ki) Choi is North Korea specialist of the *Joongang Daily*, the leading newspaper in South Korea. From 1990 onward he worked at the newspaper as an editor/researcher and covered inter-Korea relations, U.S.–Korea relations, and defense issues. Mr. Choi has written many articles on North Korea and is author of *The Longest Day on the Korean Peninsula* (2002, Japanese), *The Inter-Korea Summit: 600 Days* (2000), "In Dealing with North Korea as It Is" (1999, paper), *The Crazy*

Engineers in Silicon Valley (1999), "The Good Cop and the Bad Cop" (2001, paper), *Pyongyang Dreaming of Exile* (1996). He was selected "Journalist of the Year" by Ewha Woman's University in 2002. Also, the North Korean Workers' Party published a novel, *Mannam* (Meeting) based on his life and book in 2001. He spent one year as a visiting fellow at the Hoover Institute, Stanford University in 1996–97. Mr. Choi earned his B.A. at Myongji University and his M.A at the University of Utah.

Bruce Cumings teaches international history and East Asian political economy at the University of Chicago. He received his B.A. from Denison University in 1965 and his Ph.D. from Columbia University in 1975. He has taught at Swarthmore College (1975–77), the University of Washington (1977–86), and Northwestern University (1994–97). He is the author of the two-volume study *The Origins of the Korean War* (1981, 1990), *War and Television* (1992), *Korea's Place in the Sun: A Modern History* (1997), *Parallax Visions: Making Sense of American–East Asian Relations* (1999), and is the editor of the modern volume of the *Cambridge History of Korea* (forthcoming). He is a frequent contributor to *The Nation*, *Current History*, and the *Bulletin of the Atomic Scientists*. He was elected to the American Academy of Arts and Sciences in 1999 and is the recipient of fellowships from the National Endowment for the Humanities, the MacArthur Foundation, and the Center for Advanced Study at Stanford. He was also the principal historical consultant for the Thames Television/PBS six-hour documentary *Korea: The Unknown War.*

Meredith Woo-Cumings is professor of political science at the University of Michigan. Her teaching and research interests include international political economy, East Asian politics, and U.S.–East Asian relations. Before joining the University of Michigan, she taught at Northwestern, Columbia, and Colgate universities. She has written and edited six books, including *Race to the Swift: State and Finance in Korean Industrialization* (1991), which was published under the name Jung-en Woo; *Past as Prelude: History in the Making of the New World Order* (1991); *Capital Ungoverned: Liberalizing Finance in Interventionist States* (1996), *The Developmental State* (1999); she was also coauthor of the *Presidential Report*, *Building American Prosperity in the 21st Century: Report of the Presidential Commission on United States-Pacific Trade and Investment Policy* (1997). Her latest book, *Neoliberalism and Reform in East Asia*, published in 2003, was sponsored by the United Nations Research Institute for Social Development and the Rockefeller Foundation. She is currently finishing a manuscript entitled *Three Worlds of East Asian Capitalism.*

William M. Drennan is deputy director of the Research and Studies program at the United States Institute of Peace. He joined the Institute upon his retirement from the U.S. Air Force as a colonel in 1998. His last military assignment was as an analyst with the National Defense University's Institute for National Security Studies from 1995 to 1998, where he concentrated on Korea and Northeast Asia security issues. Prior to that he was professor of National Security Policy at the National War College. From 1990 to

1991 he was Military Fellow at the Council on Foreign Relations in New York City. He was stationed in the Republic of Korea from 1988 to 1990 as chief of the strategy and policy division, J-5, U.S. Forces Korea. In the mid-1980s he served as a squadron commander and later as the deputy commander for operations of a USAF flying training wing. From 1981 to 1984 he was assigned to the White House as the Air Force Aide to President Ronald Reagan. A command pilot, he accumulated 3,300 flying hours during his military career, including over 800 in Southeast Asia during the Vietnam War. He is a graduate of the U.S. Air Force Academy, holds a master's degree from Georgetown University, and has done doctoral work at the Catholic University of America.

James V. Feinerman is currently associate dean, International and Graduate Programs, at Georgetown University Law Center. Professor Feinerman joined the Law Center faculty as a visiting professor for the 1985–86 academic year. Immediately after law school he studied in the People's Republic of China. Subsequently, he joined the New York firm of Davis Polk & Wardwell as a corporate associate. During 1982–83, Professor Feinerman was Fulbright Lecturer on Law at Peking University. In 1986, he was a Fulbright researcher in Japan. In 1989, he was awarded a MacArthur Foundation fellowship to study China's practice of international law. During the 1992–93 academic year, he was a Fellow at the Woodrow Wilson International Center for Scholars. From 1993–95, on leave from the Law Center, Professor Feinerman was the director of the Committee on Scholarly Communication with China. Professor Feinerman served as editor-in-chief of the ABA's *China Law Reporter* from 1986 to 1998. He has coedited *The Limits of the Rule of Law in China* (2001), and coauthored *China After the WTO: What You Need to Know Now* (2001).

Yoichi Funabashi is columnist and chief diplomatic correspondent of the *Asahi Shimbun* and a leading journalist in the field of Japanese foreign policy. He is also a contributing editor of *Foreign Policy*. In 1985 he received the Vaughn-Ueda Prize for his reporting on international affairs. He won the Japan Press Award, known as Japan's "Pulitzer Prize," in 1994 for his columns on foreign policy, and his articles in *Foreign Affairs* and *Foreign Policy* won the Ishibashi Tanzan Prize in 1992. His books in English include *Alliance Tomorrow* (2001); *Alliance Adrift* (1998, winner of the Shincho Arts and Sciences Award); *Asia-Pacific Fusion: Japan's Role in APEC* (1995, winner of the Mainichi Shimbun Asia Pacific Grand Prix Award). His recent articles and papers in English include "International Perspectives on National Missile Defense: Tokyo's Temperance" (*Washington Quarterly*, Summer 2000); "Japan's Moment of Truth" (*Survival*, Winter 2000–01); "Japan's Unfinished Success Story" (*Japan Quarterly*, 2001); "Asia's Digital Challenge" (*Survival*, Spring 2002); "Northeast Asia's Strategic Dilemmas" (*Assessing the Threats*, 2002); and "Learning from Five Years of Trialogue" (*China-Japan-US: Meeting New Challenges*, 2002). He received his B.A. from the University of Tokyo in 1968 and his Ph.D. from Keio University in 1992. He has been a Nieman Fellow at Harvard University (1975–76) and an Ushiba Fellow at the Institute for International Economics (1987).

Robert L. Gallucci is dean of Georgetown University's Edmund A. Walsh School of Foreign Service. From 1998 until January 2001, he was ambassador at large on the proliferation of ballistic missiles and weapons of mass destruction concurrently with his appointment as dean. Dean Gallucci served in the Arms Control and Disarmament Agency, the Bureau of Intelligence and Research, the Policy Planning Staff, in the Bureau of Near Eastern and South Asian Affairs, and in the Bureau of Political-Military Affairs. He has served as the deputy director general of the Multinational Force and Observers of the Sinai peacekeeping force and later joined the faculty of the National War College. He was the deputy executive chairman of the UN Special Commission (UNSCOM) overseeing the disarmament of Iraq. Later, he became the senior coordinator responsible for nonproliferation and nuclear safety initiatives in the former Soviet Union in the Office of the Deputy Secretary. In July 1992, Dr. Gallucci was confirmed as the assistant secretary of state for Political-Military Affairs. Dr. Gallucci was educated at the State University of New York at Stony Brook, and holds a master's and doctorate in politics from Brandeis University. Before joining the State Department, he taught at Swarthmore College, Johns Hopkins School for Advanced International Studies and Georgetown University. He has authored a number of publications on political-military issues, including *Neither Peace Nor Honor: The Politics of American Military Policy in Vietnam* (1975).

Brad Glosserman is the director of research for the Pacific Forum CSIS (Center for Strategic and International Studies) in Honolulu and a contributing editor to the *Japan Times*, writing extensively on policy issues and international affairs. Previously, Mr. Glosserman was on the editorial board and the assistant to the chairman for the *Japan Times*. Mr. Glosserman holds a J.D. from George Washington University and an M.A. from the School of Advanced International Studies of Johns Hopkins University. He is a syndicated columnist for the *South China Morning Post*, and his commentary appears in newspapers throughout Asia.

Hahm Chaibong is professor of political science at Yonsei University. He has a B.A. in economics from Carleton College and a Ph.D. in political science from Johns Hopkins University. His main field of research is comparative political theory (Confucianism, liberalism, and postmodernism). He has been a visiting fellow at the International Forum for Democratic Studies (1999) and a visiting professor at Duke University. He is currently visiting professor at Georgetown and Princeton Universities (Spring 2003). His most recent publications in English include *Confucianism for the Modern World* (coeditor with Daniel A. Bell, 2003), "Cultural Challenge to Individualism" (*Journal of Democracy*), and "Confucian Rituals and the Technologies of the Self: A Foucaultian Perspective" (*Philosophy East & West*).

G. John Ikenberry is Peter F. Krogh professor of geopolitics and global justice at Georgetown University, and during 2002–3 he was a transatlantic fellow at the German Marshall Fund of the United States. His recent books include *After Victory: In-*

stitutions, Strategic Restraint, and the Rebuilding of Order After Major War (2001), which won the Schroeder-Jervis Prize for Best Book in History and International Relations awarded by the APSA; *American Unrivaled: The Future of the Balance of Power* (2002); and *State Power and World Markets: The International Political Economy* (2002), coauthored by Joe Grieco. His latest volume, *International Relations Theory and the Asia-Pacific* (2003) was coedited by Mike Mastanduno.

Kim Sung-han (Ph.D., University of Texas at Austin) is an associate professor and director general for American Studies at the Institute of Foreign Affairs and National Security (IFANS), Ministry of Foreign Affairs & Trade, Seoul, Korea. Currently, Dr. Kim is also teaching at Korea University, advising the ROK Joint Chiefs of Staff and the National Security Council (NSC), and serving as a guest columnist of the *Korea Herald*. He is also president of KAAP (Korean Association of American Politics). Before joining the IFANS in 1994, he had been a research fellow at the Institute of Social Sciences and an expert adviser to the Prime Minister's Committee for Globalization in 1992–94. A specialist in U.S. foreign policy and international security, Dr. Kim's recent contributed articles to scholarly journals include "The ROK-US-DPRK Trilateral Relationship," "U.S. Policy toward the Korean Peninsula and Korea-U.S. Relations," "Humanitarian Intervention, Sovereignty, and the United States," and "Security Policy of Korea: Between *Realpolitik* and *Innenpolitik*."

Uichol Kim is professor of psychology at Chung-Ang University, Seoul, Korea. He grew up in Canada and graduated from the University of Toronto (majoring in psychology and Korean studies) and Queen's University (M.A. and Ph.D. specializing in cross-cultural psychology). He taught at the University of Hawaii at Manoa (1988–93) and the University of Tokyo (1994) before returning to Korea in 1995. He has published over ninety articles and ten books, including *Indigenous Psychologies: Experience and Research in Cultural Context* (1993); *Individualism and Collectivism: Theory, Method, and Applications* (1994); *Progress in Asian Social Psychologies*, Volume 1 (1997); *Democracy, Human Rights, and Islam in Modern Iran* (2003). He is the founding editor of the *Asian Journal of Social Psychology* and currently the president of the Division of Psychology and National Development, International Association of Applied Psychology.

Chung Min Lee is associate professor of international relations at the Graduate School of International Studies, Yonsei University, in Seoul, Korea. Since 2000, he has also been the director of International Education and Exchange at Yonsei University. A graduate of Yonsei University (1982), Dr. Lee received his M.A.L.D and Ph.D. from the Fletcher School of Law and Diplomacy, Tufts University (1988). Prior to joining Yonsei in 1998, Dr. Lee was a policy analyst at RAND (1995–98); visiting fellow at the National Institute for Defense Studies (1994–95); research fellow at the Sejong Institute (1989–94); research fellow at the Institute for East and West Studies, Yonsei University (1988–89); and research fellow at the Institute for Foreign Policy Analysis

(1985–88). A specialist in international and East Asian security affairs, Dr. Lee has written widely in English and Korean; his most recent article, on North Korea's nuclear weapons program, was published in the *Pacific Review.* He has served as a member of the advisory board of the ROK Joint Chiefs of Staff and as a member of the National Security Council Secretariat. Dr. Lee is a member of the IISS (International Institute for Strategic Studies, London).

Dennis L. McNamara is Park Professor of Sociology and Korean Studies at Georgetown University. His studies of capitalism in Korea and Japan include *Colonial Origins of Korean Enterprise, 1910 to 1945* (1990), *Textiles and Industrial Transition in Japan* (1995), *Trade and Transformation in Korea, 1876–1945* (1996), *Corporatism and Korean Capitalism* (1999), and *Market and Society in Korea— Interest, Institution and the Textile Industry* (2002). An edited conference volume entitled *Borders of Korean Modernity* is now under review. He founded and continues to chair the Georgetown Conference on Korean Society, a biannual forum in Washington joining scholars from Asia with western social theorists. He is past president of the Economy and Society Research Committee of the International Sociological Association and a member of the Council on Foreign Relations in New York City. Most recently a new project, entitled "Security and Society—the Social Architecture of Economic Cooperation in Northeast Asia," has been the focus of his work as a Fulbright Research Scholar in Tokyo and Seoul.

Ronald Meinardus is presently the Resident Representative of the Friedrich-Naumann Foundation in the Philippines. Before moving to Manila in early 2002, he served his organization in South Korea for nearly six years,. There, he also taught at Hanyang University. A former journalist, Meinardus writes political commentaries for media in Asia and Europe. Prior to leaving Korea, he was awarded honorary citizenship of Seoul.

Chung-in Moon is professor of political science, Yonsei University. He is currently a visiting professor at Duke University. He is also vice president of the International Studies Association (North America). Dr. Moon has published over 19 books and 190 articles in edited volumes and scholarly journals. His most recent publications include *States, Markets, and Just Growth* (2003, coedited with Atul Kohli) and *Korean Politics: An Introduction* (2002). He is an adviser to the South Korean Ministries of Foreign Affairs and Trade and National Defense.

Katharine H.S. Moon is the Jane Bishop Associate Professor of Political Science at Wellesley College and a visiting scholar at the Woodrow Wilson International Center for Scholars and the George Washington University in Washington, DC. She is the author of *Sex Among Allies: Military Prostitution in U.S.-Korea Relations* (1997; Korean edition 2002) and other work on women and gender in international relations, migrant workers, and social movements in East Asia. She is writing a book on "anti-

Americanism" in South Korea from the perspective of democratization and social movement analysis in which she assesses the implications of these for foreign policy. Moon has served in the Office of the Senior Coordinator for Women's Issues in the U.S. Department of State and as a trustee of Smith College. She serves on the editorial boards of several journals of international relations and consults for NGOs in the United States and Korea.

David I. Steinberg Distinguished Professor and Director of Asian Studies, School of Foreign Service, Georgetown University, was previously Distinguished Professor of Korean Studies. He had been president of the Mansfield Center for Pacific Studies, a representative of the Asia Foundation in Korea (1963–68, 1994–97), Burma, Hong Kong, and Washington, and a member of the Senior Foreign Service, USAID, Department of State, in which he also served in Thailand and was director of Technical Assistance for Asia and the Middle East, as well as director for Philippines, Thailand, and Burma Affairs. Educated at Dartmouth College, Lingnan University (China), Harvard University, and the School of Oriental and African Studies, and University of London, he is the author of *Stone Mirror: Reflections on Contemporary Korea* (2002); *Burma: The State of Myanmar* (2001), *Korea: Economic Development and Social Change*, nine other books and monographs, and over eighty-five articles on Korea, Burma, and other Asian topics. He is also a columnist ("Stone Mirror") for the *Korea Times* and a frequent contributor to the international media.

William Watts is president of Potomac Associates, a policy research organization in Washington, DC. Prior to founding Potomac Associates, Watts served as Staff Secretary and Senior Staff Member of the National Security Council in the White House. Earlier, Watts served as a Foreign Service Officer in Washington, DC; Seoul, Korea; Oberammergau, Germany; and Moscow, USSR. His most recent publication is "Next Generation Leaders in the Republic of Korea: Opinion Survey Report and Analysis," May 2002.

Index